Pipe Dreams

The drying up of the Aral Sea – a major environmental catastrophe of the late twentieth century – is deeply rooted in the dreams of the irrigation age of the late nineteenth and early twentieth centuries, a time when engineers, scientists, politicians, and entrepreneurs around the world united in the belief that universal scientific knowledge, together with modern technologies, could be used to transform large areas of the planet from "wasteland" into productive agricultural land. Though ostensibly about bringing modernity, progress, and prosperity to the deserts, the transformation of Central Asia's landscapes through tsarist- and Soviet-era hydraulic projects bore the hallmarks of a colonial experiment. Examining how both regimes used irrigation-age fantasies of bringing the deserts to life as a means of claiming legitimacy in Central Asia, Maya K. Peterson brings a fresh perspective to the history of Russia's conquest and rule of Central Asia.

MAYA K. PETERSON is Assistant Professor of History at the University of California, Santa Cruz.

Studies in Environment and History

Other Books in the Series

Debjani Bhattacharyya *Empire and Ecology in the Bengal Delta: The Making of Calcutta*
Chris Courtney *The Nature of Disaster in China: The 1931 Yangzi River Flood*
Dagomar Degroot *The Frigid Golden Age: Climate Change, the Little Ice Age, and the Dutch Republic, 1560 1720*
Edmund Russell *Greyhound Nation: A Coevolutionary History of England, 1200–1900*
Timothy J. LeCain *The Matter of History: How Things Create the Past*
Ling Zhang *The River, the Plain, and the State: An Environmental Drama in Northern Song China, 1048–1128*
Abraham H. Gibson *Feral Animals in the American South: An Evolutionary History*
Andy Bruno *The Nature of Soviet Power: An Arctic Environmental History*
David A. Bello *Across Forest, Steppe, and Mountain: Environment, Identity, and Empire in Qing China's Borderlands*
Erik Loomis *Empire of Timber: Labor Unions and the Pacific Northwest Forests*
Peter Thorsheim *Waste into Weapons: Recycling in Britain during the Second World War*
Kieko Matteson *Forests in Revolutionary France: Conservation, Community, and Conflict, 1669–1848*
Micah S. Muscolino *The Ecology of War in China: Henan Province, the Yellow River, and Beyond, 1938–1950*
George Colpitts *Pemmican Empire: Food, Trade, and the Last Bison Hunts in the North American Plains, 1780–1882*
John L. Brooke *Climate Change and the Course of Global History: A Rough Journey*
Paul Josephson et al. *An Environmental History of Russia*
Emmanuel Kreike *Environmental Infrastructure in African History: Examining the Myth of Natural Resource Management*
Gregory T. Cushman *Guano and the Opening of the Pacific World: A Global Ecological History*
Sam White *The Climate of Rebellion in the Early Modern Ottoman Empire*
Edmund Russell *Evolutionary History: Uniting History and Biology to Understand Life on Earth*
Alan Mikhail *Nature and Empire in Ottoman Egypt: An Environmental History*
Richard W. Judd *The Untilled Garden: Natural History and the Spirit of Conservation in America, 1740–1840*
James L. A. Webb, Jr. *Humanity's Burden: A Global History of Malaria*

Myrna I. Santiago *The Ecology of Oil: Environment, Labor, and the Mexican Revolution, 1900–1938*

Frank Uekoetter *The Green and the Brown: A History of Conservation in Nazi Germany*

Matthew D. Evenden *Fish versus Power: An Environmental History of the Fraser River*

Alfred W. Crosby *Ecological Imperialism: The Biological Expansion of Europe, 900–1900, second edition*

Nancy J. Jacobs *Environment, Power, and Injustice: A South African History*

Edmund Russell *War and Nature: Fighting Humans and Insects with Chemicals from World War I to Silent Spring*

Adam Rome *The Bulldozer in the Countryside: Suburban Sprawl and the Rise of American Environmentalism*

Judith Shapiro *Mao's War against Nature: Politics and the Environment in Revolutionary China*

Andrew Isenberg *The Destruction of the Bison: An Environmental History*

Thomas Dunlap *Nature and the English Diaspora*

Robert B. Marks *Tigers, Rice, Silk, and Silt: Environment and Economy in Late Imperial South China*

Mark Elvin and Tsui'jung Liu *Sediments of Time: Environment and Society in Chinese History*

Richard H. Grove *Green Imperialism: Colonial Expansion, Tropical Island Edens and the Origins of Environmentalism, 1600–1860*

Thorkild Kjærgaard *The Danish Revolution, 1500–1800: An Ecohistorical Interpretation*

Donald Worster *Nature's Economy: A History of Ecological Ideas, second edition*

Elinor G. K. Melville *A Plague of Sheep: Environmental Consequences of the Conquest of Mexico*

J. R. McNeill *The Mountains of the Mediterranean World: An Environmental History*

Theodore Steinberg *Nature Incorporated: Industrialization and the Waters of New England*

Timothy Silver *A New Face on the Countryside: Indians, Colonists, and Slaves in the South Atlantic Forests, 1500–1800*

Michael Williams *Americans and Their Forests: A Historical Geography*

Donald Worster *The Ends of the Earth: Perspectives on Modern Environmental History*

Robert Harms *Games against Nature: An Eco-Cultural History of the Nunu of Equatorial Africa*

Warren Dean *Brazil and the Struggle for Rubber: A Study in Environmental History*

Samuel P. Hays *Beauty, Health, and Permanence: Environmental Politics in the United States, 1955–1985*

Arthur F. McEvoy *The Fisherman's Problem: Ecology and Law in the California Fisheries, 1850–1980*

Kenneth F. Kiple *The Caribbean Slave: A Biological History*

Pipe Dreams

Water and Empire in Central Asia's Aral Sea Basin

MAYA K. PETERSON

University of California

CAMBRIDGE
UNIVERSITY PRESS

University Printing House, Cambridge CB2 8BS, United Kingdom

One Liberty Plaza, 20th Floor, New York, NY 10006, USA

477 Williamstown Road, Port Melbourne, VIC 3207, Australia

314–321, 3rd Floor, Plot 3, Splendor Forum, Jasola District Centre, New Delhi – 110025, India

79 Anson Road, #06–04/06, Singapore 079906

Cambridge University Press is part of the University of Cambridge.

It furthers the University's mission by disseminating knowledge in the pursuit of education, learning, and research at the highest international levels of excellence.

www.cambridge.org
Information on this title: www.cambridge.org/9781108475471
DOI: 10.1017/9781108673075

First published 2019

Printed in the United Kingdom by TJ International Ltd, Padstow Cornwall

A catalogue record for this publication is available from the British Library.

Library of Congress Cataloging-in-Publication Data
NAMES: Peterson, Maya K., author.
TITLE: Pipe dreams : water and empire in Central Asia's Aral Sea Basin / Maya K. Peterson, University of California, Santa Cruz.
DESCRIPTION: Cambridge, United Kingdom ; New York, NY : Cambridge University Press, [2019] | SERIES: Studies in environment and history | Includes bibliographical references.
IDENTIFIERS: LCCN 2018052005| ISBN 9781108475471 (hardback) | ISBN 9781108468541 (pbk.)
SUBJECTS: LCSH: Water resources development–Asia, Central. | Rural development–Asia, Central. | Asia, Central–History–20th century. | Soviet Union–Politics and government.
CLASSIFICATION: LCC HD1698.A783 P48 2019 | DDC 333.91009587–dc23
LC record available at https://lccn.loc.gov/2018052005

ISBN 978-1-108-47547-1 Hardback

To my parents, for being my original source of inspiration.

Contents

List of Figures

Acknowledgments

Just as a river on its way to the sea acquires water from many different tributaries, so this book has been influenced by many different sources on its journey to its final destination, a journey that has spanned many years and half the globe. Taking on and finishing such an endeavor was made possible by the support of a vast number of colleagues and friends. Many academic communities have made this book far better, and for that I am infinitely grateful. There is not enough space here to acknowledge every contribution in so many words, but these acknowledgments are, first and foremost, a thank-you to everyone who has helped this book to completion, in ways both big and small.

My interest in Russian history began in high school, when I took the last class that Peter Viereck ever taught at Mount Holyoke College. The following fall, I showed up at Swarthmore College, ready to tackle not only Russian history, but also the Russian language. My Swarthmore professors, including Sibelan Forrester, Bruce Grant, Pieter Judson, and Bob Weinberg, have remained generous mentors through the years. In a master's program at Harvard University, I began learning Uzbek with Gulnora Aminova, and I first encountered the Aral Sea in a class taught by Laura Adams. The Davis Center for Russian and Eurasian Studies, which provided a wonderful academic home over many years, funded my first trip to the Aral Sea basin that summer.

The following fall, Terry Martin's graduate seminar on Soviet history confirmed my desire to pursue a PhD in Russian and Soviet history. Terry was a wonderful graduate advisor and mentor; he encouraged me to follow my instincts and was this project's first champion. David Blackbourn introduced me to environmental history, and though I abandoned my initial plan of writing about a river for his seminar in German history, the idea never quite went away. Over my years at Harvard, members of the Russian and East European History, Frontiers of Eurasia, Central Eurasian Studies, and Center for History and Economics workshops gave the project important critiques and helpful suggestions. Thanks go in particular to Greg Afinogenov, Misha Akulov, Bryan Averbuch, Johanna Conterio, Kathryn Dooley, Jeff Eden, Philippa Hetherington, Tom Hooker, Brendan Karch, Beth Kerley, Philipp Lehmann, Carolin Roeder, Andrey Shlyakhter, Josh Specht, Shirley Ye, and Jeremy Zallen. My thanks go also to my committee members Mark Elliott and Kelly O'Neill, and to John LeDonne for his careful reading of my work in its early stages.

Steve Caton and Ben Orlove provided direct inspiration for this work when they organized a Social Science Research Council (SSRC) Dissertation Proposal Development Fellowship (DPDF) workshop in 2007 around the theme "Water Sustainability." They taught me that water can and should be an object of inquiry, and continued to be mentors long after the workshop was finished. The DPDF program provided me with funding for a first foray into the archives, during which I discovered many of the elements at the core of this book. Without a doubt, this book would not be the same without that grant.

The bulk of the research for this book was funded by a year-long Fulbright-Hays Doctoral Dissertation Research Abroad fellowship, which provided a key support network on the ground in Moscow and Central Asia through the Fulbright program, its staff, and embassy connections. An SSRC International Dissertation Research Fellowship allowed me to spend additional time in the region, including two months in Uzbekistan, where I was able to make good use of my time in the excellent libraries while waiting for permission to access the archives. Hearty thanks go to Scott Levi for helping me to secure affiliation with the Uzbek Academy of Sciences during my stay in Tashkent. The staffs at the State Archives in Tajikistan, Kyrgyzstan, Kazakhstan, and Uzbekistan, as well as the staff at the Central State Archive of Political Documentation of the Kyrgyz Republic, were generous and welcoming, even when sometimes faced with limited resources and political pressures over allowing foreign researchers to do research in their reading rooms. In Russia, archivists at the Russian State Archive of Socio-Political History (RGASPI) and the Russian State Archive of the Economy (RGAE) were particularly helpful, while the staff at the Russian State Historical Archive (RGIA) made the newly reopened archive a delightful place to work.

Throughout my research travels, many people assisted and inspired me, kept me grounded, and made sure I had a roof over my head, including, in Dushanbe: Jessica Abenstein, Shahodat Umarova, Lisa Walker, Lisa Yountchi; in Bishkek: Medina Aitieva, the Beshimov family, Tricia Ryan, Jeff Sahadeo, Amanda Wetsel; in Almaty: Susie Armitage, David Brophy, Del Schwab, and Kadyr Toktogulov; in Moscow: Geoff and Naomi Anisman, Sam Hirst, Christine LeJeune; in St. Petersburg: the Afonins, Hassan Malik, Jennifer Siegel, Mark Soderstrom; and in Tashkent: Alisher Sobirov, Shukhrat Mukhamedov, Sardor Djurabaev, and Jalol Nasirov. Special thanks to Jalol, not only for providing help and good company in the early days of this project, but more recently for securing duplicates of the photographs from the rare books section of the Alisher Navoi State Library of Uzbekistan that appear in this book.

On my return to the United States, an SSRC Eurasia fellowship gave me uninterrupted writing time to finish my dissertation. My cohort of SSRC Eurasia fellows, in particular Pey-Yi Chu, gave vital feedback in the last stages of writing the dissertation. Harvard's Department of the History of Science gave me a place to land in the months after dissertation completion. I am indebted to my colleagues there, including Janet Browne, Anne Harrington, and Alistair Sponsel, who provided a wonderful entrée into the world of the history of science.

The following year, the Rachel Carson Center for Environment and Society at Ludwig-Maximilians-Universität in Munich, Germany, provided a stimulating environment – including field trips to the local beer gardens! – in which to begin the process of turning a PhD dissertation into a book. Thanks to Christof Mauch and Helmuth Trischler for their support for this project, to the countless wonderful fellows and visiting scholars who provided feedback and inspiration during my stints at the RCC between 2012 and 2014, and the amazing RCC staff, especially Annka Liepold. Through the RCC, I became involved in the European Society for Environmental History, as well as the International Water History Association, both of whose members have provided thoughtful and engaged audiences for my work, as well as a host of interlocutors around the world. While in Germany, I was fortunate to be not far from Julia Obertreis, who generously shared materials and read chapter drafts. Her recent book provides a valuable contribution to the history of water management in Central Asia, shedding light on aspects of that history which do not appear in this book.

In addition to the scholars mentioned above, numerous scholars of Russian and Soviet history, Central Asia, environmental history, and the history of science and technology have shared ideas and materials, given feedback, helped to organize conference panels and workshops, and provided collegiality in what otherwise might be the lonely academic world of the historian who spends her time buried in the archives and working on monographs. So thanks to Christine Bichsel, Christian Bleuer, Nick Breyfogle, Andy Bruno, Sarah Cameron, Ian Campbell, Bathsheba Demuth, Maurits Ertsen, Krista Goff, Loren Graham, Ryan Jones, Stephen Jones, Paul Josephson, Marianne Kamp, Botakoz Kassymbekova, Adeeb Khalid, Julia Lajus, Ben Loring, David Moon, Douglas Northrop, Patryk Reid, Alan Roe, Lewis Siegelbaum, and Christian Teichmann. I am especially grateful to the scholars who read a full draft of the manuscript as part of a Junior Faculty Manuscript Workshop sponsored by the University of California's Humanities Research Institute in Fall 2017: Jonathan Beecher, Choi Chatterjee, Adrienne Edgar, Peter Kenez, Louis Warren, and Paul Werth. (Thanks, too, to Melissa Brzycki for taking excellent notes on the proceedings!) Their advice improved the manuscript immensely; I hope I have done their comments justice. Thanks to John McNeill and Ed Russell for nudging me to submit the manuscript to Cambridge University Press, to Debbie Gershenowitz for agreeing to take on this project, and to all three editors, as well as the two anonymous readers, for helping me to realize that less can indeed be more. Thanks, too, to Rachel Blaifeder and Julie Hrischeva for help with images, and to Bill Nelson for the maps.

I am very lucky to have spent the last six years among brilliant, thoughtful, and generous colleagues in the History Department and surrounding academic community at the University of California, Santa Cruz. UCSC provided me with the opportunity to take the postdoctoral fellowship at the Rachel Carson Center and financed further research and writing through a generous start-up package. The Humanities Institute at UCSC provided funding and a course release to allow time to work on revisions and the maps that appear in this book. During my time at UCSC, colleagues and friends in Santa Cruz have provided not only indispensable advice, but also indispensable friendship and ever-welcome distraction, accompanied by copious amounts of home-cooked food, wine, laughter, and solace. Thanks, especially, to Anna Barry-Jester, Dorian Bell, Emily Bondor, Tim Bragg, Vilashini Cooppan, Jennifer Derr, Renee Fox, Alma Heckman, Daniel Hermstad, Sikina Jinnah, Kate Jones, Sharon Kinoshita, Marc Matera, Samantha Matherne, Grant McGuire, Greg O'Malley, Katrina Ricca, Juned Shaikh, Elaine Sullivan, Zoe Whitehouse, and Zac Zimmer. Marm Kilpatrick has not only been part of all this, but he made even the last, tedious months of revisions more joyful than I could have imagined, remaining equal parts enthusiastic and patient, while also providing the gentle prodding to get the book done so we can have more adventures. It is hard to be away, but I am exceedingly grateful to Klaus Gestwa for giving me the chance to put the finishing touches on this book in the charming university town of Tübingen, Germany.

Last, but certainly not least, no part of this would have been possible without my parents, Indira and Mark Peterson, who remain my biggest inspiration. They have always encouraged without pushing, supported without questioning, and provided models of scholarship to which I continue to aspire. They read every word of this book in an earlier form, and it is to them that I dedicate this final version.

Note on People, Places, and Institutions

This book uses the term *Central Asia* for the region described by the Soviet concept of Central Asia (the area comprised by the Uzbek, Turkmen, Tajik, and Kyrgyz Soviet Socialist Republics, along with the southern part of the Kazakh SSR), and *Central Asians* to refer to the indigenous people who inhabited the region (Kazakhs, Kyrgyz, Tajiks, Turkmen, Uzbeks, and others) in both the tsarist and Soviet periods. Likewise, *Russians* or *Slavs* is used as a shorthand to describe people coming from central parts of the empire, either in an official or unofficial capacity, to the Central Asian borderlands, though many of these people, including the governors of the Central Asian province of Russian Turkestan, were Baltic Germans or may have been ethnically Slavic, but not Russian (e.g., Ukrainians or Poles). *Russian Turkestan*, *Turkestan*, and *Turkestan krai* [border region] all refer to the region under direct Russian rule in the imperial period (that is, excluding the autonomous protectorates of Bukhara and Khiva). *Central Eurasian* describes a broader territory, including the protectorates, the Kazakh Steppe, and regions that were generally beyond the boundaries of the Russian Empire and Soviet Union, such as Persia (Iran), Afghanistan, and the Xinjiang province of northwest China.

In terms of spelling, I have generally used transliterations commonly used in English-language publications for names of places and peoples that may be familiar to the audience (e.g., Amu Darya, rather than Amu Daria; Ferghana, rather than Farghona; Kazakh, rather than Kazak or Qazaq; Bukhara, rather than Bukhoro), but I have taken the liberty of spelling other place names with transliterations that better approximate their Central Asian spellings, rather than the Russified versions of those names: e.g., Qurghonteppa for Kurgan-Tiube, Qaraqalpaq for Karakalpak, Qara Qum for Karakum. There were, of course, still choices to make. The oasis of Khorezm, for instance, may be spelled Khwarezm or Khoresm (in addition to many other spellings). In all cases, I have tried to be consistent.

Throughout this work, for simplicity, I refer to the Ministry of Agriculture, although this institution underwent several important name changes between the late nineteenth and the first half of the twentieth centuries. What was the imperial Ministry of Agriculture and State Domains (Ministerstvo Zemledeliia i Gosudarstvennykh Imushchestv) was reorganized in 1905 into the Main Administration of Land Management and Agriculture (Gosudarstvennoe Upravlenie Zemleustroistva i Zemledeliia, often abbreviated GUZiZ). Turkestan gained its own branch of the ministry in 1897; that branch, however, retained the title of Administration of Agriculture and State Domains through the end of the imperial period. In 1915, GUZiZ became the Ministry of Agriculture (Ministerstvo Zemledeliia). After the Bolshevik Revolution, the tsarist-era Ministry of Agriculture became the People's Commissariat of Agriculture. Throughout, I have given the commonly used abbreviated version of Soviet ministries (people's commissariats) when they first appear – for instance, the People's Commissariat of Agriculture (Narodnyi Kommissariat Zemledeliia) was typically referred to by its abbreviation, Narkomzem – but I have otherwise used their English translations, for those not familiar with these abbreviations or the Russian language. I have translated the tsarist-era Otdel Zemel'nykh Uluchshenii (OZU), a department of the Ministry of Agriculture, literally as Department of Land Improvement, rather than Department of Reclamation, since the term *melioratsiia* was coming to be used more frequently to mean "reclamation" in the twentieth century. Explanations of Russian and Central Asian terms that appear frequently in this work can be found in a separate glossary.

Introduction

On March 12, 1967, on the front page of *Pravda*, the main newspaper of the Communist Party of the Soviet Union, just under a headline reminding Soviet citizens that it was "election day," was a short piece entitled "On the Shores of the Aral." The piece described for Soviet readers the idyllic scene that day in Raushan, a small village in the Kungrad (Qo'ng'irot) district of the far western Qaraqalpaq region of the Uzbek Soviet Socialist Republic. Readers of the article learned that storks, "harbingers of a bounteous spring," had recently returned to the shores of the Aral Sea. These shores of the Aral, the article informed *Pravda*'s readers, had once been characterized by salt flats, swamps, and dense reed thickets, but such typical features of the Aral landscape had in recent years submitted "to the will and labor of the Soviet people." The Qaraqalpaq lands, reclaimed with Soviet labor from the marshes and lovingly cleared of weeds, now rewarded the inhabitants of Raushan's state farm (*sovkhoz*) with five thousand tons of rice annually. Thus, above the entrance to Raushan's local polling place was a banner with the words "Labor – the source of wealth." As he approached this polling place, an *aqsaqal* (elder) from Raushan's state farm could barely conceal his joy, such was his belief that "happiness has settled forever on this land." His sense of wonder over the changes brought to the region by Soviet rule was evident as he asked the *Pravda* reporter, in reference to the successful career of a local son, "Which of us could have dreamed before that an inhabitant of the Aral region would become a government figure?" before answering the question himself: "No one."[1]

[1] "Segodnia – vybory!," *P* 71 (March 12, 1967): 1. The Qaraqalpaq spelling of Kungrad is Qońırat.

Many readers of *Pravda*, never having seen the shining expanses of the Aral Sea, might have found it difficult to picture this far-off Central Asian village. The newspaper's reassuring tone, however, informed them that even in the most distant corners of the Soviet Union, Soviet power had overcome the peculiar challenges of nature and turned the regional inhabitants – in this case, the formerly semi-nomadic, Turkic-speaking Qaraqalpaqs – into modern Soviet workers. Several months later, another front-page article, entitled "The Aral Is Becoming Richer," announced to *Pravda*'s readers a new breeding ground for the local fish industry in the Aral region. Such articles told readers that Soviet power had brought modern agriculture, industry, representative government, and prosperity to what had once been one of the most "backward" and "barbaric" territories of the Russian Empire.[2]

Yet, an attentive *Pravda* reader might also have realized that beneath such confident and cheerful proclamations lurked uncertainty and tragedy. In October 1968, for instance, in an article on "our southern seas," the section on the Aral Sea began: "Today there is not yet a fully-formed notion of the damage which will be sustained by the economy of the Aral region from the significant change in the level of the sea." Already, the article told readers, the sinking of the sea level by one-and-a-half meters between 1960 and 1965 had resulted in the loss of seven million kilograms of fish annually. The forecast was for catches to be five times lower by the 1970s; by the year 2000, the level of the sea could sink as much as fourteen meters, resulting in such high salinity that "the Aral Sea would basically no longer exist."[3] With it would go the fish, as well as the way of life of many people in the Aral Sea region. If happiness had indeed settled on these lands, it had not necessarily come to stay.

Fifty years later, the prophetic vision of the "fate of the Aral Sea" sketched out in *Pravda* in October 1968 has become reality. On the sands of the former sea bed, rusting hulks of fishing ships have become a global symbol for environmental degradation. The direct cause of the disappearance of the Aral Sea – once considered the fourth-largest lake in the world – was the increasing diversion in the 1950s and 1960s of Soviet Central Asia's main rivers, the Amu Darya and the Syr Darya, away from the sea and into reservoirs and agricultural fields. By the time *Pravda* reported on the fishing outlook in 1968, Soviet readers learned, almost half the sea's input had already been diverted; the volume of diverted

[2] "Aral stanet bogache," *P* 205 (July 24, 1967): 1.
[3] "Nashi iuzhnye moria," *P* 281 (October 7, 1968): 3.

water continued to increase, until by the early 1980s there were times when almost no water flowed into the sea at all.[4]

The disappearance of the Aral Sea in the late twentieth century is not, however, simply the outcome of communist gigantomania or the consequences of Soviet disregard for nature; rather, this dramatic transformation of a Central Asian landscape has roots that stretch back into the nineteenth century and extend around the world. Russian and Soviet colonial schemes to transform the arid lands of Central Asia paralleled similar schemes undertaken in the late nineteenth and twentieth centuries across arid landscapes from North Africa to Australia, from China to the American West, driven by similar visions of modernity, and what it meant to be civilized. It is this story that lies at the heart of this book.

Well before the 1960s, Russian and Soviet projects to transform Central Asian landscapes by harnessing its water resources were embedded in a larger, global dialogue about the power of science and technology to aid the human quest for modernity and progress. In the twentieth century, as a result of this quest, the human struggle to conquer nature took place on a heretofore unimaginable – and unsustainable – scale. The Aral Sea is only one of its casualties. This story, then, is a story about nature, and the way in which human beings across the globe have engaged with the natural environment in the modern era. Yet at the same time, Central Asian landscapes today – including the Aral Sea region – reflect not just human attempts to control nature, but the legacies of a colonial experiment. The arid landscapes of the Central Asian borderlands, seemingly marked as inferior, were spaces onto which Central Asia's Russian and Soviet rulers could project imperialist notions of modernity, civilization, and progress through increasingly radical methods. Visions of transforming the Aral Sea basin into a fertile colony of the Russian and Soviet empires sometimes seemed like unattainable visions, no more tangible than the smoke from an opium pipe. But with the material transformation in the twentieth century of large swaths of Central Asia, what were dreams for some became nightmares for others, in particular for those who today still inhabit the toxic sandscapes where the Aral Sea used to be. As is the case with modernizing schemes everywhere, some

[4] Ibid.; Philip Micklin, "Irrigation and Its Future in Soviet Central Asia: A Preliminary Analysis," in eds. Lutz Holzner and Jeane M. Knapp, *Soviet Geography Studies in Our Time: A Festschrift for Paul E. Lydolph* (Milwaukee, WI: The University of Wisconsin, 1987), 249.

have stood to benefit, while others, even those in whose name such schemes were ostensibly carried out, have been left in the dust.[5]

ENVIRONMENT AND EMPIRE

In recent years, environmental historians have urged us to see "that we cannot understand human history without natural history and we cannot understand natural history without human history."[6] These historians, and others who use an environmental historical approach to the study of the past, argue that an understanding of the ways in which the natural environment has constrained and shaped human actions is crucial for understanding developments in the past. The natural environment is not merely a stage on which the drama of human history takes place; rather, humans are embedded in the natural world, and seemingly natural landscapes are themselves reflections of politics, ideologies, and culture. Indeed, over the course of time, the distinctions between what is "natural" and what is the result of human action become blurred. As human actions shape the environments in which they live, these changing environments in turn may shape the possibilities for human actions in the future. Inspired by imperial historian Alexander Morrison, who has noted that "the nature of Imperial control is determined as much, if not more, by the circumstances within the colony as it is by any particularities of metropolitan politics, culture, and economics," as well as by German historian David Blackbourn, who has argued that "the human domination of nature has a lot to tell us about the nature of human domination," this book adds to a growing number of works on Russian and Soviet environmental history arguing that understanding the nature of Russian and Soviet attempts to manage and control territory – in this case, Central Asia – requires understanding how Russians encountered the physical environments of those lands, as well as the extent to which those encounters both inspired and limited the nature of Russian and Soviet rule there.[7]

[5] Karen Piper's narrative of the history of water and racial politics in Los Angeles is aptly titled *Left in the Dust: How Race and Politics Created a Human and Environmental Tragedy in L.A.* (New York: St. Martin's Press, 2006).

[6] Richard White, *The Organic Machine: The Remaking of the Columbia River* (New York: Hill and Wang, 1995), ix.

[7] Alexander Morrison, "How 'Modern' Was Russian Imperialism?" (presented at the First Congress of the Asian Association of World Historians, Osaka, May 29–31, 2009), 16; David Blackbourn, *The Conquest of Nature: Water, Landscape, and the Making of*

In the case of Central Asia, while many Russian and Soviet officials had visions for how Central Asian landscapes ought to look – based on their own preconceived notions, rooted in European ideas about what constituted a proper use of land and water resources – their abilities to effect these transformations were very much constrained by the materialities of Central Asian environments. To an extent, one can even argue that the natural processes of the region be considered actors in this narrative. Central Asia's colonial rulers grappled with malarial mosquitoes, tigers, plagues of locusts, river flows, upwardly mobile soluble salts, and loads of silt, much as they tried to control, shape, and harness Central Asia's human population. Whereas Central Asians could be convinced of the desirability of irrigation projects to make more land available for agriculture – provided their land and food were not taken from them in this process – phenomena such as soil salinization proceeded regardless of proffered incentives or professed ideologies. At the same time, while this book recognizes that it was not only human society that was left with the deep imprint of Russian and Soviet development projects, and that nonhumans often thwarted Russian and Soviet plans for the transformation of Central Asian landscapes, its major focus is on *intentional* actors – imperialist administrators who incentivized cotton cultivation and approved irrigation projects, engineers who sought to rationalize and make more efficient existing systems of land and water use,

Modern Germany (New York: W.W. Norton, 2006), 7. Recent English-language monographs on Russian and Soviet environmental history include Stephen Brain, *Song of the Forest: Russian Forestry and Stalinist Environmentalism, 1905–1953* (Pittsburgh, PA: Pittsburgh University Press, 2011); Andy Bruno, *The Nature of Soviet Power: An Arctic Environmental History* (New York: Cambridge University Press, 2016); Ryan Jones, *Empire of Extinction: Russians and the North Pacific's Strange Beasts of the Sea, 1741–1867* (Oxford: Oxford University Press, 2014); and David Moon, *The Plough That Broke the Steppes: Agriculture and Environment on Russia's Grasslands, 1700–1914* (Oxford, UK: Oxford University Press, 2013). See also Jonathan Oldfield, Julia Lajus, and Denis B. Shaw, "Conceptualizing and Utilizing the Natural Environment: Critical Reflections from Imperial and Soviet Russia," *Slavonic and East European Review* 93, 1 (January 2015): 1–15. Even with the increase in attention to the environment among historians of the Russian Empire and Soviet Union, little attention has been paid to Central Asia. Exceptions are Sarah Cameron, *The Hungry Steppe: Famine, Violence, and the Making of Soviet Kazakhstan* (Ithaca, NY: Cornell University Press, 2018), as well as the work of Marc Elie, including "The Soviet Dust Bowl and the Canadian Erosion Experience in the New Lands of Kazakhstan, 1950s–1960s," *Global Environment* 8, 2 (2015), and Elie, "Governing by Hazard: Controlling Mudslides and Promoting Tourism in the Mountains above Alma-Ata (Kazakhstan), 1966–1977" in eds. Sandrine Revet and Julien Langumier, *Governing Disasters: Beyond Risk Culture* (London: Palgrave MacMillan, 2015), 23–57.

indigenous Central Asians who both cooperated with and subverted these tsarist and Soviet attempts to transform their lands through hydraulic management – as well as the consequences, both intended and unintended, of such actions.

The temporal setting for this book is the period from the second half of the nineteenth century, when Russia rapidly conquered the vast territory south of the Kazakh Steppe, through the first half of the twentieth century and the establishment of Soviet rule in Central Asia under Vladimir Lenin and Joseph Stalin. Because the Second World War was a seminal event in Soviet history, any work that includes a substantial section on the postwar period must cover an amount of ground that is beyond the scope of this book. However, as the epilogue makes clear, one of the central arguments of this book is that by World World Two the foundations had been laid for subsequent Soviet and post-Soviet attempts to transform Central Asian environments.

The Bolshevik Revolution of 1917 continues to serve as a dividing line for those who study the histories of the Russian Empire and Soviet Union, so this book contributes to a small, but growing body of literature that explores the continuities and ruptures between tsarist and Soviet rule. By examining hydraulic projects to transform Central Asian landscapes on both sides of 1917, this book explores the extent to which the Soviet Union can be thought of as an empire – even though it explicitly defined itself as a revolutionary, anti-imperial state – and, conversely, to what extent Central Asia remained a colony.[8] According to Jane Burbank and Frederick Cooper, a *politics of difference* in which the goal is "loyalty, not likeness" is a key defining characteristic of empires. Imperial Russian administrators in Central Asia employed this politics of difference, marking Central Asian subjects as *tuzemtsy* ("natives") – different even from the *inorodtsy* (non-Christian "aliens") who inhabited parts of the empire such as Siberia – and governing various parts of Central Asia by laws pertaining specifically to those territories.[9]

[8] For views of the Soviet Union as an empire – albeit a distinct type of empire – see Terry Martin, *The Affirmative Action Empire: Nations and Nationalisms in the Soviet Union, 1923–1939* (Ithaca, NY: Cornell University Press: 2001); Yuri Slezkine, "Imperialism as the Highest Stage of Socialism," *Russian Review* 59, 2 (April 2000): 227–234; Francine Hirsch, *Empire of Nations: Ethnographic Knowledge and the Making of the Soviet Union* (Ithaca, NY: Cornell University Press, 2005). For Central Asia in particular, see Douglas Northrop, *Veiled Empire: Gender and Power in Stalinist Central Asia* (Ithaca, NY: Cornell University Press, 2004).

[9] Jane Burbank and Frederick Cooper, *Empires in World History: Power and the Politics of Difference* (Princeton, NJ: Princeton University Press, 2010), 11–13; Adeeb Khalid, "Culture and Power in Colonial Turkestan," *Cahiers d'Asie centrale* 17/18 (2009): 418–422.

In the period after the revolution of 1917, Soviet institutions replaced local and regional Central Asian ones, while Soviet Central Asian citizens were divided into theoretically equal "nations" subject to an overarching Soviet identity and Soviet laws, just like Russians, Ukrainians, and other former tsarist subjects. From this point of view, the Soviet Union does not fit comfortably into a mold of empire in which distinctions are created to maintain difference, not to level the playing field. And yet, as Terry Martin has demonstrated, separate was not equal in the Soviet "affirmative action empire." Rather, a civilizational hierarchy was maintained which identified certain (primarily "eastern") nationalities as "culturally backward." In Central Asia, Martin has argued, where "the Bolsheviks inherited a segregated society ... [t]hey abolished legal segregation but preserved much of it in practice and even in thought."[10] Recently, historians Valerie Kivelson and Ronald Suny have similarly argued that attention to practices of governance is as important as understanding the categories through which Soviet authorities purported to rule. According to them, the "imperious quality of [Soviet] rule – with imperious defined as 'domineering, dictatorial, overbearing' – in many ways overshadowed ... rule through lateral distinction ... What had been envisioned as an egalitarian multinational state in the early Soviet years evolved rapidly into a more centralized imperial formation ..."[11]

In recent years, Adeeb Khalid and Botakoz Kassymbekova have made important arguments for the nature of early Soviet rule in Central Asia which lend nuance to this debate. For Khalid, whose work focuses on Uzbekistan, Central Asia in the 1920s and early 1930s "hung between empire and revolution."[12] In *Despite Cultures*, a work on early Soviet rule in Tajikistan, Kassymbekova, drawing on Burbank and Cooper's work, argues for thinking about imperialism and colonialism as "repertoires of power" utilized by early Soviet leaders, alongside revolutionary modernizing strategies, as "tactics of both state and empire building in Central Asia."[13]

Even if the "slippery" concept of empire does not apply to the Soviet Union in all places at all times, this book argues that from an environmental perspective, early Soviet Central Asia remained a colony of the

[10] Martin, *The Affirmative Action Empire*, 56, 153.

[11] Valerie Kivelson and Ronald Grigor Suny, *Russia's Empires* (New York: Oxford University Press, 2017), 10–11.

[12] Adeeb Khalid, *Making Uzbekistan: Nation, Empire, and Revolution in the Early USSR* (Ithaca, NY: Cornell University Press, 2015), 10.

[13] Botakoz Kassymbekova, *Despite Cultures: Early Soviet Rule in Tajikistan* (Pittsburgh, PA: University of Pittsburgh Press, 2016), 15–16, 201.

Soviet Union in spite of Soviet campaigns to modernize the region and stamp out "backwardness."[14] The Central Asian borderland region was developed as a source of raw materials for the Soviet state, and Soviet authorities exploited Central Asia's human labor resources with this goal in mind. This does not mean, however, that the Soviet Union was simply the tsarist empire in a new guise; indeed, as Khalid has pointed out in the case of Uzbekistan, Central Asia was a very different place already in 1931 than it was in 1917. Some Soviet modernizing campaigns, such as the drive for literacy and the creation of new educational opportunities, changed many Central Asian lives for the better. Simultaneously, however, the Soviet state built on the imperial foundations established in Central Asia by the eve of the Bolshevik revolution – an economy centered on agriculture tending toward a cotton monoculture, the practice of encouraging resettlement of vast numbers of people to the Central Asian borderland to more firmly bind it to the metropole, and the reshaping of indigenous lifeways by encouraging the sedentarization of nomadic peoples – to transform lands and livelihoods on a much grander scale and in a much more deliberate and intrusive manner. This environmental perspective supports Khalid's conclusions that by the 1930s in Central Asia, the violence of the Soviet state "destroyed alternatives. Collectivization and the expansion of cotton tied Central Asia … to the Soviet economy; the closing of the borders cut Central Asia off from the rest of the world," leaving it more dependent on Russia than ever before.[15] Yet, even while Soviet methods, including force and violence, served as the tools, tsarist-era dreams, anchored in global visions of modernity and progress, provided the imagination, as well as the raw materials, for the transformation of realities in Soviet Central Asia.

THE MAKING OF CENTRAL ASIA

Central Asia is not a place you will find on a standard world map. The term "Central Asia" (*Central-Asien*, *Asie centrale*) to describe a particular world region was introduced by the noted German geographer Alexander von Humboldt in 1843, based on a journey he made to the region in 1829.[16] Over the centuries, this geographical region has been home to

[14] Kivelson and Suny, *Russia's Empires*, 397. [15] Khalid, *Making Uzbekistan*, 10.

[16] Alexander von Humboldt, *Asie centrale. Recherches sur les chaines des montagnes et la climatologie comparée* (Paris: Gide, 1843); *Central-Asien: Untersuchungen über die Gebirgsketten und die vergleichende Klimatologie* (Berlin: Carl J. Klemann, 1844).

various political units and has been imagined in different ways. Like Benedict Anderson's concept of nations as *imagined communities*, however, *imagined* here does not imply *imaginary*. Central Asia had real meaning for its Russian and, later, Soviet rulers, and the ways in which Central Asia was conceptualized had real consequences for the people who lived there.[17]

Politically, the geographical region covered in this book is described by what was the Russian imperial province of Turkestan at its largest extent (around the turn of the twentieth century), together with the Central Asian states which in the late nineteenth century became autonomous protectorates of the Russian Empire: the Emirate of Bukhara and the Khanate of Khiva (a third state, the Khanate of Khoqand, was abolished to give the Russians control over the fertile Ferghana Valley). In 1924, after a brief stint as Soviet "people's republics," these protectorates were abolished by the Bolsheviks, who divided the region into what would become by 1936 the four union republics (Soviet Socialist Republics, or SSRs) of Kyrgyzstan, Tajikistan, Turkmenistan, and Uzbekistan. In the Soviet imagination, these four republics formed Middle, or Central, Asia (*Sredniaia Aziia*).[18] Politically, too, they initially were united, coming until 1934 under the jurisdiction of a single Central Asia Bureau (*Sredazbiuro*) of the Central Communist Party in Moscow. Part of the former imperial province of Turkestan became the southern part of the Kazakh SSR; in Soviet policy "Central Asia and Kazakhstan" were often considered together, though northern Kazakhstan was historically, politically, and economically more closely linked with Siberia than Turkestan.[19]

In terms of physical territory, Soviet geographers defined Central Asia as:

> the broad region (*oblast'*) located in the southeast of our country and occupying territory from the Caspian Sea in the west up to the administrative boundary with the People's Republic of China in the east, and from the Aral Sea in the north up to the administrative boundary with Iran and Afghanistan in the south.

[17] Benedict Anderson, *Imagined Communities: Reflections on the Origin and Spread of Nationalism* (New York: Verso, 1983).

[18] *Tsentral'naia Aziia*, which can also be translated as Central Asia, often refers to a larger region including Xinjiang in northwest China and Mongolia.

[19] In the imperial period, northern Kazakhstan was governed as part of the Steppe region; both tsarist and Soviet authorities, however, found "compelling similarities with ... Central Asia in the natural environment, economy, and culture of the southern oblasts [regions] of Kazakhstan," in ed. Robert Lewis, *Geographic Perspectives on Soviet Central Asia* (New York: Routledge, 1992), 5.

FIGURE I.1 Map of Turkestan under Russian rule, c. 1900.
Map by Bill Nelson.

As this particular Soviet report pointed out, "the concept of 'Turkestan', which served in the pre-October days [i.e., before the Bolshevik Revolution of 1917] as a synonym for Central Asia, unites the same physio-geographical complex occupying the same territory" as Soviet Central Asia.[20] By this definition, southern and southeastern Kazakhstan belonged to Central Asia. The southern part of the Kazakh Soviet Socialist Republic also formed part of the Aral Sea drainage basin and, thus, is implicated in the environmental story this book will tell.[21]

Central Asia is a largely arid region. Lack of rainfall and humidity, coupled with extreme heat, mean that Central Asia's rivers typically do not receive much input other than glacial melt from the high mountain peaks in the eastern part of the region, primarily the Tian Shan and Pamir Mountains on the border with China. Of the main rivers of Central Asia, only the Amu Darya and Syr Darya, fed by those high mountain streams, historically reached an outlet in the Aral Sea. The rest dwindled away in the sand and steppes, having lost all their water to irrigation and evaporation. Much of western and southern Central Asia – the Ustyurt Plateau between the Aral and Caspian Seas, the Qyzyl Qum (Red Sands) and Qara Qum (Black Sands), which make up almost three-quarters of the Central Asian region – is characterized by stony, clay, or sandy desert, where the daytime maximum temperature can reach more than 50 degrees Celsius.[22] The exceptions are a few fertile oases, such as Samarkand, Bukhara, Khorezm in the Amu Delta to the south of the Aral Sea, and the lush Ferghana Valley, around which Central Asian states have historically been organized. The arid regions surrounding these oases, as well as the northern steppe region, are mostly inhabited by peoples who over the centuries have adopted pastoral nomadism as a way to cope with aridity. There are no prominent physical features dividing the deserts of "Turkestan" from the Kazakh Steppe. Semi-nomadic and sedentary societies alike practice agriculture; however, the lack of rainfall and high rates of evaporation mean that almost everywhere in the region it is necessary to construct irrigation channels in order to make land suitable for cultivation.

[20] *IUFGOS* II (1956), 123.

[21] Philip Micklin, "The Water Crisis in Soviet Central Asia," in ed. Philip R. Pryde, *Environmental Management in the Soviet Union* (New York: Cambridge University Press, 1991), 213–215.

[22] Elena Lioubimtseva, Jahan Kariyeva, and Geoffrey Henebry, "Climate Change in Turkmenistan" in eds. Igor Zonn and Andrey Kostianoy, *The Turkmen Lake Altyn Asyr and Water Resources in Turkmenistan* (Berlin, Heidelberg: Springer, 2014), 42.

Such an overview of Central Asia's geography, topography, and climate is provided in most works about the region. But where most studies leave off is where this study begins. In this work, the physical environment, and in particular the waters of Central Asia, as they flow through rivers, streams, canals, and into steppes and lakes – including the Aral Sea – is not merely the setting for the narrative; rather, water is the guiding principle. In some ways, the narrative itself traces Central Asia's waters from the lower Amu Darya and Aral region (Chapter 1) upstream along the Syr Darya and through the Ferghana Valley (Chapters 2 and 3) to the mountainous region from which the Aral and the Syr, as well as another of Central Asia's most important rivers, the Chu (Chui) River, descend (Chapter 4). After an exploration in Chapter 5 of the changes brought by the revolution, in Chapter 6 the narrative then journeys along the Vakhsh River, an important tributary of the Amu Darya, briefly follows the waters of the Naryn River – an important tributary of the Syr Darya – back to the Ferghana Valley before, eventually, returning to the Aral Sea in the Epilogue. Along the way, the narrative investigates how scientists; military officers; central, regional, and local officials; artists; entrepreneurs; nomads; peasants; tsarist subjects; and Soviet citizens perceived, portrayed, and attempted to harness Central Asia's waters in the name of their own transformative visions, as well as how those visions were received and, at times, contested.

As a fluid and mobile resource that is, and historically has been, both crucial and contested in an arid region like Central Asia, the materiality of water makes it a fascinating object of study. Water was key to the transformation of Central Asia into a region that its Russian and Soviet rulers considered fruitful and prosperous. The waters of Central Asian rivers could be used to transport troops and goods, empower or limit the autonomy of Central Asian cities and states, grow cotton and other agricultural products, water the fields and orchards of European settlers, power machinery and industry, and provide light to rural areas. Yet in Central Asia, even the best-laid imperialist plans had to contend with the material aspects of the region's physical environment: precious water resources were trapped in glaciers at high altitudes in mountains remote from any roadway; fresh river waters disappeared into sands and steppes or saline lakes surrounded by hostile deserts; attempts to construct irrigation systems resulted in water leaching salts out of the arid soil, ruining the lands they were supposed to make productive; and undrained water, in turn, converted deserts into swamps. Central Asia's water was an unpredictable resource, whose fickle nature tsarist bureaucrats and

Soviet commissars alike came to associate with the seemingly unpredictable and uncontrollable inhabitants of the region.

At the same time, water was essential for all of Central Asia's inhabitants. Water thus formed an arena in which cooperation, compromise, and conflict were unavoidable. In Central Asia, irrigation projects encouraged – sometimes even required – cooperation between indigenous peoples, local and regional administrators, Russian and foreign engineers, migrant settlers, and laborers from the greater Central Eurasian region. Arjun Appadurai has cautioned that although cooperation "frequently implies equality between partners and equally cheerful attitudes on both sides ... more often cooperation is a state of affairs that involves ... [parties] of different economic capability and that may not be regarded as especially desirable by some of the parties involved."[23] Following Appadurai, this book investigates indigenous Central Asians who entered into irrigation projects and water-sharing agreements with the Grand Duke Nikolai Konstantinovich Romanov, an imperial intermediary who was nonetheless not a state agent, a social outcast whose story may only have been possible in Russian Turkestan (Chapter 2). It also seeks out the perspectives of Central Asian nomads, whose strategies of cooperation with both Slavic settlers as well as tsarist authorities may be better read as acts of subversion toward attempts to appropriate their land for irrigation and colonization than either docile cooperation or hostile resistance (Chapter 4). These cases, along with others in this narrative, serve as a reminder that Central Asia was a place where diverse groups of peoples – local groups with varied ethnic identities and kinship ties, imported and local officials, exiles, forced and voluntary migrants and workers, refugees, soldiers, rebels, intellectuals, revolutionaries – mixed on a daily basis. This book, thus, adds to works on the Russian Empire by, among others, Paul Werth, Robert Crews, Jeff Sahadeo, and Alexei Miller, which similarly argue that relations in non-Russian regions of the Russian Empire were far too complicated to depict with one single model of colonizer and colonized.[24]

[23] Arjun Appadurai, "Wells in Western India: Irrigation and Cooperation in an Agricultural Society," *Expedition Magazine* 26, 3 (Philadelphia: Penn Museum, 1984): 3.

[24] Robert Crews, *For Prophet and Tsar: Islam and Empire in Russia and Central Asia* (Cambridge, MA: Harvard University Press, 2006); Jeff Sahadeo, *Russian Colonial Society in Tashkent, 1865–1923* (Bloomington: Indiana University Press, 2007); Paul Werth, "From Resistance to Subversion: Imperial Power, Indigenous Opposition, and Their Entanglement," *Kritika: Explorations in Russian and Eurasian History* 1, 1 (Winter 2000): 21–43; Aleksei Miller, "Between Local and Inter-Imperial: Russian Imperial History in Search of Scope and Paradigm," *Kritika* 5, 1 (Winter 2004): 7–26.

THE IRRIGATION AGE: BACK TO THE FUTURE?

Beginning in the late nineteenth century, as Russia established its presence in Central Asia, many diverse actors recognized the importance of irrigation for the region's future. Tsarist-era visions for the colonization of Central Asia and its transformation into a productive part of the empire, as well as Soviet plans for the further transformation of that province into a prosperous and modern borderland which might serve as a model of socialism to its neighbors, were resolutely forward-looking. Tsarist elites railed against "backwardness" in Central Asian societies, particularly its nomadic ones, while Soviet authorities campaigned vigorously to extinguish any last vestiges of a "feudal" past. When it came to both cultural and economic development, by the late nineteenth and early twentieth centuries, modern science and technology seemed to offer new possibilities for "conquering" the arid environment that appeared to serve as a primary obstacle preventing Central Asians from entering the modern world. Russians, thus, became enthusiastic participants in what we might term the *irrigation age*, firm believers in the potential of water to turn the "barren" lands of Central Asia into blooming gardens. Modern irrigated agriculture was to liberate Central Asians from drudgery, make them more productive, and encourage nomads to take up a settled (and therefore "civilized") way of life. It was also intended to ensure Central Asia's place as a prosperous part of the empire, rather than a drain on imperial coffers.

Irrigation was certainly not a new art. But during the irrigation age of the last decades of the nineteenth and first decades of the twentieth centuries, an increasing number of people – engineers, scientists, politicians, entrepreneurs – circulated the arid regions of the globe, bringing with them the belief that universal scientific knowledge, together with modern technologies such as the excavator, and modern construction materials such as steel and concrete, could be used to transform large areas of the planet from "wasteland" into productive (i.e., agricultural) land by means of irrigation – which often went hand-in-hand with hydropower – and similar visions of the prosperity irrigation might bring to the deserts.[25]

[25] One of the most fantastic of these schemes was German architect Herman Sörgel's 1930s vision of Atlantropa, in which damming the Mediterranean would power all of Europe and simultaneously make the deserts of North Africa bloom (Philipp Lehmann, "Infinite Power to Change the World: Hydroelectricity and Engineered Climate Change in the Atlantropa Project," *American Historical Review* 121, 1 [February 2016]: 70–100).

As Ian Tyrrell has pointed out, "irrigation is not [just] about drains, pumps, pipes, and dams, but about dreams."[26]

At the same time, however, many of the dreams of the future that arose in this irrigation age were deeply rooted in ideas about the past. In 1909, for instance, the famous British engineer William Willcocks, the mastermind behind Egypt's first Aswan Dam, described his irrigation work in Mesopotamia thus: "I have followed the traces of the four rivers of the early chapters of Genesis. Appointed by the new Turkish Government to engage engineers and survey and level the rivers and canals of the Tigris-Euphrates delta ... I first set myself the task of mastering the ancient systems of irrigation, improving on them when I could ... I started with the Garden of Eden."[27] The modern engineers of the irrigation age were fascinated with the accomplishments of ancient "hydraulic societies," and with the idea that irrigation could be used to restore glory to places where cities and gardens – in other words, "civilization" – had once flourished.

In the Aral Sea basin, which was incorporated into the Russian Empire between the 1860s and 1880s, vast desert landscapes, inhabited by semi-nomadic Turkic-speaking peoples such as the Qaraqalpaqs, seemed to serve as a reminder of the fragility of life in the region. Foreign travelers almost always remarked on the traces of ancient buildings and waterways in Central Asia's deserts, which they cited as evidence of decline from the days when great civilizations had flourished in oases along fabled trade routes linking China and Europe. For the vast Russian Empire to the north, the newly acquired Central Asian possessions had the potential to become the jewel in the Russian tsar's crown, lands of sunshine, melon gardens, fruit orchards, and fields of grain, if only the deserts could be won.

The supposed decline of ancient trade routes and, along with them, the glory of ancient civilizations, was one which Russians in the region attributed to both the corruption of Central Asia's rulers – the emirs, khans, and begs of Bukhara, Khiva, and Khoqand, lands inhabited by sedentary Turkic- and Persian-speaking peoples (whom we would today think of as Uzbeks and Tajiks) – as well as to the presence of nomads – Turkic-speaking groups of Kazakhs, Kyrgyz, Turkmen, and

[26] Ian Tyrrell, *True Gardens of the Gods: Californian-Australian Environmental Reform, 1860–1930* (Berkeley: University of California, 1999), 103.

[27] William Willcocks, "Mesopotamia: Past, Present, and Future," read at the Royal Geographical Society, November 15, 1909, reprinted from *The Geographical Journal*, 35, 1 (January 1910), *Annual Report of the Board of Regents of the Smithsonian Institution, 1909* (Washington, DC: Government Printing Office, 1910), 401.

Qaraqalpaqs, who were popularly believed to be more interested in raiding than trade. Russians assumed that this supposed marauding lifestyle made nomads poor stewards of the land. The fact that most of these nomads were really semi-nomadic (and thus "semi-sedentary") and practiced agriculture did not seem to factor into such notions.

A myth of decline can be a useful justification for conquest, as Diana Davis has shown in her work on the Maghreb, where, she argues, French imperialists created a myth of the role of nomads in the environmental degradation of North African landscapes, in order to legitimate French plans to take over the region and restore "the granary of Rome."[28] Russians shared the widely held Euro-American belief that a sedentary lifestyle was superior to a nomadic one, which therefore justified Russian conquest of the region.[29] Russian beliefs in the urgency of reversing this supposed decline were buttressed by nineteenth-century notions that the world was drying up – for which Central Asia seemed to provide some of the best evidence – and that the *sukhovei*, hot, dry, northward-blowing winds were encroaching, along with the "Asiatic" deserts, on Russian civilization in the steppes.[30]

Like the French in North Africa, Russians in Central Asia drew on ideas about the ancient past to provide evidence for what was possible in the future. Many Russians, for instance, cited a legend about a time when the Central Asian steppes and deserts (the location varied, depending on who was telling the tale) were so densely settled that a cat could leap from rooftop to rooftop and travel hundreds of miles without ever touching the ground.[31] The traces of ancient irrigation channels in the deserts were reminders of the life such "waste" lands had once supported, just as the

[28] Diana Davis, *Resurrecting the Granary of Rome: Environmental History and French Colonial Expansion in North Africa* (Athens, OH: Ohio University Press, 2007).

[29] William Cronon, *Changes in the Land: Indians, Colonists, and the Ecology of New England* (New York: Hill and Wang, 1983), 53.

[30] On Russian interest in desiccation, see Moon, *The Plough That Broke the Steppes*, 109–63, *passim*; L. S. Berg, "Vysykhaet li Sredniaia Aziia?," *IRGO* 41 (1905); Prince Kropotkin, "The Desiccation of Eur-Asia," *GJ* 23, 6 (1904); Brower, *Turkestan and the Fate of the Russian Empire* (New York: Routledge Curzon, 2003), 76. See also, Raphael Pumpelly, *Explorations in Turkestan* (Washington, DC: Carnegie Institute, 1905), 16; Pumpelly, *My Reminiscences* II (New York: Henry Holt, 1918), 725–726; Ellsworth Huntington, *The Pulse of Asia* (Boston, MA: Houghton Mifflin, 1907).

[31] See, for instance, *Trudy s″ezda khlopkovodov v g. Tashkente s 25-go do 1-e dekabria 1912 g.*, I (Tashkent: GUZiZ, 1913): 93; A. A. Tatishchev, *Zemli i liudi: v gushche pereselencheskogo dvizheniia (1906–21)* (Moscow: Russkii put′, 2001), 91; Ekaterina Pravilova, "River of Empire: Geopolitics, Irrigation, and the Amu Darya in the Late XIXth Century," *Cahiers d'Asie centrale* 17–18 (2009): 272.

magnificent architectural complexes of the oases of Samarkand and Bukhara attested to past glories of the region, even if they had been achieved at the hands of "Oriental despots." Notions of glory amid barbarism were crucial to the legends of the irrigation age, because, in the words of Tyrrell, they "did not claim arid lands to be inherently barren. [Such lands] simply lacked water. Irrigation alone was required to bring them to life."[32]

In order to bring the "dead" lands to life, however, looking backward was not enough, for it was only through the promise of modern engineering techniques and technologies that the glorious visions of the irrigation age came to seem possible in the first place. Central Asia's Russian and Soviet rulers were not, after all, seeking to recreate the legendary hydraulic despotism of the Timurid Empire. Rather, technocrats, engineers, and entrepreneurs alike hoped that the new science of irrigation being practiced around the world would awaken the potential that had long lain dormant in the Central Asian steppes and deserts and bring new kinds of liberation to the Central Asian people. Though they drew on ancient myths and legends for inspiration, the science in which such irrigation fantasies were purportedly grounded was what distinguished them from the fiction of prophecy.[33]

COTTON AND THE CIVILIZING MISSION

The logic of science and modernity that fueled the irrigation age dictated the most rational and efficient use possible of available natural resources. In the early twentieth century, tsarist technocrats increasingly spoke of harnessing the empire's "productive forces," a concept that harmonized well with Bolshevik ideology after the revolution of 1917, since Marx himself had written about the means of production (which included raw materials as well as tools) as one of society's "productive forces."[34] In Central Asia, harnessing the region's productive forces centered on putting Central Asia's rivers to work in order to expand irrigated agriculture to the greatest possible extent. Water was to be used to grow cotton that,

[32] Tyrrell, *True Gardens of the Gods*, 113.

[33] On modernity's relationship to prophecy, see Daniel Rosenberg and Susan Harding, "Introduction," in eds. Rosenberg and Harding, *Histories of the Future* (Durham, NC: Duke University Press, 2005), 4–6.

[34] Hirsch, *Empire of Nations*, 64; Peter Holquist, "'In Accord with State Interests and the People's Wishes': The Technocratic Ideology of Imperial Russia's Resettlement Administration," *Slavic Review* 69, 1 (Spring 2010): 156–157, 162, 173.

for reasons both domestic and global (discussed in Chapters 1 and 3), became Central Asia's predominant cash crop. As more and more land in Central Asia – including that traditionally used to grow food crops – was converted to cotton, cotton began to take on a logic of its own. Cotton was not the reason for Russia's conquest of Central Asia, but it became Central Asia's *raison d'être* from the point of view of the imperial metropole; that logic continued to drive Central Asia's development after the collapse of the Russian Empire (Chapter 5), and continues to drive economies in post-Soviet Central Asia today.

The process of converting as much of Central Asia's irrigated land as possible to cotton cultivation began already in the late nineteenth century and continued – indeed, accelerated – after the revolution of 1917. Even though the Soviet state explicitly rejected the imperial past, in the Soviet imagination, as in the tsarist imagination, Central Asia's potential continued to be linked with its raw cotton resources. Soviet development of the Central Asian borderlands focused on expanding the irrigated acreage under cotton (though hydropower also became an important concern in the late twentieth century).[35] The disappearance of the Aral Sea was an unintended consequence of such development schemes, but it was not unexpected. As Donald Worster has written of the American West, the logic of the irrigation age dictated that "water or any other resource should be exploited to its maximum economic potential ... It was then rational to destroy a river completely, to send it ... to another watershed altogether ... Indeed, it was *irrational* to do otherwise ..."[36] One may disagree with their choices, but engineers, entrepreneurs, peasants, and administrators from both the Slavic, as well as Central Asian populations, were rational actors, many of whom believed in the potential of both irrigation and cotton to shape a better, more modern future in the region.

Not everyone, of course, exercised the same amount of autonomy in decision-making, nor was it just Central Asia's rivers that were put to work in the service of cotton agriculture for the nation's textile industry. Russian and Soviet administrators could and did compel subject populations (with varying degrees of success) to dig canals and grow more cotton. Some peasants opted to grow cotton, as a lucrative cash crop, and some Central Asian merchants and moneylenders became quite wealthy from their role as middlemen facilitating the transport of cotton

[35] Hirsch, *Empire of Nations*, 74–75.

[36] Donald Worster, *Rivers of Empire: Water, Aridity, and the Growth of the American West* (New York: Pantheon Books, 1985), 92.

from fields and bazaars to processing factories or from lending credit to those peasants who sought to take on the risk.[37] Both Slavs and Central Asians alike agreed on the importance of expanding irrigation in the region. Increasingly, however, the logic of cotton ensured that Central Asia's inhabitants had fewer options to decide how the region's water resources were to be used.

In the Russian imaginary, the difference between the "European" and "Asiatic" parts of the empire was perceived, as it was in European metropoles toward their colonies, "as primarily civilizational" in nature; the modernization and rationalization of cotton agriculture thus played an key role in the Russian "civilizing mission" in Central Asia.[38] On the ground in the region, where Orthodox missionaries were forbidden – for fear of provoking Muslim "fanaticism" – and Slavic settlers were (theoretically) restricted, science became the means by which Russians could "convert" Central Asians to the superiority of a European lifestyle.[39] Tsarist officials and their allies envisioned Central Asians gaining new tools to become more effective farmers for the benefit of the empire: iron plows, acclimatized American cotton seeds, concrete-lined irrigation canals with steel sluice gates. Many local and regional administrators, as well as influential figures in Russian Central Asian society, believed that through successful irrigation projects, in particular, Russia could legitimize its rule in the eyes of the indigenous population. Science could demonstrate the benefits of Russian imperial rule, and it was through scientific achievements in the borderlands that Russia could prove itself to be equal to European empires.

For the most part, however, tsarist administrators found themselves hamstrung by the legislation they had created for this military borderland, in the form of provisional statutes and instructions that often lasted much longer than their drafters had originally intended. The "ignoring" of Central Asian religious institutions and practices – for fear of provoking revolt – was accompanied by only hesitant interference in practices of

[37] Stanislav Poniatovskii, *Opyt izucheniia khlopkovodstva v Turkestane i Zakaspiiskoi oblasti* (St. Petersburg: GUZiZ, 1913), 3.

[38] Adeeb Khalid, "Russian History and the Debate over Orientalism," *Kritika* 1, 4 (Fall 2000): 696.

[39] Though the multiethnic Russian Empire had included a significant Muslim population from the sixteenth century onward, by the late nineteenth century widespread discourses of Pan-Islamism and Muslim-led uprisings in the North Caucasus and neighboring Qing China led many Russians to adopt the British notion of Muslims as "fanatics," violent and unpredictable. Sahadeo, *Russian Colonial Society in Tashkent*, 300.

water management.[40] By largely devolving affairs of water management to the local level, the nineteenth-century tsarist state thus resembled the early modern Ottoman state in Egypt as described by environmental historian Alan Mikhail; in both places, administrators depended heavily on existing systems of water management, which in turn rested on customary practices developed over centuries in accordance with local conditions. In neither case was this dependence on local knowledge due to a romanticized notion of the peasantry or its abilities, but rather, in both cases it was a highly pragmatic solution.[41]

Because most agriculture in Central Asia depended on irrigation, and because Russians had little knowledge of hydraulic engineering in arid regions, whereas indigenous Central Asians had been skillfully irrigating their lands for centuries, water management was an area in which the would-be colonizers often depended on their colonial subjects. Tsarist elites chafed against such dependence, generally asserting the superiority of European science over indigenous methods of water management, even when they admired what the "natives" had accomplished. In the last years of the empire, the minimal progress in bringing the fruits of the irrigation age to the Russian Empire – in the form of engineers and large-scale hydraulic projects – led the state to begin appropriating increasing amounts of the best irrigated land in Central Asia for colonization, and promoting the growth of cotton, rather than food crops, on lands watered by existing irrigation systems. Tensions over such practices manifested themselves in a large-scale revolt across the Central Asian region (treated in Chapter 4) on the eve of the empire's collapse.

Unlike many other aspects of life which were swept away with the revolution of 1917, belief in the power of science and technology to create a more perfect society remained a central tenet of Bolshevik ideology. Marxism-Leninism itself was viewed as a scientific means to approaching human history and future development. Even if they remained wary of the new regime's political ideology, engineers trained in the tsarist era were drawn to the the Bolsheviks' "state-sponsored modernization ideology" and applied themselves to Bolshevik transformative endeavors with

[40] Turkestan's first governor-general Konstantin von Kaufman's policy of "ignoring" local customs was less about tolerance than it was an attempt to avoid provocation and uprising. See, for instance, Khalid, "Culture and Power in Colonial Turkestan," 424–425.

[41] Alan Mikhail, *Nature and Empire in Ottoman Egypt: An Environmental History* (New York: Cambridge University Press, 2011).

zeal (Chapter 5).[42] By the 1930s, according to historian Sheila Fitzpatrick, the civilizing mission returned, "as the party came to see itself not only as a political vanguard but also as a cultural one."[43] The revolutionary modernizing campaign that was Stalin's First Five-Year Plan for the development of the economy (1928–1932), taken up in Chapter 6, was a battle for enlightenment against the dark forces of backwardness. In the Central Asian borderlands, the Bolshevik sword was turned not only against the "backwardness" of rural society, but also against the twin evils of colonialism and Oriental despotism, both of which had supposedly retarded the progress of Central Asian peoples. One of the principal means of bringing the revolution to the region was modern science and technology, for with the conquest of nature, the Bolsheviks promised, would come Central Asian liberation; indeed the liberating forces of modernity and progress were the foundations of Bolshevik legitimacy.[44] Hydraulic projects to modernize Central Asian agriculture and power Central Asian villages were intended not only to legitimate the revolution internally, but also to serve as powerful models of a socialist future for colonized peoples throughout the "East."[45]

In both the tsarist and Soviet periods, settlers also were meant to play an important role in the civilizing of the Central Asian borderlands. Tsarist-era proponents of Russian colonization in Central Asia – who began in the late nineteenth and early twentieth centuries to use more frequently the term *kolonizatsiia*, rather than the more standard *pereselenie* (resettlement) – believed that Russian settlers in Central Asia would serve a civilizing function by introducing "European" culture into the region. Few of the peasants who came to the Central Asian borderlands, however, seem to have had any notion of the noble "civilizing mission" with which they had been charged. Scholars have noted that conflicts between destitute settlers on the one hand, and indigenous Central Asians on the other, heightened ethnic tensions rather than convincing Central Asians of Slavic superiority. Jeff Sahadeo, for instance, has described how

[42] Paul Josephson, *Industrialized Nature: Brute Force Technology and the Transformation of the Natural World* (Washington, DC: Island Press, 2002), 24.

[43] Sheila Fitzpatrick, *Everyday Stalinism: Ordinary Life in Extraordinary Times: Soviet Russia in the 1930s* (New York: Oxford University Press, 1999), 15–16.

[44] Slezkine, "Imperialism as the Highest Stage of Socialism," 228–229.

[45] For more on the Soviet notion of "the East" and the role it was to play there, see Masha Kirasirova, "The 'East' as a Category of Bolshevik Ideology and Comintern Administration: The Arab Section of the Communist University of the Toilers of the East," *Kritika* 18, 1 (Winter 2017): 7–34.

"poor Russians in Tashkent developed an image as a force that subverted Russian efforts to implement scientific knowledge."[46] The scarcity of water resources was one of the primary reasons tsarist colonization efforts proceeded haphazardly, leading to both conflict as well as unofficial cooperation between Slavic settlers and indigenous Central Asians (Chapter 4). Moreover, without sufficient knowledge about the region's water resources and how those could be used, the tsarist state could not proceed with an orderly program of settlement (Chapter 3).

Soviet state planners recognized the unfortunate connotations of *kolonizatsiia* with the haphazard – and sometimes violent – resettlement of the tsarist period, yet they also saw the colonization of economically strategic regions as essential for the exploitation of resources and the building of socialism.[47] As discussed in Chapter 6, many Uzbek and Tajik cotton-growers and mountaineers were encouraged, as well as forced, to colonize valleys in the border region during the early Soviet period, displacing semi-nomadic peoples in order to establish new cotton collective farms. Through the upheavals that accompanied the demise of the Russian Empire and efforts to establish Bolshevik rule, these border regions remained porous, acting as an outlet for dissatisfied groups on both sides of the border seeking freedom, whether that was Turkmen fleeing Soviet rule by moving to Persia or Afghans drawn by the promises of socialist modernity to resettle in Soviet Central Asia. By the 1930s, however, those borders were closed, leaving Central Asians with less recourse to mobility as a strategy of seeking a better future. If the Central Asian borderlands had to that point resembled "ambiguous and often-unstable realms where boundaries are also crossroads, [and] peripheries are also central places,"[48] Soviet rule of the 1930s increasingly isolated this region from a larger Central Eurasian world, making Central Asians increasingly dependent on Moscow because their needs could not be fulfilled closer to home. Deprived of the transnational labor networks between the region and China, Afghanistan, and Persia which had sustained Russian

[46] Jeff Sahadeo, "Epidemic and Empire: Ethnicity, Class and 'Civilization' in the 1892 Tashkent Cholera Riot," *Slavic Review* 64, 1 (Spring 2005): 137–138; Daniel Brower, "Kyrgyz Nomads and Russian Pioneers: Colonization and Ethnic Conflict in the Turkestan Revolt of 1916," *Jahrbücher für Geschichte Osteuropas* 44, 1 (1996): 48–49.

[47] Hirsch, *Empire of Nations*, 78, 88–92. See also *Broad Is My Native Land: Repertoires and Regimes of Migration in Russia's Twentieth Century*, eds. Lewis Siegelbaum and Leslie Page Moch (Ithaca, NY: Cornell University Press, 2014), 35.

[48] Pekka Hämäläinen and Samuel Truett, "On Borderlands," *The Journal of American History* 48, 2 (Sept. 2011): 338.

and Central Asian hydraulic engineering projects in the nineteenth and early twentieth centuries, Soviet Central Asian irrigation projects were built increasingly with coerced labor: camp labor, settlers forcibly moved from other parts of the Soviet Union, and the mobilization of hundreds of thousands of newly collectivized farm workers.

This was one of the many tragedies of a state that was supposed to be ruled by a "dictatorship of the proletariat." On Central Asian irrigation canals and in Central Asian cotton fields, the labor potential in human bodies came to be seen as just another of the region's productive forces.[49] In contrast to the weaknesses and indecision of the tsarist state in its Central Asian borderland, by the 1930s the vast mobilizational power of the Soviet state was able to surmount deficiencies in governance, scientific knowledge, and technology through force. Much like Egyptian peasants, Central Asian peasants "were increasingly treated as laboring units to be managed and manipulated by the state."[50] In this story, however, unlike the story of Egypt, it was not the commodification of water in the service of capitalism, but, ironically, the commodification of water in the service of (a version of) communism that drove the devaluation of human labor, further evidence that modernizing states in the twentieth century undertook similarly ecologically and economically unsound projects for political purposes, whether the driving ideology was colonialism, communism, or democracy.[51] The force driving the Soviet state by the end of the 1930s to transform the Central Asian borderlands was not the machine-driven high modernism described by James Scott, but a new and thoroughly modern ability to mobilize the bodies and labor of subjugated people on a mass scale to conquer nature in one of the most impressive feats of the irrigation age.[52] There would be no turning back.

SOURCES AND METHODOLOGIES

Water management remains a key issue in Central Asia today, yet the importance of water in the history of the region has until recently received little attention in studies of Central Asia under Russian and Soviet rule in

[49] In this way, too, Central Asia's story resembles that of Ottoman Egypt. See Mikhail, *Nature and Empire*, 4.

[50] Ibid., 27.

[51] John McNeill, *Something New Under the Sun: An Environmental History of the Twentieth-Century World* (New York: W.W. Norton & Co., 2000), 157–159.

[52] James Scott, *Seeing Like a State: How Certain Schemes to Improve the Human Condition Have Failed* (New Haven, CT: Yale University Press, 1998).

any language.[53] This book has benefited from conversations over many years with two German scholars, Christian Teichmann and, in particular, Julia Obertreis, whose excellent recent studies on Central Asian water management, with a primary focus on Uzbekistan, have greatly expanded our knowledge of the subject.[54] This work extends the geographical scope for the study of water management in Central Asia under Russian and Soviet rule not only to encompass the entire Aral Sea basin, including non-cotton growing regions, but it also places the history of Russian and Soviet projects for the transformation of Central Asia within a larger global history of hydraulic schemes in other arid regions of the world during what I have termed the *irrigation age* of the late nineteenth and first decades of the twentieth centuries. This work, therefore, builds on environmental histories of irrigation in places such as North Africa, Australia, and the American West, not only by adding the Russian case, but also by tracing the ways in which Russian and Soviet actors drew direct inspiration from such places and how Central Asia under Russian and Soviet rule itself served as a node of the transnational circuits of the irrigation age.[55]

Yet, there are also stories told here that are not the standard stories about irrigation and cotton cultivation in the service of empire and

[53] Although almost twenty years old, Jonathan Michael Thurman's excellent unpublished PhD dissertation ("Modes of Organization in Central Asian Irrigation: The Ferghana Valley, 1876 to Present," PhD diss., Indiana University, 1999) remains essential reading. One chapter of Alexander Morrison's comparative study of the Russians in Central Asia and the British in India is devoted to irrigation (*Russian Rule in Samarkand, 1868–1910: A Comparison with British India* [Oxford: Oxford University Press, 2008]). Akifumi Shioya has written several detailed works on Khivan irrigation in the tsarist period using vernacular documents produced by Khivan institutions, including "*Povorot* and the Khanate of Khiva: a new canal and the birth of ethnic conflict in the Khorazm oasis, 1870s–1890s," *Central Asian Survey* 33, 2 (2014): 232–245; and "Who Should Manage the Waters of the Amu Darya? Controversy over Irrigation Concessions Between Russia and Khiva, 1913–14" in ed. Paolo Sartori, *Explorations in the Social History of Modern Central Asia (19th–Early 20th Century)* (Leiden: Brill, 2013), 111–136.

[54] Christian Teichmann's study of Stalinist rule in Central Asia includes a chapter on Tajikistan (*Macht der Unordnung: Stalins Herrschaft in Zentralasien, 1920–1950* [Berlin: Hamburger Edition, 2016]); Julia Obertreis's *Imperial Desert Dreams. Cotton Growing and Irrigation in Central Asia, 1860–1991* (Göttingen: V&R Unipress, 2017) has a secondary focus on Turkmenistan. I am grateful to Julia for her generosity in sharing materials and for her comments on initial drafts of various chapters of this manuscript.

[55] In addition to the work of Alan Mikhail and Ian Tyrrell cited above, this work also draws on the work of Mark Fiege (*Irrigated Eden: The Making of an Agricultural Landscape in the American West* [Seattle: University of Washington Press, 1999]), and Jessica Teisch (*Engineering Nature: Water, Development, and the Global Spread of American Environmental Expertise* [Chapel Hill: University of North Carolina, 2011]).

global capitalism.[56] Grand Duke Nikolai Konstantinovich's attempts to irrigate the Hungry Steppe (Chapter 2), for instance, provide an alternative imperial vision of Central Asian transformation to visions emanating from Moscow or St. Petersburg, or from engineers trained in European university settings. The weakness of the tsarist state and its lack of environmental knowledge about Central Asia combined to produce a perplexing hesitancy on the part of the empire to intervene in Central Asian water management, even while it was effective in incentivizing the planting of more cotton (Chapter 3). A study of the state-sponsored irrigation project in the Chu River Valley in what is now Kyrgyzstan (Chapter 4) illustrates the ways in which the logic of cotton had reverberations beyond the cotton-growing regions alone, as well as how irrigation served as a realm for both cooperation and conflict.[57] The sometimes-utopian visions of Bolshevik hydraulic projects in the 1920s reflect the prominent role which irrigation and cotton cultivation played in the promises of the socialist future (Chapter 5), while conditions of labor on Soviet hydraulic construction projects in the 1930s illustrate the gap between such promises and the sometimes dystopian realities of life in a revolutionary "post"colonial borderland (Chapter 6).

Wherever possible, I have tried to include the perspectives, not only of state officials, but also of engineers (Russian, as well as foreign consultants) and other imperial intermediaries, as well as the voices of indigenous Central Asians contained in letters, petitions, and contracts concerning labor, land, and water use. Almost all of the archival documents I encountered, apart from rare lists of villagers or the odd untranslated memo, were written in Russian, which privileges the perspective of the colonizer. Yet even if petitions have been translated and mediated by a class of scribes, they can be read *against the grain* to understand how Central Asians negotiated empire and tested the flexibility of social estate categories, the permanence of regional boundaries, and the nature of local authority, as well as how imperial authorities responded to such requests. Central Asians cooperated with hydraulic schemes and modernizing efforts when they believed it was in their best interest; they also subverted

56 Sven Beckert's recent magisterial work only briefly touches on the Russian and Soviet cases. *Empire of Cotton: A Global History* (New York: Alfred A. Knopf, 2015).

57 Beatrice Penati has recently called for more studies of the economic history of Central Asia which do not focus solely on cotton. "Managing Rural Landscapes in Colonial Turkestan: A View from the Margins," in ed. Paolo Sartori, *Explorations in the Social History of Modern Central Asia* (Leiden: Brill, 2013), 65–110.

and resisted such attempts to transform their lives and livelihoods when it was not.

The research for this book is based on published and unpublished materials from national archives and libraries in the Russian Federation, the Republic of Kazakhstan, the Kyrgyz Republic, the Republic of Tajikistan, and the Republic of Uzbekistan, as well as archival and library collections in the United States. These materials include books and novels; newspapers, journals, and other periodicals; statistical reports; telegrams, letters, and other personal, private, and official correspondence; diaries and memoirs; scientific surveys and reports; maps; photographs; notes from the meetings of diverse government bodies, state commissions, scientific institutions, professional organizations, and congresses; contracts and petitions; reports on popular opinion; dissertations; works of poetry; and films. By looking across so many different repositories, in so many different places, I was often able to trace the movements of individual actors, from peasants to engineers to legendary figures, who sometimes showed up in the most unexpected of places. I hope you will enjoy the journey as much as I did.

1

The Land beyond the Rivers

Russians on the Amu Darya and Syr Darya

> The execution of this plan would be of altogether tremendous significance, for this waterway, penetrating the heart of Inner Asia, would be effectively a continuation and extension of the Volga. Connected to the canals which have long existed in Russia's interior, a navigable street would be created, which would begin in St. Petersburg and have its end at the feet of the Hindu Kush!
>
> – *Globus: Illustrierte Zeitschrift für Länder und Völkerkunde* (1867)[1]

In the fall of 1848, a curious story circulated among the nomadic peoples who traversed the eastern shore of Central Asia's Aral Sea. The story told of the appearance on the sea of "a high white mountain" that approached the shore and then appeared to dive under the water. In its place remained a large boat, and from this large boat issued forth a smaller one, occupied by a Russian who "rode backwards and forwards … poking black poles into the water." Word of the appearance of this strange vessel quickly reached the ear of the local ruler, the Khan of Khiva, who ordered his mounted warrior *batyrs* to command the Qaraqalpaq people growing crops in the region of the Aral Sea to immediately remove the poles and send them to him for inspection. The Qaraqalpaqs searched diligently, but the poles had disappeared. "[T]hey must have been bewitched," concluded the story.

There was, in fact, a ship sent by the Russian government in 1848 to survey the great inland body of water south of the Kazakh Steppe known,

1 "Das Verschwinden des Aralsees in Innerasien," *GB* 12 (1867) in *Turkestanskii sbornik* [*TS*] 20, 167–169: 169.

among other names, as the Aral (Island) Sea. The "white mountain" was no mountain, but rather the sail on the Russian naval vessel *Konstantin*. The small boat and black poles made up its surveying equipment, used to take soundings. The Russian in the boat was naval officer Aleksei Ivanovich Butakov, who, in addition to searching for potential harbors and sources of fresh water along the shores of the sea and its many islands, spent time investigating the mouths of the Syr Darya and Amu Darya, the two principal rivers of Central Asia, both of which drained into the Aral. He entered the Aral from the northeast via the Syr Darya. From there, he made his way to the sea's southern shore, where he explored the broad Amu Darya delta, a mercurial world of sand, water, and marshes, characterized by the dense reeds, tamarisk, and saltwort that thrive in this saline riparian environment.[2]

In Butakov's day, the most recent Russian map of the sea was a creation of the surveyor Ivan Muravin, who had visited the Aral region more than a century prior, in 1740–1741, but such a map was of doubtful utility.[3] Indeed, when Butakov returned for a second expedition in 1858, he found that many channels had shifted during the intervening years. Such shifts were the result of both natural processes and the activities of the local inhabitants. As Munis Mirab, a Khivan chronicler in the early nineteenth century, described the delta region, "The people of Aral have everywhere dug major and minor canals (*nahr u arïgh*) from this river (*su*), and engage in agriculture."[4] The result was that surveys of the "incessantly varying" branches of the Amu delta were no longer relevant even after a decade, let alone a century.[5] The sea had earned its name from the many islands (*aral*) that made up the delta, though the Khivans also called it the "Bitter Sea" (*Achïgh Tengiz*) because "its water is very salty ... although so many rivers with sweet water flow into it."[6]

To Butakov, as well as others unfamiliar with the region, the unpredictability of the physical environment around the Aral Sea was only one

[2] A. Boutakoff, trans. John Michell, "The Delta and Mouths of the Amu-Daria, or Oxus," read at the meeting of the Royal Geographical Society in London on March 11, 1867, *JRGSL* 37 (1867), 155–156.

[3] G. Maksheev, "Opisanie Aral'skogo moria," *ZIRGO* V (St. Petersburg, 1851), 30–61: 35. The German botanist Basiner published his map of the region in the same year as Butakov's expedition (Aleksej Ivanovič Butakov, *Tagebuch der Aralsee-Expedition 1848/49*, trans. and ed. Max-Rainer Uhrig [Edition Buran Zell, 2008], 40, fn 41).

[4] Shir Muhammad Mirab Munis and Muhammad Riza Mirab Agahi, *Firdaws al-iqbāl: History of Khorezm*, trans. Yuri Bregel (Leiden: Brill, 1999), 288.

[5] L. S. Berg, "Ustroistvo poverkhnosti," *Aziatskaia Rossiia* II (St. Petersburg: GUZiZ, 1914), 39. Yuri Bregel, introduction to Munis and Agahi, *Firdaws al-iqbāl*, lxiii.

[6] Munis and Agahi, *Firdaws al-iqbāl*, 342.

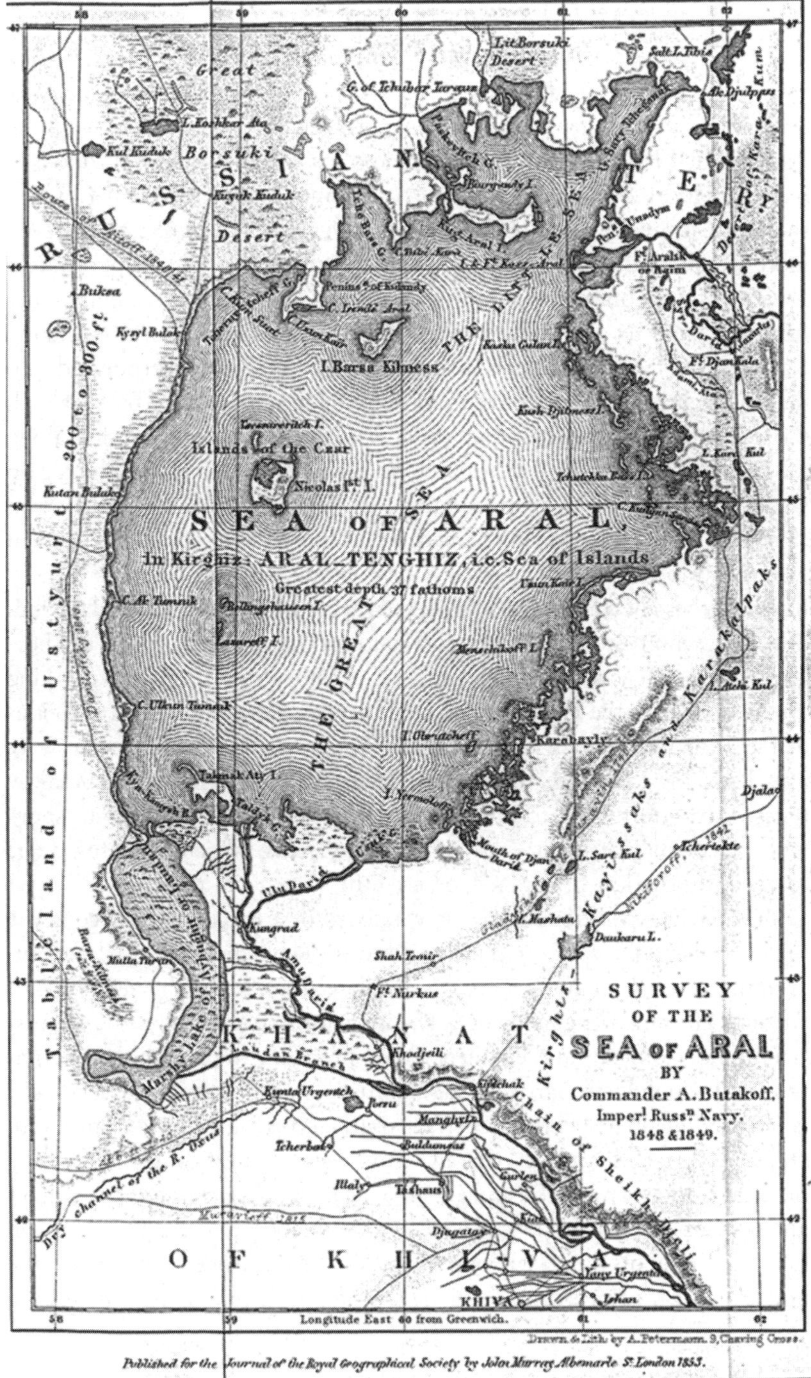

FIGURE 1.1 Butakov's map of the Aral Sea, based on his first expedition in 1848–1849, published by the Royal Geographical Society of London in 1853 to accompany "Survey of the Sea of Aral" (*JRGS* 23 [1853]) by Commander Alexey Butakoff.
Historical Maps of Russia and the Former Soviet Republics, Perry-Castañeda Library Map Collection, University of Texas at Austin.

of its many dangers. Tall forests of reeds and overgrown islands in the Amu delta concealed Caspian tigers, who occupied thickets so densely overgrown that even the light, flat-bottomed boats fashioned from wood or reeds by local fishermen could not penetrate them in summer, when shorebirds came to make their nests on the islands. To the Russians, even more fearsome than the tigers – who were known occasionally to take a cow or a sheep, but never a man – were some of the region's inhabitants.[7] Russians were to an extent familiar with the nomadic, Turkic-speaking Kazakhs, for large parts of the Kazakh Steppe had been incorporated into the empire in the eighteenth century. Butakov was even aided by a Kazakh guide. Neither did the Qaraqalpaqs engaged in fishing and hunting along the eastern shore of the Aral Sea seem to pose a great threat. But the region was also inhabited by confederations of Turkic-speaking nomads who called themselves Turkmen. Famed for their swift horses, the Turkmen were notorious in Russian circles for robbing caravans of their goods. Many of these fierce Turkmen horsemen served in the armies of the Khan of Khiva, who ruled over the region south of the Aral Sea. Aided by these Turkmen mercenaries, the Khivans, who came from a Turkic-speaking group known as the Uzbeks, managed thriving slave markets in the cities of the khanate. Though most of their captives were Persians, there were also Russians toiling in the Khivan fields. With this in mind, Butakov resisted the efforts of Turkmen nomads who tried to lure him onto shore with offers of rice, fruit, and other trade items. When he refused, he recalled, the Turkmen, enraged, entered the water with their guns.[8]

Butakov's expeditions were the vanguard of a Russian presence in the region that would not only put an end to the slave markets of Khiva but, eventually, the Khanate of Khiva itself. They also marked the beginning of Russia's sustained engagement with the waters of Central Asia, as Russian military officials and engineers, entrepreneurs and merchants, botanists and zoologists, artists and archaeologists, ethnographers and geologists, members of the imperial family and private citizens surveyed, mapped, sketched, and described Central Asia's waters, publishing many of their findings for a European audience, particularly eager for news about Central Asia, that praised Russia's cartographic achievements in filling in one of the last "blank spaces" on European maps of the nineteenth-century world.[9] Russians were not only interested in acquiring

[7] Ibid. (on birds). On tigers, see A. S. Iusupov, "Amu-dar'inskie tigry," *TV* 106 (1910) in *TS* 542, 85–86.

[8] Boutakoff, "The Delta and Mouths," 155.

[9] P. Schellwitz, "Übersicht der Russischen Landesaufnahmen bis incl. 1885," *ZGEB* 22 (1887), 479–494: 494. See also "Reise des Russischen Generalstabs-Obersten N. M.

knowledge, however; they were also interested in employing that information to utilize Central Asia's rivers for military and commercial purposes. In doing so, they soon came to realize that although the region's rivers, unlike the great rivers of northern Russia, were not ideally suited for navigation, they seemed ideally suited for irrigation.

RIVERS TO THE SEA

The appearance of Russians in the Aral Sea region in the 1840s was quickly followed by the conquest of Central Asia itself. Pushing southward its lines of fortifications in the Kazakh Steppe, in 1847 the Russian government constructed Fort Raim (today Aralsk) on the Syr Darya, just forty miles upstream from where the river emptied into the northeastern part of the Aral Sea. Besides being a point from which to conduct further exploration of the sea and neighboring Khiva, Raim lay just west of the fringes of another significant Central Asian state, the Khanate of Khoqand, and its main outpost on the lower Syr Darya, Aq Masjid (Ak Mechet). Raim, therefore, clearly signaled a new Russian presence to two of the major powers in the region.

The Russians quickly set about making this presence known, with the transportation of two ships by cart over more than nine hundred miles of the Kazakh Steppe from Orenburg to Fort Raim. The first of these two-masted ships, the *Mikhail*, was to assist the surveying of the Aral; the second, the *Nikolai*, was for a new Aral Sea fishery. A third, somewhat larger military vessel from Orenburg, the *Konstantin*, was used by Butakov for his survey of the Aral Sea in 1848 and 1849; it was this ship that had supposedly caused such a commotion among the peoples who spied it from shore. In 1850, the Russian government imported two iron steamboats from a factory in Sweden, forming the core of a new Aral Sea "flotilla," created at Butakov's initiative.[10]

Iron river steamers, as Daniel Headrick has argued, were important "tools of empire," enabling the swift expansion of a European imperial presence over a large part of the globe in the nineteenth century.[11] For the Russians, however, the steamboat was not as useful a technology of

Przewalsky von Kuldscha über den Thian-Schan an den Lob-Nor und Altyn-Tag," *Ergänzungsheft* No. 53 zu *PM* (Gotha: Justus-Perthes, 1878), iv.

10 Eugene Schuyler, *Turkistan: notes of a journey in Russian Turkistan, Khokand, Bukhara, and Kuldja*, I (London, 1876), 57; Maksheev, "Opisanie Aral'skogo moria," 37; "Aral Navy Fleet," in *The Aral Sea Encyclopedia*, eds. I. Zonn, M. Glantz, A. Kostianoy, and A. Kosarev (Berlin: Springer, 2009), 25.

11 Daniel Headrick, *Tools of Empire: Technology and European Imperialism in the Nineteenth Century* (New York: Oxford University Press, 1981).

imperial expansion in Central Asia as it was for Europeans in Africa. In 1858, for instance, Butakov and his crew found that the ship *Perovskii* was too large for the shallow waters comprising the Amu delta, where depths were sometimes no more than several feet.[12] His and subsequent expeditions attempted to take measurements of the breadth and depth of Central Asia's rivers to ensure more reliable navigation, yet these rivers seemed to change course without warning, with sandbars appearing where there had been none before, and water levels that rose and fell unpredictably. A word Russians often used to describe the Amu was "capricious"; indeed, Central Asia's rivers seemed to outside observers to be as devious and untrustworthy as its "Asiatic" inhabitants.[13] J. A. MacGahan, an American correspondent for the *New York Herald*, for instance, described the Syr Darya as "a very vagabond of a river ... [It] thinks no more of changing its course, of picking up its bed and walking off eight or ten miles with it, than does one of the Kirghiz [i.e., Kazakh nomads], who inhabit its banks."[14] Bringing Central Asia's rivers to order was thus, from the beginning, closely tied in the imperial imagination to the control of its peoples.

Large quantities of fine alluvial silt were an important cause of the seemingly temperamental nature of Central Asia's rivers. The source of Central Asia's rivers high in the mountains to the east ensured a steep and rapid initial descent, during which they acquired large amounts of sediment. Downstream in the plains, silt accumulated, causing blockages and the erosion of riverbanks, which in turn created more sediment and forced the rivers to flow in new directions; river courses might, therefore, change rapidly and often. Russian engineers remarked on the remarkably heavy sediment loads of the Amu Darya, which in recent years have been estimated to be between double and four times that of the Nile.[15] In the mid-twentieth century, it was estimated that the Amu might be the river

[12] Boutakoff, "The Delta and Mouths," 153; Schuyler, *Turkistan*, I, 57.

[13] For Russian descriptions of the caprices [*kaprizy*] and the "capricious" [*prikhotlivyi*] nature of these rivers, see, for example, N. Gavrilov, *Pereselencheskoe delo v Turkestanskom krae (oblasti Syr-Dar'inskaia, Samarkandskaia, i Ferganskaia)* (St. Petersburg: n.p., 1911), 301; "K voprosu o povorote Amu-Dar'i: Pis'mo v redaktsiiu," *M* 68 (1880) in *TS* 247, 49–57: 57; Nikolai Maev, "Topograficheskii ocherk Turkestanskogo kraia" in ed. Maev, *Russkii Turkestan: sbornik izdannyi po povodu Politekhnicheskoi vystavki*, vyp. 1 (Moscow: Universitetskaia tipografiia, 1872), 95.

[14] J. A. MacGahan, *Campaigning on the Oxus and the Fall of Khiva* (London: Sampson Low, Marston, Low, and Searle, 1874), 23.

[15] V. V. Tsinzerling, *Oroshenie na Amu-Dar'e* (Moscow: Upravlenie Vodnogo Khoziaistva Srednei Azii, 1927), 382; Igor Zonn, "Karakum Canal: Artificial River in a Desert," in Zonn and Kostianoy, *The Turkmen Lake Altyn Asyr* (Heidelberg: Springer, 2014), 98; "Amudarya" in *The Aral Sea Encyclopedia*, 14.

bearing the largest load of sediment in the world, depositing more than two hundred million tons of alluvium each year at its delta. The Syr Darya carried less silt, but also significantly less water than did the Amu, which made it even less suitable for steamship navigation.[16]

In addition to the unpredictability of silt-laden waters, other environmental challenges faced the fledgling Aral flotilla, such as the scarcity of local sources of fuel; indeed, transporting fuel became one of the flotilla's main occupations. Although Central Asia contains coal deposits, these had not yet been exploited. Instead, the ships relied on the hardy saxaul (*Haloxylon ammodendron*) plant – which thrived in the Central Asian deserts where many other plants could not maintain a foothold – or else expensive imports of anthracite coal from the Don region of what is now Ukraine. Saxaul was far from an ideal source of fuel for the steamships. Its tough wood was difficult to cut, and the resulting "crooked and knotty logs" were difficult to stow. Towing separate vessels full of fuel further hampered the progress of Russian steamships on Central Asia's rivers.[17] Saxaul, moreover, was not an efficient fuel, as it burned quickly and did not give off much heat. Because it grew slowly, Central Asian saxaul "forests" were already starting to diminish by the 1880s, when, deeming the fleet expensive and "unsuitable," the Russian government abolished the Aral Sea flotilla.[18] Yet the mere presence of Russian steamships on Central Asia's rivers carried symbolic weight, both in Central Asia and abroad. Already in 1860, the British traveler Thomas Witlam Atkinson reported that "steam has placed these States under the control of Russia, and her will must be their law."[19] By the end of that decade, the Syr

[16] Peter Sinnott, "The Physical Geography of Soviet Central Asia and the Aral Sea Problem," *Geographic Perspectives on Soviet Central Asia*, 83.

[17] Schuyler, *Turkistan*, I, 57–58; Chapter VIII in *The Russians in Central Asia: Their Occupation of the Kirghiz Steppe and the Line of the Syr-Daria: Their Political Relations with Khiva, Bokhara and Kokan: Also Descriptions of Chinese Turkestan and Dzungaria*, Capt. Valikhanof, M. Veniukof and Other Russian Travellers, trans. John and Robert Michell (London: Edward Stanton, 1865), 292–329: 328; Maev, "Topograficheskii ocherk," 95.

[18] Hugo Stumm, *Russia in Central Asia: Historical Sketch of Russia's Progress in the East up to 1873, and of the Incidents Which Led to the Campaign Against Khiva; With a Description of the Military Districts of the Caucasus, Orenburg, and Turkestan*, trans. J. W. Ozanne and Capt. H. Sachs (London: Harrison and Sons, 1885), 327; Maev, "Topograficheskii ocherk," 95–96; Nikolai Dingel'shtedt, *Opyt izucheniia irrigatsii Turkestanskogo kraia* (St. Petersburg: Min. Putei Soobshcheniia, 1893), 279; Beliavskii, *Materialy po Turkestanu*, (n.p., n.d., [St. Petersburg, 1884]), 104.

[19] Thomas Witlam Atkinson, *Travels in the Region of the Upper and Lower Amoor and the Russian Acquisitions on the Confines of India and China*, 2nd edn. (London: Hurst and Blackett, 1861), 280.

Darya was in Russian hands, and the expanse of Khoqand's influence had been reduced to the Ferghana Valley, far to the east of the Aral Sea.

The Russian government insisted on the scientific nature of imperial expeditions such as Butakov's to the Aral Sea region, yet the purportedly scientific aspects of these expeditions were inextricably entangled with political and military ones. These expeditions illuminated the topography of the region and the location of its resources, and identified points from which military campaigns could be successfully undertaken. Investigating navigability facilitated the movement of men and supplies, while the discovery of wells providing fresh water enabled the movement of troops through the desert. From a political point of view, they were useful for collecting data to fill in the blank spaces on Russian and European maps, as well as for determining borders with neighboring states, such as Persia. In 1851, the Persians sent their own scientific expedition to the Amu, with the goal of regaining Qajar control over parts of the Qara Qum and defending Persia's boundaries against potential encroachment from its neighbors.[20]

The strategic significance of ostensibly scientific expeditions was not lost on the British, who watched warily as Russian imperial troops and borders pushed ever southward, toward the oasis of Merv, only a short stage away from Herat, the "gate to India."[21] Events such as the 1853 Russian conquest of the Khoqandi fortress of Aq Masjid – quickly renamed Fort Perovskii – made it clear that Russia's intentions in the region went beyond exploration. Russian troops then rapidly achieved a series of victories that resulted in the states of Central Asia submitting to Russia with alarming speed in the 1860s and 1870s. The Emirate of Bukhara between the Amu Darya and Zarafshan Rivers was annexed as a protectorate in 1868, Khiva in 1873, and the Khanate of Khoqand lost its autonomy outright in 1876, when the Russians took over the fertile Ferghana Valley. It was unclear where this expansion would end. Frederick Fisher, a British civil servant in India, described the news in 1875 of "a [Russian] scientific exploring expedition … to 'the old bed of the Oxus' [i.e., Amu]. Instead, however, of having that innocent object,"

[20] Arash Khazeni, "Across the Black Sands and the Red: Travel Writing, Nature, and the Reclamation of the Eurasian Steppe circa 1850," *International Journal of Middle East Studies* 42, 4 (2010): 594–595.

[21] Peter Hopkirk notes wryly that while the Russians preferred the cover of the "scientific expedition," "the British preferred to send their officers, similarly engaged, on 'shooting leave', thus enabling them to be disowned if necessary" (*The Great Game: The Struggle for Empire in Central Asia* [New York: Kodansha Globe, 1994], 204).

wrote Fisher, "it turned out to be a Cossack force from Chikisliar, along the course of the Atrek, which succeeded in obtaining the submission of certain tribes in the neighborhood of that river," whom the Persians had claimed as their subjects. If Russia continued to disregard Persia's borders, Russians might soon be on the border of the British Empire itself.[22]

Many British, however, also recognized Russia's expansion into Central Asia as a sort of Manifest Destiny. Indeed, many foreign observers regarded Russia's expansion as thoroughly "natural"; in other words, to try to prevent it would be to try to counteract nature.[23] The line of the Syr Darya might have seemed a natural stopping point for Russia's southward expansion, yet just as Russian expansion into Siberia and the great Eurasian steppes in the sixteenth through eighteenth centuries had proceeded unchecked by natural obstacles, in the mid-nineteenth century there seemed nothing to prevent the Russian Empire from continuing to push its frontier farther southward. Once the Syr Darya had been wrested from Khoqand to become a "Muscovite river," it was the more southerly lying Amu that might be considered "the logical southern boundary of Russian authority," even though much of the territory on the banks of the Amu was claimed by the Khanate of Khiva and the Emirate of Bukhara.[24]

This rapid expansion into Central Asia reinforced Russian notions of the empire's special geographic destiny that had become popular following defeat in the Crimean War (1853–1856), when heightened anti-Western sentiment had given rise to a desire to define Russia as separate from Europe because of its unique historical connections with the East.[25] In 1867, the year that Russia declared the Governor-Generalship of Turkestan the newest province of the Russian Empire, centered on the formerly Khoqandi city of Tashkent, the pro-business Russian *Exchange Gazette* published an article in which the author argued that Russia's geopolitical position between Europe and Asia

22 Frederick Fisher, *Afghanistan and the Central Asian Question* (London: James Clarke, 1878), 205.

23 Chapter X in *The Russians in Central Asia*, 400, 405. W. M. Davis argued that it was the "natural" Russian expansion into Central Asia, not Siberia, that most resembled nineteenth-century American expansion ("A Summer in Turkestan," *BAGS* 36, 4 [1904]: 217–218).

24 "Das Verschwinden des Aralsees in Innerasien," 167; Richard Pierce, *Russian Central Asia, 1867–1917: A Study in Colonial Rule* (Berkeley: University of California Press, 1960), 25.

25 Vera Tolz, *Russia's Own Orient: The Politics of Identity and Oriental Studies in the Late Imperial and Early Soviet Periods* (Oxford: Oxford University Press, 2011), 8.

shaped Russia to be an ideal intermediary between the two. Believing that Russia had been "appointed by Providence" to play this mediating role, the author deplored the notion that Russia had squandered this opportunity and allowed the British to take control of Eurasian trade.[26] The Russian presence in Central Asia, according to such a perspective, would curtail British influence in the region, strengthen Russian trade, and thereby benefit the Russian Empire as a whole.

In the same year, Moscow merchant and cotton manufacturer Mikhail Alekseevich Khludov wrote to Nikolai Andreevich Kryzhanovskii, who presided over the Kazakh Steppe as Governor-General of Orenburg, with an evaluation of Central Asian markets for Russia's textile industry. Given the dangers faced by traders in the region, Khludov wrote, as well as the competition from British markets in India, the trade with Central Asia would need government protection in order to flourish.[27] Both sedentary and nomadic inhabitants of Central Asia engaged in importing foodstuffs and fabrics from their neighbors, including British India, Afghanistan, Persia, and Qing China, while goods from the Central Asian region, including livestock, circulated throughout a larger Eurasian region.[28] Russian merchants hoped to replace some of these imports to Central Asian markets with Russian goods, but caravans feared the daunting journey across the Transcaspian lands between the Aral and Caspian Seas, which, as Arash Khazeni's work on Persian expeditions to the Amu region has shown, Russians and Persians alike saw as "dangerous and frightening," waterless expanses filled with hostile Turkmen, the deserts' seemingly violent and untamed inhabitants.[29]

From the point of view of the various Turkmen tribes – who often were at odds with one another, as well as their neighbors – Russia, Persia, Bukhara, and Khiva represented powers that might be played off against

[26] "O Sibiri, kak posrednik mezhdu Rossieiu i stranami Srednei Azii," *BV* 3 (1867) in *TS* 1, 247.

[27] Cited in Muriel Joffe, "The Cotton Manufacturers in the Central Industrial Region, 1880's–1914: Merchants, Economics and Politics" (PhD diss., University of Pennsylvania, 1981), 154.

[28] Seymour Becker, *Russia's Protectorates in Central Asia: Bukhara and Khiva, 1865–1924* (Cambridge, MA: Harvard University Press, 1968), 175; M. Veniukov, "Trans-Ili and Chu Districts: Almaty, or Vernoé," in *The Russians in Central Asia*, 283–284; Khazeni, "Across the Black Sands and the Red," 604–605; Arash Khazeni, "Through an Ocean of Sand: Pastoralism and the Equestrian Culture of the Eurasian Steppe," in ed. Alan Mikhail, *Water on Sand: Environmental Histories of the Middle East and North Africa* (New York: Oxford University Press, 2013), 142.

[29] Khazeni, "Across the Black Sands and the Red," 597, 602.

one another. Like Native Americans in early modern North America, they took "advantage of occupying the lands 'in between,'" both exploiting the political rivalries between neighboring states and taking refuge across borders to escape taxation or punitive measures.[30] Though Turkmen nomads might serve the Khivan khan in the guise of military servitors or through their slave raiding, they were also known to attack Khivan fortresses, for their alliances and loyalties were not fixed.[31] The Society for the Promotion of Russian Industry and Trade lobbied for additional security for Russian caravans and the establishment of a regular port at Krasnovodsk on the eastern shore of the Caspian Sea, while hoping that the Turkmen would recognize the benefits of having Russian trade go through their land, including the opportunity to supply caravans with camels and horses. The fact that small numbers of Turkmen had asked for Russian citizenship or protection against other tribes gave Moscow merchants some hope for the feasibility of a trade route through Turkmen territory.[32]

Not all, however, were so enthusiastic about the potential for the increase of Russian trade in the Transcaspian region. The well-known Hungarian Arminius Vambery, who had spent years traveling through Central Asia, caused some furor in the Russian press when he emphatically stated that a trade route from the Russian port at Krasnovodsk on the Caspian to the Amu Darya would be impossible to realize. The Turkmen nomads would never give up their way of life, Vambery proclaimed, and it therefore made no sense for the Russians to maintain such a vital trade route through such unstable territory.[33] But because the Turkmen lands formed the only barrier between the trading oases of Central Asia and the Caspian – by means of which these goods could travel via the Volga River to central Russia and even Europe – Russian merchants were hard to dissuade.

[30] Jeremy Adelman and Stephen Aron, "From Borderlands to Borders: Empires, Nation-States, and the Peoples in between in North American History," *The American Historical Review* 104, 3 (June 1999): 816. Adrienne Lynne Edgar, *Tribal Nation: The Making of Soviet Turkmenistan* (Princeton, NJ: Princeton University Press, 2004), 20; William Wood, "The Sariq Turkmens of Merv and the Khanate of Khiva in the Early Nineteenth Century" (PhD diss., University of Indiana, 1998), 1–2.

[31] Edgar, *Tribal Nation*, 20.

[32] "Neskol'ko slov o novom torgovom puti v Sredniuiu Aziiu," *RI* 127 (1869) in *TS* 26, 109–118: 113–115.

[33] Hermann Vambery, "Die russische Handelsstrasse auf der Ostküste des Kaspischen Meeres," *AZ* 34 (extra, 1867) in *TS* 20, 209–211.

They might have been heartened by the fact that British politicians such as Sir Henry Rawlinson estimated that a reliable Russian route through the Transcaspian region was "highly probable." British business interests were not overly concerned by such a prospect, since Great Britain had the option of maintaining an overland trade route to the south of Russia, via Persia, "so that all the commerce of Asia shall not gradually be drawn to Europe through Russia, but that part ... may still be made to flow by its ancient channel of Chaldaea, Babylonia, Assyria, and Syria to the regions of the West."[34] The British also knew that the canal under construction in the Gulf of Suez would provide a great boost to maritime trade.

The construction of the Suez Canal threatened to significantly alter the contours of global trade. The trade issue that received more attention in the years of Russia's expansion into Central Asia, however, was shifts in the global cotton market. In the mid-1850s, the Crimean War struck a blow to one of the Russian Empire's growing industries, the textile industry, by cutting off large supplies of raw cotton, imported from the United States via European middlemen.[35] Just a few years later, the Northern blockade of the American South during the American Civil War caused cotton exports to Europe to plummet in a "raw materials crisis" experienced around the industrialized world as a "cotton famine."[36] Since Central Asia was another, albeit much smaller, source of Russian cotton imports, Russian attention shifted toward the region as a potential alternative supplier of raw cotton. Russians also began experimenting with developing their own sources of cotton in the Caucasus in the early 1860s.[37]

The fact that Central Asians were willing to purchase Russian cotton goods in addition to producing their own textiles meant that trade with Central Asia stimulated the Russian textile industry in two ways: by providing raw cotton for its mills and by serving as a market for the

[34] "The Sea of Aral and the Russians in Central Asia," *NMM* (1868) in *TS* 19, 363–385: 366, 370.

[35] Olive Anderson, "Economic Warfare in the Crimean War," *The Economic History Review*, New Series 14, 1 (1961): 46.

[36] Sven Beckert, "Emancipation and Empire: Reconstructing the Worldwide Web of Cotton Production in the Age of the American Civil War," *American Historical Review* 109, 5 (2004): 1406, 1410. Russians looking back on this period from the vantage point of the early twentieth century also used the language of "famine" (*golod*).

[37] Bruno Biedermann, "Die Versorgung der russischen Baumwollindustrie mit Baumwolle eigener Produktion" (PhD diss., Heidelberg University, 1907), 83.

finished product.[38] An 1869 article in the *New York Times* marveled over the rapid increase in Russia's trade with Central Asia and its detrimental effect on British trade in the region.[39] Between 1863 and the establishment of the Governor-Generalship of Turkestan in 1867, Russia's exports to Central Asia tripled, and the total value of Central Asian trade doubled, making Central Asia Russia's most important market in Asia, above China and Persia.[40] The Central Asian markets had the additional benefit of being one of the few outlets for Russian export goods, such as metal wares and tobacco, meaning that Russians could pay for Central Asian cotton with merchandise, rather than hard currency. This was a significant advantage to importing American cotton, for which Russia had been paying more than thirty million rubles annually.[41] After subjugating the Bukharan Emir in 1868, the Russians negotiated a decrease in duties on imported Russian goods in Bukhara, giving Russian textiles an edge there over those imported from Britain. By 1872, the Russian Consul in Kashgar, who had served as a commercial agent of the Ministry of Finance's Trade Department, could observe that, "Bokhara is literally filled from top to bottom with Russian cotton goods, and there seems to me to be at least six times as much of them as English goods."[42]

A GREAT EURASIAN WATERWAY

Excited by the possibility of obtaining more raw materials such as cotton from Central Asia, Russian merchants and entrepreneurs pushed for new ways to transport these materials out of Central Asia and Russian manufactured goods in. On April 28, 1869, several months after the *New York Times* marveled at the growing importance of Russia's trade with Central Asia, a Russian military officer named Aleksandr Ivanovich Glukhovskoi gave a presentation to the Society for the Promotion of Russian Industry and Trade on the importance of finding cheaper and more convenient routes for the future of Russian trade and manufactures in the region. The existing trade routes connecting the textile mills and markets of central

38 "Eine Handelsstrasse vom Kaspischen Meere nach Turkestan und die Russische Besitznahme von Krasnowodsk," *PM* 16, 2 (1870) in *TS* 20, 172–174: 172.

39 "Russia in Central Asia," *NYT* (January 27, 1869): 4.

40 "Neskol'ko slov," 109.

41 Pierce, *Russian Central Asia*, 198; "Eine Handelsstrasse," 173; "Neskol'ko slov," 111. Central Asians in turn may have traded Russian commodities for goods coming from China and India (Chapter XII, *The Russians in Central Asia*, 456–497: 464).

42 George Dobson, *Russia's Railway Advance into Central Asia* (London: W. H. Allen, 1890), 373–374; "Russia in Central Asia," *NYT*.

Russia (Moscow or Nizhnyi Novgorod) and Central Asia (Tashkent or Bukhara) took between three and five months, by way of the Volga or Kama Rivers and then overland through the steppes. In his presentation, Glukhovskoi summarized three new proposals for potential trade routes: regular steamship service on the Syr Darya, a railroad linking the Caspian and the Aral, or the opening of a new waterway from the Amu Darya.[43]

As the latter two schemes indicate, Russians were quickly coming to realize that even if regular steamship service could be established along the Syr Darya between Tashkent and the Aral Sea, the sea itself remained surrounded by arid wastes and "infested by marauding Turkmen."[44] Camel caravans between Krasnovodsk and Khiva took at least seventeen days, and often longer, while a railroad, Glukhovskoi argued, would be difficult to build in the region between the eastern shore of the Caspian and the Aral, given both the lack of wood and iron, as well as the sands of the Qara Qum desert, through which the railroad would have to be built. Glukhovskoi instead advocated the third proposal, building a canal from the Amu Darya near where it flowed into the Aral Sea to the Caspian. A waterway would allow the Russian ships sailing down the Volga to the Caspian to travel farther, via the Gulf of Krasnovodsk through the Turkmen deserts to the Khanate of Khiva, then upstream along the Amu Darya via Bukhara and overland to Tashkent, Khoqand, or even farther to Chinese Turkestan (Xinjiang).[45] Asia would, thus, be connected to Europe via Russia.

One problem an Amu–Caspian waterway could not solve, however, was the dangers of traveling through Transcaspia. Butakov had been well aware of such dangers, noting on his trip through the Amu Delta that, "three or four … [Turkmen], stationed in the bushes [above the river], might easily have shot down the whole of my party without incurring any danger themselves."[46] The potential benefits of a direct water connection, including cheap transportation costs, nevertheless seemed to outweigh the risks. An additional benefit of such a waterway was its potential use for irrigation purposes, which could turn the wasteland between the river and sea, composed of part of the Qara Qum and the Ustyurt plateau, rising steeply from the western shore of the Aral Sea, into a "fertile plain."[47]

[43] "O prolozhenii torgovykh putei v Srednei Azii," *VP*, 17 (1869) in *TS* 26: 106–108; "Neskol'ko slov," 109–111.

[44] Chapter XII, *The Russians in Central Asia*, 493.

[45] Schuyler, *Turkistan* I, 220; "O prolozhenii torgovykh putei," 106–107.

[46] Boutakoff, "The Delta and Mouths," 154.

[47] "O prolozhenii torgovykh putei," 107.

Another benefit of such a project was its prestige. A direct waterway connecting the newly acquired possessions in Russian Turkestan with the Caspian via the Amu would not only protect Russian trade in the face of increased European competition resulting from the opening of the Suez Canal, but would also help to restore ancient Central Asian trade routes linking East and West to their former glory, this time for the benefit of Russia. In the past, Glukhovskoi argued, echoing a common trope among nineteenth-century Orientalists, before the development of a maritime route between India and Europe via the Cape of Good Hope, Central Asia had held great significance in the trade between Asia and Europe. Even though Russia continued to be the beneficiary of Central Asian trade with China and India, the implication of such an argument was that the region had since entered a state of decline.[48] This sentiment was shared by Persians as well, as is evident in the lament of Riza Quli Khan, who noted in his account of the Qajar scientific expedition to the Amu in 1851 that, "Lands where settlements had once flourished ... had become a desert of sand."[49]

Writing about the history of irrigated agriculture in Turkestan, the noted Orientologist Vasilii Barthold observed that, "in this realm, perhaps more than any other, one feels the tight bond between study of the borderland's past [*proshloe kraia*] and the work being done for its future."[50] Even before the Russians took decisive control of the region, there was a sense that the building of a waterway between the Amu and the Caspian would be of benefit not only to Russia, but to the restoration of "civilization" to the region. Rawlinson believed such a waterway to be "the natural extension of civilisation," and that it "would be for the general advantage of mankind."[51] The lofty goal of restoring prosperity

[48] Ibid. Recent scholarship has demonstrated convincingly that there was a lively Eurasian trade even after the maritime Indian Ocean trade supposedly put the "Silk Road" largely out of business. Khazeni, "Across the Black Sands and the Red," 604–605; Scott C. Levi, "India, Russia and the Eighteenth-Century Transformation of the Central Asian Caravan Trade," *Journal of the Economic and Social History of the Orient* 42, 4 (1999): 519–522. Levi has argued that scholars such as V. V. Barthold were in part responsible for the persistence of such a myth of decline (ibid., 519). See also Levi, *The Rise and Fall of Khoqand: Central Asia in the Global Age, 1709–1876* (Pittsburgh, PA: University of Pittsburgh Press, 2017), 4.

[49] Quoted in Khazeni, "Across the Black Sands and the Red," 599.

[50] Vasilii Vladimirovich Barthold, *K istorii orosheniia Turkestana* (St. Petersburg: OZU GUZiZ, n.d.), 3. For more on the "new school of Orientology" to which Barthold belonged, see Tolz, *Russia's Own Orient*, 3.

[51] "The Sea of Aral and the Russians in Central Asia," 371.

was used to justify Russian intervention into a region where the indigenous rulers had supposedly squandered its potential, allowing the land to sink into decline. Though the official Russian position on an Amu–Caspian waterway was to proceed "with a view to directing the waters of the river ... to the Caspian Sea without harming meantime the economical interests of the Khanate of Khiva," Russian Colonel Nikolai Petrusevich, who took part in an expedition to the Amu in 1877, asserted that "at the current moment the fears of the Khan are hardly pertinent."[52] Another, anonymous, author wrote in the early 1870s:

> Some say that if we take away the water, we will destroy all the existing settlements in the khanate. To this I reply: Asiatic constructions are not worth a penny [*ne stoit grosha*]; it's too bad about the orchards, but for all that, by means of the new route of the Amu Darya it will be possible to settle there twice the population [...]. Even if the entire Khivan khanate is transformed into a desert, the profit gained by our merchants and our treasury by means of redirecting the Amu will far exceed the profits of the current khanate, and, in the end, all of humanity will benefit, and the inhabitants of Khiva can fashion themselves new clay nests where they are told to do so.[53]

While Russian officials continued to insist that they had no intention of taking over the Khivan khanate right up until its conquest, the idea that Khiva was an obstacle to progress and to the course of nature in the region underlay all the schemes to re-route the Amu Darya.[54]

With Khiva reduced to the status of a Russian protectorate after 1873, the opinions of the Khivans seemed of little relevance, and those of the Turkmen nomads of the region even less so. The German Hugo Stumm, who took part in the campaign against Khiva, wrote, "[W]e must in sincerity give the Russians the credit of having entered the country, not as harsh, vindictive conquerors, but as gentle mediators and true apostles of civilisation."[55] Even those who had their doubt about the potential of the Russians to serve as civilizers agreed that Central Asia under Russian rule was preferable to a self-governed Central Asia. As an article in Britain's *New Monthly Magazine* described the situation in 1869:

[52] *World's Columbian Exposition 1893 Chicago. Catalogue of the Russian Section* (St. Petersburg, 1893), No. 968, "The Expedition Organized by Imperial Order for Exploring the Ancient Beds of the River Amu-Daria between the Aral and Caspian Seas," online at: www.archive.org/stream/worldscolumbianeooruss/worldscolumbianeooruss_djvu.txt; Petrusevich, as cited in Pravilova, "River of Empire," 262.

[53] "O povorote reki Amu-Dar'i po staromu ruslu" in Maev, *Materialy dlia statistiki Turkestanskogo kraia. Ezhegodnik*, II (St. Petersburg, 1873), 24–27: 25.

[54] Pierce, *Russian Central Asia*, 179.

[55] Stumm, *Russia in Central Asia*, 236.

> Failing our power in Asia to civilise these vast countries – one of the cradles of the human race – it is unquestionably of greater advantage to a general humanity and civilisation that the Russians should bring races of bigoted, fanatic, slave-holding, predatory, and murderous propensities and practices into subjection, than that they should be for ever left to their lustful and ferocious seclusion.[56]

British hydraulic engineer Sir Colin Scott-Moncrieff, whom the Russians would invite to help develop Transcaspia, objected to the Russians' "extreme militarism," but was pleased to see that Russian rule in the region meant that "the wild Turkomans ... have settled down into respectable Russian citizens" and that the Russians were bringing "public security and order" to the region "for the good of mankind."[57] Others noted that though many nomads became "inveterate drunkards" as a "result of their contact with the Russians," it was nevertheless "gratifying to observe in these men some symptoms of civilization."[58]

As Khazeni's work demonstrates, the Persians, too, though they were ruled by the Qajars, a dynasty that "claimed the Central Eurasian steppes as part of their wild, Turanian heritage," followed the thinking of earlier Muslim geographers who placed the boundaries of civilization at the banks of the Amu River and thought of the far side (in Arabic Mā warā' al-Nahr – literally, "the other side of the river"; to the Greeks and Romans, Transoxiana – the other side of the Oxus [Amu]) as an "unsettled and unassimilated frontier." After the last Qajar expedition against Merv ended in 1860 with the enslavement of thousands of Persians, they, too, may have looked forward to the eventual Russian conquest of Khiva in 1873 and the subsequent subjugation of the Turkmen tribes following the slaughter at Göktepe in 1881.[59] Other observers felt that because the Russians were "connected by the ties of blood" to the Central Asians – an idea encapsulated in the saying, attributed to Napoleon, "Scratch a Russian, and you will find a Tartar" – they would find it easy to rule the region, unlike the British in India. Russians who believed that their people's "Asiatic" qualities made them unique among European peoples agreed.[60]

[56] "The Sea of Aral and the Russians in Central Asia," 365.

[57] Sir Colin C. Scott-Moncrieff, *The Life of Sir Colin C. Scott-Moncrieff*, ed. Mary Albright Hollings (London: John Murray, 1917), 241.

[58] *The Russians in Central Asia*, 247.

[59] Khazeni, "Across the Black Sands and the Red," 597, 600, 602, 608.

[60] Francis Henry Skrine and Edward Denison Ross, *The Heart of Asia: A History of Russian Turkestan and the Central Asian Khanates from the Earliest Times* (London: Methuen, 1899), 413; Tolz, *Russia's Own Orient*, 27; on beliefs that Russian colonization was

In addition to the political and commercial arguments for Russian intervention in Transcaspia, the arguments for a waterway connecting the Amu and the Caspian drew upon a scientific debate about the historical flow of the great river. Both Russians and Persians recorded local beliefs that the Aral and the Caspian shared a link underground; many believed, too, based on historical chronicles, that they had once shared an aboveground link as well, although it was not agreed upon when and why they had been separated. The presence of what appeared to be dry riverbeds in the lands between Aral and Caspian seemed to bear out theories that the Amu Darya had once flowed into the Caspian. Many of these theories thus hinged on what could be gleaned about the historical existence – or absence – of the Aral Sea. Whereas tenth-century Arab geographies suggested, for instance, that the Amu had already at that time flowed into the Aral, Khivan authorities in the nineteenth century asserted that the Aral had not existed at the time of Chinggis (Genghis) Khan in the early thirteenth century; according to their chronicles, the river had changed its course to flow into the Aral depression for unknown reasons around 1576.[61] Some Russians, however, were inclined to believe that the Khivans themselves had caused the Amu to flow through their lands and into the Aral, and some Khivans encouraged such ideas. Another theory was that the Amu Darya had naturally changed its course over the centuries. In any case, there seemed to be nothing unnatural about having the Amu "return" to its original bed and flow into the Caspian instead of the Aral.[62]

In 1873, inspired by the Imperial Geographical Society, Turkestan Governor-General Konstantin von Kaufman sent Glukhovskoi to investigate the Uzboi – a long, dry depression which was generally

more "tolerant" than that of other European imperialists, see Willard Sunderland, *Taming the Wild Field: Colonization and Empire on the Russian Steppe* (Ithaca, NY: Cornell University Press, 2004), 170–171.

[61] For the Persians, see Khazeni, "Across the Black Sands and the Red," 599; Maev, "Topograficheskii ocherk," 9, 113; "Amudarya," *Aral Sea Encylopedia*, 15; Ole Olufsen, *The Emir of Bokhara and his Country* (London: William Heinemann, 1911), 196–198; Khazeni, "Through an Ocean of Sand," 136; Fritz Machatschek, *Landeskunde von Russisch Turkestan* (Stuttgart: J. Engelhorns Nachf., 1921), 292–294.

[62] A theory about the desiccation of the Aral Sea was not as hopeful, however. "Zhurnal obshchego sobraniia IRGO" (April 9, 1879), *IIRGO* (1879), 143–147. Nikolai Khanikoff, *Bokhara: Its Amir and Its People*, trans. Baron Clement A. De Bode (London: James Madden, 1845), 28–34; N. I. Ivanov, *Khivinskaia ekspeditsiia, 1839–40. Ocherki i vospominaniia ochevidtsa* (St. Petersburg: Tip. T-va "Obshchestvennaia pol'za," 1873), 17; Mikhail I. Ivanin, *Khiva i reka Amu-Dar'ia* (St. Petersburg: Tip. T-va "Obshchestvennaia pol'za," 1873), 16.

believed to be the original bed of the Amu Darya – and other dry channels in the region.[63] Glukhovskoi's expedition concluded that the riverbeds had not long been dry, and that the channeling of the waters of the Amu in a different direction was the recent result of dams built by the Khivans. One explanation for his observation might have been recent efforts by the Khivan khan to deprive disloyal Turkmen of water in the years following disastrous clashes with various Turkmen groups in 1855 that had killed three successive Khivan khans.[64] Damming and diverting canals (which often merely took advantage of pre-existing dry channels in the landscape of the Amu basin) and getting a great river to flow in a different direction, however, were two entirely different things, as indeed some were quick to point out.

Military cartographer and engineer Colonel Ieronim Stebnitskii, who had traveled to the Turkmen regions in 1872, disagreed with Glukhovskoi's conclusions that the dry river beds had recently carried water. Though he agreed that "there is no doubt that a large river once flowed through the channel," based on meteorological observations and the aridity of the local atmosphere, he concluded that even if it were possible to redirect the Amu into its former bed, the likelihood of seepage and evaporation made it unlikely that the river could flow seven hundred *versts* through the old bed without any additional inflow. Nor did he see evidence of the kinds of ruins in the desert upon which travelers were so fond of remarking.[65]

Undeterred, and with the prospect of surveying work made easier by the final conquest of Khiva, proponents of an Amu–Caspian waterway among Russia's merchants, scientists, and elite society advocated a shorter route between Amu and Caspian than the Uzboi, such as by way of existing canals dug by the Khivans – the Lawzan, Polvan-ata, or Abbas Canals. Some pointed out that existing canals over a thousand versts in length did not lose excessive water to seepage and evaporation.[66] In 1878, flooding on the Amu caused Khivan dams on the Kunia Darya and the Lawzan Canal to burst, which resulted in the flowing of water from the Amu Darya into the Saryqamysh depression, in the direction

63 A. L. Kun, "Poezdka po khivinskomu khanstvu v 1873 g.," *IIRGO* X, 1 (1874) in *TS* 83, 184–189: 184.

64 Shioya, "*Povorot* and the Khanate of Khiva," 233–234.

65 "O povorote reki Amu Dar'i po staromu ruslu," 24 ; "Colonel Stebnitzky's Report on his Journey in 1872 in Central and Southern Turkomania. Summarised and translated from the Russian by E. Delmar Morgan, FRGS," *JRGSL* 44 (1874): 217–227: 218, 220.

66 "O povorote reki Amu Dar'i po staromu ruslu," 24–25.

of the Caspian Sea.[67] This convinced many that the "return" of the Amu to the Caspian was natural and inevitable.

One of the most ardent proponents of this idea was the Russian Grand Duke Nikolai Konstantinovich Romanov. The Grand Duke, whose first visit to the region was as the head of the Volynskii regiment in the Russian Army's campaign against Khiva, was captivated by the idea that the Amu could be made to flow into the Caspian. In this conviction, he felt connected to his ancestor Peter the Great, whose ill-fated expedition to the region under Prince Bekovich-Cherkasskii in 1717 had among its aims the exploration of the Amu Darya and the possibilities of making it flow into the Caspian. According to rumors that had reached Peter's court, clever Khivans had built dams to divert the waters of the Amu to the Aral Sea instead of the Caspian as a way of concealing gold deposits.[68] Before Bekovich-Cherkasskii could prove or disprove the rumors of water diversions and hidden gold, however, his expedition had been killed by forces of the Khivan khan.

The desire to realize Peter the Great's visions appealed to many Russians. The author of an article on the subject, for instance, wrote, "What Peter the Great decreed for Russia should be executed," while veterans of the campaigns against Khiva believed that the realization of "the Great Tsar's plan would bring immeasurable results."[69] But Nikolai's sense of connection to Peter was a particularly deep one. He returned to Khiva on several occasions in an attempt to bring to fruition his ancestor's dream, coming to see it, sentimentally, as his "holy duty." The starry-eyed Grand Duke imagined "mighty steamships on an American model" plying the entire length of the great river, as it flowed from the Pamir Mountains along the northern border of Afghanistan, all the way to the Aral Sea – and beyond.[70]

Beginning in 1877, Nikolai Konstantinovich began to devote himself to the question of "returning" the Amu Darya to the Uzboi, gathering all available material from Russian scientific expeditions, published histories, and oral histories. In 1879, he founded a society in Samara to study possible transportation routes through Central Asia.[71] Though he sketched out other plans to make the Russian people, "in accordance

[67] Pravilova, "River of Empire," 263. [68] Ibid., 261.
[69] "O povorote reki Amu Dar'i po staromu ruslu," 25; Ivanin, *Khiva i reka Amu-Dar'ia*, 16; Ivanov, *Khivinskaia ekspeditsiia, 1839–40*, 17.
[70] RGIA f. 435, op. 1, d. 57, l. 106; GARF f. 1155, op. 1, d. 2461, ll. 2; 4; 7–7ob.
[71] GARF f. 1155, op. 1, d. 2461, l. 2.

with the cherished dream of Peter the Great ... the mediator in the exchange of riches of East and West," such as a grand "Indo-European railway" linking Lisbon to Calcutta via Moscow, Nikolai's main interest was water.[72] Though he was unsuccessful in his appeal to Governor-General Kaufman for support, Nikolai still managed to gather for two expeditions to Khiva and the Amu some of the foremost scientists and Turkestan experts, including, on the second expedition in 1879, the geologist Ivan Mushketov and Nikolai Maev, secretary of the Turkestan statistical committee, who was chosen by the Imperial Russian Geographical Society in response to Nikolai's invitation to the society to take part in his expedition.[73] In Nikolai's mind, it was not the opening of new maritime routes that had led to Central Asian decline, but rather one "startling, unparalleled event." As he put it:

> The mighty river [i.e., the Amu] ceased to flow into the Caspian, was shortened by a thousand versts, and emptied into the Aral. Since that time, an enormous, waterless desert, cross-cut by the dry bed of the great river, has cut Asia off from Europe.[74]

The restoration of the Amu river to its "natural" course was to revive this ancient overland trade and reconnect Asia and Europe through Russia.

Deeply impressed with the ability of Central Asians to manipulate water, the Grand Duke became convinced "that the Amu Darya left the Uzboi at the will of the Khorezmians [Khivans], who were artfully able to utilize the natural peculiarities of their capricious [*prikhotlivaia*] river." He requested the opportunity to travel through the Khivan khanate to the Uzboi, as well as access to any old books that might describe the historic flow of the Amu Darya. For his investigation of the Uzboi, the Grand Duke exploited his connections as a relative of the "White Tsar" (that is, Alexander II) to obtain influential Bukharan officials to safeguard the expedition along the Amu.

On arrival in Khiva, the Grand Duke earnestly questioned as many Khivan officials and Turkmen elders as he could, "in order to know the opinion of the natives about the turn of the Amu to the Uzboi." To his frustration, he was not able to immediately get a straightforward

[72] For sketches of an Indo-European, as well as a Central Asian, railroad, see RGIA f. 426, op. 1, d. 35, ll. 6–8.

[73] GARF f. 1155, op. 1, d. 2461, l. 20b; "Zhurnaly zasedaniia Soveta IRGO," *IIRGO* (1879), 121 (March 7, 1879), 133 (March 17, 1879). Pravilova, "River of Empire," 265.

[74] GARF f. 1155, op. 1, d. 2461, ll. 3–30b.

answer about the history of the Uzboi. He recorded that in answering "questions about the reasons for the deviation of the Amu from west to north and about the significance of the dams obstructing the sacred bed, the Khivan dignitaries were unclear, inconsistent, evasive and reluctant."[75] They claimed that the river might change course over a day and that any change in its flow was the will of Allah, a game of the forces of nature, something in which humans had taken no part.[76] Since this was not the answer Nikolai wanted to hear, he was disinclined to believe it, and decided that only an audience with the khan himself would give him the information he needed. When at last the khan agreed to meet the Grand Duke at the Uzboi, Nikolai presented him with a reproduction of a portrait of Peter the Great painted in 1717, the same year in which Bekovich-Cherkasskii embarked on his fateful mission to the region.[77] Though not an official diplomatic representative of the Russian Empire, the Grand Duke perhaps hoped to use the gift to symbolize a new era in Russian–Khivan relations.

The Grand Duke was not the only Russian who believed that the khan himself was the key to the Uzboi. Colonel Petrusevich, too, believed that the main obstacle to redirecting the Amu was the khan, who blocked the flow of the river to restrict the Turkmen from access to water as a means of keeping them in check.[78] Khivan subject Khudai Bergen seemed to confirm this idea when, according to the Russians, he claimed that the khan would not allow water from the Amu to flow into its old bed for fear of the Turkmen; water was the only thing that would keep them subjugated to his rule.[79] The willingness of many Turkmen to help the Grand Duke convince the Khan of Khiva to destroy dams on the Lawzan Canal may have been a simple ruse to get water to once again flow through their land.

[75] Ibid., ll. 50b-9.

[76] An early-nineteenth century Khivan chronicler, for instance, described the "untameable" Amu and "how, by divine predestination, the dams on the Chumanay and the Changlï-Basu collapsed." Munis and Agahi, *Firdaws al-iqbāl*, 292.

[77] GARF f. 1155, op. 1, d. 2461, ll. 80b-9.

[78] Pravilova, "River of Empire," 262. See also "Melkie izvestiia: Ekspeditsiia dlia issledovaniia Sredne-aziiatskoi zheleznoi dorogi," *IIRGO* 15 (1879), 289.

[79] GARF f. 1155, op. 1, d. 2461, ll. 90b-10. For an early-nineteenth-century description of the Khivan khan damming rivers "to punish the seditious," see Munis and Agahi, *Firdaws al-iqbāl*, 288. In 1819, the Khan of Khiva seems to have dammed the Lawzan, after which "ambassadors of the Teke of Merv and of the Sarïq tribe came <to the court> expressing their submission" (ibid., 480). It was dammed again in 1857 to deprive "the rebellious Turkmens" of water (Shioya, "*Povorot* and the Khanate of Khiva," 233–234).

A similar suspicion is evident in a report from a man named Zhukov who had been hired as an assistant by the Grand Duke. Zhukov wrote:

> [I]n accordance with your order for me to journey to [the] Sarakamysh [depression] to measure the water ... it was necessary to verify all of the tales of the Turkmen ... [T]hey talked a lot about the left[-bank] dry beds, but do they exist in reality, regarding the existence of the bed it is visible from the map by Colonel Petrusevich, but could they possibly and did they actually construct such a mass of dams for directing water to Bala-Ishem, perhaps the Turkmen just wanted to have fresh water from the Darya ... at the time of the journeys of Petrusevich and others, perhaps the Turkmen just did not want to point out the main route of water to the Caspian[,] it is desirable to verify all of this.[80]

Though he did not, perhaps, express them very eloquently, Zhukov put voice to the doubts of many Russians, especially those who, in their guise as colonizers and civilizers, maintained a deep distrust for the "natives." Zhukov suspected that the Turkmen had concocted stories about the Khivan redirection of the flow of the Amu so that the Russians would draw the waters of the Amu away from the Khivans and send them flowing in the direction of the lands of the Turkmen.

In the end, in spite of considerable scientific, governmental, and popular interest, no official plan to realize the Amu–Caspian waterway was undertaken in the nineteenth century, though the idea of connecting the Amu and the Caspian continued to garner attention in the Russian and foreign press into the 1890s. As Henry Lansdell, an English clergyman, was jokingly told on his trip through Central Asia in 1885, "When you come to pay us your next visit, and the Oxus [i.e., Amu] is open, you will be able to take your ticket from London Bridge to Petro-Aleksandrovsk, in the heart of Asia, and come all the way by water!"[81]

The results of an expedition organized under the auspices of the Imperial Ministry of Ways of Communication, commanded once more by Glukhovskoi, and officially "affirm[ing] ... the possibility of directing the waters of the river Amu Darya to the Caspian sea," were displayed in the Russian section at the World's Fair in Chicago in 1893. The exhibit on the "Expedition organized by Imperial Order for exploring the ancient beds of the river Amu-Darya between the Aral and Caspian seas" contained maps of the delta and what appeared to be the ancient beds of the Amu, drafts of two potential routes to link Amu and Caspian, and

[80] RGIA f. 435, op. 1, d. 57, l. 106.

[81] Henry Lansdell, *Russian Central Asia Including Kuldja, Bokhara and Merv*, II (London: Sampson Low, Marston, Searle, and Livingston, 1885), 206.

photographs of the region.[82] By the 1890s, however, new railway projects in the region likely obviated the immediate need for such a waterway. The Trans-Caspian (Central Asian) line linked the Caspian to Charjui on the Amu Darya by the end of 1886 and extended to Bukhara and Samarkand by 1888. By 1898, rails connected the Caspian to Tashkent and the Ferghana Valley. Tashkent was connected to the Trans-Siberian railway linking Moscow and the Far East by a route across the steppes via Orenburg in 1906. But the idea for a great inland waterway did not disappear altogether; indeed, it would find a new lease on life several decades later in the imaginations of Soviet engineers.[83]

CUSTOMARY WATER USE

Before railroads, waterways had historically served the function of Russia's highways. Yet as Russian experiences in Central Asia quickly taught them, rivers in an arid region served a much greater purpose than their function as transportation arteries. Like the Khivan khan who sought to control Turkmen nomads by controlling their access to water, Russian forces had quickly subjugated the Emir of Bukhara by taking control of the headwaters of the Zarafshan River.[84] In the years that followed, the Bukharan emir himself – or his chief minister, the Kush-begi – had to write to the Russian governor of the Zarafshan *okrug* (region) about matters of water supply, which frustrated officials such as Ahmad-i Donish, who noted that Russian control of the water supply resulted in drastic changes to Bukharan agriculture and out-migration of Bukharans to Russian lands along the Syr Darya. Donish lamented that anyone petitioning for more water would have to wait so long that, when he finally received permission, he might as well throw the paper to the wind, since the emir would not decide questions of water until the river was already completely dry.[85]

Travelers to the Bukharan region in the early twentieth century remarked on the number of large canals – perhaps as many as one hundred – diverting water from the Zarafshan River.[86] Such canals were

[82] *World's Columbian Exposition 1893 ...*, 438–439.

[83] This theme is taken up again in Chapter 5.

[84] Morrison, *Russian Rule in Samarkand*, 202.

[85] Akhmad Donish, *Puteshestvie iz Bukhary v Peterburg*, revised and expanded 2nd edn. (Dushanbe: Irfon, 1976), 234, 239.

[86] Annette Meakin, *In Russian Turkestan: A Garden of Asia and its People* (London: George Allen, 1903), 14; Khanikoff, *Bokhara*, 40.

a vital feature of the habitable landscapes of Central Asia, where arable land was divided into two categories – that which could be watered by rain, and that which required irrigation. The first category was known as *lalmi* or *bahari* (from *bahar*, the Persian word for spring).[87] Bahari often referred specifically to the crop grown, rather than the land itself, since spring crops, such as wheat, millet, and barley, were the crops grown on rainfed land. The second kind of land – far more prevalent in the region – was known as *obi*, from the Persian word for water.[88] Because *obi* lands required more moisture than the available rainfall, indigenous Central Asians had over centuries worked out complex systems for the distribution of the region's water resources. These irrigation systems took advantage of the snowmelt from the vast glaciers in the mountainous regions of the Aral Sea basin, which in hot, dry summer months brought precious water into the steppes and deserts and then through irrigation canals into fields for cultivation. In fact, the very features of Central Asia's rivers that made them difficult for navigation – steep grades on their upper and middle reaches and high quantities of silt – made them suitable for irrigation, since steep grades made gravity-fed irrigation canals possible, while the silt itself made excellent fertilizer.[89]

Although irrigation was an element crucial to settled life throughout the region – and, to a lesser extent, the "semi-nomadic" lives of Turkmen, Qaraqalpaqs, and others – the sources for understanding water use in Central Asia on the eve of the Russian conquest and in the years that followed are less prevalent than one might expect. Russians who wished to understand local systems of water distribution, for instance, found that much local knowledge was transmitted orally; there were few written documents explaining customary water use, either at the level of the locality or at the level of the state. Even in the Khanate of Khiva, where two early-nineteenth-century chroniclers held the important post of canal

[87] Russians most often used *bogara*, the Russified version of *bahari*, but indigenous sources used the term *lalmi* (Penati, "Managing Rural Landscapes," 69 fn 10).

[88] Schuyler noted that the term *teremai*, like *bahari*, could be used either to refer to autumn crops or those crops which were grown on *obi* lands, or else to refer to the lands themselves. (*Turkistan,* I, 285–86; 288 fn 1). The root *ter-* is related to picking and harvesting. See also the distinction between *ak* (white) and *kok* (green) *teremai* crops mentioned by M. I. Brodovskii, "Zametki o zemledelii v Samarkandskom raione," *Russkii Turkestan. Sbornik izdannyi po povodu Politekhnicheskoi vystavki*, vyp. 2, ed. V. N. Trotskii (Moscow: Universitetskaia tipografiia, 1872), 259.

[89] Evgenii Evgenievich Skorniakov, "Iskusstvennoe oroshenie v Aziatskoi Rossii," *Aziatskaia Rossiia* (St. Petersburg: Pereselencheskoe upravlenie GUZiZ, 1914), II, 225; Sinnott, "The Physical Geography of Soviet Central Asia," 81.

overseer (*mirab*), little space in the official histories is devoted to the specifics of hydraulic engineering.[90] Even the best Russian sources often lack the kinds of details that might allow us to reconstruct indigenous irrigation systems with any kind of precision. Vasilii Barthold's *Toward a History of Irrigation in Turkestan*, for instance, which drew on the Khivan chronicles, along with other available sources in the region, explicitly avoids any discussion of matters requiring specific hydrological and technical knowledge.[91]

From another perspective, however, the lack of detailed sources explaining customary water use is not so surprising, given that water use in Turkestan, as Alan Mikhail has argued for Ottoman Egypt, "was an intensely local process."[92] While there were documents (*vasiqa*) enumerating special rights to water granted by the khans to individuals and communities, such documents were the exception, rather than the rule; on most systems, the water rights of users were at least partially renegotiated and redistributed on an annual basis according to well-established and understood local customs. In the late 1880s, state councilor Nikolai Dingel′shtedt, assistant to the military governor of Turkestan's Syr Darya region, sought to collect information from notables about such water-use customs. When he asked for documentation, he received the perplexed response from a Kazakh that, as every Kazakh community knew its spring or its irrigation channels, what use could there be for paper?[93]

From the existing descriptions it is clear that indigenous Turkestanis had sophisticated methods of agricultural water management that took into account: the water needs of different-sized plots of land planted with different crops; how to share water among different users on the same system, including upstream and downstream users; how to get water from places where it was abundant to places where there was little; how to bring water from highland areas to lowland areas, and vice versa; how to prevent evaporation; how to utilize reserves of groundwater; how to

[90] Barthold, *K istorii orosheniia*, 22–25; Munis and Agahi, *Firdaws al-iqbāl.*

[91] Barthold, *K istorii orosheniia*, 5. Other important Russian sources are the essay on irrigation by engineer Skorniakov in *Aziatskaia Rossiia*; Nikolai Dingel′shtedt's volume on irrigation in Syr Darya region (*Opyt izucheniia irrigatsiia Turkestanskogo kraia* [1893]); and the volume on irrigation of Count Konstantin Pahlen's report on conditions in Turkestan province in 1908–1909 (*Oroshenie v Turkestane*, vol. 9 of *Otchet po revizii Turkestanskogo kraia, proizvedennoi po Vysochaishemu poveleniiu* [St. Petersburg: Senatskaia tip., 1910]).

[92] Alan Mikhail, "An Irrigated Empire: The View from Ottoman Fayyum," *International Journal of Middle East Studies* 42 (2010): 570.

[93] Dingel′shtedt, *Opyt izucheniia irrigatsii*, 132.

deal with associated effects of irrigation such as soil salinization; and other issues. Water was also used to power mills (*tegirmon*) to process wheat, rice, and other grains. By using words such as "primitive" and "incorrect" to describe these systems, Russian accounts have obscured many of the complex and ingenious technologies and techniques developed by Central Asians to deal with water. Russian engineer Vladimir Tsinzerling was a rare exception when he pointed out that, "In spite of their seeming primitiveness, native irrigation is quite a complex apparatus, composed of many and very delicate parts, connected in all aspects with the surrounding nature, including soil, climate and the hydrological peculiarities of Turkestan, as well as the system of agriculture, its economy, and the lifeways of the population."[94]

In order to bring water to obi fields, Central Asians constructed canal systems consisting of channels that diminished in size as they brought water from the main source – usually a river – to individual fields. Terms such as *nahr*, the Arabic word for river, were used for some of the largest and most impressive canals, blurring the distinction between man-made watercourses and natural features of the landscape.[95] (Russians, on the other hand, preferred to make clear the distinction between "natural" channels in the landscape and irrigation canals; indeed, irrigation was often referred to as "artificial" irrigation [*iskusstvennoe oroshenie*].) Branching off of the main canal were a number of smaller feeder canals. Farmers then dug small channels from these feeder canals to their own fields. Efforts were made to construct canals and channels so that the water level was higher than the surface level of the field, allowing water to flow into the field by gravity.[96] When not being used to water the fields, small channels were "usually sealed off at one end by a diminutive dam of mud."[97] There were few permanent dams on the rivers or headworks installed to regulate the flow of water into the canals systems; in order to get water to flow into a particular channel, indigenous Turkestanis built temporary weirs of stones, wood, brush, and reeds.

94 Tsinzerling, *Oroshenie na Amu-Dar'e*, 558.

95 For a description of the ways in which "ingenuity and nature" could not be separated along the complex irrigation systems of precolonial Egypt, see Timothy Mitchell, *The Rule of Experts: Egypt, Techno-Politics, Modernity* (Berkeley, CA: University of California Press, 2002), 35.

96 V. Samolevskii, "Iz Tashkenta," *ZG*, 50 (1878) in *TS* 240, 23–27: 27.

97 Konstantin K. Pahlen, *Mission to Turkestan: Being the Memoirs of Count K. K. Pahlen, 1908–1909* (New York: Oxford University Press, 1964), 89.

Foreign observers had to admit that, though seemingly primitive in comparison with European engineering, such irrigation methods yielded results that were most often more than sufficient for their purposes. Both American traveler Eugene Schuyler and Russian explorer Alexander von Middendorf remarked on the impressive engineering skills of the indigenous population, given their "most elementary knowledge of hydraulics" and lack of scientific instruments.[98] In describing the way Central Asians planned a new canal, travelers Francis Skrine and Edward Ross wrote that a "surveyor lies prone upon his back in the direction from which he wishes to bring water, looks over his forehead, and notes the point when ground is last seen." In her description of such a practice, British travel writer Annette Meakin tried to clarify this process for her readers, noting, "If he can see it with his head in that position he knows that the water will flow to it." Skrine and Ross concluded that, "This rude substitute for the theodolite [a portable surveying instrument used in triangulation] involves a great deal of misplaced labour," but "its results are as marvellous as those of the Egyptian irrigation department."[99]

On existing canal systems, chosen and elected officials helped to oversee the distribution of water, deciding, for instance, when and for how long a farmer might bring water to his fields. With the help of these officials, water users on a given system cooperated to ensure the maintenance of the system and the correct distribution of water. In both settled and semi-nomadic regions where agriculture was practiced, village communities – usually several villages together – elected individuals to oversee the water on side canals. These overseers, known as mirabs – from the Persian *mir-e ab*, "ruler of the water" – regulated both water distribution and canal maintenance, which was carried out on an annual basis by the water users themselves. Above the mirabs were the *mirab-bashi* or *ariq aqsaqals* – elected or appointed "head mirabs" or "canal elders" – who were responsible for the maintenance of the main canal and the functioning of the irrigation system as a whole.[100] Farmers themselves were responsible for the maintenance of the smallest channels.

98 Schuyler, *Turkistan*, I, 289; A. F. Middendorf, *Ocherki Ferganskoi doliny* (St. Petersburg: Tip. Imp. Akad. Nauk, 1882), 165.

99 Meakin, *In Russian Turkestan*, 12–13. Skrine and Ross, *The Heart of Asia*, 360–361. E. R. Barts describes the same method of determining gradient, but does not accord it the same praise (*Oroshenie v doline reki Murgaba i Murgabskoe Gosudarevo imenie* [St. Petersburg: Tip. uchilishcha glukhonemykh, 1910], 137).

100 Dingel′shtedt suggests that the term *ariq-aqsaqal* came to replace *mirab-bashi* under the Russians (*Opyt izucheniia irrigatsii*, 191 fn 1; 218).

Since all users had a stake in the system, the maintenance of canals at every level was in every user's best interest. In places such as the fertile Ferghana Valley, as well as regions where water was lacking – in other words, where water distribution was a particularly complex task – water users on a system rewarded the mirab-bashi for good performance. This reward, called *kipsen*, might be the amount of grain the official could carry away in his *khalat* (robe), or else an amount considered appropriate by the water-using community.[101] Jonathan Michael Thurman has described this system as it was practiced in the Ferghana Valley under Khoqand as one of "charter and sanction," since, theoretically, communities of water users could protect themselves against abuses of power by withholding kipsen to punish overseers who were not doing their jobs properly.[102]

Determining how water was to be apportioned at any given time was a complex decision, based on the amount of water in the canal – usually estimated by observation of water levels – the number of fields watered by the canal, and what kinds of crops were being planted there. The mirab-bashi was in charge of determining annually which land could be used and which should lie fallow. The number of pairs of draft animals (*qo'sh*) owned by each villager determined the amount of land he was entitled to use. In some regions, such as along the Syr Darya, the term qo'sh referred not only to the pair of animals, but to the amount of land they could plow in one day.[103] Villagers with no animals of their own could work for a wealthy man who owned several draft pairs. Immediately before the time came for plowing the fields, the mirab-bashi would go to the villages in his jurisdiction and announce that all who wished to cultivate land that year should gather at an appointed place and time, together with their draft animals.[104] The number of draft pairs present at such meetings determined how many plots of land would be delineated in that cycle. As in the case of the Russian *mir*, the redistribution of land annually took into account losses of members of the community to death or changes in

[101] This practice was becoming more monetized under the Russians. Ibid., 192, 218, 253; Pahlen, *Oroshenie*, 170.

[102] Thurman, "Modes of Organization," 46–51.

[103] Pahlen makes this observation among the "Kirgiz" (he uses the term *kos*) (*Oroshenie*, 46).

[104] Lev F. Kostenko, *Turkestanskii Krai: Opyt Voenno-statisticheskogo voennogo okruga. Materialy dlia geografii i statistiki Rossii*, III (St. Petersburg: A. Transhel', 1880), 11.

households due to recent marriages.[105] Plots were roughly equal in size and quality, and assignment was by lottery; tokens belonging to planters were distributed at random across the plots to determine the assignments.[106] There was no set pattern of crop rotation, though farmers tended to follow certain patterns of alternating crops that could be planted and harvested in different seasons, while conventional wisdom taught that fields should be allowed to lie fallow after the harvest of crops such as tobacco.[107] Typical crops were wheat, barley, sorghum, cotton, rice, millet, soybeans, corn, alfalfa, vegetables such as pumpkin, and fruits such as grapes and melons. How much of each crop was grown depended on the suitability of the region's soil, climate, and water resources, as well as the tastes of its inhabitants.[108]

Canal overseers were responsible for making sure that water reached the correct fields at the necessary times. Particularly on canals where the volume of water was limited – or at certain times of year when less water was available on a given system – the sequence of water distribution became an important decision. Water distribution was often allotted in periods of time, rather than particular volumes of water: shifts during the day or, more rarely, night; whole days; or even periods of multiple days. This then simplified the process of creating a sequence of water users, since each group of water users knew which time had been allotted to them for taking water from the canals. Dingel′shtedt, based on his interviews of irrigation officials in Syr Darya, described the process of determining the order of water distribution as taking place, like land distribution, by lottery. In one community, for instance, the mirab-bashi divided the water users into groups and then had the groups draw lots to determine the order of water sharing. In another community in the Tashkent region, earthen mounds were marked with symbols representing particular days of water use. Each group of water users submitted a *tiubeteika*, the skullcap typically worn in the region, which were then

[105] Adrienne Edgar, "Genealogy, Class, and 'Tribal Policy' in Soviet Turkmenistan, 1924–1934," *Slavic Review* 60, 2 (Summer 2001): 274.

[106] Kostenko, *Turkestanskii Krai*, III, 13.

[107] Khanikoff, *Bokhara*, 189; Schuyler, *Turkistan*, I, 289–290; Brodovskii, "Zametki o zemledelii v Samarkandskom raione," 236–238.

[108] See, for instance, the discussion of food in chapter 5, "Occupations and Food" in Vladimir Nalivkin and Maria Nalivkina, *Muslim Women of the Fergana Valley: A 19th-Century Ethnography from Central Asia*, ed. Marianne Kamp (Bloomington: Indiana University Press, 2016), 103–119.

individually placed at random on each mound, indicating which group would receive the right to irrigate on which days.[109]

Count Konstantin Pahlen, who inspected Turkestan Province in 1908 and 1909, later recalled the process by which a group of villagers in Ferghana made sure water flowed to their fields at the appropriate time. In his recollection, a group of about fifty men rode in from a distant village, bearing "large bundles of twigs and reeds." About twenty men waded into the icy waters of the Kara Darya near the Kampyr-Ravat Dam with the bundles and weighted them down with stones passed by men on the bank. As sand, gravel, and sediment caught in the crevices of the bundles, the whole began to act as a dam, and the water began to be diverted toward the dry channel that led to their village. At last, "the aryk [channel] was opened with a blow of the *ketmen* [iron hoe] and the waters gushed into the canal." As Pahlen remembered it, the village had been allotted six hours, after which time the dam was removed, again with the help of the ketmen.[110] According to construction engineer E. R. Barts, the time allotted for water diversion was measured at night by the movement of the stars and during the day by "simple sun clocks" or water clocks.[111]

Since some crops required specially controlled types of irrigation, canal overseers were also responsible for making sure that every field received water at the correct intervals and in the correct quantities for the crops being grown. The Dane Ole Olufsen, on his journey on the Amu Darya, noted that "the natives have exact rules which prescribe how often the soil on which each species of grain is to be grown should be irrigated."[112] Schuyler noted that fields planted with alfalfa and other grains requiring water to be evenly distributed were divided into small squares, separated by borders of earth, several inches in height.[113] These individual squares could be filled with water by temporarily cutting an opening in the low earthen walls and allowing water to flow in, or by opening up a wooden pipe in the wall. The small wall would then be closed up again and the

[109] Dingel'shtedt, *Opyt izucheniia irrigatsii*, 234–236.

[110] Pahlen, *Mission to Turkestan*, 90.

[111] Barts, *Oroshenie v doline r. Murgaba*, 138. For an early-nineteenth-century description of making such fascines, see Munis and Agahi, *Firdaws al-iqbāl*, 288–289. Other devices used where water flow was particularly high due to a steep grade of the river were three- and four-legged frames known as *sipa* and *char-pay*, respectively. C. E. Bosworth and M. S. Asimov, eds., *History of Civilizations of Central Asia*, IV, 2 (Paris: UNESCO, 2000), 301. Skorniakov, "Iskusstvennoe oroshenie v Aziiatskoi Rossii," 229–30.

[112] Olufsen, *The Emir of Bokhara and His Country*, 179.

[113] Schuyler, *Turkistan*, I, 289.

water allowed to flow into a neighboring square, while the water in the first square slowly soaked into the soil.[114] The cultivation of rice, which required submersion in water for periods of several days, and therefore used three to four times more water than other crops, was limited.[115] In the Murghab Oasis in Transcaspia, for instance, rice was grown only in small quantities and was watered only after other grains.[116] In the Tashkent region, rice was grown only on low, swampy land in the Chirchiq and Angren Valleys. The Bukharan emirs, too, limited where rice was planted along the Zarafshan, a process that was disrupted when the Russians took control of the river's source.[117] As a rule, rice could not be planted near the heads of irrigation canals because it deprived downstream water users of their fair share of water. By growing rice in downstream areas already waterlogged from canal runoff, fewer inputs of water were required.[118]

In addition to regulating land use and water distribution, the other of the canal overseers' main tasks was to organize an annual cleaning of the canals. When reed fascines of the type described by Pahlen were placed in a channel, they collected large amounts of silt and debris; over the annual cycle, this material built up in the irrigation canals and had to be removed in order for the canal to keep working properly. In preparation for cleaning, water users worked together after the harvest to dam up the canals for the winter. Over the season of low water, the canals dried out, facilitating the cleaning process in the early spring in preparation for the planting season. The largest canals had water in them all year, but by winter the water level was so low that feeder canals were kept dry until spring. In the early spring, accumulated silt and sand could be removed from the feeder canals and used to build up their banks, protecting the fields from flooding and the banks from erosion in seasons of high water.[119]

Every water-using household had a duty to participate in the cleaning of the canal system, as part of a system of corvée labor known as *hashar*, in which members of a community engaged in generally unpaid collective work on public works projects. Workers were usually required to furnish their own tools and food. Veteran of the Turkestan campaigns General Mikhail Ivanin records that in Khiva, some sent paid workers in their

114 Meakin also describes this process (*In Russian Turkestan*, 16–17).

115 Thurman, "Modes of Organization," 71.

116 Barts, *Oroshenie v doline r. Murgaba*, 124.

117 Khanikoff, *Bokhara*, 190.

118 Thurman, "Modes of Organization," 71.

119 Kostenko, *Turkestanskii Krai*, III, 12.

place. In this region, canal maintenance, known as *qazu*, lasted about two weeks.[120] It was the job of the mirabs to make sure that villages furnished the correct amount of requisitioned labor and that everyone did their part. By means of this system, no one got water for free – instead, each community "paid" for its water by paying the salaries of the local mirabs and contributing to the hashar.

One of the main Russian critiques of such indigenous irrigation systems was the vast amount of physical labor they required throughout the year, from cleaning the canals to realizing water distribution. Moreover, the process of digging canals without the use of scientific instruments, Russians observed, resulted in gradients that were too steep and canals which were not straight. The water in these canals eroded the unreinforced banks of the canal and might cause flooding, particularly when vast quantities of meltwater descended from the glaciers in the late spring and summer. Nor did Central Asians seemed concerned by the question of drainage.[121] Military statistician Lev Kostenko, who wrote several important volumes on Russian Turkestan, noted that water did not disappear from an irrigation system, but returned through a different set of channels to a "central reservoir."[122] According to Pahlen, at the ends of irrigation systems in Ferghana water drained onto low-lying ground and formed swamps – thus "marshy depressions … are found in the vicinity of practically every village."[123] In Transcaspia, Barts noted that sometimes the Teke Turkmen even built new canals beginning from such swamps.[124]

Besides waterlogging from undrained runoff water, salinization of the land was another peril of "artificial" irrigation. Throughout Central Asia, the brackish quality of water and the large saline lakes – Issyk Kul, Balkhash, the Aral, the Caspian – testified to the presence of soluble salts in the environment. Like soils in other arid regions, the saline nature of Central Asian soils requires careful attention to the amounts of water added to the fields through irrigation, which draws soluble salts up

120 Ivanin, *Khiva i reka Amu-Dar'ia*, 31; Yuri Bregel, fn 607 in Munis and Agahi, *Firdaws al-iqbāl*, 609. In Samarkand, hashar on canal maintenance lasted on average eight days (Morrison, *Russian Rule in Samarkand*, 218).

121 Barts, *Oroshenie v doline r. Murgaba*, 139. Parts of Ferghana may have served as an exception – see the descriptions of a closed drainage tunnel in R. S. Igamberdyev and A. A. Razzakov, *Istoriia melioratsii v Uzbekistane (na materialakh Golodnoi stepi)* (Tashkent: Izd. FAN, 1978), 29–30.

122 Kostenko, *Turkestanskii Krai*, III, 3.

123 Pahlen, *Mission to Turkestan*, 92.

124 Barts, *Oroshenie v doline r. Murgaba*, 139–140.

through the topsoil to the surface, limiting plants' ability to absorb nutrients and water and, thus, inhibiting growth; throughout Turkestan, white patches indicated where the soil had become so salinized that it could no longer successfully grow crops. In Khiva, one solution used by farmers was to simply rake the salt off the top layer of the soil. Another common practice was to flood the entire field, in the hopes of leaching salts out of the soil; this method, however, risked merely transferring some of the salt to neighboring plots.[125] Oversaturation of the soil can also result in waterlogging and a raising of the groundwater table. On the whole, however, in spite of these challenges, many crops grew quite well in the loess soils of Central Asia with the aid of irrigation. One European observer, perhaps reluctant to give credit to the sophistication of the local irrigation techniques, claimed that "experience here has revealed the very unexpected fact that corn [i.e., grain] grows even better in saline soil than on ordinary alluvial ground!"[126]

Besides surface canals, Central Asians also employed two innovative water transportation technologies adapted to arid environments and found across a wider Afro-Eurasian region: the *chigir* and the *karez*. The chigir, a water wheel used most frequently in the Khorezm oasis (Khiva), is said to have originated in Persia. Similar water wheels are found in Egypt and North India.[127] The wooden chigir wheel was equipped with a number of bucket-like scoops or jars, made of wood or, more often, clay, attached to the outer rim. When draft animals or water turned another wheel, connected by interlocking teeth to the main wheel, the scoops retrieved water from a low-lying channel and brought it through a pipe to the desired location. Where the wheel was not powered directly by the current of the river, it drew water from a depression created specifically for the chigir, which in turn collected water from a canal; the depth of the water in the depression was carefully controlled in order to ensure the smooth working of the canal and delivery of the

[125] Ivanin, *Khiva i reka Amu-Dar'ia*, 43.

[126] Ch. VIII, *The Russians in Central Asia*, 308.

[127] Even some nomads used such water wheels (Brodovskii, "Zametki o zemledelii v Samarkandskom raione," 233). The chigir was known as *charkh palak* in Tashkent and the Ferghana Valley. Bosworth and Asimov, eds., *History of Civilizations of Central Asia*, 301. Other names for the *chigir* are *dulab* (Persia); *saqiya* (Egypt, North India); and *charkh-i abkashi (North India)*. Mikhail, *Nature and Empire*, 174 fn 8. Iqtidar Husain Siddiqui, "Water Works and Irrigation System in India during Pre-Mughal Times," *Journal of the Economic and Social History of the Orient* 29, 1 (1986): 65, 66 fn 51.

FIGURE 1.2 Chigir.
Reproduced with permission from the Willard L. Gorton Papers, Hoover Institution Archives, Stanford, CA.

proper amount of water. The chigir could also be used to remove excess water, bringing it to higher land with less water.[128]

Across the landscapes of Eurasia and North Africa, the water wheel served as a constant reminder of what a precious resource water was. A fourteenth-century Persian manuscript describes a Shaikh in Delhi who went into a state of ecstasy upon hearing the sound of the water wheel turning, together with the "melodious ... voice of the cultivator" telling his animals to speed up their labor.[129] In the early twentieth century, Count Pahlen, recalling a landscape "very reminiscent of Egypt," remembered that in Khiva the "same shrill sound of unoiled cogs [i.e., the

[128] Igamberdiev and Razzakov, *Istoriia melioratsii*, 29. Schuyler mentions a scoop as an alternative to the water wheel (*Turkistan*, I, 289), while Curzon similarly mentions a "Bokharan counterpart to the ... *shadoof*" (*Russia in Central Asia in 1889 and the Anglo-Russian Question* [London: Longmans, Green, and Co., 1889], 145), as does Henri Moser (*L'irrigation en Asie Centrale* [Paris, Société d'Éditions Scientifiques, 1894], 267–268).

[129] Siddiqui, "Water Works and Irrigation in India," 65.

turning chigir] proclaims the presence of water from afar."[130] Olufsen noted that the creaking of such water wheels was "the most typical sound heard along the canal."[131]

A less noticeable but more impressive technology that for centuries has made ingenious use of scarce hydraulic resources in arid lands is the *karez*. Like the chigir, underground systems similar to the karez are widespread; they can be found throughout the arid zone from Western China to Mesopotamia to northern Africa. Consisting of a number of borehole wells, connected by a subterranean channel, the purpose of the karez is both to take advantage of groundwater – that is, water existing below the surface of the earth – as well as to preserve water from evaporation into the dry air above the surface of the earth, since the longer a surface canal, the more water will be lost to evaporation between its head and the fields or municipal water reserves that are its endpoint. The borehole wells provided access and air to the workers who maintained them. Karez systems are constructed on a gradient so that water naturally flows to its end destination; in addition to tapping into groundwater, the karez might bring runoff water from the mountains to the plains. While average karez passages in Central Asia were between two-thirds of a mile and two-and-two-thirds miles long, one particularly notable one near Ghazni in Afghanistan was said to be thirty miles long.[132] Skrine and Ross noted "stupendous" ancient works in the region of Samarkand, with wells as deep as 420 feet, "connected by a tunnel in which a man can walk upright."[133] Most karez in Russian Central Asia, however, were in the Transcaspian region, where Persian masters were hired to construct such massive works.

Russians complained that such endeavors as building a karez were difficult and expensive, and prone to drying up or collapsing without warning, yet they recognized the technology's suitability for Turkestan. Noting the "unexpectedly propitious results" of karez irrigation, Dingel′shtedt believed that "quite solid [karez] projects" would be carried out, if only the money were available.[134] In 1894, the Russian

[130] Pahlen, *Mission to Turkestan*, 163.

[131] Olufsen, *The Emir of Bokhara and his Country*, 192.

[132] Barts, *Oroshenie v doline r. Murgaba*, 123; Fisher, *Afghanistan*, 55.

[133] Skrine and Ross, *Heart of Asia*, 406 fn 3. According to Barts, the tunnel of the average karez was just big enough to allow a person to work underground (*Oroshenie v doline r. Murgaba*, 123).

[134] N. Dingel′shtedt, "Pol′zovanie vodoiu po obychaiu," *TV* 16–18 (1887) in *TS* 461, 54–75: 64.

government did in fact undertake the construction of one of the ten karez in the immediate surroundings of Ashgabat in Transcaspia.[135] Historically, however, karez systems had been financed by private individuals, rather than the state.[136] The karez and the water it contained were then considered the property of the person or community that excavated it; the rights to use them were hereditary, an unusual occurrence in Central Asia, where water rights in general were neither owned, nor bought and sold – though there were certainly exceptions to this rule – and communities of water users collectively "owned" the water on a given irrigation system.[137]

IRRIGATING RUSSIAN TURKESTAN

In the early 1890s, Dingel′shtedt wrote, "Learning about the past fate of this now Russian land, the reader cannot help pondering the future of this land, which is in the process of drying up, dying – a land of thirst and scorching heat – a land craving moisture, craving irrigation."[138] In the first two decades of rule over the Governor-Generalship of Turkestan, other Russian administrators, too, had come to recognize the importance of Central Asia's waters not only for navigation and trade, but also for irrigated agriculture. Since Turkestani subjects were already using the irrigated lands of the region for agriculture, tsarist officials recognized the importance of expanding irrigation for the development of the province into a lucrative part of the empire, yet their first forays into water administration were tentative. Of Turkestan's early rulers, the first governor-general, Konstantin von Kaufman, was the boldest in his interventions, but had little success. In 1872, Kaufman approved plans to bring water from the Syr Darya to the region between the provincial capital at Tashkent and Jizzakh, along the newly established Russian postal road to Samarkand.[139] Called Betpaq-dala by local Kazakh

135 L. I. Tsimbalenko, *Kiarizy (vodoprovody) Zakaspiiskoi oblasti* (St. Petersburg: Izd. OZU, 1896), 50.

136 Barthold, *K istorii orosheniia*, 7.

137 For Ottoman Egypt as a comparative case, see Mikhail, *Nature and Empire*, 10–12; Skrine and Ross, *Heart of Asia*, 333. Wells and springs were occasionally private property as well. Pahlen, *Oroshenie*, 90. Pahlen reported many instances of selling water without land. Ibid., 54.

138 Dingel′shtedt, *Opyt izucheniia irrigatsii*, 2.

139 *Golodnaia Step′, 1867–1917: Istoriia kraia v dokumentakh* [*GS*] (Moscow: Izd. "Nauka," 1981), Doc. 3: 12.

nomads – *betpaq* being a word used to describe an inhospitable or largely uninhabited steppe region – this region had earned the nickname "Golodnaia step′" (Hungry Steppe) from Russians who had to cross its vast expanses.[140] Traces of ancient canals suggested that in the past the Hungry Steppe had not been as "hungry" and that irrigation could restore the past fertility of the region, creating new possibilities for agriculture as well as, eventually, settlement.[141] In 1874, the year on which construction of a new Hungry Steppe canal began, the first Russian canal-building project in Turkestan, a feeder canal from the Chirchiq into the Russian part of Tashkent, failed dismally after six years under construction.[142]

Kaufman's Hungry Steppe canal was never completed – indeed, the Hungry Steppe, true to its fearsome name, proved a formidable foe for decades to come. The money allotted to the canal project was spent on instruments and technical oversight, rather than the workers themselves, who were expected to carry out the construction of the canal as part of their "duty-in-kind," or *natural′naia povinnost′*, a Russian institution that officials in Turkestan identified with the indigenous institution of the hashar.[143] In the first year of construction, records show almost forty thousand workers from Tashkent and the surrounding districts coming for stints of between two and four weeks, while another almost thirty thousand came from neighboring Khojand *uezd*.[144] Dingel′shtedt referred to the cooptation of labor for this project as "a clear violation, not only of custom, but also of the Russian law."[145] According to one account of unknown provenance, local Central Asians called it the "pig canal" (*tonguz/to'ng 'iz ariq*).[146] Since the pig is an unclean animal for Muslims, this epithet indicates the lack of local enthusiasm for Kaufman's project.

The Russians were more successful in restoring a number of canals – such as the Zakh-ariq, an eighty-five-verst canal built by the

140 There is another "Betpaq Dala" in present-day Kazakhstan, to the north of Tashkent and west of Lake Balkhash. On the adjective *betpaq*, see Virginia Martin's note in *Law and Custom in the Steppe: The Kazakhs of the Middle Horde and Russian Colonialism in the Nineteenth Century* (Richmond, UK: Routledge Curzon, 2001), 172, note 4.

141 *GS*, Doc. 3: 12; Doc. 5: 15; Doc. 10: 28.

142 On the Chirchiq Canal, see Sahadeo, *Russian Colonial Society in Tashkent*, 87–88; on Kaufman's canal, see *GS*, Doc. 10: 25.

143 *Natural′naia povinnost′* in the form of labor service existed in Russia until 1917. Yanni Kotsonis, *States of Obligation: Taxes and Citizenship in the Russian Empire and Early Soviet Republic* (Toronto: University of Toronto, 2014), 285–286.

144 *GS*, Doc. 10: 25, 30–31.

145 Dingel′shtedt, *Opyt izucheniia irrigatsii*, 243.

146 Morrison, *Russian Rule in Samarkand*, 232.

Khoqandis in the Tashkent region – than they were in bringing water to new lands.[147] However, like Kaufman, they ignored the fact that local custom usually involved engaging those workers who had a vested interest in the irrigation system; the Russian administration, in contrast, often brought in workers from outside the irrigation region, using the indigenous administration to requisition laborers, with fines for those who did not appear.[148] Mikhail Grigor′evich Cherniaev, Turkestan's second governor-general (1882–84), turned his attention to what appeared to be an old bed of the Yangi Darya near Fort Perovskii on the Syr Darya. When he, too, tried to use unpaid corvée labor to direct water into this dry channel, the result was the flooding of an extensive swath of nearby Kazakh fields, which the *Turkestan Gazette* blamed on the "incompetent" use of "Kazakh hands, without the supervision and directives of technicians."[149] In 1887, again using corvée labor, the next governor-general, Nikolai Ottonovich von Rozenbakh (1884–89), built an eponymous canal, the Rozenbakh Ariq, in the fertile Ferghana Valley, but this, too, ultimately proved to be a failure.[150]

The largest project undertaken by the Russian administration in Turkestan before the turn of the twentieth century was upstream from the Merv Oasis in Transcaspia, using water from the Murghab River. The choice of the Merv region was logical, since irrigation, with the aid of the large Sultan-Bend Dam (Bend-i Sultan – *bend* or *band* meaning dam in Persian) – one of the only permanent dams in the region – had supported the development of agriculture there over many centuries; by restoring the dam, it was believed, this former prosperity could easily be restored. The name "Sultan" is usually associated with Sultan Sanjar, the Seljuk ruler of Khorasan who reconstructed an existing dam in the twelfth century, helping Merv to thrive as a flourishing center of trade, industry, and culture.[151] In more recent memory, Bukharans had destroyed the dam in 1784; it appears that the dam was successfully rebuilt between 1832 and 1838, probably on the initiative of a Khivan official at a spot somewhat lower on the Murghab.[152] The last destruction of Sultan-Bend occurred in 1847, when it was destroyed by the Khan of Khiva to thwart

147 Kostenko, *Turkestanskii Krai*, III, 4.

148 Dingel′shtedt, *Opyt izucheniia irrigatsii*, 243.

149 Dingel′shtedt, "Pol′zovanie vodoiu po obychaiu," 64 fn 2 [by editor].

150 Thurman, "Modes of Organization," 101.

151 Wood, "The Sariq Turkmens," 3; Svat Soucek, *A History of Inner Asia* (New York: Cambridge University Press, 2000), 96.

152 Wood, "The Sariq Turkmens," 154–155.

Salar and Sariq Turkmen; the Merv Oasis consequently declined in economic importance.[153] Before the Russians took Merv in 1884, Teke Turkmen, recent arrivals in the region, used fascine dams to irrigate nearby fields using the waters of the Murghab.[154]

The Imperial Murghab Estate, proclaimed in August 1887 by an imperial *ukase* of Alexander III, was situated on a triangular area of about 104,000 *desiatinas* on the right bank of the Murghab River in the newly proclaimed Transcaspian region of Central Asia along the newly constructed Central Asian (Trans-Caspian) Railway line. The estate was to serve as a model plantation for experimentation with seeds and modern agricultural techniques and thereby to "plant culture among the native population."[155] The Russian government enthusiastically embarked upon this scheme even though Russian officials did not know which lands in the region might be most suitable for cultivation using irrigation water from the Murghab, nor how much water was already being used by local Turkmen or across the border in Afghanistan, where the Murghab River had its source.

The Russian government initially entrusted the work to a Polish civil engineer, Jan J. Poklewski-Koziell (Poklevskii-Kozel), who had worked for a time in France. According to Pahlen's later recollections, in a chance audience with the tsar, Poklewski-Koziell had captured the monarch's imagination with his tales of the past glory of the Merv Oasis and the subsequent destruction of the Sultan Dam by a nephew of the fearsome Tamerlane (Amir Timur), as well as his promises that the glory of Merv could with little trouble be resurrected.[156] In the hopes of building the most advanced dam of its day, the government also recruited the British head of the Irrigation Department in Egypt, Sir Colin Scott-Moncrieff, to consult on the dam. Scott-Moncrieff submitted an advisory report to the Russians, but confided to his fiancée, "I don't think my opinion has been worth very much to them."[157] Poklewski-Koziell did his best to work with local conditions – constructing a series of several dams instead of a high dam that a foundation of loess soil could not support, as well as making his own bricks and hydraulic lime – but his initial attempt failed before construction of the reservoirs was even completed, much to the

[153] Barthold, *K istorii orosheniia*, 70. [154] Barts, *Oroshenie v doline r. Murgaba*, xi.

[155] Ibid., 13, Appendix One; John Whitman, "Turkestan Cotton in Imperial Russia," *American Slavic and East European Review* 15, 2 (April 1956): 195.

[156] Pahlen, *Mission to Turkestan*, 146.

[157] Scott-Moncrieff, *The Life of Sir Colin C. Scott-Moncrieff*, 257.

chagrin of the Russian administration, which had spent considerable money on the project.[158] A new dam, the Hindu Kush, was completed by Russian engineers in 1897. This dam created a large reservoir (later supplemented by additional reservoirs) and, using machinery imported from Budapest, channeled water to generate power to light the estate and run equipment for cotton processing.[159]

MUDDIED WATERS

The case of Bukhara had already demonstrated how, as the tsarist government consolidated its control over its new Central Asian possessions, existing water-sharing agreements were often disrupted. At the Murghab Estate, the fact that those involved with the project had little understanding of previously existing water-sharing customs in the region led to tension with the local Turkmen. In the fall of 1890, the head of the Transcaspian region reported to St. Petersburg that the Turkmen already used all the water in the river (according to local custom), leaving none for the estate.[160] At the same time, the Turkmen complained about the "abundant" utilization of water within the estate by the Russians.[161]

In an effort to learn more about Turkestan's water resources, as well as to assert Russian control over those resources, Governor-General Kaufman had created a position of head irrigator in the Zarafshan region already in 1872, followed by a set of "Temporary Rules for Water Use" in 1877. Zarafshan's head of irrigation was to make a list of existing canals and which villages drew water from them, as the first steps toward mapping irrigation in the region. He was also instructed to record different types of soil and crops being grown.[162] The "temporary rules" of 1877 applied to Tashkent and the surrounding regions. According to these new rules, instead of the four mirab-bashis and their teams of mirabs who had overseen water distribution in Tashkent, all rights to water distribution in the city and surrounding region now belonged to the Russian

158 Barts, *Oroshenie v doline r. Murgaba*, 39; "Irrigatsionnyi otdel na Turkestanskoi sel'sko-khoziaistvennoi vystavke," *TV* 200–201 (1909) in *TS* 513, 175–178: 178; Pahlen, *Mission to Turkestan*, 147; A. P. Davis, "Irrigation on the Royal Murghab Estate, Turkestan, Russia," *EN* 67, 14 (April 4, 1912): 621.

159 Davis, "Irrigation on the Royal Murghab Estate," 622–623.

160 Scott-Moncrieff, *The Life of Sir Colin C. Scott-Moncrieff*, 242–243.

161 Barts, *Oroshenie v doline r. Murgaba*, 141.

162 "Irrigatsionnaia sistema reki Zeravshana," 44; Morrison, *Russian Rule in Samarkand*, 210.

government, to be overseen by an official Russian irrigator. Kaufman also created positions to oversee irrigation in Samarkand and Ferghana.[163] His successor, Cherniaev, not only judged these interventions as "not fulfilling their purpose," but deemed them "an unhelpful brake on the population"; he therefore abolished the positions of head irrigator and did away with the provision that Tashkent's water belonged to the Russian government. He also decreed that ariq aqsaqals (mirab-bashis) in the Tashkent region be chosen by the people, not by the administration. In undoing Kaufman's interventions, Cherniaev claimed to be "conforming to local conditions and centuries of custom."[164]

Not everyone approved of Cherniaev's move. In 1885, his successor, Rozenbakh, brought back Kaufman's head irrigator, and over the following years further posts were created for a small irrigation administration in Turkestan. Yet the rights to water were not returned to the Russian government. In 1886, under Rozenbakh, the new statute for governing Turkestan confirmed, in a single line in Article 256, that "water in the main ariqs, streams, rivers, and lakes is made available to the population for use according to custom." Without detailed knowledge of the region's land and water resources, retaining the indigenous hierarchy of canal overseers – albeit nominally under the authority of new regional irrigation "technicians" – to oversee water distribution and irrigation maintenance seemed the most prudent strategy. The reliance on custom, however, left the Russian government's role in the management of land and water resources uncertain, since land had little value without water, and Central Asian custom gave the rights of land use to the person who could bring water to that land.

In 1887, the year the new Turkestan Statute went into effect, Dingel′shtedt posed the question which would vex Russian officials in Turkestan for years to come: "[H]ow can we resolve disputes over water according to custom if *the custom [itself] is not known*?"[165] With the assumption that Central Asian water-sharing customs – based on sharia law – must be equivalent to rigid, universally applicable, unchanging traditions, Russians set out to precisely delineate "custom." They complained about the seeming imprecision with which Central Asians regarded the distribution of precious water resources, apparently yet

[163] N. Petrov, *Ob irrigatsii v Turkestanskom krae* (Tashkent: S. I. Petukhov, 1894), 124.
[164] A. I. Dobrosmyslov, *Tashkent v proshlom i nastoiashchem* (Tashkent: O. A. Portsev, 1912) in *TS* 590, 163–164.
[165] Emphasis in the original. RGIA f. 426, op. 1, d. 19, l. 34; Pahlen, *Oroshenie*, 47–48.

another instance of the general tendency of indigenous Central Asian officials to give average figures, rather than gathering accurate scientific data about their realms.[166] In 1902, the head of irrigation in Semireche complained that the "natives" were superstitious about giving correct data, for fear of bringing misfortune upon themselves.[167] Across Central Asia, both sedentary and nomadic peoples seemed content to measure "by sight" the water necessary for their fields. As many outsiders observed despairingly, even the Bukharan emirs could only report that water was "high," "average," or "low."[168] Because officials struggled to obtain the necessary information, they often felt helpless to intervene in local affairs, and thus allowed many existing arrangements to continue and indigenous authorities to make any necessary interventions. When it came to understanding water use, they were wholly dependent on ariq aqsaqals to enlighten them as to what local custom actually entailed. As Alexander Morrison has pointed out, "this left the door wide open to extensive corruption."[169] But in their ideas about both the fixity, as well as the imprecision of local irrigation practices, Russians often missed the fact that custom was, in fact, flexible and tailored to local conditions, even as those conditions changed.

Russians hoped that the introduction of official technical oversight over Central Asian water management at the regional level would be followed by the introduction of European scientific tools, systems of measurement, and engineering methods, in order to construct canals that accorded better with what Russians thought a civilized landscape should look like. Descriptions of Central Asian canals as "tortuous" and "arbitrary," in contrast to the idealized landscapes of Europe – where rivers resembled canals, rather than the other way around – ignored the fact, however, that everywhere engineers seek to use local topographies to their advantage, and very rarely do executed projects exactly replicate the lines in the draftsman's planning book.[170] Nor did the issue in 1888 of a new set of instructions for irrigation officials in Turkestan bring the desired improvements or information about customary water management. The

[166] Pahlen, *Oroshenie*, 39; Schuyler, *Turkistan*, I, 293, On the imprecision of "Bokhariot" statistics, see also Lansdell, *Russian Central Asia*, 39.
[167] TsGA RK f. I-19, op. 1, d. 111, l. 87.
[168] Schuyler, *Turkistan*, I, 288; Morrison, *Russian Rule in Samarkand*, 207–208; "Irrigatsionnaia sistema reki Zeravshana," *GL* 166 (June 1875) in *TS* 152, 40–48: 41.
[169] Morrison, *Russian Rule in Samarkand*, 206, 226. See also Moser, *L'irrigation*, 251–252; Pahlen, *Oroshenie*, 26, 31.
[170] Barts, *Oroshenie v doline r. Murgaba*, 137; Fiege, *Irrigated Eden*, 12, 19, 22.

Irrigation Instruction required ariq aqsaqals – appointed by the Russian administration in accordance with Article 107 of the new Turkestan Statute – to write down detailed information in journals, including changes in water level on the irrigation system, as well as the number of workers and amounts of material requisitioned for canal repairs. They were also required to provide to the district head (*uezdnyi nachal'nik*) on an annual basis two copies of detailed descriptions of their systems, including an approximation of irrigated acreage and crops grown. District heads could reject unclear or incomplete descriptions and demand corrected copies; one final copy was to be forwarded to the official head of irrigation in the region. The new regulations expected district heads to make sure ariq aqsaqals and mirabs fulfilled their jobs correctly and reported accurately the conditions of the irrigation systems under their command.[171] Lack of Russian language skills, however, as well as the failure of Turkestani measurements of water to translate easily into numbers which Russian officials could recognize, hampered such efforts.[172] By the turn of the twentieth century, Russian officials still had only the most rudimentary knowledge of Central Asian water management, and – like the indigenous rulers whom they had criticized – could only provide the most approximate figures regarding the region's water resources.[173]

CONCLUSION

From the mid-nineteenth century, the Russian Empire rapidly expanded its frontier southward, first by sending out purportedly scientific missions that collected important political, military, and commercial information about the Aral Sea basin, then by annexing outright the lands that lay between the Syr and Amu Rivers. Central Asia's waterways were key both to Russian reconnaissance of the region as well as its ability to subjugate cities and states to Russian imperial power. Water was also key to Russian visions of a glorious future for its new province of Turkestan, rooted in ideas about the region's glorious past: a great Eurasian

171 "Instruktsiia o pravakh i obiazannostiakh irrigatsionnykh chinov, uezdnykh nachal'nikov, aryk-aksakalov i mirabov po zavedyvaniiu irrigatsieiu v Turkestanskom krae," Appendix 1 in Dingel'shtedt, *Opyt izucheniia Turkestanskogo kraia*, 301–305.

172 For more on indigenous water measurements, see Chapter 3.

173 When Count Pahlen conducted his inspection of Turkestan Province in 1908–1909, he reported a lack of irrigation maps, statistics, and information about how much water was necessary or available. *Oroshenie*. 195–196.

waterway could restore trade routes and boost Russia's international prestige, and the water of Central Asia's rivers could be used to reclaim lost lands from the desert and transform the province into the most fertile corner of the Russian Empire. The Russian administration's feeble effort to assert some control over the process had few, if any, positive effects on Central Asian water management, which remained based on local custom, now enshrined in the statute governing Turkestan Province. Instead, in some places such as Bukhara and the Murghab River, Russian conquest muddied the waters of Central Asian water management. The administration, however, was not alone in its visions for the establishment of empire in Central Asia and the transformation of Turkestan. There also existed an alternative late-nineteenth century vision for the future of Russian Turkestan and its place in the Russian Empire, anchored deeply in its waterways, and rooted in legends about the region's past.

2

Eastern Eden

Irrigation and Empire on the Hungry Steppe

> Casting at the holy feet of His Majesty the Emperor the fruits of my labors – several thousand desiatinas of newly irrigated land, torn away from the desert – I beg Your Excellency to tell his Imperial Highness that I consider this day the happiest day of my whole life, and the best lot that has fallen to me: to give life to the waterless deserts, in the name of the White Tsar, knowing how the Muslims revere that name as holy and how they treasure water (as the greatest gift of God).
>
> – Grand Duke Nikolai Konstantinovich Romanov (1890)[1]

Long after the Russian Empire had fallen – on the eve, in fact, of the collapse of its successor state, the Soviet Union – an ethnographer in Central Asia found that among the older inhabitants of villages near Tashkent there persisted a legend about an enigmatic figure who had lived in the region a century prior. In interviews, Ol′ga Il′inichna Brusina heard tales about how Grand Duke Nikolai Konstantinovich Romanov dressed himself in Uzbek clothing, went to the local mosque, and consulted the *aqsaqals* for help in irrigating the Hungry Steppe. According to many of Brusina's Slavic informants, it was at the Grand Duke's own invitation that their parents and grandparents had settled in Turkestan.[2]

The man whose memory lingered in the Tashkent region into the late twentieth century was that very same Grand Duke Nikolai

[1] Letter from Grand Duke Nikolai Konstantinovich to N.O. fon Rozenbakh, TsGA RU, f. 40, op. 1, d. 23, ll. 60b-7.

[2] O. I. Brusina, *Slaviane v Srednei Azii. Etnicheskie i sotsial′nye protsessy. Konets XIX-konets XX veka* (Moscow: Vostochnaia Literatura, 2001), 6, 22.

Konstantinovich Romanov, cousin to tsars Alexander III and Nicholas II, who had been involved with the campaign against Khiva and schemes to connect the Amu Darya and the Caspian. His years spent exploring the Aral basin were some of the first years he spent in exile; he eventually came to settle in Tashkent, where he would spend the last four decades of his life. Because he had been sent to Tashkent in disgrace, after 1874 Nikolai Konstantinovich's name was hardly ever invoked in court circles. But in the city where he lived more than half his life, the "forgotten" Grand Duke was one of the most recognizable and influential figures at the turn of the twentieth century. A brochure from 1909 advertising an agricultural-industrial and scientific exposition organized by the Turkestan Agricultural Society in Tashkent, for instance, listed "His Imperial Highness the Grand Duke Nikolai Konstantinovich" first among "honorable members" of the organizing committee, before the Emir of Bukhara, the Khan of Khiva, various ministers of the empire, and regional officials.[3] The palace he had built for himself still stands today, presiding over one end of Sayilgoh, more popularly known as "Broadway," the main pedestrian area in the center of Tashkent.

The path from Khiva to Tashkent had been an indirect one. After taking part in the military campaign of 1873, the Grand Duke had been embroiled in a number of scandals at the court in St. Petersburg, including a relationship with an outspoken American, Hattie Blackford, who went by the name "Fanny Lear." Besides the scandal of the relationship itself, the two were implicated in the theft of diamonds from an icon belonging to Nikolai's mother.[4] In 1874, in an attempt to spare the imperial family, already suffering from an "atmosphere of deceit and corruption," from further embarrassment, Alexander II officially declared his twenty-four-year-old nephew insane and had him placed under lifelong surveillance and removed from the capital.[5] After short stints in places scattered across the empire from Crimea on the Black Sea to Orenburg in the steppes – where in 1878, much to the imperial family's outrage, the Grand Duke managed to marry a commoner named Nadezhda von Dreyer, daughter of the local police chief – in 1881 Nikolai Konstantinovich arrived in Tashkent, where he would spend the rest of his life. Tashkent had been

[3] RGIA f. 435, op. 1, d. 35, ll. 136–136ob.

[4] Fanny Lear tells her own side of the affair in *Le Roman d'une Americaine en Russie, accompagné de lettres originales* (Brussels: A. Lacroix, 1875).

[5] Richard Wortman, *Scenarios of Power: Myth and Ceremony in Russian Monarchy*, II (Princeton, NJ: Princeton University Press, 2000), 118.

chosen as a place with a suitable climate for the "August Patient," where there was land on which he could practice agriculture, silk-making, and other small-scale activities for the benefit of the empire.[6] It was also a place the Grand Duke had grown to love, both as a participant in the campaign against Khiva and then again during his scientific expeditions to the Amu Darya.

After his arrival in Tashkent, Nikolai Konstantinovich quickly became an ardent proponent of the irrigation of Turkestan and the benefits of this irrigation for the empire. With the attention of central administrators occupied elsewhere, and with regional officials seeking vainly to learn more about Central Asian water resources and customary water use, in the 1880s and 1890s Nikolai took matters into his own hands, investing a considerable portion of his ample allowance to undertake an ambitious series of canal-building projects in the Tashkent region and the nearby Hungry Steppe, which were immediately far more effective than anything accomplished by the Russian government in Turkestan thus far. These enterprises, intended to bring water to both existing Central Asian communities and new settlements of migrants from European Russia and Siberia, managed to provide a living for hundreds of poor Slavic peasants fleeing famine and overcrowding in the central regions of the empire. By carefully establishing and maintaining a network of relationships with Central Asian notables, the Grand Duke also attempted to personally demonstrate to the local population the benefits of a benevolent Russian rule in the region. For a considerable part of the Slavic population in Tashkent and the surrounding regions – and even some indigenous Central Asians – the Grand Duke was not a recluse or a mental patient, but rather a benefactor.

Nikolai Konstantinovich was the self-appointed creator and ruler of a harmonious "Russo-Asiatic" world along his Hungry Steppe irrigation canals. For a time in the late nineteenth century, this world coexisted with official Russian attempts to take control of water management in the region. In spite of the fact that the disgraced Grand Duke was a man officially deemed mentally incompetent, he was allowed a considerable amount of autonomy in undertaking irrigation and colonization activities – two enterprises intimately linked with the Russian control of this sensitive border region – and allowed to preside over his own

[6] GARF f. 664, op. 1, d. 35, ll. 29ob-31ob. For details on the Grand Duke's many moves – and more scandals – see Rostislav Krasjukov, "Grossfürst Nikolai Konstantinowitsch, 1850–1918: Versuch einer Biographie," *Der Herold* 12 (1995): 301–318.

miniature realm on the edges of the empire. Because the military administration had to approve new canal-building projects, the government legally had a monopoly on irrigation construction, but in places such as the fertile Ferghana Valley, new irrigation construction was likely to clash with existing systems and agreements for water use (i.e., "custom") among indigenous Central Asian communities.[7] The Hungry Steppe, on the other hand – which the Russian administration had already tried in vain to irrigate in the 1870s – was relatively unpopulated, which partially explains why the Grand Duke was permitted to carry out a number of large-scale irrigation construction projects virtually without supervision.[8] Moreover, his willingness to invest in development schemes in Turkestan at a time when the regional administration worried about the colony serving as a drain on the empire's finances seems to have made regional and local administrators willing to put up with or overlook his dubious past, his eccentricities and emotional outbursts, as well as the uncertain legality of some of his decisions and the questionable actions of his associates. His irrigation exploits and role as an alternative source of authority and power in Turkestan thus illustrate the weakness of the Russian Empire in the Central Asian borderlands in the decades following conquest.

The Grand Duke's status as a member of the imperial ruling family also seems to be important for understanding his unique position in Turkestan. Though in official disgrace, as a relative of the tsar, Nikolai Konstantinovich was treated with respect and deference by tsarist administrators, including important ministers and elites in St. Petersburg. Since he was not a member of the regional administration, the Grand Duke was able to enter into personal negotiations and contracts with a wide range of people, from the Khan of Khiva to local village leaders. Here, too, his title may have earned him the respect of local elites. He also, however, professed respect for local culture and traditions in his mission to help the establishment of Russian imperial power in Turkestan.

Even those Russians who saw the traces of great civilizations in the crumbling architecture of Samarkand and in ruins in the deserts of Transcaspia tended to view Central Asia as a place of corrupt Asian despots, primitive people, and untapped resources, as a frontier region ready for exploitation and Slavic settlement. What is novel about Nikolai Konstantinovich's vision for Turkestan is that while he fully believed in

[7] Thurman, "Modes of Organization," 100. [8] GARF f. 1001, op. 1, d. 63, l. 23.

the ability – indeed, necessity – of the Russian transformation and incorporation of this imperial frontier, he always included the local Muslim peoples as full-fledged participants in this process. The idea that indigenous Turkestanis could participate in the Russian creation of a new Turkestan stood in stark contrast to the attitudes of most Russian officials, who saw the co-optation of local elites as a necessary evil and tolerated – or, more precisely, 'ignored' Islam, in Kaufman's phrasing – for fear of provoking fanaticism among the empire's Muslim subjects.

It was these legacies that persisted among Brusina's informants in the Tashkent region in the late twentieth century. What people remembered in addition to the Grand Duke's support for Slavic migrants to the region was his respect for local knowledge and culture: his adoption of local dress, his interest in the Islamic religion, his consultation of local irrigation specialists for advice, tales that harmonize surprisingly well with archival evidence. Though over the years fact may have become embellished with fiction, at its core, the picture the settlers' descendants painted of Nikolai Konstantinovich seems to be accurate. A devout Orthodox Christian, Nikolai may never have set foot in a mosque, but he did learn several simple prayers in Arabic, maintained close Central Asian friends and advisors, often dressed in local clothing, and built his canals using indigenous irrigation methods and with the consultation of local irrigation experts. At the same time, he shared Orientalist views of "the East" as a place of ancient and unchanging mystique – a place that Russians could (and should) resurrect from decline – as well as the general Euro-American belief that agriculture was the hallmark of a settled civilization and that the nomads should be sedentarized. Yet, more than most Russian administrators, he sought to learn as much as he could about Turkestan and to employ that knowledge in the region's development. In an era in which the Russian administration in Turkestan was for the most part content to leave the local population to its own devices, creating Russian districts within cities to segregate "European" residents from "natives," the Grand Duke attempted to bridge the gap between the worlds of colonizer and colonized .

One might see in the Grand Duke's life an alternative imperial vision for Russian rule of the region, a road not taken, one in which respect for local knowledge, customs, and the region's past was blended with a vision of Russia as a mighty empire with a glorious future. In a small corner of Turkestan, on the flat, open spaces of the Hungry Steppe, the Grand Duke constructed a world in which he attempted to make this vision a reality. But even this world was fraught with the misunderstandings, power inequalities, and violence that characterize imperial ventures. Moreover, frontiers, even those of the imagination, as Willard Sunderland has pointed out, eventually close.[9] The last decades of tsarist rule in the region imposed a more uniformly colonizing rule than the one existing in the decades after conquest, a regime that left no room for a liminal figure such as the Grand Duke and the hybrid world he created in the Hungry Steppe.

A NEW IRRIGATOR

From the time of his participation in the campaign against the Khanate of Khiva in 1873, Nikolai Konstantinovich immersed himself in local lore, listening to the tales and legends of villagers and gleaning as much as he could from the memories of Turkestanis themselves about the history of the region. Water, in particular the control of water, was central to the tales that he heard, tales about the adoption of Islam in the region and powerful bygone rulers.[10] When in 1881 Nikolai's movements and activities were restricted to Tashkent and the surrounding region, he set out to learn as much as possible about local water resources of the Tashkent region. Based on conversations with local inhabitants, as well as his own observations, Nikolai believed that the Syr Darya, like the Amu, might once have flowed through a different channel, and that redirecting this river would increase the possibilities for irrigating the steppes, sedentarizing nomadic Kazakhs, and establishing Russian and Cossack settlements in the province.[11]

Nikolai felt that irrigation was the perfect arena in which to demonstrate the benefits of Russian rule over Turkestan. He was critical of Governor Kaufman's rule of the region – including his failed effort to co-opt Turkestanis into building a canal in the Hungry Steppe – and agreed with the conclusions of Fedor Karlovich Girs, who led an inspection of the province after Kaufman's death and in 1883 recommended a complete overhaul of the regional administration. In a letter to his mother in January of that year, Nikolai wrote, concerning an allowance:

> I desire that this money should go towards irrigation in Turkestan, under the supervision of the chief administrator of the *krai* [borderland province] and with my personal participation. This … would create an excellent impression on the

[9] Sunderland, *Taming the Wild Field*, 2.
[10] GARF f. 1155, op. 1, d. 2461, ll. 6, 14.
[11] RGIA f. 435, op. 1, d. 15, ll. 10–10ob.

tuzemtsy [natives], whom Russian bureaucrats, unfortunately, exploited too much under the previous administration, which the current inspection by Girs has revealed … I beg of you, my Dear Mama, to support me in this.[12]

The first project to which the Grand Duke pledged the funds from his allowance was the restoration of the Khanym ariq, an old irrigation channel in the Tashkent region near the large Zakh ariq. On previous trips to the region, he had made the acquaintance of Sultan Sadyk, son of the famous Kenesary Qasimov, who had been the leader of a great uprising of Kazakhs against the Russians from 1837 to 1847. It was Sadyk who told Nikolai that the Khanym ariq might be restored with little trouble and great profit. Though he is said to have been virulently anti-Russian, Sadyk seems to have pledged his assistance to this irrigation venture, something Nikolai considered to be "very important, since he [Sadyk] exerts great influence upon the Kirgiz [Kazakhs] as a man of the white bone (descendant of Chinggiz Khan) and important batyr [warrior, hero] in Turan."[13] Like many Russians in the region, Nikolai Konstantinovich was eager to find local supporters for his projects, men who could serve as intermediaries between Russians and the local populations.[14]

For the Russians, as for other imperial rulers, cultivating a loyal class of "natives" seemed a logical way to consolidate power and increase legitimacy on the ground. For the colonized, however, entrance into such relationships was more fraught. Central Asian mediators, though they helped to maintain a sense of stability within the province – desirable to colonizers and colonized alike – had to maintain a constant balance between pleasing tsarist bureaucrats and retaining status and power within their own communities, weighing the risks of colonial projects that threatened their ways of life against the potential benefits.[15] In this case, Sultan Sadyk may have put aside his dislike of the Russians in order to participate in a project that he believed would benefit his community. It is also possible that as a member of the imperial family, the Grand Duke held a different status in the eyes of indigenous communities than did meddlesome provincial bureaucrats; this may have made his project more

[12] Ibid., ll. 28–28ob.

[13] Ibid., l. 30; Martha Brill Olcott, *The Kazakhs*, 2nd edn. (Stanford, CA: Hoover Institution Press, 1995), 79.

[14] For more on intermediaries in the Kazakh Steppe, see Ian Campbell, *Knowledge and the Ends of Empire: Kazakh Intermediaries and Russian Rule on the Steppe, 1731–1917* (Ithaca, NY: Cornell University Press, 2017).

[15] Sahadeo, *Russian Colonial Society in Tashkent*, 80.

appealing than one headed by a Russian military governor such as Kaufman.

Soon after arrival in Tashkent, the Grand Duke had already established his presence as a powerful local figure. Because the organization of water was such an essential part of life in arid Central Asia, and because Nikolai Konstantinovich – unlike Turkestan's governors-general – was willing to compensate his workers for their efforts, he seems to have had little trouble attracting local Central Asian support for his canal projects; the mutual benefits of cooperation on matters involving water were evident to many local communities. The Grand Duke also strove to take the opinions of local village elders and nomadic leaders seriously. He did not merely wish to cultivate allies; he also valued their knowledge of local conditions and history, believing that such knowledge could make his projects more successful. Although he taught himself about irrigation engineering from European publications, the Grand Duke also felt that he had much to learn from local irrigation techniques. No doubt his offer of monetary and other rewards to local notables who helped with the irrigation process provided additional incentive for collaboration.[16]

By collecting as much detailed information as possible from "prominent and honorable natives" about old channels in the Syr Darya basin near Tashkent that had fallen into disuse, and by meeting with notables from Kazakh *auls* and Uzbek villages along the Chirchiq River, a tributary of the Syr serving as the main source of water for Tashkent city as well as for much of the irrigation in the surrounding region, the Grand Duke soon came to an agreement on how the water from the restored Khanym ariq was to be divided (in his notes he used the Uzbek word *maslahat* [consultation, concurrence], indicating his understanding of the local value placed on consensus when it came to sharing water).[17] He noted with admiration that the "natives" seemed to respect the new governor-general, Cherniaev, and was even more pleased to find that Cherniaev himself shared his views on the importance of irrigation.[18] In October 1882, soon after arrival in the region, Cherniaev granted Nikolai

[16] RGIA f. 435, op. 1, dd. 15, l. 50; 57, l. 1.

[17] RGIA f. 435, op. 1, dd. 15, ll. 25ob-26; 57, l. 1; Kamoludin Abdullaev and Ravshan Nazarov argue that argue that *maslihat* [sic], or consensus, was "the key to survival" in the Ferghana Valley ("The Ferghana Valley Under Stalin, 1929–1953," in ed. S. Frederick Starr, *Ferghana Valley: The Heart of Central Asia* [New York: Routledge, 2015], 119–139: 132).

[18] RGIA f. 435, op. 1, d. 15, ll. 10, 25ob.

Konstantinovich permission to undertake canal work.[19] By the Grand Duke's own account, after securing the pledges of local villagers to help dig the canal in exchange for use of the newly irrigated land, Nikolai chose his "associate" [*priiatel'*], a man named Mulla Abduraim, to be in charge of the native work brigades, as Abduraim was "respected by Russians and natives alike."[20] They planned to begin work in the early spring of 1883.

At the same time, Nikolai also began work on another canal entirely of his own construction.[21] For the head of the canal, Nikolai chose a spot along the Chirchiq River to the northeast of Tashkent, upstream from the Khanym ariq. In the spring of 1883, he informed his parents that work on this new ariq had commenced on February 26, the birthday of Tsar Alexander III. "[T]he natives are already calling this future irrigation canal the Ak Padsha ariq, that is, the ariq of the White Tsar," he proclaimed proudly.[22] (In this letter, as in most of his writings, he preferred to use the Central Asian word *ariq* instead of the Russian *kanal.*) Instead of the Aq-Padsha Ariq, however, the canal soon came to be known as the Iskander Ariq, after another famous empire-builder, Alexander the Great of Macedonia, from whom many in the region claim to be descended, and with whom many places in the region are associated. During his early days on the Amu Darya, the Grand Duke had been fascinated by the thought that Alexander the Great had traveled along the very same river.[23] The name Iskander eventually became, at Nikolai's own request and with the tsar's approval, the hereditary name given to Nadezhda von Dreyer and bestowed upon their children together.[24]

[19] M. Iu. Iunuskhodzhaeva, *Iz istorii zemlevladeniia v dorevoliutsionnom Turkestane (na materialakh khoziaistva kniazia N.K. Romanova)* (Tashkent: Izd. FAN, 1970), 37.

[20] RGIA f. 435, op. 1, d. 15, ll. 27–27ob.

[21] It is unclear why in 1883 Nikolai simultaneously began work on two large canal-building projects so closely located. Engineer Elistratov, "Khanym-aryk," *TV* 69 (1908) in *TS* 458, 103–104.

[22] RGIA f. 435, op. 1, d. 15, l. 17. The comment may have been a dig at Kaufman for his failed "pig canal." For more on the myth of the White Tsar, see Marlène Laruelle, "'The White Tsar': Romantic Imperialism in Russia's Legitimizing of Conquering the Far East," *Acta Slavica Iaponica* 25 (2008): 113.

[23] Letter from Nikolai to Fanny Lear (March 23, 1873) cited in Lear, *Le roman d'une Americaine en Russie*, 199–200.

[24] Tatishchev, *Zemli i liudi*, 92–93; Michael, Prince of Greece, *The White Night of St. Petersburg*, trans. Franklin Philip (New York: Atlantic Monthly Press, 2004), 266. Because she and Nikolai had a morganatic marriage, Nadezhda could not take the Romanov name or associated titles.

The Grand Duke's newly asserted authority in the region was not without contestation. To his consternation, immediately after such an auspicious beginning and in spite of his attempt to appeal to Alexander III's good graces, Nikolai found himself faced with an imperial order forbidding him to undertake irrigation in Turkestan. In a telegram to his family on March 3, 1883, Nikolai implored them to see how this halt to the work would be seen by the hundreds of "natives" involved in the project, "who, at the initiation [of the canal work] prayed on the Koran for the health of the tsar ... I was informed that I would be able to practice agriculture on a large scale," he observed petulantly, "but how will I be able to improve agriculture, to develop fine cotton, if I am not allowed to dig ariqs?"[25]

The argument that a sudden halt to the construction operations would make a bad impression on the local population seems to have carried weight. On March 20, Nikolai received official word that he could resume his work, with the provision that the irrigation works be transferred to the state upon completion.[26] It is not clear why the Grand Duke was initially forbidden from undertaking the irrigation project, in spite of the regional administration's approval. It may have been that the new tsar, Alexander III, did not want the disgraced Grand Duke involved in any projects with political significance. It was one matter to indulge in the creation and maintenance of a farm in central Russia, as some in the imperial family had initially envisioned the Grand Duke's future; employing "natives" to dig canals in a military colony on the borders of the empire was another. With Russian expansion in Central Asia still underway (Merv would not be subjugated until the following year), the risk of creating dissatisfaction in Turkestan was to be avoided at all costs.

In September 1883, Governor-General Cherniaev came to inspect the progress of the Iskander Ariq and was impressed with what had been accomplished thus far. Nikolai wrote with obvious pleasure to his parents that the governor seemed to have been convinced that his frugal employment of the local method of canal-building, as opposed to hiring Russian engineers, was of "enormous utility" and should be continued.[27] The Grand Duke noted, too, with evident satisfaction, that local Kazakhs who had never before led a settled lifestyle were taking up residence in a

[25] RGIA f. 435, op. 1, d. 15, ll. 34–34ob.

[26] Ibid., l. 37; RGIA f. 426, op. 1, d. 187, l. 10.

[27] RGIA f. 435, op. 1, d. 15, ll. 21–22.

nearby valley, "in the firm belief that water will come to them in the spring."[28] It is possible that many Kazakhs were grateful for the opportunity to settle on irrigated lands, since recent winters had been particularly severe, and the phenomenon known as *dzhut* – in which an early thaw followed by freezing temperatures trapped grass under a thick layer of ice – had led to the loss of large numbers of livestock, on the heels of which came soaring grain prices.[29] Khali-bai Mambetov, member of a local Kazakh clan, many of whose members worked on the Grand Duke's canals, claims that he was commissioned to compose a song for "a great man" in St. Petersburg "on the old way of life" in the region after he was overheard singing songs in praise of the Grand Duke while working on the Iskander Ariq.[30]

Besides introducing the indigenous peoples of Turkestan to a more civilized way of life, the Russian government hoped to import civilization to Turkestan in the form of Russian farmer–colonists. Indeed, to those who had enough imagination, the vast, flat expanses of the Hungry Steppe seemed to invite transformation from a desert-like "waste" land into a "cultured" greenway supporting both agriculture and the "civilized" influence of Russian settlers. Inspired by such visions, by January 1884 Nikolai had begun a new canal from the rapids on the Syr Darya south of Tashkent, near the Uzbek settlement of Begovat, in the direction of the steppe. He called this the "Sladkaia Tsarevna Ariq" – the Sweet Princess canal. The Sweet Princess canal came to embody Nikolai's vision for the transformation of the Hungry Steppe into a bounteous land that could provide for both migrant Slavs as well as indigenous Central Asians, all through the touch of his loving hand.

Yet almost immediately, this vision seemed once again in danger. Nikolai was sorely disappointed when Cherniaev, in whom he had found an ally, left his post as governor-general in the spring of 1884. When he first heard a rumor of the governor's departure, Nikolai wrote to Petersburg, "For the good of Turkestan, let it not be so," not least because the departure of the governor dashed his ongoing schemes of returning the Amu to the Caspian, and removed an important local supporter of his

[28] Ibid., l. 22ob.

[29] Dingel'shtedt, *Opyt izucheniia irrigatsii*, 37–38; Nalivkin and Nalivkina, *Muslim Women of the Fergana Valley*, 107.

[30] N. Veselovskii, trans. and ed., *Kirgizskii razskaz o russkikh zavoevaniiakh v Turkestanskom krae* (St. Petersburg: P. O. Iablonskii, 1894), v.

irrigation projects.[31] To the Grand Duke's relief, the new governor-general, Nikolai Ottonovich von Rozenbakh, saw no harm in allowing him to continue his projects.

In 1885, after the completion of the Khanym Ariq expansion to sixty-five versts, and the new Iskander Ariq, which was seventy-five versts long, the Grand Duke began his largest and most prominent project yet, the construction of a new canal in the Hungry Steppe known as the Bukhara Ariq.[32] Russian sources often explain this name by claiming that Nikolai believed he was resurrecting an ancient canal that supposedly had brought water from the Syr Darya to Bukhara, though his writings do not indicate that this was his main motivation.[33] This canal, six years in the making, proved a colossal failure, lasting only a few days before bursting its banks. The successor to the Bukhara Ariq, the Khiva Ariq, on the other hand, was much more successful, though its proximity to the Syr Darya also posed problems. An extended version of the Khiva Ariq became the Nicholas I Canal, which was eventually expanded and re-engineered by the imperial Russian government to become the Romanov Canal.[34]

Despite constant concerns about his own health, the disgraced Grand Duke had found a place for himself in Turkestan. In the fall of 1885, he wrote to his father from the banks of the Iskander Ariq, "I am completely satisfied with my situation and . . . I have found my favorite activity."[35] In a letter to Minister of Agriculture Mikhail Nikolaevich Ostrovskii in 1889, he wrote, "I consider myself completely happy if my ideas, grounded in an accurate evaluation of and knowledge of local conditions, bring even a drop of benefit to our dear fatherland."[36] The following year he wrote:

> If . . . I am able . . . to assist in the introduction to the Krai of rational agriculture, having turned the dead steppes into cultured oases, I will consider my mission complete: to dedicate my life to the benefit of His Majesty and the fatherland."[37]

Two decades later, he would inform his brother that the former governor-general of Turkestan had written from the Caucasus with wishes of good luck "in my fruitful activities for the Krai . . . and works for bringing the

31 RGIA f. 435, op. 1, d. 15, l. 54; Pravilova, "River of Empire," 269.

32 Pahlen, *Oroshenie*, xi–xii.

33 See, for example, Andrei Matisen, "Polozhenie i nuzhdy orosheniia v Turkestane," *Ezhegodnik Otdela Zemel'nykh Uluchshenii, God Pervyi (1909)* (St. Petersburg: GUZiZ, 1910), 278.

34 Part of the system became known as the Kirov Canal in Soviet times and is the Dostyk [Friendship] Canal connecting Uzbekistan and Kazakhstan today.

35 RGIA f. 435, op. 1, d. 15, l. 78.

36 RGIA, f. 426, op. 1, d. 35, l. 30b.

37 TsGA RU, f. 40, op. 1, d. 23, l. 10.

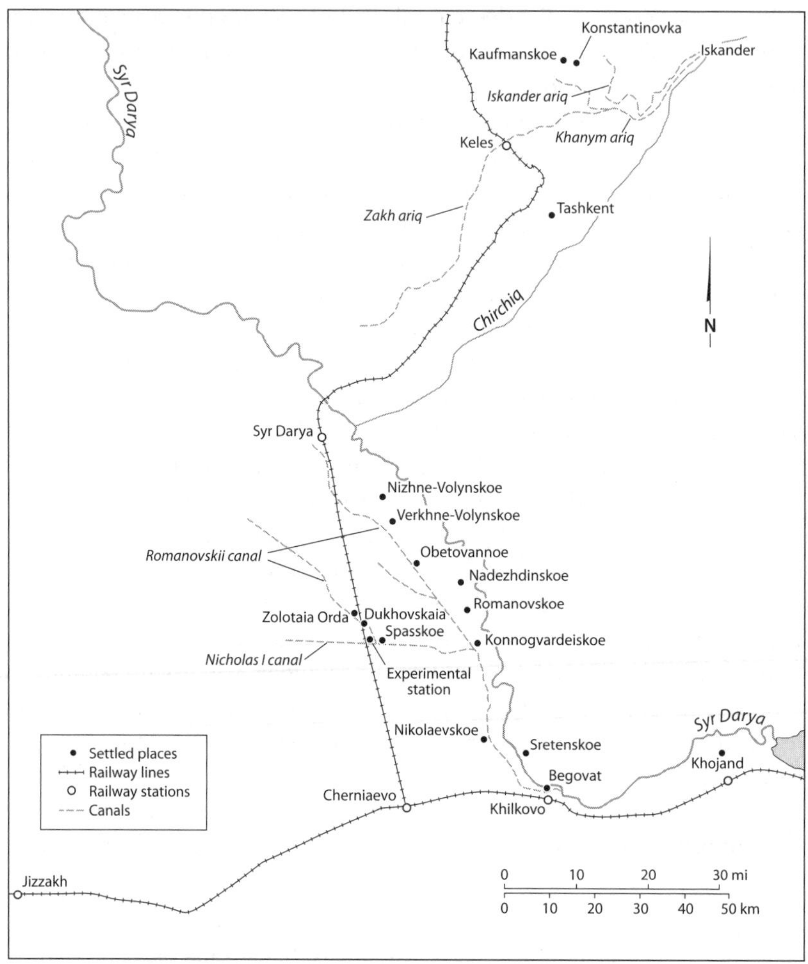

FIGURE 2.1 The Hungry Steppe, early twentieth century.
Map by Bill Nelson.

deserts of Central Asia to life"; in another telegram from the same period, he called these irrigation activities "the main goal of my life here."[38]

CANAL LABORS

On his first projects on the Chirchiq River, Nikolai Konstantinovich hired primarily local Central Asian workers, mostly from the Kazakh

[38] RGIA f. 435, op. 1, d. 35, ll. 73ob, 84.

communities inhabiting the steppes near Tashkent. At the beginning of each new canal project, the Grand Duke typically met with local leaders who pledged to provide workers, each of whom would fulfill a predetermined amount of work. The unit of volume Russians used to measure canals was the cubic *sazhen*. Each canal required a certain number of cubic sazhens of earth to be removed in order for the canal to reach its desired length, breadth, and depth. This number was calculated and divided among the *artels* (work brigades) into which the workers were organized, like peasant workers in other parts of the Russian Empire. In this case, however, each artel was headed by a leader referred to as *usta* (a Turkic term for "master"). Nikolai hired Russian overseers to coordinate the work of the artels and to pay each usta based on the amount of work accomplished by his artel, to be divided among the workers.

Each community entering into contract with the Grand Duke pledged to dig a certain number of cubic sazhens, *po krugovoiu poruku* (Russian: according to the principle of mutual responsibility) – that is, if one person did not hold up his end of the bargain, then the entire village was responsible for taking on his share. This was typical for artels in other parts of the empire, as well. Existing contracts with local Kazakh auls were drawn up in both Russian and Kazakh. The workers – often identified in the contracts by first name only – made marks or signed their names to signify agreement to the terms of the contract, which usually stipulated two to three months of work. The local aul leaders added their *tamgas* (stamps or seals) on the contracts to confirm their official nature. Though he was providing them with salaries, the Grand Duke did at times rely on the local custom whereby workers provided their own tools – typically the ketmen, the all-purpose iron hoe used for both digging and maintaining canals – and transportation to the work site.[39] Local practice generally required workers in public works projects to provide their own food as well, but the Grand Duke often paid the workers partially in kind – usually in the form of bread – since bazaars were generally far from work sites and local traders charged exorbitant prices in the Hungry Steppe. Central Asian workers were expected to find their own accommodations – which they often brought with them in the form of the nomadic felt tents known as yurts – if they did not live nearby. As work expanded into the Hungry Steppe, Nikolai began hiring Uzbeks and Tajiks from the nearby

[39] This practice was known in the Ferghana Valley, at least, as *payshkan* (Thurman, "Modes of Organization," 55); see, for example, a contract from 1896 in RGIA f. 435, op. 1, d. 75, l. 146.

FIGURE 2.2 Types of workers. "Tipy rabochikh," photograph No. 21 in *Raboty po orosheniiu 45,000 ga. v Golodnoi Stepi* [*Work on the Irrigation of 45,000 Hectares in the Hungry Steppe*] (1901–1902), 13.
Reproduced with permission of the Rare Books Section of the Alisher Navoi State Library, Tashkent, Uzbekistan.

cities of Tashkent, Khojand, and Ura-Tiube; still other workers came from Transcaspia and the Emirate of Bukhara. An early twentieth-century photo album of canal workers in the Hungry Steppe contains a composed photo labeled "Types of workers," which identifies representatives of the following ethnic groups: Uzbeks, Bukharans, Kirgiz [i.e., Kazakhs], Khivans, Ura-Tiube Tajiks, *musafirs* [travelers], Russians, Lezgin, Kazan Tatars, and Persians.[40]

[40] See Figure 2.2. *Musafir* as used by the Grand Duke seems to have referred to city-dwellers in place of *sart*, the general term applied by the Russian administration to Central Asia's urban population. It occasionally seems to have been used in the region to refer to outsiders. The Nalivkins, a Russian ethnographer couple who lived in the Ferghana Valley for several years, for instance, mention the presence of *musafirs* who had come from distant regions (*Muslim Women of the Fergana Valley*, 104). Perhaps being sensitive to the negative political connotations that the word "sart" could have for the settled peoples of the former Khanate of Khoqand, Nikolai chose to employ this term.

Though the Grand Duke's canals did draw in many ways on indigenous methods of canal construction, he also tried to introduce some innovations that did not prove popular. His system of compensating workers based on the volume of earth removed, as measured using Russian units of measurement, for instance, proved to be confusing to many Central Asians, who had difficulty conceptualizing such measurements and did not always understand the labor required. In one case, several district heads compensated workers on the Grand Duke's canals at a flat rate of seventy kopecks per day, while the majority distributed the money they had received from the Grand Duke among the various communities supplying workers to apportion as they saw fit. The senior aqsaqal of Khojand town complained to Nikolai Efremov, the Russian head of Khojand district, that local community leaders who had pledged workers were now informing him that it would be impossible for the workers to complete the task for the pay being offered, to which Efremov replied in surprise that he found the salary of seventy kopecks to be disproportionately high. Seventy kopecks was, however, the wage Nikolai had offered for digging a cubic sazhen, not a daily working wage, as some local authorities had understood it. When Efremov himself visited the work site to investigate, he found that "the district heads were not acquainted with the conditions of the work and regarded the estimated number of cubic sazhens [to be dug] with great distrust." Efremov suggested that a model cubic sazhen be dug to determine whether or not all parties could agree that the pay being offered was appropriate to the work being done.[41] As this case demonstrates, the imposition of more "scientific" methods of canal building – that is, calculating the volume of earth to be removed and measuring the labor accordingly – did not immediately prove their superiority.

As the canal networks expanded into the Hungry Steppe, so, too, did the presence of Russians on the canals. The Grand Duke began inviting Russians and Cossacks to rent land among the Kazakhs on his estates on the Iskander Ariq or to take up residence in the settler villages forming along his new canal projects in the Hungry Steppe in the 1880s and 1890s.[42] As word of the irrigation projects spread, Slavic migrants also approached the Grand Duke on their own. To those who were too poor

[41] GARF f. 1155, op. 1, d. 3689, ll. 5–9.

[42] In 1886, the first temporary provisions were made for the registration and settlement (*vodvorenie*) of migrants in Turkestan. The creation of settler villages was wholly within the purview (and dependent on the finances) of the district- and region-level administration. Gavrilov, *Pereselencheskoe delo v Turkestanskom krae*, 2–3.

to rent land along the canals, Nikolai offered the opportunity of a loan to finance the construction of a simple home, as well as a job in canal construction to repay the loan. In the new settler villages, work was often contracted on an individual basis, each settler pledging to complete an individual amount of labor in repayment for the Grand Duke's aid.

Encounters between newly arrived migrants and Central Asian workers in the Hungry Steppe were no doubt frequent. In cities such as Tashkent, where the "Asian" part of town existed separately from newer "European" quarters, Central Asians and Russians mixed on a daily basis.[43] Similarly, while for the most part Slavic and Cossack settlers lived in settlements that were separate from the Central Asian workers on the Hungry Steppe canals, migrants and locals alike rented land on the Grand Duke's estates, and all kinds of workers seem to have built temporary homes at the heads of the Hungry Steppe canals near Begovat. On the work sites, laborers were organized into separate artels by village or place of origin. However, it is likely that both Central Asian and Slavic brigades worked in the same vicinity. Already in January 1887, Nikolai observed proudly that "various Muslims (Kokandians, Bukharans, Turkmen, Uzbeks, Kirgiz [i.e., Kazakhs], Tajiks, Kashgaris) are working with their ketmens amazingly industriously and amicably alongside Russian settlers from Samara, Ukraine, and Siberia, under the supervision of foremen from among [the ranks of] retired Turkestan riflemen, artillerymen, sappers and Ural Cossacks."[44] Early twentieth-century photographs of irrigation work in the Hungry Steppe show "*sarts*" (urban Central Asians) and Russians together posing for the camera (Figure 2.3).[45]

Occasional disputes over water use between Russians and local Central Asian communities did break out in the Hungry Steppe, though low population density likely kept such clashes from being too frequent. In 1888, the Grand Duke mediated a water-sharing agreement between the residents of Begovat and the Kudrin Cotton Company, which had rented a plot of land at Begovat.[46] In 1890, the mirabs on the Iskander Ariq complained that *muzhiks* (peasant men) from nearby settler villages refused to give them water, taking advantage of the fact that there was no aqsaqal to mediate.[47] In June 1897, the Slavic inhabitants of the settler

43 Sahadeo, "Epidemic and Empire," 131; Sahadeo, *Russian Colonial Society*, 119.

44 RGIA f. 435, op. 1, d. 15, l. 94.

45 See also "Gruppa zemlekopov i rabochikh podriadchika Zimina (bol'shei chast'iu sarty i russkie)," photograph No. 23, *Raboty po orosheniiu 45,000 ga. v Golodnoi Stepi*, 3.

46 TsGA RU f. 40, op. 1, d. 21, ll. 11–11ob; RGIA f. 435, op. 1, d. 57, ll. 9–9ob.

47 RGIA f. 435, op. 1, d. 57, ll. 95–95ob.

FIGURE 2.3 Nikolaevskoe peasants and Central Asians working on the irrigation of the Hungry Steppe. "Gruppa krest′ian Nikolaevskogo poselka rabotaiushchikh na magistral′nom kanale," photograph No. 19 in *Raboty po orosheniiu 45,000 ga. v Golodnoi Stepi*, 4.
Reproduced with permission of the Rare Books Section of the Alisher Navoi State Library, Tashkent, Uzbekistan.

village of Volynskoe in the Hungry Steppe wrote to the Grand Duke asking him to "come and use Your Power to deal with our enemies," in this case a group of neighboring Kazakhs who had apparently attacked the village after the settlers dammed the ariq to water their melon fields.[48] More than a decade later, on behalf of a group of "Kazakhs and sarts" who had been granted access to land and water in the Grand Duke's domains, two Kazakh representatives from a settlement on the Khanym Ariq complained about a group of peasant muzhiks who had occupied part of the same land and refused to cede it. In these cases, both sides looked to the Grand Duke as the ultimate arbitrator (in the latter case, at least, he sided with the Kazakhs).[49] The lines were not only drawn between "Russians" and "natives," however. Clashes also took place

[48] RGIA f. 435, op. 1, d. 119, ll. 92–93. [49] TsGA RU f. 40, op. 1, d. 90, ll. 65–66.

between Central Asians from different places with different interests, such as when a deadly fight broke out between workers on the Bukhara Ariq, obliging the Grand Duke to temporarily suspend work.[50] Most squabbles among canal workers, however, seem to have been on a less-grand scale – instances of petty theft, or disagreements between artels and foremen over salaries.

Since salaries were based on the amount and type of labor performed, they often became a subject of tension. The type of work and time of year could affect pay; work in harsher weather conditions paid better wages.[51] In 1896, the Grand Duke paid the musafirs who had spent the winter living by the Padsha (Tsar) Bridge – here he used the word "*kuprik*" [*ko'prik*], Uzbek for bridge – one ruble for every cubic sazhen dug, whereas those who continued to live in their home auls and *qishloqs* (villages), as well as those who had just arrived to work in the spring, were paid only seventy kopecks.[52] This latter figure seems to have been the most typical pay offered, though it could occasionally be as high as one ruble twenty kopecks or even one ruble fifty kopecks. Under optimal circumstances, this ought to have worked out to an average daily wage in Turkestan, which was forty kopecks in 1884; in 1887, the Grand Duke's minimum wage in the Hungry Steppe was twenty-five kopecks plus a daily bread ration, with higher-end wages falling between forty and sixty kopecks.[53] Records from the Iskander Ariq in July 1884 indicate that, on average, there were between 110 and 150 workers each day, who earned between thirty-four and thirty-five kopecks a day, a wage that Efremov considered to be inadequate.[54] Such a salary, however, did fall within the low range of what peasants in central Russia might receive; in the mid-1880s, a day spent sowing the fields could earn a hired laborer on average around thirty-six kopecks.[55]

The Grand Duke appears to have been careful to emphasize the fact that he paid Slavic and indigenous workers equally. In a contract from December 19, 1896, for instance, two hundred men from the

[50] According to the Grand Duke, the "bloody fight" was between Khoqandians and Turkmen (TsGA RU f. 40, op. 1, d. 21, l. 11).

[51] RGIA f. 435, op. 1, d. 15, l. 94.

[52] RGIA f. 435, op. 1, d. 75, l. 25.

[53] RGIA f. 435, op. 1, d. 15, l. 94; Morrison, *Russian Rule in Samarkand*, 217.

[54] RGIA f. 435, op. 1, d. 57, ll. 3–7; GARF f. 1155, op. 1, d. 3689, l. 8.

[55] Stephen Wheatcroft, "Crises and Condition of the Peasantry in Late Imperial Russia," ch. 4 in eds. Esther Kingston-Mann and Timothy Mixter, *Peasant Economy, Culture, and Politics of European Russia, 1800–1921* (Princeton, NJ: Princeton University Press, 1991): 148.

communities of Zaamin and Iam, in the southern Hungry Steppe between Jizzakh and Begovat, agreed to do canal work for the Grand Duke for three months, "in exchange for the pay currently received by all Russians and Muslims in the Hungry Steppe."[56] Men and women were also paid equally. From lists of settlers who pledged to work on the canals, it does not appear that any women were contracted to assist in earth removal, but an early-twentieth-century photograph of Hungry Steppe villagers from the Slavic settlement of Nikolaevskoe does show women working alongside men.[57] Some female workers' names were never recorded. A note from Cossack sergeant Aleksei Kazachkov in June 1894, for instance, indicates that alongside fifteen men from the village of Nikolaevskoe and forty from the workers' settlement of Zaporozhskoe near Begovat, seventeen women, not included on the list of workers, had also worked four full days on the new ariq, from dawn until 11 am, and from 3 to 9 pm every day.[58] Certainly, women in the Slavic settler villages were expected to and did help repair the canals in times of emergency – when meltwater caused the canals to flood their banks, for instance – as did children, and often their Central Asian neighbors, as well. All were compensated for their labor; children, both boys and girls, were paid half of what adult men and women were paid.[59]

Sudden floods were only one challenge facing the canal builders. It is unclear just how many people died working on the Grand Duke's canals, but conditions were harsh: physical labor moving heavy loads of clayey earth and stone, long work days, the proximity to water (and, hence, the potential for drowning), and year-round climatic extremes. A contract drawn up between Nikolai and Khivan and Turkmen workers in April 1891 indicates that the workers agreed to working in any kind of conditions, "wherever we are sent, [and] at whatever time of year."[60] After almost a decade of investment in the irrigation of Turkestan, the Grand Duke had carved out a small fiefdom for himself in the Hungry Steppe, where he was determined to see his imperial visions become reality.

From the writings he has left behind, along with the accounts of those who came in contact with him over his years in exile, Grand Duke Nikolai Konstantinovich seems to have been an eccentric and impetuous figure, prone to excitability and fits of childish rage; yet he also seems, in general, to have been a humane and responsive master, relishing his paternalistic

[56] RGIA f. 435, op. 1, d. 75, l. 146.
[57] See Figure 2.3 in this volume.
[58] RGIA f. 435, op. 1, d. 57, l. 194.
[59] RGIA f. 435, op. 1, d. 75, ll. 56, 63, 72, 83.
[60] RGIA f. 435, op. 1, d. 57, ll. 121–121ob.

role and his sense of strengthening a benign Russian imperial presence in Turkestan, in part by striving to communicate his interest in local customs.[61] He enjoyed surprise gestures of benevolence, such as raising workers' salaries with no warning, or providing special treats for settlers and workers on holidays, both Orthodox and Islamic.[62] When a foreman named Tokhta Murat accidentally burned down several huts in a workers' settlement while preparing plov (rice pilaf) for the men in his artel, the Grand Duke provided for the reconstruction of these homes.[63] On more than one occasion, he held funerals for indigenous workers killed while working on the ariqs, sponsoring feasts for hundreds of workers in the local tradition and paying for mullahs to read prayers. In the case of a Turkmen worker killed while working on the Bukhara Ariq, the Grand Duke gave a donation to workers at the site "in memory of the deceased," as well as forty rubles to pay forty Turkmen to construct a *mazar* (shrine) at his grave. In the cases of several Kazakhs killed while working, he gave money to the deceased workers' relatives.[64] These expenditures are particularly noteworthy given his frugality when it came to expenditures on the canals themselves, since he continued to depend on the allowance issued by his parents in St. Petersburg. Through these rituals, he attempted to demonstrate tolerance and respect for local customs. He was also carefully building an image of legitimacy and belonging in a place where he himself was an outcast and an outsider.

THE "AUGUST BENEFACTOR"[65]

By providing work and shelter to newly arrived Slavic migrants, the Grand Duke's irrigation schemes also came to form an important support network for new arrivals in the region from other parts of the empire. Though migrants from Russia came to Turkestan throughout the 1880s, no more than three or four hundred families ever came in one year.[66] This trickle, however, turned into a veritable flood when famine swept the

[61] This fits with Fanny Lear's description of the two sides of his personality (Lear, *Le roman d'une Americaine en Russie*, 86–87).

[62] RGIA f 435, op. 1, dd. 75, ll. 90b-10, 20; 118, l. 91; TsGA RU f. 40, op. 1, d. 26, ll. 56–7.

[63] RGIA f. 435, op. 1, d. 119, ll. 88–89.

[64] RGIA f. 435, op. 1, dd. 57, ll. 10, 11, 19–190b; 118, ll. 15, 16.

[65] A reference to Nikolai Konstantinovich by Nil Sergeevich Lykoshin, head of Khojand district ("Blagopoluchie otstavnykh," *TV* 26 [1907] in *TS* 435, 68–71: 69).

[66] N. Dingel'shtedt, "Nasha kolonizatsiia Srednei Azii," *VE* 11 (1892) in *TS* 429, 59–72: 59.

black earth regions of central Russia in 1891, driving thousands of peasants to search for new places to live. Most of these peasants headed for Siberia, but many thousands headed southward to Turkestan. Prince Esper Ukhtomskii encountered some of these migrants in 1891 in the port of Uzun-Ada on the eastern shore of the Caspian. In what appears to be a jibe at the Russian administration for helping to facilitate the *hajj* (journey to Mecca) for Muslim pilgrims from the Russian Empire, Ukhtomskii contrasted the sorry economic migrants from the southern regions of Penza, Tambov, Saratov and Samara, who "themselves do not know where and why they are going, [who] helplessly await at every step support from the authorities," with the self-satisfied and well-dressed Turkestani *hajjis* on their way home from Mecca to Russian-ruled Central Asia. The Russian peasants said they were headed for the lands along the Amu Darya in Transcaspia, where "they are building *Tsarskoe Selo* [Tsar's Village]," by which they meant the tsar's estate at Murghab.[67] Rumors of a promised land in Turkestan did much to inspire this increased migration.[68] Yet unbeknownst to these peasants, much of the fertile land along the Amu Darya remained off-limits. In an attempt to stem the human tide to this sensitive region so close to the Khanate of Khiva and Emirate of Bukhara, which remained sovereign Russian protectorates, the Russian authorities closed the Amu-Darya Section – lands ceded by Khiva on the right bank of the Amu Darya – to settlement, causing many peasants to seek refuge farther eastward in the provincial capital at Tashkent.[69]

In Tashkent, the inability of the local Russian authorities to register this influx of people and provide them with places to live resulted in the formation of an extensive refugee camp on the outskirts of the city. Nikolai Dingel′shtedt reported in *The Herald of Europe* that refugees were mainly coming from the southern provinces of Voronezh and the

[67] Kniaz′ Esper E. Ukhtomskii, *Ot Kal′mytskoi stepi do Bukhary* (St. Petersburg: Kn. V.P. Meshcherskii, 1891) 49–53. N. N. Kanoda also notes that most of the peasants seeking refuge in Transcaspia were from Samara, Penza, and Tambov (*Pereselencheskie poselki v Zakaspiiskoi oblasti, konets XIX-nachalo XX vv.* [Ashgabad: Ylym, 1973], 14.)

[68] In the late 1880s, a number of Molokans (a Russian Christian sect) also expressed interest in settling in the Transcaspian region of a mythical land called "Tika" (i.e., TK, or Turkestan). Nicholas Breyfogle, *Heretics and Colonizers: Forging Russia's Empire in the South Caucasus* (Ithaca, NY: Cornell University Press, 2005), 302. They may have settled in the Hungry Steppe, where some Molokans did settle. Brusina, *Slaviane v Srednei Azii*, 28.

[69] Vasilii Vladimirovich Barthold, *Istoriia kul′turnoi zhizni Turkestana* (Leningrad: Izd. AN SSSR, 1927), 153.

lands of the Don Cossacks, but also Astrakhan, Orenburg, and Tambov.[70] In November 1891, the governor-general wrote to the war minister reporting thousands of Russian migrants "without any resources."[71] With few options, many of these migrants turned to the Grand Duke for help; as many as six hundred people found work on the Grand Duke's irrigation canals, which helped them to survive the winter.[72] A temporary list of settlers from the village of Nadezhdinskoe in the Hungry Steppe, most likely drawn up in 1891 or 1892, reflects the composition of migrants reported by Dingel'shtedt.[73]

In her autobiography, Fanny Lear wrote that Nikolai "was miserly with small expenses and generous to the point of prodigality with large ones."[74] Though Nikolai was frugal when it came to his irrigation works, he was quite generous in his attempts to support Russian civilization in Turkestan, particularly when such efforts harmonized with his own visions for the development of the krai. As early as 1887, foreshadowing Ukhtomskii's criticism that the central government was doing little to aid peasant migrants, he had written:

> [Governor-]General Rozenbakh and his family – in addition to myself – are doing everything possible to help poor migrants; we buy them cows and horses, give them shelter, clothing and flour, help them to plow the earth with our own oxen and to sow barley and wheat, supply their daughters with dowries when they marry, and clothe their children who attend school. But since the treasury is not giving them anything, and the majority of my funds goes to the construction of ariqs, aid from Russia is necessary.[75]

In the winter of 1891, the Grand Duke provided famine refugees from southern Russia with food, housing, and clothing; he also put them to work on the construction of a stone dam at Begovat.[76] He repeated his concern with the lack of government aid to the migrants and suggested to his mother a way in which both he and the peasants could profit from the situation:

[70] Dingel'shtedt, "Nasha kolonizatsiia Srednei Azii," 59. Eventually, seventeen new settler villages were formed to absorb these migrants (Gavrilov, *Pereselencheskoe delo v Turkestanskom krae*, 4).

[71] Cited in A. I. Ginzburg, *Russkoe naselenie v Turkestane (konets XIX-nachalo XX veka)* (Moscow: AN SSSR, 1991), 22.

[72] Dingel'shtedt, "Nasha kolonizatsiia Srednei Azii," 59a.

[73] TsGA RT f. I-1, op. 6, d. 24, ll. 38–43ob.

[74] Lear, *Le roman d'une Americaine en Russie*, 87.

[75] RGIA f. 435, op. 1, d. 15, ll. 98ob-99.

[76] Ibid., l. 144.

The majority of poor Russian arrivals are turning to me with the request that I give them work and bread. I try to help them as best I can, but it would be a great help if the Minister of the Interior, who is helping the starving [people] in Russia, would also send aid to the poor peasants ... Instead of the usual monetary aid, it would be best to earmark funds for the payment of salaries on the ariqs which I have begun. They [the peasants] work diligently, and their labor will bring great benefit to the culture of our krai here, bringing to life the dead lands ...[77]

Through this clever scheme, the Grand Duke would be able to aid the transformation of Turkestan by channeling government funds, rather than his own pocket money, into his beloved irrigation projects, bringing both cultivation and culture to the arid lands of the Hungry Steppe. There is no indication, however, that he ever received the desired support from the central treasury. In January 1892, he sent a telegram to the Marble Palace, stating, "All this winter I have had to support, feed and clothe a thousand peasant souls and Cossacks. [...] The expenditures are great, there is not enough money."[78]

After 1889, Russian migrants were officially entitled to state aid to help them move, but such aid varied between provinces. Peasants who left their homes without official permission usually had to make their own way, often depending on the kindness of local officials, such as Rozenbakh, to establish themselves. As historian Nicholas Breyfogle has noted, "Coming face to face with the human suffering of migrants, local and regional officials were more likely than their central counterparts to provide aid ... since the latter group ... saw them [i.e., the migrants] less as people and more as an abstraction."[79] In the Tashkent region, Grand Duke Nikolai Konstantinovich stepped in when even local officials were helpless or unwilling to provide aid.

By 1892, there were almost three thousand peasant settler households in Turkestan. More families had arrived in Tashkent in 1889–1891 than had come to Turkestan through 1888, many of them so-called *samovol'tsy*, or "self-willed" migrants, who came without official government permission.[80] To make matters worse for those seeking refuge and relief in Turkestan, a deadly cholera epidemic broke out in Tashkent in the summer of 1892. This proved to be the last straw for Russian officials who, already concerned about the influx of poor Russians, tried to put a halt to urban migration, urging Russian settlers to move to rural areas.[81]

77 Ibid., ll. 138ob-139. 78 Ibid., l. 145. 79 Breyfogle, *Heretics and Colonizers*, 51.

80 Gavrilov, *Pereselencheskoe delo v Turkestanskom krae*, 4; Dingel'shtedt, "Nasha kolonizatsiia Srednei Azii," 59; Ginzburg, *Russkoe naselenie v Turkestane*, 21.

81 Sahadeo, *Russian Colonial Society*, 117–119.

Since the administration had previously forbidden Slavic migrants to settle outside of urban areas, in an effort to forestall the possibility of conflict over land and water resources, this was clearly a measure taken out of desperation. Such "colonists," more preoccupied with daily survival than they were with boosting industry and agriculture in the region, seem to have had little, if any, notion of the lofty goal their "civilizing" presence in the borderlands was supposed to accomplish.[82] Many were simply grateful for the Grand Duke's aid.

In his description of Grand Duke Nikolai Konstantinovich, American William Eleroy Curtis wrote, "It is said that his troubles have weakened his mind, and people consider him a crank, but ... [f]ortunately, his mania is benevolence."[83] Immediately upon arrival in the region in the summer of 1881, a decade before the crisis created by famine in southern Russia, Nikolai had already taken on the role of local philanthropist, donating small sums from his allowance to those who were physically handicapped, destitute, or otherwise in need of immediate assistance. Letters he received in January and February of 1882 confirm that he was already well known as a philanthropist, among both Turkestanis and Russians, after half a year of life in the province.[84] He continued to play this role for the rest of his life, aiding illiterate peasants and the downtrodden poor, but also skilled workers, including unemployed army veterans and reserve officers, of whom there were many in this military colony far from central Russia.[85] Those in Tashkent who could think of nowhere else to turn often wrote to the Grand Duke, but letters came from afar, as well. One woman in St. Petersburg wrote to him in hopes of monetary assistance for a potential cure for her blindness.[86] Many requests for aid also came from the men working on the Grand Duke's canals.[87] The retired Russian soldier Gavriil Kozlov, for instance, who

[82] For more on the Russian "civilizing mission" in Turkestan, see Adeeb Khalid, "Culture and Power in Colonial Turkestan," 422–429. On colonists and the Russian "civilizing mission," see Willard Sunderland, "Empire without Imperialism? Ambiguities of Colonization in Tsarist Russia," *Ab Imperio* 2 (2003): 107–108; Sahadeo, "Epidemic and Empire?," 137–138.

[83] William Eleroy Curtis, *Turkestan: "The Heart of Asia"* (New York: Hodder and Stoughton, 1911), 299.

[84] RGIA f. 435, op. 1, d. 118, ll. 1–5.

[85] See, for instance, ibid., ll. 40, 57; TsGA RU f. 40, op. 1, d. 90, l. 47.

[86] RGIA f. 435, op. 1, d. 33, ll. 118ob-19.

[87] For a petition from indigenous workers, see RGIA f. 435, op. 1, d. 118, l. 12. The low number of petitions from Central Asian subjects may reflect the fact that Central Asians had their own local support networks.

lived in the village of Troitskoe on the Iskander Ariq, received ten rubles from the Grand Duke in the spring of 1889. His name appears again on lists from the spring of 1891 of villagers from Troitskoe who pledged themselves to work on the canals.[88] He was probably motivated both by a desire to repay the Grand Duke's kindness and the necessity of bringing water to his settler community to ensure successful harvests in the future.

In a similar vein, Nikolai's wife, Nadezhda Aleksandrovna, was viewed by the local Slavic population as a benefactress. Women, in particular, appealed to her. Mother of five Tat'iana Zhukova, for instance, wrote in April 1889, "I have often dreamed of seeing you in person for which purpose I would travel to Iskander [estate] but because of weak health I was not able to ... I see in you a patroness and guide on the correct path." Another woman, Anna Glotova, wrote in the summer of 1890, "I wished to come in person to press myself at the feet of Your [august] personage, but I did not have the means for that, for coming to Tashkent."[89] Russian peasants had a saying that "God is high, and the tsar is far away." It is likely that Slavic migrants had little understanding of the disgrace surrounding Nikolai and Nadezhda, seeing instead in these figures a connection to the far-off tsar himself, a connection which would serve them better than appeals to local and regional bureaucrats, whom peasants typically saw as obstacles to their connection with the tsar, rather than facilitators of that relationship.

Since there were few opportunities in Turkestan for charitable work, Nadezhda Aleksandrovna may, like her husband, have been involved in attending to the people of the Hungry Steppe; letters and collective memory suggest she may have cared for the sick.[90] Workers suffered from diarrhea, fevers, ulcers, and typhus, and it is likely that malaria was a problem even before over-watering of fields by settlers unused to irrigation, coupled with faulty irrigation systems, contributed to the swamping of a significant percentage of land in the Hungry Steppe.[91] In November 1898, Nikolai sent a telegram to his brother Grand Duke

[88] Ibid., ll. 28–28ob; as well as lists in RGIA f. 435, op. 1, d. 69, ll. 54, 55, 59, 68 (where his name is variously spelled as Govrilo and Govril).

[89] RGIA f. 435, op. 1, d. 118, ll. 24–25ob, 44.

[90] Michael, Prince of Greece, *The White Night of St. Petersburg*, 267; Brusina, *Slaviane v Srednei Azii*, 26; TsGA RU f. 40, op. 1, d. 90, l. 4. The main philanthropic organization, the Turkestan Charitable Society, had been headed by Kaufman's wife (Sahadeo, *Russian Colonial Society*, 65, 124).

[91] For malaria in the Tashkent region, see "Znachenie posevov risa na zabolevanie maliariei v Turkestanskom krae," *TV* 190–93 (1909) in *TS* 513, 108–129: 122.

Konstantin Konstantinovich in St. Petersburg, in which he expressed his concern over the "unfortunate condition of many settlers on our steppe," noting the "extraordinary disease and death [rate] among them."[92] In December 1898, the Grand Duke sent a local smallpox vaccinator, Muhamed Akhun Ibrahimov, from Khojand uezd to the canal villages, presumably in the hopes of preserving the health of his labor force.[93] Over the years, he paid dozens of hospital bills for settlers and locals.[94]

In times of sickness or hardship, peasants in Russia and Ukraine depended upon their village community, the mir; in Turkestan, at the end of an arduous journey that could take many months and all of a family's meager funds, many of these peasants, like the Saratov peasant Tat′iana Dorochova, felt completely alone. In a letter indicating how many peasant migrants may have felt in Turkestan, Dorochova wrote to the Grand Duke that, after the death of her husband and twenty-five-year-old son, she had been left in Turkestan "among strangers without aid or blood [relations]." She asked for money so that she could return to her *rodina* [homeland] – that is, Saratov province – and her kin [*rodnye*].[95]

According to historian Esther Kingston-Mann, peasants in Russia placed an:

> enormous emphasis ... upon what was *rodnoi*, native, or one's own ... In a world that their lowly social status and insecure material position rendered so uncertain, the creation of local rituals, relationships, and economic and social distinctions served ... to establish a circle of trust and control, a sort of moral community within which responsibility was shared.[96]

What was *rodnoi*, or of one's community, was contrasted to anything from the outside world. In Turkestan, this included neighbors who spoke in foreign tongues, ate strange foods, and practiced unfamiliar customs. However, though many migrants spoke longingly of "Russia" or "homeland," it is unlikely that many ever considered the possibility of returning. Having given up everything to go to Turkestan, there was nothing with which to fund such a long journey home; for those from famine-stricken areas, in particular, there may no longer have been a community to which they could return. From this perspective, the Grand Duke seemed "sent

92 RGIA f. 435, op. 1, d. 119, l. 139. 93 Ibid., 99–102.
94 See, for example, TsGA RU f. 40, op. 1, d. 119, ll. 37, 42, 82.
95 RGIA f. 435, op. 1, d. 118, ll. 10–100b.
96 Esther Kingston-Mann, "Breaking the Silence: An Introduction," in eds. Esther Kingston-Mann and Timothy Mixter, *Peasant Economy, Culture, and Politics of European Russia, 1800–1921* (Princeton, NJ: Princeton University Press, 1991), 15–16.

from heaven," as one group of grateful peasants who settled on Nikolai's land wrote to him in a note he carefully enclosed in a letter sent home to his father.[97] Word of a welcoming Slavic haven in distant Turkestan traveled throughout the empire. Nikolai received letters from as far away as Siberia from people who "heard from afar that You love toilers," asking for a chance to settle on his lands.[98]

Some migrants, disappointed with the lack of possibilities in the Tashkent region, continued to move eastward toward the region of Semireche, which during this period was governed with the Steppe Governor-Generalship to the north.[99] Peasants in Semireche, meanwhile, moved westward, thinking they might try their luck in Turkestan. Traces of their long journeys in search of a better life are scattered among archives in Russia and Central Asia. A letter contained in the Russian State Historical Archive in St. Petersburg, for instance, is from Efim Dogokhov, an illiterate thirty-six-year-old peasant from the village of Staryi Tokmak near Lake Issyk Kul in Semireche (today Kyrgyzstan). Dogokhov wrote personally – with the help of a more-literate peasant – to the Grand Duke to request aid in the resettlement of himself and his five children between the ages of two and fourteen to the Hungry Steppe.[100] Others, such as the brothers Ignat, Fedor, Vasilii, and Andrei Podmoskovnyi, along with Ivan Kolesnikov, also from the Tokmak region of Semireche, wrote to the regional authorities for permission to move to one of the Grand Duke's villages, citing the precedent set by other settlers from Tokmak who had already moved to the village of Romanovskoe in the Hungry Steppe. Their case went all the way to the military governor of the Semireche region – indeed, from evidence today in the Central State Archive of the Republic of Kazakhstan, it appears to have spent several years traveling through Semireche's bureaucratic apparatus.[101] The Posmoskovnyis were apparently successful in their petition, as was their neighbor Ivan Kolesnikov, since all of their names appear on an undated list of the residents of Romanovskoe from the 1890s, now housed in the Central State Archive of the Republic of Tajikistan. There is no trace, however, of either

97 RGIA f. 435, op. 1, d. 15, l. 113.

98 RGIA f. 435, op. 1, d. 118, ll. 33–34, 46, 58, 70-70ob. For other such peasant petitions to the imperial family, see Siegelbaum and Moch, *Broad Is My Native Land*, 27.

99 Dingel'shtedt, "Nasha kolonizatsiia Srednei Azii," 59a.

100 Nikolai agreed to the resettlement. RGIA f. 435, op. 1, d. 118, l. 68.

101 TsGA RK f. I-44, op. 1, d. 21608, ll. 4–5.

Dogokhov or his family on the lists, though other migrants from Tokmak do appear.[102]

The cases of the Tokmak peasants demonstrate that, like peasants who sought out their compatriots in the large urban centers of Moscow and St. Petersburg, it was common among peasants who journeyed to Turkestan to move either in groups with others from their home villages and provinces or to join friends and relatives who had already made the move. It is also clear that some peasants attempted to use legal means to resettle, but that bureaucratic channels might have taken longer than many desperate peasants were willing to wait. Other settler lists, as well as eyewitness accounts and oral histories, provide further evidence for this phenomenon. For instance, fifteen families from the Astrakhan region on the Caspian Sea arrived in the Hungry Steppe in November 1892, bringing the total number of families from that region in the village of Nadezhdinskoe to twenty, enough to create an *astrakhanskaia sloboda*, or Astrakhan neighborhood.[103] Though listed as separate families with separate heads of household, many of these families may have been related to one another, like the Podmoskovnyis. In 1987, Egor Ivanovich Timchenko, a resident of Krest′ianskoe (formerly Romanovskoe) told ethnographer Brusina the story of how his grandfather, parents, two elder brothers, and five bachelor uncles had left Ukraine because of a shortage of land and traveled via the Caucasus to Semireche, then back westward to Tashkent in order to work on the Nicholas I Canal in the Hungry Steppe.[104] Dingel′shtedt, who visited the canal villages in 1892, observed that "in each village *zemliaki* [compatriots] gather, not only from the

[102] The Podmoskovnyis' petition is in the Kazakh Archives since Vernyi (present-day Almaty) was at the time the capital of Semireche. Though the date provided by the archive is 1896–1897, a document in Nikolai Konstantinovich's personal files in the Russian State Historical Archive in St. Petersburg states that Fedor Podmoskovnyi was the head (*starosta*) of the village of Romanovskoe already in 1894, suggesting that the family perhaps did not wait for official permission from the regional authorities (RGIA f. 435, op. 1, d. 57, l. 196). This corroborates evidence that undated lists of the residents of Nikolaevskoe, Nadezhdinskoe, and Romanovskoe contained in the Tajik archives (Khojand district was transferred from Uzbek to Tajik territory in the 1920s) are from circa 1892, which is in keeping with other documents in the file. The Podmoskovnyis are listed as "Podmoskovnov" on the list of settlers in Romanovskoe, but the first names and place of origin are consistent. These lists probably reflect the Russian administration in Turkestan's increased concern with keeping track of migrants after the influx of 1891–1892 (TsGA RT f. I-1, op. 6, d. 24, ll. 33–37ob).

[103] RGIA f. 435, op. 1, dd. 118, ll. 88, 99–113, 175; 57, l. 172; TsGA RU f. 40, op. 1, dd. 34, ll. 1–4; 33, ll. 1–5.

[104] Brusina, *Slaviane v Srednei Azii*, 225.

same region, but even from the same district."[105] Some might even be from the same remote village, such as two peasant families from Prilogino, in Kurgan oblast′, Tobol′sk *guberniia*, a thousand miles from Tashkent, one of which moved in 1889 and one which requested to be settled in the Hungry Steppe in 1890.[106] The Hungry Steppe provided a place in which families and communities could be recreated and reunited far from home, whether they came to Turkestan legally or illegally.[107]

One of the concerns of the Russian government with regard to introducing Russian peasant farmers into the Hungry Steppe was that they would not be able to withstand the local climate, in particular the searing heat in summer.[108] The documents in the Grand Duke's files do record extremes of temperature in the Hungry Steppe, interspersed with heavy rains and flooding, as well as plagues of Moroccan locusts (*Dociostaurus maroccanus*, known in Russian as *sarancha*). These conditions affected migrants and locals alike. In the summer of 1888, for instance, winds were so strong that many workers could hardly open their eyes and some developed eye problems as a result. The spring of 1889 was characterized by heavy rains and high water, the likes of which had never before been recorded in the Hungry Steppe by Russian observers.[109] Locusts, which could lay up to ten thousand clusters of eggs over hundreds of acres, swept the region in the summer of 1893.[110] An early-twentieth-century account from the Hungry Steppe describes how, from mid-April to early May, just as crops were beginning to emerge and grow, locusts would frequently appear from the steppes: "after one or two days, instead of fields turning green, bare expanses remained."[111] In 1896, the canals and settler villages sustained major damage due to heavy rains and flooding.[112] That same summer, settlers and canal workers reeled in the extreme heat.[113] During the winter of 1898, the Syr Darya at Begovat froze for the first time in Russian memory.[114]

105 Dingel′shtedt, "Nasha kolonizatsiia Srednei Azii," 71a.

106 RGIA f. 435, op. 1, d. 118, ll. 33, 58.

107 For the importance of the family for peasants on the move, see Breyfogle, *Heretics and Colonizers*, 67.

108 *Trudy s″ezda khlopkovodov*, 68. For general European concerns about the effects of hot climates on colonizers, see Eric Jennings, *Curing the Colonizers: Hydrotherapy, Climatology, and French Colonial Spas* (Durham, NC: Duke University Press, 2006).

109 RGIA f. 435, op. 1, d. 57, ll. 15, 35–36, 59.

110 *RAE*, Series A: Agricultural, II (London, 1914), 508; RGIA f. 435, op. 1, d. 119, l. 14.

111 *Trudy khlopkovogo komiteta*, 1 (St. Petersburg: GUZiZ, 1907), 107.

112 RGIA f 435, op. 1, d. 75. ll. 56–57, 70, 72, 74.

113 RGIA f. 435, op. 1, d. 119, l. 78.

114 Another such instance of freezing was not recorded again until the winter of 1918. RGAE f. 4372, op. 27, d. 354, l. 23.

The following summer brought another plague of locusts, and the winter of 1899–1900 was again extremely cold and snowy.[115] The Tashkent musafirs, displaced from the city to the steppe, begged for supplies of rice and flour to be sent to them from Tashkent, as the difficult winter was creating problems in the delivery of supplies.[116]

Yet although the work may have been backbreaking and the living conditions difficult, and though Nikolai may not have been an easy taskmaster, the new arrivals seem to have been eager to work on the canals.[117] In 1894, the villagers of Nikolaevskoe, some of whom had been dependents of the Grand Duke for two to three years already, declared their readiness to stay with their "own patron [*rodnoi pokrovitel′*] ... forever" and to invite "all of our people [*vsekh svoikh*]."[118] The gratitude of these peasants for small kindnesses bestowed by the Grand Duke echoes the conclusion of Kingston-Mann that:

> Russian peasants who survived the demands of a difficult climate and the more or less importunate claims of landlords, tax collectors, and military recruiters ... strove persistently to protect their interests, appealing to masters ... in defense of their own notion of 'real' paternalism.[119]

Nikolai was all too happy to play the part of the paternalistic lord for these downtrodden peasants. But in spite of his sincere belief that the peasants in the Hungry Steppe would benefit the krai as a whole, his very generosity was also at odds with the Russian "civilizing mission" in the region.

Since he was not a state official, Nikolai did not request any kind of official documentation from migrants. As an outcast himself, he may even have sympathized with the plight of the peasants, but it is more likely that he was willing to engage anyone willing to work on his beloved canals. In either case, Nikolai's Hungry Steppe domains provided a refuge to those who, seeking to escape punishment or obligations, saw the Central Asian frontier as a place to start afresh. Records indicate that many of the settlers in the Hungry Steppe had no official documents, and that others had only temporary six-month passports, of the type granted to peasants in European Russia – the so-called *otkhodniki* – who traveled to other regions to do seasonal work but returned every year to their home villages. Many were samovol′tsy who came without any kind of official permission. In 1892, the Khojand district government placed the worker village of Zaporozhskoe under surveillance. The governor-general urged

[115] RGIA f. 435, op. 1, d. 75, ll. 175, 178-178ob; f. 426, op. 1, d. 187, l. 84.

[116] RGIA f. 435, op. 1, d. 75, l. 178.

[117] See, for instance, RGIA f. 435, op. 1, d. 69, ll. 54–60.

[118] TsGA RU f. 40, op. 1, d. 32, ll. 6–6ob.

[119] Kingston-Mann, "Breaking the Silence," 13–14.

local authorities to pay "special attention" to the settlement and to verify the documents of its inhabitants, ostensibly to find and remove people living illegally or taking refuge from the law there. In May 1898, the military governor of Samarkand region informed the Khojand police department that several illegal residents had been discovered in Nikolaevskoe. The police noted that it would be better not to arrest them in Nikolaevskoe, so as not to upset the Grand Duke, but rather to wait until they were on the road to Samarkand and capture them then.[120]

THE AUGUST PATIENT

The Khojand policemen's warnings are an indication that the Grand Duke's volatility was a subject of common local knowledge. Nikolai relished his role as patron, but he also relished his role as the powerful local lord, a position to which he seems to have felt entitled, in spite of his disgraced position. He made rash decisions and frequently insisted on having things his own way, even if this way was irrational. For instance, after requesting that administrators of local districts each send fifty workers to his canals, he then sent a note with a demand that they send not fifty, but one hundred. Similarly, when Efremov and the district heads tried to dispute the pay Nikolai was offering for each cubic sazhen of earth removal, the Grand Duke insisted petulantly that all local district heads fulfill their agreements, even though the original agreements had been based on a misunderstanding.[121] In 1898, the Grand Duke invited four hundred peasants to resettle from the Kuban region, then presented the regional administration with the bill for transporting them from Krasnovodsk to Samarkand.[122] Whether intentionally or not, over the 1880s and 1890s, Grand Duke Nikolai Konstantinovich had quickly built a population of several hundred – several thousand, if one considers itinerant workers – people who were almost entirely dependent upon his will. Since agriculture in the region was so dependent on irrigation, settlers had few options beyond the Grand Duke's canals. An official Tashkent commission investigating the Grand Duke concluded that perhaps "the natives find the His Highness's behavior natural, because their khans always acted that way."[123]

[120] TsGA RT f. I-1, op. 6, dd. 24, ll. 63–63ob; 20, ll. 43–46. In the wake of the large influx of migrants after the famines of 1891–1892, these matters acquired particular urgency. Renewed attention to Zaporozhskoe may have been in connection with disturbances in Andijan, Margilan, and Osh in the Ferghana Valley in May 1898.

[121] GARF f. 1155, op. 1, d. 3689, ll. 5, 8.

[122] RGIA f. 435, op. 1, d. 119, ll. 144–145.

[123] GARF f. 1001, op. 1, d. 63, l. 30.

FIGURE 2.4 Likely a photograph of Nazarmat vazir, one of Nikolai Konstantinovich's longtime servants and main assistant in irrigating the Hungry Steppe. Sergei Mikhailovich Prokudin-Gorskii, photographer. *Nazar Magomet. Golodnaia step'*. [Between 1905 and 1915].
Photograph from the Prokudin-Gorskii Collection at the Library of Congress. www.loc.gov/item/prk2000001565/.

By the 1890s, the Grand Duke's realm in the Hungry Steppe had become an alternative source of authority – and even violence – in the region, challenging that of the Russian administration. Though Nikolai himself encouraged respectful behavior toward "native" workers – he forbade the use of the word sart, for instance, regarding it as "abusive and improper," and requested instead the use of the word musafir – his men often seem to have abused their power on the canal work sites.[124] When Efremov visited a work site in 1891, for instance, he was greeted by two hundred and fifty Central Asian workers from Khojand who claimed that they had tried to leave, thinking they had fulfilled their contracts, when they were forcibly turned back by two of the Grand Duke's men, who had

[124] RGIA f 435, op. 1, d. 75, l. 54.

beaten thirty-three of them with whips. Having heard rumors of unsatisfactory conditions and "oppression" on the Grand Duke's canals, Efremov inspected the workers and admitted that though he "didn't notice [evidence of] serious blows ... the traces of whips were evident on all of these people"; he also noted that local workers approached work for the Grand Duke "with dread of his men, who managed them with the aid of sticks and whips." In another case, village heads reported a visit from "seven of the Grand Duke Nikolai Konstantinovich's *djigits* [Central Asian strongmen]," who claimed to have been sent by Nikolai himself. When Alla-Berdy Khudai-Berdyev, the head of the Yangi-Kurgon village association in the southern Hungry Steppe region near Ura-Tiube, refused to carry out the canal work demanded by the Grand Duke's men, he was allegedly beaten by a Russian named Zhukov.[125]

In 1895, the Russian Ministry of Agriculture began carrying out systematic investigations of large areas of the Syr Darya, Ferghana, and Samarkand regions for future irrigation projects. One of these plans projected the irrigation of forty-five thousand desiatinas (about 121,500 acres) in the northeastern part of the Hungry Steppe. The Grand Duke's presence in the region was now more of a nuisance than a benefit. In a letter in April 1899 from Minister of the Imperial Court Baron Fredericks to Agriculture Minister Aleksei Sergeevich Ermolov, the baron stressed that the Grand Duke should leave off his work on the canals, and "surrender them [to the state] – regardless of the [question of the] upkeep of the workers – as instructed by the Governor-General." In a letter to Finance Minister Witte the next month, Ermolov, who had his own schemes for irrigation of the Russian steppes to the north, agreed with Baron Fredericks, stating that "the implementation of the Turkestan Governor-General's plan, with regard to the transfer of the Grand Duke's works to the local branch of the Ministry of Agriculture will lead to the more independent, and for that reason more successful, accomplishment of the irrigation undertakings in the Hungry Steppe."[126]

A further sign that the regional administration may have been exasperated by the trouble caused by the Grand Duke's arbitrary actions and the havoc caused by his men is the special set of instructions sent by the military governor of Samarkand to the head of Khojand district. The instructions stated clearly that the local administration should treat the Grand Duke as an ordinary person, and not as a member of the imperial

[125] GARF f. 1155, op. 1, d. 3689, ll. 6–7, 9, 10.

[126] RGIA f. 426, op. 1, d. 187, ll. 11, 180b; for Ermolov's clashes with Witte over irrigation of the semi-arid Russian steppes, see Moon, *The Plough That Broke the Steppes*, 231–235, *passim*.

household. Any illegal actions on the part of the Grand Duke were to be reported immediately to the military government; any illegal actions on the part of those in the Grand Duke's employ taking place outside his estates should be dealt with according to existing laws and police procedures. Though controlling the Grand Duke's social interactions was something that his attendants had clearly found a difficult task – he had, after all, somehow managed to marry a commoner in Orenburg without attracting notice, and had more recently attempted to marry a Cossack schoolgirl, Valeriia Khmel'nitskaia, in a secret ceremony in his palace in Tashkent – the Samarkand governor's instruction requested that Nikolai's newly appointed superintendent, Major-General Geishtor, do everything within his means to "maintain the purity of the moral atmosphere surrounding the August Patient" and confine Nikolai's movements to Tashkent.[127]

As it turned out, Geishtor would not have to worry immediately about the resolution, for the Grand Duke was removed from Turkestan and sent back to European Russia soon afterward. For a period of several years, it appeared he would never return to the region. He did eventually return to Turkestan in 1906, where he spent the last twelve years of his life continuing to devote himself to the betterment of the province. He also continued to study the local landscapes and to send his recommendations to the local administration about irrigation until his death in 1918, but his days as the virtually unchallenged ruler of the Hungry Steppe were over.

A RUSSO-ASIATIC RULER

Since there was no solid evidence that the Hungry Steppe had ever supported people in large numbers in the past, Nikolai's settlements there were built on his imagined visions of the future: the Hungry Steppe as a Russian colony, as a "wasteland" transformed into a green oasis, as an outpost of civilization, a promised land. The fantasy of a hybrid world in Turkestan in which Russian and Asian cultures blended and settlers and "natives" lived side by side is also one threading its way through the Grand Duke's writings. As his first decade in Turkestan drew to a close, Nikolai Konstantinovich wrote, with regard to irrigation, "Having studied it carefully, I am convinced of its utility and its importance for native agriculture and for Russo-Asiatic culture overall."[128] He was adamant

[127] TsGA RT f. I-1, op. 6, d. 22, ll. 32ob-33; GARF f. 664, op. 1, d. 44, ll. 24–26. For complaints and rumors about the "dark people" with which the Grand Duke surrounded himself, GARF f. 664, op. 1, d. 43.

[128] RGIA f. 435, op. 1, d. 15, ll. 120–121.

that his newly irrigated land be for the use of both Russians and "Muslims" – that is, indigenous Turkestanis. He felt that irrigation canals would lead to both the improvement of local agriculture and the further industrialization of the region; the factories that came as a result would not only benefit the province of Turkestan, but would also "unite even more closely the Russian and native populations."[129] Irrigation, for Nikolai Konstantinovich, was not only a means by which the Russian administration in Turkestan could develop the province and incorporate it into the empire, but also a technology for successfully convincing the local population of the benefits of Russian rule. As evidenced by local legends and the influential positions held by the aqsaqals and mirabs who oversaw irrigation in Turkestan in the present, those who determined where water would flow were held in great esteem by the local population. Bringing water to the lands of Turkestan was, therefore, the best way to show off the power of the Russian Empire.

Ekaterina Pravilova has noted Nikolai Konstantinovich's predilection for local methods of canal-building as an example of his (and, by extension, other Russians') "preference for an 'Orientalist' concept of governance" by appealing "to the memory of Central Asian Khanates' glorious past rather than to the modernist concept of European civilization."[130] The ability to look both backward and forward simultaneously, however, was not unique to Russian Turkestan; rather, it was a hallmark of the irrigation age. Nikolai never rejected European science and methods, nor did he reject modern European civilization – in fact, he engaged in schemes to bring electricity to Tashkent through hydropower and established the first cinemas there.[131] He was especially enthusiastic when Russian engineers, trained in European methods, approved of his work. He reported proudly, for instance, when a "young engineer–technician" from Moscow "received the utmost delight from my hydrotechnical work" and begged St. Petersburg to send an "irrigation expert" to appraise his work in the Hungry Steppe.[132] He claimed his debt to both local Turkestani and European methods of engineering, writing:

> My teachers were the experienced ariq-aqsaqals, the *tuganchi* [dam builders] and the mirabs from among the Muslim-Uzbeks, that is, from that people that

[129] TsGA RU, f. 40, op. 1, d. 23, ll. 7–7ob. [130] Pravilova, "Rivers of Empire," 259.

[131] He used a water-powered motor to light up the grounds of his palace and schemed about using a larger turbine on the grounds of the governor's palace (RGIA f. 435, op. 1, d. 15, l. 70). For later plans for electricity and theaters for Tashkent, see TsGA RU f. 40, op. 1, d. 46.

[132] RGIA f. 435, op. 1, dd. 15, 103ob; 57, ll. 207–207 ob.

over the centuries and because of the environment has become accustomed to artificially watering its crops; I was also aided by Russian surveyors with the plane table and level.[133]

His esteem of "native" knowledge was heightened by his own sense of thrift and reinforced by the fact that he was paying for the canal projects with his own funds, which were controlled by his parents.

Indeed, there was a practical side to Nikolai's enthusiastic championing of Central Asian irrigation methods. Though in 1896 he briefly toyed with the idea of introducing an American-made excavating machine to the canal work, he ended up rejecting the idea, despite its symbolic capital, likely for reasons of cost.[134] He scoffed at what he deemed the unnecessary expenses of European engineering. Without engineers, he claimed, he could carry out irrigation works that were both simpler and cheaper, "thanks to the art of the Muslims," as he once put it.[135] With his emphasis on the experience of Central Asians with "artificially watering … crops," he was probably also aware that, even though there were Russian engineers with plenty of hydraulic expertise, these men came from St. Petersburg, the northern capital built on land reclaimed from the swamps and marshes, whose practical experience was primarily in northern Europe and Russia's water-rich interior.[136]

Nikolai worked hard to persuade the local and regional administration of the advantages of building canals using "native" methods. Most Russian administrators in Turkestan probably shared the opinion of Nil Sergeevich Lykoshin, head of Khojand district and later military governor of Samarkand region, who stated that the "local population is just waiting for the initiative on the part of the representatives of Russian science, in order to properly carry out the improvement of their irrigation."[137] In the almost complete absence of such "representatives of Russian science," however, the local administration found it expedient to allow the Grand Duke's irrigation work to continue, even in the face of spectacular failure, such as when the Bukhara Ariq burst its banks after only a few days of operation in May 1891.

[133] RGIA f. 435, op. 1, d. 15, l. 121. [134] RGIA f. 435, op. 1, d. 57, ll. 259–260ob.

[135] RGIA f. 435, op. 1, d. 15, ll. 21ob-22.

[136] Maya K. Peterson, "Engineering Empire: Russian and Foreign Hydraulic Experts in Central Asia," 1887–1917, *Cahiers du Monde Russe* 57, 1 (January-March 2016): 125–146.

[137] Nil Sergeevich Lykoshin, "Sberezhenie vody," *TV* (1907) in *TS* 435, 108–113: 113; Lykoshin, *Pol zhizni v Turkestane: ocherki byta tuzemnogo naseleniia* (Petrograd: Sklad T-va "V. A. Berezovskii" komissioner voen.-uchebn. zavedenii, 1916), 48.

In spite of his humble posturing as a student of Central Asian irrigation experts and European engineers alike, however, Nikolai clearly enjoyed the power and prestige that irrigation brought him. As one of his guardians put it, Nikolai enjoyed "playing the role of the 'small Tsar of the steppe,' punishing and rewarding according to his own discretion. His character is that of the Khan of the days of yore."[138] While Nikolai never referred to himself as a khan or tsar, he did seem to regard himself as a sort of minor ruler, if not a *padishah* (king), then a *padshazade*, the son of the king – that is, a prince – to which, indeed, his own title of *Velikii Kniaz'* (Grand Prince, usually translated as Grand Duke) could attest. In a letter written in January 1896, a man named Sheffer assigned to oversee indigenous work brigades on the Khiva Ariq confided in Nikolai, "though I am not superstitious, I am unable not to consider the following event a very happy omen." He went on to report that, several days previously, the workers, "called a mullah, and asked him to utter once more a prayer for the health and long life of our *Kniaz' Padshazade*. After about 15 minutes, I was pleased to receive the gracious telegram from your Highness that your health was improving!" Sheffer, too, found himself invoking the name of the *Padshazade* to please the local workers.[139]

The term *Kniaz'-Padshazade* reflects the way Nikolai wanted himself to be seen: as both foreign prince and local ruler, one who was European, but also sensitive to local conditions and customs and beloved by the native population. Though it cannot be said that Nikolai resembled the "white Mughals" described by William Dalrymple, who "crossed over" and were "absorbed" by the India they tried to conquer,[140] the Grand Duke prided himself on his interest in local culture and strove to display this whenever possible; his writings, for instance, are peppered with Turkic and Arabic words. He converted former servants' quarters behind his home in Tashkent into guest rooms for Muslim visitors and made a colorful figure, walking or driving, as he was said to do habitually, in "native" robes through the streets of Tashkent.[141] A *New York Times* article from 1892 reported that Nikolai's "native robe or khalat ... resembles a robe de chambre [dressing gown], and is neither rich in appearance nor free from rents."[142] A kinder eyewitness description from

[138] Cited in Pravilova, "River of Empire," 273.
[139] RGIA f. 435, op. 1, d. 75, ll. 7–7ob, 9ob.
[140] William Dalrymple, *White Mughals: Love and Betrayal in Eighteenth-Century India* (New York: Penguin, 2002), 7.
[141] TsGA RU f. 40, op. 1, d. 46, l. 65.
[142] "A Barbarous Grand Duke," *NYT* (December 31, 1892): 3.

1907 put it thus: "After lunch, the Grand Duke drives (in a red shirt and blue baggy trousers, with a wide belt; sometimes with a warm robe of local manufacture and red in color on top; on his head a felt hat) with Chesovitina [his Cossack mistress] or with his native lackey Guliam."[143]

As the *Kniaz'-Padshazade*, Nikolai requisitioned canal workers from the local population, conducted water-sharing agreements, and mediated disputes, functions that the regional Russian administration had in large part avoided by allowing local "custom" to reign in water management. Once, while away in Khiva pursuing his beloved goal of turning the flow of the Amu Darya toward the Caspian, the water-sharing system negotiated by the Grand Duke in the Begovat region was apparently overruled by Moscow merchants associated with the Kudrin Cotton Company and assisted by the district head of Khojand. The interference of the district government, though sanctioned by the Irrigation Instruction of 1888, severely vexed the Grand Duke, who thought of himself as the ultimate arbiter of custom; previously, according to him, no one had disturbed his system, since they knew that, "according to the shariat," water belongs to the person who first brings it to wastelands [*mertvye zemli*].[144] Nikolai believed that, as the local irrigator, decisions were in his hands about how the waters of his canals were to be used. In the style of a local Muslim ruler, for instance, he asserted that the "irrigation efficiency of the restored Khanym ariq will be established, like *waqf* [an Islamic charitable endowment] for all new and future ariqs in Turkestan," the gains going to cover expenses on other irrigation canals. He rewarded the lands of the best mirabs and workers along the Bukhara Ariq with water for their crops.[145]

By far his favorite reward, however, was that of a robe, or khalat. In giving khalats as rewards, Nikolai was participating in a system well-entrenched in Central Asia: the bestowal of "robes of honor" to connote fealty or to signify approval. This system was not unique to Central Asia – the giving of robes of honor had been an important ceremony at Mongol courts and had spread via Central Asia to South Asia, where the term implied a reward for service.[146] By the second half of the eighteenth century in Bengal, British East India Company leaders, in imitation of

[143] RGIA f. 435, op. 1, d. 33, ll. 147–147ob; Tatishchev similarly describes a felt Kazakh hat and asserts that the Grand Duke had a passion for the color red (*Zemli i liudi*, 93).

[144] TsGA RU f. 40, op. 1, d. 21, l. 11ob.

[145] TsGA RU f. 40, op. 1, dd. 23, l. 10b; 21, ll. 11–11ob.

[146] Morrison, *Russian Rule in Samarkand*, 90 fn 7.

indigenous rulers, took up the practice of bestowing robes upon Indian subordinates.[147] The Ottomans gave robes, as did many African and Middle Eastern rulers. While Muscovite tsars had participated in the practice, it was not part of secular rituals at the Europeanized court at St. Petersburg.[148] In fact, the practice was dying out throughout the entire "robing world," as European colonial powers abandoned the practice in favor of the bestowal of other honors, such as medals.[149] Indeed, Emir Sayyid 'Abd al-Ahad Khan of Bukhara (r. 1885–1911), in addition to "a wardrobe full of brilliant khalats," awarded medals in the European style, such as his Order of the Rising Sun medal, bestowed upon both the Russian war minister for service in building the Transcaspian Railway, as well as the first Danish mission to the Pamirs.[150]

Yet Russian administrators in Turkestan recognized the practice of giving robes as one by which mutual comprehension and coexistence could be achieved, since the "grammar" of robing was almost universal across Eurasia.[151] According to Joseph Wolff, who had traveled to Bukhara and Khiva in the early 1840s:

> The chiefs of the Turkomauns [Turkmen] came from all parts, and said to me loudly: "Write to your King of England, that if he gives us a good sum of money, we will assist him in sending an army to Bokhara … for we Turkomauns do not mind who governs those countries of Bokhara and Khiva, whether Behadur Khan, or England, or Russia; if we only get *khelats* (robes of honour) and *tillahs*, *i.e.* ducats."[152]

Aware of the significance assigned to such gestures by the inhabitants of Turkestan, Russian officials gave robes in public settings, such as at a ceremony in the Zarafshan Valley in 1871 at which Kaufman presided over the giving of khalats to aqsaqals and *qazis* [judges], who swore their

147 Bernard Cohn, *Colonialism and Its Forms of Knowledge* (Princeton, NJ: Princeton University Press, 1996), 117.

148 Stewart Gordon, "Ibn Battuta and a Region of Robing," Introduction to *Robes of Honour: Khil'at in Pre-Colonial and Colonial India* (New Delhi: Oxford University Press, 2003), 9. Peter the Great introduced European regalia to the Russian court. Elaborate robes were, however, still used within the Russian Orthodox Church.

149 Stewart Gordon, "Suitable Luxury," *Saudi Aramco World* 59, 5 (September/October 2008): 10–17. Online at http://archive.aramcoworld.com/issue/200805/suitable.luxury.htm

150 Curzon, *Russia in Central Asia in 1889*, 201; "Russia and Bokhara," *TOL* (March 11, 1889), 6; Esther Fihl, *Exploring Central Asia: From the Steppes to the High Pamirs, 1896–1899*, 1 (Seattle: University of Washington Press, 2010), 71.

151 Gordon, "Ibn Battuta and a Region of Robing," 12.

152 Reverend Joseph Wolff, *Narrative of a Mission to Bokhara, in the Years 1843–45*, I, 2nd edn. (London: John W. Parker, 1845), 275.

allegiance to the Russian tsar.[153] British geographer Edward Delmar Morgan, who observed such a ceremony in Semireche in 1880, observed that "the investiture ... might have had some resemblance to a durbar, except that it lacked the glitter and splendour of the Indian ceremony." He noted that all present – "Dungans ...Tatars, Sarts, and grimy Russian colonists" – had brought the typical Slavic welcome greeting of offerings of bread and salt, that the governor used an interpreter to exchange a few words with each recipient of a medal or khalat, and that each award was accompanied by "a document in which were recited the services for which it was bestowed."[154] Giving honorary khalats as an alternative to monetary rewards was listed in the 1886 statute governing Turkestan Krai as appropriate recognition of diligent service or knowledge of the Russian language on the part of native officials, and governors-general seem to have continued the tradition of awarding both khalats and medals into the twentieth century.[155]

The Grand Duke himself used the giving of robes to establish his own personal connections with local notables. Simple khalats were fine for ordinary occasions and for low-ranking men, such as an usta in charge of the more productive artels; more elaborate ones were reserved for special occasions. Nikolai used them especially in reward for particular services rendered or to maintain loyalty. In the case of the Kazakh district head Aibek Urmanovich, for instance, one of Nikolai's men suggested that Urmanovich ought to be given a khalat and a ring, as "he will be useful to us in the future." Urmanovich had recently supplied five hundred workers, who had dug one thousand cubic sazhens in just three weeks on the Khanym Ariq. Nikolai magnanimously agreed not only to give Urmanovich a brocade caftan but also to give twelve khalats as gifts to the aul leaders under his jurisdiction.[156] Such practices allowed Nikolai to cultivate a network of associates throughout the region, all of whom understood that their acceptance of the robe could be interpreted not only as acknowledgment of gratitude for their services, but also as recognition of the Grand Duke's power in the region and a pledge of loyalty to him in the future.[157]

[153] Morrison, *Russian Rule in Samarkand*, 104.

[154] E. Delmar Morgan, "A Journey Through Semiretchie to Kuldja in 1880," *PRGS* 3, 3 (March 1881): 160.

[155] *Polozhenie ob upravlenii Turkestanskogo kraia*, st. 106; Varvara Dukhovskaia, *The Diary of a Russian Lady* (London: John Long, 1917), 509.

[156] RGIA f. 435, op. 1, d. 57, l. 136.

[157] For the bestowal of a khalat as an act of transferring authority, see Cohn, *Colonialism and its Forms of Knowledge*, 114–115.

THE LEGEND OF THE THIRSTY STEPPE

One can get a sense of the hybrid world which the Grand Duke inhabited by imagining a journey through the villages in the Hungry Steppe just after the turn of the twentieth century. Nikolai often spoke of bringing "life" to "dead" lands (*mertvye zemli*). Here, he was not only echoing the language of Europeans and Americans in the irrigation age, but also indigenous Central Asians.[158] In Nikolai's Hungry Steppe, the life was to consist of a strong, sturdy backbone, composed of Russian settler villages running from north to south near the Syr Darya, and the network of ariqs, forming a system to carry the precious lifegiving water from the river out to fields which would flourish where the Hungry Steppe had once claimed lives. The settler villages, as beacons of Russian civilization in this former wasteland, bore Russian names, reminiscent of faith and empire – Nikolaevskoe, also known as Nikola Belyi (Nikola the White, presumably referring to the "White Tsar," Nicholas II, though it could refer to the Grand Duke himself), Romanovskoe, after the imperial rulers; Konnogvardeiskoe and Volynskoe, named after elite imperial regiments (the Grand Duke himself had been a colonel in the Volynskii regiment until his exile and used "Volynskoi" as a pseudonym); Nadezhdinskoe, which may have been named after Nadezhda von Dreyer, but also was redolent of hope (*nadezhda* means hope), Obetovannoe, which means "promised," as in *Krai Obetovannyi*, the Promised Land that Turkestan Krai was to become.[159] Indeed, many Russian settlers did hope they would find a Promised Land in the Hungry Steppe.

What connected all these fragments of empire, however – these lonely outposts of Orthodox Christianity and Russian civilization in the monotonous landscape – were the ariqs, which for Nikolai were reminiscent of another world, an ancient and romantic, Oriental world of mystique and legend. The fact that he continued to use the local Turkic word *ariq*, instead of *kanal*, for his projects embodies this understanding of the water channels in the Hungry Steppe. Constructed with the simple tools that had reshaped the land for centuries, the ariqs resurrected the ghosts of

[158] For a Khivan tale of "many dead lands being reclaimed," see Munis and Agahi, *Firdaws al-iqbāl*, 293.

[159] For a use of Volynskoi as pseudonym, see TsGA RU f. 40, op. 1, d. 532, ll. 16, 24. Volynskii also appears to be the name given to his illegimate children with Alexandra Alexandrovna Demidova (Krasjukov, "Grossfürst Nikolai Konstantinowitsch," 308–310).

the past. Nikolai had heard, for instance, that the Khanym Ariq was originally a channel dug by Amir Timur (Tamerlane) in honor of his favorite wife.[160] Nikolai's canals and estates, too, bore names redolent of history and legend. The Iskander canal and estate were linked with Alexander the Great, while his estate in the southern Hungry Steppe was called "Golden Horde." And the Sladkaia Tsarevna Canal, which originated from the Syr Darya alongside the Bukhara and Khiva canals near Begovat, was also known by its local equivalent, the "Shirin Qiz." *Shirin* is the Persian and Uzbek word for "sweet" – thus, Shirin Qiz literally means the "Sweet Girl" in Uzbek, and Sladkaia Tsarevna the "Sweet Princess" in Russian – but local inhabitants would have immediately recognized in its name a reference to the Persian legend of Farhad and Shirin.

The legend of Farhad and Shirin is the story of Khusraw II, a Sassanid king; Shirin, the Christian princess Khusraw wished to marry; and Farhad the stonemason, who also loved Shirin. Over the centuries the tale has spread across Western, South, and Central Asia, containing similar elements wherever it is told. In each of these stories, Khusraw gives Farhad a nearly impossible task, with the promise of Shirin's hand in marriage if he were capable of completing it. The task often involves tunneling through an enormous mountain or building a canal many miles long, through which water or milk would then flow. When it appears that Farhad might actually achieve the impossible, the alarmed Khusraw orders false rumors of Shirin's death to be spread. On hearing of Shirin's death, Farhad kills himself (or dies of a broken heart). When Shirin hears of her lover's death, she, too, kills herself.

In his writings, the Grand Duke often referred to a place near the rapids upstream from Begovat called "Farkhadskie skaly" – the Rocks, or Cliffs, of Farhad. His Shirin canal thus brought water from the Rocks of Farhad into the Hungry (or, as he might have thought of it, the "Thirsty") Steppe. As the constable [*uriadnik*] of Zaporozhskoe, the worker village at the Begovat rapids, wrote to him in 1892, "It's too bad that the whole canal isn't finished, so that it would be possible to see even a drop of the [Syr] Darya rushing in order to water the hungry steppe more quickly, like the Lover [here he used *ashyk*, the Russified version of the Uzbek word *oshiq*] Farkhat [rushing to bring water] to Shirin." On this letter, Nikolai wrote, "Award constable Kugerbai 25 rubles for [his work on] the Tsar Dam, in memory of the *bogatyr* Farkat and the Princess

[160] RGIA f. 435, op. 1, d. 15, l. 117.

Kyz-Shirin." On the back of the letter, with a note that the constable had received the award, he added, in Cyrillic, "*Bismil' liagi rakhmat i rakhim*" [*Bismillah al-rahman al-rahim*, Arabic for "In the name of God, most Gracious, most Compassionate"].[161] Even many years later, visitors to the villages of the Hungry Steppe were told the local version of the Farhad and Shirin story by Slavic settlers in the villages of Verkhne-Volynskoe and Zaporozhskoe.[162]

Since the legend itself is so bound up with landscapes – Farhad must literally move mountains to be with his loved one – it is quite plausible that local inhabitants near the rapids at Begovat had their own oral version of the tale associated with this landscape, particularly since this spot on the Syr Darya was associated with the fairy tale before Nikolai arrived in the region.[163] It thus appears that the Grand Duke, enamored of the tale and its local associations, inserted his own irrigation work into local tradition and the topography of the "Russo-Asiatic" world he was creating in the Hungry Steppe. A photograph of the "Rocks of Farhad" from around 1914 shows a large capital "N" carved into the rock face, surmounted by a crown.[164] This monogram was the one used by the Grand Duke in correspondence with his wife Nadezhda and seems to suggest that Nikolai was asserting his rule over the area, as a local ruler might demarcate his territory. Either way, he seems to have used the incorporation of local knowledge and legends as a way of legitimizing himself as a local ruler – of writing himself into Central Asian history.

CONCLUSION

The archives in Tashkent contain several versions of a poem on the theme of Farhad and Shirin that are heavily edited in the Grand Duke's hand

[161] RGIA f. 435, op. 1, d. 118, ll. 90–90ob.

[162] Both V. F. Karavaev and Prince Masal'skii heard a version of the story in the Hungry Steppe in which Shirin will marry whichever man can bring water to the Hungry Steppe. In this version, Khusraw tries to trick Shirin by buying reed mats from the bazaar, which resemble water as they shine in the sun where he has placed them in the steppe. Farhad, of course, pursues the real labor of bringing the river to the steppe (V. I. Masal'skii, *Turkestanskii krai*, vol. 19 of ed. V.P. Semonov-Tian-Shanskii, *Rossiia: Polnoe geograficheskoe opisanie nashego otechestva* [St. Petersburg: A. F. Devrien, 1913] 693–694). Karavaev suspected the Grand Duke's hand in this "local fantasy" (V. F. Karavaev, *Golodnaia Step' v eia proshlom i nastoiashchem* [Petrograd: GUZiZ, 1914], 31–32 fn 1).

[163] V. F. Gaidukevich, "Mogil'nik bliz Shirin-Saia v Uzbekistane," *SA* XVI (1952): 332 fn 2.

[164] Karavaev, *Golodnaia Step'*, photograph between pages 32 and 33.

and clearly display his understanding of himself as the mediator of a Russian power that could awaken the latent potential of the Central Asian land and restore it to its former glory.[165] The poem, called "Sweet Princess: A Begovat Fairy Tale," is claimed to have been written from the words of Muslims in the Hungry Steppe on the [Syr] Darya Rapids, as told in the year 7401 (1893).[166] A version of the poem was published in a "Turkestani literary collection" in 1900 under the pseudonym N. Volynskoi. The poem is introduced with quotations from Semiramis and Napoleon; thus, the Grand Duke placed his tale – and, by extension, himself – squarely between an ancient and powerful "Oriental" despot, a legendary Assyrian queen associated with the Hanging Gardens of Babylon, and a modern imperial ruler, who claimed that his greatest deeds were accomplished "in the East." Nikolai also quoted a saying "of the Turkmen, Kurds, and Arabs," which began: "A drop of water, given to one thirsting in the desert, clears away sins for one hundred years ..."[167] He made the story a particularly local one by placing the setting of the fated love story at the Begovat Rapids, where Shirin, whose beauty and kindness are known throughout the East, receives her various suitors, including the Bukharan Khosro and the Khivan Farkhat (Farhad).

Part of the section of the poem called "Shirin i Farkhat" reads, in rhyming couplets:

> Seven thousand years have passed since that time ...
> But the people still remember where the Princess lived,
> And they pray where she died,
> And thoughts of the deeds of Shirin and Farkhat,
> The River has taken with their blood to its depths ...
> And the waves roll fruitlessly to the Aral [Sea],
> And the cascades sound against the rocks in vain,

[165] Though he may have commissioned these works (Pravilova, "River of Empire," 272–273), I have primarily used the texts heavily marked with his personal edits (TsGA RU f. 40, op. 1, d. 532, "Stikhotvoreniia po povodu irrigatsionnykh rabot kniazia; s pometkami i ispravleniiami kniazia"). The published version is N. Volynskoi, "Sladkaia tsarevna: Begovadskaia skazka" in *Turkestanskii literaturnyi sbornik* (St. Petersburg: A. Benke, 1900), 57–64.

[166] The date is according to the Eastern Orthodox calendar (TsGA RU f. 40, op. 1, d. 532, l. 25). Nikolai may have been inspired by other tales he heard in Khorezm ("River of Empire," 267 fn 18); here, he takes the literary license to place Khorezm at the gates of Ferghana (which may explain his use of "Darya" without specifying the river). There is also a "Bekabad" (in Khorezmian pronunciation – Begovat) near Urgench, which may have inspired Nikolai to play around with the region's geography (Bregel, note 387 in Munis and Agahi, *Firdaws al-iqbāl*, 587).

[167] TsGA RU f. 40, op. 1, d. 532, ll. 12, 25.

The desert, as before, is somber and lifeless,
But the inhabitants believe in the prophet's words:
In the seven thousand four hundred and first year,
The River will pour its water into the steppes.
Shirin will be revived, and after her the whole country,
The desert will wake from its heavy sleep.[168]

By invoking the tale of Farhad and Shirin, Nikolai Konstantinovich gave himself the role of making the prophet's words come true; by completing the Shirin Qiz Ariq in 1893, he was waking the desert from thousands of years of slumber, restoring the world to its rightful state (while also clearing away his own sins). The end of the poem contained several verses in praise of the tsar and the changes the sovereign had brought to Central Asia, including the irrigation of the Hungry Steppe.[169] The poem, thus, features a theme resounding throughout the Russian and Soviet rule of Central Asia: that Central Asia's newest rulers were simply enabling a "natural" process, putting into motion a logical program that would make the greatest use of the natural bounty of the region. The image of rivers flowing "fruitlessly" to the Aral Sea reflects the idea shared by many in the irrigation age and beyond that Central Asia's waters were best harnessed for cultivation.

Whereas some Russians felt Turkestan would be transformed by importing European civilization, Nikolai believed that the potential of Turkestan was in the landscape itself, that the very topography of the region held clues to be deciphered by those possessing the knowledge, and that the province needed only a loving hand in order to flourish. It was a romanticized and perhaps irrational vision, but in his great love for Russia, the eccentric Grand Duke believed that Turkestan under Russian rule could indeed become the *Krai Obetovannyi* – the Promised Land. The Russian administration, however, was no longer particularly interested in what the Grand Duke thought; it had other plans. By 1900, as the empire embraced more vigorous state-sponsored programs of colonization and irrigation, projects that left little room for indigenous Central Asians and their knowledge, the days of the Kniaz′-Padshazade were virtually over, yet his memory persists to this day in the form of a legend about a harmonious lost world in the Hungry Steppe.

[168] Ibid., l. 19ob. [169] Ibid., l. 11; Volynskoi, "Sladkaia tsarevna," 64.

3

To Create a New Turkestan

Water Governance in the Irrigation Age

> The amount of reserve water could, in the cotton regions alone, irrigate at least another 3 million desiatinas – that is, an area equivalent to the amount of land currently irrigated in Turkestan, as it were creating a second Turkestan. This new Turkestan, not inferior to the old one in magnitude, would surpass it in riches and level of culture, and its new population would be Russian.
>
> – Russian Minister of Agriculture Alexander Krivoshein, 1912[1]

In the early years of the twentieth century, as the Russian administration asserted control over agricultural development and colonization in Turkestan, the issue of customary water management practices – enshrined in the Turkestan Statute of 1886 as the only legal way the waters of the province could be used – was raised repeatedly in discussions at both the regional level and at the level of the central government. On his inspection of the province in 1908 and 1909, senator Konstantin Pahlen found himself raising the same question that had vexed state councilor Dingel′shtedt more than two decades earlier: "[J]ust what, exactly," wrote Pahlen in his official report on irrigation in Turkestan, "does that customary law – whose protection from arbitrary violations forms one of the main tasks of the administration – entail?"[2] In the first decade of the twentieth century, tsarist officials in Turkestan found ways to bypass

[1] A. V. Krivoshein, *Zapiska Glavnoupravliaiushchego zemleustroistvom i zemledeliem o poezdke v Turkestanskii krai v 1912 g. Prilozhenie k vsepoddaneishemu dokladu* (Poltava, 1912), 30.

[2] Pahlen, *Oroshenie*, 6.

outright dependence on indigenous traditions and authorities – by replacing native ariq aqsaqals with Slavs, for instance – but it was clear that as the Russian Empire continued to develop Turkestan, new problems would arise for which custom had no good answers.[3] Even though most Russians agreed that more scientific methods for utilizing the region's precious water resources were highly desirable – primarily for the purposes of growing cotton, a lucrative cash crop, but also for increasing settlement – they increasingly understood that before Turkestan's "productive forces" could be efficiently harnessed and used, Russia would have to create a new set of rules by which the province's water resources were governed. In the meantime, those interested in the further development of irrigation in Turkestan would have to wait.

BRINGING ORDER TO THE HUNGRY STEPPE

In 1898, the state treasury gained possession of the Nicholas I (Khiva) Canal from Grand Duke Nikolai Konstantinovich. Yet St. Petersburg remained reluctant, as it had been in the wake of the 1891 famine, to take responsibility for the fate of poor Slavic migrants in the region. In July 1899, recently appointed Governor-General Sergei Dukhovskoi (1898–1901) begged the central government for money for the canal, noting that the imperial administration could not let existing Russian settlements go without water, and pointing out the necessity of funding the future upkeep of settler villages, as well as canal management. It appears that his exhortations went unheeded, for in October he wrote a telegram to Finance Minister Sergei Witte, stating that:

> The local branch of the Ministry of Agriculture is not receiving funds for the upkeep of ariqs. An entire series of misunderstandings threatens to precipitate needless treasury spending in future, [and] hampers colonization. The Grand Duke is curtailing his spending on those ariqs taken over by the state. There is a risk that the damage will go without repair. Newly arrived settlers refuse to take up settlement without water.[4]

The Grand Duke himself wrote a telegram to Agriculture Minister Aleksei Sergeevich Ermolov, expressing his dissatisfaction with the fact that important repairs were not being carried out, and that:

[3] Dingel'shedt, *Opyt izucheniia irrigatsii*, 58, 142–143; G. K. Gins, *Osnovnye nachala proekta vodnogo zakona dlia Turkestana* (St. Petersburg: F. Vaisberg i P. Gershunin, 1912), 30.

[4] RGIA f. 426, op. 1, d. 187, ll. 48–49, 75–75ob.

the agriculturalists whom I invited here, through my own great efforts, to the Nikolaev [sic] Steppe that I myself irrigated, are not being allowed to continue sowing, something that will cause great losses both to them and to the treasury, and I myself look on with sadness in my heart at how the fruits of my work and my great monetary expenditures over the last 15 years, all for the benefit of the motherland, are being wasted, and I beg for your magnanimous participation in the fate of these affairs ...[5]

The Ministry of Agriculture finally transferred 10,000 rubles to Tashkent for the repair of canals, including the Nicholas I Canal, but it was too little and too late. After the early and heavy snow of the "particularly severe" winter of 1899–1900, and because of the canal's proximity to the Syr Darya, in May 1900, when meltwater from high in the mountains to the east came rushing down to the lowlands, the Nicholas I Canal burst its banks, causing flooding and destruction, followed by a six-week period during which the damaged canal could not deliver water to the fields at a crucial time for the autumn harvest. The failure of the canal was followed by a plague of locusts, which descended to eat whatever crops did emerge.[6] The government failure to maintain the Grand Duke's canals threatened to undermine the illusion of Russian control, as had the earlier wave of destitute immigrants fleeing famine, or, more recently – and perhaps more alarmingly – the Andijan Rebellion of 1898, in which Madali Ishan, a Sufi leader, led a group of about two thousand, mostly Kyrgyz from the eastern Ferghana Valley, to attack the Russian garrison at Andijan in the name of *ghazawat* (holy war). Russian officials called it "the insane act of fanatics"; such "fanaticism" was a specter that Dukhovskoi was determined to stamp out.[7]

Many Russians believed that orderly colonization of the province might provide a model of civilization for the indigenous population. However, though the Russian Empire had a new Resettlement Administration, formed in order to oversee colonization throughout the empire, in 1897 Dukhovskoi's predecessor Governor-General Aleksandr Vrevskii (1889–1898) had put a halt to the official registration and

[5] Ibid., l. 89.

[6] Ibid., ll. 96, 148; Dukhovskaia, *The Diary of a Russian Lady*, 522; Pahlen, *Oroshenie*, 475. A similar thing happened in 1909, though the damage was not as severe ("Vinovaty-li russkie pereselentsy?," *NV* 11958 [1909] in *TS* 507, 190).

[7] RGIA f. 391, op. 3, d. 1484, l. 2; Dukhovskaia, *The Diary of a Russian Lady*, 509; Khalid, "Culture and Power in Colonial Turkestan," 424. Madali Ishan claimed that his goals were to halt the "decline of morals" under Russian rule; he also rued "the abolition of traditional taxes" (Beatrice Forbes Manz, "Central Asian Uprisings in the Nineteenth Century: Ferghana under the Russians," *Russian Review* 46, 3 [July 1987]: 279).

establishment (vodvorenie) of new migrants in Turkestan, until such time as the newly created Turkestan branch of the Ministry of Agriculture could identify appropriate lands for settlement.[8] Dukhovskoi's request to appropriate for new Russian settlements one hundred thousand rubles in unused regional funds was, thus, met with refusal from Witte, who insisted that such monies be devoted instead to the new government plan to irrigate the Hungry Steppe. (The unused funds themselves were from a government attempt to restore and extend the Uch-Qorghon Ariq near Namangan in Ferghana for a new Russian settler village, which had been blocked by Turkestanis with a deed claiming rights to this land.)[9]

Many of Turkestan's administrators believed that until the Ministry of Agriculture carried out land surveys, there simply were no lands where Russian settlers could be established without the expansion of existing irrigation systems at significant costs to the state. Where land was already cultivated, water rights were already apportioned by custom and, thus, were mostly in the hands of indigenous smallholders. In 1898, the head of Tashkent district wrote to the military governor of the Syr Darya region that "in the district there are no available lands suitable for Russian settlement without expenditures on the part of the State."[10] In 1900, the military governor of Ferghana similarly reported that there were "no parcels of land on which it might be possible to establish settlements without significant state expenditures on irrigation."[11]

To avoid conflict, head of the Turkestan branch of the Ministry of Agriculture Stanislav Iul'evich Rauner was adamant about the fact that in future, no one would be able to use water or land in Turkestan without prior permission from the state. When the military governor of Samarkand region granted land to five peasants who arrived in the Hungry Steppe village of Konnogvardeiskoe in the spring of 1901, he was chastised by the new governor-general, Nikolai Ivanov (1901–1904), for giving out land when there was "none available" in the village. The governor then had to be reminded on several more occasions that "without the participation of the Ministry of Agriculture, and without notifying

[8] Gavrilov, *Pereselencheskoe delo v Turkestanskom krae*, 4. For hopes of new Russian settler villages providing a model of civilization after Andijan, see "O dal'neishem zaselenii Turkestana russkimi krest'ianami," http://zerrspiegel.orientphil.uni-halle.de/t503.html

[9] RGIA f. 426, op. 1, d. 187, ll. 19, 44; Thurman, "Modes of Organization," 101; V. I. Masal'skii, *Khlopkovodstvo, oroshenie gosudarstvennykh zemel' i chastnaia predpriimchivost'* (St. Petersburg: M. M. Stasiulevich, 1908), 21.

[10] Cited in Ginzburg, *Russkoe naselenie v Turkestane*, 28.

[11] "O dal'neishem zaselenii Turkestana russkimi krest'ianami."

the ministry, no allotments can be given out."[12] The succession of governors-general in the province in the last years of the nineteenth and first years of the twentieth centuries had to contend with the frustrating situation that the civilizing mission with which they had been tasked was nearly impossible without more government support; the central government, on the other hand, felt that its lack of knowledge about the land and water resources of the province, along with its lack of full control over the governance of these resources, and a general lack of finances with which to develop this vast military colony, had tied its hands. Regional officials were simultaneously frustrated by this state of affairs as well as cognizant of the fact that there could be no more "Kniaz′-Padshahzades" who "seized" state lands, settled all manner of people on them, and subjected the lands and waters of the region to a "chaotic" system of usage, from which the administration had to rescue them.[13]

In order to determine just how much land was available for settlers in the Hungry Steppe – seen as a particularly desirable place for development because of its relative isolation from the local population – Turkestan's administrators had to clarify how much land was already being used by Russian settlers.[14] Yet they also found themselves faced with indigenous communities who claimed that the Grand Duke had given them rights to local land and water resources.[15] Like the Central Asian khans, Nikolai had issued documentation in which he, as the local "ruler" and irrigator, generously granted water-using privileges. In deference to "custom," Russian officials often honored existing agreements, such as a document bearing the Grand Duke's signature, upheld by a land assessment commission in the fall of 1903, which had been presented by the inhabitants of Begovat as their claim to water free-of-charge, having allowed the Grand Duke to build a canal through their lands that destroyed the previously existing irrigation channel they themselves had built.[16] At the same time, however, the regional administration excused itself from responsibility for ensuring that the current settlers had enough water or compensating them for any losses to their crops from any cause, including the construction of new irrigation canals through sown areas. The government also stressed that the rental of

[12] RGIA f. 426, op. 1, d. 187, l. 109; *GS*, Doc. 22: 56–59.

[13] RGIA f. 426, op. 1, d. 187, ll. 107, 109.

[14] *Trudy Khlopkovogo komiteta*, 1, 59.

[15] *GS*, Doc. 22: 58–59; RGIA f. 426, op. 1, d. 767, l. 16, *RZ* (June 7,1912).

[16] *GS* Doc. 22: 59; RGIA f. 426, op. 1, d. 767, l. 16, *RZ* (June 7, 1912).

state lands in the Hungry Steppe was a temporary arrangement, subject to change without notice.[17]

In spite of these efforts, the Turkestan branch of the Ministry of Agriculture had to admit in 1903 that, due to a lack of land surveyors, it could not report just how much land was being used by the peasants in the Russian settlements, nor could it determine exactly how much land was being irrigated by the existing Nicholas I Canal; the best guess was around six thousand desiatinas (later estimates were around nine thousand).[18] The question of how much land the Nicholas I Canal irrigated was important not for calculations of how much water each settler village received – since the ministry had already absolved itself of the burden of providing water to settlers – as it was for determining how the already existing canal could supplement the new government plan to irrigate the same region, a question that could not be solved by simple arithmetic.

Though the Hungry Steppe was often portrayed as a flat landscape, unbroken by any distinctive features, the designated area for the new government irrigation project, between the Nicholas I Canal and the Syr Darya, and to the north of the Tashkent branch of the Samarkand-Andijan railroad line, was not uniformly even, nor of consistent quality. Officials marked off hillocks, depressions that could easily turn into swamps, areas already occupied by roads, and salt flats as areas unsuitable for irrigation. The irrigators of the Hungry Steppe believed that salt flats could be reclaimed, but worried that since Russian engineers did "not yet [have] enough experience" with such lands, attempting to make salt flats into usable cropland might run the risk of the further salinization of surrounding land; thus, these lands, too, were excluded from the region slated for irrigation. The remaining area was further divided into two main regions – a region of higher steppe land and a lower-lying, swampy region of *tugay* (riparian forest), separated by a narrow terrace running parallel to the Syr Darya, on which the Grand Duke had established his settler villages.[19]

Based on a number of hasty investigations carried out by the Turkestan branch of the Ministry of Agriculture in 1900, draft plans were completed the following year for small portions of the main canal, which would have its head at the same place chosen by the Grand Duke for the Khiva Canal.

[17] *GS*, Doc. 22: 55, 58; RGIA f. 426, op. 1, d. 187, l. 109.

[18] *GS*, Doc. 23: 63. The latter figure is according to Pahlen, *Oroshenie*, 474–475.

[19] *GS*, Doc. 32: 96–97.

Though the technical plans remained incomplete "due to a lack of time and as a result of the limited number of irrigation technicians at the Ministry," with urging from Governor-General Dukhovskoi, work on the canal began in the fall of 1901. Minister Ermolov allotted one portion of the canal work to the settlers in the Hungry Steppe, since the settlers' crops had been destroyed by locusts.[20] In November 1901, the *Turkestan Gazette* reported, "Thus began the colossal affair of the irrigation of the Hungry Steppe, an affair promising a splendid future for our krai, presenting a new, expansive field for Russian colonization, which alone is able to bind this wonderful country to Russia for good."[21] The fact that the new project incorporated the Grand Duke's Nicholas I Canal was not seen as a drawback. The young engineer Stanislav Ostrovskii, for instance, who took on the project after returning from an irrigation inspection trip to British India in 1906, admitted that the Nicholas I Canal had "enormous historical value, as the first Russian canal irrigating the lifeless expanses of the Hungry Steppe and providing the impetus for the further development of irrigation ..."[22] Agriculture Minister Alexander Krivoshein would add that even though the Nicholas I Canal had been built using "typical native methods, nevertheless, as the earliest successful Russian affair in the realm of irrigation, [its significance], both economical and, in particular, moral, is beyond doubt."[23]

MANAGING WATER

Following Russian efforts to irrigate the Merv Oasis with the waters of the Murghab River, the launch of the government project to irrigate the Hungry Steppe secured Russia's place in a world with a growing interest in irrigation. By the 1890s, the idea of irrigation as a way to avoid more years of famine in the southern regions of Russia had attracted attention even in the central administration.[24] At that time, several forward-thinking Russians – even before their counterparts in Paris and Australia – had joined the newly formed American Society of Irrigation Engineers, which advertised itself as "the first of its kind in this country

[20] *GS*, Doc. 20: 51–53. It was later revealed that the soil studies were undertaken in great haste and, consequently, were neither thorough nor accurate. "K voprosu ob oroshenii Golodnoi Stepi," *TTPG* 17 (1908) in *TS* 456, 18–19.

[21] *GS*, Doc. 20: 51.

[22] *GS*, Doc. 32: 98–99.

[23] Krivoshein, *Zapiska Glavnoupravliaiushchego zemleustroistvom i zemledeliem*, 36.

[24] Dingel'shtedt, *Opyt izucheniia irrigatsii*, 141; See also chapter 7, "Irrigation," in Moon, *The Plough That Broke the Steppes*.

FIGURE 3.1 Cotton in front of the house of a settler in Veliko-Alekseevskoe in the Hungry Steppe. Photograph No. 13 in *Vidy zaseliaemoi chasti Golodnoi Stepi* [*Views of the Settled Part of the Hungry Steppe*], 7.
Reproduced with permission of the Rare Books Section of the Alisher Navoi State Library, Tashkent, Uzbekistan.

[i.e., the United States] if not in the world." Its regular activities were to be reported in an existing journal called *The Irrigation Age*, capturing the spirit of the times.[25] In the early twentieth century, Russian engineers attended irrigation congresses and conferences on the improvement of arid lands, most of which were held in the United States, and they traveled to other arid regions of the world to learn about the challenges of making the deserts bloom.[26] In Turkestan, however, lack of knowledge about the land and water resources of the region, combined with general lack of experience, made any irrigation project a major challenge. And although Article 107 of the Turkestan Statute of 1886 placed the Russian

[25] *Annual of the American Society of Irrigation Engineers for 1892–93* (Denver, 1894), 5, 223–224, 253–254.
[26] Peterson, "Engineering Empire," 139–140.

administration in charge of appointing ariq aqsaqals, the fact that these ariq aqsaqals continued to apportion water according to "custom" – as enshrined in Article 256 of the same statute – left Russian officials feeling helplessly dependent on indigenous irrigation managers. Nor had the provision of keeping journals, as detailed by the Irrigation of Instruction of 1888, enabled the state to better "see" how custom structured water use on individual systems, some of which were anyway too vast for proper oversight.[27]

The "heads of irrigation" – engineers and technicians designated to tackle "scientific and technical problems in order to aid with their knowledge and experience [*poznaniia*] irrigation affairs and their further development" – were faced with even more expansive territories, while the tedious administrative duties detailed in the Irrigation Instruction of 1888 required all technicians to spend much of their time far from the irrigation systems, which often prevented them from having any significant impact on irrigation practices.[28] Knowledgeable observers had to admit that the influence of this state-appointed technical staff over canal maintenance in Turkestan was negligible. Nor had the creation in 1892 of an administrative position to oversee all irrigation projects in Turkestan done much to change the situation. This position was replaced in 1897 with two officials within the newly created Turkestan division of the Ministry of Agriculture, who were to supervise the construction of all new irrigation canals and oversee the repair of existing ones.[29] However, the following year the governor-general upheld the right of the people to repair, clean, and use their canals as enshrined in Article 256 of the Turkestan Statute, so that even regional heads of irrigation needed to consult with the people and get approval of the district head before making any changes to irrigation systems.[30] Upper-level Russian irrigation officials were, moreover, more likely to be military topographers, or railway or mining engineers, than hydraulic engineers.[31] The lack of

[27] Pahlen, *Oroshenie*, 183–187; N. Sinel′nikov, "Uporiadochenie vodnogo khoziaistva v sviazi s kolonizatsiei oroshaemykh ploshchadei," *VK* 4 (n.d.), 134–162: 157; K. Proskuriakov, "Eshche ob irrigatsii," *TSKh* 11 (1907) in TS 455, 71–74: 71–72.

[28] Pahlen, *Oroshenie*, 6; Sinel′nikov, "Uporiadochenie vodnogo khoziaistva," 157; Skorniakov, "Iskusstvennoe oroshenie v Aziiatskoi Rossii," 243.

[29] Petrov, *Ob irrigatsii v Turkestanskom krae*, 121–122; K. A. Timaev, "Turkestanskii irrigatsionnyi otdel," *TK* 116 (1909) in *TS* 108, 105–108: 106; Matisen, "Polozhenie i nuzhdy orosheniia," 281; Pahlen, *Oroshenie*, 335.

[30] A. Babaliants, "Pervyi s″ezd gidrotekhnikov Turkestanskogo kraia i znachenie ego dlia Semirechenskoi oblasti," from *SOV* 46–52 (1908) in *TS* 471, 71–86: 84–85.

[31] Thurman, "Modes of Organization," 94; Pahlen, *Mission to Turkestan*, 92.

qualified hydraulic engineers in the Russian Empire with theoretical knowledge of or practical experience in the management of water in arid lands partially explains this situation, yet the appointment of railway engineers to important positions in the irrigation administration of Russian Turkestan also signaled that the tsarist administration placed a higher value on scientific and technical education of any kind over local Central Asian knowledge and practical experience.[32]

The Russian government also took other steps to assert control over water management. By the turn of the century, many lower-level water administrators were being replaced with representatives from the Slavic population. According to a local guide to Samarkand from 1901, for instance, in recent years the ariq aqsaqals had been chosen "primarily from the Russian people." A comparison of Samarkand directories from 1896 and 1909 shows a clear shift from the employment of indigenous ariq aqsaqals to a mix of ethnic Russians and Turkestanis.[33] Documents from the Tajik archives give a window into this process. In one case, an ordinance of the military governor of Samarkand issued in April 1899 called for replacing the ariq aqsaqal on the Ak Darya Canal, "the native Mirza Abdusait Safarov," with a certain Markov, the ariq aqsaqal from Dalverzin, just east of the Hungry Steppe. Markov's position, in turn, was to be filled by one Ivan Gavriushin. This change in staffing came about at the request of Samarkand's Head of Irrigation, who had requested that Safarov be replaced "due to lack of diligence and negligence."[34] By leveling such accusations, or by claiming that indigenous ariq aqsaqals could not fulfill the types of duties required by the kinds of changes Russians were bringing to the region, Russian authorities could ensure that more Slavs filled these positions, gradually phasing out indigenous domination of water management.[35]

In particular, Russians were frustrated by the fact that indigenous overseers did not seem to be able to fulfill certain articles of the

32 Peterson, "Engineering Empire," 132–134; Pahlen, *Mission to Turkestan*, 92.

33 *Spravochnik i adres-kalendar' Samarkandskoi oblasti na 1901 god*, ed. M. M. Virskii (Samarkand: Samarkandskoi obl. stat. komitet, 1901), 35; *Adres-kalendar' na 1896: lits, sluzhashchikh v pravitel'stvennykh, obshchestvennykh i chastnykh uchrezhdeniiakh i ustanovleniiakh Samarkandskoi oblasti, Bukhary, Chardzhuia i Kerki*, ed. M. M. Virskii (Samarkand: Samarkandskoi obl. stat. komitet, 1896), 5–11; *Spravochnik i adres-kalendar' Samarkandskoi oblasti na 1909* (Samarkand: Samarkandskoi obl. stat. komitet, 1908), otd. II ("Adres-kalendar'"), 5, 14–19, 24–28.

34 TsGA RT f. I-1, op. 2, d. 165, l. 16.

35 "K irrigatsionnym voprosam," *TK* 274 (1907) in *TS* 451, 124–126: 124; Pahlen, *Oroshenie*, 188.

instruction, such as the requirement to provide written versions of water-sharing agreements and descriptions of irrigation systems, as well as the requirement that ariq aqsaqals know how much water was flowing through an ariq at any given time; where ariq aqsaqals still came mostly from the indigenous population, such as in the agriculturally important region of Ferghana, a translator was needed to interpret entries written in the "sart language" [i.e., Turki].[36] Even though Russian administrators felt that Slavic canal overseers provided technical irrigation assistance beyond what the "natives" could give, these overseers still were dependent on the work of the mirabs in their jurisdiction, whose language they usually did not speak and whose customs they still did not understand.[37] But it was not only indigenous water administrators who were deemed incompetent; on his inspection of the province in 1908, Count Pahlen found numerous examples of "illiterate" Slavic ariq aqsaqals who submitted journals with suspiciously round numbers, improbable figures, and with considerable discrepancies from the journals submitted by other officials at other times on the same system.[38]

Nor was it was only Russians who complained about canal overseers. The same file on Samarkand region from the Tajik archives, for instance, contains numerous documents from indigenous petitioners to the local Russian authorities pointing out the shortcomings of the local mirabs, since the irrigation instruction made district heads the ultimate arbiters of conflict over irrigation. In one case, the mirab in question, Mirza Rauf Shadimirzaev, had apparently become more interested in cotton and grain sales than in the distribution of irrigation water to the fields. The water-using community on the Chorsu ariq, which had elected Shadimirzaev four years earlier, requested the right to elect a different mirab, who would be "more beneficial" for the irrigation of the community's crops.[39] In his memoirs, Lykoshin recalled having seen a satirical skit performed in Tashkent by a troupe from Samarkand, in which the actors played rival groups of Uzbeks and Tajiks, each bribing a weak-willed mirab for greater shares of water.[40]

During Count Pahlen's inspection of Turkestan, the Khoqand Exchange Committee submitted a report to the senator calling for a special Turkestan irrigation department, located in not in St. Petersburg,

[36] Pahlen, *Oroshenie*, 38–33, 187.
[37] "K irrigatsionnym voprosam," 124–125; Pahlen *Oroshenie*, 180, 444.
[38] Pahlen, *Oroshenie*, 183–187.
[39] TsGA RT f. I-1, op. 2, d. 165, l. 101.
[40] Lykoshin, *Pol zhizni v Turkestane*, 325.

but in the region itself. The report also called for following in the steps of "our teachers" from the arid American West and for inviting foreign experts to Turkestan, citing as a model the recent invitation extended by the Ottomans to "Uillok" [William Willcocks] to prepare and oversee irrigation projects on the Tigris and Euphrates Rivers.[41] Pahlen himself echoed the called for a central water agency; in the meantime, his visit resulted in the formation in 1909 of a commission to oversee the Murghab Estate.[42]

Many hopes of creating a more-qualified hydraulic administration to bring order to the region were pinned on the first hydraulic engineering school in Turkestan, which had opened in 1902. The opening of the school was an attempt by the Russian government to bring Central Asian water management into accord with the norms of European science. The school offered classes in a wide variety of subjects, including arithmetic, geometry, reading and writing in both Russian and the "sart language," religion, law, meteorology, physics, chemistry, botany, gardening, geodesy, and the art of construction, as well as classes to train joiners and turners. After completing two years of classes and a year of practical experience, the graduates became ariq aqsaqals and mirabs. The goal was that they be "not only . . . capable of serving as ariq aqsaqals, but also able to fill a technical position on the construction and maintenance of new canals."[43] In other words, though canals would still be overseen by men referred to as ariq aqsaqal, this term would now connote primarily technical expertise, rather than wisdom and the knowledge that came with years of experience supervising canal maintenance.

Though the school managed to attract a fair number of students – by 1909, seventy-five students had been accepted, and twenty-seven had graduated – it struggled through its first few years.[44] A 1909 article in the *Turkestan Gazette* reported a lack of literature in the school's library and complained that the Ministry of Agriculture only occasionally sent

41 Timaev, "Turkestanskii irrigatsionnyi otdel," 106–107.

42 Pahlen, *Oroshenie*, 462; Barts, *Oroshenie v doline reki Murgaba*, 142, and Appendix 2. A Turkestan Water Administration was included in drafts for a water law (G. N. Cherdantsev, *Vodnoe pravo Turkestana v ego nastoiashchem i v proektakh blizhaishego budushchego* [Tashkent: Tip. Turkestanskogo T-vo pechat′nogo dela, 1911], Part II, 35).

43 "S″ezd gidrotekhnikov v Tashkente v 1907," *TV* 13, 15 (1908) in *TS* 453, 144–152: 147; "Sel′sko-khoziaistvennaia gidrotekhnicheskaia shkola v Tashkente," *TV* 98 (1909) in *TS* 507, 15.

44 "Irrigatsionnyi otdel na Turkestanskoi sel′sko-khoziaistvennoi vystavke," 176.

the school journals. Even worse, the ariq used by the students for observation first passed through the army barracks; as a result, water often did not even reach the school. Moreover, the school had no relationship with the government-run experimental agricultural station near Tashkent, which doubtless could have provided beneficial experience for the students.[45] The *Tashkent Courier* reported that it was difficult for graduates of the school to get a position as an ariq aqsaqal, since local administrators tended to put forward "their own people" [*svoi liudi*] for the position, rather than those who were most qualified. Such people, the newspaper claimed, were more interested in the salary promised by the position than in irrigation.[46] On his inspection tour of Turkestan Province, Senator Pahlen verified that many district heads chose to confirm their own acquaintances as mirabs.[47] An article published in St. Petersburg in December 1907 remarked on the phenomenon of nepotism in the choosing of ariq aqsaqals, who might be railway workers, telegraph operators, or retired bureaucrats, in addition to natives who could not speak or write Russian.[48] Such practices were detrimental to local water management. As Thurman has argued in the case of the Ferghana Valley, when the election of canal overseers devolved into competitions for the highest bidder, even mirabs often were not familiar with the irrigation systems they were assigned to oversee, thus diminishing the overall efficiency of the system and divorcing the mirab's interests from those of the water users on the system.[49]

Besides favoritism, the graduates of the Tashkent hydraulic engineering school faced other challenges. A congress of hydraulic engineers that met in December 1907 in Tashkent reported that not only did the graduates lack practical experience, but they also lacked language skills. This fact, combined with their young age, meant they could not command the confidence of the indigenous population – so much for the superiority of scientific knowledge over the wisdom accumulated with age and experience![50] The conclusions of the congress were that the school

45 "Sel′sko-khoziaistvennaia gidrotekhnicheskaia shkola v Tashkente," 15.

46 "Nastoiashchee polozhenie irrigatsii v krae," *TK* 213–14 (1907) in *TS* 448, 1–4: 4; Irrigator, "K voprosu ob irrigatsii," *TK* 40 (1908) in *TS* 456, 68–71.

47 Pahlen, *Oroshenie*, 175–176.

48 "K s″ezdu gidrotekhnikov," *SPV* 269 (1907) in *TS* 450, 116–118: 117.

49 Thurman, "Modes of Organization," 81, 167–169.

50 Babaliants, "Pervyi s″ezd gidrotekhnikov," 81; Pahlen, *Mission to Turkestan*, 92–93. Though aqsaqal means "white beard," one could be elected to the position at twenty-five (Morrison, *Russian Rule in Samarkand*, 180).

required an overhaul, including raising the minimum age requirement to fifteen, increasing the years of theoretical coursework to three, and strengthening language education so that the graduates would not only be able to converse fluently in indigenous languages, but also be able to read and write in them.[51]

One of the biggest Russian frustrations with Central Asian water management – and one that the hydraulic engineering school sought to remedy – was Central Asians' seeming lack of precision when it came to measuring water. Yet, although Central Asians may not have been able to give precise measurements of how much water was in a given river or canal, this did not mean, as some observers assumed, that they did not have systems of measurement for water distribution. Russians struggled to match Central Asian terminology such as *kulak* (*quloq*, "ear") and *tegerman* ("mill") with European scientific measurements, often not realizing that instead of fixed units of volume, the amount of water allotted to a user on a given system might be measured in terms of area – how much water was needed to irrigate a plot of a certain size; or time – the amount of water that could pass through a side channel in a given period. To add to the confusion, the same term in one place might mean something different in another, and even different communities within one region seemed to have different terms for what were essentially the same processes.[52]

One of the most frequent terms encountered by outsiders was *su*, which simply means "water" in Turkic languages. According to Skrine and Ross, the *su* was the unit describing "the average quantity of water required by individual peasants." However, since that quantity was dependent on a number of different variables – including how many water users drew water from the system and what kinds of crops they were growing – the *su* could not be said to stand for any fixed quantity. They observed that the area to be irrigated by the *su* might range from one to five acres. In Merv, the *su* seemed equivalent to the amount of water "which flows in two hours through a distributory discharging water at the rate of 1 ¼ quarts per second," yet in the the Tedjen Oasis, they wrote, "it is equivalent to the needs of an average garden, or to a discharge of half a

51 Babaliants, "Pervyi s″ezd gidrotekhnikov," 81–82.

52 For the origins and histories of some of the oldest terms, see Barthold, *K istorii orosheniia*, 17–18. Pahlen notes that measurements of weight, such as *batman*, were also used (*Oroshenie*, 83).

gallon per second."[53] Such descriptions might not have clarified the meaning of *su* for their readers, but they did imply that Central Asian water managers had a better sense of the rate of flow through their irrigation systems than simply whether the water levels were "high" or "low." More importantly, Skrine and Ross did find that, though the term *su* did not seem to have a universal meaning across Central Asia, it had a well-defined and accepted meaning within a local context, such as an oasis. On his inspection of the province, Pahlen confirmed that "the concept of *su* as a precise volume of water has a definite and generally accepted connotation." While the volume designated may have varied between locations, the value of the *su* in a given locality, Pahlen noted, was "perfectly clear to every native."[54] Moreover, he observed, even if indigenous documents outlining water rights referred to units of water use, they did not guarantee an absolute, but rather a proportional, amount of water to be used in relation to the amount of water in the entire system.[55] Rather than signifying imprecision, the use of locally-specific units of time and area reflected the needs of the soil and crops being planted there, rather than fixed units that required a certain amount of water or a certain rate of water flow. To Pahlen, this seemed an appropriately flexible method of apportioning a precious resource, such as water, in an equitable manner.

The creation of the Tashkent hydraulic engineering school suggested that European science was the key to more efficient water management, yet those on the ground most familiar with irrigation methods in Turkestan, including some of Russian Turkestan's most prolific hydraulic engineers, tended to look favorably on local methods and practices in the field of irrigation engineering. In an oft-cited passage, Alexander von Middendorf, a Russian scientist who had visited the Ferghana Valley in 1878 and wrote one of the most detailed extant descriptions of irrigation practices there, asserted that Russians should learn from those who had "thousands of years of practice," and that "the foundation for the further perfection of irrigation has already been laid by the natives," praising their fervor and "elevated understanding of the needs and means of the practice of irrigation."[56] The head of the Murghab Estate praised the abilities of the Turkmen in the region as natural-born irrigators, able to accomplish by sight what most Russians would only be able to do with

[53] Skrine and Ross, *The Heart of Asia*, 332–333. [54] Pahlen, *Mission to Turkestan*, 89.
[55] Pahlen, *Oroshenie*, 37.
[56] In this case, it is taken from Dingel'shtedt, *Opyt izucheniia irrigatsii*, 196.

the aid of the level.[57] In 1887, Dingel'shtedt wrote that "customary procedure in water use satisfactorily foresees and decides all individual cases."[58] In a debate carried out in the pages of *Central Asian Life* and the *Tashkent Courier* in 1907, Iurii Fedorovich Bonch-Osmolovskii, the head of irrigation in the Syr Darya region, defended the local system of ariqs and the abilities of the ariq aqsaqals.[59] Count Pahlen, too, after his inspection of the province, noted that the work of "the native technicians ... in the main ... was faultless. One could not say as much about the efforts of our European engineers ..." Even a decade after renewed government efforts to irrigate the Hungry Steppe, Russians in Turkestan continued to depend heavily on agriculture in the Ferghana Valley made possible by the intricate and sophisticated network of irrigation channels developed under the Khoqand khanate in the eighteenth and nineteenth centuries.[60]

Recognition of the value of indigenous knowledge, however, could function at odds with claims of European scientific superiority, since there was a general sense among Russian engineers and administrators alike that European science and technology could make Central Asian irrigation systems far more efficient. Some considered European science a beneficent tool, to be used to bring maximum benefit to the local population in Turkestan. It seemed to be Russia's duty to use this knowledge, if not to help the supposedly benighted natives, then at least to maximize the profit to be gained from Turkestan as a colony. As a 1912 *Voice of Moscow* article lamented, "History has supplied us [Russians] with science and all the resources of modern culture for the conquest of nature, but we drag our feet over applying all of these forces toward the deserts ..."[61]

To be sure, even those who defended local practices did so in moderation. Dingel'shtedt saw little reason to regret the fact that the

57 Cited in Kanoda, *Pereselencheskie poselki*, 71; see also Meakin, *In Russian Turkestan*, 12–13.

58 RGIA f. 426, op. 1, d. 19, l. 47.

59 "Nastoiashchee polozhenie irrigatsii v krae"; Bonch-Osmolovskii, "Po povodu 'nastoiashchego polozheniia irrigatsii v krae', pomeshchennogo v No. 213 i 214 *Tashkentskogo kur'era*," *SZh* 224 (1907); V. A., "Eshche ob irrigatsii v krae," *TK* 236 (1907); Bonch-Osmolovskii, "Neskol'ko slov g-u V.A. po povodu irrigatsii v krae," *SZh* 260 (1907) (all in *TS* 448, 1–10).

60 Morrison, *Russian Rule in Samarkand*, 202; on irrigation in Khoqand, see Levi, *The Rise and Fall of Khoqand*, 62–70.

61 RGIA f. 426, op. 1, d. 767, l. 11, "Garantiia orositel'nykh predpriiatii," *GM* (March 2, 1912).

Russian government in Turkestan had taken irrigation matters into its own hands, rather than relying on local wisdom and experience alone. Moreover, by the time he published an extensive work on the subject of water management in Turkestan in 1893, he understood that since the Russian conquest, the customary "system" as it had existed under the khans no longer functioned in the same way.[62] Bonch-Osmolovskii was quick to assure his readers that, "I never said that the native system of irrigation was ideal, and that it can compete … with Italy, France, India. I only emphasize that with the funds that we have, the lack of a water law, irrigation capital … we have to respect the native irrigation techniques …"[63] Russian officials, engineers, and scientists, therefore, neither rejected European science in favor of local methods of irrigation engineering, nor did they discount local knowledge and its practical uses altogether. Rather, while European scientific methods remained an ideal, and while many Russians recognized the need for new legislation on water management as well as new training for water managers, on the ground in Turkestan those interested in irrigation continued to take advantage of existing irrigation systems and procedures for water management, in the hopes of developing Turkestan's agriculture to make it a profitable colony of the empire. By the early twentieth century, most of these hopes were pinned on cotton.

WHITE GOLD FEVER

The government-approved project to irrigate forty-five thousand desiatinas in the Hungry Steppe, which began construction in 1901, and the Orenburg-Tashkent Railway project, begun in the same year, were both intended to support Russia's expanding textile industry, a key component of Russia's plan for rapid industrialization championed by Finance Minister Witte. Russia's State Council had decided in 1896 to prioritize irrigation for cash crops – cotton in Central Asia, tea and tobacco in the Caucasus – over potential irrigation projects in the steppes.[64] The Orenburg-Tashkent Railroad was to connect the fields of Turkestan directly to central Russia, allowing for more efficient transport of cotton to the mills of the Moscow industrial region. In the 1870s and early 1880s, silk cultivation trials had competed for government funding with

[62] RGIA f. 426, op. 1, d. 19, l. 40ob; Dingel'shtedt, *Opyt izucheniia irrigatsii*, 59.

[63] Bonch-Osmolovskii, "Neskol'ko slov," 9.

[64] Moon, *The Plough That Broke the Steppes*, 232.

cotton, but cotton eventually proved to be more successful, in part because of the widespread sentiment in Europe in the late nineteenth and early twentieth centuries that new sources of cotton outside of the United States were both possible and desirable.[65]

While Russian manufacturers had initially been satisfied with importing the short-staple Levant cotton (*Gossypium herbaceum*) grown by indigenous smallholders in Central Asia, as a supplement to imported American cotton, in the wake of the American Civil War and following the establishment of the Governor-Generalship of Turkestan, some enterprising Russians began to experiment with the introduction of longer-staple American cotton varieties to the region, and Governor-General Kaufman sent a commission to the United States to study different methods of cotton cultivation.[66] In 1871, using his own funds, Samarkand's Russian military governor founded a cotton plantation that by 1875 produced more than thirty poods of acclimatized American cotton seeds to distribute to the local population.[67] The long-staple Sea Island variety (*Gossypium barbadense*), adapted to South Carolina's Coastal Plain, however, proved to be largely unsuitable for Central Asia's arid climate and growing season.[68] Moreover, the seeds were expensive, while the price of American cotton in the markets at Samarkand was the same as that of indigenous cotton, so that with fewer expenditures, the same profit could be reached by continuing to grow indigenous varieties. This effectively killed any enthusiasm in Turkestan for the cultivation of American varieties of cotton in the 1870s and 1880s.[69]

In 1884, the private Kudrin Central Asian Trade-Industrial Company, the major stockholders of which were the most prominent cotton manufacturers in Russia's central industrial region, including the Morozovs and Riabushinskiis, introduced its own experimental cotton plantations to grow American Upland cotton (*Gossypium hirsutum*) in the region; it was this company that had clashed with the inhabitants of Begovat over

[65] On silk, see Schuyler, *Turkistan*, I, 296; Dobrosmyslov, *Tashkent v proshlom i nastoiashchem*, 204.

[66] Biedermann, "Die Versorgung der russischen Baumwollindustrie," 34. Textile machinery required cotton varieties with a longer staple than indigenous Turkestani varieties.

[67] One pood equals thirty-six pounds. "Po povodu zavedeniia khlopchato-bumazhnoi plantatsii," *GL* 186 (1875) in *TS* 152, 50.

[68] Schuyler, *Turkistan*, I, 296; A. I. Kinze and V. I. Iuferev, "Khlopkovodstvo," in *Aziatskaia Rossiia*, II, 285.

[69] Whitman, "Turkestan Cotton in Imperial Russia," 196; "Khlopkovaia plantatsiia v Samarkande," *TV* 5 (1879) in *TS* 240, 253–265 : 263.

water-sharing in the Hungry Steppe. The Kudrin company was successful in arranging both the sale of raw Central Asian cotton in central Russia as well Russian textiles in Central Asia, but the plantations were less successful. The cause of the plantations' failure was blamed on the inability – or unwillingness – of local farmers to adopt new methods of large-scale cotton cultivation. Kudrin went into financial difficulties, and the original shareholders withdrew.[70]

In spite of the failure of large-scale plantations, the Russian production of American cotton took off dramatically in the 1890s, spurred in part by rising cotton prices worldwide. The completion in 1888 of the Central Asian Railway linking Samarkand to the Caspian greatly improved the ability of the empire to access Central Asian cotton from Turkestan, Bukhara, and Khiva, thus providing stimulation for the expansion of the Russian textile industry; this growth was also supported by Witte's new plans for the industrialization of the empire. Whereas the Russian mills processed 144,000 tons in 1890, this number had more than doubled by 1900.[71] This increase in the demand for cotton for the textile industry, in turn, spurred interest in potential new sources of raw cotton. Russian efforts to expand cotton in the Caucasus region had been largely unsuccessful, but Witte himself had visited Turkestan in 1890 and saw the potential for cotton cultivation there.[72] Turkestani *dehqans* (farmers) were increasingly encouraged to plant acclimatized varieties of Upland cotton, which began to replace grain.[73]

In order to convince Turkestanis to plant more American Upland cotton, which produced a higher yield per acre than did indigenous cotton, the Russian administration began offering dehqans tax breaks as an incentive; it also kept American cotton prices artificially high and awarded bonuses for large harvests.[74] In 1891, the Council of Ministers lowered

[70] Joffe, "The Cotton Manufacturers, 1880's–1914," 157–158, 194 fn 16; R. von der Muhlen, "Cotton Growing in Russian Central Asia and the Caucasus," *The Sixth International Congress of Delegated Representatives of Master Cotton Spinners' and Manufacturers' Associations* (Milan, 1909), 137.

[71] A. I. Kinze, "Khlopkovodstvo," *Ezhegodnik Glavnogo upravleniia zemleustroistva i zemledeliia po Departamentu zemledeliia i lesnomu departamentu (1907)* [*Ezhegodnik GUZiZ*] (St. Petersburg: GUZiZ, 1908), 321; *Statistika bumagopriadil'nogo i tkatskogo proizvodstv za 1900–1910 gg.* (St. Petersburg, 1911), xv–xvi.

[72] Moon, *The Plow That Broke the Steppes*, 235.

[73] Kinze, "Khlopkovodstvo," 325.

[74] Ravshan Abdullaev with Namoz Khotamov and Tashmanbet Kenensariev, "Colonial Rule and Indigenous Responses, 1860–1917," chapter 3 in ed. Starr, *Ferghana Valley*, 69–93: 81. On the local origins of the tax break, see Beatrice Penati, "The Cotton Boom

taxation on cotton land to be equivalent to land planted with "dry" crops (such as wheat, barley, and alfalfa), increasing the incentive to plant cotton; this became permanent in 1900 with an amendment to the Turkestan Statute of 1886.[75] Textile firms also paid more for American cotton, which may have further helped to convince some Central Asian planters to start growing the new seeds, though it was generally not the farmers themselves who profited, but rather the middlemen who transported the cotton from field to factory.[76] A significant increase in the protective tariff placed on imported cotton also served to spur the advance of domestic cotton production. Whereas the tariff was only one ruble fifteen kopecks per pood in 1887, by 1900 it had increased to four rubles and fifteen kopecks per pood. Turkestani farmers responded positively to such incentives, and in this manner American Upland cotton began to largely replace indigenous varieties across the region, except for Bukhara, where the system of estimating an assessment of the harvest for taxation only after the cotton was ready to be picked prohibited Bukharans from adopting American cotton, which had to be picked immediately after opening and could not wait for the tax officials to make their rounds.[77]

Even without much forward progress in the expansion of the region's irrigations systems, therefore, government encouragement to plant more American cotton stimulated a rapid increase in American cotton production on Turkestan's irrigated acreage by the end of the nineteenth century.[78] While American cotton was planted on only three hundred desiatinas near Tashkent in 1885, by 1900 it made up 60 percent of the cotton grown in Turkestan, most of which was in the fertile Ferghana Valley, described by the first all-Russian census of 1897 as "notable for its cotton cultivation."[79] Around that time, the Danish traveler Ole Olufsen estimated that 60 to 70 percent of some parts of Ferghana were planted with American cotton.[80] By the early twentieth century, different types of

and the Land Tax in Russian Turkestan (1880s–1915),"*Kritika: Explorations in Russian and Eurasian History* 14, 4 (Fall 2013): 741–774.

75 *Tsentral'naia Aziia v sostave Rossiiskoi imperii*, eds. S. N. Abashin, D. Iu. Arapov, and N. E. Bekmakhanova (Moscow: Novoe literaturnoe obozrenie, 2008), 147. See also Penati, "The Cotton Boom and the Land Tax," 752–758.

76 Biedermann, *Die Versorgung der russischen Baumwollindustrie*, 35; Von der Muhlen, "Cotton Growing in Russian Central Asia and the Caucasus," 138.

77 Kinze, "Khlopkovodstvo," 324, 331.

78 Thurman "Modes of Organization," 85.

79 "Ferganskaia oblast'," *Pervaia vseobshchaia perepis' naseleniia Rossiiskoi imperii*, LXXXIX (St. Petersburg: Izd. Tsentr. Stat. Komitetom MVD, 1904), iii; Kinze, "Khlopkovodstvo," 324.

80 Fihl, *Exploring Central Asia*, 2: 461.

American seeds in Turkestan already had common names based on their phenotype: *qara-chigit* for a type that had black seeds, for instance, *kok-chigit* for one with a hull that was green in color. Russians also introduced cotton ginneries to the region. Whereas native varieties of cotton could be cleaned by hand, American cotton required the technology of the cotton gin to separate the fiber from the seed. Before the advent of the Russians, cotton-cleaning machines had been used only rarely, primarily in Bukhara.[81]

The Russian expansion of the cultivation of American cotton on its own soil coincided with a general concern around the world in the early twentieth century about American monopoly of the global cotton market, as well as the fact that Americans themselves were becoming greater consumers of the material, surpassing even the British.[82] British associations of cotton spinners and weavers spearheaded the drive to reduce speculation and lessen dependence on American cotton, a drive that soon took on the characteristics of a global movement. In May 1904, the first International Congress of Delegated Representatives of Master Cotton Spinners' and Manufacturers' Associations convened in Zürich, under the impression that "[t]he cotton industry of the world has been passing through a crisis the severity of which has been rarely equalled in its history."[83] The congress became an annual event, attended by representatives from an increasing number of European countries, as well as, beginning in 1907, Japan.

Though Russian participation in these initial international congresses was intermittent, from 1904 onward Russians, too, were taking measures to ensure that their country in future would be less dependent on imports of American cotton, for which Russia paid one hundred million rubles annually.[84] In 1904, the Moscow Exchange Society organized a Commission to Develop Russian Cotton Growing.[85] By 1906, the Orenburg-Tashkent Railroad connected the cotton fields of Turkestan with the

81 Kinze "Khlopkovodstvo," 329–330.

82 Biedermann, *Die Versorgung der russischen Baumwollindustrie*, 11.

83 *Official Report of the Proceedings of the First International Congress of Delegated Representatives of Master Cotton Spinners' and Manufacturers' Associations, held at the Tonhalle, Zürich, May 23–27, 1904* (1904), 4.

84 This figure was reported in the *Turkestan Gazette* in 1910 as the figure for recent years (Cherdantsev, *Vodnoe pravo*, Part I, 18 fn 2).

85 Muriel Joffe, "Autocracy, Capitalism and Empire: The Politics of Irrigation," *Russian Review* 54, 3 (July 1995): 372.

textile mills of central Russia. The formation in 1907 of a Central Cotton Committee within the Ministry of Agriculture signaled the Russian state's further commitment to increasing the acreage under cotton cultivation. With the number of cotton spindles in Russia more than doubling between 1890 and 1905–1906, pressure was on the Turkestan branch of the Ministry of Agriculture to try to keep up by increasing cotton harvests.[86] By 1907, with a demand of 360,000 tons, Russia now represented the fifth-largest cotton consumer in the world, slightly behind India.[87]

Already in 1901, Ferghana had supplied as much as one-third of the demand of the Russian cotton industry and was home to almost 80 percent of the cotton acreage in Turkestan.[88] In that year, the military governor of Ferghana "complained of excessive conversion of grain and pasture lands to cotton."[89] As more irrigated land was converted to cotton, wheat had to be brought into the region, driving up grain prices. Prices for wheat in Ferghana at times were more than twice what they were in other parts of Russia.[90] In adjacent Samarkand, where the Hungry Steppe was located, the military governor estimated that grain prices had risen 50 percent in the last decade of the nineteenth century.[91] As an increasing amount of land was converted to cotton, nutrients were leached out of the soil and not replaced, since levels of livestock in Turkestan were generally low, due to a lack of pasture and fodder – except among the nomads – and manure for fertilizer was prohibitively expensive.[92] According to a study conducted by the Ministry of Agriculture in 1907, in the the districts of Andijan, Khoqand and Marghilan, all in the Ferghana Valley, more than 30 percent of the total land area was devoted to cotton, and there were even places where up to 70 percent of the available land was planted with cotton; a greater area

[86] Biedermann, *Die Versorgung der russischen Baumwollindustrie*, 10. This figure appears to refer only to spindles used in factories, not those used in domestic production.

[87] Kinze, "Khlopkovodstvo," 319. This still put it far behind the United States, Britain, and the rest of Europe.

[88] Thurman "Modes of Organization," 86–87; Kinze, "Khlopkovodstvo," 324.

[89] Brower, *Turkestan and the Fate of the Russian Empire*, 78.

[90] Kinze, "Khlopkovodstvo," 325 footnote.

[91] Brower, *Turkestan and the Fate of the Russian Empire*, 78.

[92] Skrine and Ross, *The Heart of Asia*, 387; Kinze, "Khlopkovodstvo," 336; *Trudy s″ezda khlopkovodov*, 104. For more on the fertilizer problem, see Beatrice Penati, "Swamps, Sorghum and Saxauls: Marginal Lands and the Fate of Russian Turkestan (c. 1880–1915)," *Central Asian Survey* 29, 1 (2010): 68.

under cotton, the study concluded, would suffer from soil exhaustion. Without improving existing irrigation systems and irrigating new lands, a further increase in cotton acreage in Ferghana was impossible, the study concluded.[93]

In this context, the Hungry Steppe irrigation and development efforts appealed to the administration, since the steppe was relatively sparsely populated, meaning that cotton did not have to compete with food crops, feed, and pastureland the way it did in the Ferghana Valley. Another appeal of the Hungry Steppe was that colonial officials did not relish putting cotton, a valuable cash crop, into the hands of the "natives." Yet the fact remained that Russian peasants had little knowledge of – and seemingly little interest in – growing cotton. Few Russian settlers in the Hungry Steppe managed to grow any cotton, leading the Turkestan Agricultural Society to conclude that Russians were "entirely unfit" for growing cotton.[94] Though some observers cited the cotton-growing villages of Spasskoe and Dukhovskoe near the Hungry Steppe Experimental Station as models, most agreed that those villages were not typical.[95] When Governor-General Pavel Ivanovich Mishchenko (1908–1909) tried to ensure that all Russian settlers renting land in the Hungry Steppe planted at least two desiatinas of land with cotton, only about a dozen families were willing to take him up on the offer. The requirement was then removed at the request of the head of the district branch of the Minsistry of Agriculture.[96]

This inversion of power – the would-be colonizers depending on the colonized – was largely symbolic, however, since the indigenous Turkestanis who possessed the irrigation and cotton-growing knowledge were in the main sharecroppers who rented land and livestock from larger landowners, and who depended on advances against the expected harvest given out by large cotton processing firms or, increasingly, by enterprising middlemen, known as *chistachi* (from the Russian word for "clean," since they cleaned the cotton themselves, thereby entirely bypassing the ginneries and selling the cotton directly to the mills). These large

[93] Kinze, "Khlopkovodstvo," 346.

[94] "Zhurnaly soveshchanii komissii, obrazovannoi pri Turkestanskom obshchestve sel′skogo khoziaistva po voprosu ob oroshenii chastnymi predprinimateliami zemel′ v Turkestanskom krae," *TSKh* 7 (1907) in *TS* 454, 145–154: 147; *Trudy s″ezda khlopkovodov*, 98, 100.

[95] *GS* Doc. 35: 105; *GS* Doc. 40: 111; "Vinovaty-li russkie pereselentsy?," 189–190.

[96] "Arendatory-pereselentsy v Golodnoi Stepi," *TK* 136 (1909) in *TS* 508, 143–145: 143–144.

FIGURE 3.2 Cotton from the state plantation. Photograph No. 32 in *Vidy zaseliaemoi chasti Golodnoi Stepi* [*Views of the Settled Part of the Hungry Steppe*], 16. Reproduced with permission of the Rare Books Section of the Alisher Navoi State Library, Tashkent, Uzbekistan.

landowners and middlemen from the local Russian, Armenian, and Bukharan Jewish populations took advantage of the small farmers' dependence on land and credit, keeping the dehqans in a vicious cycle of debt.[97] Already in 1894, the collector Henri Moser had described how "cotton fever … rages" among Europeans in Turkestan, a "game of chance … very few have been able to resist.[98]

Though the majority of Turkestani cotton growers worked only small plots of land – in the early twentieth century, 90 percent of Turkestan cotton was produced by indigenous farmers on plots of two to four desiatinas each – it seems that some Turkestanis, both those who rented

[97] Skrine and Ross, *The Heart of Asia*, 387; Brower, *Turkestan and the Fate of the Russian Empire*, 78; Kinze, "Khlopkovodstvo," 343–346.

[98] Moser, *L'irrigation*, 341.

out land, as well as those who became involved in the cotton business as middlemen, did quite well for themselves.[99] Some, such as the merchant Pulatzhon Kasymbaev, who in 1908 installed a Perkun combustion engine to pump water from the Syr Darya onto forty desiatinas near Khojand, were pioneers of new technologies and techniques in irrigation and cotton cultivation.[100] Traveling in the Ferghana Valley in the second decade of the twentieth century, Ella Christie noted that wealthy families, whether Russian or indigenous, tended to cluster together as one, leaving the less-wealthy families to live in the older, more-affordable settlements.[101] The presence of poor and downtrodden Russians who mixed with "native" society or worked for indigenous Turkestani landlords alarmed the Russians interested in the province's further development.[102] As Krivoshein put it in 1912, "the position of the Russian man as a hired man [*batrak*] on the farm of the [indigenous Turkestani] sart who is subjugated to him accords poorly with the dignity of the Russian name [and] does not provide a good moral influence on the Asian borderland ..."[103] Yet Krivoshein also realized that, having irrigated the Ferghana Valley, Turkestanis were entitled by customary practice to use these lands.

FINANCING IRRIGATION

The desire to irrigate areas outside of the Ferghana Valley, such as the Hungry Steppe, raised the issue of how to finance such projects. The prolonged fighting of the Russo–Japanese War (1904–1905) and the domestic turmoil that followed caused state funding for reclamation projects to fall by more than half from just over a million rubles in

99 On plot sizes, see Biedermann, *Die Versorgung der russischen Baumwollindustrie*, 46; Morrison, *Russian Rule in Samarkand*, 205, 234; Alexander Garland Park, *Bolshevism in Turkestan, 1917–1927* (New York: Columbia University Press, 1957), 292–293; *Khlopkovodstvo SSSR i ego perspektivy*, ed. A. V. Stoklitskii (Moscow: Biuro Pechati i Informatsii SNK i STO, 1926) 23, 76. Kinze gives the higher figure of 5–10 desiatinas for landowners; sharecroppers worked smaller plots ("Khlopkovodstvo," 332).

100 K. A. Timaev, "Oroshenie novykh zemel′ chastnymi litsami," *TK* 24 (1910) in *TS* 533, 193–194: 193.

101 Ella Christie, *From Khiva to Golden Samarkand* (London: Seeley, Service and Co., 1925), 205; for a similar observation about "newly rich sarts and Jews" living among Russians in Khoqand, while poorer Russians live in the "sart town," see Machatschek, *Landeskunde von Russisch Turkestan*, 276.

102 *Trudy s″ezda khlopkovodov*, 62–63, 154.

103 Krivoshein, *Zapiska Glavnoupravliaiushchego zemleustroistvom i zemledeliem*, 14.

1903 to just over 500,000 in 1905. These figures represented government expenditures for *all* irrigation and drainage works in the entire Russian Empire, not just in Turkestan, though the Hungry Steppe project alone was re-budgeted in 1905 at a cost of almost five million rubles, more than twice its original projected cost.[104]

Without proper funding, the Hungry Steppe was in disarray. A commission sent in 1907 by the state Hydrological Committee to investigate irrigation in Turkestan discovered that the Nicholas I Canal had not been cleaned in twelve years – that is, since its completion in 1895. In the intervening time, it had silted up; parts of the canal were completely buried in reeds. Whereas lakes through which the canal passed had originally served as filters for sediment, by 1907 these bodies of water had silted up as well, to the extent that local Kazakhs had turned the lake beds into watermelon beds (*bakhchi*).[105] The *Turkestan Gazette* published several articles drawing attention to the dismal state of affairs in the Hungry Steppe.[106] In some settler villages, the Russian peasants, unable to irrigate their crops, became almost exclusively livestock herders. Russian peasants learned to use the tugay along the banks of the Syr Darya as animal pasture, following the example set by their Kazakh neighbors.[107] Together with concerns about an increasing Russian "proletariat" in the region, as well as reports that Russian settlers, particularly poor muzhiki, had been observed converting to Islam, this state of affairs boded ill for the prestige of the Russian government, as well as the establishment of Russian "civilization" in Turkestan.[108]

One potential solution to such irrigation woes was the investment of private capital, a question that had been raised as early as 1887, when the Kudrin Cotton Company, in its effort to develop cotton plantations in Turkestan, appealed to the Russian administration for the rights to create private irrigation canals.[109] Critics of Article 256 of the Turkestan Statute believed such crucial questions could not be answered until all the water

104 As reported by N. I. Malakhovskii in *TV* 22 (January 27, 1912), reprinted in *GS* Doc. 44: 115. See also *GS*, Doc. 45: 117.

105 Pahlen, *Oroshenie*, 475.

106 See, for example, S. Ostrovskii, "K voprosu ob oroshenii Golodnoi Stepi," *TV* 145 (1907) in *TS* 442, 17–21: 17; Lykoshin, "Sberezhenie vody," 108.

107 Ostrovskii, "K voprosu ob oroshenii Golodnoi Stepi," 17.

108 "Progress v durnuiu storonu," *O* 53 (1896) in *TS* 437, 117–119; "K perekhodu pravoslavnykh v Islam," *TV* 94 (1909) in *TS* 507, 1–2; Poniatovskii, *Opyt izucheniia khlopkovodstva*, 17; *Trudy s"ezda khlopkovodov*, 71.

109 RGIA f. 426, op. 1, d. 19, l. 14.

belonged to the government. Even the Central Asian khans had not allowed water to be private proverty but had regulated its use. Particularly in regions where the water had already been divided up according to agreed-upon local customs, how could the government sanction new irrigation projects if it did not own the water?[110]

In 1890, Minister of Finance Ivan Alekseevich Vyshnegradskii, a believer in the necessity of improving Turkestan's irrigation systems in order to meet Russia's economic and cultural goals in the region, advocated private capital as a means of supplementing the meager funding available for such endeavors, but he did not receive much support. It seemed prudent to first discuss the question of the Russian colonization of the province before distributing lands to be "brought to life" by means of irrigation (*ozhivlenie*).[111] The question of involving private entrepreneurs in irrigation was taken up again in 1904 by the Department of Agriculture, which sent to the Turkestan branch of the Ministry of Agriculture a list of conditions it felt were necessary for private entrepreneurs wishing to realize "irrigation and cotton cultivation" on government lands; agriculture officials in Turkestan, however, considered most of these conditions inapplicable on the ground.[112]

Further discussion of the question took place under the auspices of a commission of the Turkestan Agricultural Society, which concluded in 1907 that Russia lagged far behind the rest of the world in irrigation matters, and that foreign capitalists might aid in the business of "bringing life to the land" in Turkestan. At the same time, however, it seemed inadvisable to grant concessions of land rights in this politically sensitive border region destined for extensive colonization. The commission's conclusion that "government land must stay government property" – with which conclusion the Governor-General's Council agreed – seemed to limit the potential for both domestic and foreign private investment.[113] The question was not, however, entirely laid to rest.

In 1910, despite engineer Stanislav Ostrovskii's trip to India to learn about cost-cutting measures, the Hungry Steppe project was faced with bills mounting to estimates of more than seven million rubles, far from the two and a quarter million rubles initially assigned to the project. Minister

110 These criticisms existed well before 1886; see, for example, the 1875 article in *Golos*, "Po povodu proekta zemel'nogo ustroistva Turkestanskogo Kraia," *GL* 56 (1875) in *TS* 152, 5–11: 11.

111 RGIA 426, op. 1, d. 19, l. 126ob.

112 Babaliants, "Pervyi s"ezd gidrotekhnikov," 72.

113 Ibid., 77; "Zhurnaly soveshchanii komissii," 146–150.

of Agriculture Krivoshein pleaded with the Council of Ministers for more money to be allocated to the project, reminding the ministers of the boost the project would give both to Russia's quest to become independent of the world cotton market and its attempt to make Turkestan a secure and stable part of the Russian Empire, arguing that action was required, "not only by 'our political, economic and cultural tasks in Central Asia, but the prestige of the Russian name among the Muslim population.'"[114] Given Krivoshein's unenviable position, it is understandable why he jumped at the opportunity presented by American entrepreneur John Hays Hammond in December 1910. The message Krivoshein received from Hammond read, in part:

> As you are aware large areas of waste land have been transformed into prosperous agricultural communities in America and in Mexico ... From an examination of reports submitted to me, I have reason to believe that there are large tracts of land in the Russian Empire which are today unproductive, but which could be rendered very productive by a suitable system of irrigation.

As part of a more general scheme of investment into the development of the Russian Empire, Hammond wished to explore the possibilities of a reclamation project in Turkestan.[115] Hammond's vision of transforming "[t]hose portions of the globe which for eons had remained comparatively barren and useless" resonated with Krivoshein, who immediately responded to Hammond that "the familiarization of foreign financial circles" with lands which could be made profitable through irrigation was "entirely desirable" and that the Russian government would render all possible assistance to such specialists as Hammond chose to send to Turkestan for reconnaissance.[116]

Though the American's expertise, good reputation, and available capital were all desirable, there remained the problem that Russian law did not easily permit foreign entrepreneurs to invest in Russian land. While imperial lands could be granted to cooperatives or joint-stock companies made up of up to one-third foreigners (or foreign capital), this only applied to lands outside of the *pogranichnaia polosa*, or border zone of the empire.

[114] Quoted in Joffe, "Autocracy, Capitalism and Empire," 370.

[115] RGIA f. 426, op. 1, d. 804, l. 5. For more on Hammond's plans, see William C. Askew, "Efforts to Improve Russo-American Relations before the First World War: The John Hays Hammond Mission," *The Slavonic and East European Review* 31, 76 (December 1952): 181–182.

[116] Quoted in Jessica Teisch, *Engineering Nature*, 9; RGIA f. 426, op. 1, d. 804, l. 7.

The lands in which Hammond was interested – a portion of the Qara Qum desert on the left bank of the Amu Darya between the Central Asian Railroad and the Afghan border – conflicted with this rule. Part of these lands, moreover, lay within the borders of the Emirate of Bukhara. Just a few months prior to Hammond's request, the Turkestan branch of the Ministry of Agriculture had received a request from Prince Mikhail Mikhailovich Andronikov, who wished to initiate a project to irrigate 80,000 desiatinas on the Karshi Steppe, within the borders of Bukhara. With no law in place to determine what such a concession might look like, the ministry decided that more information was necessary before such decisions could be made.[117] (Andronikov subsequently directly petitioned the ruler of Khiva, Isfandiyār khan, for a concession, which he was granted in 1913, sparking controversy between Russia and Khiva about who had the right to use the waters of the Amu Darya.)[118]

Andronikov and Hammond's petitions were just two of a flood of petitions concerning the irrigation of Turkestan sent to the central Russian government in the first years of the twentieth century. Many of these requests were petitions competing for the same tracts of land. For instance, Colonel M. N. Ermolaev, who had undertaken trips to the region in both 1908 and 1910, wished to use the Amu Darya to water the Merv Oasis in Transcaspia.[119] A group of Moscow industrialists representing central Russian cotton interests initially had been enthusiastic about the same region as had Ermolaev, but had come to the conclusion that this part of the Qara Qum was too hilly and, in general, not good for irrigation.[120] Colonel Aleksandr Nikolaevich Voeikov was granted permission to investigate parts of the southern Hungry Steppe and the Dal'verzin Steppe just to the east.[121] In the spring of 1911, under the leadership of a capitalist from Kiev named Al'brandt, another expedition was also researching the area.[122] Though cautious about

[117] RGIA f. 426, op. 1, dd. 804, l. 58; 785, ll. 1–40b.

[118] Shioya, "Who Should Manage the Waters of the Amu Darya?"

[119] Barts, *Oroshenie v doline r. Murgaba*, 135. According to *Karakumskii kanal i izmenenie prirodnoi sredy v zone ego vliianiia* (Moscow: Nauka, 1978), Ermolaev undertook his first investigations of the Murghab and Tedzhen basins in 1906–1907 (12).

[120] N. Shavrov, *Vodnoe khoziaistvo Turkestana i Zakaspiiskoi oblasti v sviazi s proektom vodnogo zakona* (St. Petersburg: Tip. Usmanova, 1911), 27; RGIA f. 426, op. 1, d. 804, l. 29ob.

[121] Not to be confused with Aleksandr Ivanovich Voeikov, the climatologist and geographer who warned about the harmful effects of man on the environment. RGIA f. 426, op. 1, d. 804, l. 106; "Novyi proekt" *TK* 81 (1908) in *TS* 464, 65.

[122] RGIA f. 426, op. 1, d. 767, l. 7a, *NV* (April 22, 1911); Shavrov, *Vodnoe khoziaistvo Turkestana*, 28.

granting concessions outright, on the recommendation of the commission of the Turkestan Agricultural Society convened to discuss involving private entrepreneurs in irrigation, the Russian government approved many such requests to conduct initial investigations and consult scientific data.[123] Yet, even the tsar's cousins, Grand Princes Kirill, Boris, and Andrei Vladimirovich, who hoped to irrigate a region on the left bank of the Syr Darya in Ferghana, were met in December 1911 with the statement that "granting lands currently belonging to the state for irrigation in Turkestan is impossible for lack of an appropriate law."[124]

It may therefore come as a surprise that in February 1911, in spite of Russian reservations about granting concessions in this sensitive border region, the restriction under Russian law on foreigners from making such investments, and the lack of existing legislation that would facilitate investments of private capital and concessions, the Russian government offered Hammond the condition that his syndicate would be given priority in carrying out irrigation projects in the face of any other competition, should his investigations of the Qara Qum return a favorable result. Hammond's correspondence clearly displays his general concerns about doing business with the Russian government, but once the Department of Land Improvement made it clear that the entire Qara Qum region was reserved for his team to explore, Hammond agreed to send his engineers to Turkestan.[125]

Hammond's team, which left for Turkestan in April 1911, was made up of Arthur Powell Davis, Head Engineer of the United States Reclamation Service, and William Mackie, who was, Hammond assured the Russians, "the number one American authority on the greening [translated as *ozhivlenie*] of arid lands." The Russians who joined the expedition, including engineer Ostrovskii from the Hungry Steppe, were quite impressed with both Davis and Mackie. V. V. Dubasov, the former director of the Murghab Estate, reported, "[T]hey are workers the likes of which I have never seen … they willingly listen and readily comply … [A]s people they are also amazingly kind and pleasant … I firmly believe that … whatever results they turn up will show [the way to]

123 On the recommendation, see Babaliants, "Pervyi s″ezd gidrotekhnikov," 72.

124 RGIA f. 426, op. 1, d. 817, ll. 1, 5. The law was still in draft form a year later (the text can be found in GARF f. 1001, op. 1, d. 188, ll. 12–21).

125 RGIA f. 426, op. 1, d. 804, ll. 29ob-30ob, 61, 63, 64–64ob, 67–67ob; Letter from Hammond to Grigorii Vilenkin, Box 1, Folder 10, APD.

the future."[126] The Americans, too, found much to admire in the Russian engineers.[127]

Proponents of the colonization of Turkestan with Slavic settlers, however, were skeptical about the wisdom of foreign irrigation concessions in the region. In 1910, the *Moscow Gazette* had already warned against concessions to private entrepreneurs in "one of the most important colonization regions."[128] Nikolai Nikolaevich Shavrov, a university-trained naturalist and former head of resettlement affairs in the Syr Darya region, wrote a book in 1911 on water management in Turkestan, in which he warned against introducing "alien" [*inorodcheskii*] elements into the region, which would conflict with the goal of settling these lands with Russians.[129] The fact that the "alien" element in Hammond's case was an American one particularly rankled among domestic parties wishing to invest in and profit from irrigation for the development of cotton agriculture in Turkestan. An article published in the Moscow newspaper *Russia's Morning* at the beginning of May 1911 did little to disguise the anonymous author's displeasure with the favored treatment given to Hammond. "Hammond has been promised almost the entire [Transcaspian] oblast' for his exclusive use in irrigating the Central Asian Steppes," the newspaper reported. "[I]t is remarkable that it is exactly this kind of enterprise toward which a group of Moscow capitalists – with highly respectable names that are quite familiar to Petersburg – has already been striving for several years." Though the group of Moscow capitalists had been "beating down the doors of the offices in Petersburg" for two years, Hammond had been given what he asked for with just a single visit, the article griped.[130]

The granting of irrigation privileges to Americans – the very people who potentially stood in the way of the success of the Russian textile industry – must have been a crushing blow indeed. What the proponents of domestic entrepreneurship did not know, however, was that Davis and Mackie were quickly disappointed in the results of their investigations. "[T]he country is a vast desert of sand dunes," wrote Davis, "entirely too rough for irrigation."[131] The project "would require for its irrigation

[126] RGIA f. 426, op. 1, d. 804, ll. 76–76ob, 91.
[127] Letter from Davis to Hammond (March 14, 1912), Box 1, Folder 10, APD.
[128] RGIA f. 426, op. 1, d. 767, l. 1, *MV* (June 26, 1910).
[129] Shavrov, *Vodnoe khoziaistvo Turkestana*, 99.
[130] RGIA f. 426, op. 1, d. 767, l. 7, *UR* (May 6, 1911).
[131] Letter to John Hays Hammond (May 24, 1911), handwritten copy, 4, Box 1, Folder 10, APD.

250 miles of main canal, mostly through sand dunes, which would be so costly and would lose so much water by seepage before reaching the land, as to render its feasibility out of the question."[132] After just a month of exploration in the southeastern portion of the Qara Qum desert, the American experts felt they had enough information to persuade Hammond that the scheme should be abandoned.

They were not, however, ready to abandon Central Asia altogether. In fact, Davis claimed that he had originally been given to understand that the investigations would take place along the Syr River, rather than the Amu; when he found the Qara Qum region to be "so at variance with the description given us," he lobbied for the chance to do some investigations in the Hungry Steppe, which he and Mackie had visited en route to Transcaspia, taking soil and cotton samples for analysis from the state-run experimental station there.[133] Hammond agreed, proposing that his team move to investigate the central and western portions of the steppe.[134] Krivoshein, however, informed Hammond that since there were already government investigations underway in another part of the Hungry Steppe, it was unlikely that the Russian government would grant him a concession of the type that he might secure in the Qara Qum region, and advised Hammond to choose another area of Turkestan to investigate. Despite Krivoshein's warning, Davis and Mackie spent nine days investigating the Hungry Steppe, concluding that, "with a liberal concession a profitable enterprise can be here worked out."[135] The concession was never granted, but Davis was so enthusiastic about the possibilities for irrigating the Hungry Steppe that he returned to the region almost two decades later to serve as head consulting engineer to the Soviet Cotton Committee in the region.[136]

Dubasov, who had worked so closely with Davis and Mackie in the Qara Qum desert, held out hope that a concession to Hammond in the Hungry Steppe could ultimately be successful. In an October 1911 letter to Krivoshein, apparently at the instigation of Hammond, Dubasov made four points: that the Russians still had little experience in the field of irrigation, that the Russian government could not provide the necessary

[132] Ibid., 9. [133] Ibid., 3–6; *GS*, Doc. 42: 113.

[134] RGIA f. 426, op. 1, d. 804, ll. 93–93ob.

[135] Letter to John Hays Hammond (May 24, 1911), handwritten copy, 15, Box 1, Folder 10, APD.

[136] For more, see Maya K. Peterson, "US to USSR: American Experts and the Irrigation of Soviet Central Asia, 1929–1932," *Environmental History* 21, 3 (June 2016): 451–452, as well as Chapter 6.

sums for the enormous task of bringing water to the desert, that having Hammond's work alongside the government projects could provide a beneficial influence, and that it was imperative that the "first [state-run] irrigation enterprise in Turkestan" be a success. Dubasov's impassioned reports received the response that the Hammond matter was considered closed, and that the Department of Land Improvement could see no reason for reopening the matter for discussion.[137]

Yet, the conversations continued on both sides of the Atlantic. In January 1912, Vilenkin, the Russian trade representative in the United States, wrote to Davis that he hoped "that in the end we shall be able to carry through our scheme." In February, engineer Ostrovskii wrote that he had traveled to London on his own expense to advise Hammond to continue the [irrigation] surveys, even though the "Government is not quite sure is Mr. Hammond very much interested in Turkestan irrigation." A letter in March from Davis urged Hammond to return to St. Petersburg for the negotiation of a proper concession before continuing surveys the following autumn. And in May, Hammond was apparently back in St. Petersburg, where he met with Ostrovskii, who became convinced that Hammond would receive the concession after all.[138] On May 25, Hammond requested another opportunity to investigate the Hungry Steppe, with a concession to follow. On May 28, 1912, his bid was refused for the final time.[139]

A typical Soviet interpretation of the Hammond affair focuses on the conflict between the "American businessmen," who wanted to gain control over the Russian cotton industry, and the "Russian bourgeoisie," who had to act in the protection of their interests.[140] It is quite possible that influential men from the textile industry pressured Krivoshein about his impulsive decision to grant broad privileges not only to a foreigner, but to a man from America, from whose influence the Russian cotton industry was trying to escape.[141] The extent to which textile industrialists had influence in Russian society is reflected by the fact that *Russia's Morning*, the newspaper that published the article deploring Hammond's unrestricted access to government lands in Turkestan, had been founded by two of these influential Moscow textile families, the Riabushinskiis

[137] RGIA f. 426, op. 1, d. 804, ll. 123–126ob, 129.

[138] Letters in Box 1, Folder 10, APD. [139] *GS*, 212.

[140] See, for instance, R. S. Igamberdyev, *Osushchestvlenie leninskikh idei ob oroshenii i osvoenii Golodnoi stepi* (Tashkent: Izd. FAN, 1969), 35.

[141] Krivoshein had personal ties to the Moscow textile industrialists (Joffe, "Autocracy, Capitalism and Empire," 374 fn 53).

and the Konovalovs.[142] Moreover, the government's reluctance to act quickly in the case of the Moscow entrepreneurs does, as some scholars have suggested, reflect uncertainty surrounding the kind of role private entrepreneurs should and would be able to play in the irrigation of Turkestan, an uncertainty that may have "undermined the very process of economic development it sought to encourage."[143] But the fact that Krivoshein was so quick to approve Hammond's plans – even insofar as to let him conduct studies within the Emirate of Bukhara, an act of dubious legality – suggests that St. Petersburg recognized the value that American hydraulic engineers, in contrast to Moscow entrepreneurs, could bring to Turkestan.

Hammond himself would later describe the circumstances of his coming to Russia in 1910, at the personal invitation of Finance Minister Vladimir Nikolaevich Kokovtsov, thus: "Mr. Kokovtsoff was desirous of enlisting American capital, as well as American initiative and experience – and *American initiative and experience were quite as important in his view as capital* – for the development of Russian resources."[144] Perhaps Russia wished to use American irrigation knowledge to free itself from imports of American cotton. In a letter to Prime Minister Pyotr Stolypin, Krivoshein had suggested that Hammond's expert opinion might be valuable in helping to determine a further course of action in the Qara Qum desert, where, as yet, Russians had not managed to come to an agreement on whether or not an irrigation project in the region would be either feasible or profitable. An influx of private capital would likely necessitate concessions in this politically sensitive part of the empire, but it might also finally ensure Russian self-sufficiency in terms of cotton.

There are also other factors that can explain the rejection of Hammond, as well as the rejection of the Moscow entrepreneurs, none of which is sufficiently explained by the autocratic state's hostility to private property or the desire to restrict all irrigation schemes to state-led ones. In Hammond's case, one of the factors was the global situation. In late 1911, the deterioration of trade relations with America over the Jewish passport

142 Geoffrey Hosking, *Russia: People and Empire, 1552–1917* (Cambridge, MA: Harvard University Press, 1997), 448.

143 Joffe, "Autocracy, Capitalism and Empire," 366, 373–374; see also Ian Murray Matley, "The Golodnaya Steppe: A Russian Irrigation Venture in Central Asia," *Geographical Review* 60, 3 (July 1970): 336–337.

144 Emphasis added. John Hays Hammond, Speech on the Russian Passport Question at the Hungarian Republican Club, New York, December 5, 1911, JHH, Box 11, Folder 1, 22–31: 24.

question which led to the abrogation of the Russian–American trade agreement of 1832, seems to have been the impetus needed to finally spur the Russian government to fully commit to the domestic production of cotton and to exploit Turkestan's cotton-growing potential to the maximum.[145] In February 1912, the State Duma discussed legislation advanced by the Ministry of Agriculture on increasing the Department of Land Improvement, assigning more money for hydraulic investigations in Turkestan, and developing cotton agriculture there.[146] That same month, reporting on the sudden responsiveness of the Russian government to the needs of Turkestan cotton, the *Turkestan Courier* reported that the government was now planning to send up to fifty instructors and specialists to the region.[147] In June, the State Duma acknowledged that "the rapid development of native [*otechestvennyi*] cotton is now a regular government task," and emphasized the importance of the irrigation of new lands.[148] The government also redoubled its efforts to irrigate the Hungry Steppe by contracting out work to the financier and engineer Sergei Nikolaevich Chaev, who planned to import excavators from London for the task.[149]

Another factor in explaining Hammond's rejection was more local, however. The persistence of Article 256 of the Turkestan Statute left unclear the government's ability to carry out new irrigation projects – or grant concessions – particularly in regions where water had already been apportioned according to "custom." This was the main problem with the Moscow Irrigation Company's proposal to irrigate 300,000 *desiatinas* in the Ferghana Valley; of secondary concern was that such a large irrigation project using water from the Naryn River, an

145 For criticism of John Hays Hammond's dealings with Russia because of Russia's failure to recognize the passports of Jewish-American citizens, see "Denial from Mr. Hammond" ("Senators to Back Demand on Russia") *NYT* (November 18, 1911): 2. His "Speech on the Russian Passport Question" addresses concerns about Russian anti-Semitism (25–30). For more, see Norman E. Saul, *Concord and Conflict: The United States and Russia, 1867–1914* (Lawrence, KS: University Press of Kansas, 1996), 567–584, *passim* (cotton and irrigating Central Asia, on 580).

146 *Obzor deiatel'nosti Gosudarstvennoi Dumy tret'ego sozyva, 1907–1912*, Part 2 (St. Petersburg: Gos. tip., 1912), 294–295; see also *Prilozheniia k stenograficheskim otchetam Gosudarstvennoi Dumy, Tretii sozyv, Sessiia piataia (1911–12),* V (St. Petersburg: Gos. Duma, 1912), Nos. 785, 795, 825.

147 *GS*, Doc. 46: 118. The agronomists until 1911 were not cotton specialists (Whitman, "Turkestan Cotton in Imperial Russia," 195).

148 *Obzor deiatel'nosti Gosudarstvennoi Dumy tret'ego sozyva, 1907–1912*, 2: 295.

149 According to Lykoshin, Chaev introduced the excavator to Russia (*GS*, Doc. 43: 113–114).

understudied tributary of the Syr Darya, might not leave enough water for the Hungry Steppe, and vice versa.[150] The tsarist government's official rules for private entrepreneurs, approved in 1910, pertained to investigations only – there still were no provisions for what would happen should entrepreneurs wish to invest after having carried out successful investigations.[151] Until new legislation could be drawn up, the government was hamstrung by the provisions it had made in the Turkestan Statute of 1886, which in spite of its provisional nature, continued to be the law of the land.

GOVERNING WATER

The question of investing private capital in irrigation was, thus, intimately intertwined with the question of water governance in Turkestan. In 1907, during discussions within the Ministry of Internal Affairs about Kazakh land use, at meetings of the Ministry of Agriculture's newly formed Cotton Committee, at an Extraordinary Assembly of the Members of the Turkestan Agricultural Society, and at the first congress of hydraulic engineers in Tashkent, all came to the conclusion that there had to be a law on water in Turkestan so as "to bring to strict order water use in the krai."[152] Although the majority of participants at the Congress of Hydraulic Engineers agreed that "custom" was based on centuries of experience and that it therefore should not be ignored, it was clear that not only had water management not improved under the Russian administration of Turkestan, but rather it had deteriorated.[153] Count Pahlen's inspection of the province in the following years, which discovered numerous instances of violations of custom, drove this message home.[154]

In 1909, with the idea of personally acquainting himself with the situation in Turkestan, Prince Vladislav Masal′skii, head of the Department of Land Improvement, made a trip to the province that resulted in the formation of a committee to oversee drafting a new water law for Turkestan.[155] In September, he traveled to the Hungry Steppe in a party including engineer M. P. Psarev and one of Grand Duke Nikolai

150 *Trudy s″ezda khlopkovodov*, I, 90. 151 Cherdantsev, *Vodnoe pravo*, Part I, 29–30.

152 Ibid., 22, 30; Matisen, "Polozhenie i nuzhdy orosheniia," 285; K. A. Timaev, "Ozhivlenie novykh zemel′," *TK* 120 (1909) in *TS* 508, 114–116: 114; Babaliants, "Pervyi s″ezd gidrotekhnikov," 79.

153 "S″ezd gidrotekhnikov," 149. 154 Pahlen, *Oroshenie*, 7–8, 464.

155 Matisen, "Polozhenie i nuzhdy orosheniia," 286; G. Gins, "Sovremennoe vodnoe khoziaistvo Turkestana i neobkhodimost′ vodnogo zakona," *VK* 6 (1910), 46–103: 51–52.

Konstantinovich's representatives, in order to view the progress of the government canal there. After viewing the canals and visiting the settlements near the government agricultural experiment station, Masal′skii was besieged by a crowd of Russian settlers with a written request demanding government aid, freedom from rental payments in the Hungry Steppe (granted to earlier settlers there), and pasture for their livestock. Frustrated with waiting for a response from regional authorities, the peasants were surely disappointed when the prince "rejected their request point-blank," though he indicated that the regional Ministry of Agriculture might still fulfill their requests.[156] Masal′skii's response was a reminder that although successful Russian colonization was purportedly an important goal of the state in the region, and in spite of the fact that the presence of destitute settlers continued to throw a shadow on Russian rule in Turkestan, the Russian government was preoccupied with the myriad questions of how to use scarce funds to plan the future colonization of the province – which included proper water management – rather than with assisting settlers who had somehow made their way to the region on their own.

Much of that work was being undertaken by Masal′skii's ministry, the Ministry of Agriculture and State Domains, which in 1905 had been reorganized into the Main Administration of Land Management and Agriculture, a title that reflected a new concern with the way the lands of the empire were to be used, with its emphasis on "land management" preceding agriculture. In central parts of the empire, "land management" referred to overseeing Prime Minister Stolypin's agrarian reforms in the Russian countryside. These did not extend to Turkestan, so the Turkestan branch of the ministry retained its title of Administration of Agriculture and State Domains. But land management also included overseeing the creation of settlement parcels across Russia's vast expanses, made more accessible by the railways connecting the central regions of Russia to Siberia, the Far East, and Turkestan by the early twentieth century. Thus, 1905 also saw the transfer of the Resettlement Administration to the Ministry of Agriculture (that is, the Main Administration). Turkestan also gained its own branch of the Resettlement Administration in 1905, which was actively involved in planning the future colonization of the province, including hydrological investigations.

[156] *GS*, Doc. 35: 105–106.

It was the Resettlement Administration that in 1909 assigned young law student Georgii Konstantinovich Gins to learn about the legal regulations pertaining to the distribution of water for irrigation in Turkestan. The choice of a young law student with no familiarity either with Turkestan or Russian legislation on water affairs may seem strange; it is, in part, a testament to how few people there were who were qualified for taking on such a task. (Dingel′shtedt's work on irrigation, including lengthy recommendations on how to write a water law, remained "a classic," but its author had died in 1898.)[157] The assignment to travel to Turkestan came as a shock to Gins, who in April 1909 had been preparing to pass his examinations to graduate from St. Petersburg University when one of his professors recommended him to the Resettlement Administration for the job. Gins quickly did some research and found that a law regulating water use and so-called artificial irrigation had been passed for the province of Transcaucasia already in 1890. Incredibly, the officials of the Resettlement Administration did not seem to be aware of this existing legislation, though it had been discussed for many years in Turkestan. Within a month of being approached in a university hallway – and without having taken his exams – Gins arrived in Tashkent in the guise of a "temporary hydraulic engineering agent" of the Semireche branch of the Resettlement Administration, ready to tackle the chaos of water legislation in Turkestan.[158]

In August, after reporting to Masal′skii in Vernyi, Gins returned to St. Petersburg and submitted his final report, upon which the head of the Resettlement Administration immediately offered him a job. After passing his university examinations, Gins accepted the offer. One of his first roles was to represent the Resettlement Administration on the inter-bureaucratic commission tasked with drafting a water law for Turkestan created by Masal′skii. The commission included "representatives of all government institutions interested in the development of Turkestan," including the Ministries of Finance, Justice, and State Control, the Asiatic Department of the Ministry of War, and the State Chancellery – a diverse and influential group of government bodies.[159] According to Gins, the

[157] Matisen, "Polozhenie i nuzhdy orosheniia," 280.

[158] George C. Guins [G. K. Gins], *Professor and Government Official: Russia, China and California. An Interview Conducted by Boris Raymond*, University of California Regional Oral History Office (Berkeley: Bancroft Library, 1966), 66–68. Dingel′shtedt deemed the Caucasus law unsuitable for Turkestan. *Opyt izucheniia irrigatsii*, 52.

[159] George C. Guins, *Impressions of the Russian Imperial Government: An Interview Conducted by Richard Pierce*, University of California Regional Oral History Office (Berkeley, CA: Bancroft Library, 1971), 20–21.

purpose of this commission "was to secure the government's right to use water resources for irrigation to increase the area prepared for new Russian settlements."[160] Gins's emphasis on colonization, rather than cotton, presumably reflects his position as a representative of the Resettlement Administration, though many boosters of irrigation shared the view that both from a political as well as an economic perspective, strengthening the Russian element in the krai could guarantee a firm fusion [*sliianie*] of the Turkestan borderland with the Empire.[161] Gins's emphasis on the government's right to water indicates that the new law was also aimed at curtailing the latitudes Turkestanis and individuals such as Grand Duke Nikolai Konstantinovich had enjoyed under the regime of custom, giving the state a firmer hand both in the regulation of water as well as in the exploitation of land resources. If the Russian state were recognized as the owner of Turkestan's water, it could more easily decide questions such as the investment of private capital into irrigation or where Russian colonists might profitably be settled.

Former war minister and future governor-general of Turkestan Aleksei Nikolaevich Kuropatkin visited one of the commission's meetings, claiming interest "in the organization of special institutions for exploiting water resources of Turkestan."[162] Gins was impressed by Kuropatkin's knowledge of the local conditions and needs of Turkestan, and by his emphasis on the urgent and the practical, rather than the theoretical and esoteric dimensions of legal discourse. As he later recalled, Kuropatkin stated that he was "more interested in what financial means the Turkestan government will employ and where and how soon our engineers will construct a new irrigation system than in the details of law."[163] The law would finally make possible the kinds of development that the state had thus far been reluctant or unable to undertake. Minister of Agriculture Krivoshein submitted one draft of the law to the State Duma in February 1912 and a second version in January 1913.[164] In between, he personally visited Turkestan, as Masal'skii had three years earlier. (The water law languished in various bureaus for years. It was finally set to take effect January 1, 1917; two months later, the tsar abdicated.)

160 Guins, *Professor and Government Official*, 82.
161 Babaliants, "Pervyi s"ezd gidrotekhnikov," 75.
162 Guins, *Professor and Government Official*, 83.
163 Guins, *Impressions of the Russian Imperial Government*, 22.
164 Joffe, "Autocracy, Capitalism and Empire," 381.

In his memorandum to the tsar on returning from his travels, Krivoshein made a statement to the effect that cotton plus irrigation plus colonization would equal a "new Turkestan . . . not inferior to the old one in magnitude, [and] surpass[ing] it in riches and level of culture." The notion of a "new Turkestan" was symbolic – lands colonized by Russians and planted with cotton that would "act as a counterweight to the old, Muslim Turkestan" – but it was also literal. Krivoshein calculated that by using all of the "reserve" waters of Turkestan, including those from glacial runoff and reservoirs of groundwater, the amount of land that could be irrigated in Turkestan would be equal to the acreage of irrigated land that already existed, thus doubling the amount of arable land.[165]

Krivoshein's "new Turkestan" seemed to be a neat formulation of Russia's visions for the region, yet it still did not emphasize whether cotton or colonization was more important. In some places, such as the Hungry Steppe, the two could go hand in hand. In other places, such as the Ferghana Valley, there was room only for cotton, not extensive colonization. A 1912 report addressed to the Council of Ministers recognized that "the irrigation and settlement of desert [*pustynnye*] lands has not only economic, but also political significance – the strengthening of Russian people in the borderlands [*na okraine*]."[166] When writing up his own official reports, based on this report, Krivoshein added that in Russia, "the irrigation and settlement of desert lands has not only economic significance, *as in America*, but also political significance," to emphasize that the political significance of irrigation and colonization of Russia had its own unique challenges, which could not necessarily be easily solved simply by importing American knowledge, expertise, and technology.[167] He may have been defending the government's decisions not to allow private capital investment in irrigation – as was the case in America – even when so many in Russia clearly desired it.[168]

165 Krivoshein, *Zapiska Glavnoupravliaiushchego zemleustroistvom i zemledeliem*, 30.

166 GARF f. 1001, op. 1, d. 188, l. 3.

167 Krivoshein, *Zapiska Glavnoupravliaiushchego zemleustroistvom i zemledeliem*, 39.

168 For the American case, see Cherdantsev, *Vodnoe pravo*, Part I, 32. See also E. E. Skorniakov's interest in the American Carey Act as a model for Russia: *Oroshenie i kolonizatsiia pustyn' shtata Aidago v Severnoi Amerike na osnovanii zakona Keri (Carey Act): Otchet po zagranichnoi komandirovke*, 2 volumes (St. Petersburg: GUZiZ OZU, 1911); as well as A. I. Voeikov, *Turkestan: ego vody i oroshenie* (Petrograd: Tip. T-va "Obshchestvennaia pol'za," 1915), 17.

FIGURE 3.3 Public prayer at the opening of the Romanov Canal, 1913. "Molebstvie." Photograph No. 2 in the photo album *Vidy torzhestvennogo otkrytiia Romanovskogo orositel'nogo kanala v Golodnoi Stepi 5 oktiabria 1913* [*Views of the Celebratory Opening of the Romanov Irrigation Canal in the Hungry Steppe, 5 October 1913*], 1.
Reproduced with permission from the Rare Books Section of the Alisher Navoi State Library, Tashkent, Uzbekistan.

RESTRICTING RICE

Officials such as Masal'skii, Krivoshein, and Kokovtsov believed that, by properly exploiting the resources – what were referred to as the "productive forces" (*proizvodstvennye sily*) – of Turkestan, the region could become a profitable colony of the empire, rather than a drain on the imperial coffers. Many officials in the Ministry of Agriculture and its various departments (the Departments of Agriculture and Land Improvement, as well as the Resettlement Administration), were driven by this "technocratic ethos."[169] In 1915, an official Commission for the Study of the Natural Productive Forces of Russia (KEPS) was founded, in

[169] For more, with specific reference to the Resettlement Administration, see Peter Holquist, "'In Accord with State Interests and the People's Wishes," 151–179.

order to put these principles to work for the mobilization of the country's resources for war.[170] The logic of productive forces dictated that Turkestan's water resources should be used for cultivation, and that the most beneficial crop that Turkestan could provide the empire was cotton.

Since cotton was deemed the most important beneficiary of the region's water resources, one of the crops that suffered most was rice. As a crop that demanded large amounts of water, rice was obvious competition for cotton. In fact, Russians had noted that indigenous cultivators who grew less rice typically grew more cotton, and vice versa.[171] Rice was cheaper to grow, also yielded a high profit, and, unlike cotton, was not prone to devastation by locusts.[172] There were many indications that in places such as the Ferghana Valley – where rice cultivation had successfully been limited under the Khanate of Khoqand – as well as in Zarafshan and Samarkand, where it had been restricted by the Bukharan emir, rice cultivation had, in fact, expanded under the Russians, due to the decrease in restrictions, as well as control over water management.[173] In the Hungry Steppe region, Pahlen's inspection agents found that even some Russians with fields near the head of the local ariq were stealing water for rice, to the detriment of their fellow villagers.[174] Though this gave the Russians good reasons to limit its cultivation, the implication of targeting rice – the main ingredient in Central Asian plov, consumed at all important celebrations, and even more often by those who could afford it – was that the food needs of the indigenous population were not as important as those of the newly arrived Slavic settlers, who ate mostly wheat, barley, and rye. In October 1912, *The Day*, a newspaper published in the Russian capital, reported that the Department of Land Improvement, on Masal'skii's initiative, had begun drawing up a "grandiose project" for transforming rice plantations in the Tashkent and Samarkand regions into cotton fields. The plan foresaw moving these rice fields to the Qara Qum and Qyzyl Qum deserts. How,

170 Hirsch, *Empire of Nations*, 47.

171 Brodovskii, "Zametki o zemledelii v Samarkandskom raione," 250.

172 Kinze "Khlopkovodstvo," 338, 346; Pahlen, *Oroshenie*, 10; Von der Muhlen, "Cotton Growing in Russian Central Asia and the Caucasus," 138–139. Similarly, in colonial Java, Europeans argued that sugar plantations were more lucrative for the local economy than were indigenous rice paddies (Dianne van Oosterhout, "From Colonial to Postcolonial Irrigation Technology: Technological Romanticism and the Revival of Colonial Water Tanks in Java, Indonesia," *Technology and Culture* 49, 3 [July 2008]: 701).

173 Thurman, "Modes of Organization," 71, 83; Moser, *L'irrigation*, 233–234; Dingel'shtedt, *Opyt izucheniia irrigatsii*, 125; Pahlen, *Oroshenie*, 62–68.

174 Pahlen, *Oroshenie*, 26.

precisely, the government planned to grow rice, a water-intensive crop, on arid land rejected as unfit for profitable irrigation by both American engineers and the Moscow textile industry, the article did not specify.[175]

Dingel'shtedt had cautioned against replacing local food crops in favor of a cotton monoculture, yet he also believed that Russians should follow European laws that limited the cultivation of rice near densely populated areas, for hygienic reasons.[176] In an effort to restrict rice, Russians pointed to the negative effects of rice cultivation on sanitary standards and human health. A 1909 newspaper article, for instance, argued that the "irrational" use of water on rice fields released water vapor into the air, causing the soil to remain damp, which weakened the performance of bodily organs, shortened lifespans, increased infant mortality, and enabled the development of malaria.[177] That same year, a series of articles in the *Turkestan Gazette* made the claim that the "putrid evaporations" from low-lying rice paddies meant that people who lived nearby "find themselves in completely different sanitary conditions from the point of view of air, water, soil and housing."[178] Rice cultivation, by these evaluations, seemed incompatible with modernity and its emphasis on proper hygiene and sanitation.

Malaria spread by mosquitoes breeding in areas of standing water was indeed a serious concern, and though books such as *On the Cultivation of Rice in Turkestan and Its Effects on Malarial Disease*, published in Tashkent in 1905, were right to explore the relationship between rice paddies and malaria, the disease was not caused by native rice fields alone.[179] As the Department of Agriculture noted, fevers were often just as prevalent in non-rice-growing regions.[180] Moreover, constructing rice paddies in such a manner as to encourage flowing, rather than stagnant, water was the traditional method for growing rice in Central Asia, which helped to prevent malaria.[181]

175 RGIA, f. 426, op. 1, d. 767, l. 21, "Zakonoproekt o russkom khlopke," *D* (October 25, 1912). During experiments in the early 1890s with dry-farming Chinese rice, it was hard to convince cultivators not to overwater (Dingel'shtedt, *Opyt izucheniia irrigatsii*, 177–178 fn 2). It is possible that the experimental stations had in the meantime made improvements to dry-farmed rice, but the scheme is still dubious.

176 N. A. Dingel'shtedt, *Zapiska inspektora sel'skogo khoziaistva St. sov. N.A. Dingel'shtedta* (St. Petersburg: n.p., 1897), 2–3; *Opyt izucheniia irrigatsii*, 80.

177 "O vliianii risovykh polei na zdorov'e naseleniia," *Na rubezh'* 108 (1909) in *TS* 502, 179–181: 180.

178 "Znachenie posevov risa na zabolevanie maliariei v Turkestanskom krae," *TV* 190–93 (1909) in *TS* 513, 108–129: 118.

179 Ibid., 108 fn.

180 Kinze, "Khlopkovodstvo," 346.

181 "Znachenie posevov risa na zabolevanie maliariei," 113.

There was even evidence that Russians themselves had contributed to malaria's spread, though few administrators would like to admit it. In a work published in 1914, V. A. Voshchinin, a Resettlement Administration official enamored of Krivoshein's vision of a "new Turkestan" to be realized "with the latest word in Russian engineering art," commented on the prevalence of malaria during his visit to the Hungry Steppe.[182] According to the German observer Rudolf Asmis, improper Russian irrigation work had "awakened the danger of malaria" in the previously "mosquito-free" Hungry Steppe.[183] Whether or not this is true, Asmis was correct in his observation that the Russian failure to fully study the soil and proper methods for draining it had led to a number of problems in the Hungry Steppe, including, by 1915, widespread swamping and soil salinization.[184]

In fact, rice cultivation in Turkestan was itself used to address just these kinds of problems, serving an important ecological function in addition to providing sustenance for the people of the region. Because it rarely required fertilizer, it could be planted year after year in the same place without ruining the land.[185] Moreover, through flooding, rice was used as a way of grappling with the soluble salts in the loess soils across much of the region. In Bukhara, Prince Andronikov noted that the "natives have an excellent knowledge of the properties of salt flats and gladly rent such lands, in the main planting them with rice ... [T]he irrigative water leaches the soils, which then makes it suitable for the cultivation of grain and other crops."[186] Colonel Ermolaev similarly noted that besides being "the favorite food of the population," one of the reasons that rice was so popular in Samarkand, occupying "almost half the cultivated acreage" in some parts of the region, was that planting rice on a salinized plot guaranteed a good harvest, in contrast to cotton.[187] Rice, however, could not benefit the empire in the same way that cotton could, and its high water requirements in a region in which

182 V. A. Voshchinin, *Ocherki novogo Turkestana: svet i teni russkoi kolonizatsii* (St. Petersburg: Nash vek, 1914), 19, 27, 29.

183 Rudolf Asmis, *Als Wirtschaftspionier in Russisch-Asien,* 2nd edn. (Berlin: Georg Stilke, 1926), 179–180.

184 "Khronologicheskie vypiski," *GS*, 216.

185 Dingel'shtedt, *Opyt izucheniia irrigatsii*, 177.

186 RGIA, f. 426, op. 1, d. 785, ll. 12ob-13.

187 M. N. Ermolaev, *Propusk vod r. Amu-Dar'i v Mervskii i Tedzhenskii oazisy* (St. Petersburg: Tip. uchilishcha glukhonemykh, 1908), 82; Machatschek, too, recorded up to 40 percent of land cultivated with rice in some parts of eastern Ferghana and believed the water could be better used for cotton (*Landeskunde von Russisch Turkestan*, 149, 158).

water was so precious led to its restriction, even when many parts of Turkestan were no longer self-sufficient in food.[188]

CONCLUSION

Though some present at the first conference of cotton cultivators in Turkestan warned that a cotton monoculture was "unquestionably harmful," given the scarce water resources of the province, and that the "feverish increase in cotton cultivation" could have "very serious unpleasant consequences," in the early years of the twentieth century, the acreage under cotton cultivation in Turkestan increased mainly at the expense of food crops.[189] Rice was a particularly symbolic casualty of cotton, but it was also yet another sign that the problems faced by Ferghana at the turn of the century, as cotton rapidly replaced food crops and Slavic peasants searched for places to settle, were problems that not only had not gone away, but that were set to grow and spread. The government project to irrigate the Hungry Steppe continued, but in order to avoid more trouble from both local Turkestanis and poor white settlers, settlement was to be limited to "reliable elements" – that is, to Orthodox Christians only, and only to those settlers who had at least one thousand rubles in funds.[190] The days of the Grand Duke were definitively over.

In an effort to find more land available for settlement, and with the reopening of Turkestan to official settlement in 1910, the tsarist government added a provision to the Turkestan Statute similar to one already existing in the statute governing the steppes, which allowed the government to acquire "excess" nomadic lands in the core regions of Turkestan (Samarkand, Syr Darya, and Ferghana) for the purposes of settlement. To Russia's technocrats, nomadic pastureland represented an "irrational" use of the land. Its transformation into profitable cropland would both make better use of the human population of the region – for "productive

188 V. V. Zaorskaia-Aleksandrova and I. G. Aleksandrov, *Perspektivy razvitiia orosheniia v Fergane* (Moscow: Narkomzem, 1922), 10; *Trudy s"ezda khlopkovodov*, I, 106, 171.

189 *Trudy s"ezda khlopkovodov*, I, 108, 124; Zaorskaia-Aleksandrova and Aleksandrov, *Perspektivy razvitiia orosheniia v Fergane*, 11, 15.

190 See drafts and discussions in 1913 of what became a law in 1914 in *Prilozheniia k stenograficheskim otchetam Gosudarstvennoi Dumy, Chetvertyi sozyv, Sessiia pervaia, 1912–13 gg.*, IV (St. Petersburg: Gos. Duma, 1913), No. 432, "Doklad pereselencheskoi komissii po zakonoproektu ob otvode russkim pereselentsam uchastkov kazennoi oroshennoi zemli v Golodnoi stepi, Samarkandskoi obl."

forces" included human labor, as well as natural resources – and serve the goals of the Resettlement Administration: to bring Russian settlers to Turkestan to serve as model farmers who would display the benefits of a sedentary lifestyle and raise the level of "civilization" in the province as a whole. But the fact remained that without clear legislation on Turkestan's water resources and the rights of the government and entrepreneurs to use them, that land might remain uncultivated. The creation of a "new Turkestan" advocated by Krivoshein and other technocrats seemed like a distant pipe dream.

In order to address the problems of provisioning Turkestan without curtailing cotton acreage and finding new settler parcels for Slavic colonists, the Russian government came up with an ambitious new plan: to convert the region of Semireche, in particular the Chu River Valley, into the "breadbasket" of Turkestan. A cheap source of nearby grain had the additional appeal of freeing up more land for cotton in the core regions of Turkestan.[191] Trial cotton plantations in the Chu Valley had not flourished, but fruits and grains grew exceptionally well.[192]

The Chu Valley was mainly inhabited by nomadic pastoralists. Moreover, though now once more a part of Turkestan, Semireche was still governed by the laws of the steppe provinces, which did not include any restrictions on water. Semireche, therefore, seemed an ideal place for the building of an extensive irrigation system, which could provide water to settler parcels taken from "excess" nomadic lands for Slavic settlers, as well as supply grain to the cotton regions to the west. In order to make the investment profitable, and for the valley to be able to supply the cotton regions with grain, a regional railroad connecting the two would have to be built. Without all of these pieces, the project would fail. The risks were great, but the benefits were irresistible. The consequences would be disastrous.

[191] RGIA f. 426, op. 1, d. 767, l. 8, "Razvitie khlopkovodstva," *K* (April 23, 1911).

[192] On cotton trials in Semireche, see V. N. Shnitnikov, *Poezdki po Semirech'iu* (Frunze: Kirg. Nauch.-Issled. Inst. Kraevedenie, 1930), 37. Iuferev is more ambivalent, recognizing that the trials were neither rigorous nor conclusive (*Khlopkovodstvo v Turkestane* [Leningrad, 1925], 48).

4

The Land of Bread and Honey?

Settlement and Subversion in the Land of Seven Rivers

> The Russians call this province "The Land of the Seven Rivers." It might equally well be called "The Land of Milk and Honey," for it is a region lavishly endowed by nature, where riches are to be had for the picking, where the labourer is rewarded a thousandfold for his work in field or garden, where prosperity and justice might reign with ease, where very little need be done to ensure full development, perpetuating a state of universal plenty. And yet, looking around, one is amazed at the extent of man's ineptitude, at his inefficiency, at what he can do to hem in, arrest, and even partly destroy the wonderful work of nature.
>
> – Count Konstantin Pahlen (1909)[1]

In 1913, in time for the Tercentenary of the Romanov Dynasty, the Russian government triumphantly celebrated the inauguration of its Hungry Steppe irrigation system with the opening of the Romanov Canal. The Grand Duke was present, as was Tajik poet Toshhodja Asiri, who wrote a poem in praise of the "Bekabad" Canal.[2] In September of that year, on the initiative of Military Governor Mikhail Fol′baum, the First Semireche Agricultural and Industrial Exposition was held in the center of Vernyi, capital of Turkestan's Semireche region. The exposition, one of the most significant regional exhibitions held in the Russian Empire that year, was made up of forty-three pavilions spread out over an equivalent

[1] Pahlen, *Mission to Turkestan*, 174.

[2] Toshkhodzha Asiri Khudzhandi, *Izbrannye proizvedeniia: Sostavlenie teksta, vystupitel′naia stat′ia i primechaniia Saadullo Asadullaeva* (Moscow: "Nauka," 1982), 5–6; for Asiri's views on irrigation's potential to alleviate misery, see Abdullaev, Khotamov, and Kenensariev, "Colonial Rule and Indigenous Responses," 84.

number of acres.[3] Boosters for Semireche – the Russified form of Zhetysu, which in Kazakh means "land of seven rivers" – hoped that the exposition would serve as the "best evidence of the opportune nature of those endeavors which are aimed at uniting Semireche with the cultural centers of Russia ..." These boosters, who included resettlement officials, engineers, and entrepreneurs, noted:

> Everywhere are marks of the cultured use of her natural riches, and everywhere one can glimpse the indications that in the near future our Semireche will acquire enormous economic significance. One quick overview of the exhibits of the exposition will suffice to convince [the viewer] that Semireche represents a virgin [*nepochatyi*] corner of all kinds of natural resources, and through appropriate use of these, it may become an extremely valuable pearl of the Russian state.[4]

Every exhibit at the exposition was designed not just to boast of Semireche's raw potential, but also the ways in which this "virgin" territory virtually unknown in St. Petersburg was becoming bound through its development to the empire.[5] However, in spite of the fertility implied in its very name, Semireche was not an obvious candidate for development and colonization, for it was remote not only from the central parts of Russia, but even from the urban centers of Russian Turkestan, such as Tashkent and Samarkand. According to the Resettlement Administration, any journey to the cities of Semireche, no matter the point of origin, took fifteen to twenty days.[6]

The vast Semireche region lay to the east of of Ferghana and Syr Darya, stretching between the long, sandy shores of Lake Balkhash in the Kazakh Steppe in the north to the lofty spurs of the Tian Shan Mountains in the south. Farther east, there was no natural barrier between Semireche and China; indeed, in the late nineteenth century, Russians had occupied China's Ili Valley for a decade before returning the territory to the Qing Empire in 1881. The border was henceforth demarcated in the grassy steppeland by a series of wooden or stone posts. Semireche's mountainous regions were inhabitable only by hardy nomadic peoples, though even nomadic pastoralists only spent summers in the high mountain pastures. Many of those mountain pastures had picturesque lakes. The region's

[3] TsGA RK f. I-19, op. 1, d. 230, ll. 99, 102; Iu. A. Nikitin, *Promyshlennye vystavki Rossii. XIX-nachala XX veka* (Cherepovets: Poligrafist, 2004), 194.

[4] TsGA RK f. I-19, op. 1, d. 230, l. 103.

[5] Ibid., l. 101.

[6] *Opisanie Semirechenskogo pereselencheskogo raiona: spravochnaia knizhka dlia khodokhov i pereselentsev na 1912 god* (St. Petersburg: Pereselencheskoe Upravlenie GUZiZ, 1911) in TsGA RK f. I-19, op. 1, d. 230, ll. 18–26ob: 19ob.

FIGURE 4.1 Pastoralist women milking.
Reproduced with permission from the Willard L. Gorton Papers, Hoover Institution Archives, Stanford, CA.

most famous lake was Issyk Kul (Hot Lake), the second largest alpine lake in the world, so named because its saline nature kept it from freezing in winter. Russian administrators had drawn the borders of Semireche to correspond roughly to the lands used by the Kazakh "Great Horde" (*Uly Zhuz*), yet in southern Semireche, by the shores of Issyk Kul, in the upper Chu River Valley, and farther south in the Naryn valley, Semireche's inhabitants were primarily Kyrgyz nomads. Semireche's nomads were generally referred to indiscriminately by tsarist officials as *kirgiz*, though Russian ethnographers recognized that Kazakhs and Kyrgyz did not consider themselves to be related.

Semireche had briefly been separated from the core provinces of Turkestan and governed along with the Kazakh lands of Russia's Steppe Province, becoming definitively part of Turkestan Province only in 1898.[7] Due to its history of being governed from Orenburg, Semireche continued to be governed by the Statute of the Steppe Province, rather than the Turkestan Statute. Articles 119 and 120 of the Steppe Statute made land the property of the state, which nomads had the right to use in

[7] Barthold, *Istoriia kul'turnoi zhizni Turkestana*, 148.

perpetuity; there were no specific regulations for water. Though the Turkestan Statute similarly gave nomads the right to occupy government lands, an addendum to Article 120 of the Steppe Statute from 1895 gave the Ministry of Agriculture explicit permission to take possession of any lands deemed in "excess" of nomadic use. Until 1910, therefore, when the tsarist administration approved a similar amendment to the Turkestan Statute, the Russian government could more easily claim lands suitable for Slavic settlement in Semireche, in contrast to the core areas of Turkestan, where most lands suitable for agriculture were already occupied, and custom guaranteed the rights of the indigenous people to use the water – and, therefore, any associated land.

Semireche had thus borne the brunt of the onslaught of settlers from central Russia in the late nineteenth and early twentieth centuries, even though, like the core regions of Turkestan, it had been officially closed to settlement for a decade.[8] During this time, in July 1903, Turkestan Governor-General Ivanov noted with distress that sixteen thousand samovol'tsy had entered Semireche the previous year. Many of these "self-willed" migrants had illegally seized land from local nomads upon learning that the government could not provide them with official settler plots.[9] Almost twice as many families arrived in 1908 after the region was reopened to colonization and Prime Minister Stolypin's agrarian reforms made it easier for peasants to leave the commune.[10] Like the earlier wave of migrants in the wake of the famine of 1891–1892, such settlers threatened to compromise the Russian "civilizing mission" in Turkestan.[11] On his inspection of the region, Count Pahlen found that corrupt resettlement officials, by allowing in all manner of migrants, had created a situation in which "a single Russian village was a source of more trouble than a few hundred native settlements."[12] This ran directly counter to the sentiment that the Central Asian borderland needed to be strengthened by the most reliable elements from the Russian countryside.

8 Orest Shkapskii, "Pereselentsy i agrarnyi vopros v Semirechenskoi oblasti," *VK* 1 (1907), 19–52.

9 G. F. Chirkin, *Polozhenie pereselencheskogo dela v Semirechii* (St. Petersburg: Pereselencheskoe upravlenie GUZiZ, 1908), 9.

10 Marco Buttino, *Revoliutsiia naoborot: Sredniaia Aziia mezhdu padeniem tsarskoi imperii i obrazovaniem SSSR*, trans. Nikolai Okhotin (Moscow: Zven'ia, 2007), 49; Jörn Happel, *Nomadische Lebenswelten und zarische Politik: Der Aufstand in Zentralasien 1916* (Stuttgart: Franz Steiner, 2010), 63.

11 Sahadeo, *Russian Colonial Society*, 116–119, 124.

12 Pahlen, *Mission to Turkestan*, 183.

Resettlement official Boris Shlegel′ urged the Resettlement Administration to pay "very serious attention" to the need to "fight against the independent seizure of irrigated land by resettlers" in Semireche.[13] By 1911, there were at least 85,000 peasant settlers in Semireche alone, with the samovol′tsy largely concentrated in the Chu River Valley.[14]

It was thus no accident that the First Semireche Agricultural and Industrial Exposition in 1913 was directed by S. N. Veletskii, the head of resettlement affairs in the region. A major goal of the exposition was to emphasize the positive influences of a Russian presence in a region that, many Russians felt, "until recently served only the goals of uncultured nomads with their primitive economy" – and perhaps to counteract the poor impressions created by newly arrived settlers who clashed with local nomads over land and water use.[15] There were exhibits on beekeeping (which had been introduced by the Russians), local craftsmanship, and agriculture. The Singer Company, busily engaged in hawking the modern technology of the sewing machine across Eurasia, was represented by its own pavilion.[16] At a livestock exhibit, examples of local horses and cattle bred from European Russian varieties were on display, so that "every visitor could be visually convinced of the superiority of imported breeds of livestock over native [ones]."[17] The message was that even Turkestan's fauna could not – and should not – remain immune to Russian influence.

As in the rest of Turkestan, ideas about colonization and irrigation were closely linked in Semireche, reflected in the fact that the regional Resettlement Administration had a Hydraulic Engineering department. At the Semireche Exposition in 1913, this department organized a display of hydraulic engineering technologies, which was touted by organizers of the exposition as meriting special attention. Along an existing ariq flowing through one of Vernyi's city parks, as well as in a hydraulic engineering section, were miniature versions of water-powered engines and other hydraulic engineering devices, projecting larger changes to come.[18] One of those changes – the new, state-sponsored plan to irrigate the Chu River Valley – was also featured in a brochure prepared for the Semireche Exposition, after a draft of the project had been sent to the

[13] TsGA KR f. I-54, op. 1, d. 2, ll. 50b-6.

[14] *Opisanie Semirechenskogo pereselencheskogo raiona*, 5 (TsGA RK f. I-19 op. 1, d. 230, l. 20).

[15] TsGA RK f. I-19, op. 1, d. 230, ll. 102–103. [16] Ibid., 78. [17] Ibid., l. 99.

[18] Ibid., l. 100.

Department of Land Improvement for approval in March.[19] The transformation of the Chu River Valley was the embodiment of Minister of Agriculture Krivoshein's recently articulated formula for the creation of a New Turkestan. Through irrigation the project would transform the valley into the primary supplier of food to the province's cotton-growing regions, thereby freeing up more land for cotton. It was also designed to make the valley an ideal home for newly arrived peasant migrants. As early as 1889, the military governor had determined that "the further development of colonization [of Semireche was] possible only through monetary funds from the treasury for irrigation construction ..."[20] The Chu Valley Irrigation Project would finally bring these visions to fruition. As a major irrigation project in an important borderland region of the empire, the Chu irrigation project would have the distinction not only of providing needed support for the cotton industry, but also of strengthening Russia's border with China and making that borderland indelibly Russian.[21]

Proceeding relentlessly through times of war, uprising, and revolution, the Chu Valley Irrigation Project represented the empire's attempt to use state-of-the-art technology to transform a region of Turkestan from a haven for "wild" nomads into a "cultured country." The resources invested into the project during wartime reflect the reverberations of Russia's "cotton fever" even in parts of Turkestan where no cotton was grown. Yet the Chu Valley Irrigation Project also illustrates the limits to peaceful Russian colonization of Turkestan. While it was easy for Russians to conceptualize nomadic regions such as Semireche as mostly empty, and therefore ripe for colonization, the Chu Valley had been a flourishing agricultural region, known for its gardens and orchards, already under the Khanate of Khoqand.[22] It had, therefore, attracted some of the earliest Russian settlers in the region. The attempt of the Chu Valley Irrigation Project to continue to claim even more land and water resources for colonization pushed the region to the breaking point. While in the early years of the twentieth century many nomads attempted

[19] V. A. Vasil'ev, *Proekt orosheniia doliny reki Chu* (St. Petersburg: n.p., 1913), 1–2; RGIA f. 432, op. 1, d. 15, l. 11.

[20] RGIA f. 426, op. 1, d. 34, ll. 6 ob-7.

[21] Chirkin, *Polozhenie pereselencheskogo dela v Semirechii*, 120–121. In the 1880s, the Steppe governor-general expressed the view that irrigating the steppes would be "more effective than erecting fortresses" (RGIA f. 426, op. 1, d. 34, l. 4ob).

[22] On perceptions of Semireche as relatively unpopulated, see Brower, *Turkestan and the Fate of the Russian Empire*, 128.

to subvert government attempts to gain control of their pasturelands for irrigation schemes and colonization, the irrigation project coopted them to participate in this process, leaving many with no outlet except to revolt or flee.

THE VALLEY OF THE RIVER CHU

The Chu River is formed where several minor mountain streams – the Kochkor, Shamsi and Djuvan-ariq – descend from the glaciers of the Tian Shan Mountains. It flows from the mountains in a northeasterly direction toward Issyk Kul, then abruptly changes direction as it approaches the lake to flow westward through the deep and dramatic Boom Gorge, hemmed in by red sandstone cliffs concealing myriad canyons. The river then continues in a northwesterly direction through an ever-widening valley into the Kazakh Steppe, where, like most of Turkestan's rivers (with the exceptions of the Amu and Syr), it eventually dwindles away in sand and marshland.

Russian veteran of the Turkestan campaigns Mikhail Veniukov, who had visited Semireche in the early 1860s, failed to see much potential there, describing "the monotony and paucity of the vegetable kingdom of the Chu valley, and … its little adaptability for settlements."[23] Yet, over centuries, the valley's inhabitants had taken advantage of the abundant water from the Chu River and its many tributaries for the purposes of irrigating the valley, culminating in the extensive fruit orchards that had flourished there under the rule of Khoqand. In spite of Veniukov's observation that "the majestic power of nature presents itself here in striking contrast to the impotence of man," by the early twentieth century, Russian engineers and officials alike believed that modern machinery and construction materials could be used to exploit the productive forces of the Chu Valley, particularly its rich hydrological resources and nourishing soils, for Russia's benefit.[24] As one enthusiastic booster put it in 1907, "Semireche in its nature is practically made to be the granary of the southern districts of Turkestan."[25] Pahlen also concluded that, with little effort but proper care, Semireche could become a land of "universal plenty."[26]

[23] M. Veniukov, "Trans-Ili and Chu Districts: Almaty, or Vernoé," chapter VII in *The Russians in Central Asia*, 263.

[24] Ibid., 263–264.

[25] "Zheleznyi put′ na Semirech′e," *TV* 34 (1907) in *TS*, 435, 99–100: 100.

[26] Pahlen, *Mission to Turkestan*, 174.

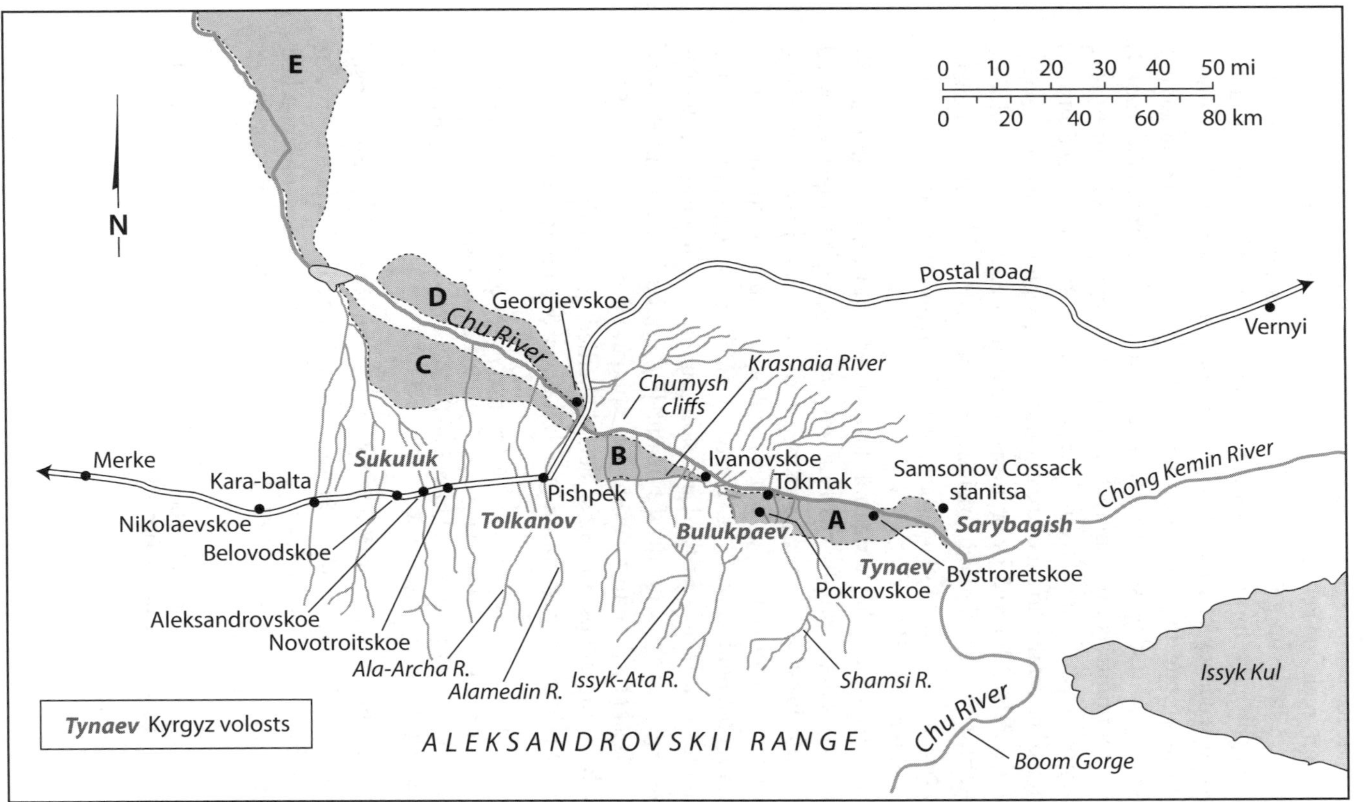

FIGURE 4.2 Map of the Chu River Valley in the early twentieth century, showing Engineer Vasil′ev's projections for irrigated areas (regions A–E), as well as the general locations of Kyrgyz volosts in the region of the Chu River Valley Irrigation Project.
Map by Bill Nelson.

Indeed, according to official calculations, in stark contrast to regions of Turkestan such as Ferghana, Semireche was overproducing grain. In 1911, a St. Petersburg newspaper reported that each inhabitant of Semireche might have forty-five poods of grain a year. By factoring in the supposed tendency of Central Asians to consume other products – milk and meat among the nomads, fruits and vegetables among the settled peoples – the article justified a calculation of almost thirty million poods of extra grain present in Semireche, which was rotting in silos or serving as livestock feed.[27] Similarly, in 1912, the Commission for New Railways estimated the total amount of excess grain in the region to be twenty-eight million poods.[28] Buoyed by enthusiasm for Semireche's grain-producing potential, engineer Vladimir Aleksandrovich Vasil′ev envisioned irrigating 220,000 desiatinas of land, in order to supply food to the cotton-growing regions of the Ferghana Valley.

Vasil′ev's Chu Valley Irrigation Project Administration established its headquarters in the rapidly growing town of Pishpek.[29] Pishpek occupied a strategic location at the juncture of the two main axes for Slavic settlement in Semireche. The first axis of settlement was the postal road from the regional capital at Vernyi, which ran southward over the mountains and then westward in a long, unbroken line toward the Syr Darya region, following the Khoqand line established by the Russian military's capture of forts from the Khoqand Khanate in the 1860s. Already in the 1890s, the most densely settled part of the postal road resembled this later description by Pavel Nazarov, a noted naturalist:

> Then came Russian settlements arranged in a very strange way; nothing more nor less than a single street extending over thirty miles! It was a series of villages with various names ... but they had all fused into this one immense uninterrupted street through which ran the postal road.[30]

The second axis of colonization was the Chu River itself. From Pishpek, another line of settlement continued in an easterly direction upstream toward the western end of Issyk Kul. Russian settler villages also marched downstream in a northwesterly direction along the banks of the Chu, to

[27] RGIA f. 426, op. 1, d. 767, l. 8, "Razvitie khlopkovodstva," *K* (April 23, 1911). On the tendency of the poor to eat principally fruit, see also Khanikoff, *Bokhara*, 62; Meakin, *In Russian Turkestan*, 23.

[28] Krivoshein, *Zapiska Glavnoupravliaiushchego zemleustroistvom i zemledeliem*, 11.

[29] V. G. Petrov, *Pishpek ischezaiushchii* (Bishkek: Literaturnyi Kyrgyzstan, 2008), 59.

[30] Paul Nazaroff, *Hunted through Central Asia: On the Run from Lenin's Secret Police*, trans. Malcolm Burr (New York: Oxford University Press, 2002), 149. The long street formed by the settlements was also described by Thomas Gaskell and William Sachtleben in *Across Asia on a Bicycle* (New York: The Century Co., 1894), 126–127.

the border of Syr Darya and beyond. Located on the postal road just south of the Chu River, and thus at the juncture of these two axes of colonization, Pishpek was an ideal location for the headquarters of the project to irrigate the Chu Valley.

The town had a diverse population of Kazakhs, Kyrgyz, Tatars, and Russians, as well as two communities of Muslims from China: a sizeable number of *Dungans* – Chinese Muslims (known in China as *Hui*) who had fled Qing repressions in the late nineteenth century and been settled by the Russian administration on nomadic lands on either bank of the Chu River – and Turki-speaking Muslim "sarts" from the Kashgar Oasis.[31] But the major change came with the influx of Russians. The *Turkestan Gazette* reported that in 1906 thousands of landless resettlers from central Russian regions had formed unofficial settlements, including one right outside Pishpek.[32] Tens of thousands of resettlers had waited years for the government to provide them with a parcel of land.[33] The arrival of large number of new Russian settlers created tensions with those who already occupied the best lands of the Chu River Valley, tensions that the Chu Valley Irrigation Project would exacerbate yet further.

The idea of linking the cotton-growing regions of Turkestan to cheaper sources of grain had been raised when the completion of the western section of the Trans-Siberian Railroad in 1897 brought thousands of new peasant settlers to southern Siberia, making the region a producer of abundant grain. Proponents of a Turkestan-Siberia railway through the Kazakh Steppe, however, had been overruled in favor of the shorter Tashkent-Orenburg line, well to the west, which facilitated the transport of Turkestan's cotton to the textile mills of the Moscow industrial region. Boosters for Semireche nevertheless continued to push for a line connecting Tashkent to the Trans-Siberian Railroad via Pishpek and Vernyi. Engineer Vasil′ev called such a railroad "the first and perhaps most important step – after the settlement of the oblast′ with Russian settlers – on the path toward the transformation of Semireche into a cultured country," since it would not only help export the products of Semireche, but would infuse the region with "cultured" people and goods.[34]

[31] Petrov, *Pishpek ischezaiushchii*, 28, 61. Today, we would think of the "Chinese sarts" as Uyghurs.

[32] "Semirech′e i pereselentsy," *TV* 5 (1907) in *TS* 435, 11–13: 13.

[33] *Zhurnal soveshchaniia o poriadke kolonizatsii Semirechenskoi oblasti (18, 20, 22, 27, 29 February 1908)*, 6.

[34] V. A. Vasil′ev, *Semirechenskaia oblast′ kak koloniia i rol′ v nei Chuiskoi doliny. Proekt orosheniia doliny reki Chu v Semirechenskoi oblasti* (Petrograd: GUZiZ OZU, 1915), ii.

Even without the link to Siberia, a railway was necessary for the Chu Valley Irrigation Project. The journey by camel or cart between Vernyi and Tashkent could take two to three months, which deprived Tashkent of the possibility of access to Semireche's cheap grain, selling on the Chinese border for only twenty kopecks per pood, one-fifth the price of a pood of grain in Tashkent. Facing pressure from Moscow industrialists, who continued to push for a connection between the cotton-growing regions of Turkestan and grain-growing regions, the Russian government – which had initially balked at the idea of another costly railroad – finally agreed in April 1912 to subsidize the Turkestan-Siberia Railroad's construction.[35] The Ministry of Ways of Communication put Muhamedjan Tynyshpaev, a Kazakh who had graduated from the St. Petersburg Institute of Ways of Communication in 1906 and had explored the mountain passes between Pishpek and Vernyi, in charge of building the stretch of the Semireche Line between Arys on the Tashkent-Orenburg Line and Pishpek.[36] Tynyshpaev was among the indigenous proponents of the railroad who hoped it might serve as a vehicle to bring change to the Kazakh Steppe. Initial construction on the Semireche Line coincided with the First Semireche Agricultural and Industrial Exposition in September 1913, and was slated to be finished within three years.[37]

The beginning of railroad construction was one of the first promising signs for the Chu Valley Irrigation Project. Senator Pahlen's inspection of Turkestan had resulted in a number of serious allegations regarding the bureaucrats involved with the Turkestan branch of the Ministry of Agriculture, particularly regarding financial matters. The new head of that branch, Alexander Vasil′evich Uspenskii, lamented that after Pahlen's report, the "careless" and "unprincipled" attitude of these bureaucrats toward government funds had become a "ceaseless topic for all kinds of gossip and newspaper articles."[38] Such concerns likely delayed government funding for the Chu project. The initial surveying party persevered, however, hastening to prepare plans for the project in time for celebrations of the Romanov Tercentenary. With the start of

[35] Matthew Payne, "Turksib: The Building of the Turkestan–Siberian Railroad and the Politics of Production during the Cultural Revolution, 1926–1931" (PhD diss., University of Chicago, 1995), 36–37, 39; Buttino, *Revoliutsiia naoborot*, 86.

[36] Fedor Osadchii, *Velikii tvorets dobra i sveta. (Stranitsy sud'by inzhenera M. Tynyshpaeva)* (Almaty: Arys, 2001), 14, 17–18.

[37] Payne, "Turksib," 39–40.

[38] TsGA KR f. I-54, op. 1, d. 1, ll. 1–10b (June 11, 1910).

construction on the railway, the first steps were taken toward a project that seemed on the surface destined to ensure the further success of Russia's expanding cotton venture in Turkestan by maximizing utilization of the province's productive forces. Cheap grain from the Chu Valley could ease the pressure on Russia's cotton-growing regions to grow grain and accept more settlers, tasks for which Semireche, in contrast, seemed ideally suited.

WHITE COAL FOR WHITE GOLD

The Ministry of Agriculture gave engineer Vasil′ev considerable authority over the project to irrigate the Chu River Valley, including autonomy in connection with questions of construction, as well as the power to decide, along with the Ministry of Agriculture, issues of land and water use connected to the "exploitation" of lands irrigated by the project.[39] From the initial surveying forays through the project's most difficult days, Vasil′ev proved to be an energetic, ambitious, and forward-thinking project director. In the fall of 1913, instead of attending the celebrations at the Semireche Exposition, he undertook a tour of Europe's recent achievements in hydraulic engineering, believing that he could learn more from the experience of Western Europeans than he could from a tour of the Russian Empire. He also continued to subscribe to foreign literature on all aspects of irrigation engineering and water management during his time as director of the project.[40] His interest in visiting French cement factories is evidence that he wanted the Chu irrigation project to be one of the most advanced projects of its day. The "First Annual Cement Show," held in December 1910 at Madison Square Garden in New York City, for instance, had been advertised as catering to "any person who desires to remain in touch with the trend of the times in building construction."[41] The International Building Exhibition in Leipzig, included on Vasil′evs European tour, also prominently featured cement. A cornerstone of Vasil′ev's plan for the Chu Valley Irrigation Project was the construction of a factory to supply Semireche with its own local source of cheap cement, for the purpose of lining irrigation canals – thus preventing seepage of water into the soil – and building massive hydraulic structures,

[39] Ibid., ll. 4–4ob.

[40] TsGA KR f. I-54, op. 2, d. 122. See also Maya K. Peterson, "Engineering Empire," 136–137.

[41] "Cement Show," Display Ad 48, *NYT* (December 18, 1910), RE4.

such as a dam to create a reservoir for times of drought. Such plans for permanent structures were intended to move engineering in Turkestan decisively away from "native" engineering and the massive amounts of labor and upkeep that such systems required on an annual basis.

Cement was also crucial for taking advantage of what Vasil′ev believed to be "one of the most favorable conditions for the development" of Semireche's resources: "enormous reserves of hydro energy – 'white coal.'"[42] The potential of "white coal" – energy harnessed from hydrological resources – excited engineers throughout America and Europe in the early twentieth century.[43] Until a railroad could give Turkestan access to the cheap and abundant lumber produced in Siberia, "white coal" could enable Semireche to provide grain to Turkestani farmers busy providing the empire with "white gold" (i.e., cotton). To exploit Semireche's "white coal," Vasil′ev ordered parts from America for the construction of a hydroelectric power plant at the Chumysh cliffs north of Pishpek, near the spot where the postal road crossed the Chu River.[44]

Vasil′ev also hoped that machine power would alleviate the need for human labor.[45] In a publication on the Chu irrigation project, he included photographs of one of these machines: the Bucyrus electric shovel "Type 25B," manufactured in Milwaukee, Wisconsin. These electric shovels had recently been used in the building of the Panama Canal, a project to which Vasil′ev proudly compared his own project.[46] The outbreak of war with Europe in the summer of 1914, however, threw a wrench into the construction of both the cement plant – and, thus, the hydroelectric plant – as well as the railroad. Vasil′ev had begun negotiations with several German manufacturers for parts for the cement plant, but when Russia entered into war with Germany, these ties had to be severed.[47] Yet, station construction outside Pishpek continued in anticipation of the opening of

[42] Vasil′ev, *Semirechenskaia oblast′ kak koloniia*, 213–214.

[43] Marc Landry, "Water as White Coal," in "On Water: Perceptions, Politics, Perils," eds. Agnes Kneitz and Marc Landry, *RCC Perspectives* 2 (2012); Blackbourn, *The Conquest of Nature*, 216.

[44] TsGA KR f. I-54, op. 1, d. 30, l. 16; Petrov, *Pishpek ischezaiushchii*, 59.

[45] TsGA KR f. I-54, op. 1, d. 58, l. 145.

[46] Vasil′ev, "Biulleten′ No. 2," 17 and end photographs. A photograph of American president Teddy Roosevelt sitting in the cab of a Bucyrus steam shovel is in Julie Greene, *The Canal Builders: Making America's Empire at the Panama Canal* (New York: Penguin, 2009), facing p. 174.

[47] TsGA KR f. I-54, op. 1, d. 58, l. 144. In 1915, a Portland cement factory evacuated from Riga because of wartime was installed near the Khilkovo station in the Hungry Steppe (near the Uzbek settlement of Begovat) (*GS*, 215–216).

the Arys-Pishpek Line, and by the fall of 1915, the *Semireche Regional Gazette* was advertising positions for workers on the "grandiose" new irrigation project underway in the Chu River Valley.[48]

SETTLERS AND NOMADS

Vasil′ev's plan to irrigate the Chu Valley divided the upper portion of the valley into five regions, in each of which site engineers would oversee the building of irrigation canals to bring water to Russian settlers' fields. Unlike the Hungry Steppe, however, the lands included in Vasil′ev's scheme were already to a large extent occupied, and even used for irrigated agriculture. Region A, for instance, encompassed land that was mostly already irrigated, including more than thirty thousand *desiatinas* being used by the Sarybagish, Tynaev and Shamsi Kyrgyz, as well as the "old settler" (*starozhil′cheskie*) villages of Bol′shoi Tokmak and Pokrovskoe, established already in the late nineteenth century. It also contained two tracts that had been more recently designated for settlement. The Krasnaia River Canal in Region B was to start from land occupied by the Shamsi Kyrgyz and then bisect lands planted and developed by the Kashgari merchant Turdi-Ahun Almazbekov. The headworks of the main canal were to use land occupied by the Kyrgyz of Uzungyr, near the Dungan village of Aleksandrovskoe. Authorities discussed granting the Kyrgyz replacement lands for those they would lose to the irrigation project, but found such a possibility doubtful, given the lack of surplus land nearby.[49]

When people spoke, therefore, of the vast tracts of unused nomadic land in Semireche, they were not describing the Chu River Valley. In a 1907 article published in the newspaper *Central Asian Life*, the author described a "huge area of land along the river Chu that lies uncultivated," adding that, "the investigation of these lands is long overdue, and it seems to me that another 5,000 Russian settlers could easily settle on the Chu." He was referring, however, to lands on lower stretches of the Chu in neighboring Syr Darya, which, after some debate, were not included in the Chu Valley Irrigation Project.[50] In the same year, the *Tashkent*

[48] *SOV* 135 (May 21, 1915), 2; *SOV* 174 (June 29, 1915), 2; *SOV* 257 (October 7, 1915), 1.

[49] TsGA KR f. I-54, op. 1, d. 4, ll. 49–50ob.

[50] "K pereselencheskomu voprosu v krae: O zemliakh po reke Chu," *SZh* 244 (1907) in *TS* 442, 92–93: 93.

Courier had published "Letters from Semireche," written by a citizen identified as G. Kolkhidskii, who had written, "[I]t is as plain as a pikestaff that today only those very nearsighted people, who cannot see anything or, more accurately, do not want to see anything, can talk about free [i.e., vacant] lands in the region." Twenty or thirty years ago, he admitted, "it was possible to speak of surplus land. But since that time ... such great changes have taken place that it is fitting to hesitate and ask the following question: is the further colonization of the region politically expedient?" According to Kolkhidskii, the only remaining unoccupied lands were unirrigated stretches of steppe or land that would never be fit for agriculture; the rest had been seized by settlers. The result, he noted, was a growing tendency of nomads to turn to a settled lifestyle.[51] This was particularly true of places such as the upper Chu Valley; indeed, even before Russian settlers had begun to arrive in Turkestan, some had warned that Russian colonization in the Chu Valley could not take place without harming the interests of the valley's indigenous inhabitants.[52]

In spite of the fact that such warnings against outright seizure of nomadic lands indicated that many Russians were well aware of the deleterious effects that colonization schemes could have on the indigenous peoples of Semireche, Russians seeking to transform the Chu River Valley acted as the benevolent bestowers of the "gift" of Russian civilization and benign Russian imperial rule on the nomads.[53] As Resettlement official Gennadyi Chirkin put it in 1908, the "resettlement question" in Semireche was "a question not just in the sense of establishing a few hundred Russian households which had happened to end up in the oblast', but of the colonization of the oblast' in the broadest sense of the word," including the "liberation of [the local population] ... from slavish dependence on a small group of powerful herdsmen."[54] The Chu Valley Irrigation Project was, therefore, intended not only to bring water to new fields, but also to bring culture, prosperity, and even a new kind of freedom to the indigenous people of the region.

It was clear from the beginning, however, that this "liberation" effort would be a delicate balancing act. In accordance with the law of the land (the 1895 addendum to Article 120 of the Steppe Statute), and following

[51] G. Kolkhidskii, "Pis'ma iz Semirech'ia," *TK* 198 (1907) in *TS* 444, 34–37: 34.

[52] See, for example, the essay by N. A. Ivanov, "Drevnyi aryk ot Syrdar'i do Bukhary," originally published in *TV* 13 (March 27, 1873) and reprinted in *GS* (Doc. 7, 16–17: 17).

[53] Bruce Grant, *The Captive and the Gift: Cultural Histories of Sovereignty in Russia and the Caucasus* (Ithaca, NY: Cornell University Press, 2009), x.

[54] Chirkin, *Polozhenie pereselencheskogo dela v Semirechii*, 120.

the model of resettlement programs in the steppes to the north, redistribution of land in the valley among nomads and settlers was based on the concept of the *izlishek* (pl: *izlishki*) – a portion of land that could be considered surplus, or extra.[55] Any lands deemed superfluous to nomadic use could be legally reclaimed by the Russian government at any time and placed at the disposal of the agriculture ministry – all that remained was to decide what quantity of land could be considered superfluous and where, exactly, those "superfluous lands" lay.

An izlishek was calculated by first determining the amount of land that an average nomadic household ostensibly needed to survive, then considering any additional land used by the household to be "surplus." Such a concept was entirely at odds with nomadic land use, since the quantity of land "needed" might vary with the season and climatic conditions; lands considered "superfluous" at one time of year might come into use at another time. To make matters more complicated, tsarist officials' estimations of how much land a nomadic household "needed" fluctuated wildly. Veletskii reported in 1907 that, while the calculations performed by the statistical committee for resettlement in neighboring Syr Darya had found that an average nomadic household in that region needed eighteen to twenty desiatinas of land, the surveys conducted by resettlement officials in Semireche yielded the result that nomads needed anywhere between forty and eighty-two desiatinas.[56]

Already in 1898, a circular had been issued in Semireche with official guidelines for expanding the "colonization fund." A "special party" formed in 1905 to hasten the division of land into settler parcels, however, complained that the circular did nothing more than "act as a brake" on the development of settler plots in Semireche. The small party, with minimal funding, had been tasked with testing soil composition, determining the "natural historical" aspects of the lands occupied by nomadic peoples, including their flora and climate, and collecting data about the economics of nomadic households in order to ensure that all surplus lands were accurately determined and that all land parcels might be usable.[57] The party had also been tasked with starting its work not in a sparsely

[55] For a slightly earlier effort to facilitate peasant migration to the Kazakh Steppe, see Ian Campbell, "Settlement Promoted, Settlement Contested: The Shcherbina Expedition of 1896–1903," *Central Asian Survey* 30, 3–4 (2011): 423–436.

[56] *Agrarnaia istoriia Kazakhstana (konets XIX – nachalo XX v.): Sbornik dokumentov i materialov* (Almaty: Daik, 2006), Doc. 80: 150–151.

[57] Ibid., 150; Chirkin, *Polozhenie pereselencheskogo dela,* 8, 12–13; *Zhurnal soveshchaniia o poriadke kolonizatsii,* 8; TsGA RK f. I-19, op. 1, d. 83. l. 88.

inhabited region, but in the densely settled Pishpek district, in the hopes of providing parcels for the samovol'tsy.[58] As a result of these onerous requirements, by the time construction on the Chu Valley Irrigation Project began, authorities still lacked much of the data necessary to determine where Russian farmers might be settled most profitably.

Acquiring detailed information about the lands of Semireche was desirable because – since not all land is equal – even if a precise size could be agreed upon for the plot of land "necessary" to the nomadic existence, the conversion of pastureland to farmland was not a simple problem to be solved by arithmetic. Statistical averages proved difficult to apply to the complexities of the uneven topography and actual patterns of land and water use existing in Semireche. Not all parties interested in the transformation of Semireche, however, had the patience to thoroughly carry out such a massive undertaking. As Count Pahlen noted, "on paper, there blossomed forth a wonderful, but purely artificial, creation supported by rows of gratifying statistical tables," yet in reality, "[t]he old truth that colonization by order cannot succeed was proved to the hilt . . ."[59] In May 1914, the military governor of Semireche, Mikhail Fol'baum, expressed his dissatisfaction with the state of affairs in the Chu Valley to resettlement official Boris Shlegel'. As Shlegel' later reported to the Resettlement Administration, even after he explained to Governor Fol'baum the obstacles hindering the successful completion of resettlement tasks, the military governor seemed to feel it was simply a matter of dividing up the land "strictly according to the number of souls" into "parcels according to the rules of resettlement and previously determined norms," with all remaining land turned over to the government.[60] The staff of the Chu Valley Irrigation Project, on the other hand, working closely with the Resettlement Administration, recognized that in many parts of the Chu River Valley, there technically were no surplus lands available, according to the recognized norms for nomadic land use. They furthermore worried that the "low level of development" of the nomadic population of the valley, together with the thus-far unsatisfactory efforts on the part of the tsarist government to determine the organization and distribution of land,

[58] Chirkin, *Polozhenie pereselencheskogo dela*, 11–13.

[59] Pahlen, *Mission to Turkestan*, 181–182.

[60] TsGA KR f I-54, op. 1, d. 4, l. 48. Fol'baum's irritation may be explained by his fears of potential conflict due to rising tensions over land (Brower, *Turkestan and the Fate of the Russian Empire*, 147).

would complicate the construction of irrigation systems on lands currently used by nomads.

Decreasing settler plot sizes – to accommodate more settlers, rather than appease the nomads (Vasil′ev himself believed that "the nomadic population should be limited in its rights to the use of land") – was an obvious solution to the problem of not enough available land in the Chu Valley, yet Shlegel′ worried that smaller plots of land would do nothing but arouse protest among already dissatisfied settlers. Still, by September 1914, he was asking the Resettlement Administration whether the temporary committee for statistical and economic investigation of the Chu settler allotments had the right to lower the land norm for new settlers, as was already the practice (whether legal or not) in many parts of the region. Vasil′ev projected that if the size of settler plots were to be reduced from established norms (between six and ten desiatinas), the Chu Valley could accommodate as many as three hundred thousand more households.[61]

As in the Hungry Steppe, delays in official matters of land distribution and irrigation construction led to Slavic settlers and indigenous communities undertaking their own unofficial negotiations over land and water resources in the region. In the absence of government aid, settlers from European Russia often came to rely on their indigenous neighbors for assistance with irrigation canals and access to fields, seeds, and livestock.[62] On traveling through Semireche as late as 1919, naturalist Pavel Nazarov wrote, "I was struck by the dependence of the Russian colonists on the Kirghiz. Everything was done by the Kirghiz: they worked in the fields, tended the cattle, hauled the coal and charcoal, and so on."[63] Digging canals was not – a Resettlement Administration pamphlet hastened to reassure inexperienced peasants – particularly difficult; nonetheless, the pamphlet claimed, Russian migrants were known to "prefer to hire natives to water their fields."[64] In his memoirs, Pahlen took a more cynical view, claiming that the "Emigration [i.e., resettlement] Authorities ... wished to settle [Slavic] emigrants on land already farmed and irrigated and then to compel the Kirgiz to make fresh areas arable by digging new irrigation

[61] Vasil′ev, *Semirechenskaia oblast′ kak koloniia*, 217–18; TsGA KR f. I-54, op. 1, d. 4, ll. 2–2ob, 48ob.

[62] For the case of Transcaspia, see Kanoda, *Pereselencheskie poselki v Zakaspiiskoi oblasti*, 70.

[63] Nazaroff, *Hunted through Central Asia*, 139.

[64] *Opisanie Semirechenskogo pereselencheskogo raiona*, 9 (TsGA RK f. I-19, op. 1, d. 230, l. 22).

systems."[65] When desperate Slavic settlers themselves submitted requests to local authorities for permission to dig their own irrigation channels, such requests often took months to be answered, which might interfere with crucial planting and growth cycles.[66]

This state of affairs suggested that Russian influence was hardly bringing about the desired transformation of the Chu Valley into a cultivated and "cultured" region. A letter to the Pishpek district administration from a settler named Semën Kir'ianov, for instance, suggested quite the opposite. Kir'ianov, who wrote on behalf of the village of Pokrovskoe, just west of Tokmak, complained that the local ariq was always dry. "In 1913 much grain withered because of a shortage of water," he wrote. "At the last *volost'* assembly our Pokrovskoe delegates earnestly begged the Tokmak delegates to increase the amount of water from the Shamsi river to irrigate up to 200 desiatinas ... lands that formerly were in the hands of the kirgiz and were irrigated."[67] Kir'ianov's plea suggests that land that had once been usable in the hands of the nomads had now fallen into disuse, likely because Russian settlers were not familiar with irrigation systems and their upkeep. In order to maximize productivity in the arid soil, some Slavic settlers in the foothills of Semireche adopted "dry farming" methods that allowed the crops to better withstand drought. Like their kinsmen in the Hungry Steppe, some Russian settlers also took up cattle breeding, along the lines of their nomadic neighbors. The Russian government may even have encouraged this transition – at least while irrigation was still a thing of the future – by creating special plots for livestock herding among the agricultural settler plots.[68]

Most Russians believed, as one Count Golovin wrote in the main regional newspaper in 1909, that "colonists here in the [Turkestan] Krai should not be pupils to the natives, but *Kulturträger* [bearers of civilization],"[69] but conditions on the ground suggested that peasant

[65] Pahlen, *Mission to Turkestan,* 208.

[66] It is possible that some of these resettlers to Semireche had experience with irrigation from Russia's southern steppes. See Moon, *The Plough That Broke the Steppes*, 236–241, *passim.*

[67] TsGA KR f. I-54, op. 1, d. 4, ll. 11–12ob. This letter is cited in O. A. Bilik, *Stanovlenie*, vol. 1 of *Irrigatsiia Kirgizii v proektakh i ob"ektakh* (Frunze: Kirgizgiprovodkhoz, 1990), 73, but without the reference to the "kirgiz."

[68] George Demko, *The Russian Colonization of Kazakhstan, 1896–1916*, Uralic and Altaic Series, 99 (Bloomington: Indiana University Press, 1969), 176, 184; Pahlen, *Mission to Turkestan*, 178.

[69] Count Golovin, "Turkestanskie kolonisty," *TV* 106–107 (1909) in *TS* 507, 32–35: 33–34.

resettlers were anything but models of cultured behavior. Slavic settlers clashed with nomads over water use, grazing boundaries, and trampled crops. The preferred stopgap solution in Semireche was to allow samovol′tsy to rent land from local nomads until the regional government could determine appropriate land plots. The practice of "renting" state lands from nomads was even made legal in 1905, before the region was officially reopened for settlement.[70] This process continued to be one of the main ways in which Russian settlers got land in Semireche, until the collapse of the empire.

A document from the Kyrgyz archives provides a record of one case – relations between the Bulukpaev Kyrgyz and the Slavic settlers of Ivanovskoe, in what came to be Region B of the irrigation project – which is revealing of the way negotiations over land and water were conducted in the Chu Valley in the early twentieth century, as well as how the coming of the irrigation project affected such relations. Russian authorities had divided the nomadic population of Turkestan into administrative-territorial units known as volosts, the same term used to denote local Russian subdistricts. For Russian-subject nomads, however, volost′ was not just a territorial designation – it also had a parallel community designation, since nomads migrated between winter and summer pastures.[71] The Bulukpaev [later Baisetov] volost′ of Pishpek district, therefore, referred to both a particular grouping of several Kyrgyz auls, or "villages" of one to two hundred yurt owners or households, as well as the designated territory where these Kyrgyz spent the winter. Many such volost′ territories in the Chu Valley had been drawn by Russian officials in the form of a long, narrow strip of land running between the Aleksandrovskii Range and the Chu River, allowing the nomads of this region access to both the river and the higher mountain pastures frequented by herders in summer. The volosts thus mimicked the many mountain streams flowing down from the glaciers and into the river. Such volosts, including Bulukpaev, were also, therefore, encroached upon by the two corridors of settlement in the Chu Valley – the post road and the Chu River – raising the potential for conflict and leading to the need for (cautious) cooperation between established and newly arrived communities.

70 Chirkin, *Polozhenie pereselencheskogo dela*, 9, 13. Governor-General Ivanov had forbidden the practice in 1901, but this ban quickly came to be seen as impractical. Buttino, *Revoliutsiia naoborot*, 370 note 77.

71 Summer pastures were "for communal use" (Martin, *Law and Custom in the Steppe*, 39).

"Verdict No. 4," dated June 13, 1908, was signed by twenty elected Bulukpaev Kyrgyz representatives in reference to lands that were part of their winter pastures – in other words, the territory on the map designated Bulukpaev volost′. It makes clear that, led by Ismailbek Suleimanov, the head of the volost′, these representatives discussed the request of eighty households in the Slavic settler village of Ivanovskoe to rent two hundred and fifty desiatinas of land from Bulukpaev volost′. The assembled Kyrgyz noted that the land in question was encircled by lands which authorities had already granted to Ivanovskoe peasants, resulting in multiple conflicts over water and the incursions of Kyrgyz livestock onto settler fields. They also noted that the Bulukpaev community had access to sufficient land even without the land desired by the village of Ivanovskoe. With these considerations in mind, the Bulukpaev Kyrgyz voted unanimously to rent out the land in question for a period of thirty years at the price of twenty kopecks per desiatina per year.[72] This money was to go toward payment of treasury and community obligations (in essence, their taxes; nomads were required to pay a tax of one ruble twenty-five kopecks per *kibitka* [nomadic tent], in place of the land tax paid by residents of settled regions).[73] The one stipulation of the Bulukpaev Kyrgyz was that a ten-sazhen-wide corridor remain along the east side of the parcel of land (bordering neighboring Shamsi volost′), so that Kyrgyz herdsmen could lead their livestock to water without trespassing on the Slavic settlers' land. It was also noted that the settlers should use water from the Krasnaia River to irrigate the new lands.[74] The agreement seems to have been satisfactory to all involved, as it would unite the disparate lands used by the peasants of Ivanovskoe, reduce conflict among neighboring groups, and ease the tax burden felt by the Kyrgyz community. Tsarist officials in the region, moreover, were more than happy to allow settlers and nomads to settle their own affairs in such ways, though a necessary stipulation of such contractual agreements was that the government administrators could terminate the contract at any time, since nomads technically used, but did not own, the land they rented out.

[72] The average rental price for a desiatina of alfalfa was calculated at between 25 and 40 rubles for a year (TsGA KR f. I-54, op. 1, d. 15, l. 95ob). The land in Bulukpaev volost′ was probably uncultivated.

[73] *Pamiatnaia knizhka i adres-kalendar′ Semirechenskoi oblasti na 1905-i god*, compiled by V. E. Nedzvytskii (Vernyi: Semireche Statistical Committee, 1905), 46.

[74] TsGA KR f. I-54, op.1, d. 15, ll. 97–100, "Prigovor No. 4" (June 13, 1908).

Locally negotiated agreements such as "Verdict No. 4" – or, worse, the outright seizure of land by Slavic peasants – complicated the task of surveyors for the planned large-scale irrigation project in the region. According to the "temporary rules for determining the basis for water use in the formation of settler parcels in Turkestan Krai in regions with irrigated agriculture," it was possible to lead water to the new settler parcels via land occupied by "natives" – thus, in this case, the main canal could legally be built through the land being rented out to Ivanovskoe on a temporary basis. However, though legal officials recognized that the Chu project could simply terminate "Verdict No. 4" without compensating the peasants – a condition that was required for the regional administration to approve such contracts in the first place – resettlement official Mikhail Terent'ev, in charge of "alienating" surplus lands for the government land fund, warned that peasants would hardly stand for such appropriations. Ill-informed about the terms of such rental contracts, and having put funds and effort into cultivation, these peasants often developed a false sense of entitlement to the land. Terent'ev suggested they be paid a "just sum that would be inoffensive to both parties."[75]

In April 1916, Terent'ev explained to the peasants of Ivanovskoe that part of the land they had rented from their Kyrgyz neighbors was necessary for the new government canal project. Following engineer Sergei Ivanovich Syromiatnikov's request that they reach a peaceful agreement with the peasants, Terent'ev then offered them up to two hundred and fifty rubles for each desiatina of rental land, in compensation for the alfalfa crop they would lose. He based his calculations on discussions throughout Pishpek district on the average annual hay yield and the harvest's potential market price. Two hundred fifty rubles for land already owned by the government – and for which the Kyrgyz of Baisetov [former Bulukpaev] volost' received only a tiny fraction of that amount. The peasants, however, claimed that with a hay harvest of ten thousand sheaves per desiatina – much higher than average yields in the district – the land was worth three thousand rubles per desiatina, figures Terent'ev called "monstrous." When he pointed out that the Chu administration could easily terminate the contract and pay the villagers nothing, the peasants supposedly answered, "The treasury is not getting poorer … They probably gave you a lot of money – why are you being stingy?!"[76]

[75] TsGA KR f. I-54, op.1, d. 15, l. 106.

[76] Ibid., ll. 106–119. The crop being grown is referred to as *klever* (clover), but was likely lucerne (alfalfa, *Medicago sativa*) – see Nazaroff, *Hunted through Central Asia*, 166.

Eventually, the Chu project's juridical consultant, Grigorii Broido, pointed out that it was rare to pay more than sixty to eighty rubles for a desiatina of land in the district; thus, it was finally decided that the government would pay the peasants of Ivanovskoe sixty-five rubles per desiatina to compensate for losses of grain on government land they had rented from their Kyrgyz neighbors. There was no mention in the discussion of compensation of the Kyrgyz, who would no longer receive payments from the settlers with whom they had signed the contract.[77]

The outcome of the case involving "Verdict No. 4" was just one indication of the ways in which the nomadic peoples of Semireche were being excluded from their traditional lands. In 1915, Engineer Vasil′ev wrote, "[T]he most important significance of the [Semireche] region in recent times is as a region for the resettlement of surplus population from European Russia."[78] For Vasil′ev, as for many others, Semireche was important not just as a colony providing raw materials for extraction, but also as a settler colony; as such, it demanded the Russian investment of both human and financial capital, in order to settle the "surplus" lands of the region with "surplus population" from central parts of the empire.

In his eagerness to bring attention to the importance of the Chu project in facilitating the colonization of Semireche, Vasil′ev may have exaggerated some of Semireche's positive attributes. A prescient reader discovered many discrepancies between Vasil′ev's *Semireche as a Colony* (1915) and his earlier writings on the Chu project put together for the Vernyi exhibition, suggesting that Vasil′ev was manipulating purportedly "scientific" data to make the Chu Valley more appealing. The reader noted that whereas in his earlier writings Vasil′ev had written about the northeasterly wind as a drawback to the region, and described the soil as clay and loam (like much of the soil across Turkestan), in *Semireche as a Colony*, he touted the Chu Valley as one of the only places in the region sheltered from the northeast winds. Vasil′ev also claimed that the soils of the Chu Valley were the best in the region; in fact, according to *Semireche as a Colony*, the local soils occupied that famous category of Russian soils, the coveted *chernozem*, or black earth.[79] A 1911 pamphlet for potential settlers confirmed the presence of chernozem in the foothills, but

[77] TsGA KR f. I-54, op. 1, d. 15, ll. 95–95ob.

[78] Vasil′ev, *Semirechenskaia oblast′ kak koloniia*, ii-iii. Vasil′ev's work, entitled *Semireche as a Colony and the Role within It of the Chu Valley*, both echoed the title of earlier works *Siberia as a Colony* (1882) and *Sakhalin as a Colony* (1905), as well as emphasized the importance of the Chu Valley scheme in this colonial enterprise.

[79] "Issledovanie Chuiskoi doliny," *SOV* 231 (October 15, 1916), 2.

described the soils in Semireche's valleys as "clay loam and loess," which seems to accord better with Vasil′ev's initial claims.[80] Whether the soils were better described as black earth or loam did not, in the end, really matter, as far as settlers were concerned. As the previous decades had shown, settlers from European Russia and Siberia would come to Turkestan whether they were welcome or not. Though at Vasil′ev's request the Department of Land Improvement and the Resettlement Administration had prepared orders for a halt to migration while the Chu project was under construction, settlers continued to come. Those who chose not to stay because of the lack of available irrigated cropland seem to have had no trouble selling off the buildings on their land to voluntary resettlers.[81]

CROSSING BOUNDARIES

As nomads in Semireche – like those further north in the Kazakh Steppe – found their grazing areas increasingly limited both by the government appropriation of "surplus" lands for the colonization land fund and by the arrival of new settlers, they began to choose one of two options: either to seek out new pastures – in regions less suitable for colonization or across the border with China, a typical nomadic strategy of adaptation to changing environmental conditions – or to adopt a settled way of life, sometimes as a means of subverting tsarist attempts to take control of their winter pastures.[82] Such a transition to a settled existence could create legal questions for both the sedentarized subjects and the local administration. The recently settled nomads of East Sukuluk volost′, for instance, wrote to the Resettlement Administration to ask if they should still pay a tent tax, as calculated when they were nomads, or a land tax, the way that peasants did. Some recently settled groups had to pay both, causing conflict in some communities between settled and still-nomadic groups.[83] Though the imperial Russian government never planned to forcibly settle the nomads, Russian administrators had no doubt of the

[80] *Opisanie Semirechenskogo pereselencheskogo raiona*, 7 (TsGA RK f. I-19, op. 1, d. 230, l. 21).

[81] RGIA f. 391, op. 5, d. 2420, ll. 1–10b.

[82] This chapter takes inspiration from Paul Werth's work on colonial governance and religious difference in the Russian Empire ("From Resistance to Subversion") by labeling nomadic strategies as *subversions* rather than resistance. RGIA f. 391, op. 4, d. 934, ll. 2–20b; TsGA RK f. I-44, op. 1, d. 21387, ll. 1–3.

[83] Pierce, *Russian Central Asia*, 149. Poniatovskii, *Opyt izucheniia khlopkovodstva*, 16. TsGA RK f. I-19, op. 1, d. 271, l. 5–50b; TsGA RK f. I-44, op. 1, d. 21387, l. 2.

inevitability of the turn to a supposedly superior settled way of life (*osedlost'*). The idea of sedentarization, moreover, resonated thoroughly with Russian notions of how land in the Chu River Valley should be used. That some nomads did express a desire for a sedentary life after Russians moved into the region served as seeming confirmation of this belief.

Like many modernizing states, the tsarist administration had practical, as well as ideological, reasons for desiring the nomadic peoples of the empire to adopt a sedentary way of life.[84] Sedentary peoples are easier to control than are ones who move, even if the movement occurs at predictable times and along predictable routes. Nomadic groups were difficult to tax, particularly because the representative officials responsible for collecting taxes from villages and volosts were also nomads.[85] By converting nomads into farmers, the Russian state gained not only more farmers, but also more land, creating space for more Russian migrants. Land norms for settlers were at most half of the estimated land needs of the nomads, meaning that one nomadic household might be replaced with multiple sedentary households. Boris Shlegel', who seems to have become more and more entranced by the idea of freeing up more land for Slavic peasants, even made the argument that one "Kirgiz" could potentially be replaced by three to four "more reliable" Russian settlers in the Chinese border region.[86] At the same time, however, some administrative officials could see the economic benefits for the empire of the vast herds of livestock tended by the nomads, which might supply the cities with meat and milk, and with leather and wool for shoes and clothing. The Russian administration, thus, occasionally expressed concern about the desire shown by some nomads to transition to a sedentary way of life. This "governmental dilemma" was compounded by the lack of survey data on land use and the slow process of demarcating official settler plots.[87] As a result, many of the Kyrgyz and Kazakhs who attempted to go through official channels to "receive sedentary status" [*poluchit' osedlost'*] were put on waiting lists, just like Russian resettlers. Some early requests in the

84 On Ottoman sedentarization policies, see, for example, Reşat Kasaba, *A Moveable Empire: Ottoman Nomads, Migrants, and Refugees* (Seattle: University of Washington Press, 2009).

85 Martin, *Law and Custom in the Steppe*, 41.

86 In February 1915, Shlegel' envisioned sending 300,000 settlers to the Ili Valley (Kulja) to defend Turkestan "from the 'yellow' peril." RGIA f. 391, op. 5, d. 2420, l. 4.

87 Steven Sabol, "'Awake Kazak!' Russian Colonization of Central Asia and the Genesis of Kazak National Consciousness, 1868–1920" (PhD diss., Georgia State University, 1998), 81.

Chu Valley were even denied until appropriate legislation could be drawn up.[88]

Under Russian rule, not only external borders – such as crossing the border to seek new pastures in China's Ili Valley – but internal borders, too, began to play an important role in nomadic communities, as the state used administrative divisions in an attempt to disunite powerful "clans."[89] Historian Virginia Martin has described the way in which Kazakh nomads learned to use administrative boundaries drawn by Russian officials – many of whom were unfamiliar with the local terrain – to support their own land claims when such claims were disputed, and the way in which these volosts came to serve as "alternative foci for group identity."[90] That many nomads recognized volost′ boundaries as demarcating the contours of a particular societal grouping is evidenced by the fact that many nomads asked to be excluded from one volost′ and instead be considered part of a different administrative district. Some petitioners requested to move to neighboring districts where they had relatives, since volost′ boundaries drawn by Russian administrators often did not correspond to local alliances; others requested permission to form their own separate district under their own leaders. Still other requests cited the need to escape from the influence of corrupt locally elected officials, from members of a different clan, or from powerful neighbors who were exhibiting "oppressive" behavior toward the group requesting to move.[91] Indeed, it seems that transferring households from one aul to another or auls from one volost′ to another was a strategy used by elected officials to maintain their power or to keep local power confined to members of the same descent line.[92]

It is not always clear what form the "oppressive" behavior alluded to by petitioners took, nor whether its cause was a fear on the part of local elites of losing their authority, or a hostility on the part of some nomads toward other nomads who desired a sedentary way of life.[93] What is clear

88 TsGA RK f. I-19, op. 1, d. 391, l. 1; TsGA RK f. I-44, op. 1, d. 21722, ll. 4–5.

89 Svetlana Jacquesson, "Reforming pastoral land use in Kyrgyzstan: from clan and custom to self-government and tradition," *Central Asian Survey* 29, 1 (2010): 106.

90 Martin, *Law and Custom in the Steppe* 82, 120.

91 See, for instance, TsGA RK f. I-44, op. 1, dd. 21722, ll. 4–5; 21387, l. 4; 21906, ll. 1–2; TsGA KR f. 130 op. 1, d. 186, l. 50b.

92 Edward Sokol, *The Revolt of 1916 in Russian Central Asia* (Baltimore, MD: Johns Hopkins Press, 1954), 50; Svetlana Jacquesson, "The Time of Dishonour: Land and Murder under Colonial Rule in the Tian Shan," *Journal of the Economic and Social History of the Orient* 55 (2012): 678–680.

93 Jacquesson, "The Time of Dishonour," 681. See also Brower, *Turkestan and the Fate of the Russian Empire,* 148.

is that tensions over the decision to sedentarize could split communities right down the middle, such as when Sukuluk volost′, to the northwest of Pishpek – where in 1907 "surplus" land had been identified for almost four thousand settlers – split in 1909 into "two enemy camps, one of which fought for sedentarization, while the other energetically sought to hinder it," leading the local administration to legally divide the region into an eastern and a western half.[94] Some nomads who had been placed in the queue with those waiting for land and the transition to sedentary status seem to have reconsidered this move, apparently as a result of hostility on the part of neighbors. They were informed by Russian officials, however, who had drawn up rules to "avoid bungling" the whole affair, that they could not be taken off the lists under any circumstances.[95] Others, seemingly regretting the decision to settle, petitioned to be returned to nomadic status – a fair claim, one Russian official noted, arguing that, "the absence in the law of guidelines on the right of kirgiz to return to the nomadic condition cannot ... serve as the basis for denying them that transition."[96]

Many nomads perceived sedentarization as offering distinct advantages. Some nomads hoped that the transfer to a settled way of life might lead to greater stability and fewer conflicts over land and water resources. In 1911, for instance, all Kyrgyz in Tolkanov volost′ of Pishpek district on the left bank of the Chu River – one of the first to be addressed by the Resettlement Administration's surveying party in 1905, and from which thousands of desiatinas had been taken for settler parcels on which thousands of new settlers now lived – petitioned the local administration with the request to be considered a settled community, provided the government regulate water usage between Kyrgyz and Russian settlers, which until that point had been characterized by illegal seizures on both sides.[97] Other nomads reasoned that if they became settled, they would remain in possession of at least some of their lands, which might otherwise be appropriated for the state's colonization fund. According to the local branch of the Resettlement Administration, the half of Sukuluk volost′ that had fought to stay nomadic "became convinced of the need

94 *Obzor Semirechenskoi oblasti za 1907* (Vernyi, 1908), 3; TsGA KR f. 130, op. 1, d. 186, l. 50b.

95 RGIA f. I-19, op. 1, d. 391, l. 1.

96 GARF f. 1797, op. 1, d. 148, ll. 2–20b, 4.

97 *Obzor Semirechenskoi oblasti za 1906* (Vernyi, 1907), 10, 14–15; *Obzor Semirechenskoi oblasti za 1907*, 2–3; TsGA KR f. 130, op. 1, d. 133, ll. 6–18ob. They had also been limited by Pishpek's water needs (Pahlen, *Oroshenie*, 281–282).

to have permanent allotments [*nadely*] ... [after the state] appropriation of surplus lands carried out in 1910 ..."[98] Shortage of winter pastures was a frequent refrain in the petitions from nomadic groups to the Russian administration.[99] One faction of the Sarybagish Kyrgyz, for instance, hoped that as a "*kishlak*" (*qishloq*, settled village) they might retain some of the best and well-watered lands in the district, to the distress of other members of the community.[100]

Some Russians assumed that nomads who desired to be enumerated among the sedentary population of the empire were making a conscious decision to become more "civilized," yet as these cases indicate, many nomads saw the decision to transition to a sedentary way of life as a strategic one. In a report to Fol′baum in September 1913, the head of Pishpek district noted that cases of returning to a nomadic way of life would likely be rare, "since it is already clear that the kirgiz highly value the lands that have been set aside for them."[101] Perhaps Russian officials took pride in being able to offer their nomadic subjects a "gift" of land, but they could not change the fact that nomads were subverting the tsarist civilizing mission by accepting sedentary status not in order to follow the model set by Russian colonists (such as that may have been), but rather seeking to retain possession of land that they had traditionally considered their own. For the most part, the Russian state seems to have upheld many petitions for the crossing of volost′ boundaries, as well as nomads' "right to join all village communities, regardless of their tribal makeup." As for those Russians who wished to join settled Kyrgyz villages, Fol′baum could only approve of such cases if large numbers wished to make such a move, given "that Russian people, for the most part uncultured and ignorant ... would hardly fulfill their lofty mission of planting Russian civilization [*grazhdanstvennost′*] among the nomads"; to the contrary, they might "Kirgizify [*okirgizit′sia*]," losing their traditions.[102]

[98] TsGA KR f. 130, op. 1, d. 186, l. 5ob.

[99] Jacquesson, "The Time of Dishonour," 681.

[100] TsGA RK f. I-44, op. 1, d. 21906, ll. 1–2ob.

[101] TsGA RK f. I-19, op. 1, d. 391, l. 1ob.

[102] RGIA f. 391, op. 4, d. 249, ll. 2, 3ob-4. *Grazhdanstvennost′* can be translated as "citizenship," but as Austin Jersild has pointed out, "'Grazhdanstvennost′ was an idealized Russian image of proper social and cultural behavior that was derived from ideas about life in a more civilized West" ("From Savagery to Citizenship: Caucasian Mountaineers and Muslims in the Russian Empire," in eds. Daniel Brower and Edward Lazzerini, *Russia's Orient: Imperial Borderlands and Peoples*, 1700–1917 [Bloomington: Indiana University Press, 1997], 108).

Some nomads may also have had more self-aggrandizing motives in their championing of sedentarization. In 1912, for instance, Olzhebai Mamyrov, who identified himself both as a peasant from the (Kyrgyz) settlement of Tash-Tiube (formed in 1898) and as the [official] elder of Baitek volost′ (both in Pishpek district), as well as a sedentarization pioneer who had convinced dozens of Tolkanov Kyrgyz households to form new settlements, filed an official complaint that his efforts had not been recognized, unlike the Kyrgyz from East Sukuluk, who had been awarded medals for "showing the way" to sedentarization. (His request for a medal was denied.)[103] Mamyrov's document indicates that literal borders were not the only kind of boundaries that the nomadic peoples of Semireche tried to cross; by trying to identify themselves legally as sedentary, rather than nomadic peoples, some nomads hoped to be able to gain status within the Russian Empire, rather than losing it.

The Kazakh archives contain dozens of petitions from Central Asian nomads requesting to be considered a member of yet other socio-legal categories. Some nomads wished to be considered a member of the *meshchanin* social estate [*soslovie*], roughly equivalent to petit bourgeois.[104] In 1912, Orthodox priest Simeon Tregubov expressed his hopes that "the recently strengthening aspiration among the kirgiz to transition to a settled existence might prompt them to change their faith in Mohammedanism to the Orthodox Christian doctrine ..."[105] Though there was no concerted effort to convert settled nomads to Orthodoxy, some nomads did, in fact, desire conversion as an accompaniment to their transition to settled town life.[106]

There were also nomads who petitioned to be considered part of the Cossack estate.[107] Though it can be argued that Cossacks' identity rested on their existence as a separate estate with a particular imperial function – Cossacks served as the borderguards of the empire – in practice in Semireche, at least, the Cossack estate was identified more with land than with imperial service. Cossacks were allotted thirty desiatinas, fewer than what most nomads purportedly needed, but at least two and more often three times as many as ordinary peasants. Nomadic petitions for Cossack status indicate that nomads were aware that this status was both land-based and flexible. They also indicate that crossing boundaries between nomad and peasant, Islam and Orthodoxy, Kyrgyz and Cossack, was a legal adaptive strategy utilized by nomads in Semireche in response

[103] TsGA RK f. I-19, op. 1, d. 371, ll. 5, 8. [104] TsGA RK f. I-44, op. 1, d. 21387, l. 2ob.
[105] RGIA f. 391, op. 4, d. 1663, l. 1.
[106] See, for instance, TsGA RK f. I-44, op. 1, d 22580.
[107] See, for instance, TsGA RK f. I-44, op. 1, dd. 21387, ll. 2ob-4; 21989; 22594; 22606; 22620.

FIGURE 4.3 Semireche Cossack officers. From the album *Vidy Semirech'ia i Kul'dzhi* [*Views of Semireche and Kulja*], 5.
Reproduced with permission of the Rare Books Section of the Alisher Navoi State Library, Tashkent, Uzbekistan.

to pressure on the environment in which they lived. On the question of nomads becoming Cossacks, one official opined, "it is impossible to rank them among the Cossacks because Cossack land allotments are very great and it would not do to give these to the kirgiz."[108] From this statement, it is clear that this official, at least, objected to nomads becoming Cossacks not on the grounds of ethnicity (i.e., Kyrgyz cannot become Cossacks), heritage, social standing, or occupation, but rather on issues of land use. Whether or not a Kyrgyz nomad could legally become a Cossack, the mere fact that Russian officials considered such propositions – and felt the need to justify their decisions – is notable.[109]

[108] TsGA RK f. I-44, op. 1, d. 21387, ll. 20b-3.

[109] Pahlen also noted instances where the Resettlement Administration had "rechristened" Cossack settlements as peasant villages in order to expropriate their land with the result that the inhabitants "were neither real peasants nor real Cossacks" (*Mission to Turkestan*, 219).

Petitions from Kazakhs and Kyrgyz were usually mediated by a class of scribes whose function was not only to translate their requests into Russian, but also to translate the language of ordinary people into the language of a bureaucracy; in so doing, these scribes may also have changed the nature and language of the requests themselves. Yet, whatever the language used, and whether or not their wishes were fulfilled, the fact that the nomadic petitioners engaged with official Russian categories such as social estate and administrative district in creative ways indicates that they understood these categories as flexible, and ones that they could employ in order to further their own self interest. The fact that many of these cases created significant amounts of paperwork is evidence that the tsarist officials took such petitions seriously. The project to develop the Chu River Valley into a prosperous colony of the empire, however, left the indigenous inhabitants of the valley with fewer such choices. In February 1915, in a report given to the Turkestan governor-general, resettlement official Boris Shlegel′ wrote:

> [A]t first the kirgiz attempted to protest against the requisitioning of their lands for the colonization fund, but their protests were, in most cases, not answered, as [being] unworthy of recognition. The kirgiz tried to show resistance to the colonists by every means, but in the end they saw that it was not within their power to stop the surging wave of resettlers. The majority understood that the only salvation of the kirgiz was in the move to sedentarism …

WAR AND REVOLT

By the end of 1915, both the Great War and the Chu Valley Irrigation Project were in full swing. In July, an order of the Council of Ministers governing emergency funds in wartime designated the irrigation project the recipient of special funding, in view of its remote location, the lack of reliable contractors, and its importance in supplying the cotton-growing regions of Turkestan with grain and feed. Of a total of 6.75 million rubles allocated to hydraulic projects in the empire in 1915, almost 1 million were assigned to the Chu Valley.[110] Though a key component of the irrigation project's success, the Semireche railroad did not receive the same special wartime considerations; financial aid was reassigned to railroad projects seen as having more strategic importance, such as the Murmansk Railroad in Russia's Far North.[111]

With many able-bodied men in Semireche drafted into the army – including Boris Shlegel′, who was assigned to hydraulic work on

[110] RGIA f. 426, op. 3, d. 165, ll. 42–43. [111] Payne, "Turksib," 40.

the western front – the Department of Land Improvement appealed to the War Ministry to have workers in reclamation projects be considered exempt from the draft.[112] Many of the technical staff on which the Chu project now relied were students. Unskilled labor was also in short supply. While ostensibly a convenient source of labor, the price of hiring Austro-Hungarian prisoners-of-war in the region was prohibitive, even when they were paid only twenty-five kopecks for a ten-hour day – the standard pay for POWs employed in agricultural work in Turkestan in May 1915 – due to the need to feed, clothe, and house them. Many of the POWs in Pishpek were in poor health, some perhaps having contracted malaria from POW camps in the Hungry Steppe. The need for surveillance increased the price of hired prisoner labor still further. Even though some POWs might provide useful technical and craft skills that were in short supply in Turkestan in wartime, it seemed to make little sense to hire such expensive and potentially unsuitable labor.[113]

In the face of such obstacles, the Chu administration turned to a place that had long supplied the Russian Empire with cheap seasonal labor: Kashgaria, just to the east in China's Xinjiang province.[114] Though Krivoshein on principle objected to the use of cheap Afghan and Kashgari seasonal labor – since he felt such workers were draining vital funds out of Russia – war had altered the landscape; cheap labor was better than the prospects of no laborers at all.[115] The Chu project administration, therefore, took on a special recruiter, hired for the specific purpose of traveling to Xinjiang and persuading workers to come to Semireche and dig canals. Several local residents – including Chu foreman Ivan Ignat′evich Pavlov, who recommended hiring workers from Kashgar and claimed to be "excellently familiar" with the conditions of hiring workers throughout the surrounding Altishahr region – offered their services to the Chu project. In the end, the Chu administration selected Galii Muhamedjanov Toktarov, a peasant from Tokmak, who claimed that with his connections – including influential relatives – he could recruit a number of laborers in the Kashgar region.[116] In December 1915, he signed a contract with the Chu administration, pledging to provide three hundred workers from Kashgar by the first of April. He was to receive two rubles for each recruit who made it to Pishpek, a journey of twelve days across the Tian

112 Tatishchev, *Zemli i liudi*, 217.

113 TsGA KR f. I-54, op. 1, dd. 71, ll. 2, 6–6a, 34–6, 46; 12, ll. 84, 188.

114 TsGA KR f. I-54, op. 3, d. 2, l. 2/16 (page numbers start over at 1 on page 15); op. 1, d. 71, l. 40.

115 Krivoshein, *Zapiska Glavnoupravliaiushchego zemleustroistvom i zemledeliem*, 14.

116 RGIA f. 426, op. 3, d. 198, ll. 67–73ob.

Shan Mountains via Naryn, and an additional two rubles for each worker who completed fifty days of labor. He was to supply the recruits with an advance of twenty rubles for the journey to the Chu Valley, which included five rubles for a passport.[117]

The war threatened even this enterprise, however, when Toktarov, who was subject to the draft, was called to military service in early 1916. Vasil′ev's assistant Nikolai Fedorovich Nefedov wrote a letter to the military head of Pishpek district, stating that sending Toktarov into military service "would cause damage to the cause of the project which would be difficult to remedy... depriving it of workers in the upcoming construction season ..."[118] On his first trip, Toktarov had managed to recruit two hundred and fifty-seven Kashgaris for stints on the Chu Valley canals, and there seemed to be no doubt that he would be able to find more.[119] It appears that Nefedov's argument was persuasive, since Toktarov continued his recruitment efforts.

However, just as Grand Duke Nikolai Konstantinovich's indigenous workers had sometimes been confused by the conditions of work on Russian canal projects, so the hired Kashgari laborers, too, misunderstood the nature of the work to which they had pledged their labor. One group of Kashgaris, for instance, envisioned earning a monthly salary of fifty-four rubles. Like the Turkestani workers in the Hungry Steppe, they understood the promise of one ruble eighty kopecks for the removal of one cubic sazhen of earth to be a daily working wage. When it became clear that most workers could only dig about one-third of a cubic sazhen in a day – reducing their daily wage to about seventy kopecks – all of these Kashgari workers left their construction site in the Chu Valley "without any warning" in the middle of the night; rumors were that they had left to seek work on the Semireche railroad.[120] As long as there were competing projects present in the region, the labor force would continue to be mobile. Toktarov instructed the Chu administration to articulate the proposed salaries more clearly – if unspecified, he assured them, the "undeveloped" Kashgaris would demand no less than ten rubles per cubic sazhen.[121]

Toktarov unexpectedly found his second expedition in search of local labor much more difficult, due to misapprehensions among relatives and friends of the recruited workers. In May, in reply to a request for three hundred more workers, Toktarov reported having trouble recruiting

117 Ibid., ll. 67, 70, 73ob; TsGA KR f. I-54, op. 3, d. 2, l. 1 (unnumbered).

118 TsGA KR f. I-54, op. 1, d. 45, l. 124.

119 TsGA KR f. I-54, op. 1, d. 71, l. 38.

120 Ibid., l. 58.

121 Ibid., ll. 69–69ob.

workers in the city of Kashgar itself, and that he was trying to get permission from the Russian Consulate to try the surrounding region. He urged the Chu administrators to have the Kashgari workers send letters home, via Toktarov himself, so as to assure their families that they were being well treated and well paid, and to limit the spread of false rumors that might jeopardize future recruiting trips. This latter request was prompted, Toktarov claimed, by an encounter with the parents of men working in Russian Turkestan, who had come to him "with tears in their eyes," having heard the rumor that some of the workers had died on the road in the mountains, while those who had reached their destination were working underground in terrible conditions. "[I]n view of their dimness," Toktarov wrote, only personal letters would suffice to convince the parents that their sons were safe and sound.[122] By the middle of July, Toktarov had sent almost six hundred workers from Kashgar to the Chu Valley.[123]

Once in Semireche, in addition to the Chu administration, the Kashgari workers were subject to administration by one of a network of officials known as *aqsaqals*, who governed Chinese subjects in Russian Turkestan.[124] Already in June 1916, Nefedov suggested that the Tokmak aqsaqal, the merchant Turdi-Ahun Almazbekov, be given a silver medal for the assistance he had given the Chu project, wielding his authority and influence to help settle various misunderstandings.[125] Moreover, that spring Almazbekov had allowed the destruction of trees on his land in Shamsi volost' so that the Krasnaia River Canal could proceed.[126] Even with Almazbekov's assistance, however, not all was smooth. In late June, Syromiatnikov, the site-engineer in the Krasnaia River region (Region B), reported a fight between the Kashgaris and the villagers of Ivanovskoe. The Tokmak police chief (*pristav*) had three of the "Chinese sarts" placed under arrest, "although their guilt has by no means been established." Though he did not appear to particularly sympathize with the men subjected to this unjust treatment, Syromiatnikov feared keeping them under arrest might hinder further recruitment of workers.[127] Little did he realize that in just a few short weeks, the Chu administration would have to face much greater problems than worker recruitment and morale.

[122] TsGA KR f. I-54, op. 1, d. 71, ll. 61, 69–69ob; op. 3, d. 2, l. 8.

[123] TsGA KR f. I-54, op. 1, d. 71, ll. 85, 93, 94–94ob.

[124] David Brophy, *Uyghur Nation: Reform and Revolution on the Russia-China Frontier* (Cambridge, MA: Harvard University Press, 2016), 123.

[125] TsGA KR f. I-54, op. 1, d. 71, l. 66. [126] TsGA KR f. I-54, op. 3, d. 8, l. 13.

[127] TsGA KR f. I-54, op. 1, d. 71, ll. 81–82; op. 3, d. 2, ll. 33–34, 38–38ob.

In 1916, Vasil′ev reported optimistically to the Department of Land Improvement that he planned to have finished the main canal in the Samsonov region by the end of the year, most of the Krasnaia River works by the end of 1917, and all of the main parts of the system by 1918. He also noted, however, that as the government consolidated its hold on the lands in the Chu region, questions about water use would increase in number, due to large amounts of pastureland being transferred to the irrigation system.[128] New contracts with Kyrgyz occupying lands in the region of the main canal, and in Region B of the Chu project, provided monetary compensation for the cessation of rice planting near the Chu irrigation project (even though one previous excuse for taking land for the Krasnaia River irrigation system had been that the Kyrgyz in Region B "do not use the land intensively enough").[129] Yet, monetary compensation could not offset the losses of land and food crops necessary for sustaining local communities. The burdensome impositions of the wartime economy, and the requisition of food, goods, and payments for the war effort from all subjects of the empire, further exacerbated matters. Conditions were set for unrest, and the summer of 1916 would expose the fault lines present in Semireche, as it did all across Turkestan.

On June 25, 1916, Tsar Nicholas II issued an imperial decree announcing a general mobilization of all "natives" between the ages of eighteen and forty-three who had previously been exempt from wartime service, including the Muslims of the Caucasus, Turkestan, and the Kazakh Steppe. The mobilization was aimed specifically at bolstering the ranks of labor on essential projects on the home front, so the Chu administration quickly petitioned the General Staff to allow 2,300 "natives" [*inorodtsy*] to work for the project.[130] The mobilization was not entirely unexpected. Former Duma representative Alikhan Bukeikhanov and other members of the Kazakh intelligentsia circle and nascent political movement known as Alash Orda, had gone to Petrograd (the new name for St. Petersburg, now that Russia was at war with Germany) to try to persuade the government that, if Muslims were to be called up for service, the Kazakhs, as skilled horsemen, be able to serve in the cavalry, rather than the infantry. Alash Orda also called for Kazakhs to be given Cossack status, clearly phrasing Cossack status not in ethnic terms, but in terms of

[128] TsGA KR f. I-54, op. 1, d. 60, ll. 72–73.
[129] TsGA KR f. I-54, op. 1, dd. 60, ll. 51, 76; 4, ll. 49ob-50.
[130] TsGA KR f. I-54, op. 1, d. 71, l. 100.

land allotments.[131] The *jadids*, Muslim reformers mostly located in urban parts of Central Asia, supported Muslim participation in the army.[132]

Predictably, however, among many others in Turkestan, the decree provoked great concern. In mid-July, violence broke out first in the Jizzakh region near the Hungry Steppe and in Samarkand. On July 19, Syromiatnikov reported doubts about the possibility of a peaceful draft of the local population of the Chu River Valley into labor on the home front. Not only were there rumors circulating throughout Semireche that Kazakhs and Kyrgyz were refusing the draft and moving toward the Chinese border in large numbers, but the two hundred Kazakhs and Kyrgyz working until that point on the Krasnaia River irrigation canal had also suddenly left the project en masse, "out of a feeling of solidarity." In spite of the fact that they had been informed that service on the Chu irrigation project, as an important component of the effort to defend the homeland, exempted them from the draft, not a single indigenous worker remained.[133] Many Kashgari workers left without fulfilling their contracts after a "Muslim holiday" was declared on July 23, 1916.[134] Nomadic inhabitants of the Chu Valley and surrounding areas may have been particularly upset because the tsarist government lowered the number of men to be requisitioned from the cotton-growing region of Ferghana from 77,000 to 50,000, while simultaneously increasing the number in Semireche from 43,000 to 60,000.[135]

In late July, in the Lepsinsk district of Semireche near the Chinese border, the rumor began to circulate that local Kazakhs were planning to slaughter settlers, since the Russian troops were "broken," and the peasants had been left defenseless.[136] Rumors of an impending attack were swirling in southern Semireche by early August. On August 5 in the Chu River Valley, the Tokmak district police officer ordered the arrest of Bektursun Begaliev from Shamsi volost′ (straddling Regions A and B of the Chu Valley Irrigation Project) for "spreading lying rumors about the

[131] Sokol, *The Revolt of 1916*, 103–104. For the Kazakhs' call for the same land and water rights as Cossacks, see Tomohiko Uyama, "A Particularist Empire: The Russian Policies of Christianization and Military Conscription in Central Asia" in ed. Tomohiko Uyama, *Empire, Islam, and Politics in Central Eurasia* (Sapporo: Slavic Research Center, Hokkaido University, 2007), 55–56.

[132] Adeeb Khalid, *The Politics of Muslim Cultural Reform: Jadidism in Central Asia* (Berkeley: University of California Press, 1998), 241.

[133] TsGA KR f. I-54, op. 1, d. 71, l. 95.

[134] TsGA KR f. I-54, op. 3, d. 2, l. 64.

[135] Buttino, *Revoliutsiia naoborot*, 373 note 132. After the uprising of 1916, the figures for Semireche were readjusted once again to 43,000 (Ibid., 73).

[136] TsGA KR f. I-87, op. 1, d. 4, l. 4.

demonstration [*vystuplenie*] of Kyrgyz against Russians" (district head Putintsev freed him a month later, since the rumors had been substantiated).[137] According to Ivanovskoe village head Demian Vasil'evich Rostovskii, Kyrgyz laborers and visitors to the settler village had been talking about a Kyrgyz uprising for a long time, and how "things would go badly for the Russians ... What that meant we understood poorly and [we] did not exactly believe that an uprising was possible," Rostovskii would later testify. In early August, alarmed villagers asked their Kyrgyz neighbors whether the rumors of an uprising in the region were true; they were answered in the negative. The following week, according to these settlers' testimony, Kyrgyz from nearby Nurmambetov volost' asked if the Russians were well armed.[138] In fact, the Berdan rifles given by the government to Russian settlers for defense of their villages had been collected months before for the war effort.[139] It is possible that the Lepsinsk rumor about the "defenseless" peasants and this query about arms possession were related to local knowledge that the Russians of the region were less well protected than they once had been. That same week, violence broke out in the Chu River Valley.[140]

On the night of August 8, 1916, in the region around Tokmak, there was a nighttime attack on the recently formed settler village of Novo-Aleksandrovskoe. That same night, several of the Chu project workers went on strike, calling for an increase in pay and issue of advance payments. The next night, according to Russian accounts, around three hundred Kyrgyz drove off the horses and oxen that had been left at one of the project sites by the striking workers. The Russian workers housed in nearby barracks fled the scene, while the Kazakh and Kyrgyz workers joined the attackers, setting fire to the warehouses and hay storage; from there the fire spread to the stables, the blacksmith's, the saddle-maker's, the wagon repair shop, and the workers' housing.[141] On August 9, settlers from the village of Belotsarskoe reported its destruction; remaining residents fled to the local schoolhouse, where, according to eyewitness testimony, they held out against their attackers for eight days.[142]

137 TsGA KR f I-6, op. 1, d. 2, ll. 31–31ob.
138 TsGA KR f. I-87, op. 1, d. 4, ll. 3–4, 18–18ob.
139 Sokol, *The Revolt of 1916*, 114.
140 Happel, *Nomadische Lebenswelten*, 130.
141 TsGA KR f. I-54, op. 1, d. 30, ll. 75–75ob.
142 TsGA KR f. I-87, op. 1, d. 7, ll. 12–13.

By August 10, the Sarybagish Kyrgyz volosts of Tynaev and Shamsi near the Krasnaia River Canal worksite had joined the uprising.[143] On August 11, according to the testimony of Russian settlers, the residents of Ivanovskoe were informed by a Kyrgyz man named Suleiman Korchenov that all would be quiet, but that very day, at his orders, Kyrgyz attacked the nearby settlement of Santash (Iur′evskoe). The next day, another Kyrgyz man, Alim Davletov, warned Ivanovskoe residents that if they did not leave, they would be slaughtered [*pererezhut*]. Though some Kyrgyz tried to dispel the rumors, another Kyrgyz named Tubaldai Bajibaev confirmed to an Ivanovskoe settler with whom he was acquainted that the Kyrgyz were indeed planning to attack. With several such warnings, Rostovskii called on one of the technicians from the Chu irrigation project, Efraim Bagirov, for help. Rostovskii himself would later testify that he had personally learned about preparations for the uprising from an acquaintance named Saltabai from Nurbambetov volost′, whom he also identified among the attackers. Three days later, on August 14, at the request of the village, the Pishpek commanding officer sent ten soldiers from the reserve cavalry to defend Ivanovskoe in case of an attack.[144]

The next morning, Ivanovskoe was attacked by "a large mob" of Kyrgyz armed with rifles and lances, and bearing emblems [*so znachkami*]. One of the attackers was technician Bagirov's former translator; another was reported as Suleiman Korchin, likely the same "Suleiman Korchenov" who had visited Ivanovskoe several days prior.[145] The cavalry reserves sent to the village seem to have been poor marksmen, and were, thus, of little use in protecting the village. By 8 am, according to eyewitnesses, the town had been surrounded and several villagers who were out working in the fields had been killed. One, a man named Kolmantsev, had his eyes gouged out and his tongue and penis cut off; another, the eighteen-year-old Vera Solomatina also had her "sexual organs cut out" and her braid cut off. According to the villagers, around fifty Kyrgyz attacked from the east, with shouts of "Allah!" setting homes on fire. They also burned the barrack at marker No. 52 on the main canal near the village, which was used by the Chu irrigation project to store construction tools, as well as shops that supplied provisions to the Kashgari workers. Technicians from the irrigation project set up brigades to help defend Ivanovskoe, since one of their accounting offices was

[143] TsGA KR f. 54, op. 1, d. 30, l. 103. [144] TsGA KR f. I-87, op. 1, d. 4, ll. 3, 18–20.

[145] Ibid., ll. 3, 20, 22. Korchin was said to be the head of Baisetov volost′ (Happel, *Nomadische Lebenswelten*, 244 fn 320).

located in the village. On this occasion, the Kyrgyz did not lay siege to the village, but instead returned on August 17, only to find Ivanovskoe protected by tsarist troops. They returned one more time on September 8, in a raid that killed eleven villagers.[146]

The raids against Slavic settler villages marked a severe change in relations between neighbors in the Chu River Valley. In spite of the fact that eyewitnesses in the villages recalled large numbers of Kyrgyz attacking their village (according to the technician Bagirov, six hundred "kirgiz" attacked Ivanovskoe at 7 am on September 8), they also claimed to recognize their attackers' faces. Many settlers testified using the names of the attackers – sometimes a first name only – and often they also knew from where the attackers had come. In testimony to the Pishpek Procuracy, the villagers of Ivanovskoe reported that the attackers in the raid of August 15 had come from Nurmambetov, Shamsi, Baisetov, and Tynaev volosts, though they were not as sure about the latter, since Tynaev volost′ was farther away, and so they did not know those Kyrgyz so well. In testimony about the raid of September 8, Ivanovskoe villagers identified their attackers as coming, once more, from Baisetov and Nurmambetov volosts.[147] Indeed, they should have been quite familiar with the Kyrgyz of Baisetov volost′, since it was with these neighbors that they had negotiated the land contract entitled "Verdict No. 4" just eight years previously. Ismail Suleimanov, who had led the process of negotiation, was reported to have been among the attackers in August.[148]

The Slavic settlers' testimony indicates that those involved in the violence of 1916 in the Chu River Valley and surrounding regions were neighbors who had extensive dealings with one another. Some settlers had turned to their Kyrgyz neighbors to disprove the rumors. Some Kyrgyz had warned their Slavic neighbors of planned atrocities. Nor was it just nomads and settlers who were faced with the decision to revolt or stay loyal to the Russian government. Many Dungans joined nomadic resistance to the mobilization, while the aqsaqal administrators of Chinese-subject Kashgaris, many of whom worked on the irrigation project, counseled their subjects not to take part in the violence.[149] It is clear that

[146] TsGA KR f. I-87, op. 1, d. 4, ll. 3–4, 7, 20; TsGA KR f. I-54, op.1, d. 30, l. 103.

[147] TsGA KR f. I-87, op. 1, dd. 4, ll. 30b, 20, 220b, 28; 11, l. 110b.

[148] Likely the father of Suleiman Korchin. TsGA KR f. I-87, op. 1, d. 4, l. 22.

[149] Tokmak aqsaqal Almazbekov's silver medal was in part for ensuring that the Kashgaris showed allegiance to Russian authorities (TsGA KR f. I-54, op. 1, d. 52, ll. 74–75). One of the leaders of the uprising in Semireche was Bular Moguev [Mogui], head of the Dungan village of Alexandrovskoe in Pishpek district.

many Kyrgyz felt conflicted – even horrified – at the decisions of their kinsmen and neighbors to attack Slavic settlers and workers in the region. Diur Saurumbaev, head of Tynaev volost′, for instance, testified about the effects of the events of August 1916 on his district, whose summer and winter pastures were located on the slopes of the Alexandrov Ridge and in the Chu River Valley. At the time of the uprising, he reported, many Tynaev Kyrgyz were in the summer pastures, while others were in the valley to harvest grain and to help the families of Russian soldiers away at the front. According to Saurumbaev, the main trouble was caused by the participation of the neighboring Sarybagish Kyrgyz who lived across the river Taldy-Bulak from Tynaev volost′. By the time Saurumbaev got word of the Sarybagish attack on the village of Bystroretskoe, they had already taken control of the mountain passes, trapping his people in their summer pastures. According to Saurumbaev, some Tynaev Kyrgyz joined the Sarybagish in the hopes of gaining booty, others joined up with rebel Kyrgyz from Shamsi volost′, and the remaining Tynaev Kyrgyz gathered in the summer pastures from August 9 to 11 to discuss the situation. When one of the local leaders of the uprising, Kanat Abukin, approached "with his forces," he threatened the Tynaev Kyrgyz to join them or face "pillage and death." Accordingly, many Tynaev Kyrgyz took part in the siege of Tokmak from August 12–20 (as well as, perhaps, the attack on Ivanovskoe). Supposedly, the instigators returned one more time to the Tynaev summer pastures and "spread among the Tynaev people a panicked fear of the Russian people." (Incidentally, this was not the first time the people of Tynaev had felt oppressed by their neighbors: some Tynaev Kyrgyz had reported in 1897 that they were afraid to settle because of the hostility of neighboring nomadic groups to the settled condition.) In early October, Saurumbaev provided to Russian authorities the names of the main instigators from his community.[150]

The efforts of many Kyrgyz to aid their Slavic neighbors was noted by the Slavic inhabitants of Semireche as well, who made an effort to separate those Kyrgyz who attacked their villages from those who had helped them. A cattle trader from Ivanovskoe, for instance, later testified that he had "heard long before its start that a Kyrgyz revolt was being prepared." Noticing an unusually large gathering of Kyrgyz, he had asked a Kyrgyz man named Dauliudov, with whom he had conducted many

[150] TsGA RK f. I-44, op. 1, dd. 20075, l. 43–43ob; 21722, l. 4. Four men from Tynaev volost′ appear on a list from early October of mutiny leaders. TsGA KR f. I-6, op. 1, d. 2, l. 32; TsGA KR f. I-87, op. 1, d. 9, l. 9.

business deals, what the gathering was about, only to learn that the Kyrgyz were planning to revolt after the harvest, probably around the middle of September. Dauliudov refused to accompany the villager to Lepsinsk on business as he had in the past – though the villager assured him that they would be home before September 15 – but he did send his son in his stead. On their return, Dauliudov warned once more about the preparations for an uprising, but the villager, fearing the police would take him for a fool, did not report the matter. He did, however, warn his fellow villagers.[151]

Scholars of the 1916 Turkestan uprising have noted that some of the worst violence occurred in Semireche.[152] The Chu Valley was certainly not the only place in Semireche where violence broke out in 1916, but a close look at the relationships here between government, technical workers, nomads, and settlers reveals the intimacy of this violence. In Pishpek district, the uprising of 1916 was not abstract and faceless, but savage and personal; Kyrgyz participants were not content with killing their neighbors, but had mutilated them as well. While some felt compelled to warn their neighbors, others lied to their faces. Nor was the composition of the attackers random – the volosts that attacked Ivanovskoe, for instance, were the volosts that made up the Chu irrigation project's Krasnaia River canal-building site. Many of them, too, were intimately acquainted with those involved in irrigation construction, having served as translators, contractors, and technicians' assistants. When violence broke out, the nomads of Pishpek district attacked not only the material manifestations of the project, but also its representatives – the technicians and surveyors with whom many of them had worked – as well as their Slavic settler neighbors with whom they had extensive daily dealings.[153]

PATCHING FAULT LINES

The tensions that erupted in 1916 across Central Asia can be explained by many factors, among them the strains of wartime requisitions. The case of the Chu Valley supports the claims of other scholars that the taking of excess land resources was at the heart of much of the violence.[154] But just

151 TsGA KR, f. I-87, op. 1, d. 4, ll. 20ob-22ob.

152 See Brower, "Kyrgyz Nomads and Russian Pioneers," 42.

153 TsGA KR f. I-87, op. 1, dd. 7, l. 32; 4, ll. 18–22ob.

154 Happel, *Nomadische Lebenswelten*, 55; Brower, *Turkestan and the Fate of the Russian Empire*, 139.

what that process looked like has been missing from those accounts. The problems in the Chu Valley were not just tensions between the indigenous inhabitants of Semireche and the "new settlers" of the early twentieth century.[155] After all, Ivanovskoe had been founded already in 1892. Rather, the violence was due to the increasingly intrusive role of the state as it embarked on a program of colonization in a land of scarce water resources.

It is important to remember that in an arid region, not all land is equal. As Mark Fiege has pointed out, where it is water that makes land valuable, both cooperation and conflict exist together, as if built into the irrigation systems themselves. Irrigation is by its nature "a largely cooperative enterprise," and yet, due to the material nature of water, "[d]ividing this fluid, mobile, scarce substance ... was difficult and created ample opportunities for error."[156] The Chu River Valley was an attractive place for the settlement of Russian peasants because of the abundant availability of water, but this was precisely the characteristic that made it so attractive to the region's nomadic population, as well. Irrigation required hard labor, and the fruits of that labor were, therefore, highly contested. Count Pahlen had realized this on his inspection of the region, when he observed that the ongoing practice of depriving "the Kirgiz of all of the arable land they had irrigated and were now farming," if followed through to its logical conclusion, "would have amounted to condemning the Kirgiz to death, as to grow cereals in the mountains was impossible ..."[157] Krivoshein, too, on his visit to the region in 1912, had recognized that "the most urgent resettlement question even here, in the northern, non-cotton-growing, nomadic regions of Turkestan, is a question not of land, but of water. It seems that the whole future of the Russian settlement of Turkestan is inseparable from the question of water."[158] For a time, both settlers and nomads tried to cooperate, but conflicts over the best lands – those that could be watered – were inevitable. Nomads did not resort immediately to violent resistance, however. Negotiations with peasant settlers over land and water, and with the government over sedentary status, are examples of ways in which Kyrgyz in the Chu River Valley attempted to subvert tsarist impositions of taxes

[155] Happel, *Nomadische Lebenswelten*, 55. [156] Fiege, *Irrigated Eden*, 83–84.

[157] Pahlen, *Mission to Turkestan*, 92.

[158] Krivoshein, *Zapiska Glavnoupravliaiushchego zemleustroistvom i zemledeliem*, 54. See also A. A. Kaufman's earlier expression of a similar sentiment in *Pereselenie i kolonizatsiia* (St. Petersburg: Tip. T-va "Obshchestvennaia pol'za," 1905), 262–264.

and land requisitions for irrigation and colonization. But pressure was mounting, and the mobilization of indigenous peoples forced a breaking point. The warnings some Kyrgyz gave their neighbors in the summer of 1916 may have been their last call for peaceful resolution before violent conflict broke out, exposing fault lines throughout the valley and beyond.

Nomads in Semireche still had one option available to them after the violence of 1916, and that was to cross the border to seek their fortunes in China. Edward Sokol has argued that proximity to the safety valve of the border may even have encouraged many nomads to resort to violence.[159] By the fall of 1916, crossing the border was the only choice remaining for many of Semireche's indigenous inhabitants, even if it meant giving up any chance at holding onto their ancestral lands. The violent actions of participants in the uprising had jeopardized the lives even of those members of their communities who chose not to participate. Staying meant facing the punitive detachments sent by the tsarist army to quell rebellion in the borderlands. But for the Kyrgyz of southern Semireche, crossing the border was a difficult and dangerous option, as the shortest route for many was not through the grasslands to the Ili Valley, but rather through the high mountain peaks to the east of Issyk Kul. Many were to lose their livestock during the flight to China, while others were to perish in the mountains.

Ultimately, while the Chu irrigation project mourned the loss of staff members – including several students and recent graduates from the Petrograd Polytechnical Institute – it estimated its losses in rubles: around 106,365 rubles 85 kopecks. The regional Russian administration estimated that losses in the nomadic population in the wake of the uprising (including through flight) were between 150,000 and 270,000 nomads, or a total of almost one-third of the nomadic population; the Russian losses, in contrast, were estimated at 2,325 Russians dead, 1,384 disappeared in Semireche.[160] Perhaps the last casualty was Fol′baum himself. Rumors circulated, as they did in Petrograd, of ties to Germany among the ruling elite, including Fol′baum and Governor-General Fedor Vladimirovich (Von) Martson. According to some, as a German sympathizer, Fol′baum had consciously caused the uprising of the nomads, in order to contribute

159 Sokol, *The Revolt of 1916*, 110–111.

160 TsGA KR f. I-54, op. 1, d. 30, ll. 18, 23, 94; for the figures, see Buttino, *Revoliutsiia naoborot*, 79–80, 375–376 note 216. These numbers represented the vast majority of Slavic victims in Turkestan. Sokol, *The Revolt of 1916*, 120–121.

to the weakness of the empire from within.[161] In the wake of the uprising, Fol′baum legally changed his surname to Sokolov-Sokolinskii (a name from his mother's side), but it was not enough; on his fiftieth birthday in October 1916, he died of a heart attack, presumably brought on by the stresses of recent months.[162]

With Central Asia quiescent, the question remained how to restore peace there while the empire was still at war in Europe. In the wake of the uprising, onetime governor of Transcaspia and former war minister Kuropatkin was relieved of his duties as Commander of the Northern Front and reassigned to Turkestan, where he felt it strongly necessary to divide the Slavic from the indigenous Central Asian populations in the regions where the uprising had taken its most widespread and violent form; he planned to set aside certain areas, such as the shores of Lake Issyk Kul and the Chu Valley, for Russians only, while disloyal nomadic populations were to be deported to the mountainous areas of the Naryn River basin farther south.[163] However, the empire still lacked laborers for important projects on the home front, and in October the mobilization of indigenous Central Asians, delayed by the uprising and ensuing violence, was finally set in motion. This move ensured that Russians and Central Asians would continue to live and work in close proximity.

According to the "Procedural rules for using natives requisitioned to work internally within the Empire in defense of the state," the mobilized "natives" were not to leave the projects to which they had been assigned; those who did not fulfill their duties were subject to imprisonment for up to three months or a three-thousand-ruble fine. By early November 1916, there were more than two thousand Central Asians working at Chu from the Pishpek region alone. Documents from the Chu project's archive suggest that even though violent resistance had died down, ethnic tensions continued to simmer. Vasil′ev reported worker demoralization due to what seems to be subversive behavior among "translators" and elected representatives from among the requisitioned workers, who were "completely useless … or even directly harmful" to the project, encouraging workers to turn against the administration.[164]

161 Buttino, *Revolutsiia naoborot*, 83; for more on supposed links between German agents and POWs and the uprising, see Happel, *Nomadische Lebenswelten*, 168–175.

162 On the name change, *SOV* 217 (September 28, 1916), 1–2. On Fol′baum's death, *SOV* 239 (October 25, 1916), 1; *SOV* 244 (October 30, 1916), 3.

163 Buttino, *Revoliutsiia naoborot*, 73–74.

164 TsGA KR f. I-54, op. 1, dd. 49, ll. 1, 20–22ob; 48, ll. 2, 45; 15, l. 84.

The reluctance of the project administration to treat the requisitioned workers well may have exacerbated such tensions. The procedural rules specified that any desires expressed by the "natives" – for food, firewood, housing with heat and light – should be fulfilled.[165] In spite of this, and even though a standard daily wage of one ruble plus twenty-eight kopecks for food had been established by the governor-general, the issue of Kyrgyz and Kazakh workers' pay became the subject of a heated debate among Chu administrators in a series of meetings at the end of October 1916. Some suggested that the daily wage of one ruble could be raised or lowered "in connection with the diligence of the worker." Others referred to a circular of the Turkestan governor-general from 1882 that suggested that more workers were necessary for projects in Turkestan because the harsh climatic conditions in the region lowered worker productivity. By this kind of arithmetic, each Turkestani laborer was worth only a fraction of a worker outside of Turkestan, which argued for a *decrease* in salaries for Turkestan natives from one ruble to seventy-five kopecks. It was further suggested that "clumsy" workers be paid only 70 percent of the already reduced rate, meaning that even with a food allowance, the total daily pay for Turkestani workers designated "clumsy" would be a meager eighty kopecks. Eventually, it was decided to postpone this issue, as well as the question of what kinds of measures could be taken to force "kirgiz and dungans" who refused to obey or who worked poorly until word came from the governor-general.[166] Foreseeing work stoppages because of the bitter cold as winter approached, Vasil′ev requested advances for food, as well as permission to let some of the requisitioned workers go.[167]

As foreseen, many of those who stayed on the project fell ill with smallpox and typhus, malaria and bronchitis; even those who were young and ostensibly in good health died in the harsh working conditions in places such as the remote logging site in the Kemin Valley, the ancestral home of Shabdan-batyr of the Sarybagish Kyrgyz, who had long negotiated with the Russian government for those lands, and whose sons had been among the instigators of the uprising in Semireche.[168] In late January 1917, Vasil′ev reported a typhus outbreak to the governor-general in

[165] TsGA KR f. I-54, op. 1, d. 49, ll. 20–22ob: 21ob.

[166] TsGA KR f. I-54, op. 1, dd. 12, l. 218; 48, ll. 23–28.

[167] TsGA KR f. I-54, op. 1, dd. 48, ll. 2–3; 49, l. 78.

[168] TsGA KR f. I-54, op. 1, dd. 48, ll. 62–69, 84–85ob; 14, l. 15. For more on Shabdan Jantai (Dzhantaev), see Tetsu Akiyama, "On the Authority of a Kyrgyz Tribal Chieftain: The Funeral Ceremonies of Shabdan Jantai." www.orientphil.uni-halle.de/sais/pdf/2009-12-11/On_the_Authority_of_a_Kyrgyz_Tribal_Chieftain.pdf.

Tashkent and requested the aid of medical personnel, noting the absence of a Russian doctor and the lack of beds. Regional authorities were aware that showing paternal concern for the health of the local population would cause this news to "spread among the kirgiz workers" and might act to restore the local population's faith in the Russian government. Yet even the settler hospital in Pishpek had only six beds, and district officials feared infecting the troops in the city. The governor-general recognized the role of poor food and poor accommodations in worsening the typhus epidemic at the Chu Valley Irrigation Project, but in wartime conditions it was difficult to ameliorate the situation.[169] Even when ration allowances in Turkestan were raised to thirty-one kopecks, a Kazakh named Sargazy Itkuchukov wrote that, "In view of the rise in prices of all necessities at the current time [the allowance] is by no means sufficient ..." Confirming the governor-general's suspicions, he reported that in the earthen dugouts at the worksites, many workers fell ill because of the "spoiled [*isporchennyi*]" air, lack of food, and the difficult work; sick workers were not isolated from healthy ones, causing disease to spread. Vasil'ev could give no satisfactory reponses to Itkuchukov's calls for change.[170]

Another sign of continuing tensions between Russians and Central Asians in Semireche was the Chu project administration's call for soldiers to provide guard services and oversight at the worksites, and its request for additional rifles, revolvers, and bullets from the state artillery warehouses at any price.[171] The requisitioned workers continued to display subversive behavior, taking advantage of the reigning climate of fear to resist orders and drag their feet over their forced labor tasks. In December 1916, for instance, Vasil'ev had noted that the three hundred "kirgiz" working near Samsonovskoe were working particularly sluggishly, but that the technical personnel in the region would not take any forceful measures to ensure better work, for fear of further clashes.[172] In the spring of 1917, two groups of Kazakhs from Kargalinsk in Vernyi district who were requested to remain behind on the irrigation project while others were let go for two months to return home and work in the fields, refused to split up voluntarily. When requested to send a group of eighty-five workers to complete a specific task, none showed up. When asked which of them were best with horses and cattle, they replied that not a

169 TsGA KR f. I-54, op. 1, d. 49, ll. 35, 38, 40, 113.
170 TsGA KR f. I-54, op. 1, d. 59, ll. 46–46ob.
171 TsGA KR f I-54, op. 1, dd. 48, l. 7; 52, l. 100.
172 TsGA KR f. I-54, op. 1, d. 48, ll. 47–47ob.

single one of them knew how to deal with horses. (The perplexed Chu administrator's response to such a declaration coming from people who were ostensibly nomadic horsemen was: "In my opinion, a lie?") That evening, a rumor circulated that they were returning their tools and planned to report to Pishpek on their own for another service assignment.[173]

But the workers also had to be protected. One Kyrgyz worker from Kanaev volost′, for instance, who had been elected as a worksite leader, recounted an incident that had occurred while he was out looking for requisitioned workers who had been granted temporary home leave but had not yet returned. On his way, he met four shepherds, who recognized from a pin in his cap that he was doing military service. They beat him and took his horse, one hundred rubles, and his yellow *chapan* (robe). These were not unknown bandits; he knew each of them by name.[174] As this episode demonstrates, divisions in local society that had manifested themselves in the tensions over sedentarization and the uprising against the Russian government continued to play out over participation in and resistance to wartime service in the fall of 1916 and into 1917. In some cases, those summoned tried to find ways to evade service. A Dungan from Nikolaevskoe near Tokmak, for instance, reported that he had been signed up for work on the Chu project by a relative who was loath to send his own son. In other cases, relatives were simply signed onto the project in lieu of those who were absent on the day the mobilization lists were drawn up.[175]

Frustration with the way the entire mobilization affair had been conducted is evident in the report written up by another group of Dungans from Nikolaevskoe, who had just been released from the project, apparently for "poor work [performance]." They explained that they had been chosen "not by means of a legal list," since "those who could pay were not chosen" and claimed that this lack of legality had made them not want to work. They requested a "second draft [*prizyv*] by means of legal lists, [this time] not omitting the merchants . . ."[176] Like earlier complaints of nomads about the oppression of powerful volost′ officials, these complaints reflect tensions within indigenous communities over the local distribution of wealth and power, which emerged as individuals and communities attempted to negotiate the changes brought by Russian rule.

[173] TsGA KR f. I-54, op. 1, d. 83, ll. 185-ob.
[174] TsGA KR f. I-54, op. 1, d. 14, l. 83.
[175] TsGA KR f. I-54, op. 1, dd. 48, l. 1; 59, l. 138.
[176] TsGA KR f. I-54, op. 1, d. 49, l. 99.

Some Semireche inhabitants, on the other hand, may have been relieved to have the opportunity to fulfill their service so close to home, and not in the European trenches, as had been widely feared. A group of two hundred and twelve members of Botpaev volost′ in Vernyi district, for instance, wrote to Vasil′ev requesting work at the Chu project, even though they had heard that quotas had already been filled. They volunteered to bring their own yurts, sleeping pads, shovels, and hoes (ketmen) to supplement the Chu project's supplies.[177] A few even offered to sign up for active military duty, rather than working on the home front. The Semireche military governor's refusal to accept a petition to join the active ranks of the army from five Kyrgyz who were engaged on the Chu construction site suggests that, while their labor was accepted as necessary for the home front, overall distrust of the "natives" prevailed.[178]

In spite of the tensions in the Chu Valley, the restrictions of the wartime economy, and the bitter winter, Vasil′ev was determined to have the Chu Valley Irrigation Project succeed, as evidenced by the arrival in early 1917 of a foreign visitor who provided a ray of hope in these otherwise-dismal times. The visitor was a Dane named Hans Rützou, representative of concrete industry pioneer F. L. Smidth & Co., who was traveling in fulfillment of a contract from October 1915. Wartime restrictions and the freezing of the Baltic Sea had delayed the shipment of an expensive cement kiln and turbines from Denmark. With the arrival of the equipment in Russia, Rützou finally began the arduous journey to Semireche to help with its assembly, returning to Petrograd on February 21, 1917. After a brief detainment for "not having permission" to exit the Russian Empire, he somehow managed to leave on February 26, in the midst of the revolutionary activity that brought to an end the rule of the Romanov dynasty just four years after the triumphant celebration of its tercentenary.[179]

Vasil′ev continued to spend money on parts and expertise to make the cement kiln operational, yet as the spring of 1917 wore on, morale on the Chu Valley Irrigation Project was slipping, as it was in the empire as a whole.[180] Some administrative personnel banded together to form a "mutual aid union" with the workers, which clamored for (at least, Slavic) workers' recognition and sent its own greetings to recognize the Provisional Government formed in the wake of the tsar's abdication,

[177] TsGA KR f. I-54, op. 1, d. 59, l. 102. [178] TsGA KR f. I-54, op. 1, d. 49, l. 74.
[179] TsGA KR f. 1246, op. 1, d. 22, l. 13; f. I-54, op. 1, d. 64.
[180] TsGA KR f. I-54, op. 1, d. 64

along with seventy-four rubles and five kopecks "for a monument to freedom [*svoboda*]."[181] Toward the end of April, all forty-five of the remaining indigenous workers at one of the five worksites suddenly left. On May 7, 1917, the head of logging in the Kemin Valley reported that "recently all the kirgiz performing their military service, without exception, have been starting to behave extremely defiantly ..." and that between May 2 and 6 almost all had fled the logging site.[182] That same night, forty-three workers from Vernyi district fled another of the worksites. Since artels were organized by volost′, mass flight of workers to their home district was made easier and more likely. The widespread nature of the subversive behavior suggests the power of unofficial communication to spread quickly across the construction project. Concessions to workers, such as a later start to the workday, seemed to have little effect on labor retention.[183]

In fact, the requisitioned workers were completely justified in leaving, for on April 24, the Provisional Government of Russia had decreed that all "requisitioned sarts" were to be freed from military labor and sent home. "Sarts" technically referred only to the sedentary peoples of Turkestan, and not nomads, so the decree was officially extended to all inorodtsy on May 5 and publicized in Semireche by mid-month; it is possible that rumors, which spread more quickly in Turkestan than the telegraph wires could carry the news, had caused the mass exodus of indigenous workers in late April and early May.[184] By the end of May, Vasil′ev was requested to release all Central Asian workers from service, except for those who voluntarily wished to stay. Railroad engineer Tynyshpaev, who now represented the Provisional Government in Semireche, suggested that the requisitioned workers be replaced with Kyrgyz and Kazakhs who had fled to China in the aftermath of the violence of 1916, some of whom were now returning to find their abandoned lands seized by overeager settlers.[185] In anticipation of layoffs, some Chu engineers offered their "forces and knowledge" to the Provisional Government "for defense needs."[186]

[181] TsGA KR f. I-54, op. 2, d. 76, ll. 8, 14.
[182] TsGA KR, f. I-54, op. 1, d. 89, ll 19, 48.
[183] Ibid., ll. 23–23ob; TsGA KR f. I-54, op. 1, d. 81, ll. 158, 189.
[184] On the ability of nomads to spread news as if by telegraph, see Georgii K. Gins, "V Kirgizskikh aulakh," *IV* 134 (October 1913): 285–332: 296.
[185] TsGA KR f. I-54, op. 1, d. 59, ll. 55, 66, 80–80ob. On Tynyshpaev's mediation, see Olcott, *The Kazakhs*, 131.
[186] TsGA KR f. I-54, op. 2, d. 76, ll. 23, 33.

The chaotic political mood that characterized Petrograd and Moscow in the wake of the February Revolution penetrated even distant Semireche, where a distorted socialist rhetoric resounded through the streets of Pishpek. In April, an engineer named Lakomkin, formerly connected with the project, denounced Vasil′ev, claiming that the engineer continued to appropriate government funds for useless schemes to irrigate empty steppeland, solely in order to further his own career. Lakomkin helped stage a rally in Pishpek on April 30 to mobilize the local population against the "Vasil′ev party." According to one rather improbable account, seven thousand citizens and soldiers attended. Lakomkin claimed that settlers had been waiting nine years for water, while the "serf" labor of "kirgiz" and Dungans, who could have been sent to the front, had been used to water the empty steppe. In the aftermath of the violence of 1916, claimed Lakomkin, the land formerly occupied by nomads should go to the settlers, solving Semireche's problems. Yet, that would also mean an end to Vasil′ev's career, which is why Vasil′ev continued to trick "the People and the Ministers" into thinking that the Chu irrigation project was necessary. Iakov Fedorov, a representative of a local soldiers' council, stated that the "Vasil′ev party" had only caused harm to the defense of the empire and was keeping large tracts of land out of the hands of the people. He advised that the Provisional Government send the whole Chu administration to the front and liquidate the enterprise.[187] On May 13, a fire at a warehouse in Pishpek owned by Vasil′ev caused several thousand more rubles in damage to the already beleaguered project. The cause of the fire is not clear, but given the heated political climate, arson is not out of the question.[188]

In June, the *Turkestan Courier* printed an article about the "sorry state" of the Chu project and the money that had "flowed like a river" into – and out of – the hands of the project administration. Some of the accusations – such as there being no exact plan of the Chu irrigation system – seem to have been true, though the accusations are for the most part better reflections of the difficulties faced by the Chu administration, rather than its corruption. In what was an unauthorized sale of state property, for instance, Vasil′ev's assistant Petr Weymarn had conducted an auction of livestock that could no longer be fed by the shrinking project staff and budget. The money from the sale was put toward other aspects of the irrigation project. In another instance, Vasil′ev, who had

[187] RGIA f. 426, op. 3, d. 208, ll. 109, 170–171, 235–244ob.
[188] TsGA KR f. I-54, op. 1, d. 88, ll. 113, 146.

taken on the role of the head of Pishpek's "Public Committee," formed after the February Revolution, advanced fifty thousand rubles from the Chu project to the Public Committee, in order to help aid the spring 1917 sowing campaign. Though the Turkestan treasury board recognized that the act had been "beneficial for the well-being of the population of the krai," it had nonetheless been unauthorized.[189]

CONCLUSION

In the summer of 1917, as the Chu Valley Irrigation Project struggled to stay afloat through the political upheavals taking place far to the north, Russian settlers came together with local nomadic leaders to discuss the possibilities for reconciliation and the necessity of continuing the irrigation project in order to meet the needs of all. One Kyrgyz leader expressed his inability to understand why the Kyrgyz and the Russians could not live peacefully, as they had in the nineteenth century, under Semireche's first governor, Gerasim Alekseevich Kolpakovskii, who was said to have taken special measures to ensure friendly relations between Russians and the indigenous nomads.[190] To this, Slavs and Central Asians alike could now contrast the reign of Mikhail Fol'baum and his administration, a time of increased land seizures, haphazard Russian settlement, war privations, and violence, and a far cry from the fertile and abundant colony envisioned by Vasil'ev and other boosters for Semireche in 1913.[191] The atrocities on both sides had been horrific, yet some inhabitants of the Chu Valley persisted in hoping that the possibilities for mutual cooperation – and perhaps even mutual understanding – remained. It is impossible to know how Semireche would have continued to evolve, had the Bolsheviks not taken over in the region in 1918; as it was, the violence of Russian civil war and the resulting new regime only served to deepen existing rifts and create new ones.

189 RGIA f. 426, op. 3, d. 208, ll. 246, 275–277, 299. For more on the formation of such committees in the power vacuum after the February Revolution, see Buttino, *Revoliutsiia naoborot*, 143.

190 RGIA f. 432, op. 1, d. 5, ll. 17–19; Pahlen, *Mission to Turkestan*, 180.

191 *SOV* 244 (October 30, 1916), 2–3.

5

Sundering the Chains of Nature

Bolshevik Visions for Central Asia

> Nature had set up a barrier: native technology was not capable of surmounting it, and only the aid of the [Soviet] Union makes it possible to eternally tear asunder the many chains of slavery with which nature has fettered an entire people, and at the same time put in motion the complete liberation of our textile industry from the foreign cotton market.
>
> – Soviet engineer V. Poslavskii[1]

In the fall of 1923, the All-Russia Agricultural and Cottage Industrial Exhibition opened in Moscow. One of the most visible and visited buildings at the exhibition was the Turkestan Pavilion, with its eye-catching turquoise, yellow, and green mosaics. Visitors to the Turkestan Pavilion, like visitors to the First Semireche Agricultural and Industrial Exposition a decade earlier, would likely have noticed the prominent emphasis on irrigation. Even before entering the building, they passed models of irrigated areas in Turkestan. These models of "native" irrigation systems, placed next to "engineered" ones – that is, ones built using European engineering techniques – were reported to have drawn particular attention.[2] The contrast between the two models was intended to clearly demonstrate both the accuracy of water distribution along "engineered" systems, as well as how canal systems built using European engineering required only minimal funds and labor

[1] RGAE f. 4372, op. 16, d. 183, l. 33.

[2] K. M. Zubrik, "Turkvodkhoz na Vserossiiskoi sel'sko-khoziaistvennyi i kustarno-promyshlennoi vystavke," *VI* 9 (December 1923), 118–120: 118.

during operation.[3] This was contrasted to the large amounts of labor and labor-hours needed to build and maintain a "native" Turkestani irrigation system. The exhibition thus gave the impression that the new Bolshevik rulers of Russia were not only freeing the peoples of Turkestan from the oppressive forces of capitalism and colonialism; by means of engineering technologies, they were also freeing Central Asians from the onerous burdens of the physical environments in which they lived. By liberating the peoples of Central Asia from the drudgery of irrigation maintenance, the exhibition intimated, the Bolsheviks were setting in motion a process by which these supposedly "backward" Central Asians could at last join the modern world.

Abstract models could not hide the fact, however, that the Turkestan pavilion at the agricultural exhibition displayed few existing hydraulic engineering accomplishments. The only models of large-scale hydraulic projects were of the Hindu Kush dam at the Murghab Estate and the sluice gates of the main Hungry Steppe Canal, both achievements of tsarist engineers.[4] In the five years since the Bolsheviks had seized power, little had been done to improve the irrigation systems of Turkestan. Indeed, the process of consolidating Bolshevik rule in Turkestan had taken longer than in other parts of the former Russian Empire. Moreover, the chaos of civil war following the Bolshevik takeover in late 1917 had disrupted local cycles of canal observation and maintenance, leading to a rapid deterioration of many irrigation systems. In spite of Bolshevik financial support for irrigation construction in Turkestan, the large-scale hydraulic projects begun before the revolution – including the Chu Valley Irrigation Project – hampered by a lack of personnel, workers, and supplies, proceeded only haltingly.[5] This lack of progress was visible on a large irrigation map of the region displayed at the Turkestan Pavilion. Bolshevik hydraulic engineers stressed instead the potential for the future irrigation of Turkestan, which awaited only "the cultured hand of the engineer." Like Turkestan's irrigators before the revolution, as well as other enthusiastic denizens of the irrigation age, the pavilion's designers suggested the potential inherent in the Central Asian deserts which, with the right touch, could be made to spring to life. These messages were further conveyed by a photo kiosk emphasizing the modern nature of the

[3] A. Bykov, "Melioratsiia na Vserossiiskoi sel′sko-khoziaistvennoi vystavke," *VI* 2 (February 1924), 76–87: 85.

[4] Zubrik, "Turkvodkhoz na Vserossiiskoi . . .," 118.

[5] For Chu's predicament, see, for instance, TsGA KR, f. 486, op. 1, dd. 1; 2, ll. 19, 39, 68.

new regime. The kiosk displayed photographs of the latest innovations in hydraulic management – soon (ostensibly) to be introduced to Turkestan – accompanied, like other parts of the pavilion, by captions printed in the "Muslim language," to make sure Central Asians fully understood this new Bolshevik vision of progress.[6]

How "engineered" irrigation systems were to transform Central Asia under Bolshevik rule, however, was not entirely clear to all of the pavilion's visitors. Some excursion leaders informed their groups that canals existed to make Turkestan's dry climate "moist and cool." Others reported that the "native" systems had been accompanied by "great exploitation" (of the local population), whereas the "engineered" canals functioned "without exploitation." This confusion was apparently caused by *ekspluatatsiia*, the Russian word used to refer to the operation and maintenance of canals. Since the entire model was constructed from concrete, some explanation was also necessary to remind visitors that "in nature, everything is [made of] earth."[7]

According to an article about the exhibition, Russian peasant visitors were particularly interested in the model of a chigir brought from Khorezm. The peasants "touched, observed, sketched" the chigir, and asked about its cost and how it functioned. The chigir was not meant to be an object of fascination; rather, Turkestan's wooden water wheel was meant to represent the older, more primitive way of life giving way to the modern technology introduced by the Bolsheviks. Indeed, even though at least one prominent Soviet engineer argued that chigir irrigation utilized less water and led to less risk of salinization and waterlogging, an early goal of Bolshevik water management was to transform the exisiting chigir-driven irrigation in the Khorezm oasis to gravity irrigation.[8] And yet, grumbled the author of the article, even "with a good bucket chain excavator as part of the neighboring reclamation section ... the simplicity of ... [the chigir's] construction and materials, and its low price won over the heart of the peasant."[9] The supposed advantages of sophisticated engineering technologies were by no means evident to the peasant's practical eye.

Irrigation was also the theme of the pavilion of the Reclamation Department of the new People's Commissariat (i.e., Ministry) of Agriculture. On its exterior was printed the following verse, attributed to the

[6] Zubrik, "Turkvodkhoz na Vserossiiskoi ...," 119–120. [7] Ibid., 119.
[8] GARF f. 5674, op. 6, d. 666, l. 44ob; Tsinzerling, *Oroshenie na Amu-Dar'e*, 585–590.
[9] Zubrik, "Turkvodkhoz na Vserossiiskoi ...," 119.

legendary Assyrian queen Semiramis, who, it is said, confined the river Euphrates to its banks:

I made the rivers flow where I desired them to flow,

And I desired that they would flow only where they would be of use.

I transformed the barren land into fertile land,

Irrigating it with the rivers.[10]

The choice of the words of an ancient "Oriental despot" to adorn the pavilion designed to display the new and highly modern Soviet visions for the transformation of Turkestan may seem strange, but it was in keeping with the romanticized visions held by proponents of the irrigation age around the world of the ability of irrigation to unlock the potential of even the most barren-seeming earth. The same quotation had graced the frontispiece of the first annual publication of the American Society of Irrigation Engineers – of which Nikolai Dingel′shtedt had been an early member – in the early 1890s.[11] Grand Duke Nikolai Konstantinovich, who had died of natural causes shortly after the revolution, had used it to introduce his "Begovat Fairy Tale," in which he inscribed himself as an irrigator into a local version of the legend of Farhad and Shirin.[12] Prince Masal′skii quoted it, as well; he, too, had fantasized about a day when Russia could boast about "having brought to life dead lands with the water of the rivers, which presently are being lost to an ocean of air, [and of] having given our Fatherland a new, broad and rich country …," a new Turkestan.[13]

But whereas visions of tsarist-era irrigation proponents had been confined largely to imaginings of a glorious future based on legends about a glorious past, the Bolsheviks made it clear that their transformative vision

[10] Bykov, "Melioratsiia na Vserossiiskoi sel′sko-khoziaistvennoi vystavke," 76.

[11] *Annual of the American Society of Irrigation Engineers for 1892–93*, title page. The original source of this legend seems to be the French engineer François-Jacques Jaubert de Passa's *Les arrosages chez les Peuples Anciens* (1846), vol. 1; Jaubert de Passa in turn took it from Polyaenus the Macedonian's *Stratagems in War*.

[12] See Chapter 2. Based on archival materials, the Grand Duke appears to have died of illness, rather than being shot by the Bolsheviks. His death announcement in *Nasha Gazeta* in the "Local Chronicle" section, reads: "The funeral of citizen Romanov: Yesterday in Tashkent [was] the funeral of the former grand prince, citizen Nikolai Romanov, who died Sunday, January 14, at six am. Romanov's body was laid in the ground within the enclosure of the military cathedral. *NG* (13) (January 17, 1918), 2.

[13] Masal′skii, Vladislav Ivanovich *Amerikanskaia monopoliia i russkoe khlopkovodstvo* (Petrograd 1914), 25.

was an immediate and deeply practical one, as evidenced by the slogans adorning the interior of the pavilion: "Reclamation improves health and extends the life of the rural population," "There is no bad land – only bad farmers," "Knowledge and labor will bring life to the desert."[14] Health and productivity were hallmarks of a modern industrial society, and these slogans reflected the modernizing campaign of Turkestan's new rulers: a campaign that was to arm the people with new scientific knowledge, technology, and new forms of labor with which to "master" the obstacles of nature. This last idea of "mastering" the natural environment was particularly important in a region in which it was argued that the environment had halted the progress of the people who lived there, even if this emphasis on the importance of geography and climate to cultural development in part "contradicted the revolution's optimism."[15] Soviet rule was to transform lands that had for too long suffered under inept caretakers. At the same time, through modernizing the Soviet Central Asian environment, Central Asia's inhabitants would become modern, efficient, and productive, as well. Since modernity and progress were fundamental to the new regime's legitimacy, in Central Asia, successful mastery of nature as a means of defeating "backwardness" was a cornerstone of the Bolshevik program of transformation.[16]

WATER MANAGEMENT, SOVIET-STYLE

The 1923 All-Russia Agricultural and Cottage Industrial Exhibition was just one of many topics covered in the first issues of a new Tashkent-based journal, *The Irrigation Herald*. Beginning in 1923, it served as the free monthly publication of Vodkhoz, the Central Asian Water Administration. (Vodkhoz, an amalgamation of the two words in the phrase *vodnoe khoziaistvo* [water economy] was typical of the truncations, as well as acronyms, that quickly became part of a bewildering Bolshevik newspeak filling the pages of newspapers and echoing from loudpeakers across the Soviet Union in the 1920s.) Through the creation of this central organ of water management in Soviet Central Asia, the Bolsheviks fulfilled the wishes of those in Turkestan who before the revolution had called for more order and control to be brought to water management in the region. Theoretically, this institution should have helped to do away with the

[14] Bykov, "Melioratsiia na Vserossiiskoi sel'sko-khoziaistvennoi vystavke," 76–77.
[15] Francine Hirsch, "Getting to Know 'The Peoples of the USSR': Ethnographic Exhibits as Soviet Virtual Tourism, 1923–1934," *Slavic Review* 62, 4 (Winter 2003): 689.
[16] Slezkine, "Imperialism as the Highest Stage of Socialism," 228–229.

many uncertainties regarding water use that had plagued tsarist administrators and engineers, as well as streamline the procedures for overseeing both existing and new hydraulic projects in the region. From the beginning, however, Vodkhoz did not have a clear position within the Soviet administrative structure; instead, it had to compete with other governmental bodies overseeing hydraulic issues.

If the multitude of new organs of government introduced after 1917 and their catchy acronyms were not confusing enough, the plethora of government committees involved in decisions on the irrigation of Turkestan in the 1920s and early 1930s is bewildering. The irrigation of Turkestan, intimately tied to its economic role within the Soviet Union, as well as visions for the modernization and transformation of the region, was an undertaking in which almost every government body had an interest – interests that often conflicted. Perhaps unsurprisingly, therefore, through the 1920s Central Asian water management remained far from early Soviet hopes for the nationalization and centralized control of water resources in the region.

An initial vision of a streamlined system, under which the entire system of water management was to be coordinated at each level between a local or regional water management organ and the the corresponding organ of the administration, creating a uniform hierarchy from the Council of People's Commissars (Sovnarkom), the highest executive body in the Soviet government, at the center down to the mirabs in each locality, never was realized in practice.[17] Rather, from the summer of 1918 through 1924, a kaleidoscope of administrative bodies and construction agencies with shifting names and allegiances to the Supreme Soviet (Council) of the National Economy (VSNKh or Vesenkha), the Council of Labor and Defense (STO), and the People's Commissariat of Agriculture (Narkomzem) were responsible for water management in Turkestan.[18] Different branches of Turkestan's centralized water management dealing with sanitation, reclamation, transport, energy, and water reserves were handled by the respective ministries that normally handled such affairs. In the summer of 1925, the State Planning Committee (Gosplan), which was responsible for economic planning, reported

[17] See the 1922 "organizational scheme" for water management in RGAE f. 478, op. 3, d. 1644.

[18] GARF f. 5674, op. 6, d. 666, ll. 94ob-95; RGAE f. 4372, op. 16, d. 31a, l. 1; f. 2276, op. 1, d. 5, ll. 7–8; RGASPI f. 71, op. 34, d. 1642a, ll. 63–67; Bykov, "Melioratsiia na Vserossiiskoi sel'sko-khoziaistvennoi vystavke," 77–78.

that the scattering of these responsibilities across the people's commissariats (Bolshevik-speak for ministries) had led to "a diffusion of hydraulic specialists across various agencies, where the branches of Vodkhoz eke out a meager existence ..." A lack of unified legislation, moreover, was "serving as a brake on the rational use of the water resources of the [Soviet] Union."[19] The State Planning Committee itself, along with its rival, the People's Commissariat of Finance (Narkomfin), was involved in approving irrigation design and construction in Central Asia.[20]

In May 1927, the Workers' and Peasants' Inspectorate (Rabkrin) – which also played an important role in Soviet economic planning and construction in the 1920s and had its own "irrigation group" to help recruit specialists and experts for Vodkhoz – liquidated the Moscow Vodkhoz office, which until that point had been responsible for issues of supply, and transferred its responsibilities to an irrigation committee under the Council of People's Commissars (Sovnarkom). This irrigation committee, in turn, had been formed in August of the previous year "for the unification and regulation of the activities of water management in the cotton-growing regions of the USSR," and contained representatives from the federated regions of Central Asia, the Caucasus, and Russia, the People's Commissariat of Finance, and two other economic organs under the Council of People's Commissars, the Supreme Soviet of the National Economy, and the Economic Council (EKOSO). Functions of this irrigation committee included introducing legislation on water issues, undertaking large-scale irrigation construction projects, planning and budgeting hydraulic projects, and publishing reports and journals on issues of water management.[21] The emphasis on the cotton-growing regions demonstrates their importance within plans for the development of the Soviet economy and explains why the irrigation committee was subsumed to the highest executive body in the Soviet government.

The Council of Labor and Defense (STO) also created a special commission in 1924, formed from representatives of many of the same government organs listed above, as well as the OGPU (secret police), and sent in late 1925 to Turkestan specifically to review irrigation practices and

[19] RGAE f. 4372, op. 16, d. 15, l. 149.

[20] Christian Teichmann, "Canals, Cotton and the Limits of De-colonization," *Central Asian Survey* 26, 4 (2007): 505. Attempts were made in 1928 to more clearly delineate the separate roles of these institutions in irrigation planning. "Moskva – Sredniaia Aziia," *PV* 42 (February 20, 1928), 2.

[21] GARF f. 374, op. 19, d. 4, l. 105; f. 3292, introduction to Opis′ 1, ll. 1–3; Teichmann, *Macht der Unordnung*, 101–102.

spending.[22] From the beginning, the Central Cotton Committee (Glavkhlopkom), formed in 1921 under the Supreme Soviet of the National Economy, placed a particular emphasis on improvement of existing irrigation systems in cotton regions and the irrigation of new lands.[23] This followed tsarist-era precedent in which the Ministry of Agriculture's Central Cotton Committee had been consulted when devising legislation and procedures regarding the irrigation of new lands in Turkestan. Finally, with the restoration of irrigation in Central Asia closely tied to the improvement of health in the region, representatives from the People's Commissariat of Health (Narkomzdrav) were tasked with reviewing the technical drafts of all pending hydraulic engineering projects in Central Asia.[24]

One point on which all interested bodies could agree was that the restoration of irrigation systems was crucial to restoring order and ensuring stability in Turkestan, as well as furthering the region's development. In the wake of the Bolshevik Revolution, provisions were quickly made to ensure that irrigation work in Turkestan continue, in spite of political upheavals. The newspaper *Sword of the People*, a publication of the Council of Workers', Soldiers', Peasants', and Muslims' Deputies in Tashkent, reported in March 1918 that all hydraulic and irrigation projects in Turkestan were to come under the direct control of the People's Commissariat of Agriculture. All officials were required to stay at their posts and maintain their responsibilities, under threat of arrest and sentencing in a revolutionary court.[25]

Two months later, in May 1918, a decree approved by chairman of the Council of People's Commissars and Communist Party leader Vladimir Lenin made provisions for an administration of irrigation projects in Turkestan (IRTUR) under the Supreme Council of the National Economy. To promote the continuation of cotton agriculture, the Council of People's Commissars allocated fifty million rubles for irrigation projects in Turkestan, to be given in six installments over the course of 1918, and to be aimed at the large-scale projects that were already under construction in the region, including the projects to irrigate the Hungry Steppe and the Chu River Valley, the latter of which was to receive three

[22] GARF f. 7817, introduction to Opis' 1, l. 1; f. 5674 op. 6, d. 666, ll. 3, 5, 8.

[23] *Polozhenie o Glavnom khlopkovom komitete* (Moscow: VSNKh, 1924), 4; Iuferev, *Khlopkovodstvo v Turkestane* (Leningrad: RAN, 1925), 122–124.

[24] Cassandra Marie Cavanaugh, "Backwardness and Biology: Medicine and Power in Russian and Soviet Central Asia, 1868–1934" (PhD diss., Columbia University, 2001), 173.

[25] RGASPI f. 71, op. 34, d. 1642a, ll. 48–49, excerpt from *ShchN* (March 26, 1918).

million rubles that summer.[26] The conditions of civil war, however, isolated Turkestan from central Russia, which prevented IRTUR from immediately moving its headquarters to Tashkent. According to Bolshevik officials in Central Asia, through the summer of 1920 a trip from Moscow to Tashkent could take ten to fifteen weeks.[27]

Because questions of Central Asia's water resources remained intimately bound up with issues of land use, in December 1917, the Tashkent Council of People's Commissars called for the formation of "Committees for Land and Water" (*zemel'no-vodnye komitety*) that were to be the first step toward state-led land and water reform.[28] The land-water committees were introduced region-wide by the Turkestan commissar of agriculture in January 1918; by October, there were forty water committees operating on small-scale irrigation systems that sent their representatives to a district-level water committee, which in turn sent its representatives to a regional water committee.[29] Private property was not abolished, however, and the Red Army's struggle to consolidate control in Central Asia hampered Bolshevik attempts to enact revolutionary measures in land and water governance in the region.[30] A water law drafted by a multi-bureau commission – like the one that had worked to devise a water law in the years before the collapse of the tsarist empire – became the "Decree on the utilization of water in the Turkestan Soviet Socialist Republic" in 1921, but this law was never put into action and was replaced by another law in August 1922.[31] This second law was "far more modest"; in it, as well as in the April 1924 "Temporary Rules Concerning Water in the Turkestan Republic," the goals of nationalization and the central control of water resources were temporarily abandoned in favor of water use based on "custom," provided that custom did not conflict with new Soviet laws.[32]

Vodkhoz continued to place the main burden of water distribution on elected and appointed officials at the community and irrigation system level – junior and senior mirabs, elected by communities of water users and confirmed by the local branch of the party's executive committee

[26] RGASPI f. 71, op. 34, d. 1642a, ll. 59–60 (May 17, 1918); for the continued necessity of Chu for the cotton-growing regions, see GARF f. 5674, op. 5, d. 146, l. 1.

[27] RGASPI f. 670, op. 1, d. 57, l. 142.

[28] Niccolò Pianciola, and Paolo Sartori, "Waqf in Turkestan: The colonial legacy and the fate of an Islamic institution in early Soviet Central Asia, 1917–24," *Central Asian Survey* 26, 4 (December 2007): 480.

[29] I. E. Semenov and A. I. Rakhimov, *Razvitie irrigatsii v Kirgizii* (Frunze, 1987), 14–15.

[30] Waqf as property was not abolished until the late 1920s throughout Central Asia (Pianciola and Sartori, "Waqf in Turkestan," 489).

[31] RGAE f. 4372, op. 16, d. 30, l. 400b.

[32] Thurman, "Modes of Organization," 129.

(though in 1924 there was a move toward appointing senior mirabs, rather than electing them); and ariq aqsaqals, who were appointed and confirmed by the heads of district and regional branches of Vodkhoz.[33] Ariq aqsaqals were still responsible for oversight of both the main canal on an irrigation system as well as the activities of the mirabs engaged on its branches. In a continuation of the tsarist attempt to standardize water management by giving it a scientific foundation, courses for the scientific training of water overseers were introduced to the curriculum of the Technical Department of the newly formed Turkestan People's University. Like the Tashkent hydraulic engineering school, the Technical Department offered courses in arithmetic and geometry, geodesy, hydrometry, agricultural hydraulic engineering, meteorological observation, and drafting.[34] While it is not clear how many indigenous pupils such courses attracted, one change brought with the revolution was that by the late 1920s, at least in the Ferghana Valley, some women were elected to mirab positions; in other places, large numbers of women showed up for the elections.[35]

Overall, however, the revolution brought few immediate changes to water use in Turkestan. Maintenance of water distribution systems continued to be carried out by able-bodied, male water users in the form of a "duty-in-kind" (*natural'naia povinnost'*). As laid out in Decree Number 60 of the Turkestan Council of People's Commissars in April 1923, the "duty-in-kind" was the "usual, necessary, and unavoidable work of every water user" – that is, a fixed amount of unpaid labor directed toward the maintenance of the irrigation system. "Water users" required to spend time on the upkeep of the canal continued to be men between the ages of eighteen and forty-five using their own tools.[36] Though there were discussions about replacing the old system, desire for the smooth functioning of irrigation systems dictated continuity until such tasks could be transferred to hired workers.[37] In some places, while waiting for official instructions, local inhabitants took matters into their own hands, using their own funds and labor to keep canals functioning.[38]

33 STO's December 1924 resolution on appointment was not fulfilled in 1925 (GARF f. 5674, op. 6, d. 666, l. 111); Thurman, "Modes of Organization," 145–146.

34 *Obzor prepodavaniia na kursakh mirabov po podgotovke masterov-polival'shchikov vodomershchikov, vodnykh nadziratelei, vodnykh starost i t.p.*, 2nd edn. (Tashkent: Turkestanskii Narodnyi Universitet, Tekhnicheskii fakul'tet, 1918), 3–4.

35 RGASPI f. 62, op. 2, dd. 1431, ll. 4–5, 9; 1497, l. 14ob.

36 "Postanovlenie SNK Turkestanskoi Respubliki (April 5, 1923, No. 60)," *VI* 1 (April 1923), 92–94: 92. A TsIK decree of December 1920 had declared a "trudovaia povinnost'" for all men between 16 and 50. RGASPI f. 122, op. 1, d. 131, l. 53.

37 GARF f. 5674, op. 6, d. 666, ll. 51ob-52.

38 See, for example, "Bezvod'e v poselke Sretenskom," *NG* 8 (January 11, 1918), 2; GARF f. 5674, op. 5, d. 146, ll. 1–1ob.

FIGURE 5.1 Khivan irrigation official [1920s?]. "Native engineer, the chief irrigator of the Khivinsky khan."
Reproduced with permission from the Willard L. Gorton Papers, Hoover Institution Archives, Stanford, CA.

HUNGER IN TURKESTAN

With local governance in flux, a large percentage of Turkestan's existing irrigation systems deteriorated. The All-Russia Agricultural and Cottage Industrial Exhibition in Moscow in 1923 strove to show the strength and potential of a united Russia that was "not in ruins" after years of war and violence.[39] Yet, much of Turkestan – in particular its irrigation

[39] Zubrik, "Turkvodkhoz na Vserossiiskoi …," 120.

systems – was, in fact, in ruins. It has been estimated that between 1915 and 1920, the amount of cultivated land declined by half and the amount of livestock decreased by almost two-thirds.[40] A report of the Turkestan Commission, the central Bolshevik government organ formed to oversee matters pertaining to the region, stated that "anarchy has placed its heavy stamp on the existing [irrigation] system. Drainage systems are partially destroyed, partially non-functioning."[41] Much of the previously usable land in Turkestan became unusable, and cotton production virtually ceased. In 1921, there were also particularly severe spring floods, which washed out the control mechanisms on a number of irrigation systems. Soviet engineers assigned a higher priority to canal repair than to reclamation of salinized and waterlogged lands, with the result that in the early 1920s many settlers either left the Hungry Steppe for other parts of Russia or abandoned salinized plots, only to repeat the same process of ruining the land elsewhere. Even where fields were in reasonable condition, the precipitous decline in livestock made it harder to plow the fields, while simultaneously depriving fields of much-needed fertilizer.[42]

Alongside the decline in Turkestan's cultivated acreage, other factors threatened the region's food supply. The many years of war and political upheavals had slowed the project to turn Semireche into a granary that could supply the cotton-growing regions of Turkestan with food. The difficult political circumstances of 1916–1917 were exacerbated by weather: that winter had been particularly dry, meaning less water from the mountains for the fields in the summer of 1917. In 1919, Pavel Nazarov, a scientist and naturalist fleeing Bolshevik rule, headed toward the Chinese border under the pretense of undertaking "'hydrotechnical investigations,' a rather artful term which would be incomprehensible to the half-educated Bolsheviks and place me in a position of superiority," as he wryly put it. He noted that many of the irrigation canals in former

40 Marco Buttino, "Study of the Economic Crisis and Depopulation in Turkestan, 1917–1920," *Central Asian Survey* 9, 4 (1990): 61; Alexander Park estimates that the total irrigated acreage in Turkestan declined by almost four million acres between 1915 and 1922 in all of Central Asia, and in Turkestan (excluding Bukhara and Khiva) from 6,523,400 to 3,212,300 acres. Park, *Bolshevism in Turkestan*, 299.

41 RGASPI f. 122, op. 1, d. 106, l. 110b.

42 "K voprosu o bor′be s solonchakami v Golodnoi stepi," *VI* 6 (September 1923), 11–19; P. Putilov, "Sovremennoe polozhenie Golodnoi Stepi," *VI* 1 (January 1924), 6–13: 8; RGASPI f. 71, op. 34, d. 1642a, l. 69; RGAE f. 478, op. 3, d. 1645, l. 9.

Kyrgyz regions of the Chu River Valley had been destroyed by vengeful Slavic settlers following the uprising of 1916.[43] When combined with Turkestan's isolation from Russia, the food situation in the region turned dire.

In the upheavals of the civil war, disruptions to government and railway transport deprived Central Asia of crucial grain shipments, with the result that already in 1918 – well before the better-known famine in southern Russia in 1921 – Turkestan teetered on the brink of starvation. Even where railway lines were intact, a fuel shortage hindered the transport of essential food supplies. Saxaul became scarce, and in Pishpek it was reported that saltwort (tumbleweed) was being sold for one thousand rubles per bundle.[44] Railway locomotives may have burned anything from cottonseed oil to dried fish in an attempt to continue operations.[45]

The flourishing of a black market further complicated efforts to provision Central Asia. In 1917 and 1918, a Bolshevik named Liapin, who in the guise of a "Provisions Commissar" was charged with ensuring that shipments of grain reached Turkestan, recorded that every day he received up to fifty telegrams from Turkestan entreating him to send grain. So-called *meshochniki* ("bagmen"), who were keeping Russian cities alive by exchanging household goods in rural areas for food, were willing to pay twenty times the normal price for a pood of grain, making it nearly impossible for officials such as Liapin to secure grain for cash. Liapin reported offering peasants in the steppes south of Orenburg hundreds of meters of cloth, as well as hundreds of pounds each of sugar, soap, butter, tea, kerosene, and petroleum, in exchange for one thousand poods of grain, but was met with the demand for a million rubles, or else the equivalent in goods. Peasants in Siberia were confiscating goods destined for Turkestan and, thus, had no need for what he was offering.[46] In April 1918, the *Sword of the People* reported masses of starving people in the streets of Skobelev in the Ferghana Valley, and in May it reported on systematic theft in Russia of grain bound for Central Asia. In an attempt to prevent "a grain crisis in the near future," the Tashkent City

[43] RGAE f. 4372, op. 27, d. 354, l. 25ob; Nazaroff, *Hunted through Central Asia*, 128, 166.
[44] TsGA KR f. 89, op. 1, d. 191, ll. 11–11ob.
[45] Ian Murray Matley, "Agricultural Development (1865–1963)," in ed. Edward Allworth, *Central Asia: 130 Years of Russian Dominance, a Historical Overview*, 3rd edn. (Durham, NC: Duke University Press, 1994), 284.
[46] RGASPI f. 71, op. 34, d. 1638, ll. 1–7.

Provisions Committee lowered grain allowances for citizens to a quarter pound per day.[47]

Yet, in spite of the fact that Turkestan was starving, as in other parts of Bolshevik Russia local party officials instituted a policy that became known as war communism, an attempt to bring about a communist system through the forced requisitioning of grain, livestock, and other commodities. In Turkestan, this policy was meant to ensure that farmers had no incentive to replace cotton with grain or rice, since the entire harvest of any crop went to the state for redistribution. Support for cotton was further strengthened by a 1920 decree of the Russian Council of People's Commissars, "On the resurrection of cotton culture in the Turkestan and Azerbaijan SSRs."[48] Desperate farmers still replaced the cotton crop with food, but it was not enough. In a report to Lenin in September 1920, Red Army commander on the Eastern Front Mikhail Frunze reported that "the question of provisioning Turkestan is close to a catastrophic situation. The disruption of agriculture is so great that Turkestan cannot supply itself with grain, even [though] ... the entire area that once was planted with cotton is now planted with cereals."[49] All told, according to historian Marco Buttino, food shortages, epidemics, and conflict between 1917 and 1920 led to the deaths of fully one-quarter of the indigenous Central Asian population.[50]

Like others throughout the country after the revolution, Central Asians displayed fierce resistance to requisitioning. In Central Asia, such resistance became conflated with anti-Bolshevik opposition. Assuming all such opposition to be unified, the Bolsheviks labeled them *basmachi* (bandits). (Organized resistance groups themselves used *qo'rboshi*, a military title.[51]) Though these *basmachi* have been described as destroying infrastructure, including irrigation networks, even those who were opposed to Bolshevik rule needed to eat. The "systematic burning of cotton reserves and cotton-cleaning factories" observed by the Bolsheviks was symbolic

47 Ibid., 20; "Prodovol'stvie," *ShchN* 98 (May 25 [12], 1918), 2.

48 *Irrigatsiia Uzbekistana v chertyekh tomakh*, 1 (Tashkent: Izd. FAN UzSSR, 1975), 6.

49 RGASPI f. 71, op. 34, d. 1607, l. 8.

50 Around 1,600,000 people. Marco Buttino, "Politics and Social Conflict during a Famine: Turkestan Immediately after the Revolution" in ed. Marco Buttino, *In a Collapsing Empire: Underdevelopment, Ethnic Conflicts and Nationalisms in the Soviet Union* (Milan: Fondazione Giangiacomo Feltrinelli, 1993), 258. Ian Murray Matley places the figure for famine deaths between 1919 and 1923 at "well over a million" ("Agricultural Development," 286).

51 Northrop, *Veiled Empire*, 15.

of indigenous frustration, yet destroying factories may also have had the goal, as Jonathan Michael Thurman has argued, of "capturing" water by diverting it away from the factory.[52] Certainly, the replacement of cotton with foodstuffs was more a practical measure than a sign of ideological resistance to the new regime.[53]

Seeing all resistance to Bolshevik policies in Turkestan as coherent also ignores the persistence of fault lines running through Turkestani society that did not clearly separate Soviet partisans from "natives." Bolshevik officials themselves noted in-fighting among various qo'rboshi.[54] And while some Central Asians attempted to subvert Soviet rule, as they had attempted to subvert tsarist rule, other Central Asians sided with the Bolsheviks. As Adeeb Khalid's work has shown, the modernist reformers known as the jadids found much in common with Bolshevik visions for modernizing the region. There were groups of qo'rboshi and their leaders who fought for the Bolsheviks, as well as Central Asian Red Army units.[55] On the other side were Russians who wished to see the restoration of imperial rule, as well as White Army troops fighting at the head of "bandit" groups against the Bolsheviks. One Bolshevik report claimed that White Army officers – who were usually from the former tsarist army – were training rebels in Ferghana and helping them to destroy cotton and stores of provisions.[56] Some Central Asians simply supported whichever side might bring stability to the chaos and violence following years of war and upheaval. In 1920, for instance, two Central Asians, in a letter to "Citizen proletarians and subjugated and oppressed Muslims," urged their neighbors in Ferghana to restore order to the region by supporting Soviet power, "the only power that exists at the present time and [one] which has been chosen by the people," rather than aiding the destructive, looting activities of the "basmachi," whose murderous activities, they argued, were against sharia law.[57]

Among those who did not accept the legitimacy of the new regime were the Semireche Cossacks who, in the wake of the Bolshevik seizure of power in October 1917, had claimed powers of self-government, "until the resurrection of communications with the center and the legal power of

[52] Thurman, "Modes of Organization," 136–137; RGASPI f. 670, op. 1, dd. 51, l. 226; 57, l. 50.

[53] Iuferev, *Khlopkovodstvo v Turkestane*, 107.

[54] RGASPI f. 670, op. 1, d. 57, l. 101ob.

[55] Khalid, *The Politics of Muslim Cultural Reform*, 288; RGASPI f. 71, op. 34, d. 1607, ll. 6, 12–13.

[56] RGASPI f. 670, op. 1, d. 51, l. 236.

[57] Ibid., l. 255.

the Provisional Government." According to Frunze, through 1920 Semireche continued to conduct its own policies, some of which were in conflict with orders issuing from Tashkent.[58] One Semireche Cossack who styled himself "Qo'rboshi Vasilii Donets [of the Don]" was said to have become a hero in Ferghana when he and his "Russian kulak division" joined the rebels there.[59] Cossack leader Alexander Dutov, from his refuge in neighboring Xinjiang, voiced his support for the anti-Soviet activities of these groups. Russian peasants, who like Turkestanis objected to confiscation of their grain, often felt more affinity with the violent resistance of the so-called basmachi and their slaughtering of "provisions workers" than with the violent requisitioning tactics of the Red Army.[60]

As Khalid and Buttino have demonstrated, in spite of the Bolshevik trumpeting of equality and liberation, indigenous Turkestanis were subjected to deliberate and ongoing measures on the part of the new Soviet government that favored the Slavic population.[61] In 1921, famine resulting from the requisitioning policies of war communism, and exacerbated by drought, once again gripped the central and southern regions of Russia. Peasants fleeing central Russia, like their predecessors in the 1890s, once again saw Turkestan as a haven. In spite of the fact that Turkestanis themselves did not have enough food, and although Bolshevik officials privately admitted that some of the trouble in Turkestan was due to the fact that as early as 1918, "Russians got grain, but the sarts didn't get so much as a pound," the Bolshevik government directed starving migrants from central Russia to Turkestan.[62] In the summer of 1921, a Bolshevik propaganda train traveled through Turkestan, no doubt extolling the virtues of Bolshevik rule to an audience that had yet to see any real transformation in their lives for the better. Paid only half their wages and facing starvation themselves, the actors put on at least fifty-seven performances over the course of four months.[63] At the end of the summer, the Central Economic Council of Turkestan reported Turkestan's acceptance of 200,000 starving migrants from other parts of Soviet Russia, in spite of the fact that in November 1920, in an effort to contain conflict, the Turkestan Central Executive Committee and the Council of

[58] TsGA KR f. I-54, op. 1, d. 15, l. 79; RGASPI f. 71, op. 34, d. 1607, l. 4.

[59] RGASPI f. 670, op. 1, d. 51, ll. 228, 236, 247.

[60] Ibid., ll. 226, 236.

[61] Adeeb Khalid, "Tashkent 1917: Muslim Politics in Revolutionary Turkestan," *Slavic Review* 55, 2 (Summer 1996): 290; Buttino, "Politics and Social Conflict during a Famine," 259.

[62] RGASPI f. 670, op. 1, d. 51, l. 266ob.

[63] RGASPI f. 122, op. 1, d. 70, ll. 177–178.

People's Commissars had forbidden settlers from entering Turkestan, as well as any "voluntary" (i.e., unsanctioned) occupation of land.[64]

The arrival of such large numbers of migrants threatened to drive Turkestan even deeper into the arms of starvation. To the world, however, the Bolsheviks announced that Russia was counting on the levy of tons of food from Turkestan.[65] Such reports led foreign aid organizations to assume that Turkestan had surplus grain for export. Directed by Herbert Hoover, the American Relief Association (ARA) sent sixty million dollars to Soviet Russia in aid. Though central party leaders were well aware that "the financial situation of Turkestan is catastrophic," no monetary aid went to Turkestan.[66] Soup kitchens were set up throughout central and southern Russia that would feed people until 1923, yet no soup kitchens were established in Turkestan, whose plight remained invisible to the eyes of the world.[67]

Walter Duranty, the Moscow bureau chief for the *New York Times* who would later come under fire for underreporting Soviet atrocities, seems to have made only oblique reference to Turkestan in the context of the Volga famine, when he reported in January 1922 that Soviet authorities had halted trains going to Turkestan because of the prevalence of typhus there.[68] That spring, the newspaper published a report by the Reverend Julius Hecker, who, when touring famine-ravaged central Russia, found that "the situation surpassed even his worst expectations ... I have seen refugee trains," Hecker wrote, "that for four months were creeping toward the southeast to the promised land of Turkestan. How many of these unfortunates will survive the privations of the long journey I do not venture even to guess."[69] He apparently did not know that there would be little food for them at their destination.

In June 1922, the members of the executive committee of the Tokmak subdistrict party committee (*raikom*) in Turkestan's Chu River Valley noted the circulation of distressing rumors. They feared that new arrivals from central Russia might believe "cannibalism" (the agitated secretary was not even sure how to spell the term) to be a local custom. Deciding

64 RGASPI f. 122, op. 1, dd. 149, l. 27; 90, l. 56.

65 Cyril Brown, "Russia's Only Hope in New Food Levy," *NYT* (July 20, 1921), 2.

66 RGASPI f. 122, op. 1, d. 42, l. 1.

67 Hakan Kirimli, "The Famine of 1921–22 in the Crimea and the Volga Basin and the Relief from Turkey," *Middle Eastern Studies* 39, 1 (January 2003): 39.

68 Walter Duranty, "Plague of Typhus Sweeps over Russia," *NYT* (January 6, 1922), 6.

69 "Tells of Deaths on Famine Trains: Dr. Hecker, After Tour of Stricken Russia, Describes Ravages of Hunger and Typhus," *NYT* (March 26, 1922), 33.

that the rumors were clearly an act of counterrevolution designed to undermine Soviet rule, the *raikom* executive committee urged its members to hasten to assure both the local Russian and Muslim populations that the rumors were not true.[70] Whether or not the rumors were true, the fact that the rumor was credible enough to be a subject for discussion at a local party meeting is significant. In a telegram to the Kremlin, Bolshevik officials reported "massive cases of hunger deaths" in Tashkent and other regions, "primarily among poor Muslims," along with gatherings of workers to protest the "massive export of grain outside the borders of Turkestan." After Red Army raids, many bazaars had to close for lack of provisions. "No one is regulating this bacchanalian export of provisions out of Turkestan," they concluded. Meanwhile, thousands of starving people were stranded at the stations of Turkestan; they could not be moved without the Turkestan Commission's official approval.[71]

Famine and disease went hand-in-hand. In spite of the fact that in December 1921 the Central Executive Committee ordered a halt on selling railway tickets to private citizens on the Turkestan line, the Extraordinary Commission on the Fight against Epidemics noted in early 1922 that "large numbers of refugees from the starving provinces are continuing to come into Turkestan, the majority of whom are infected with typhus."[72] In Turkestan, particularly in the hot summer months, many susceptible famine refugees from places like the Volga, often already suffering from diseases such as cholera and typhus, encountered a different strain of malaria from that to which they had previously been exposed.[73] In places such as the Hungry Steppe, in particular, but also farther downstream in Perovsk district on the Syr Darya, the arrival of new bodies susceptible to the disease was a factor in helping severe strains of malaria to propagate, even when it was dissipating elsewhere.[74] In the Hungry Steppe, the waterlogging of irrigation systems (itself a result of neglect) meant that malaria had "grown monstrously … and taken on a terrible tropical form that results in the death of the afflicted," according

[70] TsGA PD KR f. 1, op. 1, d. 4, ll. 92ob-93ob.

[71] RGASPI f. 122, op. 1, d. 42, ll. 76, 121–122, 135 ob.

[72] Ibid., l. 33.

[73] "Khronika," *TMZh* 3 (March 1925), 194; Cavanaugh, "Backwardness and Biology," 170; TsGA KR f. 20, op. 1, d. 313, l. 10ob, table on malaria in Frunze in 1925–1926.

[74] N. I. Khodukin, "Vodnyi faktor i epidemiologiia maliarii v Golodnoi stepi za sezon 1924," as cited in a review in *TMZh* 4, 4 (April 1925), 240; Dr. V. A. Dobrokhotov, "Zabolevaemost′ naseleniia Perovskogo uezda [Ak-Mechetskogo]," *TMZh* 4, 6 (June 1925), 369–380: 375; M. F. Mirochnik, "Immunitet i reaktsiia komplementa pri maliarii," *TMZh* 4, 1 (January 1925), 1–10: 2.

to the Turkestan Commission. Comparing the Hungry Steppe to a hospital, the commission reported that 90 percent of the technicians in the Hungry Steppe had fallen ill, and "there is not a single house without a malarial patient."[75] Even indigenous Central Asians reported higher numbers of malaria cases in the region of the Hungry Steppe.[76] The newly formed swamps, which served as breeding grounds for mosquitoes, became part of a vicious cycle, since the disease they helped spread further prevented proper oversight of the irrigation system.[77]

The lack of an extensive hospital network in Turkestan and inadequate supplies of quinine led physicians to advocate addressing water management as a way to help prevent the spread of malaria.[78] The restoration of the irrigation system was, thus, deemed crucial not only for economic recovery in the region, but also for the population's health and well-being, as encapsulated in the phrase "Reclamation improves health and extends the life of the rural population."[79] However, Bolshevik officials, in their haste to restore irrigation systems, often allowed Vodkhoz officials to overrule anti-malarial restrictions in economic priority areas, such as the Hungry Steppe and the Merv Oasis.[80] Since central authorities believed rice in some regions was interfering with cotton cultivation, the image of the rice plantation as a breeding ground for malaria continued to serve as a convenient official justification for attacking local rice production.[81]

Soviet engineers argued that the "malarial nature [*malariinost'*] of Central Asia [was a] legacy of the past, and an indicator of the cultural and economic backwardness of the province [*krai*]." They were confident that, with the aid of "a collective of water workers, in contact with malariologists under the conditions of Soviet power," malaria could be beaten. Malaria was simply the "dues" to be paid "for the primitive condition of irrigation which had arisen and existed under the conditions of man's oppression of man." The "first and last task of a water

75 RGASPI f. 122, op. 1, d. 106, ll. 11 ob-12. On health care for irrigation workers in the Hungry Steppe, see Cavanaugh, "Backwardness and Biology," 176–177. See also "K voprosu o bor'be s solonchakami v Golodnoi stepi."

76 G. I. Demov, "Maliariia i irrigatsiia v Turkestane," *VI* 6 (June 1924): 38–45: 42–43.

77 RGASPI f. 122, op. 1, d. 106, ll. 11 ob-12; Demov, "Maliariia i irrigatsiia v Turkestane," 44.

78 Cavanaugh, "Backwardness and Biology," 172.

79 RGAE f. 4372, op. 16, d. 30, l. 49.

80 Cavanaugh, "Backwardness and Biology," 167, 173–174.

81 RGASPI f. 62, op. 2, d. 1431, l. 7; GARF f. 374, op. 1, d. 236, l. 19.

manager" was "to deliver water without malaria." Once the irrigation system could be improved, malaria, like other obstacles to progress, would disappear as well. "The fight against malaria is the fight for water," an article in the *Irrigation Herald* concluded."[82] This called for the continued mobilization of all of Turkestan's available resources to restore the region's irrigation systems.

IRRIGATION RECONSTRUCTION

The *Irrigation Herald* proclaimed that, unlike other branches of the economy, water management in Turkestan would not be content with a mere return to "prewar conditions," since "the state of water management before the war was unsatisfactory." Water management needed to be "not only thoroughly rebuilt, but created practically anew ..."[83] But even the basic reconstruction of Turkestan's irrigation systems was a massive undertaking. In April 1919, all specialists in Turkestan between the ages of twenty and fifty with skills useful for the restoration of irrigation systems had been mobilized by Turkestan's Council of People's Commissars. Any economists, statisticians, engineers, and technicians residing in the region who refused to show up for registration to the local organ of water management or the construction projects in the Hungry Steppe and the Chu Valley were to be subject to the "laws governing wartime conditions."[84] The country was still at war – no longer with Europe, but with itself. Even with this "mobilization," however, there were not enough water specialists to complete the enormous task of restoring and maintaining Central Asia's irrigation systems. A January 1920 Turkestan Commission report warned that "*irrigation is in danger*," underlining the urgency of the need for rapid Soviet transformation. As the report put it:

> If in the current conditions it is not possible to increase irrigation of these spaces, then the preservation and maintenance of the irrigation of this land – the base of all kinds of life in Turkestan – is a task of the first order, and there is no other matter in Turkestan which may compare in this regard with irrigation. This truth was fully understood even by Asiatic despots, striving even in the midst of their eternal bloodshed to increase the area of land under irrigation.[85]

[82] L. M. Isaev, "Irrigatsiia i maliariia v Srednei Azii," *VI* 3 (March 1926), 3–14: 13–14.

[83] "Ot redaktsii," *VI* 1 (April 1923), 1.

[84] "Prikaz SNK Turkrespubliki o mobilizatsii spetsialistov irrigatorov dlia raboty v irrigatsionnykh uchrezhdeniiakh" (April 26, 1919), Doc. 171 in *Pervye sotsialisticheskie preobrazovaniia v Kirgizii. Sbornik dokumentov 1918–20* (Frunze, 1990), 199–200.

[85] RGASPI f. 122, op. 1, d. 106. l. 9. Emphasis in the original.

In 1921, the Bolshevik Party decreed that that the Turkestani population, too, was required to take part in the irrigation reconstruction process by providing building materials and labor.[86] That same year, in a letter to the leaders of the Caucasus, Lenin wrote: "Immediately try to improve the condition of the peasantry and begin large-scale works of electrification and irrigation. Irrigation is necessary more than anything, and more than anything it will radically change [*peresozdast*] the borderland [*krai*], revitalize it, bury the past, and strengthen the transition to socialism."[87]

Even with such exhortations, the area of irrigated land in 1922 remained only half of what it had been.[88] The region lacked sources of cheap labor for reconstruction, particularly as prisoners of war departed and the work brigades from neighboring Afghanistan, Persia, and Kashgaria, on whom tsarist engineers had been so dependent, "almost completely disappeared from the domestic labor market."[89] Mechanization was one proposed solution, particularly since the idea of getting machines to take the place of human labor harmonized with a growing "cult of the machine" and the Bolshevik belief that technology could conquer the obstacles that nature put in the way of human progress, while simultaneously liberating workers for leisure and spiritual development.[90] Many engineers trained before the revolution rejoiced (if cautiously) at the increased attention to the promises of mechanization and the rational order of a planned socialist economy.[91] In Turkestan, however, since Soviet Russia did not produce its own excavators, and

86 Thurman, "Modes of Organization," 133.

87 V. I. Lenin, "Tovarishcham kommunistam Azerbaidzhana, Gruzii, Armenii, Dagestana, Gorskoi Respubliki" (April 14, 1921) in *V. I. Lenin: Polnoe sobranie sochinenii*, 43, 5th edn. (Moscow: Izdatel'stvo Politicheskoi Literatury, 1970), 198–200: 200.

88 GARF f. 5674, op. 6, d. 666, l. 42.

89 Engineer M. P. Psarev, "Ob izyskaniiakh, stroitel'nykh rabotakh, rabochikh i materialakh v Turkestanskom krae," *KhD* 5–6 (May–June 1922), 36–53: 43; E. G. Pospelov, "K probleme rabochego voprosa v irrigatsii Srednei Azii," *VI* 6 (June 1925), 153–158: 153, 155. Many fled already in the winter of 1917–1918 (RGASPI f. 122, op. 1, d. 106, l. 10)

90 N. I. Khrustalev, "Mekhanizatsiia zemlianykh rabot v oroshenii," *VI* 5 (May 1925), 3–34; Richard Stites, *Revolutionary Dreams: Utopian Vision and Experimental Life in the Russian Revolution* (New York: Oxford University Press, 1989), 43, 145; Paul Josephson, *Would Trotsky Wear a Bluetooth? Technological Utopianism under Socialism, 1917–1989* (Baltimore, MD: Johns Hopkins University Press, 2010).

91 Kendall Bailes, "The Politics of Technology: Stalin and Technocratic Thinking among Soviet Engineers," *The American Historical Review* 79, 2 (April 1974): 451–453, 457; Loren Graham, *The Ghost of the Executed Engineer: Technology and the Fall of the Soviet Union* (Cambridge, MA: Harvard University Press, 1993), 50.

since it was difficult both to import these machines to regions far from reliable transport, and to find the skilled labor and parts to repair them, the mechanization of irrigation projects was not a simple fix; given these difficulties, it was not even clear that mechanized work would be cheaper than manual labor. In addition, noted Engineer Syromiatnikov, who had returned to Transcaspia – now Soviet Turkmenistan – after years of working as a site engineer on the Chu irrigation project, there was an important political argument *against* the mechanization of labor. Particularly in a borderland such as the Kerki region of Turkmenistan, where over half of the population had fled to Afghanistan out of fear of the Bolsheviks, the improvement of irrigation systems through the use of local labor could serve both to provide the remaining population with much needed income, while also creating a positive impression of Soviet power on the local population, in the hopes of inducing some emigrants to return.[92]

A more diabolical solution to the labor problem, and an early Bolshevik attempt to use human labor power more efficiently, was the introduction in Turkestan, as in other parts of the former Russian Empire, of concentration camps [*kontslageri*]. Before the creation of the infamous Gulag, political prisoners sentenced by revolutionary tribunals for alleged crimes against the new Bolshevik regime were herded into concentration camps, which served as pools of labor for projects aimed at restoring infrastructure. A 1919 decree stated that such camps should be opened "in all regional [*guberniia*] cities ... [and have] no fewer than 300 people each." Draft legislation for such camps was discussed by the Turkestan Council of People's Commissars in 1920.[93] Judging from lists of the five hundred inmates present in the Pishpek concentration camp in the fall of 1921, most of these prisoners were Slavic and male, though women – even, occasionally, accompanied by their children – also went through the camps.[94] In 1921, most detainees at the concentration camp were put to work on a new hydroelectric station in the Chu River Valley. This project aimed to realize Vasil′ev's dream of harnessing the power of so-called white coal, now conveniently aligned with Lenin's newly declared

[92] S. I. Syromiatnikov, "Organizatsiia truda na postroike Kerkinskogo kanala," *VI* 1 (January 1927), 62–66: 62–63.

[93] "O lageriakh prinuditel′nykh rabot," *Sbornik dekretov 1919 goda. Sobranie uzakonenii i rasporiazhenii rabochego i krest′ianskogo pravitel′stva* (Petrograd 1920), 128; RGASPI f. 122, op. 1, d. 90, l. 39.

[94] TsGA KR f. 89, op. 1, dd. 191; 209, ll. 6 ob, 9; TsGA KR f. 486, op. 10, d. 100, ll. 1–4.

"second party program" for the physical and metaphorical enlightenment of the entire country through electricity.[95]

The example of the Pishpek concentration camp illustrates the early Bolshevik attitude toward organizing prison labor. In writing about early twentieth-century concentration camps, Peter Holquist has noted that, "while not intentionally lethal, these camps were deadly nonetheless."[96] Although there were calls to make Bolshevik camps sanitary and hygienic, these measures were left up to the local camp administrators. Considering the lack of fuel and food throughout Turkestan, one can only imagine the miserable conditions of the political prisoners in Pishpek, who worked barefoot, slept outside, dressed in rags, and endured the whims of an "arbitrary" and violent camp director.[97] When in December local authorities proposed liquidating the camp, regional authorities overruled it, citing the need to "exert the maximum energy in the restoration of the irrigation system in the Chu Valley." Bolsheviks praised the concentration camp as a way of "using the accumulated criminal element as a labor force" and its ability to bring "culture and progress by means of the electrification ... of the central part of Semireche."[98] Apparently, the regime saw no irony in bringing "enlightenment" to the masses by means of forced labor; rather, the camp was a new kind of technology, a more modern – though coercive, even violent – form of labor organization than anything existing under the tsarist regime. It also served the redemptive function of reshaping political miscreants into ideologically correct citizens of the new regime. The "educational" function of Soviet labor was repeatedly touted to Central Asians as a benefit of Soviet rule, though on the ground it often resembled anything but education.

While forced labor was one way of cutting costs, Vodkhoz also needed to find new ways of financing irrigation. In 1923, water administrators suggested two solutions: taxes on land and water, and attracting private – including foreign – capital investment.[99] In the interests of "the creation of a solid base for [the supply of] cotton," the Central Cotton Committee was requested to formulate irrigation concessions, a task that involved

95 TsGA KR f. 89, op. 1, d. 191, ll. 11, 15ob, 30–30ob.

96 Peter Holquist, "Violent Russia, Deadly Marxism? Russia in the Epoch of Violence, 1905–21," *Kritika* 4, 3 (Summer 2003): 635.

97 "O lageriakh prinuditel'nykh rabot," 132; TsGA KR f. 89, op. 1, d. 191, ll. 4, 11–11ob, 13, 30–30ob.

98 TsGA KR f. 89, op. 1, d. 191, ll. 6, 30ob.

99 Trombachev, "K voprosu vosstanovleniia Turkestanskogo vodnogo khoziaistva," *VI* 1 (April 1923), 3–14.

determining the value of water, the nature of privileges to be granted to investors, and an appropriate length of time for such concessions.[100] Just as legal restrictions had hindered irrigation concessions in the early twentieth century, protection for Soviet industry was written into the basic laws on concessions, which limited foreigners' rights and maintained the supremacy of Soviet law in governing foreigners operating on Soviet soil.[101] The regime's introduction in 1921 of the New Economic Policy (NEP) – a scheme to partially liberalize the economy – had eased the anxieties of many foreign observers, but potential foreign investors remained wary, particularly since many who had invested in the Russian Empire had lost "every cent . . . as a result of the revolution."[102] For their part, worries about foreign dependence and the potential ideological contradictions of attracting aid from "hostile" capitalist countries led Turkestan's irrigators to advise concessions "only in cases of the utter impossibility of finding the necessary means in the state budget of the USSR or obtaining funds by means of special loans."[103] Ultimately, most foreign concessions were on a small scale only; such concessions would not be an immediate answer to Turkestan's irrigation needs.[104]

Nor could taxes be the only solution to financing irrigation in Turkestan. In 1922, the Central Executive Committee of the Soviet Union had announced an irrigation tax to be applied to both irrigated land and the water used to power industry. Although fixed rates for the tax had not yet been established in 1923, Vodkhoz estimated that it could collect about three-quarters of a million rubles in taxes.[105] This revenue was intended to cover all aspects of irrigation (except for large-scale irrigation construction, which was subsidized by Moscow), including the salaries of canal overseers, who numbered anywhere between eight and eleven thousand in the mid-1920s; the estimated cost to the population of supporting one

[100] *Polozhenie o Glavnom khlopkovom komitete*, 5; Prof. I. G. Aleksandrov, "Ob orositel'nykh kontsessiakh," *KhD* 5–6 (May–June 1922): 20–32.

[101] Anthony Heywood, "Soviet Economic Concessions Policy and Industrial Development in the 1920s: The Case of the Moscow Railway Repair Factory," *Europe-Asia Studies* 52, 3 (May 2000): 551–552.

[102] Ibid., 549; Walter Duranty, "Soviet Concessions in Dazzling Array," *NYT* (October 14, 1928), E3.

[103] B. Lodygin, "K voprosu ob irrigatsionnykh kontsessiiakh v Turkestane," *VI* 3 (March 1924), 3–16: 16; "Organizuite vodnye tovarishchestva!," *VI* 2 (May 1923), 3–8: 3; Heywood, "Soviet Economic Concessions Policy," 549; Graham, *The Ghost of the Executed Engineer*, 37.

[104] Heywood, "Soviet Economic Concessions Policy," 550.

[105] Trombachev, "K voprosu vosstanovleniia," 8–9.

mirab alone was around five hundred rubles.[106] In addition, Vodkhoz officials also recognized that many people would be unable to pay the tax, and that even if taxes were collected, the expenditures required to properly restore regional irrigation systems were much more than the paltry sum the people could provide; in 1922–1923, the Soviet administration had spent four and a half million rubles on restoring irrigation, which included neither labor nor the upkeep of mirabs.[107] In 1924, Vodkhoz amassed about 100,000 rubles through taxation, only a fraction of projected revenue.[108] Many local officials reported problems collecting the tax. Officials in the Kara-Kirgiz [Kyrgyz] autonomous region, for instance, which included the Chu Valley Irrigation Project, reported that the local population did not take the tax campaign of 1924–1925 seriously and that only one-half (only one-third in Pishpek district) of the tax had been collected. In a move to "bring Vodkhoz closer to the population" – that is, to explain the importance of the restoration work being undertaken on local irrigation systems – Vodkhoz exhorted all technical personnel working in rural areas to give monthly public reports on their activities both to the local executive committees as well as the general population.[109]

The irrigation tax was itself a stopgap measure to create an "irrigation credit fund" in the absence of other sources of funding. This proposed credit fund, the result of a conference on irrigation within the Turkestan Economic Council headed by engineer Georgii Rizenkampf, was to serve as a means of easing the burden on the population of financing irrigation construction and maintenance. Small groups of citizens would form local "reclamation associations," which would receive credit from this fund for canal reconstruction.[110] In the fall of 1924, with the help of an additional 150,000 rubles in grants promised by the People's Commissariat of Finance and the All-Russian Cooperative Bank, there were twenty-nine reclamation associations, primarily in the Tashkent region, most of which

[106] Thurman, "Modes of Organization," 149–150; GARF f. 5674, op. 6, d. 666, ll. 42 ob, 51. The government gave a mirab only a small sum for himself and upkeep for his horse; the rest fell on the population. "Iz raboty s″ezda rabotnikov po eksploatatsii Sr. Azii i KSSR 18/XII-28 g.," *VI* 11–12 (November–December 1928), 72–78: 74–75.

[107] Trombachev, "K voprosu vosstanovleniia," 8–9; GARF f. 5674, op. 6, d. 666, ll. 42 ob, 51.

[108] V. I. Iuferev, "Meliorativnye tovarishchestva v Srednei Azii," *KhD* 1–2 (January–February 1925), 61–66: 63.

[109] TsGA KR f. 20, op. 1, d. 27, ll. 29, 34–35.

[110] Trombachev, "K voprosu vosstanovleniia," 13.

had proposed short-term irrigation restoration projects. In some cases, calculations of human labor-hours, rather than loans, "financed" well over half of the projects.[111] By 1925, the number of associations had risen to sixty-two, and it was estimated that more than forty thousand people were members of such reclamation associations in Soviet Central Asia's newly formed Uzbek Soviet Socialist Republic alone; by 1926–1927 this number had more than quintupled.[112] By devolving much of the irrigation restoration work to the local level, the reclamation associations scheme gave Vodkhoz more latitude to work on large-scale projects. In 1927, Faizulla Khojaev, chairman of the Uzbek Council of People's Commissars, declared that "only the largest projects … connected with the resettlement of an enormous number of people … should be carried out using funds from the Union budget." As Thurman has argued, the reclamation associations basically functioned as "a construction department of Vodkhoz."[113]

Vodkhoz was candid about the fact that the reclamation associations were to be an extension of the duty-in-kind, a service by ordinary citizens to the new Soviet state. By creating an institution supposedly based on popular initiative, however, Soviet officials hoped to make participation in irrigation reconstruction more efficient than the corvée labor of the tsarist "duty-in-kind" or the indigenous system of hashar, which the Bolsheviks associated with the "arbitrary" rule of the former khans and beks. Under the exhortation to "Organize water associations!" the *Irrigation Herald* pointed out that forming such water cooperatives ought to be easy, since water was in everyone's interest.[114] This idea of inducing participation in irrigation by introducing hydraulic projects that were supposedly in the best interests of "the people" was a strategy the Soviet rulers of Central Asia continued to employ in the decades to come.

The reclamation associations also seemed to be aimed at reducing the power of the mirabs, who, Vodkhoz officials complained, in an echo of tsarist-era laments, controlled water distribution on secondary systems without oversight by water management organs, "driven not by the interests of the population itself, but by their own profit."[115] In reports reminiscent of Count Pahlen's inspection of Turkestan in 1908–1909, Uzbek party officials reported bribery, nepotism, and even occasional

[111] Iuferev, "Meliorativnye tovarishchestva," 64–65 and pull-out table (unnumbered page).
[112] GARF f. 5674, op. 6, d. 666, l. 45; RGASPI f. 85, op. 27, d. 344, l. 7.
[113] RGASPI, f. 85, op. 27, l. 344; Thurman, "Modes of Organization," 152.
[114] "Organizuite vodnye tovarishchestva!," 6.
[115] GARF f. 5674, op. 6, d. 666, l. 51.

fistfights in the election of mirabs. Fights also continued to break out between upstream and downstream users over unfair allocation of water.[116] Because mirabs continued to be paid for their labor by water users, not the state, there was little incentive for them to adhere to a resolution on mirabs drawn up by Vodkhoz, nor could Vodkhoz enforce the resolution until they were subject to the bureaucracy and local party organs. The *Irrigation Herald* griped that even the junior technicians – not to speak of the mirabs – hired from among the local population were "technically illiterate" and "in need of constant instruction"; unlike good Bolsheviks, they were seemingly unable to imagine "the possibility of a more economical and profitable utilization of irrigation systems."[117] Subsuming small-scale irrigation systems to water user associations, and subordinating mirabs to local executive committees and water management organs was an attempt to "eradicate this evil," even though Boris Shlegel′, now vice-supervisor of Vodkhoz, estimated in 1925 that a mirab was responsible for supervising an average territory of more than two hundred and fifty hectares, which made any kind of oversight difficult.[118]

NATIONALIZING WATER MANAGEMENT

Vodkhoz itself was not immune to criticism. In 1924, in an article for the *Irrigation Herald* entitled "General Landmarks for the Activity of Vodkhoz in the Near Future," Shlegel′ admitted that the main organ of water management in Turkestan had no clear goals, and no perspective, that there had been mismanagement of government funds and materials, negligence when it came to estimating costs, and execution of projects without approved plans and budgets. Moreover, Vodkhoz staff were guilty of drafting plans that were not firmly grounded, either from a technical or from an economic point of view. These may have seemed like grave accusations, but for Shlegel′, with his long career in Turkestan, it probably seemed like business as usual. In the article, Shlegel′ also called on the Bolsheviks to address the question of land management [*zemleustroistvo*] at important irrigation sites such as Murghab, the Chu Valley,

[116] Ibid., 50ob; RGASPI f. 62, op. 2, d. 1431, l. 8.

[117] Pospelov, "K probleme rabochego voprosa," 155–156; GARF f. 5674, op. 6, d. 666, ll. 51–51ob.

[118] B. Kh. Shlegel′, *Vodnoe khoziaistvo Srednei Azii* (Moscow, 1926), 59.

and the Hungry Steppe, an issue to which he was particularly sensitive, having formerly served as the head of resettlement affairs in Semireche.[119]

Shlegel′'s article was published on the eve of a major change in territorial organization and land governance in the region. In 1924, after a brief period of existence as "people's Soviet republics," Bukhara and Khorezm (Khiva) ceased to exist. Their lands were incorporated into the newly declared Soviet Socialist Republics (SSRs) of Uzbekistan and Turkmenistan, whose borders were drawn along putatively national lines. This division of the former Turkestan krai – which since the revolution had been known as the Turkestan Autonomous Soviet Socialist Republic (ASSR) of the Russian Soviet Federative Socialist Republic (RSFSR) – into such "national" republics has been interpreted by some scholars as an effort by the Bolsheviks to "divide and rule" the Central Asian population. Recent work, however, has concluded that Communist Party officials, aided by ethnographers, seem to have drawn the borders of the Uzbek, Turkmen, and Kirgiz (in 1925 renamed the Kazakh) SSRs, as well as the autonomous republics and regions – the Kara-Kirgiz Autonomous Oblast′ (which became the Kyrgyz AO in 1925 and the Kyrgyz SSR in 1936), the Kara-Kalpak AO, and the Tajik ASSR (which became the Tajik SSR in 1929) – to correspond as closely as possible with the geographic areas inhabited by discrete ethnic groups, as the Bolsheviks understood them (though political decisions also had to be made, particularly when it came to multiethnic border regions), and that Central Asians themselves played an important role in the so-called national-territorial delimitation process.[120]

While it has been argued that in places such as the Ferghana Valley, "being transferred to another administrative unit did not produce immediate changes in people's everyday lives, nor did it seriously affect their interests," the delimitation of the territory of Turkestan into separate "national" units created divisions in ecologically coherent regions and

[119] B. Kh. Shlegel′, "Obshchie vekhi dlia deiatel′nosti Upravleniia Vodnogo Khoziaistva na blizhaishchie vremia," *VI* 1 (January 1924), 125–131.

[120] On the national delimitation, see Arne Haugen, *The Establishment of the National Republics in Soviet Central Asia* (New York: Palgrave Macmillan 2003); and Khalid, *The Politics of Muslim Cultural Reform*, 298–299. On the older view of divide-and-rule, see works by Baymirza Hayit, in particular *"Basmatschi": nationaler Kampf Turkestans in den Jahren 1917 bis 1934* (Cologne: Dreisam Verlag, 1992); and Olivier Roy, *The New Central Asia: Geopolitics and the Birth of Nations* (New York: New York University Press, 2000), 72–73. On Bolshevik ethnographers and nationalities policy, see Hirsch, *Empire of Nations*, and Martin, *The Affirmative Action Empire*.

watersheds which had once been politically unified.[121] In particular, the segregation of upstream and downstream water users into separate political units with their own interests was bound to cause problems. The projects to irrigate the Hungry Steppe and the Chu River Valley became "inter-republican" projects overnight, with separate "national" governments and populations to satisfy.

The Council of People's Commissars' Irrigation Committee justified these watershed divisions by pointing out that large-scale irrigation projects such as the Hungry Steppe were considered to have "all-union importance"; thus, it would hardly do to "isolate newly irrigated regions for particular nationalities," just because the land now fell within the borders of a given national republic.[122] But the People's Commissariat of Finance found that the creation of new "national" water management organizations complicated and "bureaucratized" water management, leading to unnecessary expenditures on such projects.[123] So-called parity commissions had to be created under the Central Asian Economic Council to oversee water conflicts on inter-republican systems, resolve land and water conflicts among settlements on republican borders, and set up land and water rights commissions at the district and subdistrict levels.[124] In spite of such complications, some regional party members welcomed the division of Turkestan into national units. In a report on the need to attract specialists to Kyrgyzstan, for instance, a member of the Kyrgyz Communist Party's executive committee hoped that the newly created national republics would be assigned some of the specialists that, he claimed, Tashkent had for years been withholding.[125]

After the national delimitation, however, water management continued to be uneven. Five republican administrations of water management were created under the umbrella of the renamed Central Asian Water Management Administration (Sredazvodkhoz) in Tashkent, which was directly subject to the Council of Labor and Defense.[126] Uzbekistan,

[121] Sergei Abashin, with Kamoludin Abdullaev, Ravshan Abdullaev, and Arslan Koichiev, "Soviet Rule and the Delineation of Borders in the Ferghana Valley, 1917–1930," in Starr, *Ferghana Valley*, 94–118: 114.

[122] GARF f. 3292, op. 1, d. 42, l. 4.

[123] GARF f. 5674, op. 6, d. 666, l. 61ob.

[124] These institutions did not always fulfill their functions, and tensions between different republics over water allocation continued throughout the Soviet period. Thurman, "Modes of Organization," 169–170; RGASPI f. 62, op. 2, d. 1290, ll. 1–10b; 6–7. The tensions in the early 1930s between the Kazakh and Kyrgyz governments over the Chu project are described in TsGA PD KR f. 10, op. 1, d. 430, ll. 1–3.

[125] TsGA KR f. 20, op. 1, d. 321, l. 37.

[126] GARF f. 5674, op. 6, d. 666, l. 95.

with its capital at Tashkent, had by far the most well-developed water administration, with seven water management units at the regional (oblast′)-level, eleven at the district (okrug) level, forty-eight at the sub-district (*raion*) level, and seven hundred and sixty water management "sections" at the local level. The autonomous republic of Tajikistan within the Uzbek SSR, however, had only one water management unit at the sub-district level, while the Kara-Kalpak (Qaraqalpaq) autonomous region of the Uzbek SSR had three district-level units and none at the regional or sub-district level.[127] Because Tajikistan, which was comprised of former Eastern Bukhara and the mountainous Pamir region, was considered so remote and its water management apparatus so weak, in 1926 the Central Asian Water Management Administration was tasked with establishing a water administration in Tajikistan and directly supervising its activities.[128] Eventually, these units would become more standardized.[129]

Staffing the various Vodkhoz branches proved to be a challenge, since the low prestige and level of comfort of a position in Central Asia, as compared to Moscow or Leningrad, continued to be a reason few engineers and other technical specialists came to the region; some even demanded monetary compensation for such a move. Fel′dman, the Vodkhoz representative in Moscow, reported that specialists who were paid 350 rubles in the Moscow region wanted a guarantee of more than twice as much to work in Central Asia. According to the People's Commissariat of Labor (Narkomtrud), however, even the most qualified and experienced engineers in Central Asia were paid salaries of 650 rubles a year, meaning that the demands of the Moscow specialists for such hardship pay were untenable.[130] Since a limited number of institutions trained engineers, and the number of available employment opportunities for engineers had increased with the new regime, there was little incentive to take up positions in such a remote region. In 1925, the *Irrigation Herald* reported that in spite of the fact that Vodkhoz had specially invited more than one hundred engineers and technicians to Central Asia, there were still numerous spots waiting to be filled.[131] In April 1927,

[127] Shlegel′, *Vodnoe khoziaistvo v Srednei Azii,* 59.
[128] GARF f. 374, op. 1, d. 236, l. 15.
[129] For the accompanying 1920s debate on the regionalization of Central Asia by ethnonational territory or economically based territory, see Hirsch, *Empire of Nations,* 70–87, *passim.*
[130] GARF f. 374, op. 9, d. 561, l. 41.
[131] Pospelov, "K probleme rabochego voprosa," 155.

Vodkhoz engineer Dunaev sent an angry telegram to Sergo Ordzhonikidze in the Workers' and Peasants' Inspectorate, complaining that Moscow was sending specialists working for Vodkhoz in Central Asia to the parallel organization in the Caucasus.[132] The fact that, reminiscent of the irrigation bureaucracy in the tsarist period, only three specialists on the staff of Turkmenistan's Vodkhoz had irrigation experience, while fully one-quarter were railway specialists, reflects Vodkhoz's staffing woes.[133]

Starting in 1924, Vodkhoz organized day and evening training classes for lower-level hydraulic technicians. This was a step toward providing trained specialists from the indigenous population – the "muslimization [*musul'manizatsiia*] of the technical apparatus," as one report by a Council of Labor and Defense commission referred to it – similar to Bolshevik "affirmative action" policies throughout the country designed to suppress so-called great Russian chauvinism and promote local non-Russian cadres. The courses attracted several hundred students, even though certification as a hydraulic technician took three and a half years, and training to become a foreman took two.[134] Language issues, however, continued to be a problem in communicating knowledge, complicated further by Bolsheviks efforts at script reform and the standardization of Central Asian languages. One report complained that in geography books, terms such as "river, river basin, delta, high plateau" were sometimes translated into Russian, sometimes into Arabic, or even into "newly invented Tajik. The intrusion of Uzbek terminology is noticeable," the complaint concluded.[135]

The Central Asian State University (SAGU, the new name for the Turkestan People's University) in Tashkent also provided small numbers of locally-trained specialists, though it is not clear whether any were from the indigenous population. In the fall of 1927, thirteen students prepared to graduate from the reclamation division of SAGU's Department of Reclamation Engineering, while four were scheduled to graduate from the hydropower division. In the meantime, many of the construction projects filled their spots with student interns from the main polytechnical institutes in Russia, just as they had before the revolution. In 1928, for instance, the Chu irrigation project had sixteen paid spots available for

[132] GARF f. 374, op. 2, d. 6, l. 7. [133] GARF f. 5674, op. 6, d. 666, l. 96ob.

[134] RGAE f. 4372, op. 16, d. 30, ll. 39 ob, 52–52ob. For more on such policies, see Martin, *The Affirmative Action Empire*.

[135] GARF f. 374, op. 9, d. 578, l. 24.

students, as well as sixteen one-year internships. Students turned up for such opportunities "in groups, with and without documents," from Leningrad, Moscow, Tomsk, and Kazan, from the Don and Siberian Polytechnical Institutes, as well as the Timiriazev Agricultural Institute, to the point at which Kyrgyz water management authorities wrote to the central Vodkhoz administration, requesting that no more students be sent. Like students everywhere, some were interested and worked well; others were inadequately prepared and apathetic. All required constant supervision.[136] Even students, however, were not always willing to go just anywhere. A report by the Workers' and Peasants' Inspectorate from early 1930 noted that the Leningrad Polytechnical Institute was placing its students in Leningrad instead of sending them to Central Asia, since the students "stubbornly do not want to go to the periphery [*v periferiiu*]," even if staying in the Leningrad region meant not working in their area of specialization.[137]

REFORMING LAND AND WATER

A corollary to the consolidation of Central Asians into modern "national" rather than "tribal" groups was the enactment of a series of land and water reforms, in an attempt to undermine existing systems of land and water distribution based on indigenous forms of societal organization. If there were "no bad land, only bad farmers," Central Asians would need to be taught to be good farmers and proper stewards of their land; only then could this arid land be brought to life and made to bloom. What Soviet rule promised to achieve was the goal toward which late-tsarist-era technocrats had striven as well: the rational and efficient use of all of Central Asia's "productive forces."

Unlike the insistence on land surveying that accompanied the amassing of the colonization land fund in the tsarist period, however, the Soviet land-water reforms of the 1920s were to be undertaken immediately. The reforms were, thus, carried out initially in areas considered to be most "developed" – that is, in those core areas for which the Bolsheviks already possessed statistics about land and water use. Mostly nomadic regions of Turkmenistan were omitted from the early campaign for land and water reform, as were regions of Uzbekistan and Turkmenistan that had been part of the Emirate of Bukhara and Khanate of Khiva. Such regions were

[136] TsGA KR f. 332, op. 1, d. 764, ll. 2, 16, 41, 80ob-81, 104, 109.
[137] GARF f. 374, op. 9, d. 561, l. 10.

declared to be not "politically ready."[138] Land-water reforms were subsequently carried out in the Kazakh SSR and the Kyrgyz AO in 1928–1929, as well as in the more "backward" regions of Uzbekistan and Turkmenistan.

According to the initial proposal for the land-water reforms ratified by a commission of the Politburo of the Communist Party's Central Committee on October 15, 1925, the reforms were intended to support the process of the nationalization of water, as well as establish procedures of water use designed to eliminate the "holdovers" or "survivals" [*perezhitki*] of feudal custom and the private ownership of land and water.[139] Eliminating "survivals" of the feudal past, assumed to be a key aspect of modernization, was used to justify Bolshevik interference even in places where the urgent need for land and water reform was not evident. Bolsheviks acknowledged, for instance, that there was less need for land in the Turkmen oasis of Merv than in more densely settled regions, but claimed that "traditional landholding [*sanashik*] has a deleterious effect nonetheless."[140] Bolsheviks, furthermore, claimed that ethnic tensions were inextricable from both land and water use and that a more equitable distribution of land and water, governed by the state and not by genealogical relationships, would solve any inter- and intra-ethnic tensions remaining after the national delimitation. As David Iul'evich Gopner, the plenipotentiary of the People's Commissariat of Foreign Affairs (Narkomindel, NKID) in Turkestan, had put it in 1920, "In the area of economics, irrigation enterprises and agrarian reform are the only means of solving the 'Iomud [Turkmen] question' and the legal equalization of them with the Uzbeks."[141] Or as a Soviet engineer put it, "The entire history of the Turkmen is a complicated history of bloody wars with the Uzbeks, the Persians and each other. It was not the slogan 'war for war's sake' which instigated the Turkmen to engage in these malicious affairs, but rather a hopeless situation ... Only water might save this situation and establish peace in the country."[142] By positing the Bolsheviks as the only rulers who could at last free the Turkmen people from centuries of

[138] Edgar, "Genealogy, Class, and 'Tribal Policy,'" 276.

[139] "Zemel'no Vodnaia Reforma v Srednei Azii: Doklad Sredazbiuro TsK VKP(b) Tsentral'nomu Komitetu Vsesoiuznoi Kommunisticheskoi Partii (bol'shevikov)" (Tashkent 1926) (in TsGA PD KR f. 10, op. 1, d. 68, ll. 81–91), 3. Six hundred copies of this brochure were printed and distributed to various party organs in September 1926. TsGA PD KR f. 10, op. 1, d. 68, l. 82ob.

[140] "Zemel'no Vodnaia Reforma," 5.

[141] RGASPI f. 670, op. 1, d. 52, l. 52.

[142] RGAE f. 4372, op. 16, d. 183, l. 13.

oppression and backwardness, land and water reform in such regions was intended to "create a group of peasants dependent on Soviet patronage instead of on their lineage for land and economic benefits."[143]

There had already been one radical attempt at land reform in Central Asia in the first years of Bolshevik rule, one that did indeed seem inextricable from ethnic tensions. Under the slogan of decolonization, the Bolshevik authorities had pledged to restore indigenous lands seized by Russian settlers after the disturbances of 1916. Though the original decree in March 1920 was aimed explicitly at the Ferghana Valley and Samarkand region, Semireche was added to the cotton-growing regions later that month, likely taking into account reports from officials near the Chinese border that they expected up to twelve thousand returnees with no means of subsistence.[144] With Semireche overwhelmed with returning refugees, Pishpek, Karakol (former Przheval′sk) and Alma-Ata (former Vernyi) districts, in particular, were declared "shock districts" [*udarnye uezdy*] where unsanctioned settlers were slated for eviction in the spring of 1921. As Niccolò Pianciola's research has found, however, in Pishpek district it proved to be difficult to restore lands to the rightful inhabitants; the lands requisitioned from Slavic settlers, instead of being immediately transferred to returnees, were subordinated to a general plan aimed at sedentarizing nomadic peoples.[145] Like their tsarist predecessors, Bolshevik officials saw nomadic land use as "inefficient." Nomadic pastoralism was the lifestyle of a "backward" people, and therefore incompatible with Soviet progress and the full utilization of Central Asia's "productive forces." Many nomads were left with no choice but to sedentarize. At a conference of Muslims in February 1920 in Karakol district, for instance, delegates decided that the entire population of the district would adopt sedentary status, since they had been deprived of their herds and, thus, any possibility of a nomadic lifestyle.[146]

By August 1922, the experiment in decolonization had come to an end. Bolshevik officials were concerned that instead of resulting in "leveling" on a class – or even national – basis, depriving the "European" population of land and water resources for transfer to the indigenous people of the region seemed merely to have resurrected ethnic hostilities in

[143] Edgar, "Genealogy, Class, and 'Tribal Policy,'" 275.

[144] Niccolò Pianciola, "Décoloniser l'Asie centrale? Bolcheviks et colons au Semirech′e (1920–1922)," *Cahiers du monde russe* 49, 1 (2008), 110; RGASPI f. 122, op. 1, d. 60, ll. 4–4b.

[145] Pianciola, "Décoloniser l'Asie centrale?," 124; RGASPI f. 670, op. 1, d. 51, ll. 82–83.

[146] RGASPI f. 122, op. 1, d. 60, ll. 4–40b (no date, after February 1920).

Semireche just a few short years after the atrocities of 1916.[147] Inhabitants of one village reported that returning "kirgiz" had set fire to a Russian settler village and "are carrying out real pogroms." A Turkestan Communist Party report stated that simmering ethnic tensions had been further exacerbated by the "colonialist mindset" of Russian workers and their "peculiar communist actions, which were seen by the subjugated native population as a continuation of the actions of agents of the old tsarist rule."[148] According to historian Terry Martin, when regional officials called for measures putting indigenous land and water needs first, Moscow "insisted on equal rights for all remaining Slavic settlers."[149] Railing against "great power chauvinism" – something Lenin was determined to stamp out – in order to win the favor of the indigenous population was one thing; an all-out crusade against the Russian peasantry was another, as Ian Rudzutak, head of the central Communist Party's Turkestan Bureau was the first to admit.[150] Martin and Pianciola concluded that although the Bolsheviks called for worldwide revolution and the end to imperialism, the redistribution of land in Turkestan did not succeed in any substantial redistribution of wealth between the former colonizers and the formerly colonized; instead, the halt to the process of land reform in 1922 confirmed the episode as a one-time occurrence and not the beginning of a thorough process of decolonization in non-Russian regions.[151]

In the Ferghana Valley in the early 1920s, the Bolsheviks tried to undertake a different form of land reform – and early form of collectivization of agriculture – aimed at eliminating local practices of sharecropping and the use of hired labor that had characterized cotton and other agriculture in the region. This reform was based on the principle that each person should have exactly as much land as he could effectively work, and no more. The idea of "labor use" [*trudopol'zovanie*] of land was to do away with absentee landowners and ensure an equitable distribution of land. The Central Cotton Committee apparently hired Central Asians sympathetic to the Bolshevik cause to go into villages in

[147] RGASPI f. 670, op. 1, d. 57, ll. 101, 125–125ob; TsGA RU, f. 756, op. 1, d. 1669, ll. 1–2; RGAE f. 478, op. 1, d. 1836.

[148] RGASPI f. 670, op. 1, dd. 57, l. 125ob; 56, ll. 11ob-12.

[149] Martin, *The Affirmative Action Empire*, 61.

[150] Genis, "Deportatsiia russkikh iz Turkestana v 1921 godu ('Delo Safarova')," *VIst* 1 (January 1998), 49.

[151] Pianciola, "Décoloniser l'Asie centrale?," 140; Martin, *The Affirmative Action Empire*, 128.

FIGURE 5.2 Cotton bazaar, Old Andijan (Soviet postcard).
Reproduced with permission from the Willard L. Gorton Papers, Hoover Institution Archives, Stanford, CA.

Ferghana where it might be "risky for Europeans" and try to assess the cotton situation.[152] Though local resistance seems to have hindered this early attempt at land reform, along with many early Bolshevik attempts to penetrate the cotton-growing regions, the idea of labor use, in keeping with the principle of maximum exploitation of the productive forces of the region, formed the basis for the land-water reforms undertaken in Central Asia beginning in 1925.[153]

As part of the land-water reforms of 1925–1926, a new codex was to establish procedures for the labor use of land and bring rules on hiring labor into correspondence with rules for other parts of the Soviet Union, with the eventual goal of creating a law on rental relations and sharecropping that would protect the interests of "average" and "poor" peasants (*seredniaks* and *bedniaks*, contrasted to the *kulaks*, or "wealthy" peasants). The land codex was also to ensure that land belonging to people living in cities would be redistributed to those who worked the land, while unused land could go to the urban poor, workers, craftsmen, or petty

[152] N. P. Utkin, "Polozhenie v Turkestane," *KhD* 5–6 (May–June 1922), 91–96: 92–93.
[153] Thurman, "Modes of Organization," 124–125; "Zemel'no Vodnaia Reforma," 3.

merchants. The committees responsible for carrying out the land reforms were to establish norms of labor land use, based on local conditions.[154] Because practices of renting land and hiring labor differed between regions in Central Asia, however – and even within regions like the Ferghana Valley – such blanket legal regulation proved difficult to enact.[155]

The Central Asia Bureau (the reincarnation of the Turkestan Bureau after the national delimitation) had to concede that the land-water reforms did not resolve all aspects of the "land question."[156] Just as the "decolonization" reforms in Kazakhstan and Kyrgyzstan in 1920–1922 had not resulted in a major redistribution of land, the land reforms of 1925–1926 did not result in a significant redistribution of wealth, principally because Bolshevik beliefs about class difference did not map easily onto Central Asian patterns of land ownership and use. In 1926, the Council of People's Commissars' Irrigation Committee similarly concluded that the cotton-growing regions had not benefited particularly from the reforms.[157] Additionally, authorities concluded that in certain regions of Turkmenistan, "wealthy" households had not been deprived of land and water rights; while there had been a transfer of rights of access to water, this was useless without the accompanying land.[158] In fact, the "water" aspect of the "land-water reforms" was mostly incidental. The reform of water use was only insofar as irrigated plots of land were parceled out in new ways, not through any thoroughgoing reform of water laws or management practices.[159]

Since no complete sets of official statistics were published (and Soviet statistics are themselves notoriously problematic), it is difficult even in hindsight to fully evaluate the effects of the land-water reforms[160] Joshua Kunitz, an American socialist writer who visited Central Asia in the early 1930s, recorded that he met an enthusiastic Uzbek peasant who had named his son "Er-Islokhaty" (Yer-Islohoti, "Land Reform"), in honor of the great undertaking.[161] Yet, rather than reacting with enthusiasm,

[154] "Zemel'no Vodnaia Reforma," 3.

[155] L. I. Dembo, "Zemel'no-vodnoi kodeks i chairikerstvo," *VI* 1 (January 1925), 65–68: 66.

[156] "Zemel'no Vodnaia Reforma," 18. [157] GARF f. 3292, op. 1, d. 42, ll. 38–39.

[158] RGASPI f. 62, op. 2, d. 1284, ll. 62–64.

[159] Edgar, "Genealogy, Class, and 'Tribal Policy,'" 274.

[160] A. Gurevich, "Zemel'no-vodnaia reforma v Uzbekskoi SSR (1925–1929)," *VIst* 11 (November 1948), 50.

[161] Joshua Kunitz, *Dawn over Samarkand: The Rebirth of Central Asia* (New York: International Publishers, 1935), 196.

many rural Central Asians, like their counterparts in other parts of the Soviet Union who resisted Bolshevik interference, likely attempted to subvert the land-water reforms of the 1920s. Adrienne Edgar and Benjamin Loring's findings for Turkmenistan and the Kyrgyz part of the Ferghana Valley, respectively, support such conclusions. In Turkmenistan, land redistributions took place within communities in anticipation of the reform commissions; the commissions themselves, often made up of influential people in local society, undermined the land reforms by refusing to dispossess their own relations. In the Ferghana Valley, peasants redistributed property among their poorer neighbors and undertook other efforts to deceive the local officials charged with carrying out the reforms.[162] The land-water reforms might even have had a counterproductive effect on agriculture. By demonstrating what would happen to productive farmers – the so-called kulaks (in Central Asia often called *kulak-biys*, *biy* being a reference to local wealthy landowners) – the reforms seem to have served as a disincentive to farmers to increase productivity.[163] Authorities in Turkmenistan, for instance, observed a decrease in the area of land planted under grapes, as a result of land reform. Rumors circulated that the reform would be carried out every year and that farmers would, therefore, suffer continual losses in future, depriving them of any incentive to develop their plots.[164]

Many rural Central Asian inhabitants viewed the land reforms with distrust, believing the Bolsheviks were attempting to register the local population for the purposes of control. They were not far wrong. As Edgar has argued in the case of Turkmenistan, the reforms served as a basis for determining the economic status of individuals; as in other parts of the Soviet Union, the label of "kulak" or "clergy" had important political ramifications in the late 1920s and early 1930s.[165] In his study of the land reform in the part of the Ferghana Valley belonging to the Kyrgyz ASSR, Loring posited that through the reforms, the state merely replaced "private exploitation with a state version," making farmers indebted to state-owned credit cooperatives, rather than private lenders and landowners.[166]

[162] Edgar, "Genealogy, Class, and 'Tribal Policy,'" 277; Benjamin Loring, "Rural Dynamics and Peasant Resistance in Southern Kyrgyzstan, 1929–1930," *Cahiers du monde russe* 49, 1 (2008): 190.
[163] Thurman, "Modes of Organization," 160–161.
[164] RGASPI f. 62, op. 2, d. 1284, ll. 69–69ob.
[165] Edgar "Genealogy, Class, and 'Tribal Policy,'" 278.
[166] Loring, "Rural Dynamics and Peasant Resistance," 190.

Dissatisfaction with the land and water reforms, combined with other intrusive policies introduced into Central Asia in 1927, even before widespread cultural revolution in other parts of the Soviet Union – policies such as the *hujum* ("attack") campaign to unveil Central Asian women, the anti-religious campaign and accompanying destruction of mosques and madrasas, and the Latinization of Central Asian Arabic scripts – resulted in increasing dissatisfaction with Soviet rule. Attacks on the old way of life were not accompanied by a significant increase in quality of life. Central Asians continued to chafe at the lack of provisions in the region and the Bolsheviks' emphasis on planting cotton, rather than grain, in what amounted to an extension of tsarist-era policies, even if liberation from the global cotton market now carried the ideological justification of freedom from dependence on hostile capitalist countries. Reports of the Central Asia Bureau make it clear that dehqans were willing to plant cotton only as long as there was a "timely and sufficient supply" of crops not planted in their regions.[167] With provisions remaining in short supply, OGPU reports depicted an "anti-cotton mood" in the Central Asian countryside and even instances of people being forced to plant cotton.[168] Spurred by a general war scare in the Soviet Union in 1927, rumors circulated in bazaars and teahouses throughout Central Asia that Soviet rule was only temporary.[169] Many Central Asians sought refuge in Persia, Afghanistan, and China as an alternative to Soviet rule; the last years of the 1920s witnessed thousands of Central Asians crossing the border. The plenipotentiary of the People's Commissariat of Foreign Affairs in the region, Andrei Znamenskii, noted unhappily in 1928 that foreign newspapers were reporting disturbances in Samarkand and Ferghana over the new Soviet agrarian laws and that "administrative organs in Afghanistan, Persia and Western China view the land-water reform in an entirely negative light."[170] While censure from Britain was unpleasant, censure from the Soviet Union's neighbors in Asia was even more disheartening, as the Soviet Union had high hopes for winning over its neighbors in "the East" to the Soviet cause through

167 RGASPI f. 62, op. 2, d. 1431, l. 7.

168 RGASPI f. 62, op. 2, dd. 1349, l. 7; 1350, ll. 12–13, 79, 85; 1808, ll. 50–51, 135. These documents are from 1928 to 1929, but there is not much reason to suppose that conditions in the countryside were much better in 1926–1927.

169 See RGASPI f. 62, op. 2, dd. 1350, ll. 5–6, 45, 48; 1351, ll. 74, 80, 83, 90; 1352, l. 72; 1430, l. 9; 1808, ll. 9–10, 131; 1809, l. 74.

170 RGASPI f. 62, op. 2, d. 1284, ll. 50, 54.

the visible transformation of the landscapes of Central Asia and the lives of its inhabitants.

GREENING THE DESERTS

In their promises to transform Central Asia, Soviet engineers claimed that it was time for the Bolsheviks to "eternally tear asunder the many chains of slavery with which nature has fettered an entire people."[171] Victor Turin's 1929 film *Turksib*, based on the contemporaneous construction of the the Turkestan-Siberia Railway (Turksib) – itself based on tsarist-era plans to build a railroad through the Kazakh Steppe connecting the cotton fields of Central Asia with the grain and timber of Siberia – vividly conveys this message of liberation and modernization from oppressive nature. The film's opening scenes portray "Turkestan – in Central Asia – a land of burning heat." People pick cotton "in the parched fields of Turkestan" and hoe the cracked earth, which gives off clouds of dust, while others sit apprehensively. A dog pants, a calf lies on its side, empty vessels wait for water, tumbleweeds drift across the landscape. Clouds gather, but no rain appears. The water, as the viewer soon finds out, is "high above the thirsting fields." As the water descends from the mountains, it sends people scurrying and prompts water wheels to spring into motion. The rushing water is interspersed with whirling cotton spindles until the blurred motions of the two can hardly be distinguished. Unfortunately – the viewer is informed – this water is not for the cotton, for there is only enough for grain.

> "BRING GRAIN TO TURKESTAN"
> "FREE THE LAND FOR COTTON"
> "COTTON FOR ALL RUSSIA"

the intertitles command the viewer. The crooked sticks of saxaul collected by Central Asians for fuel are contrasted to the great, straight logs from the timber yards in Siberia. A camel caravan fights in vain against the fierce desert winds, which rip open sacks of cotton and scatter the precious cargo across the sands.

At last, "the attack begins!" an airplane appears, and then a man with surveying instruments, maps, rolls of plans and numbers, "the advance guard of a new civilisation." Finally, excavators come to break the "dour earth," which is:

[171] RGAE f. 4372, op. 16, d. 183, l. 33.

"TORN ASUNDER"
"BY THE LABOR OF MAN" "THE WEIGHT OF A THOUSAND YEARS – LIFTED."

Nomads pack up their belongings and race to see the first locomotive, which, the viewer is told, will be operating by 1930. The activity of the men and machines conquering nature with the railway is interspersed with water rushing toward the cotton fields, now being plowed by mechanical cultivators. "WAR/ON THE PRIMITIVE," the intertitles proclaim, and the cotton spindles again begin to whirl.[172]

It was the transformative aspect of Turksib – more than the technology of the railroad itself – that gave it such appeal. Soviet art and literature of the 1920s indicates that everyone, from children to adults, was encouraged to dream about the utopian Soviet future that would be made possible by scientific advances and the development of new technologies to make modern life more efficient and comfortable and to enable the human conquest of nature.[173] Yet, transformation did not necessarily require technologies that had not yet been invented; in Central Asia, the Bolsheviks planned to use the technology of the railroad in a new way – to change Central Asian lives, landscapes, and the entire economy of the region. But Turin's film was also deceptive. Not only did it obscure any connection to the railways of the tsarist past, which had helped Russians to subjugate and colonize Central Asia, but the film also seemed to imply that the railway itself could bring water to the cotton fields.[174] Building a railway, however, could not make the deserts bloom.

In the mid-1920s, Bolshevik engineers turned their attention to Central Asia's deserts, perhaps most symbolic of the obstacles nature had ostensibly placed in the path of Central Asia's development. Optimists believed that with the advent of Bolshevik planning and Western technology, even this obstacle could finally be removed, opening the way for Central Asia's progress toward modernity. Yet, despite the fact that in 1912 the Imperial

[172] *Turksib* (57 min, B/W), USSR 1929, dir. Victor Turin, prod. Vostok-Kino, produced for video by David Shepard (Kino Video, NY, 1997).

[173] Richard Stites, *Revolutionary Dreams*; Asif A. Siddiqi, "Imagining the Cosmos: Utopians, Mystics, and the Popular Culture of Spaceflight in Revolutionary Russia," *Osiris* 23 (2008): 260–288; John McCannon, "Technological and Scientific Utopias in Soviet Children's Literature, 1921–1932," *The Journal of Popular Culture* 34, 4 (Spring 2001): 153-169; Douglas Weiner, *Models of Nature: Ecology, Conservation, and Cultural Revolution in Soviet Russia* (Pittsburgh, PA: University of Pittsburgh, 2000), 168–169.

[174] Oksana Sarkisova, *Screening Soviet Nationalities: Kulturfilms from the Far North to Central Asia* (London: I.B. Tauris, 2016), 181.

Russian Geographical Society had established a scientific station devoted to the study of sand in the Qara Qum, Soviet engineers and scientists remained uncertain about the process of building canals across the deserts that covered 80 percent of the new Soviet Republic of Turkmenistan. In a report presented by the All-Union Institute of Applied Botany and New Cultures to the irrigation committee of the Council of People's Commissars, the author asked whether it was even possible to build canals through sand, how they would be protected, and how the lands irrigated by these desert canals would themselves be protected from encroaching sand, particularly given the widespread harvesting of saxaul for fuel. "In the practice of irrigation worldwide," he wrote, "we do not have answers to these questions, since up until now nowhere in the world has irrigation so nearly approached such bodies of sand, nor has it intertwined so closely with sands of different varieties as it has in our Central Asian Republics."[175] In 1925, Vodkhoz requested that the desert station start work again, and academician Aleksandr Fersman took a preliminary trip to the Qara Qum that would serve as preparation for his much publicized "attack" on the desert in 1929.[176] Describing Soviet progress among the peoples of the Qara Qum region, Fersman wrote, "The Qara Qum is coming to life. It is already not a desert, but 'sands' with their own kind of economy and way of life."[177]

Even if few of the engineers who came up with such schemes fully embraced the Bolshevik cause, the enthusiasm of the new regime for transformative projects stood in stark opposition to the caution of the tsarist government, making the Bolshevik government in some ways a better fit for tsarist engineers who saw the advent of the Bolsheviks as an opportunity to put their more grandiose ideas in motion. In June 1925, the Water Section of the State Planning Committee held a meeting on the possibility of rerouting the Amu Darya so that it no longer flowed into the Aral Sea, but rather found its outlet in the Caspian. Those in support of the plan noted that the idea of channeling the Amu Darya into what was believed to be its old bed and thus "returning the [Khivan] oasis to

[175] GARF, f. 3292, op. 1, d. 5, ll. 191ob-92. The author is presumably Professor Vladimir Andreevich Dubianskii (compare to TsGA RU f. 756, op. 1, d. 1207, l. 1). For the role of saxaul in preventing shifting sands, see Pierce, *Russian Central Asia*, 196.

[176] GARF, f. 3292, op. 1, d. 5, ll. 192–93; f. 3316, op. 23, d. 650; "V pustyne Kara-Kum ... (Pis'mo iz Srednei Azii)," *KZh* (August 13, 1929) and "Nastuplenie na Kara-Kumy," *TI* (October 28, 1929) in GARF f. 3316, op. 23, d. 650, ll. 34–35.

[177] A. E. Fersman, *Moi puteshestviia* (Moscow: Molodaia gvardiia, 1949), 34.

cultured life is not a new one."[178] Indeed, the scheme was a revival of Glukhovskoi's 1893 plan to connect the Amu Darya to the Caspian, though many of Glukhovskoi's original reports and findings had been lost, partly due to the chaos of the civil war, and partly due to a flood in 1924.[179]

A similar proposal was made in 1924 for a canal that would connect Kazakhstan with the Black Sea, and thus even Western Europe. In a report on the "Kirgiz [i.e., Kazakh]-Turkestan canal," engineer V.A. Monastyrev pointed out that the idea of building a canal from Altai to the Black Sea might appear utopian, "the game of a diseased mind," but that such ideas found many supporters, who dreamed of the "future ocean harbors" on the Caspian shores of Kazakhstan, by means of which it would be possible to get foreign goods to the region more directly. To those who criticized the ambitious scope of the project, including engineer Vladimir Tsinzerling, engineer Bushinskii from the Reclamation Department declared that "from the scientific point of view it is entirely possible," though probably too expensive.[180]

Proponents of river diversion stressed not simply navigation, but also the potential of new canals to transform arid climates and bring "cultured" life to the deserts. A professor named Rybnikov described the positive aspects of the Kazakh-Turkestan Canal as creating a greenbelt to protect the local inhabitants from the heat and wind where, at present, "everything living dies under ... [the Asian desert's] burning and oppressive breath." With the construction of the canal, according to Rybnikov, "it follows that their periodic famines and crop failures will disappear."[181] Georgii Rizenkampf's new plans for a Transcaspian Canal stressed its irrigation potential in addition to its utility for navigation, ensuring that not a drop of water would be wasted. Rizenkampf, like his colleague Fedor Morgunenkov, foresaw the transformation of Transcaspia into "Russia's California and Russia's Egypt," a land of subtropical cultures, in particular cotton. "Cotton will be the fulcrum of life in Transcaspia," Rizenkampf predicted, "and it will remain that way for a long time."[182]

178 RGAE f. 4372, op. 16, d. 183, ll. 72, 54, 33; GARF f. 5674, op. 7, d. 82, ll. 7–7ob.

179 Tsinzerling, *Oroshenie na Amu-Dar'e*, 22 fn 2.

180 RGAE f. 4372, op. 15, d. 307, ll. 81, 74, 67.

181 Ibid., ll. 74–73.

182 Georgii Rizenkampf, *Trans-Kaspiiskii Kanal (Problema orosheniia Zakaspiia)* (Moscow: Vysshii Sovet Narodnogo Khoziaistva, Trudy Upravleniia irrigatsionnykh rabot v Turkestane, 1921), 50–51, 66, 81. Aleksandr Voeikov had also stated that Russia "can and should, if it finds the means, embark on irrigation work in Transcaspia,

Rizenkampf's plans for settlement in the Hungry Steppe provide a window into how tsarist-era engineers adapted their schemes in the years after the Bolshevik revolution. Rizenkampf's sketches for a pre-revolutionary "Golodnostepska [Hungry Steppe-ville]," dating to around the time of the revolution and preserved in the imperial archives in St. Petersburg, reflect both colonial attitudes toward the urban spaces of Russian Turkestan, as well as the technocratic ethos prevailing among tsarist bureaucrats on the eve of the empire's collapse. Rizenkampf's Golodnostepska mirrors the layout of colonial Tashkent, with streets radiating fan-like out of a central point (imitating the layout of the imperial capital at St. Petersburg), and separate "European" and "Muslim" neighborhoods. The orderly European part of town is centered around parks and a commercial area; it also contains the hospital. The Muslim part of town, about one-quarter the size of the European part of town, does not reflect such rational ordering principles, though it does include two small parks, as well as a mosque. The settlement was to be provided with ariqs and trees, as well as paved sidewalks, light from hydroelectric stations, and modern conveniences such as telegraph lines, permanent cinemas, shops, and a fire station.[183]

Soviet-era plans that emerged under Rizenkampf's guidance in the late 1920s, now preserved in the Russian State Archive for the Economy in Moscow, were similar in design, but stressed the communal character of Hungry Steppe settlements. Villages were reorganized into "belts of life" running along the canals, divided into equal plots with roads and canals as the boundaries, with each "colonization quadrant" receiving an equal amount of water. In the center of each quadrant were commercial areas, schools, and hospitals. There were no longer separate quarters for "Europeans" and indigenous Central Asians. Water was now the main organizing principle of the Soviet settlements in the Hungry Steppe.[184]

In 1929, eighteen years after his first trip to the region, Arthur Powell Davis returned to the Hungry Steppe. He described Rizenkampf's plans as "an ideal scheme for distribution and use of water ... which seems hard to improve." Moreover, he wrote, the vast area of land relatively free from topographic inequalities, "together with the construction of new

and progressive desiccation will not exist in the krai." A. I. Voeikov, "Oroshenie Zakaspiiskoi oblasti s tochki zreniia geografii i klimatologii," *Vozdeistvie cheloveka na prirodu* (Moscow, 1949), 157–178: 158.

[183] RGIA f. 432, op. 1, d. 768a, plan for "Golodnostepska" (n.d., after October 18, 1916; the file is labeled 1918).

[184] RGAE f. 4372, op. 27, d. 354, particularly ll. 89ob-90.

railroads proposed, and plenty of good roads throughout the project, will make possible high and profitable production and the development of an ideal rural life and excellent citizenship in the Golodnaya [Hungry] Steppe ..."[185] What Davis likely did not realize was that by 1929, Rizenkampf was struggling to adjust his plans to incorporate Stalin's new plans for the collectivization of Soviet agriculture. How the collective (*kolkhoz*) farms and state (sovkhoz) farms were to fit into the new village model proposed for the Hungry Steppe was not yet clear.[186] Indeed, nothing about the future was clear for hydraulic engineers in Central Asia.

WATER MANAGEMENT ON TRIAL

In September 1925, the *Irrigation Herald* reported the "tragic deaths" of an engineer and technician in southern Uzbekistan – murdered, apparently by basmachi.[187] But another murder – that of Vodkhoz engineer Grigorii Mitrofanovich Maksimov at the hands of a railway worker and Communist Party member of peasant origin who targeted "harmful specialists" for threatening the revolution – is a better illustration of the challenges facing engineers under the Bolshevik regime.[188] This railway worker's crusade against prominent "specialists" illustrates the tensions between engineers, technicians, and others who had been educated in tsarist institutions and often had worked for the tsarist government, and the new ranks of ardent Bolsheviks, many of whom were illiterate peasants, who had devoted themselves to advancing the goals of the party, as they understood them. The fact that few engineers joined the Communist Party caused loyal Bolsheviks, particularly those who had recently joined the party, to question their loyalty and to feel resentful at the power wielded by these non-party men.

A clear signal to engineers and technicians throughout the Soviet Union that their ambitions had limits was the campaign against the so-called "bourgeois specialists," technical experts trained before the

[185] TsGA RU f. 756, op. 1, d. 3226, l. 21.

[186] G. K. Rizenkampf, *K novomu proektu orosheniia Golodnoi stepi*, Part 1 (Leningrad: GUVKh Srednei Azii, 1930), 132 fn 2.

[187] "Tragicheskaia gibel' inzhenera Tseitlina i tekhnika Iurchenko," *VI* 9 (September 1925), i–iii.

[188] "Grigorii Mitrofanovich Maksimov, nekrolog," *VI* 2 (May 1923), 109; "Prigovor po delu ob ubiistve inzhenera Upravleniia vodnogo khoziaistva GM Maksimov," *VI* 5 (August 1923), 93.

revolution. The conventional beginning of this attack is taken to be the Shakhty Trial of May 1928, in which coal industry engineers in the North Caucasus were publicly arrested and made to stand trial, accused of sabotage and collaborating with the Germans. The campaign against technical specialists culminated two years later in the Industrial Party Affair, in which thousands more specialists throughout the Soviet Union were implicated and arrested.[189] Yet, the trial in February and March 1928 of sixteen employees of the Central Asian water management administration preceded the Shakhty Trial by several months, indicating that the attack on Central Asian hydraulic engineers might be considered a trial run in the borderlands for a larger attack on more prominent specialists.[190]

In his study of the Industrial Party Trial, Kendall Bailes wrote that "a prime intention of the trial ... was to divert the attention of an uncritical public from the mistakes of the Stalinist leadership ... and to find scapegoats among the engineers."[191] It is likely that the earlier Vodkhoz trial similarly aimed to distract from Soviet failings and find scapegoats, which may explain why the trial was held in Tashkent, rather than Moscow, even though, as an affair of all-Union importance, it was prosecuted by the Supreme Court. "According to the indictment," reported the London *Times*, "the officials concerned devised 'intentionally fantastic projects,'... disorganizing the entire irrigation system, and creating discontent amongst the native masses. Until recently the authorities in Moscow boasted of these 'fantastic projects,' but now apparently they need scapegoats to mollify the native population."[192]

In border regions, where Bolshevik rule was weaker, and in a place like Central Asia in particular, where many inhabitants had kinship and linguistic ties with their neighbors across foreign borders, Bolshevik officials felt a particularly urgent need to portray Soviet rule as successful. Victory in Central Asia could be the key to the liberation of the entire "Orient," the spark for revolution in the East. In the face of rumors that Soviet rule was only temporary, portraying the specialists in charge of water affairs in Central Asia as inept and anti-Soviet was far easier than making any kind of immediately significant improvements to irrigation

[189] Bailes, "The Politics of Technology," 447–448.

[190] The Shakhty Affair began in March, but the trial – much hyped in the Soviet media – took place only in May.

[191] Bailes, "The Politics of Technology," 447.

[192] "Trial of Soviet Officials: Charges of corruption in Central Asia," *TOL* (February 9, 1928), 13.

and water management on the ground. As Terry Martin's work on the Bolshevik nationalities policy has shown, the existence of contradictory policies – on the one hand, to develop Central Asian irrigation as quickly as possible, in order to free the Soviet Union from the world cotton market; on the other hand, to blame and remove from power all those who were capable of implementing such a policy – was not unusual in the Soviet Union.[193] Hydraulic engineers were, thus, accused of daring to aim too high, of focusing on "fantastic" schemes that could never come to pass, rather than on the practical tasks at hand. The Tashkent newspaper *Pravda Vostoka*, for instance, scoffed at engineer Morgunenkov's revival of tsarist-era plans to redirect the Amu Darya to the Caspian; fantasies of seeing French and English ships sailing in the Qara Qum, the paper claimed, had led the employees of Turkmenistan's Vodkhoz to begin constructing the Kerki Canal in defiance of the State Planning Committee's orders.[194]

The condescending attitude of many Bolsheviks to engineers and other specialists can also be heard in the scornful tone of procurator Kondurushkin's testimony during the trial, his sarcasm, and his boredom with the "empty speeches" of the defense attorneys. When the defense lawyer Michurina asked to be able to provide photographic evidence of hydraulic projects in order to dispute accusations of utopian fantasizing, for instance, Kondurushkin scoffed at such an idea, asking for project costs and results, which could only be obtained through "proper evaluations." He pushed aside the enumerations of projects from 1923 to 1925, asking to see documents that could prove how much had been spent and what had actually been accomplished. The fact that there seemed to be no documents for 1925–1926 – no indication of what had been built or where the money had gone – could be the most incriminating factor yet, he argued. The specialists, Kondurushkin proclaimed, "need to deal with the fact that those to whom they used to bow their heads are no longer in power – they can't expect their supervisors to get down on all fours."[195]

Yet the trial was not only aimed at "old specialists"; even those who had begun their careers under Soviet rule were not safe. On February 21, 1928, *Pravda Vostoka* published an article entitled "Millions scattered to the winds," containing testimony that *all* employees of Vodkhoz

193 Martin, *The Affirmative Action Empire*, 22–23.

194 "Delo rabotnikov Vodnogo khoziaistva," *PV* 31 (February 7, 1928), 1; conclusion to "Milliony broshennye na veter," *PV* 44 (February 22, 1928), 3.

195 RGASPI f. 62, op. 2, d. 1289, ll. 25–39.

embezzled funds and falsified budgets to cover up the discrepancies.[196] In a list of specialists employed by the Turkmen Water Administration who had been implicated in the trial, four had been working only since 1924; the fifth, Syromiatnikov, had been working since 1910 on some of the largest irrigation projects in the region, including the Murghab Estate and the project to irrigate the Chu River Valley, and was generally deemed to be "the most experienced hydraulic construction engineer in Central Asia."[197] Several of the most prominent officials who determined policy in Soviet Central Asia were also implicated in the show trial and accused of having supported Vodkhoz's utopian plans. Faizulla Khojaev, for instance, was criticized for his call to revisit tsarist-era plans for the Karshi Steppe and "striving to create with all-Union funds something grandiose and entirely ephemeral ... something *stunning*, his own Volkhovstroi [a reference to the recent completion of the Volkhov hydroelectric dam and station after almost a decade of construction]," against which accusation he vigorously defended himself.[198]

By implicating both Soviet engineers and their failures, as well as members of the regional government, the Vodkhoz trial may have had the consequence of undermining Soviet rule in the region still further. OGPU reports collected in March 1928 suggested that the trial sparked "anti-Soviet conversations" among workers about the "abnormalities in the Soviet bureaucracy" that became more frequent after the Shakhty Affair was publicized. One report stated that people were inclined to help the accused Vodkhoz workers; there were murmurs that it was the party that was to blame, rather than the engineers themselves.[199] Whether or not these reports were accurate, it seems likely that such reports reflected the regime's anxieties.[200] In the end, Central Asia desperately needed irrigation specialists; as a result, many of the engineers got off with only light sentences, unlike those implicated in the Shakhty Trial later that spring.

Despite the scapegoating aspects of the trial, the accusations were not entirely misplaced. From all accounts – even the accounts of the hydraulic engineers themselves contained in the pages of the *Irrigation*

196 "Milliony broshennye na veter," *PV* 43 (February 21, 1928), 3.

197 RGASPI f. 62, op. 2, d. 1289, l. 20.

198 RGASPI f. 85, op. 27, d. 344, ll. 1–2. For the links between Central Asian Bolsheviks and the water administration, see Teichmann, *Macht der Unordnung*, 111–113.

199 RGASPI f. 62, op. 2, d. 1349, ll. 173, 176.

200 For a critical take on *svodki* (digests of reports) of the Soviet political police as sources for Central Asian history at this time, see Khalid, *Making Uzbekistan*, 25.

Herald – water was not managed efficiently in Soviet Central Asia in the 1920s. At the end of 1928, only 2 percent of Central Asian irrigation systems could be said to consist of "engineered," rather than "native," systems.[201] The lack of qualified specialists that had plagued hydraulic engineering projects in the tsarist period continued to characterize water management into the Soviet period. The Council of Labor and Defense's investigation of Central Asian irrigation in 1925, for instance, discovered that Vodkhoz had hired staff without requesting official documentation to confirm the qualifications stated by candidates on their applications, resulting in "a series of cases of imposture [*samozvanstvo*]."[202] At the same time, a perusal of the pages of the *Irrigation Herald* hardly betrays any utopian leanings. For the most part, large-scale irrigation projects from the tsarist era were continued with few amendments, except, perhaps, in the technical details. An important goal of the new Soviet project to irrigate the Chu Valley, for instance – which was still deemed important for its role in providing grain to the cotton-growing regions – was to conduct new scientific investigations in the valley in order to "make necessary corrections to engineer Vasil′ev's drafts."[203]

CONCLUSION

Although the Soviet government officially proclaimed the reconstruction of Central Asian irrigation systems and the restoration of cotton production complete by 1928, it came at a cost. The poor planning and haphazard nature of construction and maintenance – in many ways simply a continuation of tsarist-era practices – resulted in the increasing degradation of land in places like the Hungry Steppe and the Ferghana Valley. The continual attempt to grow more cotton, without any opportunity for the land to lie fallow, and without the presence of nitrous fertilizer or the rotation of cotton with nitrogen-fixing crops that might postpone soil degradation, resulted in increasing salinization of the land. Cotton was privileged more than ever, as the OGPU reports of "anti-cotton moods" throughout Central Asia could attest. The Bolsheviks had made almost no headway in their promise to liberate Central Asians from the double burden of oppressive rule and oppressive nature; rather, by adopting policies that continued to deprive Central Asians of vital food sources,

201 "Iz raboty s″ezda rabotnikov," 72.

202 GARF f. 5674, op. 6, d. 666, l. 97.

203 TsGA KR f. 20, op. 1, d. 27, l. 57; f. 99, op. 2, d. 62, l. 27; GARF f. 5674, op. 5, d. 146, l. 1; f. 7817, op. 1, d. 11.

the Bolsheviks prolonged the years of ill health and famine that they had pledged to eradicate. The construction of Turksib by the end of the decade was one positive step in the direction of provisioning Turkestan, but it also gave impetus to the further development of cotton in the region at the expense of local sources of food, furthering Central Asian dependence on the country's Slavic population.[204] Nor had the land and water reforms done much to create more equality on the ground. In the wake of the show trial of Central Asian water managers – which put on display all the faults of tsarist-era engineers and their planning mistakes – and facing continued land constraints in the cotton-growing regions, it became clear that new enthusiasm and new methods were required to demonstrate to Central Asians how the revolution had changed their lives for the better. This need for change seemed evident throughout the Soviet Union; Stalin's response was to replace Lenin's New Economic Policy with the first in a series of five-year plans for the development of the economy. In Central Asia, the First Five-Year Plan dictated a new commitment to cotton, which in turn required new kinds of irrigation projects built with new kinds of labor.

204 GARF f. 5674, op. 7, d. 155. See, for example, the correspondence about drought and the threat of famine in Turkmenistan (ll. 6–7), appeals for grain from the Caucasus (l. 11), and the "catastrophic" situation of grain in Uzbekistan (l. 15).

6

From Shockwork to People's Construction

Socialist Labor on Stalin's Canals

Russia may be a workman's paradise but it is Soviet Engineer's Hell.
– Willard Livermore Gorton[1]

On August 1, 1929, from his home in Boise, Idaho, engineer Willard Livermore Gorton wrote to former United States Bureau of Reclamation head Arthur Powell Davis in Oakland, California, inquiring whether Davis needed any "experienced assistants" in his new position as "Consulting Engineer for the Irrigation Work of Russian Soviet Government."[2] Six weeks later, Davis replied from Moscow's Grand Hotel that the Central Asian Water Administration had, indeed, inquired about "some experienced American engineers," that he hoped Gorton would come, and that the Soviet government had:

> plans for undertaking a very ambitious program of irrigation construction in Turkestan ... during the next 6 or 8 years. ... The living conditions there are primitive, but doubtless will be made comfortable and sanitary on construction jobs ... The Soviet authorities have a high opinion of the capacity and reliability of American Engineers, and I have found them willing and anxious to live up to their contracts.[3]

Six months later, having signed a two-year contract with Vodkhoz via the New York-based Amtorg Trading Corporation, Gorton was en route to the Soviet Union, his bags bursting with technical tomes on

[1] Manuscript beginning "In most instances...," WLG, Box 1, Folder F.
[2] Letter from W. L. Gorton to A. P. Davis (August 1, 1929), WLG, Box 1, Folder B.
[3] Letters from Davis to Gorton (September 15 and 17, 1929), WLG, Box 1, Folder B.

engineering; foreign-language dictionaries for Spanish, German, and Russian; several pairs of rubber boots; and "5 summer union suits of Rayon."[4] Gorton wrote home to his wife:

> The Russians seemed to be interested in what would weigh as much as my baggage did . . . I think from the remarks that any books except *Das Kapital* by Carl Marx are considered suspicious. I don't know how Shakespeare and Victor Hugo will go with them.[5]

By the time Gorton signed a contract with the "Middle Asian Reclamation Service" in February 1930, the Soviet experiment had new appeal for a world caught in the spiral of a global depression that seemed to confirm Soviet boasts that capitalism could not survive. Unlike many of the foreigners who took up residence in the Soviet Union in the 1920s and 1930s, Gorton was not a communist. Yet, like many at the time, he was curious about the events taking place in the Soviet Union and intrigued by the possibility of witnessing firsthand the great upheavals transforming the Russian Empire into the world's first socialist state. Engineer Zara Witkin, on the eve of his departure from the United States to the Soviet Union in the spring of 1932, wrote that he "encountered everywhere tremendous interest in the USSR."[6] With the Great Depression limiting the possibilities of employment elsewhere, many engineers chose to fulfill their contracts in the Soviet Union simply because such positions promised a steady source of income, though the Soviet government often had trouble keeping its promises to pay foreign engineers through deposits of hard currency into their bank accounts abroad.[7]

Bolshevik efforts to recruit men such as Davis, Gorton, and Witkin to help build socialism signaled a shift from a brief attempt in the fall of 1928 to revive foreign interest in Soviet investment to a direct importation of foreign expertise, rather than capital. The invitation of foreign

[4] Inventories of Gorton's steamer trunks, WLG, Box 1, Folder B; Letter from Davis to Gorton (September 17, 1929), WLG, Box 1, Folder B.

[5] Letter from Gorton to his wife (March 6, 1930), WLG, Box 1, Folder B.

[6] Zara Witkin, *An American Engineer in Stalin's Russia: The Memoirs of Zara Witkin, 1932–1934* (Berkeley, CA: University of California Press, 1991), 36. On the widespread foreign interest in Soviet economic modernization, including among non-Communists, see David Engerman, *Modernization from the Other Shore: American Intellectuals and the Romance of Russian Development* (Cambridge, MA: Harvard University Press, 2003), 9, 155–158.

[7] The hard currency (*valiuta*) crisis of 1933 further exacerbated tensions over salaries and payment. Davis to Gorton (November 22, 1932), WLG, Box 1, Folder B; Antony Sutton, *Western Technology and Soviet Economic Development, 1930–1945* (Stanford, CA: Hoover Institution, 1971), 39–40, 43.

specialists, including hydraulic engineers, was a crucial element in the First Five-Year Plan to industrialize the country, which included the reorganization of agriculture to support industrialization. Such far-reaching goals required foreign technology and the knowledge of how to use it, knowledge that experts could bring with them to the Soviet Union. The scholars who have investigated American engineers and others who traveled to the Soviet Union during the First Five-Year Plan have shown that these foreign specialists in many ways enabled the Soviet drive for industrialization and collectivization of agriculture.[8]

In the wake of the show trial of Vodkhoz specialists in Tashkent in the spring of 1928, and with discussions of the First Five-Year plan in full swing, the Bolsheviks debated measures to improve water management in the cotton-growing regions of the USSR. In August, Vodkhoz wrote to the Supreme Council of the National Economy requesting foreign specialists with experience in America and Egypt to come to Central Asia.[9] In October, in connection with "bringing order" to water management in the cotton-growing regions, the Council of People's Commissars suggested expert competitions to come up with new hydraulic schemes and sending no fewer than ten young hydraulic specialists abroad to increase their qualifications.[10] The Central Cotton Committee sent one of its representatives, V. V. Chikov, to New York to work with Amtorg on recruiting engineers to come to Central Asian worksites. In early 1929, the irrigation group of the Workers' and Peasants' Inspectorate wrote to Chikov that Arthur Davis's assistance, in particular, was "extremely necessary" for the needed work in Central Asia, though the group's head, Suren Shadunts, fretted that "the conditions proposed by the best experts [were] very difficult" for the Soviet government to meet.[11] In July 1929, the Central Committee of the Communist Party rubber-stamped this ongoing attempt to recruit foreigners to improve cotton irrigation by approving a resolution of the Central Cotton Committee calling for

[8] Andrea Graziosi, "'Visitors from other times': Foreign workers in the prewar piatiletki," *Cahiers du monde russe et soviétique* 29, 2 (April–June 1988): 161; Dana Dalrymple, "American Technology and Soviet Agricultural Development, 1924–1933," *Agricultural History* 40, 3 (July 1966): 190, 192–193; Deborah Fitzgerald, "Blinded by Technology: American Agriculture in the Soviet Union, 1928–32," *Agricultural History* 70, 3 (Summer 1996): 460; Anne D. Rassweiler, *The Generation of Power: The History of Dneprostroi* (New York: Oxford University Press, 1988). Foreign techical assistance received, however, almost no attention in Soviet publications (Sutton, *Western Technology*, 34–35 fn 8).

[9] GARF f. 374, op. 9, d. 561, l. 133.

[10] RGAE f. 4372, op. 27, d. 281, ll. 26–25.

[11] GARF f. 374, op. 9, d. 561, ll. 118, 132; op. 7, d. 824, l. 4.

"utilizing foreign technical experience by means of attracting powerful specialists from abroad," particularly those already acquainted with Central Asia.[12] Within the Soviet Union, Vodkhoz still struggled to compete against "more attractive regions of the Soviet Union than Central Asia."[13] But with Davis, who remembered fondly his trip to the Hungry Steppe in 1911, Vodkhoz was in luck; by the summer of 1929, Davis was in Tashkent, where he was given "engineering responsibility for the irrigation program in Turkestan."[14]

In Soviet history, 1929 is known as the "Great Break," the year Stalin called the "year of great change." In Central Asia, this break ushered in a new project that would at last embody the promises of the revolution and, through the very latest in scientific knowledge and technology, put Soviet modernity on display for not only the peoples of the Soviet Union, but for the peoples of "the East" who lived just beyond Soviet borders. With the collaboration of the consulting engineers who made up the Central Cotton Committee's newly formed American Bureau (Ambureau), headed by Davis, Tajikistan's Vakhsh River Valley was to be transformed into a producer of Egyptian cotton, which was even more desirable than the American cotton introduced under the tsars. In the visions of modernization shared by both Soviet and American engineers, machines would do the labor into which Oriental despots had once forced their subject populations; engineering would release Central Asians from constant upkeep of their irrigation systems; and Soviet Central Asia, transformed into a cotton garden, would be more productive and more bountiful than could ever have been imagined under the rule of the emirs and the khans. For the Bolsheviks, by training camel drivers to be truck drivers and shepherds to be engineers, the Vakhsh Irrigation Construction Project was also to be Lenin's nationality policy embodied and the forge for new Soviet Central Asian men and women. These promises of the Vakhsh Valley, however, were not to be realized. Though Tajik authorities believed irrigation and cotton would bring freedom to the previously oppressed peoples of the region, the irrigation project motivated the forcible resettlement of thousands of people to the Vakhsh Valley to grow cotton. Moreover, though Soviet authorities trumpeted the evolution of

[12] RGASPI f. 62, op. 2, d. 1840, l. 8. The shift from concessions to contracts for technical assistance had begun in 1928. Dalrymple, "American Technology and Soviet Agricultural Development," 190.

[13] GARF f. 374, op. 9, d. 561, ll. 41, 103.

[14] Diary entry for August 26, 1929, Box 11, Folder 2, APD.

new forms of Soviet labor over the course of the 1930s, Vakhsh itself tells a different story: by the final years of the decade, it was almost entirely built by forced labor. The shift from an emphasis on machines to an emphasis on the human body itself as a "productive force" by the end of the decade presaged new projects in the Ferghana Valley and beyond, which claimed to be the pinnacle of Soviet labor, but in which the lines between forced and free labor no longer could be so easily distinguished. Based on his experiences in Central Asia in 1930, Willard Gorton might not have been all that surprised.

TAMING THE WILD RIVER

On March 31, 1930, Gorton arrived in Tashkent, where he was immediately assigned to work not on construction, as he had been led to expect by his contract, but as an engineering consultant to the newly organized Vakhsh Designing and Investigating Party, a committee that was to furnish the plans for an ambitious new construction project in the Vakhsh River Valley in southern Tajikistan, several days' journey to the south. If Gorton had set off from America looking for a bit of adventure, he had found it. En route to Tashkent, he had met two American engineers in Moscow who had helped to devise the most recent three-year irrigation plan for the Hungry Steppe, yet by the time he joined Davis in Uzbekistan:

> the job had gone cold. The Russian Engineer who had been in charge [i.e., Georgii Rizenkampf] had disappeared under rather mysterious circumstances without any official explanation other than that he was ill ... [Instead], a new project some 200 miles to the south of the Golodnaya [Hungry] Steppe was feverishly being examined.[15]

Five days after arrival in Soviet Central Asia, Gorton was transported by plane to Stalinabad, the capital of the newly established Tajik Soviet Socialist Republic, and then sixty-five miles by car along what he described as "a muddy mountain road" to a valley where the inhabitants still made river crossings on rafts of inflated skins, rather than bridges.[16] The destination was the future headquarters of the new Vakhsh Irrigation Construction Project, better known as Vakhshstroi.

[15] From the manuscript, "The 5 year plan, which is our child...," WLG, Box 2, Folder 2a, 5.

[16] Gorton, "The Vaksh project in Tadjikistan is near the Afgan frontier...," undated manuscript, section that has been crossed out (WLG, Box 1, Folder F); for descriptions and photographs of the rafts, see Egon Erwin Kisch, *Changing Asia*, trans. Rita Reil (New York: A. A. Knopf, 1935), 228–230, photographs opposite p. 330.

FIGURE 6.1 Map of Soviet Central Asia, 1940s.
Map by Bill Nelson.

The assignment of Gorton to a grand irrigation project in southern Tajikistan came as a surprise to Arthur Davis, as well. In September 1929, when he first wrote to Gorton, Davis had been working his way through a list of fourteen problems that Vodkhoz hoped he might help solve. After several long conferences with Rizenkampf, Davis had approved his latest plans for a large-scale irrigation project in the Hungry Steppe, writing to his brother, "[I]f they do not get a model community there the fault will be with the human element."[17] To Gorton, he wrote, "It is possible that they are considering placing this construction under your charge."[18] Yet the Vodkhoz Trial had raised grave suspicions in the central government about Rizenkampf's undue influence on water management in Central Asia, as well as grave doubts about his competence. After twelve years of working on the Hungry Steppe, his critics complained, Rizenkampf had little to show.[19]

In contrast to the Hungry Steppe, the Vakhsh Valley had not even figured on the "formidable document" given to Davis when he arrived in Tashkent.[20] For those involved in Soviet economic planning, however, the shift in emphasis with the First Five-Year Plan from the Hungry Steppe to the Vakhsh Valley was not a secret. In June, Shadunts had met with the head of the Tajik branch of Vodkhoz and the People's Commissar of Agriculture and became convinced that the valley was one of the most suitable in all of Central Asia for the rapid development of both irrigation and cotton. Shadunts recommended the acceleration (*forsirovanie*, a favorite term of the First Five-Year Plan) of researching and drafting a plan for the valley's development, to be followed by equally rapid construction. Even though the technical council of Vodkhoz warned about the potential errors of such haste, advocates of "forcing" the Vakhsh River Valley's development won the day.[21] The Hungry Steppe was omitted from the 1929–1930 irrigation plan, and planning organizations worked to bring new plans for cotton sovkhozes into line with the

[17] Letter from Davis to his brother "K" (March 5, 1930), Box 5, Folder 4, APD; diary entries from August–Sept. 1929 (Box 11, Folder 2, APD). For the plan itself, see RGAE f. 4372, op. 27, d. 354, "Zakliuchenie chlena Vysshego technicheskogo soveta B.Kh. Shlegelia po skeme orosheniia Golodnoi stepi, sostavlennyi Prof. G.K. Rizenkampfym" (1929).

[18] Letter from Davis to Gorton (September 17, 1929), Box 5, Folder 4, APD.

[19] GARF f. 374, op. 28, d. 2913, ll. 121–122. See also Nelson-Skorniakov's testimony in *PV* 47 (February 25, 1928), 3 and 48 (February 27, 1928), 3.

[20] Arthur P. Davis, diary entry from July 14, 1929, Box 11, Folder 2, APD; "List of Problems to be Studied by AP Davis" (July 1929), Box 5, Folder 4, APD.

[21] GARF f. 374, op. 9, d. 539, ll. 5, 13, 15–16, 20–21.

new five-year plan for the irrigation of Central Asia.[22] In January 1930, just before Gorton committed to the job, the Soviet government abolished the central Vodkhoz organization in Tashkent and gave its administrative functions to the Central Cotton Committee, a move that indicated a shift in Moscow to an even greater emphasis on cotton production as the main goal of water management in Central Asia.[23]

Few Soviet citizens had visited the Vakhsh Valley, which until the national delimitation of 1924 had belonged to the territory of eastern Bukhara. It is a long, narrow river valley in the southwest of Tajikistan, extending from the mountains north of Qurghonteppa (known to the Soviets as Kurgan-Tiube) eighty-five kilometers southward to the Panj River at the Afghan border, where together the Vakhsh and Panj become the Amu Darya. Foreign descriptions of the valley in the late nineteenth and early twentieth centuries alternated between describing it as a tangled jungle where tigers and boars roamed wild and an empty wasteland, waiting for the touch of a civilizing hand. As recently as 1879, the Vakhsh Valley remained virtually unknown territory on European maps. Nikolai Maev, who, after leaving the Grand Duke's expedition to the Uzboi, made the journey from Dushambe (the village the Bolsheviks would designate the capital of the Soviet Republic of Tajikistan and rename Stalinabad in 1929), described the difficulties of accessing the valley from the north – only local nomads used the existing road at the time. This mountainous part of the Bukharan Emirate, he wrote, had "only recently emerged from obscurity."[24] The name Vakhsh itself was said to mean "wild."[25] Such descriptions do more to give us a sense of Russian perspectives on Central Asia than a clear picture of the Vakhsh Valley. In his readings of seventeenth-century Europeans' descriptions of the New England

[22] RGAE f. 4372, op. 27, d. 430, l. 28.

[23] From the introduction to Opis' 1 of TsGA RU f. 756, 14–15. A Central Water Administration (Glavvodkhoz) was formed under Narkomzem SSSR in February 1930 to oversee all matters of water management in the Soviet Union. This organ existed until March 15, 1946.

[24] Nikolai Maev, "Doliny Vakhsha i Kafirnigana," under "Geograficheskie izvestiia," *IIRGO* 17, 3 (1881; publ. 1887), 179–192: 179, 189–190.

[25] Abdurahim Khojibaev, *Tadzhikistan: Kratkii politiko-ekonomicheskii ocherk Tadzhikskoi SSR* (Moscow: Tip. Khoz. Otdela VTsIK, 1929), 14. A December 1929 article from the newspaper *Soviet Tajikistan* claimed that in Tajik the word "Vakhsh" meant "fertile," perhaps in an effort to attract people to settle there. "Gory i liudi," *ST* 29 (December 6, 1929), 2."Vakhsh" is related to the word "Oxus" (the Greco-Roman name for the Amu Darya), and is most likely related to the ancient Sanskrit/Vedic verb *vaksh*, which means "to grow, increase, be powerful." Classical Sanskrit texts refer to a river called Vankshu, which later scholars identified as the Oxus.

landscape, William Cronon found that such descriptions "testify as much to their own cultural preconceptions as to the actual environments they encountered,"[26] a caveat that could easily apply to nineteenth-century Russian descriptions of the Vakhsh Valley, as well.

The valley was certainly not empty, though it experienced fluctuations in population, in part due to changes in political rule. Far from the cultural and political centers to the west, Qurghonteppa, which became part of the Emirate of Bukhara in the 1870s, was a relatively insignificant Bukharan province. Most of the inhabitants of the region were Turkic-speaking nomadic peoples identified as Uzbeks or Lakai (Loqay), though there were also representatives of many other ethnic groups, as is typical of a border region. It is difficult to know exactly how many people lived in the region, since the Bukharan emirate did not keep detailed demographic statistics. In the early twentieth century, the valley may have been depopulated as its residents sought to escape onerous tax burdens.[27]

In 1909, Russian geographer Dmitry Nikolaevich Logofet published an article entitled "New Lands," in which he discussed the possibility of irrigating the Vakhsh River Valley. He estimated that as the waters of the Amu Darya and its tributaries passed through the Bukharan emirate, they irrigated only about one one-thousandth of the land they might be profitably employed to irrigate. "Not to investigate these vacant [*pustuiushchie*] lands is a sin," he wrote, "and because of this it is urgently necessary to pursue this question, which could lead to the creation of a new cotton region, renewing the arid border zone of the Bukharan domains." Like other travelers through Central Asia, Logofet had noticed the traces of old ariqs in the Vakhsh Valley and come to the conclusion that in the past the valley had supported more agriculture than at present, fueling his dream of the region's "renewal" through irrigation.[28] A hydrometric gaging station was established near the mouth of the Vakhsh in October 1913, and several Russians, including Engineer Sergei Nikolaevich Chaev, who had overseen the completion of the Romanov Canal in the Hungry Steppe, negotiated with the Emir of Bukhara for concessions in the region. The outbreak of revolution, however, put an end to such schemes.[29] For several years, the unpublished records of investigations of the Vakhsh

[26] Cronon, *Changes in the Land*, 22.

[27] Sh. Iusupov, *Vakhshskaia dolina nakanune ustanovleniia sovetskoi vlasti* (Dushanbe: Akademiia Nauk, 1975), 9–17, 20, 22. For the difficulties of calculating population figues for Bukhara in the nineteenth century, see Khanikoff, *Bokhara*, 94.

[28] D. N. Logofet, "Novye zemli," *TV* 4 (1909) in *TS* 497, 109–112: 111–112.

[29] Tsinzerling, *Oroshenie na Amu-Dar'e*, 37; TsGA KR f. 332, op. 1, d. 1865, l. 14.

River south of Qurghonteppa, carried out by a Russian engineer named Blumberg, languished in the Uzbek city of Termez.[30]

The idea of irrigating the Vakhsh Valley was revived in the second half of the 1920s. The Tajik water administration concluded in 1925 that Qurghonteppa's sub-districts of Kurgan-Tiube and Djilikul along the left bank of the Vakhsh River comprised "the best parcel of land in Tajikistan for agriculture," the future of which "doubtless will be great." A surveying party in the region marveled at the yield of cotton per desiatina and the copious numbers of watermelons in the fields. The chief technician of the Tajik branch of Vodkhoz estimated that the Vakhsh River could irrigate more than two hundred thousand hectares of land in the Vakhsh Valley (including up to thirty thousand that had previously been irrigated), and noted that "the question of the irrigation of this [Qurghonteppa] *vilayat* is of the utmost importance." Someone, likely the recipient of the letter, Vodkhoz director Mikhail Rykunov in Tashkent, highlighted this part of the report, noting in the margins, "pay attention."[31] In September 1928, an article in the *Irrigation Herald* reiterated that in the Qurghonteppa region, "the abundantly rich water resources – [including] the river Vakhsh ... the no less rich soil ... and the climatic conditions which are extremely favorable for growing cotton – make this region, as well as the adjacent districts of Djilikul and Kum-Sangir the center of the economic rebirth of Tajikistan." Yet, the engineers who wrote the article also admitted that, "in light of the fact that there are not complete enough investigative materials pertaining to this region, it is not possible to speak in more exact detail about the plan to irrigate it."[32]

Despite the fact that investigations had not yet concluded, the First Five-Year Plan provided the needed impetus for proceeding with plans to develop the valley. On July 18, 1929, the Central Committee of the Communist Party declared that all measures were to be taken in the next five years to force the maximum production of cotton in the Soviet Union. While the original version of the First Five-Year Plan demanded a yield of 590,400 tons of cotton by 1932, the Central Cotton Committee increased

[30] Tsinzerling, *Oroshenie na Amu-Dar'e*, 32.

[31] TsGA RU f. 756, op. 1, d. 832, l. 12. Other marginal comments bear the notation "MR," Rykunov's initials.

[32] Engineer V. Ia. Moiseev, "Ocherki po irrigatsii Tadzhikistana," *VI* 9 (September 1928), 53–88: 65–66. It was not on a list of ongoing investigations in 1926 (GARF f. 5674, op. 6, d. 666, ll. 43–44ob).

this goal by one-third to 787,200 tons.[33] In the same month, in conjunction with the call for increased levels of cotton production, the party urged the State Planning Committee to consider the economic utility of irrigating the Vakhsh Valley, and to calculate the possibilities for growing Egyptian cotton there, a variety of fine, long-staple cotton that required up to 20 percent more water than did American varieties, as well as a longer growing season. Initial trials growing Egyptian cotton at Bairam Ali – the old Murghab Estate – in Turkmenistan in 1926 had proved successful; the whole of the Vakhsh Valley, similarly located south of the 38th parallel, but with abundant water resources, appeared better suited still, though just which variety of Egyptian cotton should be grown there remained to be determined.[34] Stalin, who was one of the driving forces behind the shift to a heavier emphasis on cotton production in Central Asia, significantly reorganized the Central Cotton Committee to support his new plans, having:

> received information that members of the Cotton Committee as well as State Planning Committee workers ... *don't believe* in the correctness of the Politburo *decisions* regarding the increase in the cotton production five-year plan and want to *defeat* it in practice in order to show they are right.[35]

In spite of the fact that the Bolsheviks had identified Tajikistan's *bezdorozh'e*, or "roadlessness," as a pressing problem in the development of the valley, the plans to transform the Vakhsh River Valley into the center for Egyptian cotton in the Soviet Union forged ahead without the construction of better roads or a planned railroad between Dushanbe and Qurghonteppa.[36]

[33] *Stalin's Letters to Molotov, 1925–1936*, eds. Lars T. Lih, Oleg V. Naumov, and Oleg V. Khlevniuk, trans. Catherine A. Fitzpatrick (New Haven, CT: Yale University Press, 1995), 172 fn 19.

[34] Agronomist Artemov, "Razvedochnye posevy egipetskogo khlopka v Tadzhikistane v 1929," *KhD* 2–3 (February–March 1930), 304–323: 304, 322; Agronomist R. Sh. Liberman, "Egipetskie khlopchatniki v SSSR v proshlom, nastoiashchem i blizhaishem budushchem," *KhD* 1 (January 1930), 123–126: 124; TsGA KR f. 332, op. 1, d. 1865, 114, 125.

[35] Emphasis in the original. *Stalin's Letters to Molotov*, Letter No. 42 (August 21, 1929), 169, 172 fn 20–21. For more on Stalin's shift to a "cotton offensive" in 1929, see Teichmann, *Macht der Unordnung*, 121–127.

[36] Botakoz Kassymbekova, "Humans as Territory: Forced Resettlement and the Making of Soviet Tajikistan, 1920–38," *Central Asian Survey* 30, 3–4 (2011): 353; Peterson, "US to USSR," 457; GARF f. 374, op. 9, d. 552, ll. 20–21ob.

THE VAKHSH IRRIGATION CONSTRUCTION PROJECT

At its core, the Vakhsh plan was to rehabilitate the existing irrigation system of the Vakhsh Valley, which, like irrigation systems across Central Asia, had fallen into disrepair in the years of violence and emigration following the Russian Civil War. A 1928 map in the *Irrigation Herald* shows that together with their feeder canals, the existing Djilikul and Djuibor Canals, which by that year had been at least partially restored, covered a good portion of the valley.[37] The development plan would extend this system by building new canals in order to incorporate more than eighty thousand hectares of newly irrigated land on the left bank of the river. Gorton approved of the incorporation of the existing canals, with the caveat that "this would seem to be desirable if it can be accomplished without the expenditure of considerable sums of money for work that would later be thrown away when the new canal is constructed."[38]

By the time construction started in 1931, however, the irrigation plan had expanded into a much larger enterprise, the Vakhsh Agro-Industrial Complex, a vision fueled by the goals of the First Five-Year Plan to achieve both rapid industrialization and the modernization of agriculture. The new plan, therefore, included cotton-processing factories and a nitrous fertilizer plant.[39] Simultaneously, thousands of households were to be resettled from throughout the region to settle on new cotton collective farms, in what the Bolsheviks called *osvoenie* – "mastering" the valley (the word means "making it our own"). The agricultural side of the Vakhsh project, much like the project to irrigate the Chu River Valley, thus had a program of irrigation that was closely linked to a program of agricultural resettlement.

Even before the First Five-Year Plan, resettlement was already underway. Thousands of the valley's inhabitants had fled to Afghanistan in 1924 after the abolition of the state of Bukhara. In spite of a Bolshevik campaign to encourage these former Bukharans to return, whole villages remained empty, particularly in places such as the Qurghonteppa region.[40] The Bolsheviks used this opportunity to resettle Tajiks from

37 GARF f. 5674, op. 6, d. 666, l. 58; *VI* 9 (September 1928), after page 88.

38 Letter from Gorton to Chairman of Sredazvodproiz Trust Dunaev (July 8, 1930), WLG, Box 1, Folder B.

39 *Narodno-khoziaistvennyi plan Tadzhikskoi SSR na 1932 god (kontrol'nye tsifry). Doklad Gosplana TajSSR* (Stalinabad, 1931), 149.

40 Kurbanova, Shirin I. *Pereselenie: kak eto bylo* (Dushanbe: Irfon, 1993), 21; Beatrice Penati, "The reconquest of East Bukhara: the struggle against the Basmachi as a prelude to Sovietization," *Central Asian Survey* 26, 4 (December 2007), 528.

other regions, particularly mountainous ones, in order to replace the semi-nomadic peoples of the region with sedentary ones and to thereby "stabilize" the border region. Thousands of households were moved between 1925 and 1928, and the plan called for tens of thousands more by the end of 1931. As justification for the internal resettlements, some argued that Persian-speaking Tajiks had been driven from the Vakhsh Valley into the mountains by the semi-nomadic Turkic-speaking Uzbeks and Lakai; the repopulation of the now "empty" valley with highlanders would, thus, "correct a 'historical injustice.'"[41] Stabilizing the borderland and proving the superiority of the Soviet experiment took on an additional urgency in January 1929, when the reigning sovereign of Afghanistan, Amanullah Khan, was deposed by a rebel leader. Rumors spread among the teahouses and *gaps* (community meetings of men) of the Uzbek SSR that the British were on their way to do away with Bolshevik rule and that the Emir of Bukhara might return from his hiding place in Afghanistan.[42]

The first cotton state farm in Tajikistan, organized in that year, did not bode well for the region's future as the stable and prosperous center of Egyptian cotton in the Soviet Union. In its first years of existence, the "Vakhsh" state farm fulfilled only 14 percent of its Egyptian cotton plan. The "cotton-irrigation group" of the Workers' and Peasants' Inspectorate reported "cases of great Russian chauvinism, beatings, and derision aimed toward local workers by Russians," who made up more than half of the farm workers, and even a case of drunken Russian policemen shooting into a crowd of Tajiks, causing more than one hundred Tajiks to flee the farm.[43]

Such lawlessness and chaos was typical in descriptions of Tajikistan in the 1920s. A commission investigating Central Asian irrigation in 1924 had discovered that remote organs of water management such as those in Tajikistan were "virtually outside of the influence of central Vodkhoz organs" in Tashkent. Even raising the salaries of engineers and technicians could not attract qualified workers to Tajikistan, in light

[41] Kassymbekova, "Humans as Territory," 354–355; GARF f. 374, op. 9, d. 552, l. 34; Christian Bleuer and Kirill Nourzhanov, *Tajikistan: A Political and Social History* (Canberra: Australian National University E Press, 2013), 71. On resettlement, see also Pavel Polian, *Against Their Will: The History and Geography of Forced Migrations in the USSR* (New York: Central European University Press, 2004), 67; Christian Bleuer, "State-building, migration and economic development on the frontiers of northern Afghanistan and southern Tajikistan," *Journal of Eurasian Studies* 3 (2012): 76–77.

[42] RGASPI f. 62, op. 2, d. 1808, ll. 9–10.

[43] GARF f. 374, op. 9, d. 552, ll. 24, 27.

of the "high cost of living, as well as the peculiar local conditions."[44] Tajik water administrators were described as living in "earthen huts [*kibitki*] of the native type"; technical specialists sent out into the field suffered from "constant illness"; and workers employed on Vodkhoz *ariq* restoration projects in the Qurghonteppa region chafed at low salaries, poor living conditions, and lack of provisions.[45]

In 1925, a senior technical specialist named Babkin working for the Tajik water administration wrote a lengthy letter to his superior in Tashkent describing the daunting conditions of working in the Tajik Autonomous Republic. In his letter, Babkin described Tajikistan after seven years of civil war and "basmachi" violence as a "completely ruined borderland [krai]." Dushambe was in the throes of transformation from a provincial village known for its Monday market into an urban center worthy of being a Soviet capital. Yet, transformation did not happen overnight. The staff of the Tajik water administration both worked and slept in the private home of a local merchant, which was miserable in cold and rainy weather. They slept on the floor, since beds and other comforts remained in transit three months after leaving Tashkent. Noting that the "record speed" for "urgent correspondence" sent from Tashkent to Dushambe was eighty days, Babkin added wryly, "It is said that in the 19th century Jules Verne traveled around the world in this time, [and he] even had adventures [along the way]." Outside of the capital, difficult living conditions were exacerbated by the unpredictability of basmachi violence. A party of water administrators sent to survey the lands in the region around the capital in 1924 had been surrounded a few kilometers outside of town, apparently only narrowly escaping with their lives.[46] Some of the last surviving rebel groups, who had established a stronghold on the other side of the Panj in Afghanistan, attacked the surveying parties undertaking preliminary investigations for the Vakhsh Irrigation Construction Project in the fall of 1929 and the spring of 1930.[47]

On April 20, 1930, three weeks after Gorton's arrival in the region, a group of representatives from the Cotton Committee and the design trust responsible for overseeing the hydraulic project, along with irrigation engineers, listened attentively to reports on the conclusions of the Cotton Committee's Technical Council and Arthur P. Davis about the irrigation

[44] RGAE, f. 4372, op. 16, d. 31a, ll. 9, 33; GARF f. 5674, op. 6, d. 666, l. 57
[45] GARF f. 5674, op. 6, d. 666, ll. 58, 99; RGASPI f. 62, op. 2, d. 1808, ll. 66, 107.
[46] TsGA RU f. 756, op. 1, d. 832, ll. 7–7ob, 9–11ob.
[47] TsGA RT f. 18, op. 1, d. 152, ll. 36–37.

of the Vakhsh Valley. They called for the technical drafts of the Vakhsh main canal and its head works to be finished by July.[48] Committees were formed at the republican and Central Asian regional levels to assist the future construction site in every way possible, and in early 1931, with the spot for the head of the main canal confirmed, construction began.[49]

Yet grave concerns about the project remained. In January 1930, a team of economists called upon to evaluate the irrigation scheme had raised its doubts about the profitability of the proposed project. The economists' report had stated that:

> We have called this report "The Economic Aspect of the Vakhsh Problem" – instead of the usual heading, "Economic Foundations (of the Vakhsh Irrigation Project)" ... because ... the technical project cannot, from any economic point of view – from, let's say, the point of view of profitability – be justified, substantiated. However, this does not mean that the planned irrigation enterprise should not be realized, since – besides profitability – other considerations may be stimuli for hydraulic enterprises, both economic (national economic, socioeconomic), and also other considerations (political, etc.).[50]

As the Vakhsh economists' report reveals, both the economic and political significance of Vakhsh were so intertwined that despite the objection that the Vakhsh irrigation project was financially irrational, the economists approved it.[51]

The awkward position of the economists faced with justifying on ideological grounds a hastily planned irrigation project reveals the ugly side of Soviet planning. In the case of Vakhshstroi, "planning," in the sense of rational development and distribution of resources, gave way again and again to "planning" in the Soviet sense – the need to meet certain production quotas and development targets within a fixed (and usually very short) amount of time, regardless of the financial, human, and ecological costs. Though the Vodkhoz Trial of 1928 had exposed these kinds of shortcomings in irrigation work in Central Asia for all to see, by 1930 the planned economy trumped all other

48 RGAE f. 4372, op. 29, d. 451, l. 51.

49 Kurbanova, *Pereselenie*, 36.

50 TsGA KR f. 332, op. 1, d. 1865, l. 1. The two extant copies I have found of the economists' report are both contained in the Central State Archive of the Kyrgyz Republic, in the files of the Kyrgyz Water Management Administration ("Ekonomicheskaia zapiska po Vakhshu," TsGA KR f. 332, op. 1, dd. 1865, 1868 [1930]). It is not clear how the reports came to be filed with the Kyrgyz papers, nor which group produced the report (possibly the economists associated with the Vakhsh Designing and Investigating Party, to which Gorton served as a consultant).

51 This supports Kassymbekova's conclusions on the resettlement drive to the southern borderlands during this period ("Humans as Territory," 351).

considerations – "forcing" through a symbolic project like the Vakhsh plan was more important than considerations of profitability and loss.

Gorton later described the planned Vakhsh Irrigation Construction Project thus:

> Remote from sources of labor, material, equipment and supplies + 65 miles from the nearest railroad terminal, with only the crudest roads, there was nothing to commend it from the standpoint of rapid construction, and yet the plan was to complete the job involving the irrigation of some 200,000 acres of land at a cost at that time estimated to be around 30 million dollars. No plans had been made and the investigations were in the most preliminary stage. The idea of completing the project in one year was utterly impracticable ...[52]

As with previous Russian and Soviet irrigation schemes in the region, the plan to irrigate the Vakhsh Valley addressed these challenges by merely acknowledging that problems existed that would have to be overcome, and suggesting only the vaguest solutions to overcome these obstacles on the ground. The economists euphemistically referred to these sketchy plans as "working hypotheses."[53] Gorton himself suspected that irrigation "programs were made out in detail before the Designs for the job were completed and were based on mere hypotheses."[54]

The grandiosity of the scale of the construction project, and the seeming carelessness with which work was proceeding, caused the Vakhsh irrigation project's American consulting engineer a great deal of concern. In late October 1930, Gorton was invited to give a speech at a meeting of the Tajik Council of People's Commissars in Stalinabad.[55] The incident became a legend incorporated into Soviet narratives about Vakhshstroi. According to Lev Ish, who in 1932 wrote a book about cotton production entitled *The End of the Gold Drain* (referring to the need to stop importing cotton from the United States), the "talented engineer irrigator Mister Gordon [sic]" stood up at the meeting, saying, dramatically:

> Friends – you are all big dreamers, you are talented fantasy-makers! I have worked on the great world irrigation systems "Imperial Viley" [sic] and "India" ... I have seen the gold seekers of California ... I know and have spoken with Herbert

[52] W. L. Gorton, undated manuscript. This appears to be a continuation of his description of his first trip to the Vakhsh Valley, cited above (WLG, Box 1, Folder F).

[53] TsGA KR f. 332, op. 1, d. 1865, l. 232.

[54] Manuscript starting "In most instances..." (WLG, Box 1, Folder F).

[55] Handwritten manuscript starting with "The five year plan, which is our child," WLG, Box 2, Folder 2a, 12.

Wells, the influential novelist of our time. They, my friends, have daring thoughts, terrible plans. But what you have thought up on the Vakhsh is a whole head above all of this! I confirm that mankind does not know similar works in similar conditions. Forgive me, but this seems impracticable.[56]

This speech also appears verbatim in Semën Liakhovich's 1934 book on Vakhshstroi. Neither Ish nor Liakhovich explains the source of Gorton's speech.[57] The account is certainly embellished, since there is no evidence that Gorton, born in Wisconsin in 1881, ever worked in California's Imperial Valley or India, nor did he witness the California gold rush. The British author H. G. Wells was most likely invoked as an example of a popular utopian dreamer that most Soviet readers would recognize. What is possible, however, is that Gorton chided the Bolsheviks on their fantastical plan to irrigate a vast area of the Vakhsh Valley by 1933. Gorton took his duties as irrigation consultant seriously, and he sincerely wished to be of use to the Soviet engineers, in whom he recognized professional counterparts, whatever their political beliefs; he could not, however, in good conscience approve such a scheme, even if he did indeed find it without parallel, a sense one certainly gets from his notes on his frustrations at dealing with the Soviet system. Almost without a doubt, the last sentence is his, for the word "impracticable" is one he used several times in his own consulting notes.

Gorton's own account of the report he delivered in Stalinabad in October 1930 (having had it translated into Russian beforehand) records how the Bolsheviks "listened attentively to my conclusions" about how the rapid removal of more than two and a half million cubic yards of heavy gravel, "as well as a headgate for the proposed canal, was practically impossible," particularly given the challenges of transporting food and supplies sixty-five miles over the muddy mountain roads in winter. "No heavy equipment was available with the exception of one steam shovel," he recalled. And yet, "During the course of the debate on the subject of whether it was possible to get the work done[,] one of the Russian Engineers made a speech in which he disagreed violently with me. This surprised me, because just a few days before he had agreed with my

[56] Lev Ish, *Konets zolotogo potoka. Chto takoe Vakhsh?* (Moscow-Tashkent: Ob″edinenie gosudarstvennykh izdatel′stv, Sredneaziatskoe otdelenie, 1932), 4–5.

[57] Semen Liakhovich, *Vakhshstroi: ekonomicheskoe i politicheskoe znachenie* (Kurgan-Tiube: Partkom Vakhshskogo udarnogo irrigatsionnogo stroitel′stva, 1933), 42. There may also have been a third, unnamed source. See also M. Abdurakhmanov, *Vakhshskaia dolina: putevoditel′* (Dushanbe: Irfon, 1982), pages unnumbered; and Pavel Luknitsky, *Soviet Tajikistan* (Moscow: Foreign Languages Publishing House, 1954), 191.

conclusions." According to Gorton, this Russian engineer "made a very eloquent speech in which he called attention to the fact that I came from a capitalist country and did not understand how the Russian laborer could work with his hands, under the leadership of Communist Shock brigades."[58]

The fact that the Soviet engineer privately agreed with Gorton and publicly disagreed with him is an indication of the pressure on engineers, like economists, to push forward construction projects in order to meet the objectives of the five-year plans. Yet the content of his objection is also an important aspect of the story. The one sentence contained in Ish's version of Gorton's presentation and not in Liakhovich's later account is the following, which comes at the end of the speech: "However, I am not familiar with the application of your manual labor. If it proves to be more productive than machine [labor], it seems I will be mistaken." Here, the criticism that, in Gorton's own account of the episode, the Russian engineer leveled at him – his failure to understand the unique nature of Soviet labor, with an emphasis on manual labor, rather than machine technology – becomes in Ish's account something Gorton himself admits.

Indeed, it was precisely Gorton's objection to Bolshevik methods that led him to caution against the irrigation scheme, not any objection to the irrigation and development of the Vakhsh River Valley. He himself pointed out to the engineers and technicians that, until recently, even Americans had used mostly draft power rather than machine power on such projects.[59] What he objected to was the rapid tempo at which the Bolsheviks wished to proceed in a region lacking the roads, necessary supplies, and scientific data to make the project successful. Davis supported his consulting engineer, writing to the Central Cotton Committee that he "fully concur[red] in all the comments and recommendations of Mr. Gorton."[60]

For the Bolsheviks, however, it was not only grandiose new construction sites that would display to the world the superiority of

58 "Attending a Meeting in Tajikistan," WLG, Box 2, Folder F.

59 W. L. Gorton, "Report on the Assignment 'General Conclusions and Recommendations on Questions Concerning Irrigation Construction on the Basis of Your Two Years Work in the American Consulting Bureau," WLG, Box 1, Folder D, 7. Davis, too, had advised the importation of fewer "Ruth" dredgers "on account of their inadaptability to hard ground" (Diary entry for September 18, 1929, Box 11, Folder 2, APD), though he also noted the scarcity of draft animals (Letter from Davis to Sobolev [December 18, 1929], Box 5, Folder 4, APD).

60 Davis to Glavkhlopkom (March 16, 1931), Box 5, Folder 5, APD.

socialism. It was also new forms of Soviet labor that would be able to achieve the impossible, and in record time. On construction sites throughout the Soviet Union in the early 1930s, brigades engaged in "socialist competition" to see which one could finish more work in less time. "Shockworkers" (*udarniki*, highly productive workers) and, later, "Stakhanovites" (named after coal miner Alexei Stakhanov, who in 1935 famously mined fourteen times what his quota required), performed at an almost superhuman level. A popular novel of the years of the First Five-Year Plan was Valentin Kataev's 1932 *Vremia vpered!* (*Time Forward!*), suggesting that with new methods of Soviet labor, time itself would accelerate, allowing Soviet workers to accomplish in a matter of months what previously would have taken years. Indeed, one of the famous slogans of the First Five-Year Plan was "The Five-Year Plan in Four Years!" Even such optimism, however, could not change the material conditions with which the builders of Vakhsh and a modern Tajikistan had to contend.

BUILDING A MODERN SOVIET SOCIALIST REPUBLIC

If the Bolsheviks knew about the difficulties of irrigating the Vakhsh Valley, economists advised that it was utterly unjustifiable from a financial point of view, and the very expert hired to advise the project warned against proceeding; and if, moreover, there existed another, expert-approved project in a well-studied region served by the railroad and near the regional capital, why was Vakhshstroi rammed through? Historian of science Loren Graham has pointed out that many early large-scale Soviet construction projects, such as the hydroelectric dam at Dneprostroi – built to power the metallurgical industry in Ukraine while simultaneously providing increased irrigation and transport possibilities – and the massive steel plant at Magnitogorsk in the Urals, were carried out with almost complete disregard for local conditions and often against the advice of the specialists who had been hired to plan the projects.[61] Stalin's noted fondness for canals, as well as the wishes of top party officials to undertake rapid and grandiose projects the likes of which the world had never seen, were likely other factors contributing to the realization of the Vakhsh scheme. Moreover, compared to some of the projects proposed in the 1920s, in its basic elements of transforming a warm and water-rich

[61] Graham, *The Ghost of the Executed Engineer*, 49–66.

valley into a site for cotton farms, Vakhshstroi no doubt seemed far less ambitious and utopian. What it had instead was a politically significant potential that harmonized better with the Bolsheviks goals in Central Asia than the renewal of tsarist-era plans to irrigate the Hungry Steppe, even if those plans were reworked to better fit Soviet ideological frameworks.

The Vakhsh Valley's geographical position may have been inconvenient in terms of transportation, labor, and supplies, but it was of great strategic importance. Stalin had declared in 1925 that the Tajik republic's geopolitical position "at the gates of Hindustan" – that is, on the Afghan border – made it perfectly poised to spread revolution to the oppressed peoples of British India and Afghanistan. After he gave this speech, Tajik party officials often urged fellow Tajiks to fulfill comrade Stalin's words and turn Tajikistan into a "model Soviet Socialist Republic at the gates of Hindustan."[62] By the end of the 1920s, the prospect of imminent worldwide revolution had subsided; Stalin's new directive was to build "socialism in one country," shifting the focus from exporting revolution to attracting attention to the Soviet Union's achievements. Vakhshstroi, a great canal system using modern engineering methods, built directly on the border of Afghanistan, would both provide visual evidence to the outside world that socialism was indeed being built, and at the same time demonstrate the superiority of the socialist way of life to the Soviet Union's neighbors to the south and east.

The idea of creating a model state on the Afghan border was one that had intrigued Bolsheviks since the revolution. In an October 1920 report on "Our immediate tasks in Central Asia," Gopner, the plenipotentiary of the People's Commissariat of Foreign Affairs in Turkestan, wrote: "Our most important task in Bukhara is to transform it into a model workers' republic, into an object of imitation for adjacent Afghanistan and for Persia, to which it is connected by many threads."[63] With the Emir of Bukhara in hiding in Afghanistan, a Bukharan republic could have provided a rallying point for those who wished to see the restoration of the emirate; indeed, the Bukharan People's Republic had based its legitimacy

[62] See, for instance, Tajikistan Central Executive Committee Chairman Nusratullo Maksum's exhortation from June 1932 (TsGA RT f. 18, op. 1, d. 411, l. 133); Chairman of the Tajik Council of People's Commissars Abdurahim Khojibaev's introduction to *Tadzhikistan* (4); and Tajik party secretary Grigorii Broido's speech reprinted as "Vysoko derzhat' znamia partii (rech' sekretaria TsK KP(b) Tadzhikistana tov. Broido na sobranii Stalinabadskogo partaktiva 7 iiunia 1934)," *UV* 63 (263) (June 27, 1934), 1.

[63] RGASPI f. 670, op. 1, d. 52, l. 57.

on its claim to be the regeneration of the Bukharan nation.[64] In contrast, historically there had never existed a place called "Tajikistan." With its lack of schools, factories, roads and other modern infrastructure, Tajikistan hardly seemed the ideal candidate to serve as a model of Soviet socialist modernity. It didn't even have a proper city to serve as its capital. But it was exactly these drawbacks that made the daring potential of Vakhshstroi so appealing. In describing the Soviet Arctic of the 1930s, historian John McCannon has written, "Uncivilized and unknown, the Arctic was the Soviet Union's ultimate frontier, the very end of the world."[65] This description could be applied to Tajikistan as well. For a state founded with the goal of transforming the world in a revolutionary manner, Tajikistan represented the ultimate challenge.

As the Bolsheviks saw it, by launching one of the most backward areas of the entire country headlong into socialism, Vakhshstroi represented an important step in the transformation of the empire of the tsars into a truly modern state. Just as earlier tsarist administrators had sought to show the nomadic peoples of the steppes the virtues of European civilization, the Bolsheviks were determined to bring culture to the "wild" lands along the Vakhsh River. Francine Hirsch has observed that in this "postcolonial multinational state that was the sum of all of its parts ... the Soviet socialist future depended on the rapid economic and social modernization of *all* the lands and peoples within Soviet borders."[66] For the Soviet Union to be a modern state, Tajikistan would have to become modern as well. Vakhshstroi also supports Kassymbekova's conclusions that the resettlement drive to southern Tajikistan had both external, as well as internal goals in securing this unstable borderland region.[67] Though much of the hype surrounding Vakhshstroi focused on displaying Soviet superiority to its neighbors, often using the metaphor of a beacon shining its light on the supposedly benighted peoples of the East, this outward display of socialist triumphs also concealed more practical motives.[68] Vakhshstroi was intended to demonstrate the superiority of the Soviet system to the formerly colonized peoples of Central Asia who already lived on Soviet territory. Modernity did not have to be an abstract

64 Adeeb Khalid, "The Bukharan People's Soviet Republic in the Light of Muslim Sources," *Die Welt des Islams* 50 (2010): 347–348.

65 John McCannon, "To Storm the Arctic: Polar Exploration and Public Visions of Nature in the USSR, 1932–39" *Ecumene* 2, 1 (January 1995): 26.

66 Hirsch, "Getting to Know 'The Peoples of the USSR,'" 684.

67 Kassymbekova, "Humans as Territory," 349.

68 See, for example, Ish, *Konets zolotogo potoka*, 3.

concept. When Tajiks and Uzbeks themselves were able to experience the benefits of modern civilization, through engineer-built canals, collective farms, and electricity, Soviet rule in the borderland would be secured.

Visitors to Soviet Tajikistan in the 1920s and early 1930s were convinced that the modernization drive embodied in Vakhshstroi was the only way forward. Vodkhoz technician Babkin, for instance, while griping about the slowness of the postal system and his miserable living and working conditions, praised this "new and uninhabited territory … with a good economic future." He described the "feverish haste and nervousness" that one could feel everywhere, comparing it to "Colorado" during the gold rush.[69] (Gorton, on the other hand, ridiculed this excitement, remarking, "My idea is that the appearance of feverishness is due to the utter confusion, bordering on chaos, which obtains practically everywhere.")[70] The writer Boris Pilniak called Stalinabad the "Soviet Klondike."[71] In 1931, the young Davud Guseinov, party secretary of Tajikistan, wrote to Politburo member Sergo Ordzhonikidze that he struggled with the difficulties of his position, yet recognized that he had been sent to Tajikistan to take part in its transformation.[72] In the same year, Joshua Kunitz, an American socialist professor and editor of the journal *New Masses*, who visited Tajikistan as part of an international "literary brigade," commented:

> Even those who cling to the old cannot resist the magnificent upsurge of the new. History has executed a sudden *volte face*: the West is carrying its civilization back to its place of origin. Western revolutionary scientific ideas have been hurled against eastern tradition with unparalleled daring, and the emotional overtones of this collision of two world systems are surely the most dramatic aspects of the epoch-making advance of Bolshevism in the Orient.[73]

Perhaps nowhere else in the Soviet Union did promises of revolutionary transformation resonate more than in southern Tajikistan. Vakhshstroi was a key element in both the taming of this "wild" and "exotic" borderland and its transformation into a model of Soviet socialist modernity. In July 1929, the month in which the party's Central Committee advocated forcing the maximum production of cotton and urged the State Planning Committee to evaluate the "Vakhsh question," the decision

[69] TsGA RU f. 756, op. 1, d. 832, l. 90b.

[70] Manuscript beginning with "In most instances…," WLG, Box 1, Folder F.

[71] Boris Pilniak, *Tadzhikistan: Sed'maia sovetskaia* (Leningrad: Izd-vo pisatelei v Leningrade, 1931), 9.

[72] RGASPI f. 85, op. 27, d. 456, l. 13.

[73] Kunitz, *Dawn over Samarkand*, 14.

was also made to convert Tajikistan from an autonomous republic within the Uzbek Soviet Socialist Republic into a full-fledged republic in its own right, the seventh such republic in the union.[74] A London *Times* article reporting on the ascension of Tajikistan to union republic status and Soviet efforts to make Tajikistan a "model republic at the gates of Hindustan" included a statement by Avel Enukidze, secretary of the Central Executive Committee of the Congress of Soviets, who claimed that, "Peoples akin to the Tajiks inhabiting India, Afghanistan, Persia and Western China will watch our constructive work in Tajikistan with great interest."[75]

Writers who visited the nascent Vakhsh construction site as part of the international literary brigade, including Kunitz, noted that Afghans did seem to evince interest in Bolshevik activities on the other side of the River Panj.[76] The French socialist writer Paul Vaillant-Couturier formed the opinion that "one of the worst outrages of the Soviet Union is that even here, in view of the oppressed peoples across the border, socialism is being built. Not a day goes by that Afghans do not flee from their land to the Soviet Union ..."[77] Their tales are enhanced by the account of the construction project worker Ivan Kurochkin, who recalled a "massive pilgrimage" of Afghans to the villages of the border region. He wrote:

> It could be seen from the Soviet shore, how the Afghan border patrol opened fire on those gathered and with the power of their weapons forced the farmers to disperse. Borderguards beat and bloodied the farmers who had beaten their way through the thickets of reeds along the banks of the Panj in order to observe what was being done on the mysterious and alluring free Soviet banks.[78]

Whether or not such tales are true, the version of Vakhshstroi that greeted the literary brigade was one which OGPU officials and administrators had doctored for consumption, like the Potemkin villages supposedly engineered to present Empress Catherine the Great with a false sense of prosperity as she toured her domains.[79] Aleksandr Rudol'fovich

[74] For more on the making of the Tajik SSR, see Paul Bergne, *The Birth of Tajikistan: National Identity and the Origins of the Republic* (New York: I. B. Tauris, 2007); Khalid, *Making Uzbekistan*, 369–371; Kassymbekova, *Despite Cultures*, chapters 2 and 3.

[75] "New Soviet Republic 'At the Gates of India,'" *TOL* (December 9, 1929), 12.

[76] Kunitz, *Dawn over Samarkand*, 15–16.

[77] Paul Vaillant-Couturier, *Mittelasien Erwacht: Ein Reisebericht* (Moscow: Co-op. Pub. Soc. Of Foreign Workers in the USSR, 1932), 46–47.

[78] Ivan Kurochkin, *Vakhshstroi: Ocherki i putevye zametki* (Tashkent-Samarkand, 1934), 20.

[79] American Fred Beal made similar observations about foreign visitors in his observation of the Kharkov Tractor Factory in 1931. *Proletarian Journey: New England, Gastonia, Moscow* (New York: Hillman-Curl, 1937), 287, 318. Large industrial centers and

Trushnovich, a doctor who arrived in the region in 1932, found that people remembered the visit of the brigade with fondness as a time when they were well fed and supplied with tobacco. Many had hoped the brigade would stay longer.[80] The brigade itself was divided in its opinions on the project. Egon Kisch, an Austrian journalist, deemed the transformation of the "stony waste" of the Vakhsh Valley into a cotton garden a phantasmagoria.[81] But others were more enthusiastic. Kunitz admired the cotton collective farm as a way to absorb superfluous labor; he dedicated his book on the marvelous changes taking place "to the Negro people of the United States," apparently finding no irony in the fact that the Bolsheviks wished to free the oppressed peoples of the East by making Central Asia into a cotton plantation.[82]

CONSTRUCTING STALIN'S CANALS

The actual construction project got off to a shaky start. The haste with which preliminary investigations were undertaken resulted in wild underestimates of costs, labor, and time. The short-lived "Vakhsh Agro-Industrial Complex" was scrapped by the end of 1931, and Ivan Tolstopiatov, the former deputy director of the People's Commissariat of Labor, was appointed the project's new director.[83] While news reports boasted that various parts of the system were near completion, privately the word used most frequently at the site to describe conditions in the first half of the decade was "catastrophic." In 1935, writing in *Irrigation and Hydraulic Technology*, the journal of the newly formed Central Asian Scientific Research Institute for Irrigation (SANIIRI), engineer E. Pospelov wrote: "The realization of a construction project can be divided into two

achievements such as the dam at Dneprostroi were included on tours designed to acquaint foreigners with the Soviet Union in the early 1930s. *Party to USSR* (Moscow: Intourist, 1930), 7.

80 A. R. Trushnovich, *Vospominaniia kornilovtsa* (Moscow-Frankfurt: Posen, 2004), from the section "Bruno Iasenskii i Vakhshstroi." Thanks to Andrey Shlyakhter for sharing this source with me.

81 Kisch, *Changing Asia*, 245.

82 The International Publishers edition of *Dawn over Samarkand* has this dedication. The Covici Friede version (also New York, 1935) is dedicated to Angelo Herndon. There were, in fact, attempts by the Soviets to attract black cotton workers from America (Kassymbekova, *Despite Cultures*, 76). Agronomists from the Tuskegee Institute in Alabama worked in Tashkent on developing a new variety of cotton with a shorter maturation time. For more on the Tuskegee experts, see Peterson, "US to USSR."

83 TsGA RT f. 18, op. 1, d. 486, ll. 2, 100b; GARF f. 3316 op. 23, d. 175, l. 9.

stages: preparation for initial construction and fulfillment of the construction itself. The experience of Vakhshstroi," he admitted ruefully, "has demonstrated that the first stage is no less important than the second ..."[84]

Vakhshstroi was declared an all-union shock construction site in October 1931, which made it a national priority, alongside other famous construction sites, such as the steel production complex at Magnitogorsk in the Urals.[85] As the largest construction project in Central Asia, it was truly an all-union effort, supplied with auto parts from Nizhnyi Novgorod; locomotives, steam shovel parts, and wire rods from the Leningrad region; cement from Novorossiisk; nails and spikes from Saratov; and other supplies from far-off cities such as Yaroslavl', Smolensk, Kaluga and Kostroma. Vakhshstroi representatives were sent as far as Odessa and Murom to ask questions about supplies of tarred roofing paper and the possibility of obtaining the latest construction technologies.[86] Yet, a shortage economy reigned throughout the country, meaning such construction materials were scarce everywhere. Those supplies assigned to Vakhshstroi came via boat – when such were available – on the Amu Darya and Panj. From there, they had to be transported northward over extremely rough roads. The construction of a narrow-gauge railway system from the dock at Nizhnyi Piandzh (Panj-i Poyon) to the project site was not completed until 1933; even after completion, the railway often sat idle for lack of locomotives and wagons. Such shipping delays cost the project millions of rubles.[87] In hopes that creating more awareness about the project throughout the Soviet Union might help with supplies as well as labor recruitment, in 1932, chairman of the Tajik Council of People's Commissars Abdurahim Khojibaev alerted the Vakhshstroi administration that several central newspapers, including *Izvestiia*, had agreed to publish daily information about the construction progress.[88]

Whatever the central newspapers might have reported, the local newspaper at the construction site, the *Vakhshstroi Shockworker* (*Udarnik Vakhshstroia*), paints a grim picture of the construction project in the

[84] E. Pospelov, "Proektirovanie organizatsii i proizvodstva rabot v irrigatsii," *IG* 1, 3 (1935), 3–16: 8.

[85] RGASPI f. 62, op. 2, d. 2523, l. 31.

[86] TsGA RT f. 268, op. 1, d. 31, ll. 10, 19.

[87] TsGA RT f. 268, op. 2, d. 123, ll. 3–4. For the narrow gauge railway, see Patryk Reid, "'Tajikistan's Turksib': infrastructure and improvisation in economic growth of the Vakhsh River valley," *Central Asian Survey* 36, 1 (2016): 19–36.

[88] TsGA RT f. 18, op. 1, d. 400, l. 31.

early 1930s. This newspaper is one of the few insights available into the lives of workers at Vakhshstroi. Unionwide newspapers could inspire workers with tales of overfulfillment of the plan and the heroic deeds of tractor brigades in distant corners of the country, but the *Vakhshstroi Shockworker* could not lie to its readership about conditions at the construction site. Local newspapers, thus, provide a fascinating record not only of local events and happenings, but also of how citizens reacted to what was going on around them, and what kinds of responses they received in return from those in positions of power.

Like newspapers in other parts of the Soviet Union during the First Five-Year Plan, as Matthew Lenoe has argued, the *Vakhshstroi Shockworker* aimed to serve as an instrument of mobilization. Every issue was festooned with the latest slogans and party dicta, and every headline strove to goad its readers into entering into socialist competition with one another or seeking out and punishing the "wreckers" who were holding the project back from meeting party goals. Lenoe noted that "Soviet newspapers received a volume of mail probably unprecedented in world history"; the *Vakhshstroi Shockworker*, too, encouraged individuals to write in with their criticisms, suggestions, and opinions, giving readers a sense that they were actively participating in building socialism by participating in a consistent and ongoing dialogue with local officials, administrators, and editorial boards.[89] There are numerous cases of Semën Liakhovich, the editor of the *Vakhshstroi Shockworker*, forcing dialogue, pressing administrators for answers to urgent questions, and even rejecting the given answers as insufficient. Lenoe's portrayal of Soviet journalists in the early 1930s as collaborating with party officials in bringing about the indoctrination of the masses does not capture the kind of dynamic force that a local Soviet newspaper editor could be. Liakhovich's comments interspersed throughout the pages of the *Vakhshstroi Shockworker* demonstrate that he interpreted his job of editor as serving as a mediator between workers and the project administration by providing a forum in which both sides could participate in dialogue. In early 1932, for instance, a local party committee advised, on the basis of an article in the *Vakhshstroi Shockworker* about "great power chauvinism," that two Vakhshstroi employees – Kopkin, the head of the garage, and Lykachev, a senior mechanic – be removed from their posts. The party protocol went on to recommend that the editorial board of the

[89] Matthew Lenoe, *Closer to the Masses: Stalinist Culture, Social Revolution and Soviet Newspapers* (Cambridge, MA: Harvard University Press, 2004), 83.

FIGURE 6.2 An imported German Menk excavator at work in the Vakhsh Valley, 1930s. From the photo album *Vakhshskoe irrigatsionnoe stroitel'stvo v Tadzhikskoi SSR* [*Vakhsh Irrigation Construction in the Tajik SSR*], RGAE f. 8390, op. 1, d. 1098, l. 5.

Vakhshstroi Shockworker take measures to increase the fight against such great power chauvinism. For his efforts to expose the ills of the project and increase the tempo of work, as well as its quality, the committee recommended editor Liakhovich for the Order of Lenin. (In spite of this, similar cases were still being reported in party committee protocols in 1935.)[90]

Increasing the tempo of work was difficult without the machines on which Vakhshstroi's plans for rapid construction had been based. Many of the imported excavators sat idle for lack of fuel or spare parts.[91] When they did work, they proved unable to dig through the clay-rich soil at Vakhsh. Without machines, more human power was needed. Labor, however, proved difficult to attract. The enormous turnover in labor force was one of the biggest problems at Vakhshstroi, as it was at other major construction sites in the Soviet Union, where poor living and working conditions similarly contributed to *tekuchest'*, or labor "leakage."[92] According to Tajik historian Shirin Kurbanova, party records indicate that almost twelve thousand laborers came in 1931, but more than seven thousand of those workers also left.[93]

[90] TsGA RT f. 268, op. 4, dd. 2, ll. 1–2; 6, ll. 7, 14; RGASPI f. 62, op. 2, d. 2999, l. 69.
[91] TsGA RT f. 268, op. 1, d. 45, ll. 143, 153.
[92] Stephen Kotkin, *Magnetic Mountain: Stalinism as a Civilization* (Berkeley, CA: University of California Press, 1995), 95–99.
[93] Cited in Kurbanova, *Pereselenie*, 39.

In 1930, Moscow authorities had offered a 10 percent hardship pay increase to workers who stayed in "remote places" for one year.[94] But there were also other ways to combat the hemorrhaging of dissatisfied workers who were able to "vote with their feet" and move on to the next construction site. Stephen Kotkin has suggested that the reintroduction of the tsarist-era internal passport system in early 1933 was in part a measure designed to bring order to construction sites.[95] Already in late 1932, however, when recruiters failed to provide the requisite numbers of workers to the construction site, director Tolstopiatov appealed to the secret police to get workers from OGPU forced-labor camps in other parts of Central Asia. By December, twelve hundred had been sent and were assigned to the most difficult work on the cliff above the river. In the following years, forced laborers continued to do some of the worst work in the most brutal conditions on the Vakhsh Irrigation Construction Project.[96]

The Vakhsh administration did, however, continue to conduct extensive and expensive recruiting campaigns all over the Soviet Union, such as an eight-person brigade sent to Kuybyshev in October 1935 to bring in workers from the Russian Republic.[97] As is often the case with such campaigns, recruiters talked up the project and the conditions awaiting people at Vakhsh, simply to fulfill quotas. In most cases, authorities turned a blind eye toward unscrupulous recruitment agents; they may even have aided in their activities, as they did in the case of a Soviet official, documented by Jonathan Bone, whose fabricated stories about the life awaiting migrants in the Far East were knowingly distributed in print by the Political Administration of the Red Army in the early 1930s.[98]

Stories abounded of greedy Vakhshstroi agents who took advantage of their recruits' naiveté, since many in the Soviet Union had only the vaguest idea of where Tajikistan was and what to expect. One agent in Orenburg promised his recruits that they would arrive at Vakhsh on the ninth day. Instead, the journey took more than a month, by which time eight out of ten had given up.[99] If they were not supplied with the proper advances, recruiters often turned corrupt. A Vakhshstroi recruiter in

[94] TsGA RT f. 268, op. 2, d. 123, l. 70. [95] Kotkin, *Magnetic Mountain*, 99.

[96] RGASPI f. 62, op. 2, d. 2999, l. 10. [97] TsGA RT f. 268, op. 2, d. 123, l. 28.

[98] Jonathan Bone, "Socialism in a Far Country: Stalinist Population Politics and the Making of the Soviet Far East, 1929–1939" (PhD diss., University of Chicago, 2003), 59–61. For the tactics used by Magnitostroi recruiters, see Kotkin, *Magnetic Mountain*, 78–79.

[99] "S plenuma Postroikoma," *UV* (June 12, 1934), 3.

Ukraine, for instance, charged tickets for accompanying wives and children – even nursing infants – claiming repayment would take place at the construction site. He sold off recruits' provisions along the way, bought and resold goods that he transported disguised as the recruits' baggage, including vodka to sell at the construction site, something that was strictly forbidden. One recruit claimed that after three days' wait in Stalinabad in January 1933, he and his family, including small children, were abandoned by a drunken driver and forced to spend a night in the freezing cold. To be fair to the driver, it was perhaps the dirty, leaky Vakhshstroi drivers' barrack with no firewood, hot water, or beds that drove him to put a bottle in each pocket and disappear for days at a time. Many who reached the construction site promptly turned around, either because they were so distressed at the conditions or because, on arrival, no one was there to provide them with housing or food, forcing them to give up.[100]

Director Tolstopiatov blamed lazy recruiters for going not to the collective farms, but to the cities and railway stations, where "as a result, they enlisted a large percentage of the 'lumpen' [*deklassirovannyi*] element, unfit for work at Vakhshstroi." Unlike Galii Toktarov, the Chu irrigation project's recruiting agent in Kashgar in 1915, the recruiters employed by Vakhshstroi do not seem to have been chosen for any special abilities or connections; many were spectacularly unsuccessful in finding recruits. Tolstopiatov further complained about recruiting agents from other projects, claiming that they "intercepted" new recruits on their way to Vakhsh, causing the loss of hundreds of workers.[101]

Whether or not recruiters were to blame, there was no doubt that the administration struggled to hold up its end of the bargain spelled out in a 1931 "collective agreement" between representatives of the Union of Construction Workers and the Vakhsh project administration. In this collective agreement, the administration pledged to provide workers with proper food and water, housing, bath houses for use at least once a week, two weeks vacation after ten months of work, education for workers' children, regular notices about work plans, regular updates about construction progress, and to organize work brigades and socialist competitions, with prizes for the best and hardest-working groups. The

[100] TsGA RT f. 18, op. 1, d. 400, l. 90; "Istoriia odnoi poezdki (pis'mo rabochego)," *UV* 13 (146) (January 28, 1933), 4; "Byvaet li rabochkom v barakakh?" *UV* 17 (148) (February 6, 1933), 3; Kurochkin, *Vakhshstroi*, 25.

[101] TsGA RT f. 268, op. 1, d. 94b, l. 22.

workers, in turn, pledged to handle the machines carefully, to economize fuel and materials, and to work toward fulfilling the five-year plan in four.[102] Without machines, fuel, and other supplies, however, it was hard for them, too, to uphold their end of the bargain.

Like other large-scale endeavors throughout the Soviet Union, Vakhshstroi suffered from a lack of labor discipline. Official records indicate that drunkenness, sometimes for days on end, brought to a standstill the transport of urgently needed supplies. Bolshevik exhortations could not change the situation.[103] Yet, although drunkenness, lack of discipline, and failure to appear for work were common problems, they rarely seem to have led to dismissal from the project. Documents from the middle of the decade indicate that by far the largest reason for dismissal was the worker's own request (eighty-four such requests in the first half of 1936 alone). The second-highest category during that period was "no reason given" (eighteen requests).[104]

Archival materials corroborate the many stories in the *Vakhshstroi Shockworker* demanding attention to the quantity and quality of food being served in Vakhshstroi cafeterias. These documents chronicle decreases in rations to three hundred grams of bread a day for workers in December 1932, when temperatures hit twenty-five below and workers were forced to melt snow to get drinking water. They also record director Tolstopiatov's fears of sabotage when he reported in January that white-collar workers and junior technicians were getting only two hundred grams.[105] In spite of requests for additional shipments of sugar, oil, tea, and cloth, as well as meat from nearby regions, and guaranteeing small luxuries to every worker, such as low-quality tobacco [*makhorka*], cigarettes [*papirosy*], and soap, the Economic Council in 1934 reported lack of fats, low caloric value, and lack of variety in the food at Vakhsh as major contributors to poor labor retention. The People's Commissariat of Provisioning replied that it was powerless to increase the norms for Vakhshstroi workers.[106] In the fall of 1935, the administration reported that the price of lunches had gone up so much that the lowest-paid workers could

[102] TsGA RT f. 268, op. 1, d. 8, ll. 1–11.

[103] TsGA RT f. 268, op. 1 dd. 123, l. 34; 135, ll. 19, 160.

[104] Based on "Prikazy po lichnomu sostavu Upravleniia Vakhshstroia," TsGA RT f. 268, op. 2, d. 123 (1935) and TsGA RT f. 268 op. 2, d. 135 (1936).

[105] RGASPI f. 62, op. 2, d. 2999, ll. 13–14, 19.

[106] RGASPI f. 62, op. 2, d. 2523, l. 18; TsGA RT f. 268, op. 1, d. 42a, l. 162; TsGA RU f. 9 op. 1, d. 2130, ll. 13–14.

not afford it, even while the quality had declined.[107] Vakhshstroi workers might even be considered lucky, considering the fact that in early 1930s, thousands of people were starving in Ukraine and Kazakhstan, some of whom even fled to the Vakhsh Valley.[108]

Like construction sites elsewhere in the country, proper protective clothing was also lacking. Every worker was guaranteed a new pair of shoes on an annual basis, but in winter 1933 there were no shoes in the entire Tajik Republic, meaning that the party could not fulfill Vakhshstroi's demands, even though workers could hardly be expected to work barefoot in the water in winter. The project administration called for sending a comrade to Tashkent or even Moscow to obtain not fewer than three thousand pairs of leather boots. Such problems were persistent; as late as the end of October 1937, there were no rubber boots at the construction site for the forced laborers working in cold weather in slippery clay mud.[109]

Poor living conditions, in temperatures which were freezing in winter and scorching in summer, also took a toll on workers. The *Vakhshstroi Shockworker* published countless articles about the wretched state of the workers' barracks (it is unknown if conditions were better in the tents and yurts commandeered from local nomads due to a lack of sufficient housing). On March 29, 1934, the editorial board enacted a "raid" on some of the workers' barracks, where distressed newspaper staff found that the "barracks resembled not workers' quarters but rather some kind of dark burrow." One barrack was infested with parasites, had no mattresses, washstands, or lamps, and had holes in the windows. The workers bathed in the local irrigation canal. The tents visited by the self-appointed inspection team were deemed "not fit for habitation."[110]

A particularly pitiful attestation to conditions at Vakhshstroi from the summer of 1933 is a letter from a worker named Semën Ivanovich Rodin. In the letter, Rodin begged his son Stepan, a Red Army soldier, for help. Rodin's wife and daughter were sick with malaria, and he himself had been transferred to difficult earthwork operations, where, he claimed, the administration was neither paying nor feeding him:

107 TsGA RT f. 268, op. 2, dd. 123, l. 35; 135, l. 35.

108 On famine refugees from Kazakhstan, see Teichmann, *Macht der Unordnung*, 149.

109 RGASPI f. 62, op. 2, d. 2523, l. 18; TsGA RT f. 268, op. 1, dd. 41, l. 23; 45, l. 29; 133, l. 160.

110 "Na 4-om prorabstve baraki plokho prisposobleny dlia zhil'ia," *UV* 30 (330) (April 1, 1930), 3.

(I)n a word they are mocking us ... we are in a bad situation we are starving I beg you dear son Styopa cant you petition your supervisors to rescue us from misfortune otherwise our death [is nigh] if possible then as soon as possible so that they pay us otherwise they do not pay us or give us bread if possible petition as soon as possible to rescue us from misfortune write us your answer immediately ...

A Red Army official in Stalinabad did contact the construction site, but no one knew what had become of Rodin or his family.[111] As Rodin's letter indicates, epidemics of malaria, as well as typhus, swept the construction site and the surrounding collective farms, as they did large-scale construction sites throughout the Soviet Union.[112] 60 percent of the population in the cotton-growing areas of Tajikistan was reported to have fallen ill with malaria in 1932, to fight against which six tons of petroleum were imported to Djilikul, yet in 1935, it was reported that up to 90 percent of workers still got sick in the summer, when the mosquitoes were rampant.[113] In the reports of the construction project and various government and party organizations, diseases among animals receive more attention than human epidemics, as if their lives and labor were valued more than human ones. Vakhshstroi documents attest to the skeletons of camels and horses littering the project, and an outbreak in 1934 of equinia that affected horses, donkeys, mules, and camels on the collective farms and at the project. In 1935, an outbreak of epizootic paratyphus at the pig farm owned by the Department of Workers' Provisioning led to a hasty quarantining of the farm.[114] The archives are for the most part silent, however, on the number of humans who may have become ill and died during work at Vakhsh.

FORGING NEW SOVIET PEOPLE

Historian Stephen Kotkin has ably chronicled the difficulties of Magnitostroi, another large-scale construction site during the first five-year plan, which beginning in 1929 was designed to create a vast steel

[111] Original letter is TsGA RT f. 268, op. 4, d. 4, l. 13; correspondence about Rodin is ibid., 35, 37–37ob.

[112] TsGA RT f. 268 op. 1, d. 39, l. 1. Graham, *Ghost of the Executed Engineer*, 54–55; Graziosi, "Visitors from other times," 176, note 11; Kotkin, *Magnetic Mountain*, 139–140.

[113] TsGA RT f. 268, op. 1, dd. 42a, ll. 165–166; 94b, l. 24.

[114] TsGA RT f. 18, op. 1, d. 881, l. 54; TsGA RT f. 268, op. 2, d. 123, l. 148; op 1, d. 94b, l. 42.

complex in the Urals mountain region.[115] The same problems that plagued "Magnitka" – constant replacement of the administration in the early years, huge labor turnover, difficult working conditions – plagued Vakhshstroi, only magnified. If Russian and Ukrainian workers felt that the Urals were the end of the earth, one can imagine how they felt about Tajikistan, a region that had difficulty retaining even committed party officials.[116]

The Vakhsh administration believed that if the workers could but understand how vital this project was for the Soviet Union's economic progress, they would be more likely to come, as well as to stay. Though Bolshevik rhetoric of decolonization and emancipation did resonate with many Central Asians in the 1920s, in the 1930s Vakhshstroi repeatedly failed in its efforts to attract Central Asians to the construction site and to the farms of the Vakhsh Valley. The fact that only twenty of seven hundred registered unemployed workers in the region had come to Vakhshstroi in February 1933 reinforced to the administration the distance between the project and the indigenous population.[117] Having Nasrulla Abdulaev, a twenty-five-year-old Komsomol (communist youth group) member, on the editorial board of the *Vakhshstroi Shockworker*, as well as, eventually, a (somewhat reduced) Tajik-language version of the paper (*Zarbdori sokhtmoni Vakhsh*) were meant to help with communication issues.[118] The newspaper did provide a forum for some Central Asian workers, by means of a "comrade Kurbanov," to complain on behalf of the other indigenous workers that no one bothered to pursue "cultural work" or meet with them, nor could they understand the meetings organized by Russians. Kurbanov expressed their desire for the administration and party organizations to explain to them the situation at the entire construction site.[119]

In 1933, editor Liakhovich claimed that Vakhshstroi's "most important significance" was in serving as "the greatest achievement of Lenin's

115 Kotkin describes these difficulties in his magisterial *Magnetic Mountain* (1995).

116 Bergne, *The Birth of Tajikistan*, 57.

117 "Shire verbovku rabsily," *UV* 20 (151) (February 12, 1933), 1.

118 TsGA RT f. 268, op. 4, d. 2, ll. 3, 14. The *Vakhshstroi Shockworker* reported in June 1934 that there was no newspaper in the "national" language ("S plenuma Postroikoma," *UV* 57 [357][June 12, 1934], 3). Only part of the print-run of the Russian-language version from 1933 to 1934, along with a handful of issues of *Zarbdori sokhtmoni Vakhsh*, has been preserved at the Firdawsi National Library of the Republic of Tajikistan in Dushanbe.

119 "Tekhpersonal sovershenno ne rukovodit nashimi rabotami," *UV* 14 (145) (January 30, 1933), 1.

nationality policy," yet he admitted that Vakhshstroi's efforts to serve as the "forge for qualified proletarian cadres from the local population" were "of a completely inadequate degree." Over the span of three years, he could not find more than fifty-five Central Asians who attended courses to learn to drive trucks and tractors, even though the administration had pledged to immediately train no fewer than seventy adult workers from the indigenous population, as well as a number of youth through a special construction school, whose students would be mainly Central Asians. Even though Liakhovich adopted the party line that Vakhshstroi itself was to serve as a school for uncultured laborers, his newspaper told a different story.[120]

If, as Kotkin claims, workers at Magnitogorsk in the Urals soon found themselves "speaking Bolshevik" as a means of survival, Central Asians at Vakhshstroi often could not even understand Russian.[121] Some Central Asian workers who were fortunate enough to receive training as truck drivers and mechanics found themselves unable to fill out reports at the end of the day because they did not know the Cyrillic alphabet; others languished indefinitely in the garages, having been deliberately assigned to drive trucks lacking engines and wheels.[122] Reports from both the newspaper and the archives confirm that there was little education offered to Central Asians in technical skills, Soviet ideology, or even basic literacy. Moreover, Central Asians often were assigned to worse housing than Russians and Ukrainians, and treated with contempt and even violence by their Slavic overseers. In spite of the urgings of the Communist Party, Vakhshstroi found it impossible to train cadres from the local population and keep them on the construction project. In 1935, there was still not a single Tajik or Uzbek member of the trade union organization or the Vakhsh administration.[123] It is likely that, as frustrations with the technical failings of Vakhshstroi grew, efforts to improve opportunities for the

[120] Liakhovich, *Vakhshstroi*, 16, 26–7; TsGA RT f. 268, op. 1, d. 8, ll. 5–6.

[121] Kotkin, "Speaking Bolshevik" in chapter 5 in *Magnetic Mountain.*

[122] See "Tekhpersonal sovershenno ne rukovodit nashimi rabotami"; "S natsionalami rabota ne vedetsia," *UV* 17 (148) (February 6, 1933), 1; "Prekratite izdevatel'stvo nad 'Stroiuchem' i kursami shoferov," *UV* 69 (369) (July 15, 1934), 1; "Zlochastnaia putevka," *UV* 62 (362) (June 24, 1934), 4; Kurochkin, *Vakhshstroi*, 80.

[123] TsGA RT f. 268, op. 4, d. 6, ll. 7–8, 14, 49–50; "Na 5-oe prorabstve nuzhdy natsionalov zabyti," *UV* 14 (145) (January 30, 1933), 1; "S natsionalami rabota ne vedetsia"; "O natsionalakh ne dumaiut: Zhilishchno-bytovye usloviia na 6-m prorabstve trebuiut uluchsheniia," *UV* 21 (152) (February 14, 1933), 1.

"nationals" decreased. "Cultural opportunities" would always be second to issues of labor and supply.

Perhaps the most detailed published narrative of a life in the Vakhsh Valley of the 1930s is not a firsthand account, but a reconstruction of the life of Saidkul Turdiev, supposedly written at the request of his friends and published half a century after construction on Vakhshstroi began. According to this account, ostensibly based on extensive interviews with people who were close to him, Turdiev was a simple village boy from a poor family who, through his involvement with Vakhshstroi, went from being an illiterate orphan born in Eastern Bukhara at the twilight of the Russian Empire to becoming a deputy to the Supreme Soviet of the USSR and a Hero of the Soviet Union. After a short stint helping to build canals in the Vakhsh Valley, he became a cattle herder for the newly founded Vakhsh state farm – that same state farm where, according to official reports, violence and "great Russian chauvinism" abounded in the early 1930s. Turdiev's life story makes no mention of such matters, however. He quickly became the leader of a cotton brigade and fell in love with a Russian shock worker who had come to Tajikistan from the Volga; their marriage was said to be the first Komsomol wedding celebrated at the farm. He was then given the opportunity to study at a technical institute in Tashkent, where he earned the qualifications of an agronomist. In 1935, he was sent as part of a Tajik delegation to Moscow, where awards were given to representatives of progress in agriculture from around the Union, followed by an appointment in 1937 as district representative to the Council of Nationalities of the Supreme Soviet of the USSR. He went on to die a heroic death in World War II.[124] His story is one that embodies the fulfillment of what might be called the "Soviet dream," as it was represented by Vakhshstroi. It is difficult, however, to compare his life to that of others, since most of the laborers, both on the construction site, as well as the collective farms, remain anonymous, their voices coming through only rarely in the records preserved in archives and libraries. From what can be pieced together, most indigenous lives in the Vakhsh Valley of the 1930s were starkly different from that of Saidkul Turdiev.

Bruno Jasieński, a Polish-born communist and member of the international literary brigade that visited the Vakhsh Valley in 1931, popularized another version of the Soviet dream as it was embodied in

[124] R. Safarov, *Geroi Vakhsha i Dnepra* (Dushanbe: Irfon, 1982).

Vakhshstroi in his novel *Man Changes His Skin* (1932), which was later made into both a film and a television series. *Man Changes His Skin* took its place among the ranks of a genre of socialist realist fiction that emerged during the First Five-Year Plan: the industrial novel. The plots of Soviet industrial novels centered on great construction projects such as Dneprostroi, the subject of Fedor Gladkov's 1932 novel *Energiia* [*Energy*], and Magnitostroi, the subject of *Time, Forward!*, published in the same year. These works glorified the industrialization and technology embodied in these large construction projects, but also – in contrast to similar novels in the West – stressed the transformative power of Soviet labor and its "educational value" as it turned peasants, workers, and sometimes even members of the pre-revolutionary intelligentsia "into conscious builders of socialism." Like other industrial novels, *Man Changes His Skin* focuses on the collective over the making of the new Soviet individual.[125] Yet, surely one of the striking features of the novel – one that draws attention to the great changes taking place on the frontiers of the Soviet Union – is that one of its heroes is Said Urtabaev, an energetic young Tajik engineer. Unlike the American engineers in the novel, who may have been inspired by Davis and Gorton, Urtabaev was not based on any of the engineers Jasieński met when he visited Vakhshstroi; rather, he represents the promise inherent in the Vakhsh enterprise.

Socialist realist novels were not intended to depict the world as it was – they were to depict the world as it was becoming. Vakhshstroi was the perfect subject for socialist realism, for it seemed to embody the promise of a new form of labor. This labor would transform people who were said to be hampered by two kinds of backwardness: on the one hand, they were peasants, and on the other they were Central Asian, a category that for the Bolsheviks, like their tsarist predecessors, carried connotations of backwardness. The transformation was to be violent and total. An indication of the expectations of such change is the fact that although Jasieński's novel received a mostly favorable review in the *Vakhshstroi Shockworker* in the spring of 1933, the review's author lamented the choice of title, since socialist construction was to change the whole man, not just his "skin."[126] The slogan at Magnitogorsk was, "It is not only the mountain and the steppe that are being rebuilt. Man

[125] Nina Kolesnikoff, *Bruno Jasieński: His Evolution from Futurism to Socialist Realism* (Waterloo, Ont., Canada: Wilfrid Laurier University Press, 1983), 93–96.

[126] V. Doroshev, "Vakhshstroi v khudozhestvennoi literature," *UV* 53 (184) (April 20, 1933), 2–3.

himself is being rebuilt."[127] Yet, over the course of the 1930s, Magnitostroi, Vakhshstroi, and other massive projects to transform Soviet lives and landscapes were less concerned with the transformation of the individual than they were with amassing bodies with which to carry out the collective labor deemed necessary for building a socialist society.

MASTERS OF THE VALLEY

By 1933, the year in which Vakhshstroi was supposed to have been completed, the end was still a long way off. In February of that year it was estimated that 70 percent of the cotton fields in two major growing areas of the Vakhsh Valley suffered from salinization or swamping. Not only would such fields be unable to guarantee an average harvest of Egyptian cotton, but they might also have to lie fallow in 1933. The organization of a drainage system involving spillways and catchment areas was, therefore, marked an urgent task, yet Tolstopiatov refused to let workers from the main irrigation project begin working on the drainage system until late May.[128] Even worse, the site for the head sluice gates of the main canal had been poorly chosen and work was proceeding more slowly than planned. A series of telegrams from Karl Bauman, head of the Central Asia Bureau, to party leaders from August of 1933 urged special measures to be taken to finish the drainage networks and warned that September 20, the date chosen for the celebratory first release of water into the main canal, named after Stalin, appeared to be premature. At least two to three months' worth of labor remained, and Bauman worried that because of the canal's "great political and economic importance," a "festive opening of the canal at the given moment, when it is not yet finished, will only demobilize workers and distract from its real completion."[129]

In July 1934, the *Vakhshstroi Shockworker* published an article by an engineer named Kuznetsov, who wrote:

> At the end of the second five-year plan the Vakhsh Valley is to be a great source of Egyptian cotton ... However, by means of unskillful and destructive use of water, by means of a singular striving towards the development of only the irrigation system, without the construction of a network of drainage canals and collectors, and moreover an indifferent attitude toward the question of the drainage of

[127] Kotkin, *Magnetic Mountain*, 73. [128] TsGA RT f. 268, op. 1, d. 42a, ll. 1–2, 12, 56.
[129] RGASPI f. 17, op. 120, d. 95, ll. 72, 74. Thanks to Botakoz Kassymbekova for alerting me to this file's existence.

waterlogged land, it is possible that, in a short period of time, the Vakhsh Valley will transformed into "Death Valley" ...[130]

In his report from 1935 on the state of affairs at Vakhsh, Tolstopiatov claimed that reports by an inspection brigade about the rapid decline of soil conditions due to waterlogging were untrue. Catchment areas had been constructed, he reported, that had transformed a series of swampy areas into "cultured" ones; these lands, he wrote, had already been "mastered."[131]

"Mastering" the valley meant not only irrigating it, but also resettling tens of thousands of Soviet citizens to new collective farms in the valley. The collectivization of agriculture that accompanied the First Five-Year Plan was one of the most brutal policies carried out by the Soviet state. The "working hypothesis" for the Vakhsh cotton sovkhozes and kolkhozes, included with the economists' evaluation of the Vakhshstroi plan in January 1930, gives a glimpse into the vision for collective farmers in the valley. The initial plans foresaw workers, most of whom were to be Central Asians, engaging in almost entirely manual labor, working ten-hour days throughout the year – and longer in June and October – to raise cotton. In spite of the promises of the revolution to do away with traditional gender roles, domestic work continued to be seen as "women's work," though children and the elderly – and even, if necessary, men – could also help out. Women were also to do most of the cotton harvesting in October, as some Central Asian women had before the revolution.[132] Initial plans for the state farms foresaw "a cotton monoculture," with room for "neither gardens, nor orchards." The call in July 1929 to increase cotton production had also been accompanied by a call to reduce acreage of "non-cotton cultures" in the cotton-growing regions; thus, on Vakhsh state farms, alfalfa was to be planted "exclusively as a companion crop," because of its potential to restore overworked and salinized soils for cotton. Rice, widely grown in the valley until that point, was seen as "only a temporary crop in our region," though future rice sovkhozes might be possible. Though by the early 1930s rice occupied less

130 Engineer Kuznetsov, "O zabolachivanii i rassolenii Vakhshskoi doliny," *UV* 66 (366) (July 4, 1934), 2. For more on salinization and waterlogging in 1934, see TsGA RT f. 268, op. 1, d. 39.

131 TsGA RT f. 268, op. 1, d. 94b, ll. 16.

132 Poniatovskii, *Opyt izucheniia khlopkovodstva*, 9; Nalivkin and Nalivkina, *Muslim Women of the Fergana Valley*, 105–106, 109; Ivanin, *Khiva i reka Amu-Dar'ia*, 47–48. For the Russian view that harvesting cotton was "women's work," see *Trudy s"ezda khlopkovodov*, 61.

than half of its prerevolutionary acreage, it contined to be seen as a competitor for cotton – particularly since Turksib was now complete – and, therefore, had no place in the new plan to develop the Vakhsh River Valley. Calculations for nutrition foresaw bringing in most of the food from outside the valley.[133]

In an attempt to attract settlers to the Vakhsh Valley, benefits offered to resettlers included three years of freedom from taxes beginning with the first harvest, as long as they settled on a collective farm, and as long as at least half the plot they farmed were planted with Egyptian cotton (which suggests that the initial plans for a cotton monoculture may not have been implemented on state farms). Until 1936, the process of "mastering the valley" was overseen by a department of Vakhshstroi; afterward, it became its own independent organization with its own funds, directly under the People's Commissariat of Agriculture.[134] Although official Tajik government documents stressed that resettlement should take place "on a strictly voluntary basis and with the full consent of the resettlers themselves," there are many references in extant correspondence to "perversions." Reports on the "violation of the principle of voluntariness" include accusations that local party leaders, in their efforts to fill quotas, had forced people to move. Documents regarding the need to "return" peasants who had left the cotton-growing regions to their places of resettlement (*vodvorenie*) also may have led to the use of force.[135] Recruiters working to find suitable peasants for the collective farms reported that some households absconded with the credit funds provided to them by the Resettlement Administration, without ever reaching the places they were supposed to settle. One recruiter encountered his own recruits fleeing from Stalinabad back to Leninabad in the north. Some resettlers who had been "recruited" in the northern regions were already registered in the Vakhsh Valley and were happy to accept more money to return.[136]

Along with moving thousands of demobilized Red Army soldiers, many of those targeted for resettlement were "experienced cotton-growers" from northern Tajikistan or Uzbekistan, particularly those with

[133] TsGA KR f. 332, op. 1, d. 1865, ll. 79, 95, 112–113, 118–119, 124–125, 153, 207–208, 233. For figures on rice acreage and the Soviet view of rice as a competitor for cotton, see "K voprosu o perspektivakh razvitiia risoseianiia v SSSR," *IG* 2, 6 (1936), 1–30: 5, 10. See also RGASPI f. 62, op. 2, d. 1840, l, 4.

[134] TsGA RT f. 282, op. 8, d. 4, l. 29; op. 2, d. 22, ll. 19, 26.

[135] TsGA RT f. 18, op. 1, d. 370, l. 355; TsGA RT f. 18, op. 1, d. 359, ll. 42, 90, 153–154.

[136] TsGA RT f. 18, op. 1, d. 1625, ll. 157, 160, 163.

large families; the party instructed the sovkhozes to use the workers' families to help bring in the cotton harvest.[137] In later years, when not enough farmers could be recruited from northern Tajikistan, Tajik authorities turned eastward to the Pamirs. The Ferghana Valley was also encouraged to "give more households."[138] By the end of 1935, slightly more than one-third of the newly arrived settlers had been successfully settled, only one-quarter of them on newly irrigated lands; in total, fewer than fifteen thousand hectares of new land had been "mastered."[139]

In addition to these supposedly "voluntary" settlers, many of those resettled were so-called special settlers, including many Russians and Ukrainians accused of being kulaks (rich peasants). (Bolsheviks who had criticized tsarist-era "colonization" of the borderlands with kulaks do not appear to have appreciated this irony.) In the spring of 1935, more than half of the households resettled to the Vakhsh Valley were (special) labor settlers [*trudposelentsy*] from the European part of the Soviet Union, some of them "from the urban element," with little knowledge of agriculture. Advantages of getting these households were that no money had to be spent on their recruitment, no special measures were taken to transport them in sanitary conditions, and they could be housed in temporary barracks on arrival. A call for fifteen hundred so-called kulaks to be resettled from Ukraine in August 1935, for instance, requested that they be housed in large tents holding up to fifty people.[140] Their experiences contrast sharply with Soviet claims about collective and socialist labor as a means of educating – or reeducating – former tsarist subjects to become modern Soviet citizens. As historian Lynne Viola has observed, "In the end, special resettlement was primarily about punishment, isolation, and the most brutal – and distinctly noneducational – exploitation of labor."[141]

Leaving rates among settlers, especially in the first years, were significant – 23 percent of recruited households left in 1933 and 28 percent in 1935. Almost the only regions of settlement that did not record any

[137] Demobilized Red Army soldiers and their families were an "attractive alternative to the Cossacks" used to settle the borderlands in the tsarist era (*Broad Is My Native Land*, 42). TsGA RT f. 18, op. 1, dd. 486, ll. 13–13ob; 1626, l. 40; f. 268, op. 1, d. 42a, ll. 114–115, 162; f. 282, op. 8, d. 4, l. 28.

[138] TsGA RT f. 18, op. 1, d. 1623, l. 38; f. 282, op. 2, d. 22, l. 80.

[139] TsGA RT f. 18, op. 1, d. 1626, l. 78.

[140] TsGA RT f. 18, op. 1, dd. 1625, ll. 34–37; 1622, l. 8; f. 282, op. 8, d. 4, l. 27; op. 2, d. 22, l. 35.

[141] Lynne Viola, *The Unknown Gulag: The Lost World of Stalin's Special Settlements* (New York: Oxford University Press, 2007), 187.

outflow were Molotov and Ak-Gaza, the two regions predominantly populated by special (non-voluntary) settlers. In total, between 1933 and 1937, slightly more than eighteen thousand families moved to Kurgan-Tiube (Qurghonteppa) and the Vakhsh Valley, of whom thirty-five hundred (around 20 percent) left.[142] Lack of housing, livestock, farm implements, and food were all reasons for settlers to pack their bags.[143] As of early 1937, harvests of Egyptian cotton in the "resettlement border zone" [*pereselencheskaia pogranichnaia zona*] were still low.[144] Nor was there was any denying that in order to combat salinization and swamping, Vakhshstroi had created Karalang, an artificial lake that Tolstopiatov claimed had already "shrunk several-fold" in 1934, but in 1937 measured fifteen hundred hectares of newly irrigated land meant for cotton.[145]

THE LEGACY OF VAKHSHSTROI

One can still see a bit of the Vakhsh Valley as it once was, preserved as a *zapovednik* (nature reserve) established in 1938 by the Bolsheviks as a reaction to the encroachment of agriculture in the valley and the rapid destruction of riparian woodland for firewood and building materials for Vakhshstroi and the surrounding state and collective farms. The name of the reserve is "Tigrovaia Balka" – Tiger Gully – but those who come here looking for tigers will be disappointed, for a Caspian tiger has not been seen here since 1958.[146] In the early years of Soviet rule, Vaillant-Couturier and Kisch both recorded being proudly informed about how many tigers had been killed and how few remained; "nests of tigers" were making way for productive agricultural land, a sentiment captured in Kisch's chapter "From Tigers to Cotton Collectives."[147] An early draft

142 TsGA RT f. 18, op. 1, d. 1626, l. 40.

143 On lack of housing, see TsGA RT f. 18, op. 1, dd. 1626, l. 82; 1625, l. 82; 1623, l. 137. See also Polian, *Against Their Will*, 67.

144 TsGA RT f. 18, op. 1, d. 1384, l. 80.

145 TsGA RT f. 268, op. 1, d. 94b, l. 16; f. 18, op. 1, d. 1771, ll. 14, 101.

146 As Doug Weiner has pointed out, "frequently, zapovedniki became the only remaining patches of the original virgin nature that once covered the entire region" (*Models of Nature*, 97). For the large numbers of tigers killed here in the early 1930s, see Kurochkin, *Vakhshstroi*, 23–24. Solid evidence for the last Caspian tiger sightings in the wild is difficult to find. The last one is said to have been killed in 1970, though new evidence suggests that the Amur tiger is, in fact, descended from the Caspian tiger. Cheryl Lyn Dybas, "The Once and Future Tiger," *BioScience* 60, 11 (Dec. 2010), 872.

147 Vaillant-Couturier, *Mittelasien Erwacht*, 47–48; Kisch, chapter 10, *Changing Asia*, 147–166.

of the park rules even contained a three hundred-ruble reward for killing a tiger. As a Comrade Livaev of the Tajik agriculture ministry had asserted on the park's establishment, "Tiger Gully" was only ever meant to be understood as "a romantic name."[148] Life was useful only when it served some economic purpose. There was no room for wild tigers in the rational vision of modernity Soviet planners held for the Vakhsh Valley.

That vision is captured on the cover of a celebratory photo album from Vakhshstroi dating to around 1937, which features a fanciful drawing on its cover of the head gates of the main Stalin Canal, framed by excavators and ornamental cotton bolls. The excavators hold aloft a banner that reads, "Vakhsh is conquered [*Vakhsh pokoren*]. Its waters have been summoned to the service of the socialist agriculture of the valley." Photos of the work inside the album are more realistic – muddy troughs, dusty fields plowed by horses, lone excavators belching smoke. A meeting held on top of the completed sluice gates shows hundreds of Central Asians gathered beneath a banner that reads, "Vakhshstroi is a mighty weapon in the [fight?] for the cotton independence of the Soviet Union."[149]

Internally, however, Vakhshstroi's mood in 1937 was less triumphant. In 1933, Tolstopiatov had fired engineer Syromiatnikov, who had survived the trial of 1928 to become head engineer at Vakhshstroi, but he himself was not immune. Like Tolstopiatov's own predecessors, people were expendable; the plan was not. Soviet and post-Soviet accounts of Vakhshstroi mention Tolstopiatov as the strong-willed director who was brought in to assist the ailing construction project. None of these accounts mentions his arrest in 1936 and probable death by firing squad in 1937, along with the directors of several other large-scale hydraulic projects in Central Asia, as part of the general Great Terror carried out across Stalinist Russia in the late 1930s. The archives, however, are clear. An indication that the writing was on the wall can be seen in a decree of Tajikistan's Council of People's Commmisars, from May 31, 1936, in which Deputy Chairman Nusratullo Maksum stated that any further "mistakes" made in the development of irrigation in the already irrigated regions of the Vakhsh Valley would fall personally on Tolstopiatov.[150] Project documents from the following year refer to Tolstopiatov as a

148 TsGA RT f. 18, op. 1, d. 1870, ll. 49, 60.

149 The cover of the photo album is on the cover of this book. RGAE, f. 8390, op. 1, d. 1098.

150 TsGA RT f. 18, op. 1, d. 986, l. 36.

FIGURE 6.3. Meeting on the [Vakhsh canal] headworks, 1930s. From the photo album *Vakhsh Irrigation Construction in the Tajik SSR*, RGAE f. 8390, op. 1, d. 1098, l. 100b.
Reproduced with permission from the Russian State Archive of the Economy.

Trotskyite and spy.[151] As Gorton remarked on his return to the United States, "Russia may be a workman's paradise but it is Soviet Engineer's Hell."[152] For engineers, he wrote, having to adhere to the five-year plan, always with the fear of the secret police lurking, "is tantamount to forced labor."[153]

But Gorton also had his doubts about the claim of a workman's paradise. He recognized the hypocrisy in Soviet claims that new forms of Soviet labor differed significantly from capitalist labor in their

151 TsGA RT f. 268, op. 4, dd. 9, l. 43; 10, l. 33. According to Teichmann, he was arrested in August 1936 (*Macht der Unordnung*, 169). See also the lists with Tolstopiatov's name, preserved by the Russian organization Memorial ("Spisok lits, podlezhashchikh sudu Voennoi kollegii Verkhovnogo suda Soiuza SSR") from October 21 and November 1, 1937. (*Stalinskie spiski*, http://stalin.memo.ru/names/p372.htm). Accessed June 23, 2018.

152 Manuscript beginning "In most instances...," WLG, Box 1, Folder F.

153 Manuscript beginning "The Vakhsh Project in Tadjikistan is near the Afgan frontier...," WLG, Box 1, Folder F.

capability to free human beings from drudgery. Among the items Gorton kept from his time in the Soviet Union are a newspaper clipping from a Soviet English-language newspaper with a photograph of a Chinese "coolie" as an example of capitalist oppression and a very similar photograph of a Turkestani man weighted down by a great load on his back. On the back of the second photograph, Gorton wrote, "This shows how labor is exploited where I have been, not as the capitalists exploit it, but in a spirit of brotherly love, blinding humanity with the torch of civilization." (In his 1929 book on Tajikistan, Tajik official Khojibaev had included a similar picture of a man with a burden on his back with the caption "Backwardness vanishing.")[154] In the era of the First Five-Year Plans, with their emphasis on speeding up time itself, when machines did not work, men became the machines. Human labor became a substitute for time and technology alike. The ends were always more important than the means. This was the legacy of Vakhshstroi, as the great hydraulic projects undertaken in Central Asia beginning in 1939 would make all too clear.

MAKING HISTORY ON THE GREAT CANALS

By 1938, Vakhshstroi had brought water to less than half of the area it was to have irrigated by 1933. Almost all of Vakhshstroi's voluntary labor had disappeared, and officials reported that trying to recruit more workers was nothing but a waste of time and money. In 1939, the forced laborers of the local OGPU camp moved from a remote location to the main headquarters of the construction site. It is hard to know what conditions for them were like, though Vladimir Andrle has argued that in the 1930s there may very well have been little difference between the conditions of free and forced labor on construction sites. A 1939 project report concluded, perhaps in an effort to justify the abandonment of Vakhshstroi's revolutionary promises, that manual labor was, in fact, more precise – and, in some cases, more efficient – than was machine labor. There remained no rationale for the further existence of Vakhshstroi as a separate organization.[155]

[154] Newspaper clipping, WLG, Envelope B; photograph of a man carrying a burden, Envelope D; Khojibaev, *Tadzhikistan*, 49.

[155] RGAE, f. 8378, op. 1, d. 671, ll. 16, 24; Vladimir Andrle, *Workers in Stalin's Russia: Industrialization and Social Change in a Planned Economy* (New York: St. Martin's Press, 1988), 206.

It was not only at Vakhshstroi, however, that in 1939, the power of Soviet manual labor – touted to Willard Gorton as early as 1930 – came back to occupy center stage in Soviet Central Asia. That year, on September 19, the Central Committee of the Communist Party of Uzbekistan, along with the Council of People's Commissars, pronounced that digging on the Great Ferghana Canal had ceased. In total, official reports claimed, more than one hundred and sixty thousand collective farm workers had worked for forty-five days to move sixteen million cubic meters of earth. They had created a two-hundred-and-seventy-kilometer-long canal spanning the fertile Ferghana Valley from the Kyrgyz border into neighboring Tajikistan, which would provide water from the Naryn River to new cotton fields.[156] By December 31, all regulating structures were complete, and water entered the canal for the first time, just four months after initial construction had begun. The wild success of the Great Ferghana Canal inspired the immediate construction of other "great" canals to transform the landscapes of Soviet Central Asia: the Great Chui Canal in the Chu River Valley on the border of the Kyrgyz and Kazakh Soviet Socialist Republics, and the Great Hissar Canal that, like the Great Ferghana Canal, brought water to the collective farms of the Uzbek and Tajik SSRs.

While official reports about the Great Ferghana Canal resemble typical Soviet propaganda in their emphasis on numbers – volume of earth moved, number of collective farmers involved – the "tremendous preoccupation with the machine" evident in the projects of the First Five-Year Plan is strangely absent.[157] In contrast, propaganda about the Great Canals emphasized that almost no modern technology was to be employed in construction; rather, tens of thousands of farmers, "using their own initiative and their own resources," worked without pay, in the blazing sun – in the case of the Great Ferghana Canal in temperatures reaching forty-five degrees Celsius in the shade – employing hoes and shovels to built a gigantic canal for the state.[158] The local newspaper indicated that excavators would be used only in the most difficult sections of the Great Ferghana Canal, where manual labor could not be employed; archival documents also indicate that the plan from the beginning was for more than sixteen million cubic meters of earth to be removed manually, while blasting, scrapers, and excavators were to remove the remaining

156 "Tovarishcham Stalinu i Molotovu," *P* 261 (September 20, 1939), 1.

157 John McCannon, "Technological and Scientific Utopias, 1921–1932," 159.

158 U. Iusupov, "Bol'shoi Ferganskoi Kanal proryt," *P* 262 (September 21, 1939), 3.

one million cubic meters.[159] An official volume dedicated to the construction of the Great Chui Canal – intended to increase production of sugar beets in the Chu Valley – similarly noted that "all of this great work . . . will be mainly fulfilled by the labor of kolkhoz workers . . . and only an insignificant part will be carried out mechanically."[160] Officials estimated that half the local population was to participate in building the canal.[161] More than sixty thousand collective farmers worked in the spring of 1941 and the following year to complete the project. A similar canal project begun in 1940 to irrigate forty thousand hectares in the Hissar Valley of Tajikistan and the Surkhondaryo region of the Uzbek SSR foundered due to the Soviet entrance into war with Germany, but was nevertheless reported to be a success – in part, perhaps, because it was a convenient way to forget about the swamping and salinization of land in the Vakhsh Valley.[162]

What distinguished these mass mobilizations for the "great canals" from the projects of earlier Central Asian rulers – the khans, emirs, and beks – who, according to both Russian tsarist and Bolshevik officials, had forcibly driven their populations to dig the extensive irrigation networks that were still visible across the landscapes of Stalin's Central Asia?[163] What was it that had led the Soviet state to abandon its focus on modern technology and retreat to what appeared to be indigenous Central Asian techniques of irrigation construction? Some clues may be found in the stories woven around the construction of the Great Canals.

The first story told about the Great Canals was their origin in a triumphant "popular" initiative, in which collective farm workers in the Ferghana Valley had demonstrated their dedication to Stalin through an enormous feat of labor. According to this narrative, a group of inspired collective farmers, driven by their desire to free the cotton harvest from dependence upon the whims of nature, had decided to build a nine-kilometer canal in the spring of 1939, which then inspired many others

159 RGAE f. 8378, op. 1, d. 678, ll. 8–8ob. *NSS* 3 (July 27, 1939), 4.

160 S. P. Petrov, *Bol'shoi Chuiskii Kanal i Orto-Tokoiskoe vodokhranilishche* (Frunze: Uprav. stroit. BchK i Orto-Tokoi vodokhranilishcha, 1941), 37. Another key component of the plan was the construction of the Orto-Tokoi (Ortokoi) Reservoir, the very reservoir that engineer Vasil'ev had imagined back in 1913.

161 RGAE f. 4372, op. 41, d. 1234, l. 2.

162 RGAE f. 8378, op. 1, d. 663, ll. 39–40.

163 For a Soviet criticism of Central Asian rulers forcing tens of thousands of their subjects to dig by hand canals up to one hundred versts in length, see the article by Vodkhoz director Rykunov, "Blizhaishie zadachi po irrigatsii Srednei Azii," *VI* 4 (April 1925), 3–13: 3.

to follow their lead. In honor of the supreme leader, the Great Ferghana Canal, like the main Vakhsh canal, was named after Stalin.[164]

The Great Canals were not, however, simply successful demonstrations of Soviet patriotism; rather, they represented a significant achievement in the age-old struggle of the Central Asian people for water. In this version of the story, of all the rulers of Central Asia, it was only Soviet Communist Party leadership that had been able to fulfill the water needs of the people. In highlighting the role of the Soviet government, official propaganda about the Great Chui Canal, for instance, insisted that "the tsarist government was not interested in the irrigation of the rich Chu Valley," a message intended to be spread to the people not only in writing, but also by means of discussions and lectures.[165] According to the Communist Party, "The Kyrgyz people has dreamt for centuries of conquering [*pokorenie*] the River Chu, dreamed of the transformation of the Chu Valley into a valley of rich harvests, orchards, and vineyards. But it was only a dream."[166] Admitting that the khans of Khoqand had developed flourishing orchards in the Chu Valley, or that a large-scale irrigation project had already been well underway there before the collapse of the Russian Empire would undermine the Soviet claims to legitimacy in the region as the only government able to help the people fulfill their age-old desire for water. Moreover, linking the Soviet administration to the project might recall the atrocities of 1916 and might raise questions of how different Soviet policies were from the tsarist colonization of the borderlands, even if the Soviet government had reverted once more to using the word resettlement (*pereselenie*), rather than *kolonizatsiia*.[167] Instead, by the end of the 1930s, the Soviet government claimed to have sundered the chains of slavery forged by nature and despotic rulers alike, seting in motion the process by which the Great Canals could at last provide the water for which the people had clamored for centuries.[168]

Yet, even more important than Stalin's leadership and the ability of the Soviet state to provide water to the people of Central Asia was an emphasis on *how* this was achieved. This was the third victory of the Great Ferghana Canal and its successors: the fact that they were built

[164] For the role of "popular initiative" in the construction of the Great Chui Canal, see Petrov, *Bol'shoi Chuiskii Kanal,* 5.
[165] Ibid., 3; TsGA PD KR f. 56, op. 4, d. 300, l. 110.
[166] TsGA PD KR f. 56, op. 4, d. 301, l. 24. [167] *Broad Is My Native Land*, 35.
[168] Gepner, *Bol'shoi Ferganskii Kanal im. Stalina* (Tashkent: Partizdat TsK KP(b) Uzbekistana, 1940), 7, 27.

using a new method of Soviet labor.[169] According to this version of the story, it was an entirely new form of "free, conscious, socialist labor" that had made the rapid construction of these canals possible.[170] This interpretation may at last explain the apparent paradox posed by the fact that what were touted as the greatest irrigation achievements in Central Asia since the advent of Russian rule, in a country infatuated with technology and relentless forward progress, used methods that seemed no different from those ostensibly used by the pharaohs of ancient Egypt. (Indeed, some even explicitly made the comparison, but pointed out how many had died in the construction of the massive works of ancient Egypt, in contrast to those of the Soviet Union!)[171]

By emphasizing the effectiveness of labor brigade organization on the Ferghana Canal, the Soviet Union could essentially claim that by means of Soviet organizational methods, human labor had become more efficient than a machine. Whereas Marx had written about workers in capitalist societies becoming "depressed spiritually and physically to the condition of a machine," a century later Soviet labor had solved this dilemma. Unlike oppressed capitalist laborers, Soviet workers on the Great Ferghana Canal were conscious workers, imbued with a sense of the purpose for which they worked and a sense of involvement with a revolutionary project that would free them from drudgery.[172]

Unlike projects such as Vakhshstroi, which differed little from their counterparts in other parts of the Soviet Union, the Great Canals tried to make history by infusing the construction sites with revolutionary elan. By eliminating costly housing and machinery, and by mobilizing collective farm workers, who already owed the state a set number of labor hours, the Soviet state could invest money in cultural productions intended to raise the consciousness of workers and increase their motivation to work. Moving cinemas traveled with work brigades along the Great Ferghana Canal, showing popular new films, such as Sergei Eisenstein's *Alexander Nevsky* and *Lenin in 1918*, dubbed into Uzbek. Breakfast and lunch breaks during the ten-hour day were utilized to to spread propaganda,

169 See, for instance, the speech of Engineer Siniavskii, TsGA RU, f. 837, op. 32, d. 1523, ll. 101–107: 107. I thank Lewis Siegelbaum for generously sharing his materials from this *fond* with me.

170 "Plody narodnoi initsiativy," *P* 361 (December 30, 1940), 1; RGAE f. 8378, op. 1, d. 663, l. 4.

171 Gepner, *Bol'shoi Ferganskii Kanal*, 79.

172 Karl Marx, "Wages of Labor," *Economic and Philosophic Manuscripts of 1844*, ed. Dirk J. Struik, trans. Martin Milligan (New York: International, 1964), 68.

through radio broadcasts, and to stamp out religion and illiteracy; to this end, twenty-one agitators and twelve lecturers were hired to promote the anti-religion campaign, and workers had access to libraries, classrooms, and teachers. According to an official report, more than fifty thousand people attended forty-five minutes of "school" each day (though only six thousand "completed" the program).[173]

Through relentless articles on the novelty of the construction project, *On the Stalinist Construction Site*, the free daily newspaper on the Ferghana Canal, helped to instill the notion that canal workers were, quite literally, "constructing" history. The newspaper was brought daily by airplane to the construction site and distributed in both Russian (*Na stalinskoi stroike*) and Uzbek (*Stalincha Qurulishda*) versions.[174] Authorities suggested inviting delegations from other republics to see how entertainment and leisure were provided on the construction site.[175] When building the Great Chui Canal, the Kyrgyz Party followed Ferghana's lead by stressing that the construction should be accompanied by moving cinemas; "red yurts" with newspapers, chess, and checkers; literacy classes; and a free newspaper so that workers could see history being made.[176]

To further the sense of historical importance, a proposal for a "Great Ferghana Canal Museum" was announced on August 1, 1939 – the very day that construction began – in order "to give visitors the opportunity to learn what the Great Ferghana Canal has given the Uzbek people." Exhibits documenting the preparation and progress on the construction project opened at points along the canal and in Ferghana's city parks.[177] The production of new plays, which officials intended to connect the promise of the future canal to examples from the past highlighting the lack of water, further enhanced the drama of this historical juncture. *Orzular* (which can be translated as "hopes" or "dreams"), for instance, was a dramatic work that began with an 1895 uprising of peasant-

[173] RGAE f. 8378, op. 1, d. 678, ll. 24–27; Gepner, *Bol'shoi Ferganskii Kanal*, 76; TsGA RU f. 837, op. 32, d. 1523, l. 58; *NSS* 8 (August 2, 1939), 1.

[174] The Uzbek version is visible in Max Penson's photo "Agitator Sakduleijev distributes newspapers to the workers of a kolkhoz on the canal of Fergana" (1939) in Erika Billeter, *Usbekistan: Dokumentarfotografie 1925–1945 von Max Penson* (Bern: Benteli, 1996), 103. Gepner, *Bol'shoi Ferganskii Kanal*, 84–86.

[175] TsGA RU, f. 837, op. 32, d. 1523, l. 15.

[176] TsGA PD KR f. 56, op. 4, d. 300, ll. 111–113.

[177] "Muzei Bol'shogo Ferganskogo kanala," *NSS* 7 (August 1, 1939), 4; *NSS* 37 (September 5, 1939), 4.

farmers in the Ferghana Valley over lack of access to water from the Uch-Qorghon *ariq* and culminated with the Great Ferghana Canal.[178] The prizes given for the best work included robes of honor (khalats), just the way Grand Duke Nikolai Konstantinovich Romanov had given them out to recognize distinguished contributions to his efforts to irrigate the Hungry Steppe. Three artists on the banks of the canal produced hundreds of drawings of the best workers and of key moments of the work as it was taking place, which were then displayed in a mobile exhibition.[179]

Even though technology was for the most part absent from the worksite itself, technology was used to record the construction process for posterity. The great photographers Max Penson, Mikhail Grachev, and Max Alpert produced stunning photomontages of the Great Ferghana Canal worksite, which resembled a vast Hollywood movie set. The canal was immortalized in film, as well, by famed Soviet director Sergei Eisenstein himself, accompanied by the twenty-eight-year-old Uzbek filmmaker Malik Kayumov. Though Eisenstein abandoned his original idea for a full-length feature film that would begin with Tamerlane (Amir Timur), continue through the tragic episodes of the rules of the khans and the tsars, and end with "the great joy of communist labor," the footage he and Kayumov recorded became part of an award-winning shorter-length documentary called *Moguchii Potok* (*Mighty Torrent*).[180] These uses of technology as propaganda, as well as documenting and recording history while it was being made, were not new. But the scale was. And compared to earlier projects, the vivid and explicit emphasis on the power of a mass of human bodies engaged in manual labor was striking.

There were certainly practical reasons for not employing expensive technology on the site. Vakhshstroi had shown that complex machines such as excavators, which still had to be imported from abroad, were expensive to maintain and repair, and generally did poorly on the rough terrain and soft soils at Central Asian construction sites. The puzzle now

[178] RGAE f. 8378, op. 1, d. 678, l. 27; TsGA RU f. 837, op. 32, d. 1523, l. 52; "Novaia p″esa," *NSS* 41 (September 10, 1939), 2. The history of tsarist attempts to use water from the Naryn to irrigate the Uch-Qorghon steppe was told in "Voploshchenie mechty [Realization of Dreams]," *NSS* 30 (August 28, 1939), 3.

[179] Gepner, *Bol'shoi Ferganskii Kanal*, 106; RGAE f. 8378, op. 1, d. 678, l. 27.

[180] The first part of Eisenstein's original script is published as "Ferghana Canal, Reel 1" in Sergei Eisenstein, *The Film Sense*, trans. Jay Leyda, revised edn. (New York: Harcourt Brace Jovanovich, 1975), 256–268. *NSS* 18 (August 14, 1939), 4. Kayumov's *Mighty Torrent*, which Kyrgyz officials mistakenly thought featured road construction, was one of the films recommended to be shown at kolkhozes involved in the construction of the Great Chui Canal (TsGA PD KR f. 56, op. 4, d. 300, l. 110).

facing Soviet authorities was how to make the absence of technology a sign of progress. The answer was an emphasis on "new rapid methods" of construction, realized by means of a new phenomenon, the *narodnaia stroika*, or "people's construction project."[181]

The *narodnaia stroika* was the latest method by which the new Soviet people were to be forged. Its key characteristic was its efficiency in mobilizing the local population for irrigation construction. No longer would laborers have to be recruited from all corners of the Soviet Union by means of expensive and inefficient recruitment brigades. In the people's construction projects of 1939–1941, moreover, the collective attained an even greater symbolism, since the units adopted in structuring people's work brigades were the units of the kolkhoz, or collective farm, the result of the great – and, for many, traumatic – collectivization drive of Stalin's First Five-Year Plan.[182] In what today sounds like a parody, an issue of *On the Stalinist Construction Site* in August 1939 celebrated "Free Kolkhozistan."[183] Collective farm workers already present in the region simply had to shoulder the ketmen, using the tool of their ancestors and the knowledge of generations to bring water to the inherently fertile lands with support from the Soviet leadership. The triumph of the collective farm workers' "popular initiative" in the building of the Great Ferghana Canal, thus, seemed to justify the entire collectivization experiment of the First Five-Year Plan, which was deemed to have both made such grandiose projects practicable for the first time, as well as raised the cultural level, consciousness, and confidence of the peasant masses to the point at which people's construction became possible.[184] (The fact that the "popular initiative" behind these canals arose from the state's failure to provide adequate water was conveniently overlooked in official Soviet propaganda.[185])

It was, therefore, not technology, but the supremacy of Soviet labor itself which would "hasten the transition to communism."[186] In what appears to be the first full-length article on the new phenomenon of the people's construction project, featured on the front page of *Pravda* at the

[181] RGAE f. 8378, op. 1, d. 663, l. 3.
[182] "Plody narodnoi initsiativy"; "Slavnye traditsii stalinskoi stroiki," *NSS* 41 (September 10, 1939), 1.
[183] "Svobodnyi kolkhozistan," *NSS* 9 (August 3, 1939).
[184] "Moguchaia sila kollektivnogo truda," *P* 129 (May 11, 1941), 1; Gepner, *Bol'shoi Ferganskii Kanal*, 29, 37.
[185] See, for instance, Iusupov, "Bol'shoi Ferganskoi Kanal proryt."
[186] RGAE, f. 8378, op. 1, d. 663, l. 4.

end of 1940, the author wrote that the "new relationship to labor" demonstrated on the worksite of the Great Ferghana Canal had evolved from previous socialist initiatives, including Lenin's *subbotniki*, or voluntary days of labor, followed by "socialist competition," and then that infamous form of competitive labor, the Stakhanovite movement.[187] This genealogy was sufficiently well-established in the popular imagination in Central Asia that in 1941 a schoolteacher in Tashkent suggested that an appropriate essay topic for tenth-form students would be "From the first subbotnik to the mass people's construction projects," citing the Great Ferghana Canal as an appropriate example.[188]

CONCLUSION

During the First Five-Year Plan, disasters could be written off as necessary sacrifices for the cause of building socialism. But, by 1936, socialism had officially been achieved and it was no longer so easy to hide the fact that life was not necessarily getting better or more joyous, whatever Stalin might have said to the contrary.[189] In the wake of the failure of the great shockwork construction project in the Vakhsh Valley to transform Central Asian workers and collective cotton farmers into joyful new Soviet people, the people's construction projects attempted to claim that this transformation had already been accomplished, by portraying as a joyous community affair an enormous irrigation project based on the mass mobilization of the unfree labor of collective farmers. Whereas Vakhshstroi by the end of the decade could only feebly justify the use of camp labor instead of expensive imported machinery, people's construction celebrated both the power of conscious Soviet labor over that of machines, as well as the power of the initiative of the Soviet people when placed under the guidance of the Soviet state, a clever strategy that the Soviet state continued to invoke in the decades to come.

Historians of Soviet labor have noted the profound shifts that took place among the "free" (that is, non-Gulag) labor force in the late 1930s. Lewis Siegelbaum, for instance, has documented a distinct near--

[187] "Plody narodnoi initsiativy."

[188] Iu. Sokolov, "Pis'mennye raboty po istorii v srednei shkole," *IZh* 6 (June 1941), 107–111: 109–110.

[189] In a late 1935 speech about the Stakhanovite movement, Stalin famously declared, "Life has become better, comrades. Life has become more joyous."

militarization of the labor force between 1938 and 1941.[190] Collective farm workers represented a captive population that could be mobilized like military units, and without which – and here, those who stressed the essential role of collectivization were right – the people's construction projects would not have been possible. The year of the Great Ferghana Canal, 1939, was also the year in which the Soviet state began to tighten its grip on the Soviet workforce in what Donald Filtzer has argued was "its first legal response to what it saw as its deteriorating control over the so-called 'free' labour force."[191] By early 1939, being twenty minutes late to work was grounds for dismissal from a job. On collective farms, as well, labor discipline increased with the introduction of "a compulsory minimum of labour-days (the arbitrary unit defining the amount of work done on the collective farms)," which was much higher in the cotton-growing regions than in the central regions.[192]

Yet, the years between 1938 and 1941 were also years in which qualitatively different changes were introduced to the organization of production.[193] A particularly innovative approach to labor during this period was the notion of people's construction that took shape along the Great Canals. Politically, times were tense following Stalin's widespread purges of Soviet society and with war looming on the horizon, yet official descriptions of the brutal work along the Great Ferghana Canal often reduced the scene to a festive holiday mood, a joyful celebration of socialist labor, emphasizing the concerts, theatricals, movies, and other leisure activities at the workers' disposal.[194] As one planning report put it, "On this canal a holiday will literally be organized. Of course, not a holiday in the literal sense, but a holiday of skillful [*umelyi*] labor ..."[195] The Great Ferghana Canal was presented to the local Central Asian

190 Lewis Siegelbaum, *Stakhanovism and the Politics of Productivity in the USSR, 1935–41* (Cambridge: Cambridge University Press, 1988), 285.

191 Donald Filtzer, *Soviet Workers and Stalinist Industrialization: The Formation of Modern Soviet Production Relations, 1928–1941* (London: Pluto, 1991), 233.

192 Jean Lévesque, "Foremen in the Field: Collective Farm Chairmen and the Fate of Labour Discipline after Collectivization, 1932–1953," in *A Dream Deferred: New Studies in Russian and Soviet Labour History*, eds. Donald Filtzer, Wendy Z. Goldman, Gijs Kessler, and Simon Pirani (Bern: Peter Lang, 2008): 252–253, 253 fn 31.

193 Siegelbaum, *Stakhanovism and the Politics of Productivity*, 285.

194 RGAE, f. 8378, op. 1, d. 663, l. 30b; TsGA RU, f. 837, op. 32, d. 1523, l. 39; "Ferganskii pochin," *P* 215 (August 5, 1939), 6; Gepner, *Bol'shoi Ferganskii Kanal*, 4, 51.

195 TsGA RU, f. 837, op. 32, d. 1523, l. 14.

people as an instance of hashar, the indigenous system whereby all households had to contribute to public works projects, now transformed into a joyful occasion. As a later Soviet Uzbek writer put it, "*Khashar* is an old Uzbek tradition. When a *khashar* is announced, the whole of the village turns out for work as if for a great holiday. In Soviet times this tradition has developed new aspects. The Great Ferghana Canal was the first republic-wide *khashar*."[196]

According to the official Soviet narrative, what made this hashar different from the corvée labor of the past was that it was not the whim of the ruler that was being fulfilled, but rather the will of the people. By invoking the hashar, Soviet authorities thus claimed to invoke something that was "nationally" Uzbek and in keeping with what "the people" wanted. As a 1941 *Pravda* article entitled "The Mighty Power of Collective Labor" put it, "In the Soviet Union, the interests of the government and the interests of the people coincide."[197] In this narrative, it was indigenous Central Asian rulers who had twisted the hashar – a community-based institution intended to mobilize labor resources based on mutual interest and collective benefit – to serve their own interests. Thus, Soviet leaders claimed the return of the hashar to its original community-based roots as the outcome of "popular initiative," even though in reality the Great Canals were a centralized, state-sponsored mobilization of a captive population for the advancement of Soviet economic and political goals in the region, in keeping with the overall shift toward greater labor discipline. Over the early Soviet period, community input in Central Asian water management had been replaced by centralized state decision-making, but the invocation of the hashar and the emphasis on a new form of labor were clever ways to disguise this distinction. The reports of "enthusiasm," "popular initiative," and "free, conscious, socialist labor" among the workers could not conceal the fact that the people's construction projects essentially used conscripted labor, yet unlike the Belomor (White Sea) Canal, which was explicitly touted as a means of reforging criminals through labor, the Great Canals claimed to use a new form of labor as a means of transforming people through transforming landscapes, mobilized under the watchful and caring eye of the

196 S. K. Tatur, *From the Great Fergana to the Kara-Kum Canal* (Moscow: Novosti, 1976), 8.

197 "Moguchaia sila kollektivnogo truda."

Soviet state.[198] Like other projects of the irrigation age, the Great Canals also looked backward – in this case at the water that previous Central Asian rulers had denied to the people – in order to look forward, projecting a vision of the future in which happiness had at last settled on Central Asian lands under Soviet socialist rule.

198 Cynthia Ann Ruder, *Making History for Stalin: The Story of the Belomor Canal* (Gainesville: University Press of Florida, 1998). The Belomor Canal was constructed by mostly manual labor between 1931 and 1933.

Epilogue

The Fate of the Aral Sea

An early report on the Great Ferghana Canal suggested that the "new rapid construction" of the people's construction projects could be fruitfully applied to other areas of the economy. In 1940, the "methods of Ferghana" were used throughout the Soviet borderlands and beyond to undertake not only irrigation canals, but also the construction of reservoirs and roads.[1] The mobilization for such people's construction projects blended seamlessly into wartime mobilization. While World War II itself put a temporary damper on large-scale irrigation projects in the Central Asian borderlands, by the end of the 1940s, such projects were pursued again with renewed vigor.

The year 1948 marked a century after Butakov had conducted his first investigation of the Aral delta; it also marked the introduction of Stalin's own "Great Plan for the Transformation of Nature." A major goal of the Great Plan, on the heels of another famine in 1946–1947, was an afforestation program to improve the climate of the southern Russian steppes by planting shelterbelts to protect them from harmful winds arising in Central Asia.[2] In an article entitled "Changing Nature to Aid Man," a Soviet writer described how "[r]oughly three times every decade … the winds from the Central Asian deserts shrivel the [wheat] fields" of the southern steppe region, "in the worst years raising the temperature to 50 degrees centigrade and driving enormous clouds of

[1] RGAE f. 8378, op. 1, d. 663, l. 4; "Plody narodnoi initsiativy."

[2] Klaus Gestwa, *Die Stalinschen Grossbauten des Kommunismus: Sowjetische Technik- und Umweltgeschichte, 1948–1967* (Munich: Oldenbourg, 2010), 230; Brain, *Song of the Forest*, chapter 6.

dust over the scorched landscape."[3] Discussion of how to limit the hot Central Asian winds (called *sukhovei*) in order to improve the climate of the steppes raised a parallel discussion about how irrigation might be used to improve the climate of the Aralo-Caspian Basin – where the winds supposedly originated in the first place – by changing the vegetation forming the ground cover and bringing more moisture to the air.[4] Such ideas built on a long history of fears about the desiccation of the Eurasian steppes and deserts. In the postwar period, therefore, even though the Soviet Union had triumphed in the cataclysmic armed conflict still known today as the "Great Patriotic War," the war on nature, and in particular, the deserts, continued to hold sway.

These campaigns to conquer nature were portrayed vividly in the pages of the 1948 issues of the popular illustrated youth magazine *Around the World*.[5] In the year of Stalin's Great Plan, at the site where the Grand Duke's Shirin Canal had drawn water from the rushing waters of the Syr Darya at the foot of the Rocks of Farhad, the Farhad Hydroelectric Station and dam triumphantly opened. As reported in *Around the World*, the postwar film *Day of a Victorious Country*, shot at locations all over the Soviet Union on August 14, 1947, blended tradition and modernity in its portrayal of the construction site at Farhadstroi by showing thousands of collective farmers hard at work, accompanied by the poetry of the fifteenth-century poet Mīr 'Ali-Shir Nava'i, who had written his own version of *Farhod wa Shirin*.[6] The poetic accompaniment emphasized the longstanding nature of the Central Asian desire for water, while the vision of thousands of collective farmers emphasized the supposedly popular nature of the construction of the reservoir and hydroelectric station.

Two photographs by Soviet photographer Max Penson clearly illustrate further continuities between the Great Canals and the construction of the Farhad Hydroelectric Station. In one, a smiling group of Uzbek men, women, and youth, several of them holding the ketmen on high, stands in a truck bed adorned with a portrait of Stalin and a large placard reading, in Uzbek, "*Salaam* [Greetings] to the kolkhoz workers who have

[3] *USSRIB* VII, 9 (May 28, 1947), 6.

[4] Mitrofan Mikhailovich Davydov, *Enisei-Ob-Aralo-Kaspiiskaia vodokhoziaistvenno-energeticheskaia problema* (Moscow: Glavgidroenergostroi, 1949), 9–11, 21–22, 40.

[5] See, for example, "O chem rasskazyvaet karta," *VS* 1 (January 1948), inside front cover; Mikhail Il'in, "U Farkhadskikh skal," *VS* 1 (January 1948), 4–8; L. Khvat, "Vokrug ozera Issyk-Kul," *VS* 5 (May 1948), 43–47.

[6] V. Popov, "Den' pobedivshei strany," *VS* 1 (January 1948), 52–54: 52.

come to the Farhod Hydroelectric Station construction project, to the mass hashar!" In another photo, two men appear to be reading an Uzbek newspaper – a nod to the literacy programs on such projects – the title of which, clearly displayed, is *Halq Qurilishi* ("People's Construction").[7] The existence of "people's construction" after the war suggests that the mass projects conducted in the borderlands on the eve of World War II did not find popularity among the Soviet leadership merely because of a climate of impending war or as an extension of the repressive policies of the Stalinist Great Terror, but rather were an expedient way for the Soviet state to draw attention away from its weaknesses, while at the same time mobilizing popular support for the regime through the idea of the superiority and unique potential of Soviet labor. In 1955, Nikita Khrushchev's campaign to liquidate the housing shortage engaged ordinary Soviet citizens in a "people's construction" movement to build their own apartments – adequate living space in central Russia, like water in Central Asia, being a crucial good that the Soviet state historically could not (or would not) provide.[8]

In the first year of the Great Stalin Plan, the spirit of Georgii Rizenkampf – who had been sent in the 1930s to work with the prison laborers on the Belomor Canal – reappeared with the resurrection of his Hungry Steppe irrigation plans. Construction of a 126-kilometer-long Southern Hungry Steppe Canal (the Romanov Canal, renamed the Kirov Canal, served as a "Northern" Hungry Steppe Canal) began in 1948 and progressed slowly until its completion in 1963. In 1956, Khrushchev promoted the irrigation of five hundred thousand hectares in the Hungry Steppe, as had Rizenkampf in his plans of 1912 and 1921; the project was touted as a scheme for the transformation of "virgin lands" to

[7] "Farkhadstroy": "Rabochie v gruzovoi mashine na stroitel'stve Farkhadskoi GES" (Image 15–6540) and "Dva stroitelia chitaiut gazety" (Image 15–6587) at maxpenson.com.

[8] Steven Harris, *Communism on Tomorrow Street: Mass Housing and Everyday Life after Stalin* (Baltimore, MD: Johns Hopkins University Press, 2013), 154–155. The 1955 campaign, rather than marking the start of the people's construction movement (Lewis Siegelbaum, *Cars for Comrades: The Life of the Soviet Automobile* [Ithaca, NY: Cornell University Press, 2008], 69), or even a revival, seems rather to be a more prominent national application of an existing and continuously used organizational technique. A 1951 Tel Aviv lecture series included a lecture on "People's Construction Projects in the USSR." Document 395, "Report on VOKS Activities in Israel" (January 1, 1952) in *Documents on Israeli-Soviet Relations, 1941–53*, II (London: Frank Cass, 2000), 767–768: 768.

cotton-growing land, paralleling the more well-known 1954 Khrushchev scheme to grow grain in the steppes to the north.[9]

In these years, emphasis continued to be placed on the notion of Soviet power as solely responsible for the "life awakening in the great, dead expanses of Central Asia" and for making Central Asian dreams come true, whether it was describing the changes wrought by "the expansive works to irrigate the Chu Valley," "the cherished dream [*zavetnaia mechta*] of the peoples of Khorezm" to "overcome the opposition of nature," or an ancient Tajik yearning for "a permanent irrigation system in the Vakhsh Valley."[10] In 1949, *Izvestiia* reported that the Stalinabad Documentary Film Studios were finishing work on a film called *Land of Our Fathers*, which depicted the centuries of struggle of Tajik mountaineers to defend their land against nomadic invaders. In an effort, no doubt, to justify the renewed effort to remove these mountain people from their homes and force them into agricultural labor, the film contrasted "the hard, colorless life of the mountaineers in the past ... with life on new collective cotton farms of the Vakhsh Valley."[11]

A February 1948 article in *Around the World* about a people's construction project harnessing the labor of seventy thousand collective farmers from Uzbekistan, Turkmenistan, and Qaraqalpaqstan on the construction of a railway in the Qara Qum from Charjui to the lower reaches of the Amu Darya and beyond to the Volga reported that the railway would release the Amu Darya from the burdens of transport to "fulfill its main duties: to irrigate the fields, to supply hydroelectric stations with energy." The river itself would be put to work. In words reminiscent of that darling of the irrigation age, the legendary Queen Semiramis, the article noted that the new railway, by taking over the duties of transport, would "bring the unruly [*nepokornyi*] river to flow where the people wanted it to flow," emphasizing once again the supposedly popular nature of such initiatives.[12]

The idea of harnessing the waters of the Amu Darya for the irrigation of the Qara Qum drove one of the biggest projects in subsequent decades. The July 1948 issue of *Around the World* resurrected the issue of rechanneling the Amu Darya to flow through the Uzboi and into the Caspian,

[9] For more, see Obertreis, "The Hungry Steppe: A Microstudy," in *Imperial Desert Dreams*, 273–321.

[10] Il'in, "U Farkhadskikh skal," *VS* 1: 4–5; A. Shakhov, "Priroda i kniga," *VS* 6 (June 1948), 63; Viktorin Popov, "Trassa v pustyne," *VS* 2 (February 1948), 27–33: 27; Luknitsky, *Soviet Tajikistan*, 190.

[11] *CDSP* I, 34 (September 20, 1949), 60.

[12] Popov, "Trassa v pustyne," 30–31.

the question that had been so earnestly debated by Russians in the late nineteenth century and then again by Soviet engineers in the 1920s. Plans for a Main Turkmen Canal were approved by the Soviet Council of Ministers in 1950 and touted in *Pravda* as "the realization of the centuries-old popular dream of transforming the desert into blooming fields and gardens."[13] After Stalin's death in March 1953, a new plan emerged for a Qaraqum Canal, completed in 1962, which followed a southerly route through the Qara Qum (as opposed to the northerly route proposed by Soviet engineers in the early 1920s), utilizing the eastern part of the Uzboi.[14] Over the following decades, this Qaraqum Canal was extended to the shores of the Caspian, reaching a length of 1,375 kilometers in 1988, which makes it the second-longest canal in the world. From at least the 1970s – and more frequently in the years following the collapse of the Soviet Union – it has been referred to as the Qaraqum or Turkmen River (Turkmendarya), rather than the Qaraqum Canal, much as indigenous Turkestanis had for centuries used interchangeable words to describe rivers and their largest canal constructions, blurring the boundaries between what was "natural" and what had been shaped by human hands.[15] This new blurring of boundaries, however, deliberately indicated a "natural" destiny for the water resources of the region – what was "meant to be" has come to pass.

The waters of the Qaraqum Canal were to help redistribute the resources of Turkmenistan and expand agriculture into the desert for "subtropical" cultures including, first and foremost, cotton.[16] A shift in economic emphasis in the years after Stalin's death away from heavy industry and toward the production of consumer goods brought renewed focus on the Soviet textile industry. While other countries shifted toward synthetic materials for clothing, Khrushchev emphasized cotton. Within Central Asia, procurement of cotton continued to be encouraged by artificially low prices, in contrast to livestock and food production, which were de-incentivized by procurement prices that were often lower than the actual costs of production. At the same time, Khrushchev's failures to grow grain and increase meat and milk production in the promised

[13] "Glavnyi Turkmenskii Kanal – velikaia stroika kommunizma," *P* 257 (September 14, 1950), 2.

[14] Geoffrey Wheeler, *The Modern History of Soviet Central Asia* (New York: Praeger, 1964), 172; Zonn, "Karakum Canal," 99.

[15] See, for example, "Reka vozrozhdeniia," *P* 270 (September 27, 1977), 3.

[16] A. S. Kes′, "Sud′ba Uzboia," *VS* 7 (July 1948), 46–47; Davydov, *Enisei-Ob-Aralo-Kaspiiskaia vodokhoziaistvenno-energeticheskaia problema*, 8, 16–17.

quantities resulted in pressure on the Central Asian republics to simultaneously increase the amount of land planted with cotton as well as become more self-sufficient in food production, resurrecting the tension between cotton and food production that had existed since tsarist times.[17] By the 1960s, pressure to grow both more cotton and more rice resulted in the target area for irrigation being raised from four million hectares to seven million for cotton alone, while the figures for the amount of cultivable land in the region as a whole were first doubled and then, by the early 1970s, more than tripled from estimates of the amount of land suitable for irrigation dating to the early twentieth century.[18] Cotton in the Qaraqum Canal zone increased four and a half times between 1958 and 1990.[19]

In the 1970s, the Uzbek Academy of Sciences admitted that the "rather one-sided use of irrigated land for cotton cultivation" resulted in not enough land being planted with food crops.[20] The high birth rate in Soviet Central Asia had led to population growth, resulting in lower averages of food production per person compared to other parts of the Soviet Union.[21] In the 1980s, the Central Asian republics, along with the Caucasus, were more dependent than other Soviet republics on imports of food and consumer goods.[22] Nearly all of the Soviet Union's raw cotton came from Central Asia; by 1980, the Soviet Union was second only to China in world cotton production.[23]

Since the Aral Sea basin is an endorheic (closed) basin, in the 1960s, with the continuing expansion of irrigated acreage and the Qaraqum and Southern Hungry Steppe Canals drawing water from the Amu and Syr

17 Grey Hodnett, "Technology and Social Change in Soviet Central Asia: The Politics of Cotton Growing," in eds. Henry W. Morton and Rudolf Tökés, *Soviet Politics and Society in the 1970s* (New York: The Free Press, 1974): 67–68, 70.

18 Igor Zonn, "Reasons for the Environmental and Socio-Economic Crisis," in eds. Andrey Kostianoy and Alexey Kosarev,*The Aral Sea Environment* (Berlin, Heidelberg: Springer, 2010): 76, 78.

19 Zonn, "Karakum Canal," 104.

20 *Irrigatsiia Uzbekistana*, 1 (Tashkent: FAN, 1975), 119.

21 Micklin, "Irrigation and Its Future in Soviet Central Asia," 240–241; *Irrigatsiia Uzbekistana*, 1, 118.

22 Gertrude Schroeder, "Economic Relations Among the Soviet Republics," in eds. Michael P. Claudon and Tamar L. Gutner, *Investing in Reform: Doing Business in a Changing Soviet Union* (New York: New York University Press, 1991), 25.

23 Gertrude Schroeder, "Regional Economic Disparities, Gorbachev's Policies, and the Disintegration of the Soviet Union," in *The Former Soviet Union in Transition*, I, Study Papers Submitted to the Joint Economic Committee, Congress of the United States (February 1993), 129; Beckert, *Empire of Cotton*, 435–436.

Darya, respectively, the increasing consumptive withdrawals of water – that is, water not returned to the system – began to have an observable effect on the level of the Aral Sea.[24] These losses became more noticeable in the dry years of the 1970s. The Qaraqum Canal, in particular, has been a culprit; to this day unlined, it loses large percentages of water to seepage, while the water it diverts for irrigation is deposited in the desert, where it evaporates or forms small swamps and ponds in old riverbeds and other depressions – what has been described as a "Karakum Venice" – rather than returning to the Amu Darya.[25] While particularly egregious, however, the seepage from the Qaraqum Canal is not the only case of inefficiency and water wastage in Central Asian irrigation systems today. In recent years, leakage in Uzbek irrigation systems caused the loss of as much as 70 percent of irrigation water. In Tajikistan, where 64 percent of water is diverted to the agricultural sector, it is thought that only half of this water reaches the crops.[26]

The dumping of irrigation drainage water in the deserts has continued the problem that plagued tsarist engineers as well as their Soviet successors: deterioration of the soil due to salinization, as salts are leached to the surface. Rather than extending the areas of irrigated land, increasing consumptive withdrawals of water seem to have resulted in increased application of water to both newly irrigated lands as well as areas of old irrigation. The oversaturation of these soils – sometimes as an intended corrective to surface salinization – has resulted in waterlogging and a raising of the groundwater table. Already in the 1960s, for instance, increased applications of water to the Hungry Steppe attempted to leach excess salt from the ground. By the 1980s, one-third of lands in Uzbekistan were affected by secondary salinization (that is, salinization occurring as a result of human activities) and crop yields across Central Asia had fallen 20 to 25 percent.[27]

In more recent years, the International Crisis Group (ICG) has blamed "inappropriate irrigation practices" for affecting more than 50 percent of

[24] Philip Micklin, "Aral Sea Basin Water Resources and the Changing Aral Water Balance," in eds. Philip Micklin, N. V. Aladin, and Igor Plotnikov,*The Aral Sea: The Devastation and Partial Rehabilitation of a Great Lake* (Berlin, Heidelberg: Springer, 2014): 121.

[25] Zonn, "Karakum Canal," 105; Micklin, "Aral Sea Basin Water Resources," 123–124.

[26] "The Curse of Cotton: Central Asia's Destructive Monoculture," International Crisis Group, *Asia Report* 93 (February 28, 2005), 28; "Water Pressures in Central Asia," *ICG Europe and Central Asia Report* 233 (September 11, 2014), 4.

[27] Micklin, "Irrigation and Its Future in Soviet Central Asia," 245; Micklin, "Aral Sea Basin Water Resources," 123.

irrigated land in Uzbekistan.[28] In the Vakhsh Valley, where the main crop is still cotton, secondary salinization has been a significant problem; a major culprit has been the Djuibor Canal, an integral part of the Vakhsh Valley irrigation system since the 1930s.[29] In Turkmenistan, where more than half the labor force continues to be employed in cotton agriculture, and cotton makes up one-quarter of the country's GDP, subsidies have resulted in a situation in which the country uses twice as much water as neighboring Uzbekistan, which already uses more than ten times as much as arid regions of the Middle East, such as Israel and Jordan. By the early twenty-first century, salinization caused by waterlogging affected nearly all of the irrigated cropland in Turkmenistan; today, "comprehensive rehabilitation of the irrigation network" is badly needed.[30] Across Central Asia, cotton yields – the very reason for most of the increasing water withdrawals in the first place – on salinized lands are 50–80 percent lower, and agricultural production losses due to salinization are estimated at two billion dollars annually.[31] Waterlogging and salinization are the first two steps toward desertification, and today the Aral Sea is often aptly described as Aralkum, the Aral Desert.[32]

In an attempt to reduce the waterlogging and salinization of Turkmen lands, the first president of post-Soviet, independent Turkmenistan, Saparmurat Niyazov, popularly known as Turkmenbashi (Father of the Turkmen People), unveiled a new scheme at the beginning of the twenty-first century: the creation of the Altyn Asyr (Golden Age) Lake, a project that has been continued by his successor Gurbanguly Berdymukhamedov. This new lake is to unite all of the drainage water from the entire country, which is currently being funneled there by large collectors, including the Dashoguz, which follows the bed of the old Uzboi. The hope is that the

28 "Water Pressures in Central Asia," 4.

29 Sherali Dzhuraevich Safarov, "Agrotekhnicheskie mery bor′by s protsessami vtorichnogo zasoleniia pochv v usloviiakh ogranichennogo drenazha agrolandshafta Vakhshskoi doliny," Aftoreferat dissertatsii na soiskanie uchenoi stepeni kandidata sel′sko-khoziaistvennykh nauk (Dushanbe, 2006), 3–4.

30 G. Winckler, E. Kleinn, and S.-W. Breckle, "The Aralkum Situation under Climate Change Related to Its Broader Regional Context" in eds. Siegmar-W. Breckle, Walter Wucherer, Liliya A. Dimeyeva, and Nathalia P. Ogar, *Aralkum – A Man-Made Desert: The Desiccated Floor of the Aral Sea (Central Asia)* (Berlin/Heidelberg: Springer, 2012), 435; "Curse of Cotton," 10; Paltamet E. Esenov,"Groundwaters and Salinization of Soils in Turkmenistan," *The Turkmen Lake Altyn Asyr*, 149.

31 Zonn, "Reasons for the Environmental and Socio-Economic Crisis," 81; Winckler et al., "The Aralkum Situation under Climate Change," 433.

32 "Curse of Cotton," 29; "Aralkum," *The Aral Sea Encyclopedia*, 41.

lake will serve as a recreational site and even a fishery. With the creation of the Golden Age Lake, another lake, the Saryqamysh, will likely rapidly disappear. Saryqamysh itself is a manmade product, which expanded in area from twelve square kilometers to almost four thousand in the years from 1962 to 2006, forming a water body full of salts, pesticides, fertilizers, and defoliants from irrigation runoff.[33]

As Lake Saryqamysh expanded, the Aral Sea shrank. The push for more cotton and large, wasteful projects such as the Qaraqum Canal led to the sea's rapid disappearance in the decades from 1961 onward, exposing vast expanses of the sea bed. Further contributors to the drop in the level of the Aral Sea were two reservoirs constructed in the 1960s – Charvak on the Chirchiq River near Tashkent and Toktogul on the Naryn River in Kyrgzystan (both feeders of the Syr Darya) – as well as two more upstream from Farhad on the Syr Darya itself. By the 1980s, water no longer flowed into the Aral through the main channel of the Amu Darya, and for several years in the mid-1980s, no water from the Syr Darya reached the sea at all.[34]

There was no question that irrigation was the culprit. As Philip Micklin reported on the eve of the collapse of the Soviet Union, "The fundamental cause of the water crisis in Central Asia is irrigation; water use by other sectors is, by comparison, insignificant."[35] In spite of the fact that Soviet leader Mikhail Gorbachev advocated for intensive, rather than extensive agricultural development, the Twelfth Five-Year Plan (1986–1990) called for 8.5 percent growth in irrigated regions in Central Asia and 19 percent in Kazakhstan. Cotton, all of which was grown on irrigated land, continued to be "far and away the region's most important crop," much of which was still shipped to the central industrial region around Moscow, though a portion of the crop was also exported by the 1980s.[36]

By September 2011, the Aral Sea had lost 85 percent of its surface area and 92 percent of its volume.[37] The ancient oasis of Khorezm has largely been replaced by sand. Gone is much of the tugay, which had been cut in

[33] Leah Orlovsky, Offir Matsrafi, Nikolai Orlovsky, and Michael Kouznetsov, "Sarykamysh Lake: Collector of Drainage Water – The Past, the Present, and the Future," *The Turkmen Lake Altyn Asyr*, 107–109.

[34] Micklin, "Irrigation and Its Future in Soviet Central Asia," 249; "Aral Sea Basin Water Resources," 121–24.

[35] Micklin, "The Water Crisis in Soviet Central Asia," 217.

[36] Ibid., 217–219; "Irrigation and Its Future in Soviet Central Asia," 230, 234–239, 242.

[37] Philip Micklin, "Introduction," *The Aral Sea*, 2.

half already by 1980, and with it the tigers; other fauna, such as the saiga and the hyena, have largely disappeared as well.[38] There is little water for migratory waterfowl. Gone, too, are the fish: twenty of the twenty-four species native to the region were gone by the early 1980s, and all endemic fish had disappeared by the time the Soviet Union collapsed.[39] With the bream, carp, and roach went the fishing industry that had provided many Central Asians with their livelihood, though the cannery at Muynak managed to operate a little longer by importing fish from the Baltic Sea.[40] Many of those fishermen were the sedentarized and collectivized descendants of the nomads who had roamed the shores of the Aral when Butakov investigated the region in the mid-nineteenth century; others had fled famine in Kazakhstan in the 1930s. Others, still, who had been resettled to the region to aid in its industrialization found themselves uprooted once more, as whole villages had to move because there was no longer any water.[41] In the meantime, the balneological resorts formed to take advantage of the supposed curative properties of the Aral, the pioneer camps, and rest and recreation areas constructed in the region from the 1950s onward, have disappeared with the receding waters.[42]

Cotton remains the dominant cash crop in the region today.[43] In 2011, independent Uzbekistan was the world's fifth-largest exporter of cotton. The Uzbek government requires farmers to meet an annual cotton quota by dedicating a percentage of their land to cotton cultivation and then selling the cotton to the government at a fixed price.[44] In the fall of 2009, when I was briefly given permission to work in the central state archives

[38] Reimov and Fayzieva, "The Present State of the South Aral Sea Area," *The Aral Sea*, 173; Micklin, "The Water Crisis in Soviet Central Asia," 226; Dybas, "The Once and Future Tiger."

[39] Micklin, "The Water Crisis in Soviet Central Asia," 225.

[40] Igor Zonn, "Socio-Economic Conditions of the Aral Sea Region before 1960," in eds. Andrey Kostianoy and Alexey Kosarev, *The Aral Sea Environment*, 68–69; Reimov and Fayzieva, "The Present State of the South Aral Sea Area," 173; McNeill, *Something New under the Sun*, 165.

[41] Olaf Günther, "Žetis Ötgenov: Ein Lehrer und sein Museum am Ende der Sowjetunion," in eds. Askar Dzhumashev, Olaf Günther, and Thomas Loy, *Aral Histories: Geschichte und Erinnerung im Delta des Amudarja* (Wiesbaden: Reichert Verlag, 2013), 50; Medet Davletjarov and Olaf Günther, "Wasser bewegt – Migration im Amudarja-Delta" in ibid., 59–60, 64, 67.

[42] Zonn, "Socio-Economic Conditions of the Aral Sea Region before 1960," 72.

[43] Winckler et al., "The Aralkum Situation under Climate Change," 432.

[44] "Uzbekistan: Forced Labor Widespread in Cotton Harvest," Human Rights Watch (January 25, 2013), online at www.hrw.org/news/2013/01/25/uzbekistan-forced-labor-widespread-cotton-harvest.

in Tashkent, the director was working in the cotton fields, as all government employees are expected to do. While work in the cotton fields continues to be described as voluntary, it is virtually impossible for citizens of Uzbekistan, Turkmenistan, and Tajikistan to refuse this service; orders come orally, so that there is no official record of the summons. Even children take their turn – though child labor is officially forbidden – often working alongside their teachers, when local officials close schools and universities during harvest time, in order to fulfill their quotas.[45] In spite of the fact that students have been expelled for refusing to pick cotton, government officials portray the cotton harvest as a "voluntary" act of children aiding their parents and communities, or, in the case of older students, "practical training that is needed for professional development."[46] Sometimes, in a striking parallel with Soviet "people's construction," what International Crisis Group has described as "almost free forced labour . . . is portrayed as an example of the Central Asian tradition of hashar, collective work for the benefit of the community."[47] Some now distinguish between (mandatory) hashar for the state "and 'little' hashar for the community or the family."[48] Geographer Christine Bichsel has noted that, like the Soviet state, successor states in the region "have altered and often incorporated such institutions as part of governance strategies," even though "the institutions themselves appear timeless, static and uniform" in their portrayal by the state.[49]

Besides the backbreaking labor involved in its harvest, the cotton monoculture has had other deleterious effects on human health in the region. Instead of the healthy landscapes promised by Bolshevik slogans in the 1920s, late-Soviet landscapes in the Aral Sea region were toxic zones that remain highly polluted to this day. Chemicals used to protect the cotton crop have been detected throughout ecosystems in the Aral region – in the air, water, and soil, as well as in local food products; storms of toxic dust from the exposed sea bed, first observed in 1975 by Soviet cosmonauts, have increased in frequency and magnitude as the sea

[45] Ibid. [46] Ibid.; "Curse of Cotton," 18, 23. [47] "Curse of Cotton," 18, 25.

[48] Tommaso Trevisani, *Land and Power in Khorezm: Farmers, Communities and the State in Uzbekistan's Decollectivisation* (Berlin: LIT Verlag, 2010), 52 fn 60.

[49] Christine Bichsel, *Conflict Transformation in Central Asia: Irrigation Disputes in the Ferghana Valley* (New York: Routledge, 2009), 71. Even international aid organizations have invoked hashar in construction projects, expecting it to "increase the community's sense of ownership toward the outcome of the project" (Ibid., 70).

has shrunk, and are believed to cause major health problems.[50] In the 1980s, Central Asians took advantage of Gorbachev's promotion of transparency to speak out against these injustices. Writer Muhammad Solih, born after the war in Uzbekistan's Khorezm region, wrote an essay in 1988 called "Give Health to Women." Although he did not use the word "cotton," Solih nonetheless clearly stated that the problems of the Aral Sea region had been caused by discriminatory policies emanating from Moscow, even though central administrators claimed to have changed their ways and now spoke of "openness" [*oshkoralik*, i.e., *glasnost'*]. They did not want to admit, he wrote, that the people's health had fallen victim to fulfilling the plan.[51] Today in the Aral Sea region, anemia, hepatitis, and diarrhea; lung, endocrine, and gastrointestinal diseases; cancers and hormonal dysfunctions; and chronic and infectious diseases remain widespread. Contamination of the water supply in Turkmenistan has been particularly dire. Many still rely on the Amu Darya for their water supply, even though the water is highly salinized and contaminated with bacteria.[52]

The disappearance of the Aral Sea in the late twentieth century was the unintended, but not entirely unexpected, result of the dreams of the irrigation age. As early as 1867, the German geographical publication *Globus* had published an article on "The Disappearance of the Aral Sea in Inner Asia." Based on the fluctuations of the sea throughout history, the article concluded, together with the important role played by its tributaries, "as soon as these have been redirected away from the sea for a period of time, the sea must dry up over the course of only a few years and thus become again what it actually is, a depression in the desert."[53] Almost sixty years later, Soviet engineers came to a similar conclusion. In one of the first issues of the *Irrigation Herald*, in an article on utilizing "available" Central Asian water resources, hydraulic engineer Fedor Morgunenkov, editor of the journal and one of the main proponents of the plan to redirect the Amu into the Uzboi, discussed

50 Reimov and Fayzieva, "The Present State of the South Aral Sea Area," 183, 187, 191; Zonn, "Reasons for the Environmental and Socio-Economic Crisis," 79; Micklin, "The Water Crisis in Soviet Central Asia," 224.

51 Muhammad Solih, "Ayollarga sog'liq bering," *Iqror (Maqolalar)*, II (Istanbul: Ihlas Gazetecilik, 2013), 125.

52 Reimov and Fayzieva, "The Present State of the South Aral Sea Area," 187, 192–193, 196; Pryde, *Environmental Management in the Soviet Union*, 77.

53 "Das Verschwinden des Aralsees in Innerasien," 168.

the consequences of Soviet water planning in a section entitled "The Fate of the Aral Sea":

> After putting into motion the entire above-mentioned program [which will end up] using almost completely the waters of the Amu and Syr Darya, the level of the Aral Sea, no longer receiving water from the rivers, will quickly begin to drop – at the rate of one meter a year. In light of the fact that the sea ... is twenty meters deep at its deepest point, it follows that the Aral Sea will completely dry up in twenty years.

In reality, Morgunenkov went on, the desiccation of the sea would take quite a bit longer. And, indeed, there was more good news for his readers:

> Instead of the Aral Sea ... a new sea will form in the Sary-Kamysh depression, with an area seven times smaller ... but with regard to shipping, the new sea will have much greater significance, because it will have a water connection to the Caspian Sea on the one hand and to the Amu Darya and railway ... on the other.[54]

Arthur P. Davis, on his return to the United States, could find no fault with a plan that would "uncover a considerable area of alluvial lands which will add materially to the irrigable area of the desert."[55]

In the postwar years, Soviet scientists reiterated the idea that existing plans for irrigation and hydropower using the waters of the Aralo-Caspian Basin would lead to the desiccation [*vysykhanie*] of the sea with effects on its hydrologic regime, salinity, and ichthyofauna.[56] In conjunction with the Great Stalin Plan for the Transformation of Nature, discussions were raised about the transfer of water from the northward-flowing rivers of Siberia – the Enisei and the Ob – to the Aralo-Caspian Basin for transport, hydropower, and irrigation purposes, a scheme that resembled the "Kazakh-Turkestan Canal" of 1924. Though 90 percent of the water was to go to irrigation, it was recognized that these waters could also be used to maintain the level of the Aral Sea.[57] Like the schemes in the 1920s to transform the deserts between the Urals and the Caspian, river diversion

[54] F. P. Morgunenkov, "Ispol'zovanie svobodnykh vodo-zemel'nykh ressursov v Turkestane, Khive i Bukhare," *VI* 3–4 (June–July 1923): 3–16: 15.

[55] "Arthur Powell Davis Relates Story of Two Years He Spent in Turkestan," *The University Hatchet* (Georgetown, 1932), Box 5, Folder 5, APD.

[56] Davydov, *Enisei-Ob-Aralo-Kaspiiskaia vodokhoziaistvenno-energeticheskaia problema,* 25; B. D. Zaikov, *Vodnyi balans i uroven' Aralskogo moria v sviazi so stroitel'stvom Glavnogo Turkmenskogo Kanala,* Trudy Gosudarstvennogo Gidrologicheskogo Instituta, 16 (Leningrad: Gidrometeoizdat, 1952), 3.

[57] Micklin, "The Water Crisis in Soviet Central Asia," 228; Davydov, *Enisei-Ob-Aralo-Kaspiiskaia vodokhoziaistvenno-energeticheskaia problema,* 25–26.

as a way to mitigate Central Asia's climate was also discussed. In recent years, the drying of the Aral Sea has led to an amplification of seasonal droughts and more days with temperatures over forty degrees Celsius.[58] The river diversion scheme is periodically resurrected, most notoriously by former Moscow mayor Yuri Luzhkov, who has suggested that Russia sell its water to Central Asia.[59] In Qaraqalpaqstan – including, perhaps, in Raushan – villagers recalling the memories of their parents and ancestors who inhabited the same land, and who believed that water comes and goes, as it had always come and gone in the past, still hold out hope that, one way or another, water will return to the Aral Sea.[60]

[58] Reimov and Fayzieva, "The Present State of the South Aral Sea Area," 173.

[59] Iurii Luzhkov, *Voda i mir* (Moscow: Moskovskie uchebniki i kartolitografiia, 2008), 21, 46–47.

[60] Burul Shaimkulova, "Gründe zu bleiben. Alltags- und Lebensgeschichten aus Mojnaq," *Aral Histories*, 125.

Conclusion

The transformation of Central Asia in the late twentieth century was deeply rooted in the dreams of an earlier irrigation age. Technocrats and modernizers around the world believed that harnessing the earth's water resources to reclaim "barren" land for agriculture was what would lead humankind to a better future; it was what they meant by the notion of *progress*. With the conquest of Central Asia in the second half of the nineteenth century, inhabitants of the Russian Empire, too, joined the rank of irrigation age dreamers, envisioning how, with the help of scientific knowledge and technology, water might restore past glory to the region and turn its deserts green. Russians wanted their empire to be a modern one, the equal of other European empires; participating in irrigation projects was one way of realizing that vision.

Though Russian Turkestan attracted a number of irrigation enthusiasts, from regional administrators to Russian and foreign engineers to an outcast member of the imperial family who devoted his life to bringing life to the Central Asian deserts, Russia's central administration was slow to recognize the importance of irrigation for the arid southern regions of the empire. In the meantime, like the attempt to colonize and "civilize" the Central Asian borderlands, Russian attempts to establish oversight and control over Turkestani irrigation systems, or to "bring them to order" by means of science, foundered on a lack of knowledge of Central Asian environments: which lands were suitable for irrigation, where the water resources were located, and how best to bring water to those lands without making the land unusable through salinization and swamping. The most advanced project of the tsarist period, the project to irrigate the Chu River Valley, suffered from wartime deprivations as well as its location, since the coveted lands of the valley were already home to numerous semi-nomadic and sedentary peoples. The expropriation of land at the expense of the indigenous peoples for the purposes of both irrigation and further colonization of the region put the Chu River Valley at the heart of some of the worst violence during the revolt that shook Central Asia on the eve of the Russian Empire's collapse.

The Chu Valley Irrigation Project was designed to make the southern part of Turkestan's Semireche region into the breadbasket of Turkestan. Most of the projects examined in this work, however, were for cotton. In the late nineteenth century, environmental and historical junctures – a global panic over the American monopoly on the cotton market, a domestic concern about the outflow of currency for raw materials for the Russian textile industry, the fact that there were already native varieties of cotton grown in Central Asia, and new advances in the science of irrigation – caused many in the Russian Empire to believe that Central Asia's destiny lay in its development into Russia's main source of cotton. As tsarist administrators hesitated to intervene in local systems of water management and engineers struggled to bring water to new lands, many scientists and officials warned about the dangers of a cotton monoculture. Their successors, however, who believed in the ability of technology and the planned economy to overcome any obstacles nature might place in their way, paid those warnings little heed, carrying forward the visions of the irrigation age – maximum exploitation of water resources for cotton for a glorious, prosperous, and thoroughly modern future – into a new era.

Sven Beckert's recent work on the global "empire of cotton," of which Russia was a part, has drawn attention to the role cotton played in the development of global capitalism.[1] It seems particularly tragic, then, that with all of their inventiveness and revolutionary spirit, the creators of the world's first socialist state could come up with no other vision for Central Asia than continuing to develop the region into that global symbol of slavery and capitalist oppression, a cotton plantation. And yet by the 1930s, Soviet hydraulic schemes in Central Asia were not merely colonial projects seeking to extract resources for the metropole. New educational institutions and construction jobs provided new opportunities for many Central Asians, including women, even if ethnic tensions and gendered relations had not disappeared with the revolution. Beginning at the end of

[1] Beckert, *Empire of Cotton.*

the 1930s, the people's construction projects did more than shockwork construction sites such as Vakhshstroi in aiming to educate and entertain workers between and after hours. Moreover, while appearing to step backward from technology as a means of liberation, the Great Canals were nonetheless far more successful in bringing water to Central Asian fields than was anything accomplished under the tsars. Having moved tens of thousands of people to and within the borderlands, the ability to mobilize these vast numbers of bodies to accomplish what perhaps even expensive machines could not was not exactly high modernism, but it was, in fact, highly modern. Soviet rule in Central Asia was by no means simply a reincarnation of tsarist rule.

The disappearance of the Aral Sea is one of the unintended consequences of this modernization drive, yet Soviet authorities also made telling choices when it came to transforming the "backward" empire of the tsars into a modern socialist state. Klaus Gestwa has argued that the border zones of the Soviet Union, viewed by the center as the "sphere of the unmodern," became "surfaces onto which to project utopias and spaces for experiments in brute social engineering."[2] Under the rule of the Bolsheviks, the utopian visions of the irrigation age evolved from pipe dreams to intensive, intrusive, and at times violent attempts at radical transformation. The Central Asian borderlands, with their inhabitants already marked in tsarist times as "unmodern," "backward," and subject to the whims of nature, provided the perfect experimental space to develop what would become a tool in the modern Soviet regime's arsenal of mobilizational techniques, a convenient way to distract from continuing state weakness in the borderlands and to boost support for the regime, even in more central parts of the country.

Cleverly, with the notion of people's construction developed along the Great Canals, the Soviet state masked its colonialist schemes to extract more cotton from Central Asia with an appeal not only to "modernity" (a new form of distinctly Soviet labor, enabled by Soviet organization and providing cultural and educational opportunities alongside backbreaking manual work) but also to "tradition" (the hashar) and popular initiative, which allowed the state to rely on cost-saving indigenous canal-building techniques and to give the impression of supporting an indigenous way of life. Thus, the Soviet state was perversely able to carry out what were essentially extractive projects fueled by forced labor in the tradition of the

[2] Klaus Gestwa, "Raum-Macht-Geschichte: Making Sense of Soviet Space," *Osteuropa* 55, 3 (2005): 48.

best "Oriental despots" and European imperialists, which simultaneously allowed it to cover up its own weaknesses and previous failings in irrigation construction, while maintaining the notion that only modern Soviet rule could liberate the Central Asian people on two fronts: politically, from the despotism and imperialism of past rulers, and, ecologically, from the oppressive arid environments in which they lived.

It was in part the cutting off of traditional paths of resistance that allowed these projects, as well as the grand hydraulic projects of the postwar years, to be successfully undertaken. The ability in the late nineteenth and early twentieth centuries of peasants and nomads to cross borders and undertake subversive strategies in the hopes of securing a better future, as well as the existence of spaces for alternative and competing sources of authority, such as the Grand Duke in the Hungry Steppe or the qo'rboshi in the Ferghana Valley and Tajik borderlands, had disappeared by the 1930s. The modernization of Central Asia was realized by means of the Soviet state's single-minded focus on economic planning, based on the maximum exploitation of the "productive forces" of the region, and regardless of the human and ecological costs. The results of such uneven development bear resemblance to a colonial experiment, even though today it is Central Asians who have taken over the cotton plantations.

The unintended consequences of the changes to Central Asian landscapes wrought by decades of Russian and Soviet hydraulic schemes have themselves engendered ever more costly and improbable technological "fixes," which continue to be debated in post-Soviet Central Asia to this day. In a world in which water is disappearing (as I write these words in 2018, Cape Town, South Africa, has narrowly escaped running out of water, and although it threatened to be the first modern city to run out of water, it certainly will not be the last); in which climate change makes the future of water uncertain in many parts of the world; and in which from Standing Rock to the Aral Sea, colonized and formerly colonized peoples clamor for environmental justice and access to safe drinking water, technological fixes are not an adequate solution. Though Soviet-era schemes and Soviet-style solutions to Central Asia's water problems are periodically raised, such schemes cannot reverse the fact that moving water from one place to another will always cause conflict and will always cause some to lose out while others gain, that quick fixes are not sustainable, and that the mentalities, the social, economic, and political structures, as well as the ecological landscapes that have been established in Central Asia over the course of more than a century, will be more difficult to reverse than any river.

Glossary

aqsaqal (Russ: *aksakal*) – lit. "white beard"; elder, village head
ariq (Russ: *aryk*) – irrigation channel, canal
ariq aqsaqal (Russ: *aryk-aksakal*) – upper-level water administrator, a person in charge of overseeing an irrigation system, including lower-level water administrators (*mirabs*); see also *mirab-bashi*
artel – work collective
aryk – see *ariq*
aul – group of one to two hundred nomadic households; in the tsarist period, several *auls* formed a *volost'*
bahari (Russ: *bogara*) – adjective pertaining to rainfed lands or the spring crops grown on that land
basmachi – armed groups in Central Asia during the Russian Civil War; also used to refer to general resistance to the Bolsheviks in Central Asia through the 1920s; see also *qo'rboshi*
batyr – in Central Asian tradition, a warrior, hero
bogatyr – in Russian tradition, a mythical warrior hero
chigir – water- or animal-powered wheel used to deliver water from a low-lying place to a higher one
Cossacks – self-governing communities in southern Russia, originally formed by people seeking freedom from Russia and Poland-Lithuania in the steppes and borderlands; by the nineteenth century, Cossacks resembled a military estate and served as the border guards of the Russian Empire
dehqan (also *dehqon*; Russ: *dekhkan*) – indigenous peasant-farmers in Central Asia

desiatina – Russian unit of area equivalent to 2,400 square *sazhens*, or 1.0925 hectares (2.7 acres)
djigit (*dzhigit*) – brave man, strongman
Dungan – Chinese-speaking Muslims from China (known in China as the *Hui*)
great power chauvinism – Bolshevik term for overt nationalism expressed by a (formerly) dominant ethnic group (e.g., Russians) against another (e.g., Uzbeks)
guberniia – province of the Russian Empire; Turkestan, however, was designated a governor-generalship and also a *krai* (borderland)
hashar (also *ashar*; Russ: *khashar*) – collective labor used in Central Asia for community construction and maintenance tasks, such as the cleaning of irrigation systems
inorodtsy – lit. "of other birth"; non-Orthodox peoples of the Russian Empire; in Turkestan, the sedentary peoples were generally designated *tuzemtsy* (natives), rather than *inorodtsy*
izlishek (pl. *izlishki*) – a unit of land considered to be "surplus," or in excess of what nomadic peoples required to sustain their way of life; *izlishki* were identified in order to free more land for settler-colonists
jadid – "new school" Muslim modernizing reformer in Central Asia (early twentieth century)
karez (also *kariz*; Russ: *kiariz*) – a series of borehole wells connected by an underground gallery designed to channel water by gravity for drinking or irrigation purposes without losing that water to evaporation
Kashgari – Turkic-speaking Muslim from the Kashgar Oasis of eastern Turkestan in China's Xinjiang province. Today, we would think of Kashgaris as Uyghurs.
Kazakh – Turkic-speaking, traditionally nomadic or semi-nomadic people of the steppes. The term *Kazakh* did not come into widespread usage, outside of nationalist intelligentsia circles, until the Soviet period. Russians used the spelling "Kazakh," rather than "Kazak" to distinguish them from the Cossacks (*kazaki*). In 2018, a process of script reform underway in Kazakhstan from Cyrillic to Latin characters is set to render Kazakhstan as Qazaqstan. See also *kirgiz*
ketmen – all-purpose Central Asian farm implement that served as both spade and hoe
khalat – robe, often in the sense of a robe of honor, bestowed by a ruler as a reward for loyal service

kibitka – caravan, tent or yurt; a nomadic household
kipsen (also: *kapsan, kepsan, kifsen*) – reward to an *ariq aqsaqal* for good service in kind (usually the amount of grain he could carry in his *khalat*), or in cash (increasingly so by the twentieth century)
kirgiz – Russian term for the Turkic-speaking nomadic peoples in the Kazakh steppe and northern Turkestan. Russians occasionally distinguished between *kirgiz-kaisak* (the people who later would be designated Kazakhs by Soviet ethnographers) and *kara-kirgiz* ("black" *kirgiz*) or *dikokamennye kirgiz* ("wild stone" *kirgiz*) (those who would become known in the Soviet period as the Kyrgyz).
kishlak – see *qishloq*
kolkhoz – abbreviation for "collective farm"; in the Soviet period, a farm nominally owned by workers who owed a set-number of labor-hours to the farm, which determined how much they were paid. Along with the sovkhoz, the kolkhoz was one of the main organizations of life in the rural countryside after collectivization during Stalin's First Five-Year Plan (1928–1932).
kolonizatsiia – colonization; often used interchangeably with *pereselenie*.
krai – borderland, border region. The Governor-Generalship of Turkestan was officially called Turkestan Krai after 1886.
kulak – Russian for "fist"; a wealthy peasant-farmer. During the Soviet period, *kulak* was a label used to remove undesirable elements from the countryside (a process known as "dekulakization").
Kyrgyz – Turkic-speaking nomadic or semi-nomadic peoples of the Tian Shan mountain region; see also *kirgiz*
lalmi – adjective pertaining to rainfed lands, usually referred to as *bogara* by the Russians (see *bahari*)
mir – the Russian peasant commune
mirab – lower-level water administrator, oversaw side canals on an irrigation system, reported to the *ariq aqsaqal*
mirab-bashi – head of the *mirabs*, head overseer on an irrigation system; during the Russian period usually referred to as *ariq aqsaqal*
musafir – foreigner, traveler
muzhik – Russian peasant (male)
narodnaia stroika – people's construction; beginning in 1939, a movement mobilizing vast number of of Soviet citizens (often collective farmers) for manual labor on construction projects, usually carried out over a short period of time
obi – adjective pertaining to irrigated land

oblast' – region into which Russian provinces were divided. Turkestan was divided into the three core *oblasts* of Ferghana, Samarkand, and Syr Darya, which by 1898 were joined by Transcaspia and Semireche.
okrug – a type of district in both the tsarist empire (e.g., the Zarafshan Okrug) and Soviet Union
osvoenie – making one's own, mastering
ozhivlenie – "bringing to life," greening of arid regions through irrigation
pereselenie – resettlement; also referred to as *kolonizatsiia* (colonization)
plov – rice pilaf, a dish traditionally prepared by Central Asians on festive occasions (though eaten more often by those who had the means)
pood – a Russian unit of weight equal to 16.38 kilograms or 36.11 pounds
qishloq (Russ: *kishlak*) – a Central Asian settlement or village
qoʻrboshi – *basmachi* leaders
qoʻsh – pair of oxen or the amount of land a pair of draft animals could plow in one day
raion – a sub-district in the Soviet period
rodina – motherland, homeland; from *rod-* , birth (as in *rodnoi* – kin, one's own)
samovol'tsy – "self-willed" or voluntary migrants in the Russian Empire who moved without official permission
sarancha – plague of locusts, usually Moroccan locusts (*Dociostaurus maroccanus*)
sart – a term for the mixed, Turkic- and Tajik-speaking sedentary peoples of Turkestani towns, sometimes with pejorative connotations
saxaul (*Haloxylon ammodendron*) – a large shrub or small tree which grows in the sandy deserts and steppes of Central Eurasia; important source of fuel
sazhen – a Russian measure of length equal to 7 feet or 2.1336 meters
shockworker (Russ: *udarnik*) – Soviet term for a highly productive worker; high-priority construction projects were known as shockwork construction sites and were generally better supplied and expected to have higher outputs
soslovie – social estate in the Russian Empire; subjects of the tsar belonged to either the nobility, clergy, townspeople, or peasantry; indigenous Central Asians were included with the peasantry.
sovkhoz – Soviet state-owned farm in which the workers received wages; one of the main institutions of the rural Soviet countryside after collectivization during the First Five-Year Plan (1928–1932)

Stakhanovite – a prestigious title awarded to Soviet workers with particularly high productivity levels; named after Aleksei Stakhanov, a coal miner who in 1935 famously mined fourteen times his required quota
sukhovei – the name of a hot, dry wind said to originate in Central Asia
Tajiks – settled Persian-speaking people of southern Central Asia
tugay (*to'qay; tugai*) – riparian woodland in semi-arid regions
Turkestan – the Central Asian province of the Russian Empire
Turkmen – Turkic-speaking nomadic or semi-nomadic people of western Central Asia
tuzemtsy – "natives," the word used for sedentary inhabitants of Turkestan
uezd – district of the Russian Empire
usta – master
Uzbeks – settled Turkic-speaking people of Central Asia
verst (Russ: *versta*) – a Russian unit of distance equal to 3,500 feet or 1.0668 kilometers
vilayat – district in Soviet Tajikistan, as well as Bukhara
vodvorenie – the process of becoming established in a resettlement district
Vodkhoz – short form for various Soviet ministries of water management; from *vodnoe khoziaistvo*, water economy
volost' – sub-district in the Russian Empire; groupings of nomadic *auls* were also referred to as *volosts*, with geographic boundaries based on their winter pastures
zemleustroistvo – land management, land organization

Bibliography

ARCHIVAL SOURCES AND SPECIAL COLLECTIONS

Notations for archival documents from the former Soviet Union indicate the name of the archive, the collection (*fond*, abbreviated "f."), the subdivision of the collection (*opis'*, abbreviated "op."), the file (*delo* ["d."], plural *dela* ["dd."]), and the page numbers (*list* ["l"], plural *listy* ["ll."]).

APD – Arthur Powell Davis Collection, circa 1865–1974, Collection Number 01366, American Heritage Center, University of Wyoming

GARF – Gosudarstvennyi arkhiv Rossiiskoi Federatsii (State Archive of the Russian Federation)

- f. 374 – NK RKI SSSR (Narodnyi komissariat raboch'e-krest'ianskoi inspektsii)
- f. 664 – Nikolai Konstantinovich Romanov, syn Velikogo Kniazia Konstantin Nikolaevich, vnuk Imperatora Nikolaia I
- f. 1001 – Mosolov, Aleksandr Aleksandrovich, 1854–1931
- f. 1155 – Rostovtsevy, grafy
- f. 1797 – Ministerstvo Zemledeliia Vremennogo Pravitel'stva
- f. 3292 – Irrigatsionnoi komitet pri Sovete narodnykh kommisarov
- f. 3316 – Tsentral'nyi ispol'nitel'nyi komitet
- f. 5674 – STO (Sovet truda i oborony pri SNK SSSR)
- f. 7817 – Kommissiia STO SSSR po Revizii irrigatsii Turkestana (1923–1928)

JHH – John Hays Hammond Papers, Yale University MS 259, Yale University Archives, New Haven, CT

RGAE – Rossiiskii gosudarstvennyi arkhiv ekonomiki (Russian State Archive of the Economy)

- f. 478 – Narkomzem (Narodnyi komissariat zemledeliia)
- f. 2276 – IRTUR
- f. 4372 – Gosplan (Gosudarstvennyi planovyi komitet Soveta Ministrov SSSR)

f. 8390 – VASKhNIL (Vsesoiuznaia ordena Lenina Akademiia sel'skokhoziaistvennykh nauk im. V. I. Lenina Gosagroproma SSSR)
f. 8378 – Glavvodkhoz (Glavnoe upravlenie vodnogo khoziaistva)
RGASPI – Rossiiskii gosudarstvennyi arkhiv sotsial'no-politicheskoi istorii (Russian State Archive of Socio-Political History)
f. 17 – Tsentral'nyi Komitet KPSS (TsK SSSR)
f. 62 – Sredazbiuro (Sredneaziatskoe biuro TsK VKP(b))
f. 71 – Institut Marksizma-Leninizma pri TsK KPSS
f. 85 – Ordzhonikidze, Georgii Konstantinovich
f. 122 – Turkkomissiia (Komissiia VTsIK i SNK RSFSR po delam Turkestana)
f. 670 – Sokol'nikov, Grigorii Iakovlevich
RGIA – Rossiiskii gosudarstvennyi istoricheskii arkhiv (Russian State Historical Archive)
f. 391 – Glavnoe upravlenie zemleustroistva, Pereselencheskoe upravlenie
f. 426 – Otdel zemel'nykh uluchshenii Ministerstva zemledeliia
f. 432 – Izyskatel'nye partii po sostavleniiu proektov orosheniia v Turkestane Otdela zemel'nykh uluchshenii MZ
f. 435 – Opeka nad Vel. Kn. Nikolaem Konstantinovichem MIDV
TS – *Turkestanskii Sbornik* (594 volumes), Alisher Navo'i State Library, Tashkent, Uzbekistan
TsGA KR – Tsentral'nyi gosudarstvennyi arkhiv Kirgizskoi Respubliki (Central State Archive of the Kyrgyz Republic)
f. I-6 – Pishpekskoe
f. 20 – Ispolnitel'nyi komitet Sovetov rabochikh, dekhkanskikh i krasnoarmeiskikh deputatov KAO
f. I-54 – Nachal'nik rabot po orosheniiu doliny reki Chu Komiteta zemel'nykh uluchshenii Ministerstva zemledeliia
f. I-87 – Frunzenskii Sovet rabochikh, dekhkanskih i krasnoarmeiskikh deputatov
f. 89 – Pishpekskii Sovet rabochikh, dekhkanskikh i krasnoarmeiskikh deputatov
f. 99 – Gosplan Kirgizskoi SSR
f. 130 – Starshii gidrotekhnik Pishkpekskogo podraiona Semirechenskoi pereselencheskoi organizatsii
f. 332 – Upravlenie vodnogo khoziastva pri SNK "Kirvodkhoz"
f. 486 – Krasnorechenskii stroitel'nyi uchastok Upravleniia rabot po orosheniiu doliny r Chu
f. 1246 – Post. Pred. Soveta Ministrov KirgSSR pri Sovete Ministrov SSSR
TsGA PD KR – Tsentral'nyi gosudarstvennyi arkhiv politicheskoi dokumentatsii Kirgizskoi Respubliki (Central State Archive of Political Documentation of the Kyrgyz Republic)
f. 1 – Tokmakskii komitet kommunisticheskoi partii Turkestana
f. 10 – Kirgizskii oblastnoi komitet VKP(b)
f. 56 – TsK Kompartii Kirgizstana
TsGA RK – Tsentral'nyi gosudarstvennyi arkhiv Respubliki Kazakhstan (Central State Archive of the Republic of Kazakhstan)

f. I-19 – Zaveduiushchii Pereselencheskim upravleniem Semirechenskoi oblasti

f. I-44 – Semirechenskoe oblastnoe pravlenie

TsGA RT – Tsentral'nyi gosudarstvennyi arkhiv Respubliki Tadzhikistan (Central State Archive of the Republic of Tajikistan)

f. I-1 – Khodzhentskii uezd

f. 18 – Sovnarkom (Sovet narodnykh komissarov) TSSR

f. 268 – Upravlenie Vakhshskogo irrigatsionnogo stroitel'stva TadzhSSR pri sredneaziatskom Gosudarstvennom stroitel'nom tresta irrigatsionnykh sooruzhenii (Vakhshstroi) g. Kurgan-Tiube

f. 282 – Postoiannoe predstavitel'stvo TadzhSSR pri pravitel'stve SSSR

TsGA RU – Tsentral'nyi gosudarstvennyi arkhiv Respubliki Uzbekistan (Central State Archive of the Republic of Uzbekistan)

f. 9 – Sredazekoso

f. 40 – Upravlenie delami Velikogo kniazia N. K. Romanova

f. 756 – Upravlenie vodnogo khoziaistva Srednei Azii i Kazakhstana pri Upolnomochennom STO SSSR

f. 837 – Sovnarkom UzSSR

WLG – Willard L. Gorton Papers, Hoover Institution Archives, Stanford, CA

HISTORICAL NEWSPAPERS, JOURNALS, AND OTHER PERIODICALS

AZ *Allgemeine Zeitung*

BAGS *Bulletin of the American Geographical Society*

BV *Birzhevye vedomosti*

CDSP *Current Digest of the Soviet Press*

D *Den'*

EN *Engineering News*

GB *Globus: Illustrierte Zeitschrift für Länder- und Völkerkunde*

GJ *Geographical Journal*

GL *Golos*

GM *Golos Moskvy*

IG *Irrigatsiia i Gidrotekhnika*

IIRGO *Izvestiia Imperatorskogo russkogo geograficheskogo obshchestva*

IUFGOS *Izvestiia Uzbekistanskogo filiala Geograficheskogo obshchestva SSSR*

IV *Istoricheskii vestnik*

IZh *Istoricheskii zhurnal*

JRGSL *Journal of the Royal Geographical Society of London*

K	*Kolokol'*
KhD	*Khlopkovoe delo*
KZh	*Kooperativnaia zhizn'*
M	*Molva*
MV	*Moskovskie vedomosti*
NG	*Nasha gazeta: Organ ispolkoma Tashkentskogo soveta rabochikh i soldatskikh deputatov*
NMM	*New Monthly Magazine*
NR	*Na rubezh'*
NSS	*Na stalinskoi stroike*
NV	*Novoe vremia*
NYT	*The New York Times*
O	*Okraina* (Tashkent)
P	*Pravda*
PM	*Petermann's Mitteilungen aus Justus Perthes' Geographischer Anstalt*
PV	*Pravda Vostoka*
PRGS	*Proceedings of the Royal Geographical Society and Monthly Record of Geography*
RAE	*Review of Applied Entomology*
RI	*Russkii invalid*
RR	*Russische Revue: Monatsschrift für die Kunde Russlands*
RZ	*Russkoe znamia*
SA	*Sovetskaia arkheologiia*
ShchN	*Shchit naroda*
SOV	*Semirechenskie oblastnye vedomosti*
SPV	*Sankt-Peterburgskie vedomosti*
ST	*Sovetskii Tadzhikistan*
SZh	*Sredneaziatskaiia zhizn'*
TI	*Turkmenskaia iskra*
TK	*Turkestanskii kur'er (Tashkentskii kur'er)*
TOL	*The Times* (of London)
TTPG	*Turkestanskaia torgovo-promyshlennaia gazeta*
TV	*Turkestanskie vedomosti*
TMZh	*Turkestanskii meditsinskii zhurnal*
TSKh	*Turkestanskoe sel'skoe khoziaistvo*
UR	*Utro Rossii*
USSRIB	*USSR Information Bulletin*
UV	*Udarnik Vakhshstroia*
VE	*Vestnik Evropy*

VI	*Vestnik irrigatsii*
VIst	*Voprosy istorii*
VK	*Voprosy kolonizatsii*
VP	*Vsemirnyi puteshestvennik*
VS	*Vokrug sveta*
ZGEB	*Zeitschrift der Gesellschaft für Erdkunde zu Berlin*
ZIRGO	*Zapiski Imperatorskogo russkogo geograficheskogo obshchestva*
ZG	*Zemledel'cheskaia gazeta*

PUBLISHED WORKS

Primary Sources and Document Collections

Abdurakhmanov, M. *Vakhshskaia dolina: putevoditel'*. Dushanbe: Irfon, 1982.

Adres-kalendar' na 1896: lits, sluzhashchikh v pravitel'stvennykh, obshchestvennykh i chastnykh uchrezhdeniiakh i ustanovleniiakh Samarkandskoi oblasti, Bukhary, Chardzhuia i Kerki. Edited by M. M. Virskii. Samarkand: Samarkand oblastnoi statisticheskii komitet, 1896.

Agrarnaia istoriia Kazakhstana (konets XIX – nachalo XX v.): Sbornik dokumentov i materialov. Almaty: Daik, 2006.

Annual of the American Society of Irrigation Engineers for 1892–93. Denver: n. p., 1894.

Asmis, Rudolf. *Als Wirtschaftspionier in Russisch-Asien*, 2nd edn. Berlin: Georg Stilke, 1926.

Atkinson, Thomas Witlam. *Travels in the Region of the Upper and Lower Amoor and the Russian Acquisitions on the Confines of India and China*, 2nd edn. London: Hurst and Blackett, 1861.

Aziatskaia Rossiia (izdanie Pereselencheskogo upravleniia Glavnogo upravleniia zemleustroistva i zemledeliia). St. Petersburg: Pereselencheskoe upravlenie GUZiZ, 1914.

Barthold, Vasilii Vladimirovich. *Istoriia kul'turnoi zhizni Turkestana*. Leningrad: Izd. AN SSSR, 1927.

K istorii orosheniia Turkestana. St. Petersburg: OZU GUZiZ, n.d.

Barts, E. R. *Oroshenie v doline r. Murgaba i Murgabskoe Gosudarevo imenie*. St. Petersburg: Tip. uchilishcha glukhonemykh, 1910.

Beal, Fred. *Proletarian Journey: New England, Gastonia, Moscow*. New York: Hillman-Curl, 1937.

Beliavskii. *Materialy po Turkestanu*. St. Petersburg: n.p., 1884.

Berg, L. S. "Ustroistvo poverkhnosti." *Aziatskaia Rossiia*. Vol. II. St. Petersburg: Pereselencheskoe upravlenie GUZiZ, 1914. 25–103.

Biedermann, Bruno. "Die Versorgung der russischen Baumwollindustrie mit Baumwolle eigener Produktion." PhD diss., Heidelberg University, 1907.

Billeter, Erika. *Usbekistan: Dokumentarfotografie 1925–1945 von Max Penson.* Bern: Benteli, 1996.

Brodovskii, M. I. "Zametki o zemledelii v Samarkandskom raione." Edited by V. N. Trotskii. *Russkii Turkestan. Sbornik izdannyi po povodu Politekhnicheskoi vystavki.* Vyp. 2. Moscow: Universitetskaia tipografiia, 1872. 233–261.

Butakov, Aleksej Ivanovič. *Tagebuch der Aralsee-Expedition 1848/49.* Translated and edited by Max-Rainer Uhrig. Zell: Edition Buran, 2008.

Cherdantsev, G. N. *Vodnoe pravo Turkestana v ego nastoiashchem i v proektakh blizhaishego budushchego.* Tashkent: Tip. Turkestanskogo T-vo pechat'nogo dela, 1911.

Chirkin, G. F. *Polozhenie pereselencheskogo dela v Semirechii: Zapiska komandirovannogo v Semirechenskuiu oblast' letom 1908 goda revizora zemleustroistva GF Chirkina.* St. Petersburg: Pereselencheskoe Upravlenie GUZiZ, 1908.

Christie, Ella. *From Khiva to Golden Samarkand.* London: Seeley, Service and Co., 1925.

Curtis, William Eleroy. *Turkestan: "The Heart of Asia."* New York: Hodder and Stoughton, 1911.

Curzon, George N. *Russia in Central Asia in 1889 and the Anglo-Russian Question.* London: Longmans, Green, and Co., 1889.

Davis, W. M. "A Summer in Turkestan." *Bulletin of the American Geographical Society* 36, 4 (1904): 217–228.

Davydov, Mitrofan Mikhailovich. *Enisei-Ob-Aralo-Kaspiiskaia vodokhoziaistvenno-energeticheskaia problema.* Moscow: Glavgidroenergostroi, 1949. Online at www.cawater-info.net/library/rus/hist/davydov3.

Dingel'shtedt, Nikolai A. *Opyt izucheniia irrigatsii Turkestanskogo kraia.* St. Petersburg: Min. Putei Soobshcheniia, 1893.

Zapiska inspektora sel'skogo khoziaistva St. sov. N. A. Dingel'shtedta (Gen.-leit.-u Zhilinskomu po povodu proektov orositel'nykh rabot v Turkestanskom krae). St. Petersburg: n.p., 1897.

Dobrosmyslov, A. I. *Tashkent v proshlom i nastoiashchem: istoricheskii ocherk.* Tashkent: O. A. Portsev, 1912.

Dobson, George. *Russia's Railway Advance into Central Asia.* London: W. H. Allen, 1890.

Documents on Israeli–Soviet Relations, 1941–53, Vol. II. London: Frank Cass, 2000.

Donish, Akhmad (Ahmad-i). *Puteshestvie iz Bukhary v Peterburg.* Revised and expanded 2nd edn. Dushanbe: Irfon, 1976.

Dukhovskaia, Varvara. *The Diary of a Russian Lady: Reminiscences of Barbara Doukhovskoy (née Princesse Galitzine).* London: John Long, 1917.

Eisenstein, Sergei. "Ferghana Canal, Reel 1." *The Film Sense.* Trans. Jay Leyda. Revised edn. New York: Harcourt Brace Jovanovich, 1975. 256–268

Ermolaev, M. N. *Propusk vod r. Amu-Dar'i v Mervskii i Tedzhenskii oazisy.* St. Petersburg: Tip. uchilishcha glukhonemykh, 1908.

"Ferganskaia oblast'." *Pervaia vseobshchaia perepis' naseleniia Rossiiskoi imperii*, Vol. LXXXIX. St. Petersburg: Izd. Tsentr. Stat. Komitetom MVD, 1904.

Fersman, A. E. *Moi puteshestviia.* Moscow: Molodaia gvardiia, 1949.

Fisher, Frederick. *Afghanistan and the Central Asian Question.* London: James Clarke, 1878.

Gaskell, Thomas, and William Sachtleben, *Across Asia on a Bicycle*. New York: The Century Co., 1894.

Gavrilov, N. *Pereselencheskoe delo v Turkestanskom krae (oblasti Syr-Dar'inskaia, Samarkandskaia, i Ferganskaia)*. St. Petersburg: n.p., 1911.

Gepner, D. *Bol'shoi Ferganskii Kanal im. Stalina*. Tashkent: Partizdat TsK KP(b) Uzbekistana, 1940.

Gins, G. K. *Osnovnye nachala proekta vodnogo zakona dlia Turkestana*. St. Petersburg: F. Vaisberg i P. Gershunin, 1912.

Golodnaia step' 1867–1917: Istoriia kraia v dokumentakh. Moscow: Izd. "Nauka," 1981.

Guins (Gins), George C. *Impressions of the Russian Imperial Government: An Interview Conducted by Richard Pierce*. University of California Regional Oral History Office. Berkeley, CA: Bancroft Library, 1971.

Professor and Government Official: Russia, China and California. An Interview Conducted by Boris Raymond. University of California Regional Oral History Office. Berkeley, CA: Bancroft Library, 1966.

Humboldt, Alexander von. *Asie centrale. Recherches sur les chaines des montagnes et la climatologie comparée*. Paris: Gide, 1843.

Central-Asien: Untersuchungen über die Gebirgsketten und die vergleichende Klimatologie. Berlin: Carl J. Klemann, 1844.

Huntington, Ellsworth. *The Pulse of Asia*. Boston: Houghton Mifflin, 1907.

Ish, Lev. *Konets zolotogo potoka. Chto takoe Vakhsh?* Moscow-Tashkent: Ob"edinenie gosudarstvennykh izdatel'stv, Sredneaziatskoe otdelenie, 1932.

Iuferev, V. I. *Khlopkovodstvo v Turkestane*. Leningrad: n.p., 1925.

Ivanin, Mikhail I. *Khiva i reka Amu-Dar'ia*. St. Petersburg: Tip. T-va "Obshchestvennaia pol'za," 1873.

Ivanov, N. I. *Khivinskaia ekspeditsiia, 1839–40. Ocherki i vospominaniia ochevidtsa*. St. Petersburg: Tip. T-va "Obshchestvennaia pol'za," 1873.

Karakumskii kanal i izmenenie prirodnoi sredy v zone ego vliianiia. Moscow: Nauka, 1978.

Karavaev, V. F. *Golodnaia Step' v eia proshlom i nastoiashchem. Statistiko-ekonomicheskii ocherk (po issledovaniiu 1914 g.)*. Petrograd: GUZiZ, 1914.

Kaufman, A. A. *Pereselenie i kolonizatsiia*. St. Petersburg: Tip. T-va "Obshchestvennaia pol'za," 1905.

Khanikoff, Nikolai. *Bokhara: Its Amir and Its People*. Translated by Baron Clement A. De Bode. London: James Madden, 1845.

Khlopkovodstvo SSSR i ego perspektivy. Edited by A. V. Stoklitskii. Moscow: Biuro Pechati i Informatsii SNK i STO, 1926.

Khojibaev, Abdurahim. *Tadzhikistan: Kratkii politiko-ekonomicheskii ocherk Tadzhikskoi SSR*. Moscow: Tip. Khoz. Otdela VTsIK, 1929.

Kinze, A. I. "Khlopkovodstvo." *Ezhegodnik Glavnogo upravleniia zemleustroistva i zemledeliia po Departamentu zemledeliia i lesnomu departamentu. (izdanie Pereselencheskogo upravleniia Glavnogo upravleniia zemleustroistva i zemledeliia)*. St. Petersburg, 1908. 315–361.

Kinze, A. I., and V. I. Iuferev, "Khlopkovodstvo." *Aziatskaia Rossiia*. Vol. II. St. Petersburg: Pereselencheskoe Upravlenie GUZiZ OZU, 1914. 275–298.

Kisch, Egon Erwin. *Changing Asia*. Translated by Rita Reil. New York: A.A. Knopf, 1935.

Kostenko, Lev F. *Turkestanskii Krai: Opyt Voenno-statisticheskogo voennogo okruga. Materialy dlia geografii i statistiki Rossii*. St. Petersburg: A. Transhel', 1880.

Krivoshein, Aleksandr V. *Zapiska Glavnoupravliaushchego Zemleustroistvom i Zemledeliem o poezdke v Turkestanskii krai v 1912 g. Prilozhenie k vsepoddaneishemu dokladu*. Poltava: n. p., 1912.

Kunitz, Joshua. *Dawn over Samarkand: The Rebirth of Central Asia*. New York: International Publishers, 1935.

Kurochkin, Ivan. *Vakhshstroi: Ocherki i putevye zametki*. Tashkent-Samarkand: n.p., 1934.

Lansdell, Henry. *Russian Central Asia Including Kuldja, Bokhara and Merv*. Vol. II. London: Sampson Low, Marson, Searle, and Livingston, 1885.

Lear, Fanny. *Le Roman d'une Americaine en Russie, accompagné de lettres originales*. Brussels: A. Lacroix, 1875.

Lenin, V. I. *V. I. Lenin: Polnoe sobranie sochinenii*. Vol. 43, 5th edn. Moscow: Izdatel'stvo Politicheskoi Literatury, 1970.

Liakhovich, Semën. *Vakhshstroi: ekonomicheskoe i politicheskoe znachenie*. Kurgan-Tiube: Partkom Vakhshskogo udarnogo irrigatsionnogo stroitel'stva, 1933.

Luknitsky, Pavel. *Soviet Tajikistan*. Moscow: Foreign Languages Publishing House, 1954.

Luzhkov, Iurii. *Voda i mir*. Moscow: Moskovskie uchebniki i kartolitografiia, 2008.

Lykoshin, Nil Sergeevich. *Pol zhizni v Turkestane: ocherki byta tuzemnogo naseleniia*. Petrograd: Sklad T-va "V. A. Berezovskii" komissioner voen.-uchebn. zavedenii, 1916.

MacGahan, J. A. *Campaigning on the Oxus and the Fall of Khiva*. London: Sampson Low, Marson, Low, and Searle, 1874.

Machatschek, Fritz. *Landeskunde von Russisch Turkestan*. Stuttgart: J. Engelhorns Nachf., 1921.

Maev, Nikolai, "Topograficheskii ocherk Turkestanskogo kraia." Edited by N. Maev, *Russkii Turkestan: sbornik izdannyi po povodu Politekhnicheskoi vystavki*. Vyp. 1. Moscow: Universitetskaia tipografiia, 1872. 1–115.

Marx, Karl. "Wages of Labor." *Economic and Philosophic Manuscripts of 1844*. Edited by Dirk J. Struik, translated by Martin Milligan. New York: International, 1964. 65–77.

Masal'skii, Vladislav Ivanovich. *Amerikanskaia monopoliia i russkoe khlopkovodstvo*. Read at the general meeting of the Imperial Russian Geographical Society, May 7, 1912. Petrograd: n.p., 1914.

Khlopkovodstvo, oroshenie gosudarstvennykh zemel' i chastnaia predpriimchivost'. St. Petersburg: M. M. Stasiulevich, 1908.

Turkestanskii krai. Vol. 19 of *Rossiia: Polnoe geograficheskoe opisanie nashego otechestva*. Edited by V. P. Semenov-Tian-Shanskii. St. Petersburg: A. F. Devrien, 1913.

Materialy dlia statistiki Turkestanskogo kraia (Ezhegodnik, Izdanie Turkestanskogo statisticheskogo komiteta). Edited by N. A. Maev. 2nd edn. St. Petersburg: n.p., 1873.

Matisen, Andrei. "Polozhenie i nuzhdy orosheniia v Turkestane." *Ezhegodnik Otdela Zemel'nykh Uluchshenii, God Pervyi (1909).* St. Petersburg: GUZiZ, 1910. 274–301.

Meakin, Annette. *In Russian Turkestan: A Garden of Asia and Its People.* London: George Allen, 1903.

Middendorf, A. F. *Ocherki Ferganskoi doliny.* St. Petersburg: Tip. Imp. Akad. Nauk, 1882.

Morgan, E. Delmar. "A Journey through Semiretchie to Kuldja in 1880." *Proceedings of the Royal Geographical Society and Monthly Record of Geography* 3, 3 (March 1881): 150–169.

Moser, Henri. *L'irrigation en Asie Centrale.* Paris, 1894.

Munis, Shir Muhammad Mirab, and Muhammad Riza Mirab Agahi. *Firdaws al-iqbāl: History of Khorezm.* Translated by Yuri Bregel. Leiden: Brill, 1999.

Nalivkin, Vladimir, and Maria Nalivkina. *Muslim Women of the Fergana Valley: A 19th-Century Ethnography from Central Asia.* Edited by Marianne Kamp. Bloomington: Indiana University Press, 2016.

Narodno-khoziaistvennyi plan TadzhSSR na 1932 god (kontrol'nye tsifry). Doklad Gosplana TadzhSSR. Stalinabad: n.p., 1931.

Nazaroff, Paul. *Hunted through Central Asia: On the Run from Lenin's Secret Police.* Translated by Malcolm Burr. New York: Oxford University Press, 2002.

Obzor deiatel'nosti Gosudarstvennoi Dumy tret'ego sozyva, 1907–1912. St. Petersburg: Gos. Tip., 1912.

Obzor prepodavaniia na kursakh mirabov po podgotovke masterov-polival'shchikov vodomershchikov, vodnykh nadziratelei, vodnykh starost' i t.p., 2nd edn. Tashkent: Turkestanskii narodnyi Universitet, Tekhnicheskii fakul'tet, 1918.

Official Report of the Proceedings of the First International Congress of Delegated Representatives of Master Cotton Spinners' and Manufacturers' Associations, held at the Tonhalle, Zürich, May 23–27, 1904. n.p., 1904.

Olufsen, Ole. *The Emir of Bokhara and His Country.* London: William Heinemann, 1911.

Raboty po orosheniiu 45,000 ga. v Golodnoi Stepi. Tashkent: n.p., 1902.

Pahlen, Count K. K. *Mission to Turkestan: Being the Memoirs of Count K. K. Pahlen, 1908–1909.* Edited by Richard A. Pierce. Translated by N. J. Couriss. New York: Oxford University Press, 1964.

Oroshenie v Turkestane. Vol. 9 of *Otchet po revizii Turkestanskogo kraia, proizvedennoi po Vysochaishemu poveleniiu.* St. Petersburg: Senatskaia tip., 1910.

Pamiatnaia knizhka i adres-kalendar' Semirechenskoi oblasti na 1905-i god. Compiled by V. E. Nedzvytskii (Vernyi: Semirech'e Statistical Committee, 1905).

Party to USSR. Moscow: Intourist, 1930.

Pervye sotsialisticheskie preobrazovaniia v Kirgizii. Sbornik dokumentov 1918–20. Frunze: n.p., 1990.

Petrov, N. *Ob irrigatsii v Turkestanskom krae.* Tashkent: S. I. Petukhov, 1894.

Petrov, S. P. *Bol'shoi Chuiskii Kanal i Orto-Tokoiskoe vodokhranilishche.* Frunze: n.p., 1941.

Pilniak, Boris. *Tadzhikistan: Sed'maia sovetskaia.* Leningrad: Izd-vo pisatelei v Leningrade, 1931.

Polozhenie o Glavnom khlopkovom komitete. Moscow: VSNKh, 1924.

Poniatovskii, S. *Opyt izucheniia khlopkovodstva v Turkestane i Zakaspiiskoi obl.* St. Petersburg: GUZiZ, 1913.

Prilozheniia k stenograficheskim otchetam Gosudarstvennoi Dumy. St. Petersburg: Gos. Tip., 1912–1913.

Pumpelly, Raphael. *Explorations in Turkestan.* Washington, DC: Carnegie Institute, 1905.

My Reminiscences. Vol. II. New York: Henry Holt, 1918.

Rizenkampf, G. K. *K novomu proektu orosheniia Golodnoi stepi*, Part 1. Leningrad: GUVKh Srednei Azii, 1930.

Trans-Kaspiiskii Kanal (Problema orosheniia Zakaspiia). Moscow: Vysshii Sovet Narodnogo Khoziaistva, Trudy Upravleniia irrigatsionnykh rabot v Turkestane, 1921.

The Russians in Central Asia: Their Occupation of the Kirghiz Steppe and the Line of the Syr-Daria: Their Political Relations with Khiva, Bokhara and Kokan: Also Descriptions of Chinese Turkestan and Dzungaria. By Capt. Valikhanof, M. Veniukof and Other Russian Travellers. Translated by John and Robert Michell. London: Edward Stanton, 1865.

Safarov, R. *Geroi Vakhsha i Dnepra.* Dushanbe: Irfon, 1982.

Sbornik dekretov 1919 goda. Sobranie uzakonenii i rasporiazhenii rabochego i krest'ianskogo pravitel'stva. Petrograd: n.p., 1920.

Schuyler, Eugene. *Turkistan: Notes of a Journey in Russian Turkistan, Khokand, Bukhara, and Kuldja.* London: n.p., 1876.

Scott-Moncrieff, Sir Colin C. *The Life of Sir Colin C. Scott-Moncrieff.* Edited by Mary Albright Hollings. London: John Murray, 1917.

Shavrov, N. *Vodnoe khoziaistvo Turkestana i Zakaspiiskoi oblasti v sviazi s proektom vodnogo zakona.* St. Petersburg: Tip. Usmanova, 1911.

Shlegel', B. Kh. *Vodnoe khoziaistvo Srednei Azii.* Moscow: n.p., 1926.

Shnitnikov, V. N. *Poezdki po Semirech'iu.* Frunze: Nauch.-issled. Inst. Kraevedenie, 1930.

Skorniakov, Evgenii Evgenievich. "Iskusstvennoe oroshenie v Aziatskoi Rossii." *Aziatskaia Rossiia.* Vol. II. St. Petersburg: Pereselencheskoe Upravlenie GUZiZ, 1914. 219–255.

Oroshenie i kolonizatsiia pustyn' shtata Aidago v Severnoi Amerike na osnovanii zakona Keri (Carey Act): Otchet po zagranichnoi komandirovke. St. Petersburg: n.p., 1911.

Skrine, Francis Henry and Edward Denison Ross. *The Heart of Asia: A History of Russian Turkestan and the Central Asian Khanates from the Earliest Times.* London: Methuen, 1899.

Solih, Muhammad. "Ayollarga sog'liq bering." *Iqror (Maqolalar)*, II. Istanbul: Ihlas Gazetecilik, 2013. 125–29.

Spravochnik i adres-kalendar' Samarkandskoi oblasti na 1909 g. Samarkand: Samarkandskoi obl. stat. komitet, 1908.

Spravochnik i adres-kalendar' Samarkandskoi oblasti na 1901 god. Edited by M. M. Virskii. Samarkand: Samarkandskoi obl. stat. komitet, 1901.

Stalin's Letters to Molotov, 1925–1936. Edited by Lars T. Lih, Oleg V. Naumov, and Oleg V. Khlevniuk. Translated by Catherine A. Fitzpatrick. New Haven, CT: Yale University Press, 1995.

Statistika bumagopriadil'nogo i tkatskogo proizvodstv za 1900–1910 gg. St. Petersburg: n.p., 1911.

Stumm, Hugo. *Russia in Central Asia: Historical Sketch of Russia's Progress in the East up to 1873, and of the Incidents Which Led to the Campaign Against Khiva; with a Description of the Military Districts of the Caucasus, Orenburg, and Turkestan*. Translated by J. W. Ozanne and Capt. H. Sachs. London: Harrison and Sons, 1885.

Tatishchev, Aleksei Alekseevich. *Zemli i liudi: v gushche pereselencheskogo dvizheniia (1906–21)*. Moscow: Russkii Put', 2001.

Tatur, S. K. *From the Great Fergana to the Kara-Kum Canal*. Moscow: Novosti, 1976.

Trudy Khlopkovogo komiteta. Vol. 1. *Zhurnal vtorogo zasedaniia Khlopkovogo Komiteta 16 aprelia 1907 g*. St. Petersburg: G.U.Z.Z. Departament Zemledeliia, 1907.

Trudy s''ezda khlopkovodov v g. Tashkente s 25-go do 1-e dekabria 1912 g. Vol. I. Tashkent: GUZiZ, 1913.

Trushnovich, Aleksandr Rudol'fovich. *Vospominaniia kornilovtsa*. Moscow-Frankfurt: Posev, 2004.

Tsimbalenko, L. I. *Kiarizy (vodoprovody) Zakaspiiskoi oblasti*. St. Petersburg: Izd. OZU, 1896.

Tsinzerling, V.V. *Oroshenie na Amu-Dar'e*. Moscow: Upravlenie vodnogo khoziaistva, 1927.

Turksib (57 min, B/W). USSR, 1929. Director Victor Turin. Produced by Vostok-Kino. Produced for video by David Shepard. Kino Video, NY, 1997.

Ukhtomskii, Esper E. *Ot Kal'mytskoi stepi do Bukhary*. St. Petersburg: n.p., 1891.

Vasil'ev, V.A. "Biulleten' No. 2." n.p, n.p., 1916.

Proekt orosheniia doliny reki Chu. St. Petersburg: n.p., 1913.

Semirechenskaia oblast' kak koloniia i rol' v nei Chuiskoi doliny. Proekt orosheniia doliny reki Chu v Semirechenskoi oblasti. Vvedenie k proektu s kartoi Semirechenskoi oblasti i 59-iu fotografiiami. Petrograd: GUZiZ OZU, 1915.

Veselovskii, N., translator and editor. *Kirgizskii razskaz o russkikh zavoevaniiakh v Turkestanskom krae*. St. Petersburg: P. O. Iablonskii, 1894.

Vaillant-Couturier, Paul. *Mittelasien Erwacht: Ein Reisebericht*. Moscow: Co-op. Pub. Soc. of Foreign Workers in the USSR, 1932.

Voeikov, A. I. *Turkestan: ego vody i oroshenie*. Petrograd: Tip. T-va "Obshchestvennaia pol'za," 1915.

Vozdeistvie cheloveka na prirodu. Moscow: n.p., 1949.

Volynskoi, N. "Sladkaia tsarevna: Begovadskaia skazka." *Turkestanksii literaturnyi sbornik*. St. Petersburg: A. Benke, 1900.

Von der Muhlen, R. "Cotton Growing in Russian Central Asia and the Caucasus." *The Sixth International Congress of Delegated Representatives of*

Master Cotton Spinners' and Manufacturers' Associations. Milan: n.p., 1909. 135–142.

Voshchinin, V. A. *Ocherki novogo Turkestana: svet i teni russkoi kolonizatsii.* St. Petersburg: Nash vek, 1914.

Willcocks, William. "Mesopotamia: Past, Present, and Future." Read at the Royal Geographical Society, November 15, 1909. Reprinted from *The Geographical Journal* 35, 1 (January 1910). *Annual Report of the Board of Regents of the Smithsonian Institution, 1909* (Washington, DC: Government Printing Office, 1910). 410–416.

Witkin, Zara. *An American Engineer in Stalin's Russia: The Memoirs of Zara Witkin, 1932–1934*. Edited by Michael Gelb. Berkeley: University of California Press, 1991.

Wolff, Reverend Joseph. *Narrative of a Mission to Bokhara, in the Years 1843–45*. Vol. 1. 2nd edn. London: John Parker, 1845.

World's Columbian Exposition 1893 Chicago, Catalogue of the Russian Section. St. Petersburg, 1893. Full text available online at: www.archive.org/stream/worldscolumbianeooruss/worldscolumbianeooruss_djvu.txt

Zaikov, B. D. *Vodnyi balans i uroven' Aralskogo moria v sviazi so stroitel'stvom Glavnogo Turkmenskogo Kanala.* Trudy Gosudarstvennogo Gidrologicheskogo Instituta. Vol. 16. Leningrad: Gidrometeoizdat, 1952.

Zaorskaia-Aleksandrova, V. V., and I. G. Aleksandrov. *Perspektivy razvitiia orosheniia v Fergane*. Moscow: Narkomzem, 1922.

Zhurnal soveshchaniia o poriadke kolonizatsii Semirechenskoi oblasti (18, 20, 22, 27, 29 fevralia). n.p., n.p., 1908.

Secondary Works

Adelman, Jeremy, and Stephen Aron. "From Borderlands to Borders: Empires, Nation-States, and the Peoples in between in North American History." *The American Historical Review* 104, 3 (June 1999): 814–861.

Akiyama, Tetsu. "On the Authority of a Kyrgyz Tribal Chieftain: The Funeral Ceremonies of Shabdan Jantai." Paper presented at the workshop "Social History of Modern Central Asia: A Focus on Arabic-Script Documents (18th–20th Centuries)." Oriental Institute, Martin Luther University Halle-Wittenberg. December 11–12, 2009. www.orientphil.uni-halle.de/sais/pdf/2009-12-11/On_the_Authority_of_a_Kyrgyz_Tribal_Chieftain.pdf

Anderson, Benedict. *Imagined Communities: Reflections on the Origin and Spread of Nationalism*. New York: Verso, 1983.

Anderson, Olive. "Economic Warfare in the Crimean War." *The Economic History Review, New Series* 14, 1 (1961): 34–47.

Andrle, Vladimir. *Workers in Stalin's Russia: Industrialization and Social Change in a Planned Economy*. New York: St. Martin's Press, 1988.

Appadurai, Arjun. "Wells in Western India: Irrigation and Cooperation in an Agricultural Society." *Expedition Magazine* 26, 3 (Philadelphia: Penn Museum, 1984): 3–14.

The Aral Sea: The Devastation and Partial Rehabilitation of a Great Lake. Edited by Philip Micklin, N. V. Aladin, Igor Plotnikov. Berlin, Heidelberg: Springer, 2014.

The Aral Sea Encyclopedia. Edited by Igor S. Zonn, Michael H. Glantz, Andrey G. Kostianoy, and Aleksey N. Kosarev. Berlin: Springer, 2009.

The Aral Sea Environment. Edited by Andrey Kostianoy and Alexey Kosarev. Handbook of Environmental Chemistry 7. Berlin, Heidelberg: Springer, 2010.

Askew, William C. "Efforts to Improve Russo-American Relations before the First World War: The John Hays Hammond Mission." *The Slavonic and East European Review* 31, 76 (December 1952): 179–185.

Bailes, Kendall. "The Politics of Technology: Stalin and Technocratic Thinking among Soviet Engineers." *The American Historical Review* 79, 2 (April 1974): 445–469.

Becker, Seymour. *Russia's Protectorates in Central Asia: Bukhara and Khiva, 1865–1924*. Cambridge, MA: Harvard University Press, 1968.

Beckert, Sven. "Emancipation and Empire: Reconstructing the Worldwide Web of Cotton Production in the Age of the American Civil War." *The American Historical Review* 109, 5 (2004): 1405–1438.

The Empire of Cotton: A Global History. New York: Alfred A. Knopf, 2015.

Bergne, Paul. *The Birth of Tajikistan: National Identity and the Origins of the Republic*. New York: I. B. Tauris, 2007.

Bichsel, Christine. *Conflict Transformation in Central Asia: Irrigation Disputes in the Ferghana Valley*. New York: Routledge, 2009.

Bilik, O. A. *Stanovlenie: Ot feodalizma k sotsializmu, Leninskie dekrety, pervye piatiletki, Velikaia Otechestvennaia voina. Irrigatsiia Kirgizii v proektakh i ob"ektakh. Ot proshlogo k nastoiashchemu*. Vol. 1. Edited by T. Sarbaev. Frunze: Kirgizgiprovodkhoz, 1990.

Blackbourn, David. *The Conquest of Nature: Water, Landscape, and the Making of Modern Germany*. New York: W.W. Norton, 2006.

Bleuer, Christian. "State-Building, Migration and Economic Development on the Frontiers of Northern Afghanistan and Southern Tajikistan." *Journal of Eurasian Studies* 3 (2012): 69–79.

Bleuer, Christian, and Kirill Nourzhanov. *Tajikistan: A Political and Social History*. Canberra: Australian National University E Press, 2013.

Bone, Jonathan. "Socialism in a Far Country: Stalinist Population Politics and the Making of the Soviet Far East, 1929–1939." PhD diss., University of Chicago, 2003.

Brain, Stephen. *Song of the Forest: Russian Forestry and Stalinist Environmentalism, 1905–1953*. Pittsburgh, PA: Pittsburgh University Press, 2011.

Breyfogle, Nicholas. *Heretics and Colonizers: Forging Russia's Empire in the South Caucasus*. Ithaca, NY: Cornell University Press, 2005.

Broad Is My Native Land: Repertoires and Regimes of Migration in Russia's Twentieth Century. Edited by Lewis Siegelbaum and Leslie Page Moch. Ithaca, NY: Cornell University Press, 2014.

Brophy, David. *Uyghur Nation: Reform and Revolution on the Russia-China Frontier*. Cambridge, MA: Harvard University Press, 2016.

Brower, Daniel. *Turkestan and the Fate of the Russian Empire*. New York: Routledge Curzon, 2003.

"Kyrgyz Nomads and Russian Pioneers: Colonization and Ethnic Conflict in the Turkestan Revolt of 1916." *Jahrbücher für Geschichte Osteuropas* 44, 1 (1996): 41–53.

Bruno, Andy. *The Nature of Soviet Power: An Arctic Environmental History*. New York: Cambridge University Press, 2016.

Brusina, O. I. *Slaviane v Srednei Azii. Etnicheskie i sotsial'nye protsessy. Konets XIX-konets XX veka*. Moscow: Vostochnaia Literatura, 2001.

Burbank, Jane, and Frederick Cooper. *Empires in World History: Power and the Politics of Difference*. Princeton, NJ: Princeton University Press, 2010.

Buttino, Marco. "Politics and Social Conflict during a Famine: Turkestan Immediately after the Revolution." *In a Collapsing Empire: Underdevelopment, Ethnic Conflicts and Nationalisms in the Soviet Union*. Edited by Marco Buttino. Milan: Fondazione Giangiacomo Feltrinelli, 1993. 257–277.

Revoliutsiia naoborot: Sredniaia Aziia mezhdu padeniem tsarskoi imperii i obrazovaniem SSSR [Russian translation of *La rivoluzione capovolta*]. Trans. Nikolai Okhotin. Moscow: Zven'ia, 2007.

"Study of the Economic Crisis and Depopulation in Turkestan, 1917–1920." *Central Asian Survey* 9, 4 (1990): 59–74.

Cameron, Sarah. *The Hungry Steppe: Famine, Violence, and the Making of Soviet Kazakhstan*. Ithaca, NY: Cornell University Press, 2018.

Campbell, Ian. *Knowledge and the Ends of Empire: Kazakh Intermediaries and Russian Rule on the Steppe, 1731–1917*. Ithaca, NY: Cornell University Press, 2017.

"Settlement Promoted, Settlement Contested: The Shcherbina Expedition of 1896–1903." *Central Asian Survey* 30, 3–4 (2011): 423–436.

Cavanaugh, Cassandra Marie. "Backwardness and Biology: Medicine and Power in Russian and Soviet Central Asia, 1868–1934." PhD diss., Columbia University, 2001.

Cohn, Bernard. *Colonialism and Its Forms of Knowledge*. Princeton, NJ: Princeton University Press, 1996.

Crews, Robert. *For Prophet and Tsar: Islam and Empire in Russia and Central Asia*. Cambridge, MA: Harvard University Press, 2006.

Cronon, William. *Changes in the Land: Indians, Colonists, and the Ecology of New England*. New York: Hill and Wang, 1983.

"The Curse of Cotton: Central Asia's Destructive Monoculture." International Crisis Group, *Asia Report* No. 93 (February 28, 2005).

Dalrymple, Dana. "American Technology and Soviet Agricultural Development, 1924–1933." *Agricultural History* 40, 3 (July 1966): 187–206.

Dalrymple, William. *White Mughals: Love and Betrayal in Eighteenth-Century India*. New York: Penguin, 2002.

Davis, Diana. *Resurrecting the Granary of Rome: Environmental History and French Colonial Expansion in North Africa*. Athens, OH: Ohio University Press, 2007.

Davletjarov, Medet, and Olaf Günther. "Wasser bewegt – Migration im Amudarja-Delta." *Aral Histories: Geschichte und Erinnerung im Delta des*

Amudarja (Erinerrungen an Zentralasien). Edited by Askar Dzhumashev, Olaf Günther, and Thomas Loy. Wiesbaden: Reichert Verlag, 2013. 59–74.

Demko, George. *The Russian Colonization of Kazakhstan, 1896–1916*. Uralic and Altaic Series, v. 99. Bloomington: Indiana University Press, 1969.

Dybas, Cheryl Lyn. "The Once and Future Tiger." *BioScience* 60, 11 (December 2010): 872–877.

Edgar, Adrienne Lynn. "Genealogy, Class, and 'Tribal Policy' in Soviet Turkmenistan, 1924–1934." *Slavic Review* 60, 2 (Summer 2001): 266–288.

Tribal Nation: The Making of Soviet Turkmenistan. Princeton, NJ: Princeton University Press, 2004.

Elie, Marc. "Governing by Hazard: Controlling Mudslides and Promoting Tourism in the Mountains above Alma-Ata (Kazakhstan), 1966–1977." *Governing Disasters: Beyond Risk Culture*. Edited by Sandrine Revet and Julien Langumier. London: Palgrave MacMillan, 2015. 23–57.

"The Soviet Dust Bowl and the Canadian Erosion Experience in the New Lands of Kazakhstan, 1950s-1960s." *Global Environment* 8, 2 (2015): 259–292.

Engerman, David. *Modernization from the Other Shore: American Intellectuals and the Romance of Russian Development*. Cambridge, MA: Harvard University Press, 2003.

Esenov, Paltamet E. "Groundwaters and Salinization of Soils in Turkmenistan." *The Turkmen Lake Altyn Asyr and Water Resources in Turkmenistan*. Edited by Igor Zonn and Andrey Kostianoy. Berlin, Heidelberg: Springer, 2014. 141–150.

Fiege, Mark. *Irrigated Eden: The Making of an Agricultural Landscape in the American West*. Seattle: University of Washington Press, 1999.

Fihl, Esther. *Exploring Central Asia: From the Steppes to the High Pamirs, 1896–1899*. Vol. 1 & 2. Edited by Ida Nicolaisen. Seattle: University of Washington, 2010.

Filtzer, Donald. *Soviet Workers and Stalinist Industrialization: The Formation of Modern Soviet Production Relations, 1928–1941*. London: Pluto, 1991.

Fitzgerald, Deborah. "Blinded by Technology: American Agriculture in the Soviet Union, 1928–32." *Agricultural History* 70, 3 (Summer 1996): 459–486.

Fitzpatrick, Sheila. *Everyday Stalinism: Ordinary Life in Extraordinary Times: Soviet Russia in the 1930s*. New York: Oxford University Press, 1999.

Gaidukovich, V.F. "Mogil'nik bliz Shirin-Saia v Uzbekistane." *Sovetskaia arkheologiia* XVI (1952): 331–359.

Genis, Vladimir. "Deportatsiia russkikh iz Turkestana v 1921 godu ('Delo Safarova')." *Voprosy istorii* 1 (January 1998): 44–58.

Geographic Perspectives on Soviet Central Asia. Edited by Robert Lewis. New York: Routledge, 1992.

Gestwa, Klaus. "Raum-Macht-Geschichte: Making Sense of Soviet Space." *Osteuropa* 55, 3 (March 2005): 46–69.

Die Stalinschen Grossbauten des Kommunismus: Sowjetische Technik- und Umweltgeschichte, 1948–1967. Munich: Oldenbourg, 2010.

Ginzburg, A. I. *Russkoe naselenie v Turkestane (konets XIX-nachalo XX veka)*. Moscow: Akademiia Nauk SSSR, 1991.

Gordon, Stewart. "Ibn Battuta and a Region of Robing." Introduction to *Robes of Honour: Khil'at in Pre-Colonial and Colonial India*. Edited by Stewart Gordon. New Delhi: Oxford University Press, 2003. 1–30.

"Suitable Luxury." *Saudi Aramco World* 59, 5 (Sept./Oct. 2008): 10–17. Online at http://archive.aramcoworld.com/issue/200805/suitable.luxury.htm

Graham, Loren. *The Ghost of the Executed Engineer: Technology and the Fall of the Soviet Union*. Cambridge, MA: Harvard University Press, 1993.

Grant, Bruce. *The Captive and the Gift: Cultural Histories of Sovereignty in Russia and the Caucasus*. Ithaca, NY: Cornell University Press, 2009.

Graziosi, Andrea. "'Visitors from Other Times': Foreign Workers in the Prewar Piatiletki." *Cahiers du monde russe et soviétique* 29, 2 (April–June 1988): 161–180.

Greene, Julie. *The Canal Builders: Making America's Empire at the Panama Canal*. New York: Penguin, 2009.

Günther, Olaf. "Žetis Ötgenov: Ein Lehrer und sein Museum am Ende der Sowjetunion." *Aral Histories: Geschichte und Erinnerung im Delta des Amudarja (Erinerrungen an Zentralasien)*. Edited by Askar Dzhumashev, Olaf Günther, and Thomas Loy. Wiesbaden: Reichert Verlag, 2013. 49–58.

Gurevich, A. "Zemel'no-vodnaia reforma v Uzbekskoi SSR (1925–1929)." *Voprosy istorii* 11 (November 1948): 50–69.

Hämäläinen, Pekka, and Samuel Truett. "On Borderlands." *The Journal of American History* 98, 2 (September 2011): 338–361.

Happel, Jörn. *Nomadische Lebenswelten und zarische Politik: Der Aufstand in Zentralasien 1916*. Stuttgart: Franz Steiner, 2010.

Harris, Steven. *Communism on Tomorrow Street: Mass Housing and Everyday Life after Stalin*. Baltimore, MD: Johns Hopkins University Press, 2013.

Haugen, Arne. *The Establishment of National Republics in Soviet Central Asia*. New York: Palgrave Macmillan, 2003.

Hayit, Baymirza. *"Basmatschi": nationaler Kampf Turkestans in den Jahren 1917 bis 1934*. Cologne: Dreisam Verlag, 1992.

Headrick, Daniel. *The Tools of Empire: Technology and European Imperialism in the Nineteenth Century*. New York: Oxford University Press, 1981.

Heywood, Anthony. "Soviet Economic Concessions Policy and Industrial Development in the 1920s: The Case of the Moscow Railway Repair Factory." *Europe-Asia Studies* 52, 3 (May 2000): 549–569.

Hirsch, Francine. *Empire of Nations: Ethnographic Knowledge and the Making of the Soviet Union*. Ithaca, NY: Cornell University Press, 2005.

"Getting to Know 'The Peoples of the USSR': Ethnographic Exhibits as Soviet Virtual Tourism, 1923–1934." *Slavic Review* 62, 4 (Winter 2003): 683–709.

History of Civilizations of Central Asia. Vol. IV, Part 2. Edited by C. E. Bosworth and M. S. Asimov. Paris: UNESCO, 2000.

Hodnett, Grey. "Technology and Social Change in Soviet Central Asia: The Politics of Cotton Growing." *Soviet Politics and Society in the 1970's*. Edited by Henry W. Morton and Rudolf L. Tökés. New York: The Free Press, 1974. 60–117.

Holquist, Peter. "'In Accord with State Interests and the People's Wishes': The Technocratic Ideology of Imperial Russia's Resettlement Administration." *Slavic Review* 69, 1 (Spring 2010): 151–179.

"Violent Russia, Deadly Marxism? Russia in the Epoch of Violence, 1905–21." *Kritika* 4, 3 (Summer 2003): 627–652.

Hopkirk, Peter. *The Great Game: The Struggle for Empire in Central Asia*. New York: Kodansha Globe, 1994.

Hosking, Geoffrey. *Russia: People and Empire, 1552–1917*. Cambridge, MA: Harvard University Press, 1997.

Igamberdyev, R. S. *Osushchestvlenie leninskikh idei ob oroshenii i osvoenii Golodnoi stepi*. Tashkent: Izd. FAN, 1969.

Igamberdyev R. S. and A. A. Razzakov. *Istoriia melioratsii v Uzbekistane (na materialakh Golodnoi stepi)*. Tashkent: Izd. FAN, 1978.

Irrigatsiia Kirgizii v proektakh i ob"ektakh. Ot proshlogo k nastoiashchemu. Edited by T. Sarbaev. Frunze: n.p., 1990.

Irrigatsiia Uzbekistana v chertyrekh tomakh. Tashkent: Izd. FAN, 1975–1981.

Iunuskhodzhaeva, M. Iu. *Iz istorii zemlevladeniia v dorevoliutsionnom Turkestane (na materialiakh khoziaistva kniazia N.K. Romanova*. Tashkent: Izd. FAN, 1970.

Iusupov, Sh. *Vakhshskaia dolina nakanune ustanovleniia sovetskoi vlasti*. Dushanbe: Akademiia Nauk, 1975.

Jacquesson, Svetlana. "Reforming pastoral land use in Kyrgyzstan: from clan and custom to self-government and tradition." *Central Asian Survey* 29, 1 (2010): 103–118.

"The Time of Dishonour: Land and Murder under Colonial Rule in the Tian Shan." *Journal of the Economic and Social History of the Orient* 55 (2012): 664–687.

Jennings, Eric. *Curing the Colonizers: Hydrotherapy, Climatology, and French Colonial Spas*. Durham, NC: Duke University Press, 2006.

Jersild, Austin. "From Savagery to Citizenship: Caucasian Mountaineers and Muslims in the Russian Empire." *Russia's Orient: Imperial Borderlands and Peoples*, 1700–1917. Edited by Daniel Brower and Edward Lazzerini. Bloomington: Indiana University Press, 1997. 101–114.

Joffe, Muriel. "Autocracy, Capitalism and Empire: The Politics of Irrigation." *Russian Review* 54, 3 (July 1995): 365–388.

"The Cotton Manufacturers in the Central Industrial Region, 1880's–1914: Merchants, Economics and Politics." PhD diss., University of Pennsylvania, 1981.

Jones, Ryan. *Empire of Extinction: Russians and the North Pacific's Strange Beasts of the Sea, 1741–1867*. Oxford, UK: Oxford University Press, 2014.

Josephson, Paul. *Industrialized Nature: Brute Force Technology and the Transformation of the Natural World*. Washington, D.C.:Island Press, 2002.

Would Trotsky Wear a Bluetooth? Technological Utopianism under Socialism, 1917–1989. Baltimore, MD: The Johns Hopkins University Press, 2009.

Kanoda, N. N. *Pereselencheskie poselki v Zakaspiiskoi oblasti, konets XIX-nachalo XX vv*. Ashgabad: Ylym, 1973.

Karakumskii kanal i izmenenie prirodnoi sredy v zone ego vliianiia. Moscow: Nauka, 1978.

Kasaba, Reşat. *A Moveable Empire: Ottoman Nomads, Migrants, and Refugees.* Seattle: University of Washington Press, 2009.

Kassymbekova, Botakoz. *Despite Cultures: Early Soviet Rule in Tajikistan.* Pittsburgh, PA: University of Pittsburgh Press, 2016.

"Humans as Territory: Forced Resettlement and the Making of Soviet Tajikistan, 1920–38." *Central Asian Survey* 30, 3–4 (2011): 349–370.

Khalid, Adeeb. "The Bukharan People's Soviet Republic in the Light of Muslim Sources." *Die Welt des Islams* 50 (2010): 335–361.

"Culture and Power in Colonial Turkestan." *Cahiers d'Asie centrale* 17/18 (2009): 413–447.

Making Uzbekistan: Nation, Empire, and Revolution in the Early USSR. Ithaca, NY: Cornell University Press, 2015.

The Politics of Muslim Cultural Reform: Jadidism in Central Asia. Berkeley: University of California Press, 1998.

"Russian History and the Debate over Orientalism." *Kritika: Explorations in Russian and Eurasian History* 1, 4 (Fall 2000): 691–699.

"Tashkent 1917: Muslim Politics in Revolutionary Turkestan." *Slavic Review* 55, 2 (Summer 1996): 270–296.

Khazeni, Arash. "Across the Black Sands and the Red: Travel Writing, Nature, and the Reclamation of the Eurasian Steppe circa 1850." *International Journal of Middle East Studies* 42, 4 (2010): 591–614.

"Through an Ocean of Sand: Pastoralism and the Equestrian Culture of the Eurasian Steppe." *Water on Sand: Environmental Histories of the Middle East and North Africa.* Edited by Alan Mikhail. New York: Oxford University Press, 2013. 133–158.

Khudzhandi, Toshkhodzha Asiri. *Izbrannye proizvedeniia: Sostavlenie teksta, vystupitel'naia stat'ia i primechaniia Saadullo Asadullaeva.* Moscow: "Nauka," 1982.

Kingston-Mann, Esther. "Breaking the Silence: An Introduction." *Peasant Economy, Culture, and Politics of European Russia, 1800–1921.* Edited by Esther Kingston-Mann and Timothy Mixter. Princeton, NJ: Princeton University Press, 1991. 3–20.

Kirasirova, Masha. "The 'East' as a Category of Bolshevik Ideology and Comintern Administration: The Arab Section of the Communist University of the Toilers of the East." *Kritika: Explorations in Russian and Eurasian History* 18, 1 (Winter 2017): 7–34.

Kirimli, Hakan. "The Famine of 1921–22 in the Crimea and the Volga Basin and the Relief from Turkey." *Middle Eastern Studies* 39, 1 (January 2003): 37–88.

Kivelson, Valerie, and Ronald Grigor Suny. *Russia's Empires.* New York: Oxford University Press, 2017.

Kolesnikoff, Nina. *Bruno Jasieński: His Evolution from Futurism to Socialist Realism.* Waterloo, Ont., Canada: Wilfrid Laurier University Press, 1982.

Kotkin, Stephen. *Magnetic Mountain: Stalinism as a Civilization.* Berkeley: University of California Press, 1995.

Kotsonis, Yanni. *States of Obligation: Taxes and Citizenship in the Russian Empire and Early Soviet Republic.* Toronto, Canada: University of Toronto, 2014.

Krasjukov, Rostislav. "Grossfürst Nikolai Konstantinowitsch, 1850–1918: Versuch einer Biographie." *Der Herold* 12 (1995): 301–318.

Kurbanova, Shirin I. *Pereselenie: kak eto bylo*. Dushanbe: Irfon, 1993.

Landry, Marc. "Water as White Coal" in "On Water: Perceptions, Politics, Peril." Edited by Agnes Kneitz and Marc Landry. *RCC Perspectives* 2 (2012): 7–11.

Laruelle, Marlène. "'The White Tsar': Romantic Imperialism in Russia's Legitimizing of Conquering the Far East." *Acta Slavica Iaponica* 25 (2008): 113–134.

Lenoe, Matthew. *Closer to the Masses: Stalinist Culture, Social Revolution and Soviet Newspapers*. Cambridge, MA: Harvard University Press, 2004.

Lehmann, Philipp. "Infinite Power to Change the World: Hydroelectricity and Engineered Climate Change in the Atlantropa Project." *The American Historical Review* 121, 1 (February 2016): 70–100.

Lévesque, Jean. "Foremen in the Field: Collective Farm Chairmen and the Fate of Labour Discipline after Collectivization, 1932–1953." *A Dream Deferred: New Studies in Russian and Soviet Labour History*. Edited by Donald Filtzer, Wendy Z. Goldman, Gijs Kessler, and Simon Pirani. Bern: Peter Lang, 2008. 243–264.

Levi, Scott C. "India, Russia and the Eighteenth-Century Transformation of the Central Asian Caravan Trade." *Journal of the Economic and Social History of the Orient* 42, 4 (1999): 519–548.

The Rise and Fall of Khoqand: Central Asia in the Global Age, 1709–1876. Pittsburgh, PA: University of Pittsburgh Press, 2017.

Lioubimtseva, Elena, Jahan Kariyeva, and Geoffrey Henebry. "Climate Change in Turkmenistan." *The Turkmen Lake Altyn Asyr and Water Resources in Turkmenistan*. Edited by Igor Zonn and Andrey Kostianoy. Berlin, Heidelberg: Springer, 2014. 39–57.

Loring, Benjamin. "Rural Dynamics and Peasant Resistance in Southern Kyrgyzstan, 1929–1930." *Cahiers du monde russe* 49, 1 (2008): 183–210.

Manz, Beatrice Forbes. "Central Asian Uprisings in the Nineteenth Century: Ferghana under the Russians." *Russian Review* 46, 3 (July 1987): 267–281.

Martin, Terry. *The Affirmative Action Empire: Nations and Nationalisms in the Soviet Union, 1923–1939*. Ithaca, NY: Cornell University Press, 2001.

Martin, Virginia. *Law and Custom in the Steppe: The Kazakhs of the Middle Horde and Russian Colonialism in the Nineteenth Century*. Richmond, UK: Routledge Curzon, 2001.

Matley, Ian Murray. "Agricultural Development (1865–1963)." *Central Asia: 130 Years of Russian Dominance, a Historical Overview*. Edited by Edward Allworth. 3rd edn. Durham, NC: Duke University Press, 1994. 266–308.

"The Golodnaya Steppe: A Russian Irrigation Venture in Central Asia." *Geographical Review* 60, 3 (July 1970): 328–346.

McCannon, John. "To Storm the Arctic: Polar Exploration and Public Visions of Nature in the USSR." *Ecumene* 2, 1 (January 1995). 15–31.

"Technological and Scientific Utopias in Soviet Children's Literature, 1921–1932." *The Journal of Popular Culture* 34, 4 (Spring 2001): 153–169.

McNeill, John R. *Something New under the Sun: An Environmental History of the Twentieth-Century World*. New York: W.W. Norton & Co., 2000.

Michael, Prince of Greece. *The White Night of St. Petersburg*. Trans. Franklin Philip. New York: Atlantic Monthly Press, 2004.

Micklin, Philip. "Aral Sea Basin Water Resources and the Changing Aral Water Balance." *The Aral Sea: The Devastation and Partial Rehabilitation of a Great Lake*. Edited by Philip Micklin, N. V. Aladin, and Igor Plotnikov. Berlin, Heidelberg: Springer, 2014. 111–136.

Introduction to *The Aral Sea: The Devastation and Partial Rehabilitation of a Great Lake*. Edited by Philip Micklin, N. V. Aladin, and Igor Plotnikov. Berlin, Heidelberg: Springer, 2014. 1–14.

"Irrigation and Its Future in Soviet Central Asia: A Preliminary Analysis." *Soviet Geography Studies in Our Time: A Festschrift for Paul E. Lydolph*. Edited by Lutz Holzner and Jeane M. Knapp. Milwaukee: The University of Wisconsin, 1987. 229–261.

"The Water Crisis in Central Asia." *Environmental Management in the Soviet Union*. Edited by Philip R. Pryde. New York: Cambridge University Press, 1991. 213–232.

Mikhail, Alan. "An Irrigated Empire: The View from Ottoman Fayyum." *International Journal of Middle East Studies* 42 (2010): 569–590.

Nature and Empire in Ottoman Egypt: An Environmental History. New York: Cambridge University Press, 2011.

Miller, Aleksei. "Between Local and Inter-Imperial: Russian Imperial History in Search of Scope and Paradigm," *Kritika: Explorations in Russian and Eurasian History* 5, 1 (Winter 2004): 7–26.

Mitchell, Timothy. *The Rule of Experts: Egypt, Techno-Politics, Modernity*. Berkeley: University of California Press, 2002.

Moon, David. *The Plough That Broke the Steppes: Agriculture and Environment on Russia's Grasslands, 1700–1914*. Oxford, UK: Oxford University Press, 2013.

Morrison, Alexander. "How 'Modern' Was Russian Imperialism?" Paper presented at the First Congress of the Asian Association of World Historians, Osaka, May 2009.

Russian Rule in Samarkand, 1868–1910: A Comparison with British India. New York: Oxford University Press, 2008.

Nikitin, Iu. A. *Promyshlennye vystavki Rossii. XIX-nachala XX veka*. Cherepovets: Poligrafist, 2004.

Northrop, Douglas T. *Veiled Empire: Gender and Power in Stalinist Central Asia*. Ithaca, NY: Cornell University Press, 2004.

Obertreis, Julia. *Imperial Desert Dreams. Cotton Growing and Irrigation in Central Asia, 1860–1991*. V&R Unipress, 2017.

Olcott, Martha Brill. *The Kazakhs*. 2nd edn. Stanford, CA: Hoover Institution Press, 1995.

Oldfield, Jonathan, Julia Lajus, and Denis B. Shaw. "Conceptualizing and Utilizing the Natural Environment: Critical Reflections from Imperial and Soviet Russia." *Slavonic and East European Review* 93, 1 (January 2015): 1–15.

Oosterhout, Dianne van. "From Colonial to Postcolonial Irrigation Technology: Technological Romanticism and the Revival of Colonial Water Tanks in Java, Indonesia." *Technology and Culture* 49, 3 (July 2008): 701–726.

Orlovsky, Leah, Offir Matsrafi, Nikolai Orlovsky, and Michael Kouznetsov. "Sarykamysh Lake: Collector of Drainage Water – The Past, the Present, and the Future." *The Turkmen Lake Altyn Asyr and Water Resources in Turkmenistan*. Edited by Igor Zonn and Andrey Kostianoy. Berlin, Heidelberg: Springer, 2014. 107–140.

Osadchii, Fedor. *Velikii tvorets dobra i sveta (Stranitsy sud'by inzhenera M. Tynyshpaeva)*. Almaty: Arys, 2001.

Park, Alexander Garland. *Bolshevism in Turkestan, 1917–1927*. New York: Columbia University Press, 1957.

Payne, Matthew J. "Turksib: The Building of the Turkestan-Siberian Railroad and the Politics of Production during the Cultural Revolution, 1926–1931." PhD diss., University of Chicago, 1995.

Penati, Beatrice. "The Cotton Boom and the Land Tax in Russian Turkestan (1880s–1915)." *Kritika: Explorations in Russian and Eurasian History* 14, 4 (Fall 2013): 741–774.

"Managing Rural Landscapes in Colonial Turkestan: A View from the Margins." *Explorations in the Social History of Modern Central Asia (19th–Early 20th Century)*. Edited by Paolo Sartori. Leiden: Brill 2013. 65–110.

"The Reconquest of East Bukhara: The Struggle against the Basmachi as a Prelude to Sovietization." *Central Asian Survey* 26, 4 (December 2007): 521–538.

"Swamps, sorghum and saxauls. marginal lands and the fate of Russian turkestan (c. 1880–1915)." *Central Asian Survey* 29, 1 (March 2010): 61–78.

Peterson, Maya K. "Engineering Empire: Russian and Foreign Hydraulic Experts in Central Asia, 1887–1917." *Cahiers du Monde Russe* 57, 1 (January–March 2016): 125–146.

"US to USSR: American Experts and the Irrigation of Soviet Central Asia, 1929–1932." *Environmental History* 21, 3 (June 2016): 442–466.

Petrov, V. G. *Pishpek ischezaiushchii*. Bishkek: Literaturnyi Kyrgyzstan, 2008.

Pianciola, Niccolò. "Décoloniser l'Asie centrale? Bolcheviks et colons au Semirech'e (1920–1922)." *Cahiers du monde russe* 49, 1 (2008): 101–144.

Pianciola, Niccolò, and Paolo Sartori. "Waqf in Turkestan: The Colonial Legacy and the Fate of an Islamic Institution in Early Soviet Central Asia, 1917–24." *Central Asian Survey* 26, 4 (December 2007): 475–498.

Pierce, Richard. *Russian Central Asia, 1867–1917: A Study in Colonial Rule*. Berkeley: University of California Press, 1960.

Piper, Karen. *Left in the Dust: How Race and Politics Created a Human and Environmental Tragedy in L.A.* New York: St. Martins Press, 2006.

Polian, Pavel. *Against Their Will: The History and Geography of Forced Migrations in the USSR*. New York: Central European University Press, 2004.

Pravilova, Ekaterina. "River of Empire: Geopolitics, Irrigation, and the Amu Darya in the Late XIXth Century." *Cahiers d'Asie centrale* 17/18 (2009): 255–287.

Pryde, Philip R. *Environmental Management in the Soviet Union*. New York: Cambridge University Press, 1991.

Rassweiler, Anne Dickason. *The Generation of Power: The History of Dneprostroi*. New York: Oxford University Press, 1988.

Reid, Patryk. "'Tajikistan's Turksib': Infrastructure and Improvisation in Economic Growth of the Vakhsh River Valley." *Central Asian Survey* 36, 1 (2016): 19–36.

Reimov, Polat, and Dilorom Fayzieva. "The Present State of the South Aral Sea Area." *The Aral Sea: The Devastation and Partial Rehabilitation of a Great Lake*. Edited by Philip Micklin, N. V. Aladin, and Igor Plotnikov. Berlin, Heidelberg: Springer, 2014. 171–206.

Rosenberg, Daniel, and Susan Harding, eds. *Histories of the Future*. Durham, NC: Duke University Press, 2005.

Roy, Olivier. *The New Central Asia: Geopolitics and the Birth of Nations*. New York: New York University Press, 2000.

Ruder, Cynthia Ann. *Making History for Stalin: The Story of the Belomor Canal*. Gainesville: University Press of Florida, 1998.

Sabol, Steven. "'Awake Kazak!' Russian Colonization of Central Asia and the Genesis of Kazak National Consciousness, 1868–1920." PhD diss., Georgia State University, 1998.

Safarov, Sherali Dzhuraevich. "Agrotekhnicheskie mery bor'by s protsessami vtorichnogo zasoleniia pochv v usloviiakh ogranichennogo drenazha agrolandshafta Vakshskoi doliny." Aftoreferat dissertatsii na soiskanie uchenoi stepeni kandidata sel'sko-khoziaistvennykh nauk. Dushanbe: n.p., 2006.

Sahadeo, Jeff. "Epidemic and Empire: Ethnicity, Class and 'Civilization' in the 1892 Tashkent Cholera Riot." *Slavic Review* 64, 1 (Spring 2005): 117–139.

Russian Colonial Society in Tashkent, 1865–1923. Bloomington: Indiana University Press, 2007.

Sarkisova, Oksana. *Screening Soviet Nationalities: Kulturfilms from the Far North to Central Asia*. London: I. B. Tauris, 2016.

Saul, Norman E. *Concord and Conflict: The United States and Russia, 1867–1914*. Lawrence, KS: University Press of Kansas, 1996.

Schroeder, Gertrude. "Economic Relations among the Republics." *Investing in Reform: Doing Business in a Changing Soviet Union*. Edited by Michael P. Claudon and Tamar L. Gutner. New York: New York University Press, 1991. 19–37.

"Regional Economic Disparities, Gorbachev's Policies, and the Disintegration of the Soviet Union." *The Former Soviet Union in Transition*. Volume I. Study Papers Submitted to the Joint Economic Committee, Congress of the United States. February 1993. 121–145.

Scott, James. *Seeing Like a State: How Certain Schemes to Improve the Human Condition Have Failed*. New Haven, CT: Yale University Press, 1998.

Semenov, I. E., and A. I. Rakhimov. *Razvitie irrigatsii v Kirgizii*. Frunze: n.p., 1987.

Shaimkulova, Burul. "Gründe zu bleiben. Alltags- und Lebensgeschichten aus Mojnaq." *Aral Histories: Geschichte und Erinnerung im Delta des Amudarja (Erinerrungen an Zentralasien)*. Edited by Askar Dzhumashev, Olaf Günther, and Thomas Loy. Wiesbaden: Reichert Verlag, 2013. 112–127.

Shioya, Akifumi. "*Povorot* and the Khanate of Khiva: A New Canal and the Birth of Ethnic Conflict in the Khorazm Oasis, 1870s–1890s." *Central Asian Survey* 33, 2 (2014): 232–245.

"Who Should Manage the Waters of the Amu Darya? Controversy over Irrigation Concessions between Russia and Khiva, 1913–14." *Explorations in the Social History of Modern Central Asia (19th–Early 20th Century)*. Edited by Paolo Sartori. Leiden: Brill 2013. 111–136.

Siddiqi, Asif A. "Imagining the Cosmos: Utopians, Mystics, and the Popular Culture of Spaceflight in Revolutionary Russia." *Osiris* 23 (2008): 260–288.

Siddiqui, Iqtidar Husain. "Water Works and Irrigation System in India during Pre-Mughal Times." *Journal of the Economic and Social History of the Orient* 29, 1 (1986): 52–77.

Siegelbaum, Lewis. *Cars for Comrades: The Life of the Soviet Automobile*. Ithaca, NY: Cornell University Press, 2008.

Stakhanovism and the Politics of Productivity in the USSR, 1935–41. Cambridge, UK: Cambridge University Press, 1988.

Sinnott, Peter. "The Physical Geography of Soviet Central Asia and the Aral Sea Problem." *Geographic Perspectives on Soviet Central Asia*. Edited by Robert Lewis. New York: Routledge, 1992. 73–95.

Slezkine, Yuri. "Imperialism as the Highest Stage of Socialism." *The Russian Review* 59, 2 (April 2000): 227–234.

Sokol, Edward. *The Revolt of 1916 in Russian Central Asia*. Baltimore, MD: Johns Hopkins Press, 1954.

Soucek, Svat. *A History of Inner Asia*. New York: Cambridge University Press, 2000.

Starr, S. Frederick, ed. *Ferghana Valley: The Heart of Central Asia*. New York: Routledge, 2015.

Stites, Richard. *Revolutionary Dreams: Utopian Vision and Experimental Life in the Russian Revolution*. New York: Oxford University Press, 1989.

Sunderland, Willard. "Empire without Imperialism? Ambiguities of Colonization in Tsarist Russia." *Ab Imperio* 2 (2003): 101–114.

Taming the Wild Field: Colonization and Empire on the Russian Steppe. Ithaca, NY: Cornell University Press, 2004.

Sutton, Antony. *Western Technology and Soviet Economic Development, 1930–1945*. Stanford, CA: Hoover Institution, 1971.

Teichmann, Christian. "Canals, Cotton and Colonization." *Central Asian Survey* 26, 4 (2007): 499–519.

Macht der Unordnung: Stalins Herrschaft in Zentralasien, 1920–1950. Berlin: Hamburger Edition, 2016.

Teisch, Jessica. *Engineering Nature: Water, Development, and the Global Spread of American Environmental Expertise*. Chapel Hill, NC: University of North Carolina, 2011.

Thurman, Jonathan Michael. "Modes of Organization in Central Asian Irrigation: The Ferghana Valley, 1876 to Present." PhD diss., Indiana University, 1999.

Tolz, Vera. *Russia's Own Orient: The Politics of Identity and Oriental Studies in the Late Imperial and Early Soviet Periods*. Oxford, UK: Oxford University Press, 2011.

Trevisani, Tommaso. *Land and Power in Khorezm: Farmers, Communities and the State in Uzbekistan's Decollectivisation*. Berlin: LIT Verlag, 2010.

Tsentral'naia Aziia v sostave Rossiiskoi imperii. Edited by S. N. Abashin, D. Iu. Arapov, and N. E. Bekmakhanova. *Historica Rossica: Okrainy Rossiiskoi Imperii*. Series editors A. I. Miller, A. V. Remnev, and A. Rieber. Moscow: Novoe literaturnoe obozrenie, 2008.

The Turkmen Lake Altyn Asyr and Water Resources in Turkmenistan. Edited by Igor Zonn and Andrey Kostianoy. Heidelberg: Springer, 2014

Tyrrell, Ian. *True Gardens of the Gods: Californian-Australian Environmental Reform, 1860–1930*. Berkeley: University of California Press, 1999.

Uyama, Tomohiko. "A Particularist Empire: The Russian Policies of Christianization and Military Conscription in Central Asia." *Empire, Islam, and Politics in Central Eurasia*. Edited by Tomohiko Uyama. Sapporo, Japan: Slavic Research Center, Hokkaido University, 2007. 23–63.

Viola, Lynne. *The Unknown Gulag: The Lost World of Stalin's Special Settlements*. New York: Oxford University Press, 2007.

"Water Pressures in Central Asia." International Crisis Group, *Europe and Central Asia Report* 233 (September 11, 2014).

Weiner, Douglas. *Models of Nature: Ecology, Conservation, and Cultural Revolution in Soviet Russia*. Pittsburgh, PA: University of Pittsburgh, 2000.

Werth, Paul. "From Resistance to Subversion: Imperial Power, Indigenous Opposition, and their Entanglement." *Kritika: Explorations in Russian and Eurasian History* 1, 1 (Winter 2000): 21–43.

Wheatcroft, Stephen. "Crises and Condition of the Peasantry in Late Imperial Russia." *Peasant Economy, Culture, and Politics of European Russia, 1800–1921*. Edited by Esther Kingston-Mann and Timothy Mixter. Princeton, NJ: Princeton University Press, 1991. 128–172.

Wheeler, Geoffrey. *The Modern History of Soviet Central Asia*. New York: Praeger, 1964.

White, Richard. *The Organic Machine*. New York: Hill and Wang, 1995.

Whitman, John. "Turkestan Cotton in Imperial Russia." *American Slavic and East European Review* 15, 2 (April 1956): 190–205.

Winckler, G., E. Kleinn, and S.-W. Breckle. "The Aralkum Situation Under Climate Change Related to Its Broader Regional Context." *Aralkum – A Man-Made Desert: The Desiccated Floor of the Aral Sea (Central Asia)*. Edited by Siegmar-W. Breckle, Walter Wucherer, Liliya A. Dimeyeva, and Nathalia P. Ogar. Berlin-Heidelberg: Springer, 2012. 431–458.

Wood, William. "The Sariq Turkmens of Merv and the Khanate of Khiva in the Early Nineteenth Century." PhD diss., University of Indiana, 1998.

Worster, Donald. *Rivers of Empire: Water, Aridity, and the Growth of the American West*. New York: Pantheon Books, 1985.

Wortman, Richard. *Scenarios of Power: Myth and Ceremony in Russian Monarchy*. Princeton, NJ: Princeton University Press, 2000.

Zonn, Igor. "Karakum Canal: Artificial River in a Desert." *The Turkmen Lake Altyn Asyr and Water Resources in Turkmenistan*. Edited by Igor Zonn and Andrey Kostianoy. Heidelberg: Springer, 2014. 95–106.

"Reasons for the Environmental and Socio-Economic Crisis." *The Aral Sea Environment*. Edited by Andrey Kostianoy and Alexey Kosarev. Berlin, Heidelberg: Springer, 2010. 75–82.

"Socio-Economic Conditions of the Aral Sea Region before 1960." *The Aral Sea Environment*. Edited by Andrey Kostianoy and Alexey Kosarev. Berlin, Heidelberg: Springer, 2010. 65–74.

Index